BECAUSE
THE MEDICINE
RAN OUT

BECAUSE
THE MEDICINE
RAN OUT

THE STORY BEHIND THE
CREATION OF
INTERVIEWGIRL.COM AND
THE INTERVIEW GIRL
FOUNDATION

Victoria Hagerty

Why and How this nonprofit organization
believes that it can change the world
through STORIES

Because the Medicine Ran Out
Copyright © 2014 by Victoria Hagerty. All rights reserved.
First Print Edition: March 2014
ISBN-13: 978-0-692-29713-1
ISBN-10: 0-692-29713-8

Blue Valley Author Publishing Company

Table of Contents

v

My Mom and Dad are the most impactful individuals in my life ... and they join me in dedicating this book to the billions of people, part of our larger human family, who live in misery. This book is for them. May they know that we want to tell their stories because we believe there is *hope* for a better tomorrow.

"God has not called me to be successful; He has called me to be faithful."

—Blessed Teresa of Calcutta

"As water reflects the face, so one's life reflects the heart."

—Proverbs 27:19

"Let light shine out of darkness."

—2 Corinthians 4:6

"*Ubuntu*"—the only way for me to be human is for you to reflect my humanity back at me.

CHAPTER ONE

What Kpando, Ghana Taught Me About Perspective

What is Your Perspective?

"Why did she die?" I ask demanding to know an answer. "Because the medicines ran out that particular week," the orphanage director from Ghana, Africa responds. I wake up sweating in the middle of the night with that moment running through my head. From that point in Ghana, where the director of the children's home told me that someone died of a treatable disease because monetarily she lacked the financial means for medicine, my perspective about our world was never the same from that second forward.

I grew up in the suburbs of Chicago in a well off middle class family. Everyone has heard the phrase, "we all have problems." Well, in my "subculture" at home in Chicago's suburbia, the biggest problems for most people my age are that they *have* to sit all day at their desk at their job and then fit in 30 minutes of exercise on a treadmill after work. The problems in various Chicagoan twenty-something's reality (in their world or how they experience the world), that I have heard individuals lament about time and time again, are that they *have* to get up and go to work day after day or that they *have* to go work out. Everyone's reality in this world is different based on his/her circumstances and where he/

she comes from. According to *Merriam Webster's Dictionary*, reality is the state or quality of being real, resemblance to what is real, or a real thing or fact. People throughout the world all experience different realities. Depending on our perspective, we see reality a certain way.

Perspective. It all comes down to perspective. In the past year, I've pondered about what shapes and defines one's perspective. Learning to look at situations from different perspectives allows us to understand the world and people better. One's perspective is what makes us see things in this world in one light or another. This is important because the way that we see the world determines how we live our lives. When I graduated high school, reality to me was that mostly everyone went away to college. It is just the next step after senior year of high school, but I once heard an interesting analogy. There are 7 billion people living on planet Earth today. In *Our Lives Change When Our Habits Change*, Matthew Kelly elucidates that if we were to reduce the world's population to 100 people proportionately: 57 of those 100 people would come from Asia, 21 from Europe, 14 from North and South America and 8 from Africa. 51 of those 100 people would be women, 49 would be men, 68 of those 100 people wouldn't be able to read and write. 6 of those 100 people would own or control more than 50% of the world's wealth. 5 of those 6 people would be U.S. citizens, 3 of those 5 people would live on the same street on the north shore of Long Island, 1 of those 100 people would have just been born, 1 of those 100 people would be just about to die, and only 1 of those 100 people would have been to college. Maybe in your world, everyone goes to college, but on planet earth 1 in 100 people have a college experience. 1/3 of the world's population is dying from lack of bread, 1/3 of the world's population is dying from lack of justice, and 1/3 of the world's population is dying from overeating. Kelly's description of the breakdown of the population on planet Earth challenges one's view of the world. How do you see the world? In your world does everyone go to college, because the majority of the people on the planet still can't read and write. 50% of the world's population lives on less than \$2.50 a day, 22,000 children die each day due to poverty, 1.1 billion people in developing countries have inadequate access to water, and 270 million (1 in 7) children have no access to health services.[1]

We all have a tendency to get caught up in our own little world. Experiencing new circumstances and meeting new people in person, or through stories, challenges what we are concerned about and brings us the gift of perspective. Perspective is exigent for varied reasons, but it's important to step back and ask ourselves, "How do we see the world?," because the way we see the world determines the way we live our lives and how we react to the world.

A New Perspective

I have countless explanations as to why I am grateful for my time in Ghana, Africa, but I am most grateful because I procured a new perspective about resources and health from visiting Africa. Rewind to my time volunteering in Kpando, Ghana to discover just how my life changed. My life was transformed from this experience because my perspective about the world expanded. Late on a Monday evening in July, I paced up and down the aisle at the Washington, Dulles international airport while I waited to board the plane to go to Accra, Ghana. I had that butterfly feeling in my stomach before I boarded the plane. I ended up at this airport heading to Ghana because I decided that I wanted to travel to Africa. I had always loved to travel, and I remember after one of my favorite screen writers gave the advice to travel and see as much as you could, I then made it more of a priority to travel to places that I had never been—places diverse to my subculture back home. I concentrated on graduate school the prior summer, and I now wanted to dedicate this summer to service. I did not know what I really meant by that, and as friend of mine said to me when I told him my plans to go to Africa, "I think you are using serving as an excuse just to see a new place and check it off your to travel list." I don't know why it was that I decided to volunteer that summer at an orphanage in Ghana, Africa, but that's where I was headed that July evening.

I remember texting "I love you" one last time to all of those close to me before I had to turn off my cell phone for take-off. While on the flight to Africa, I met a monk who was doing missionary work in Africa (I wasn't sure that monks actually existed in this modern world). My upcoming volunteer work would introduce me to a plethora of distinctive perspectives. Speaking with this monk was the beginning of these new perspectives that I would harvest whilst in Africa. After conversing with him in flight, I was touched and inspired by what he and the Catholic Church were aspiring to do with their charity in Africa. This is just what I needed while on the flight too. We had a tremendous conversation. I did not realize it then, but some of his words would speak to me in the months to come as the Interview Girl Foundation became an actualization. As he was describing his missionary work, at one point I asked him what was the best thing that I could do to "help the Africans" (yes I used these general terms). He replied, "To help anyone, you need to listen to them. Ask them, not me." His inspiriting words took my mind off the nervousness of what I was really doing – heading to a strange country where I did not know anyone and would be living without running water, electricity, a cell phone, or the internet for a month.

After ten long hours, the plane touched down at the Accra airport in Ghana. As I descended from the airplane, I found myself walking down the stairs of the aircraft onto what seemed like a dirt road with cracked and broken cement, and then walking into the airport. No gate to get you from the plane to inside the airport when you get off a plane, was the first of many differences that I noticed in Africa from how things are done in the United States. I entered the airport to find chaos and the smell of sweat. I stood in a long, crowded line leading up to a desk with a glass-encased box. When I finally made my way to the front of the line, I was instructed that I had to place my passport in the box.

4

I could not understand what the man in the uniform behind the desk was saying, but through hand motions and gestures, I figured out that he was indicating that I had to pay some sort of fee. I did not understand, I paid for my VISA and completed everything else that I had to do before entering Africa before I left Chicago. Confused, I took out the little bit of money that I changed to Ghana Cedis before I left the United States. The man then took whatever fee I needed to pay and shortly after, he stamped my passport.

I entered the frenzied Accra airport and after finally retrieving my luggage, I came across a row of about 18 to 20 African males holding signs with various names. They were obviously all waiting to pick up foreigners who arrived in Accra. Before boarding the plane, I read an article from the U.S. travel alert website about how people pretend to be an airport pick up service and then abduct people. So, as I saw a young man with a sign that said my name, I hoped it was actually David, the young man that the organization I was volunteering for told me to expect, and not a pseudo phony who hijacked the "Victoria" sign pretending to be David. I stood there in an unfamiliar environment, gazing at the line of guys, one who had a sign with my name, I said a quick Hail Mary and then decided that there was nothing left to do, but to walk up to the guy holding a sign saying "Victoria."

I approached him and he warmly greeted me, "Victoria from Chicago." I smiled and acknowledged that I was Victoria. We walked quite a ways from the airport as we made our way toward a parked car that another man was driving. We got into the dilapidated car and drove to what seemed like a bus depot. People were everywhere. They had baskets of food on their heads and were wearing long robes and dresses wrapped in various ways. It was a hot, sticky afternoon. I heard unfamiliar languages, constant chatter, car horns, animal sounds and I kept noticing all the people in bright colors carrying baskets of various items on top of their heads. We waited at this busy center for what seemed like a very long time. Individuals and animals fluttered past me. I stood there mesmerized watching the women walk past as their hips gracefully swayed in their flowing dresses all the while balancing these baskets of bananas on top of their heads. I waited amidst my various roller luggage and could not even keep all of them standing upright. I thought that the women, who were balancing baskets of food and other goods on top of their heads, possessed an impressive skill which was foreign to me. Eventually, David pointed toward a large van and told me that it would take me to Kpando. I entered and sat with about 12 other people. It was so tight in there—I mean indubitably tight. The smell of sweat infiltrated the van. It was hot, and with all of the people close together and sweating, it did not smell great. What I was told would be a four hour commute to Kpando began.

I stared out the window and to me, it seemed like we were just driving across wide open dirt roads and fields at various times. It was not a highway with paved roads and lanes like I was used to driving on if I had to make a four hour commute at home. After about two hours, the van pulled over and I overheard someone in front of me say something about a bathroom break. It took some time for all of us to descend from the van, since we were packed so tightly inside. I stepped down from the van onto the ground outside. My legs were tight from being cramped and sitting. Rivulets of sweat ran down the side of my face. I looked around wondering where the bathroom was. All I could see was nature; I didn't see any buildings in sight. I noticed my fellow passengers going off in different directions and squatting and urinating. I stood there in my long pants, socks up to my knees and tightly tied gym shoes, observing people using the washroom by spreading open their legs. This was one of those moments where I was introduced to a new perspective. I now understood why the women wore long dresses and sandals. My outfit was not conducive to urinating with people all around me. I really had to pee. As a modest American out of her element, I would not dream of pulling my pants down and revealing my bottom for strangers to see, no matter how bad I did have to go. I stood there feeling really uncomfortable as the only white person in the van, the only individual in long pants, and everyone around me urinating. I just stood there. It was one of those moments in my life where I was not sure if I should smile. I'm a huge proponent of smiling and I try to do it as much as possible. In this particular case, I did not know if it would seem weird if I was smiling at people as they were urinating, so as I said, I literally just stood there attempting to emote no emotion.

Eventually everyone got back into the van and the commute to Kpando continued. After a few more hours, the van dropped me off and I was told to wait for James. By now my needing to pee was almost intolerable. I felt as if I was going to burst. It was now dark outside. I was on the busy street (which was a dirt road) with all of my luggage just waiting. A foul stench surrounded me as I stood there with people staring at me. I was so terrified of dying of malaria while in Africa because of all the travel alert warnings that I read. I was given every shot imaginable, I had my bed net, and about 15 bottles of various insect repellents in my luggage. I was wearing a baseball cap with my long blond hair coming out the back, socks up to my knees, a long sleeve shirt, and long pants. Mind you—it's very hot in Africa which is why none of the locals dress this way, but I was scared of becoming sick with malaria that despite my full body sweating, for the first week, I wore long pants and long sleeves every day. Eventually James came and before he could finish introducing himself, I was practically in tears pleading that I had to use the bathroom. He calmly assured me the Children's Home was close and that I could go to the bathroom there. He escorted me to the Children's Home where I would be volunteering for the next month. When we arrived, I was ready to run to the nearest stall, but James pointed to the field on the other side of the gate that was the entrance to the home. I hurried to the field trying to get out of visible sight and pulled my pants and underwear down, holding my pants as far forward as possible, so the urine that at this point was now gushing out of me would not hit my clothes. After relieving my bladder for what was now about 8 hours of not using the washroom, I went back to the Children's Home and met James. Probably because he could tell without me ever saying so that peeing in the dark field was awkward and uncomfortable for me, James assured me that there was an outhouse in the place where I would be sleeping. I kindly smiled while sarcastically thinking in my head, "An outhouse? Much better."

I went to sleep with a mosquito net around me and just as I fell asleep, I awoke to chickens, roosters, and a host of other animal sounds before the sun had even risen. As much as I would love to continue describing play by play moments in Kpando about what I experienced there, I will give you a general feeling of the Children's Home where I was volunteering, so that we can move onto discussing the reason for this book: the purpose of InterviewGirl. com. About twenty children live at the Children's Home in Kpando, Ghana. On any given day you enter the Children's Home, you would see a few small, frail, Ghanaian boys between 6 and 11 years old sweeping loose stones and other particles off the dirty, cracked cement ground with thin branches tied together with twine (what looks like a brush that was made from tree branches). Donkur, a 14 year old orphan may be stirring a pot of what looked like mush to me, but it is really called Banku. It is cooked fermented corn dough and cassava dough. Asantewa, a four year old, most likely is pulling on the American volunteer's arm to read her the book, *Curious George* yet again, even though she and the volunteer read that same book, that old, dirty falling apart book 15 other times that same day. Broken cement, the ground, rocks, stones, dirt, and maybe a few old toys and books (that were donations that had been there for years) would be what you see available for the children.

The children did not have anything by materialistic standards, yet the children with whom I was privileged enough to get to spend that month with, were some of the most gracious, amusing, kind, and gentle people whom I've ever had the pleasure of meeting. Two sisters (as the children called them) worked at the home and took care of the children. Volunteers, like me, would come and then go after our month, week, or year of service was over. Depending on donations, the children received food and/or medicine. These were not even guaranteed to the children, children who lived at the Children's Home because they were orphans whose parents had died of AIDS.

A Story that Changed My Life

Amara was a fourteen year old girl living at the orphanage in Kpando, Africa. I noticed her during my first week there. She was a quiet girl with an angelic like face who always had a book in hand. I was struck immediately by the fact that she was always carrying a book. As someone who loves to read, one of the first things that I noticed about her was how she always had a book with her. The book that she was constantly working with and reading was a geology textbook from the United States from the 1970's. This was a textbook that any school teacher in the USA would not even consider using, and yet Amara was determined to learn all that she could from this book because it was all that she had. The book must have been a donation that was given to the orphanage at some point. She would point to the charts displayed in the old textbook and ask me questions about the material, "Auntie Victoria, please explain this to me?" The politeness of the children in Kpando, their continually using "please" and "thank you" when they asked me questions and always referring to me as "Auntie" was so endearing. As any young, new teacher can attest to having done, I played off like I knew what I was talking about (fully admitting not to be an expert in Geology) as I threw out every bold vocabulary word that I could remember from the science text book back from when I studied Geology years ago (paleontology, systematics, evolutionary theory, meteorics, etc.) and wove them into my answers to Amara's questions. Over the course of several days, big-eyed and curious, Amara's questions continued, "What causes drought? How does the Earth's core generate a magnetic field? What is mineralogy and what does a mineralogist do? How are mountains formed? Is aluminum harder than gold?" I did the best that I could to answer her questions. I did not know if aluminum was harder than gold. I missed my internet connection and the ability to find out instantaneously. I told Amara that most likely gold was harder, but I wasn't 100% sure. When I came home to Chicago, I looked up if aluminum is harder than gold. It turns out that aluminum is slightly harder than gold. It depends on the purity and the age of both metals (So, in a way yes and in a way no). Even in just spending a few short days with Amara, it was evident that she was desperately thirsting for knowledge, always hoping to learn something.

A couple days passed and I noticed that Amara was not at the orphanage. I asked one of the women caregivers of the children where she was, and she told me that Amara had to go to the hospital (the children at the home called the women who took care of them "Sisters" and they called volunteers like me, "Auntie"). I made a worried look on my face. Sister Tawiah told me that it was nothing to worry about, she said that this was routine. Many of the children would go to the hospital for days at a time and then come home, so I didn't think much of the situation and continued on with my volunteer work in Ghana. About two weeks into volunteering, I asked the sisters when Amara would return. They told me soon. I was anxious to see her yet again. I was inspired by this fourteen year old that would do all that she could to learn anything from anyone. Many students in well-funded U.S. schools take for granted the amalgamation of resources that are within their schools. The students have access to state of the art textbooks and innovative technology, and many go through their school days and never bother to ask questions. Amara had an outdated book on a subject that would not interest most and she was determined to take advantage of the volunteer there and ask all that she could. Sadly for her, I was her Geology expert, but her inquiry about Geology, and her determination to learn made an impression on me.

When I was on my way to the airport at the end of my volunteer trip, the founder and director of the orphanage, Edem shared with me that Amara had died at the hospital. My face cringed. It was heartbreaking to hear this. I asked Edem why; he explained, "Because the medicines ran out." He continued, "If there had been donations, Amara could have received her medicines. She passed away because she didn't get the medicines" (The adults I interacted with in Ghana always referred to medicine as "medicines").[2] As I stood there with over 200 Ghana cedis in my pocket, I felt so guilty. Had Amara had that money, she could have received her medicine and she may still be living.

There was no way for me to know the situation at the time because no one had explained it to me, but I felt a profound sense of guilt. Edem revealed that the children at the orphanage didn't know yet and he would have to break this news to them, that one of their fellow brothers and sisters died. The kindness and gentleness in Amara's face was not something that I would or could ever forget. I could not forget her quizzically asking me those geology questions. Edem saying to me, "because the medicines ran out" permeates through my mind what seems like at all times. For months after the conversation, that conversation with Edem would run through my mind. "Because the medicines ran out," "Because the medicines ran out," "Because the medicines ran out," I just kept thinking, "what could we do to change this? How can we get the medicine not to run out?"

Months later when I was back in Chicago, I interviewed a WWII vet, Fred, who served in the Pacific and after his tenure in the army; he had a successful career as a geophysicist.[3] After our interview finished, I went onto my next interview. As I was walking down the hall to exit the retirement village after I finished my second interview, there sat Fred waiting for me. "I wanted to give you this." He handed me a copy of *The Leading Edge*, a publication from the Society of Exploration Geophysicists (the international society of applied geophysics). I smiled and thanked Fred. I watched him slowly walk back to his room as he took one step at a time and pushed his walker forward with each step. I stood there frozen in the middle of the hallway. My interview with Fred introduced me to a geophysicist, which reminded me of Amara and the geology textbook. Fred's story combined with Amara's struck a chord that seemed to go through the center of my heart. In that moment, I was touched by Fred's story and his service for the United States in World War II and also by all that he did in his life after serving in the war in the field of Geophysics. Geophysicists determine geology by studying electromagnetic waves, seismic waves and other methods that cannot be seen directly. Conjointly, I was also moved in that moment in the retirement community because I thought of Amara. I flipped through *The Leading Edge* and right away I saw the word, aluminum, reminding me of one of Amara's questions.

But ... You Knew This

"In the middle of the journey of life I found myself in a forest so dark that I could not tell where the straight path lay."

—Dante Alighieri, *Inferno*

It's not like I don't know that situations like this exist in Africa. I am aware that children die from AIDS. I mean I was completing "service" there for a reason. As I already mentioned, I asked the monk whom I met on the plane what I could do to "help" these people I was going to volunteer to help. In the past year, my idea of how to best help someone has evolved in all respects since I sat on that plane impressed by the diminutive man wearing a robe, sitting next to me who was unraveling tails about his missionary work. As the monk shared with me, the people know what they need, not me. I would never help anyone if I thought that they needed me to help them. Although I did not understand it all in that moment, the monk's words and stories about his life's work stayed with me. Initially I thought people like the monk go to places far away from their homes to "help" people, but the more stories that I read about the AIDS epidemic, charities, developing countries, and foreign aid, I now understand that this "mentality," although perhaps intentions are in the right place, this type of ideology makes it seem as if someone is "saving" someone else. This will never change the world. People being able to fulfill their own potential will make the world a better place. Charities, NGO's, governments, and nonprofit organizations that can assist people in creating systems able to do that will ultimately transform destitution into a better world. Anyway, more on how to effectively make a difference in this world in the coming pages. My point, however, is that I must have been aware that misery exists if I was going somewhere to complete "service" in the first place.

It's not as if the world's misery is a secret to most of us in the population. If this is the case, why isn't more done to end it? Misery exists. We all know it, yet ... for much of the population, we dismiss it. Individuals dismiss human suffering that happens throughout the world either because they are not fully aware (even if they have heard statistics) of what a certain misery entails or people dismiss it because they believe that it is not their responsibility or problem to deal with misery. In *I Am Because We Are*, Dr. Jeffrey D. Sachs, the special adviser to United Nations Secretary-General Ban Ki-moon on the Millennium Development Goals, gives the example of a woman who is poor and dying of something that we know is treatable, but she does not have money. He urges, "We have to say that humans actually deserve this as a right. Disease coming from ecology causes poverty, poverty causes disease. It goes around in a vicious circle." Dr. Sachs' words made so much sense to me as I pictured Amara. I thought, yes, it is a human right to be treated when an illness is treatable. The fact of the matter about Amara's disease is that with the proper medication, it would have been treated and she did not need to die. Perhaps a bit of a stretch on the analogy, but, if a child with dyslexia is diagnosed early enough; the interventions can help the child to succeed in school. If the child with dyslexia does not get interventions, he/she will most likely struggle through school. With the proper medication no child has to die from AIDS, the more advanced stage of HIV infection. This is the truth. This is the part about it that constantly haunts me. If Amara would have had medication, she would be living. There is not yet a cure for HIV/AIDS. However with the medications available today, it is possible to have a normal lifespan with little or minimal interruption in quality of life. There are ways to help people stay healthy and live longer.[4]

My life in Chicago is surrounded by abundance, a plethora of materialistic things, stuff and more stuff. The refrigerator is constantly stocked with food. So stocked in fact that many weeks food gets thrown out. I have closets upon closets of clothes and shoes. I have enough books that I could literally start a library. I have multiple gym memberships. In order to ensure that I eat the best quality foods, I am fortune enough to shop at places like *Trader Joe's* and *Whole Foods*. I frequent weddings to what seems like is a monthly affair. Comparing my life in Chicago to a dirt floor covered with little pebble stones, no electricity or running water was an eye opening experience in itself for me. Before Amara's passing away, I never really reflected on all that I had because everyone around me had the same possessions or people in my reality had even more than I had. Amara's story affected me eminently because I knew if she would have had the resources to get medication, she would still be living.

Again, it's not like my story about an orphan in Africa dying due to lack of medicine is a reality that you weren't aware of. As did I, you know that these disheartening situations exist. You've heard it again and again. You know as did I that Africa is the place in the world that is hit hardest by the AIDS epidemic. It's not like we do not know that there is a disparity between life in America and life in underdeveloped nations, yet without meeting someone directly affected by one of these miseries, I never would have attained the "perspective" that I did. As a student in a social studies classroom, you read and jot down statistics in your notebook. The numbers you wrote in your notebook that often represent people dying, begin to fade away from your memories after your test. Looking back to my days as a student, I remember students reflecting more upon their test score than the millions of people who lost their lives in one of the world wars. One's GPA is often the reflection point not the millions of lives lost to preserve freedom and order in the world during WWII. After the test is completed, no one is thinking about how this generation sacrificed on the front lines of battle and back home in the factories that produced what was needed to wage war. The units about World War One and World War Two are completed in History class, but do students legitimately comprehend the millions of casualties that happened during these wars? When you are watching a documentary, you learn statistics that make your mouth drop. These figures sound horrific and you feel bad when you become aware of these grave realities, but then class or the documentary ends and you go on and go about your normal life.

From the class in school or the documentary, you learn and then think to yourself that it's unjust that 9 million children under age 5 die every year. You cannot comprehend that more than 1,000,000 children worldwide will become victims of child trafficking this year.[5] In some parts of the world, right this very minute, women are locked in brothels and teenage girls with fistulas can be found curled up on the floor of isolated huts.[6] It's hard to understand why 25,000 people die every day of hunger-related causes.[7] It's not fair that 1.2 million children in Sub-Saharan Africa alone die of AIDS every year.[8] How can 34 million people worldwide be living with HIV and almost 70% of them live in sub-Saharan Africa?[9] To continue with some of the statistics related to AIDS in Africa, it is estimated that 28.5 million people are infected with HIV in sub-Saharan Africa, and 11 million African children are thought to have been orphaned by AIDS. At the end of 2001, it was estimated that only 30,000 of the 28.5 million people living with HIV / AIDS in Africa had access to antiretroviral drugs.[10]

In June 2000, at the thirteenth International AIDS Conference, held in Durban, South Africa, Dr. Piot maintained it would take $3 billion per year to take basic measures to deal with AIDS in Africa and tens of billions in additional yearly funds to provide Africa with the standard drugs used to combat the diseases in developed nations. Merely $300 million was spent annually on AIDS in Africa in 2001.[11] In the amount of time that it takes you to read one page of this book, a child will die. AIDS kills one child every minute.[12]

Documentary after documentary, the news every evening, book after book, many sources reveal the miseries that scads of people in this world deal with each day. No one likes to hear these atrocious things and we all feel god-awful when we do. We just think that there's nothing that we can do to change those disconsolate, bitter, irremediable things that plague some parts of the world. We think: what could we possibly do to help someone across the world? After all, we ourselves have a salary that at times it seems hard enough to even support our own family. How could we possibly even begin to help those 9 million children under age 5 who die every year? What could *we* (one person in this huge world) ever do to help an enormous and wretched situation such as that? In *More Than Good Intentions*, Dean Karlan and Jacob Appel express that people feel discouraged when it comes to wanting to help a large scale global problem such as poverty, because they feel like there isn't anything that they can do anyway. Dean Karlan and Jacob Appel describe an experiment where two fliers were passed out asking people to help with hunger issues to demonstrate people's thinking about large scale global issues. One flier spoke about how food shortages in Malawi are affecting more than 3 million children.[13] The other flier explained that Rokia, a 7 year old girl from Mali, Africa is poor and she faces a threat of severe hunger or even starvation. The first flier raised an average of $1.16 from each student. The second flier raised $2.83 from each student. With the second flier, the plight of millions became the plight of one. Karlan and Appel's explanation clarifies that many people feel like the fight against poverty is too overwhelming. They describe that the students' reaction is typical of how most of us feel when we are confronted with problems like poverty. "We feel as if our contribution would be a drop in the bucket, and the bucket probably leaks."[14] Misery undeniably exists in our world. Most of us are aware that it exists. Is there anything that an ordinary person just trying to make it by can actually do to change some of the misery that exists in the world?

"Things which matter most must never be at the mercy of things which matter least."
—Johann Wolfgang von Goethe

How my trip to Kpando, Ghana motivated me to start InterviewGirl.com

"Inevitably, an individual is measured by his or her largest concerns."
—from *Human Options*, Norman Cousins

My trip to Kpando, Ghana changed the type of thinking emblematic in the experiment where the two fliers were passed out and asked people to help with hunger issues. I went from thinking, "what can I really do to help, anyway?" to "I cannot not help." What brought about this change in my mentality? The people whom I met in Ghana who became my friends were the catalyst that started this project: InterviewGirl.com. A statistic is radically altered when a face and a name match that statistic. Human contact and relationships are the cornerstone of society and cannot be replaced. There is new interesting research in the field of psychology on happiness. From Daniel Gilbert to Malcolm Gladwell to Sonja Lyubomirsky to Daniel Pink to Martin Seligman to Jonathan Haidt, some interesting books have been written on the science and practice of happiness. Of course, happiness was written about long before modern psychology. Epicurus, Aristotle, Cicero, St. Thomas Aquinas, William James, and the Dalai Lama are all contributors to those works that we have in the history of happiness. From the studies of contemporary psychologists and scientists to the ancient philosophers listed above, having strong social bonds is probably the most meaningful contributor to happiness. Martin Seligman makes known that "of the 24 character strengths, those that best predict life satisfaction are the interpersonal ones."[15] In Epicurus', *A Guide To Happiness*, he states, "Of all the means to insure happiness throughout the whole life, by far the most important is the acquisition of friends."[16] These classic works about happiness demonstrate that it is the quality of our relationships that make us happy or not.

In putting together one of InterviewGirl.com's compilations, I had a phone interview with Jean Vanier. Vanier is the founder of the *L'Arche* communities. Vanier informed me about how interpersonal relationships are paramount in humans' lives. *L'Arche* works closely with people who have an intellectual disability. This community was created so that each person can play their full role in society. In *The Miracle, the Message, the Story: Jean Vanier and L'Arche*, Kathryn Spink sets forth that *L'Arche* communities bear witness to the reality that persons with intellectual disabilities possess inherent qualities of welcome, wonderment, spirituality and friendship. The communities make explicit the dignity of every human being by building inclusive communities of faith and friendship where people with and without intellectual disabilities share life together. *L'Arche* exists to strengthen local communities, welcome more people into people's lives and work, engage in advocacy on behalf of those often on the margins of society, and to raise awareness of the gifts of persons with intellectual disabilities.[17] The late Pope John Paul II called *L'Arche*, "a providential seed of the civilization of love, *L'Arche* is a sign of hope in a divided world." In Vanier's provocative work, *Becoming Human*, he shares his profoundly human vision for creating a common good that radically changes our communities, our relationships, and ourselves. He proposes that by opening ourselves to outsiders, those that we perceive as weak, different, or inferior, we can achieve pure personal and societal freedom. In writing about what people need, Vanier maintains,

> "There is something intolerable about pain and suffering when we cannot cure the person. No one wants to be with people in pain, unless they can do something to alleviate the pain ...When all is said and done, in *L'Arche* there are no cures. What people need when all the therapy has been tried, is a friend who is faithful, who stands by them, a loving milieu where they are respected as full human beings."[18]

The story about Jean Vanier and the founding of *L'Arche* communities is another example of the importance of relationships in humans' lives. Interpersonal relationships between individuals are nonpareil.

> "The secret of *L'Arche* is relationship: meeting people, not through the filters of certitudes, ideologies, idealism or judgments, but heart to heart; listening to people with their pain, their joy, their hope, their history, listening to their heart beats."
> —Jean Vanier, *L'Arche* founder

Statistics about HIV / AIDS, I had heard, but in creating bonds and relationships with the children at the Children's Home, those discouraging statistics became intolerable. They had to be changed. Take Bill Gates, for example, he knew of the downcast situations in Africa, but when he and his wife, Melinda began traveling there, it was then that they truly began to understand the misery there. In his blog entry, *The Power of Catalytic Philanthropy* from September 2012, Bill Gates writes,

> "But when my wife Melinda and I made our first trip to Africa in 1993, it was really our first encounter

with deep poverty and it had a profound impact on us. Not long after we returned, we read that millions of poor children on that continent were dying every year from diseases that, essentially, nobody dies from in this country: measles, malaria, hepatitis B, yellow fever. Rotavirus, a disease I had never even heard of, was killing half a million kids each year – none of them in the United States. We assumed that if millions of children were dying, there would be massive worldwide effort to save them. But we were wrong."[19]

It was after that trip to Africa that the perspective of Bill Gates changed. Since 1993, the Gates Foundation has focused on improving people's health and giving them the chance to lift themselves out of hunger and poverty in developing countries. Although I apprehended statistics about the AIDS epidemic, I heard what was happening in the news, I took current events courses about global issues in college and I saw *Invisible Children*; it was while I volunteered in Ghana, Africa this past summer that I was introduced to some stories that legitimately had a transformative effect upon my life, because I met people and learned their stories. When I read "9 million children under age 5 die every year," the 20 children that I spent a month with at the Children's Home pop into my mind and suddenly the world needs to be changed because I CANNOT imagine 9 million Taycutays, (one of the boys at the children's home) dying before they reach age five. When I see "1.2 million children in Sub-Saharan Africa die of AIDS every year," the images of millions of young, inquisitive Amaras fill my mind. I am determined that statistic cannot remain the same. Such a misery in our world needs to be erased, or at least, we need to work on it becoming less of a misery. I was now on a quest to discover how to make sure someone like Amara could get medication.

Thinking is Not Driven by Answers ... But by Questions

"Judge a person by their questions, rather than their answers."

—Voltaire

Forlorn as it may be, many of us know that the miserable actualities discussed above exist. We understand that AIDS and human trafficking are problems in Africa and problems in this modern world, in general. We cringe when we hear these heart wrenching stories on a dateline special or some other documentary, but then we go on and go about our normal lives. We figure what is my $10 donation going to do anyway? I was that way too, but then I went there and I saw misery and now I have to do something about it. As you very well know from what you have read up to this point, the "there" I am speaking of, is Africa, but I would like to expand that "there" to mean any place on this Earth where a community within a country is developing and an individual does not have access to means that are necessary for basic survival. I can no longer just stand by. What poverty means took on a new meaning for me. When I wrote to the director of the Children's Home months after I was home, I asked him to fill me in on the children's backgrounds. These questions led to me realizing how many of the orphans that I spent time with that summer were HIV positive. Children who were playfully playing with their peers who seemed healthy were in fact chronically ill—HIV positive. Although in the weeks that I spent with them, you couldn't physically see their sickness, it was there and if it wasn't treated, eventually it would kill them. These are realities that I learned before I even did any major research from scholarly articles, academic journals, and books. Not long after I wrote to the director and asked him to share with me the biographies of the children there (to tell me the stories of why the kids were in the home), I began to research in earnest the AIDS epidemic in Africa, human trafficking around the world, and world poverty.

As my research unfolded, I stumbled upon even more inconsolable and saddening statistics. A door had been opened. I could not go back. I found a huge problem. It was not just from soaking up the statistics regarding these global issues, but my impetus to do something about all of this really came from the umpteen stories that I read, heard, and learned about all the people affected by these miseries. The problem was that all these people in our world were living in misery. Peter Singer, a professor of bioethics at the University of Melbourne and author of *Practical Ethics,* tells a story about how a child was killed in China because he was ran over by a truck and people just walked past the child on the street. Singer poses the question, asking what you would do if you saw a child laying in the street who was just ran over by a truck? Then he poses another question,

> "Nineteen thousand children are dying every day. Does it really matter that we're not walking past them in the street? Does it really matter that they're far away? I don't think it does make a morally relevant difference."[20]

Singer raises a brilliant question; just because we do not see these miseries taking place before our very own eyes does not mean that they do not exist. They are still happening even if we do not see them happening. A common thread throughout this book is that if you study any human being in history who accomplished something that his/her peers at the time believed was impossible, that person started with asking a clear question. Had no questions been asked by those who laid the foundation for a field or made a discovery—the field/ discovery would never have been developed in the first place. Anything in this world that at one time seemed unimaginable to surmount or to achieve from peers of the doer in the place and time that a new discovery was made, was something that started with an individual asking the correct questions. When you break it down, when you look back, you discover that what people consider to be someone's extraordinary feat within History began with the individual asking precise questions. As Albert Einstein understood,

> "The mere formulation of a problem is far more often essential than its solution, which may be merely a matter of mathematical or experimental skill. To raise new questions, new possibilities, to regard old problems from a new angle requires creative imagination and marks real advances in science."[21]

Historians discovered that Charles Darwin's notebooks were filled with questions. In a letter from Charles Darwin to C. Lyell in *The life and letters of Charles Darwin*, Darwin writes, "Looking back, I think it was more difficult to see what the problems were than to solve them."[22] G.K. Chesterton observed, "It isn't that they can't see the solution. It is that they can't see the problem." In *Borrowing Brilliance*, David Murray imparts, "A problem is the foundation of a creative idea. In other words, a creative idea is built upon the problem one is trying to solve."[23] It's the starting point. Murray describes, "Every subject presents a series of interrelated problems, often creating a highly complex hierarchy of problems and solutions. It's this hierarchy that forms the foundation you build upon."[24] Understanding that there are many problems woven together and in order to alleviate one problem, you must address another problem is how you understand the scope of your problem. A person begins to solve these problems Murray discusses as he/she raises intense questions. Michael Novak, a professor from Ave Maria University, points to a human's ability to question as one of his/her greatest capabilities. Novak informed,

> "Alert human beings ask an endless stream of questions: Why are conscious beings such as we on this earth, under this great sky, with the wind on our faces? What ought we to do? What ought we to hope for? Our endless drive to ask questions is the clearest sign in our own nature that we are driven by the infinite.

We grow tired of anything less than the infinite, as we seek higher and deeper. There is also the capacity in us to love infinitely. To love purely. To love un-self-centeredly. Another sign of the divine in us."[25]

Michael Novak, Albert Einstein, Charles Darwin, G.K. Chesterton, and David Murray all affirm the value of questions.

I countlessly admire economist, Esther Duflo's work because she takes economics out of the lab and into the field to discover the causes of poverty and means to eradicate it.[26] The *Jameel Poverty Action Lab* is a network that evaluates social programs. It's concerned less with wide-ranging policy than with specific questions. In this lab that Duflo founded, randomized trials offer new insights toward creating global equity and prosperity. Duflo's work is not just economics, but it is activism. In a talk Duflo delivered at the highly acclaimed *TED* conference, she explains,

"It's not the middle ages anymore. It's the 21st century. In the 20th century, randomized controlled trials have revolutionized medicine by allowing us to distinguish between drugs that work and drugs that don't work. You can do the same randomized controlled trials for social policy. You can put social innovation to the same rigorous scientific tests that we do for drugs. In this way, you can take the guess work out of social policy so you can know what works and what doesn't work and why."[27]

In looking at specific questions like: *If school kids could get their uniforms for free, would attendance go up?* and *what's an effective way to reward mothers for immunizing their babies?*, the *Jameel Poverty Action Lab* is able to look at which development efforts help and which hurt. They do this by testing solutions with randomized trials.[28] The strides that the *Jameel Poverty Action Lab* has made against poverty began with the members of the lab asking questions and from the solutions that they found, they then asked better questions.

From the moment that I had that conversation with Edem in Africa about Amara's death, I was stirred to help play a role in eliminating the misery that the HIV virus creates in Africa (and my examination looking into this type of misery that some experience has not ceased since I've returned home). This all started with the questions: What could I do to change the misery that people suffering from HIV/ AIDS who do not have access to medication live with? What could be done to prevent a teenage girl like Amara from dying from AIDS? Strewn throughout my room and around my desk in my parent's basement (my desk in my parent's basement is what I refer to as my office) are post-it notes and note cards with questions. Every book that I read and every story that I learn about these miseries (AIDS, poverty, human trafficking) poses new questions for me. Each story that I take in becomes a part of me and inspires me to keep working at coming up with answers to these questions. I had no idea as to where to begin with answering these complex questions, but every time I learned a disheartening statistic about poverty, AIDS, or human trafficking, I pulled out a post-it note and jotted down my new question. Usually the question started with why, how, or what. I wanted to know how I could do something to help change certain miseries in the world, what I could do to help prevent certain miseries from happening, and/or why these miseries were happening? I am reminded of a part from Terry Pratchett's *Mort*:

> Albert grunted. "Do you know what happens to lads who ask too many questions?"
> Mort thought for a moment.
> "No," he said eventually, "what?"
> There was silence.
> Then Albert straightened up and said, "Damned if I know. Probably they get answers, and serve 'em right."[29]

Questions were everywhere throughout my room, office and car. I was now frantic to find some meaningful answers.

How Do You See It?

I came home from Africa and I was overwhelmed. Months after the experience passed, the children's faces with whom I had spent time at the orphanage still constantly popped into my mind. I would see those faces and I knew that I had to do something to make sure that those children who were sick had access to medicine. I had never experienced anything quite like this. From all the research that I was doing and from the questions I was coming up with, I was inundated with a profusion of new data. I began to share statistics about poverty, AIDS, and human trafficking around the world with people whom I came into contact. I would brainstorm ideas and share them with people and I would hear, "Those problems are too big. You'll never do anything to change them. You need money to make changes like that." These responses just made me think: we can and we will. In *Poor Economics*, Abhijit Banerjee and Ester Duflo give the statistic that every year 9 million children die before their fifth birthday. They go onto to explain, "To read this kind of paragraph might want to make you forget about the whole business of world poverty because the problem seems too big, too intractable." Their goal with *Poor Economics* is to persuade people not to give up even though the problem seems so big.[30] In *Six Months in Sudan*, a humanitarian doctor shares a story about an ill infant. He shows the audience a picture of the baby. His story details how fifteen minutes after that picture was taken; the mother wrapped the body that once held her daughter, and walked slowly down the hospital road. He asks the audience, "What is this to us as humans?" He questions, "It's possible that because you were too far to feel its ripples, it doesn't matter at all. But if I can make it seem closer maybe you can sense that it does."

I wanted to make the miseries that people throughout the world experience "matter" to those who are not affected by their miseries.

I was determined to come up with a way to make money in order to create programs that would help orphans who had AIDS (and no medication) have a better chance of surviving. I did not understand why everyone believed that these problems were irreversible. Why did so many people think certain problems were too immense or beyond our scope? I have always believed that an optimistic attitude can go a long way. Why not try to see the positive side of things? In the case of the miseries that I was focusing on, why not look at the possibility of what could be done instead of how difficult it would be to achieve the plight against AIDS, poverty and human trafficking.[31] One of the things that I admire about Thomas Edison was his optimism. Even when a situation appeared catastrophic, Edison remained optimistic. Edison was 37 in 1914 and his response to a fire illustrates his optimism. Michael Gelb and Sarah Caldicott describe how Edison reacted to this fire,

> "He watched calmly while a raging fire burned six new phonograph factory buildings to the ground and gutted seven others at the West Orange complex. A small wooden shed holding inflammable motion picture film somehow had caught fire, casting flames onto the original wooden Phonograph Works building, and then spreading rapidly to several surrounding structures made of cement—a material believed to be fireproof in the early years of the twentieth century. How did Edison respond? He proclaimed that he would resume manufacturing phonograph records within ten days and began mapping out his rebuilding campaign immediately."[32]

Where others viewed disaster or failure, he saw the possibilities for new direction and improvement. Edison did not let the fire ruin his desire to manufacture phonograph records. His optimism is why he persevered until his invention of the incandescent light bulb even when he kept failing in his experiments to refine the light bulb. As I studied statistics about AIDS, I decided that it was not okay just to think those are walloping problems, there is nothing that we can do, or philanthropic entities like the Gates Foundation or UNICEF will solve problems that the spread of AIDS has created. What could I (one person in a world of 7 billion people) possibly do to help this HUGE problem? The line of thinking that there was nothing that I could do to help such an enormous problem was not all right with me. Instead of hearing the naysayers, I was inspired by Thomas Edison's optimism. In Dr. Martin Seligman's *Learned Optimism: How to Change Your Mind and Your Life*, he points to optimism not only as a means to individual well-being, but also as a powerful aid in finding your purpose and contributing to the world. Seligman's powerful words resonated with me, "Optimism is invaluable for the meaningful life. With a firm belief in a positive future you can throw yourself into the service of that which is larger than you are."

"I have not failed 10,000 times. I have not failed once. I have succeeded in proving that those 10,000 ways will not work. When I have eliminated the ways that will not work, I will find the way that will work."

—Thomas Edison

CHAPTER TWO

How InterviewGirl.com Came To Be

Development Economics

So there I was, home from Africa, with everyone around me telling me that the problems that I was worried about were "too big" for an average person like me to ever even begin to make any sort of difference. They told me that I was lucky to have been able to travel there and now it was time to return to my "normal" life. The school year started and I began teaching my classes and finishing my graduate degree in European History. On top of school (being a teacher and a student), I went to the library and began to research poverty, AIDS and human trafficking within the continent of Africa.

I came to two realizations as I learned about these miseries to a greater extent. 1.) I realized that there was a great need for relief there when it came to AIDS. As I read about AIDS in Africa, it seemed like impossible odds. People seemed to be living in the nadir of despair in certain areas. I thought that it was not fair that some people lived like this. *What can be done to change this?* and *How could anyone stem the HIV epidemic in the developing world?* were questions that guided me as I continued to complete research. The research illuminated that the HIV epidemic was happening because there were too many impoverished people, too little infrastructure, and lack of consistent medical care in remote areas. 2.) Although, I knew misery needed to be alleviated, at the same time, I learned about the altruistic efforts of many individuals and non-profit organizations. I became aware that although the HIV epidemic was a misery that existed, it had made progress in the last twenty years. There were people who had completed initiatives to conquer the problem and people who are currently working to overcome the AIDS epidemic. I wanted to know *what efforts people had taken to alleviate the AIDS crisis?* and *if these efforts were working?* Researching what efforts were working (doing good beyond intentions) turned out to be one of the most critical questions I asked.

Quickly it became my supposition that to get to the root of issues like poverty or AIDS, sending money to someone experiencing a misery would not be enough. The questions that I was asking led to a discovery about humanitarian efforts that were being made across the globe. Surely, I was not the first individual to try and decide to make a difference in someone's life—someone who was less fortunate than me. Then I began the research and it seemed like aid had been given. People were working to eliminate misery. Why then were there so many people that fell into those atrocious statistics if various aid efforts had been made? This is where the questions that I was asking took on a different dimension. Alleviating miseries like extreme poverty and AIDS in Africa was what I wanted to work toward achieving, but I yearned to figure out a way where people could sustain the alleviation of misery even when the donor was gone. Recent research illuminated that aid given directly to governments has been problematic in the past, therefore that type of aid needed to be replaced with direct investment in African nations.[33] This made sense to me, but the question was how or what could someone here in the United States do to help with direct investment in Africa? In *28 Stories of AIDS in Africa*, Stephanie Nolen explains how "trade not aid" became a mantra for international donors. She describes how an African woman who lived in Kitwe explained to her,

> "Frustrated that poverty in Africa remained unsolved by the influx of $500 billion in aid money since the late 1960's, they began to cut grants, and instead championed foreign investment and private-sector driven growth in the hope that these would have a more lasting effect. It was a good theory in the abstract but one that breaks down entirely in the face of the reality of Kitwe. Who would invest here? You have a workforce with high rates of HIV, no infrastructure, the only lucrative industry is extractive and it could leave at any moment."[34]

The woman speaking with Nolen raises a good point. Government to government aid has proved to be problematic in the last sixty years and this needed to be replaced with direct investment in African nations, but how could this be done? And what could I possibly ever do to help this cause?

There is a long standing ideological debate when it comes to the perennial issue of donor aid. Leaders in the discussion about aid, Dambisa Moyo and Jeffrey Sachs view the argument differently. Originally from Zambia, Moyo argues against the ills of aid in its current disbursement form. Sachs contends that aid is needed. In *The End of Poverty*, Jeffrey Sachs maintains, "opponents of foreign assistance today claim erroneously and tendentiously that it does more harm than good."[35] There is merit in both Sachs and Moyo's viewpoints. Moyo is right that development is the only long term solution and Sachs is right that you can't develop while people are struggling to survive. As I grasped a better understanding of what was currently being done in Africa already in regards to aid, my ideas about how a person could contribute to eliminating miseries began to form. The questions were there. From my experience in Africa and from my research, I began to formulate what I hoped were the correct questions. This was an integral first step for me. Think about it. Even with just a Google search you have the possibility to learn scads of information, but without typing in the correct question or key word, the information that you are searching to discover does not come to you. The questions were there: 1.) What could I do to help to eliminate a misery like AIDS in Africa? 2.) Was there a way to come up with a product or a system to eliminate someone's misery when a person was experiencing misery? 3.) What were others currently doing to alleviate people's misery? Were these efforts working or not working?

Hamilton and Worobey's Story

I gleaned a new perspective during my time in Africa and the experience introduced me to stories that I never encountered before while living in suburbia outside of Chicago. As I began to try and make sense of trying to help others and humanitarian efforts, I wanted to somehow contribute to making the world a place with a little less misery. I decided this plan that I had to "help eliminate someone's misery" needed to begin with my taking an initiative to help provide medication to orphans (like Amara) without access to medication. With an unfaltering optimism and mission to provide medication to the orphans, I had plans. Plans yes. My room was filled with books about AIDS, Africa, History's greatest humanitarian efforts, books on how to get good ideas, statistics about HIV and AIDS were written on sheets of paper throughout my room, and a myriad of other things that point in the direction of starting some sort of nonprofit organization. I now felt compelled to get a degree in science in a field such as: virology or epidemiology and go to Africa and complete research on HIV like I learned that Hamilton and Worobey did when I read *Tinderbox*. Hamilton and Worobey are scientists and the two went to Africa to research the birth of HIV. Before continuing with explaining "my plan," a quick side note, I'd like to share a story that I learned about Hamilton and Worobey. Their story influenced me.

William Hamilton was an Oxford University scholar who was a renowned scientist in evolutionary biology. Hamilton was interested in how mass vaccination campaigns triggered the AIDS epidemic. Hamilton co-authored *The River: A Journey to the Source of HIV and AIDS*. Michael Worobey, a young Rhodes Scholar from Canada read *The River*. Worobey was also an evolutionary biologist with an interest in the origin of HIV. Worobey had an interest in the microscopic world of genomes. Worobey's aptitude in this kind of work was what formed the basis for an unlikely partnership between the two scientists. Hamilton and Worobey went to Africa to complete research about the birth of HIV. Once in Africa, hunters helped Hamilton and Worobey to collect chimp feces. From these collections they would then be able to test the vaccine theory of HIV's birth. However, early on, Hamilton came down with a fever. It turned out that he had gotten malaria. This fever turned into a medical nightmare. Hamilton suffered a gastrointestinal hemorrhage that was most likely caused by medicine he had taken to combat the malaria. He died in March of 2000. He was sixty-three. He died just two months after he had departed on his final, thrilling intellectual journey. As Timberg and Halperin write, "The questions that drove him to Central Africa remained, for all Hamilton's brilliance, beyond his mortal reach." Worobey was devastated by the loss. Between hospital visits and the funeral, the research project was sidetracked for months. Worobey eventually continued the lab work. When it was done, Worobey discovered that none of the chimp feces that Hamilton and the hunters helped collect showed signs of SIV. The same was true for the vials of chimp urine, except for two. These samples that contained just a few drops each reacted weakly to an antibody test for HIV-1. It was the first enticing evidence of SIV in the jungle near Kisangani.[36]

Stories like these stirred me as I continued with my research. Hamilton was a brilliant scientist who asked vital questions and he went to Africa to test these questions. Developing the right questions and pursuing learning the stories and answers that come from these questions is how scientific progress is made when we boil down the complicated scientific process. In proactively pursuing this methodical process, Hamilton came down with malaria and lost his life. As I added William Hamilton, Oxford University scholar and Michael Worobey, a young Rhodes scholar to my list of people who were making a difference in what it was that we knew about AIDS, I stared at Hamilton's name on my sheet of paper and was inspired not only by his intellect as a scientist from Oxford, but by the sacrifice he suffered as he set out to answer questions that needed to be answered in order to find out about HIV's birth. Answering this question about the birth of HIV is important because as scientists learn about where the disease was born, they can better figure out ways to combat the disease. Learning somebody's story always brings us a deeper level of understanding. The samples reaction to the antibody test for HIV-1 was a question that the scientists needed to answer, but Hamilton becoming ill with malaria in his intellectual journey to understand the birth of HIV was now a story that I could not forget. It was a story about an individual's personal sacrifice as he was working to help a greater cause.

I was gaining more knowledge, more insight. The science behind HIV/AIDS was fascinating, but I needed to focus on ways to help those with the disease that did not have access to medication. I learned what efforts were happening to alleviate the AIDS crisis. I was encouraged by humanitarian efforts people were taking, but it wasn't enough to just read about these public policy issues, raise some money and then send it to one of the organizations already in place. Development economics has long been a contentious field tied up with geopolitics and ideology. There are those who believe that the poor simply need more resources and there are those who believe that top-down aid programs don't work. As I was reading, it seemed like the articles and books went on endlessly to debate ideology. It occurred to me that analyzing empirical evidence was necessary and I knew that strides had been made in the last several years doing just this. I needed to find out when it comes to aiding someone, what is it that works? I was restless. I knew that I could do something more, or more accurately maybe I couldn't, but society could. I wanted to contribute to alleviating the miseries that exist in our world (ones like Amara experienced) in more of a way than sending a donation to a nonprofit that already existed.

"Dare to reach out your hand into the darkness, to pull another hand into the light."

—Norman B. Rice

Right Place, Right Time: Whole Foods

"A journey of a thousand miles begins with a single step."

—Lao Tzu

Bringing it all back to reality, yes I was moved to help make a change in parts of the world where things did not seem fair when I came home from Africa, yet, to be honest, my lifestyle had not changed much since I left Africa and returned to my life in Chicago. I felt extremely awful about Amara's death and the disparity of experiences between kids' lives in some parts of the world and the orphans that I met in Africa. I had this unpleasant feeling, yet there I was at *Whole Foods* spending way too much money for organic tofu and bread that was flourless. I now felt guilty that I had luxuries like *Whole Foods*, yet I did not know what to do to help make life for the orphans without access to medication better. On the spot, I wanted to splurge at *Whole Foods*, yet it made my heart ache that children throughout the world do not even have access to clean water. The statistics I learned from my research into poverty were no longer something that I saw as "too overwhelming." I thought of the few people whom I had met affected by these miseries and I was beginning to imagine "millions" of stories to go along with the enormous figures that the statistics exemplified. According to AfricaAlive.org, 34 to 46 million people worldwide are infected with AIDS. In 2003 alone, more than 3 million people died. That same year, Africa whose population is only 11% of the world population, was home to 2/3 of all patients with HIV in the world. 34 to 46 million people are living with the misery of HIV. The largeness of this global problem unmistakably began to constantly infiltrate my mind. I stood there in the checkout line at *Whole Foods* holding my hormone free, all natural free range chicken that cost $11.00 for 2 pieces of chicken and all I could picture was what I learned while researching a few weeks back: 3 billion people live on less than $2.50 a day.[37] That number—3 *billion* kept popping up in my mind. Something had to be done. I just did not know what.

Contrary to the typical reaction that Dean Karlan and Jacob Appel describe in *More than Good Intentions*, I did not feel like these problems were so big that I could not make a difference anyway, quite the opposite, learning about these problems made me feel compelled to do something. The largeness of the problem did not push me away, rather because of the vast amount of people that these problems affected, I was more inspired to try and do something to make some sort of a difference. Certain circumstances that we can no longer tolerate force us to take certain actions to mitigate and/or change these circumstances. Vera Cordeiro's story validates this notion. Cordeiro founded *Associação Saúde Criança Renascer* because she could no longer stand to see so many children discharged from the hospital only to return weeks later, sick again. In her work as a physician in a public hospital in Rio de Janeiro, Cordeiro felt helpless when children who were successfully treated for an infectious disease returned to the hospital and died from the same disease after being infected again at home. Cordeiro realized that to save these children, she must help their entire family. She raffled off her own belongings to start *Associação Saúde Criança Renascer* (Brazil Child Health Association) in 1991. Despite early resistance from social workers who felt she was interfering, Cordeiro persevered, recruiting and training volunteers who, together with the staff of *Saúde Criança*, worked one-on-one with poor families to give them dignity and self-sustainability.[38] The circumstances that the sick children dealt with at the hospital in Rio DE Janeiro propelled Cordeiro to act in order to better these miserable circumstances.

As I left *Whole Foods*, I noticed a sign at the checkout that said, "Changing the world one dime at a time." It seems like every time you turn around, there is a motivational saying or sign that says, "one person at time, one dollar at a time, one trip at a time (you get the idea) …. We can change the world." Can these types of efforts genuinely pay off? Could we change the world one dime at a time? I think these types of efforts can pay off because if you think about it, the only way large scale projects are ever completed is by smaller tasks being completed one step at a time. Starting small, helping one person, hearing one person's story, and moving forward from there are integral concepts in InterviewGirl.com's mission. As a historical figure, St. Therese of Lisieux demonstrates the power of doing small things. Gretchen Rubin artfully expresses why St. Thérèse is known for her "Little Way" in the *Happiness Project*. In her quest for sanctity, she realized that it was not necessary to accomplish heroic acts or "great deeds" in order to attain holiness and to express her love of God. St. Therese of Lisieux wrote,

> "Love proves itself by deeds, so how am I to show my love? Great deeds are forbidden to me. The only way I can prove my love is by scattering flowers and these flowers are every little sacrifice, every glance and word, and the doing of the least actions for love."

What is captivating about Therese's story is that her achievement of sainthood happened through the perfection of small, ordinary acts. That was her "Little Way"—holiness achieved in a little way by little souls rather than by great deeds performed by great souls.[39]

I knew that I had to come up with a strategy (by this point, I knew that I wanted to found a nonprofit organization) where my reach would begin by my helping individuals in a small way. I thought of my graduate research and my love for stories. I wondered if I could somehow use these passions to eliminate problems like poverty, AIDS, or human trafficking. I laughed as these thoughts crossed my mind because it was such a stretch to think that my unique set of passions (love of learning and stories) had anything to do with the necessary measures needed to begin to make a dent in extensive miseries such as these. To make any sort of impact in the fight against poverty, AIDS, or human trafficking, I thought that the solutions had to lie in fields such as science and development economics where individuals focus on how antiretroviral drugs treat HIV-positive people, how HIV drugs, such as AZT and Tenofovir work, the merit in microfinance institutions, and the goals of the UN Millennium Project and the United Nations Development Program (UNDP). I was hesitant that my strong background in the humanities could be of any help, but I knew that I markedly wanted to somehow play a part in helping orphans who carried the HIV virus without access to medication to have access to medicine. It was as simple as that. I knew that whatever I came up with would help the capacious misery (AIDS orphans with no medication) in a minor way, but that small gesture whatever it would be could make an immense difference overtime. Not long after that afternoon at *Whole Foods*, my plan would transform into InterviewGirl.com and the Interview Girl Foundation. As InterviewGirl.com shares one story at time, the Interview Girl Foundation helps one orphan at a time by eliminating the misery that orphan experiences. These "little" initial steps that InterviewGirl.com and the Interview Girl Foundation take help to make the world a better place. Small acts when they all come together have the ability to make a big difference. As with any idea, a whole slew of things came together as InterviewGirl.com was created, but this concept of "one person at a time" was a central tenet of the organization's focus from the very beginning in my journey to come up with a way to help eliminate misery that people in our world experience.

"If everyone gives a thread, the poor man will have a shirt."

—Russian Proverb

Right Place, Right Time: Tampa

Sometimes in life you'll come across just what you need at a particular moment in your life. Maybe it's serendipity? Or maybe things in your brain begin to connect in a certain way because of other things that you have come into contact with prior to the present. Well I found myself back to reality, feeling guilty I had so much, wanting to help orphans without access to medication, yet the truth was I could not even afford my own rent (hence why I was living with my parents). How could I possibly give back to others? One particular weekend that fall, I was in Florida for a conference through a professional organization, the Italian American Studies Association, that I am a part of. One evening after the sessions ended, I decided to go for a walk around Tampa. I was in the center of town and a former homeless man approached me. Now I know this is any parent or boyfriend's worst nightmare for their daughter/girlfriend. She is alone in a strange state, it's late at night and a homeless person is "bothering" her. I sat there on the bench holding a bag. I had my bag of pamphlets that I gathered at the conference. I did not go drop off this bag in my hotel room before I went for my walk. Dan approached me and said, "Do you need a place to sleep tonight? Are you looking for shelter?" With a puzzled look on my face, I looked back at him and responded, "No, I don't. I am in town for a conference. I have a place to stay." Dan laughed, "Sorry I saw you here with a bag and figured you needed somewhere to stay."

Now looking back, the fact that I was not more bothered that he thought I was homeless makes me think, but what came from this situation was a conversation with Dan about his experiences of being homeless in the past. In the middle of our conversation, I pulled out my IPhone and began to record our conversation (this turned into one of my interviews). This is one example of many of how interviews that will be shared in projects produced at InterviewGirl.com came about. I was speaking with someone and in the process I heard an exceptional story. Dan was homeless for over ten years when a family helped him to get back on his feet. No longer homeless, in the spirit of "paying it forward,"[40] Dan was now helping other homeless people in Tampa. He thought that I was homeless and offered me a place to sleep. The point of bringing up this situation is because Dan's journey from homelessness to stability and his quest to help other homeless people is inspiring and because at one point in our interview, I opened up to Dan and tried to somehow put into words as crazy as I'm sure it would sound to a stranger how my time in Kpando affected me and how I now wanted to change the world. It came out something like, "I have some ideas about endeavors and undertakings that I'd like to accomplish in this world, yet I don't know where to begin." Dan listened carefully to me as if what I was rambling on about actually made some sort of sense and he poignantly told me something that I needed to hear, "begin with the end in mind and move your way forward from there." My conversation with Dan is an example of giving your time to someone who is a stranger and from that person sharing their story with you, you grow infinitely.

"Beginning with the end in mind" was the perfect guidance that I needed to hear at this exact point in InterviewGirl.com's path to realization. Dan's assistance that evening in a local Tampa park helped to shape at this point my still cloudy ideas into a more coherent indication of what I was hoping to do. I continued to have a conversation with Dan that evening in the local park and his personal story galvanized me and the advice that he gave me provoked me. We all have those stories from when we meet someone new and from that individual we hear an unbelievable story or a story we cannot forget. Well, I was filled with stories like this – stories like the one that I just heard from Dan. I wanted to be able to help alleviate miseries through sharing stories. At this point the idea (InterviewGirl.com) was not fully developed, but I knew that even though I did not have a lot of money, some sort of effort could be set up to reach people and help people: one person at a time, out of all ways, none other than that of sharing stories.

From traveling to Africa and then delving into research about some of these miseries that I was introduced to, I was presented with some startling realities and the truth is that when we look further into these statistics surrounding these miseries, it is hard to just stand by. The figures jump out. There is a colossal disparity between the lives that individuals live in certain parts of the world. There are roughly 2.2 billion children in the world and 1 billion (every second child) live in poverty. According to UNICEF, 22,000 children die each day due to poverty. And they "die quietly in some of the poorest villages on earth, far removed from the scrutiny and the conscience of the world. Being meek and weak in life makes these dying multitudes even more invisible in death."[41]About 25,000 people die every day of hunger or hunger-related causes, according to the United Nations. This is one person every three and a half seconds. Unfortunately, it is children who die most often. AIDS is now second only to the Black Death as the largest epidemic in history. AIDS kills over 1.5 million people a year, or about one person every 20 seconds. This death toll surprisingly includes a lot of children, who are often infected with the HIV virus during pregnancy or through breast-feeding. The toll is worst in Africa, where millions of parents have died, leaving children as orphans. Often teachers have died as well, leaving schools empty. Doctors and nurses have died, leaving hospitals and medical clinics with nothing. Farmers have died, leaving crops in the fields. Entire villages have been devastated.[42] I now read and see the above statistics and it is just unacceptable. The statistics themselves are dispiriting, but in the past year, I reached out to people throughout the world and asked questions about these miseries, I read case studies about individuals experiencing these miseries, I read books with stories about people who encounter these miseries and I read books about people who are working to help some of these problems. It was when I learned all these peoples' stories that their stories became part of my world. My perspective about the world shifted after I became conversant with these stories. We have all heard statistics through the years. Behind the disheartening statistics are peoples' stories. As we learn an individual's story, a demoralizing statistic becomes even more of a nightmare.

We hate to hear that atrocities like poverty, disease, hunger, or child trafficking happen in this world. I too had studied global issues before my time in Kpando and I knew how certain places in the world struggle with the AIDS epidemic, human trafficking, and poverty, but when you put a face, a name, a child you bonded with—the idea of that child being sold into slavery for human trafficking, the magnification of the awfulness of the situation is increased by 100%. You know that child. You see their potential and you think, "what if, he wasn't rescued, then what?" And you hate to think about that. Taycutay is a six year old orphan who was rescued from child trafficking whom I had the privilege of meeting because he now lives at the Children's Home that I volunteered at this past summer. The sincerity of Taycutay, the welcoming presence of him, his courtesy, his creative wit, and the beautiful honesty and playfulness of Taycutay made him someone who profoundly affected my life. He was one of those people whom I met and I would never be the same. There are millions of other children around the world who are starving, who are victims of human trafficking, who are disabled, who suffer from some sort of illness, and who are orphans with the HIV virus that will turn into AIDS if they don't get the proper medicine (antiretroviral treatment). This list of agonizing experiences that children around the world live with could enduringly continue. As I picture Taycutay and his sweet personality and academic potential, the idea of Taycutay or any child like him being a victim of child trafficking is deplorable. My unwavering determination to be an individual who plays a role in helping to eliminate these miseries that exist happened because I was privileged enough to meet someone like Taycutay and learn his story. The stories of people like Taycutay, Amara and the many other stories that my research brought into my world are what encouraged me to found InterviewGirl.com.

Moving toward a plan

"If I had eight hours to chop down a tree, I'd spend six hours sharpening my axe."

—Abraham Lincoln

I have attempted to articulate the thoughts that went through my mind in those months when I came back from Kpando. As Dr. James Orbinski perfectly rationalizes in *Triage: Dr. James Orbinski's Humanitarian Dilemma*,

"For me, one of the most important knowings I have now.... it's literally beyond words. It comes from a place of silence. There's no way in words to capture what it is. And so the challenge of writing is how do you capture what has no words? Because in the expression, you lose it."

This has been the challenge for me throughout writing this book. How do I put into words these far-reaching stories that so impacted my life? What words can possibly convey the affect meeting Amara had on me or how my friendship with Taycutay or Amara made statistics from a book about the suffering of millions become a cause where indifference is not an option in my opinion? What words could I conceivably use to justly share the beautiful stories that Jim Mallers, Frank Loos, Curtis Hale, Eda D'Amico, Guido Barini, Elaine Stapleton, or countless other individuals who lived through WWII shared with me as they told me their stories?[43] As Orbinski put it, "it's literally beyond words." The stories that I learned in Kpando encouraged the subsequent thoughts that overran my mind after the trip. My increased perspectives about peoples' realities that I became familiar with while I was in Kpando is what encouraged me to found InterviewGirl.com, but at the same time, coming up with what exactly I could actually do to help those existent miseries that I was so distraught over was an adventure and a process.

From sitting at my computer months after I returned home from Africa, I felt helpless. I felt like these problems were so big, problems with substantial overlapping causes and reasons as to why the problems were happening. What could I do to help? I didn't want to be one of those people that thought the problem was beyond help, but I worried because large organizations and countries could not seem to alleviate poverty. What could I really do? I didn't know what to do, but I knew that I had to do something. I decided that my doing a little something won't solve the large issues that upset me, but as I did a little something and other individuals and organizations also did their little something, together we could all make a difference. The more I read, the more stories I learned. It did not make me want to give up. Every new detail that I consumed added to the stories I was learning and with every passing day, the knowledge I obtained was moving how I saw these miseries farther and farther away from just being a statistic in a book. Each story I learned elucidated on the problems and made them more and more real and despite the grandness of the problems, I was motivated to try and do something.

Shortly after I came home from Florida after my conversation with the former homeless man, Dan, I was out to dinner at a Chinese restaurant with some friends. We were each given a fortune cookie at the end of dinner. I cracked open the cookie to read my fortune and it said, "The simplest answer is to act."

I smiled as I folded the fortune and tucked it into the pocket of my over $200 chic Burberry skinny jeans that I bought years ago. I bought those jeans a few years back because everyone around me bought them. A part of my worldview at the time consisted of wearing top of the line jeans, but now the idea of spending so much money on pants is of no interest to me. Fortunes from fortune cookies can seem vague. For example, for this particular fortune one might ask, answer to what? Or how should I act?, but these five simple words spoke to me. I knew exactly what I was meant to act on. My girlfriends drove me home from dinner that evening. I remember sitting in the back seat, looking out the window of my friend's new Lexus as we drove through the suburbs outside of Chicago. The moon was shining bright that evening. Boston's *More Than A Feeling* was playing off of from my friend's iPod that was connected to her dashboard and we heard the music through the car's speaker. I heard the lead singer as he sang, "it's more than a feeling ...." and the great instrumentals that followed. I gazed at the moon through the car window knowing that Taycutay and Asantuwa saw the same moon from their environment in Kpando back at the Children's Home. I felt in my heart that this surely was more than a feeling. All the questions, the overwhelming odds, not having a clue how I could make a difference in helping to provide a sick person across the world with medication, not knowing any clear cut answers, despite all of this, as my fortune from the cookie I received at the end of our meal set forth, it was necessary to act. This was the simplest answer: to act.

"Do not wait for leaders; do it alone, person to person."
—Mother Teresa

How Do You See Africa?

I don't know what is much worse than allowing children on this planet to die of vaccine preventable diseases. Millions of children die every year from these preventable diseases. This perspective, this glimpse into the knowledge about these deaths galvanizes deep inside me this need to act in order to help stop millions of children from dying like this. Seeing poverty, what it is like to live on less than $2 a day and learning stories about people like sweet Amara enlightened me that misery does exist, and the point of InterviewGirl.com and the Interview Girl Foundation is to help eliminate a person's misery, but we need to remember that as humans, we all have dignity, and the idea of someone saving someone else is not InterviewGirl.com's focus or mission.[44] The Interview Girl Foundation's mission is to play a role in creating an HIV and AIDS and poverty free society where every person is valued and treated equally before the law. The Interview Girl Foundation creates programs that help people experiencing miseries to be able to overcome these miseries. In essence, the Interview Girl Foundation is working to make sure that all humans can live a life filled with dignity.

It would be unquestionably short sighted of me to have traveled to one little community within the entire huge continent of Africa for a month and to seem as if I understand the social policies, economic policies, and cultural entities of the continent. First of all, Africa is a continent with 54 different countries comprising the continent. I know that the Interview Girl Foundation or any nonprofit organization in this world cannot have one plan to cure the problems within any continent or region on this earth. Each country and communities within those countries have diverse needs. To paint one picture of an entire continent is an injustice to the people who live within the continent. Much of the literature pertaining to Africa incites how Americans portraying the entire continent in one particular light is problematic.

I read a blog that spoke of the continent of Africa so generally as many books do and perhaps as even this book is, but I recognize the fact that we need to acknowledge the diversity of stories within Africa and we cannot represent a continent with one story. This particular blog introduced Africa along the lines of,

"In most parts of Africa, the citizens are hungry, they hardly get 3 square meal a day, they don't have light and water, then their president comes in a 9 motorcade convoy with $30,000 cars and they cheer and dance their hunger away, there are no ambulances, when there's an accident the immediate people around cut branches of trees and put it on the dead human beings."

Yes, there may be truth in those statements, but it does not encompass the whole continent. There are stories where people do not experience hunger, as well. No blanket statement can ever represent an entire continent of people. The Interview Girl Foundation was created to erase miseries that exist in the world. There is not one blanket plan or solution in dealing with these miseries. Micro-finance, training health care professionals, lessening the price of antiretroviral drugs to treat HIV infection, the role of small businesses in development and poverty alleviation, school-based deworming initiatives, providing chlorine dispensers for safe water, and/or changing education policies are all solutions when dealing with poverty and disease. There is not just one solution. Various projects will be created within the Interview Girl Foundation in order to help alleviate specific miseries.

As humans we tend to create certain images about certain places in our minds. We must realize that it is not healthy to "stereotype" any specific geographical place as being a certain way. I think this because as I told people I was going to "volunteer" in Africa, people said off putting things to me like, "What is you going to Africa and volunteering with an orphan kid going to do to change the backwardness of the continent of Africa?" "Why would you go there? It's stupid. You are putting yourself in a dangerous situation," and many other things along these lines. Those conversations struck me at the nerve for two reasons. First of all, as I said to assume all of Africa is in a state of anarchy and despair is very short sighted of us as Global citizens. For example, when I was told that it was stupid to go "there," it was necessary for me to enlighten my companions that Ghana was one of the most stable countries in Africa with its new democracy and successful democratic elections from 2008. One of the reasons that I was so affected by this trip to Africa is because I knew Ghana was stable and one of Africa's development success stories, yet I still witnessed poverty and difficulties such as Amara dying because she did not have medicine. Secondly, yes, there is misery in some parts of Africa and to assume that I, as one person could not ever make a difference in changing those miseries was irritating, as well. One of my all-time favorite quotes from Mother Teresa is, "We cannot do great things only small things with great love." If we all had that attitude that the problems in Africa or problems anywhere in the world for that matter are too great and we can't do anything, then no progress would ever be made. If we all have the attitude that anyone who has an illness is doomed, no one would ever recover. If we believe that people are stuck in certain circumstances, well then, they will remain there. We must have faith, hope, and persevere. We must spread love. Progress can be made. Even by one person doing something small, he/she can make a difference and help other people.

Maybe my initial volunteer trip to Africa was not going to make major changes in any African's life as those around me warned me before I left to volunteer, but what is done through InterviewGirl.com and the Interview Girl Foundation can make a major difference in the lives of those suffering with AIDS in Africa. The Interview Girl Foundation can make a difference in the world in which we live because the point of our projects is to help eliminate different miseries. My trip to Ghana had an indelible mark on me. It provided me with an experience of a lifetime because I gained a new perspective. I came home from Africa and I was motivated to somehow make a difference by helping to eliminate a misery that someone experiences. As you most likely have, I too had heard the statistics about some of the issues that are problematic in Africa. I knew that some of the people there were living in misery, but seeing it and experiencing it made me want to make Mother Teresa's words a reality. To be honest, maybe I went to Africa to see the world, to check another place off my "to travel to" list. Why did I volunteer there? Did I really want to volunteer? Well regardless, I came back changed. I learned a reality that was different than mine and I couldn't go back. Maybe I did go there to see more of the world, and I achieved just that. I saw a world that was different from my world and my perspective would never be the same.

Dr. James Orbinski perfectly articulates, "What I've experienced is that I can't know the future. I can't know if anything that I do will change what happens tomorrow. I can't know with certainty, but what I do know is if I do nothing, nothing will change."[45] I can no longer just read disheartening statistics like the ones explained in the beginning of this book. Something has to be done. Many people see the type of problems like the spreading of the HIV virus, poverty, or child trafficking in Africa as too overwhelming because they are massive in scale. We feel that our little efforts will not make a difference anyway. Many people think, "That is just how it is." The little thing that I can do won't change those huge injustices. Or they think that enough other people will contribute to helping the problem that they do not have to. N. Jambunathan Iyer from India shares a story about the problem with everyone assuming that everyone else will step up and help in the *Motivate Us* blog and website,

> "Once there was a king who told some of his workers to dig a pond. Once the pond was dug, the king made an announcement to his people saying that one person from each household has to bring a glass of milk during the night and pour it into the pond. So, the pond should be full of milk by the morning. After receiving the order, everyone went home. One man prepared to take the milk during the night. He thought that since everyone will bring milk, he could just hide a glass of water and pour that inside the pond. Because it will be

dark at night, no one will notice. So he quickly went and poured the water in the pond and came back. In the morning, the king came to visit the pond and to his surprise the pond was only filled with water! What happened is that everyone was thinking like the other man that "I don't have to put the milk, someone else will do it."[46]

Each of us needs to act. We cannot assume that everyone else will. Dave Morley explains why *Doctors Without Borders* does what it does, "We would like to see a more just world, but we have to focus on what we can do. And what we can do is something simple, small and profound." Dan Bortolotti writes about Morley and his work through *MSF*. Bortolotti delineates Morley's work as a humanitarian doctor, "That's more than a drop in the ocean; it's a lifeboat. It may not stop the ship from going down, but it saves lives and, more important, it promises hope."[47] If InterviewGirl. com does nothing else other than spread the message that the little things you do can and will make a big difference in this world, I will consider this idea to be a success.

From Want to Do

"Don't Make Excuses, Make Changes"

—Tony Gaskin

As Interview Girl always does, let's look back throughout human history and garner what we can from those lessons where history has witnessed wrongs being undone. The movements against slavery, colonialism, and racism all have commonalities. To start, as Jeffrey Sachs enlightens,

"They looked quixotic, perhaps even hopeless at the start, as calls to the richest and most powerful in the world to extend justice for the poorest and most helpless. They required a mix of political action, real politics, and mass education to succeed. They took decades to bring to fruition; perseverance was key."[48]

To the people living during the time of slavery, abolition seemed like a cause that idealists hoped for, but most believed that it would never actually come to fruition. Abolition of the slave trade seemed noble and good, but too far out of reach. However, from what started with the actions of a few individuals: William Wilberforce and Thomas Clarkson, in time, society saw and now we as history students study about the abolition of the slave trade and of slavery itself in European colonies. To the individuals living in the 1800's, ending slavery seemed impractical, but it eventually happened because individuals took actions.

"Act as if what you do makes a difference. It does."
—William James

Every time I look at my Facebook, it motivates me more than you can imagine. You most likely are thinking, "Why is that?" I read an article in *Upfront* magazine about Facebook and I had a vision for InterviewGirl.com. Back in 2005, Facebook was a new Internet start-up. A young graffiti artist named David Choe was hired by Facebook to paint murals on the walls of its California offices. As a payment, Facebook offered Choe either $60,000 in cash or company stock, then worth about the same amount. Choe chose the stock. It was a smart decision. Choe's shares were expected to be worth about $200 million when Facebook stock began trading publicly. In February of 2012, Facebook announced that it would go public in the spring by offering $5 billion worth of stock for sale to the general public. When Google went public, its stock opened at $85 and now trades at about $600. David Choe made an even better investment than the Google scenario explained above. "This is like a godlike amount of money," Choe told ABC News, "where I could actually change the world." Choe's words resonated with me. What if I could somehow make some "real" money and start a movement. I once heard that the only way to change the world is to change your world. This past summer, I stepped out of my comfort zone and I went to Africa. For someone who is not used to living without modern American amenities, it was difficult to live without running water and electricity while in Africa, but from this experience came a passion, a mission, an idea and a desire to make a change for those that did not experience the luxuries that I did. It takes money to make real changes in this world and I believe that through selling stories, I can help to make some real changes in two ways. The stories will positively affect those who read them because knowledge and know-how is a powerful gift and the revenues generated from the stories can make real changes to eliminate a person's misery within this world. I just need YOU to share your stories with InterviewGirl.com and once you do: one story at a time, we'll begin to change the world.

CHAPTER THREE

What is InterviewGirl.com?

What is this project, InterviewGirl.com, anyway?

At InterviewGirl.com, we collect stories and then share those stories with the world. There are two ways that InterviewGirl.com serves individuals through using stories. The first way that InterviewGirl.com helps people is by using profits that come from InterviewGirl.com's projects to make a difference in the lives of others (eliminate misery), and the other way InterviewGirl.com serves people is by sharing remarkable stories and valuable content and advice with the public through our various projects and compilations. You never know whose life a story can touch. The *content of the stories* will help people and the *profits from the stories* will help people.

At InterviewGirl.com, we hear your story, document it, compile it within one of our compilations or other projects and then projects are created featuring peoples' stories (compilations of stories) with the goal of making a profit from the stories, so that we can help those in this world living in misery. The profits from the compilations of stories and projects that are produced at InterviewGirl.com go toward those in this world who experience some type of misfortune. The profits from undertakings completed at InterviewGirl.com are given to the Interview Girl Foundation, which is a nonprofit organization that is a part of InterviewGirl. com. The Interview Girl Foundation creates specific ventures to erase miseries that exist in the world. For example, *Operation A²* is a project through the Interview Girl Foundation that was specifically created to erase the misery that orphans with HIV/AIDS without access to medication experience. As InterviewGirl. com expands, a multitude of other projects will be created and each one can target a different cause in order to help alleviate miseries throughout the world.

InterviewGirl.com is a social media platform where people can share stories, advice, tips, and information. The internet and Social Media have changed the world. How we receive information has been altered due to these platforms. Pam Hendricks informs in the *Make Money Launch* webinar (February 2012) that we consume an equivalent of 73 newspapers per person per day. Day in and day out, people share ideas via the internet with one another. Individuals share pictures on *Pinterest*, people post recipes on *Recipes.com* and other nutrition/cooking websites, *Twitter* feeds are constantly blasted, people post comments on their favorite *Facebook* pages, people post pictures to *Instagram*, people upload videos to *Vine*, *YouTube*, and *Instagram,* and this list could most definitely continue.

Social Media has altered how we communicate. In an article, *What's Next? Social media is changing the way we communicate,* Erica Perdue elucidates that "there's no doubt that social media sites have changed the way we communicate. "Friending" and "following" now are verbs commonly used in the English language, and we post pictures on our profile walls instead of the walls in our homes."[48] Social media platforms and how we ingest information is continually changing. Staying abreast with these changes is important for InterviewGirl.com. To effectively disseminate meaningful stories into the world, we need to understand how the public is consuming stories. In July of 2013, *Fortune* magazine's cover story was: "How YouTube Changes Everything." Miguel

Helft spoke about how *YouTube* grew 50 percent in 2013 and how it continues to make money and change the media world. Changes such as *YouTube's* popularity are important for InterviewGirl.com because we must share stories with the public in a way in which the public wants to receive stories.

InterviewGirl.com was created to get people to share their stories. These stories can be shared through numerous different mediums. Typing out a story is only one way out of various choices for people to share their stories on InterviewGirl.com. With how easy communication overseas has become and with how easily individuals can upload videos, InterviewGirl.com will be able to hear peoples' stories in a variety of ways. InterviewGirl.com is a place to share stories, messages, and ideas because as these stories are disseminated out into the world, we'll make the world a better place.

Other projects besides compilations of stories are completed at InterviewGirl.com, but compilations are our biggest focus. Other projects that InterviewGirl.com completes include putting together exhaustive research lists of books, articles, websites, and resources for you in various categories in order to help you to achieve what it is that you hope to achieve. Some of our compilations will feature hundreds of web sites, books, resources, and other sources about a certain topic, so that you will have access to the most current information on a particular topic all together in one book or all together via a digital platform. As you have this information all curated together in one spot, it will allow you to have a better grasp on the subject from the vast knowledge compiled together for you.

InterviewGirl.com also sponsors speakers as well as events and panels of select individuals to give speeches and complete interviews. The proceeds from these events are also donated to various causes that the Interview Girl Foundation is helping just as the proceeds from the compilations are donated to these causes. In a project completed at InterviewGirl.com, a distinct topic will be discussed within the project and the project shares diverse information about the topic. The information shared in the InterviewGirl.com project is garnered from interviews with individuals, interviews with various organizations, and investigating a wide array of other resources.

Mission of InterviewGirl.com

The mission of InterviewGirl.com is: to make the world a better place through sharing stories. Although it is a simplistic analogy, to understand InterviewGirl.com's mission better, picture slicing a birthday cake. After you slice the first piece of cake, you continue to slice the cake, you then hand out a slice of the cake to someone and then you hand a slice to someone else. Piece by piece, you hand a slice of cake to people. As you hand out slices, eventually the cake would be gone. When everyone chips in, together, we can make a difference in this world. If the world were a cake, each of us can take one slice and with us doing this, we'll then begin to slice off, piece by piece, the misery within this world. Each story submitted to InterviewGirl.com is a "slice of cake." One story at a time, we can change humanity for the better. This idea can work, but it'll take many hands coming together. If you take the time and share a story, piece of advice, message, or idea on InterviewGirl.com, you'll be making a difference in someone's life. By sharing your story, you are taking your slice of the cake.

Interview Girl's purpose: learn more (live more), earn more and give more

Can learning more equate to earning more? As Interview Girl, my motto is learn more (live more), earn more, and then give more because the more that I learn, the more that I can share with you. The more that we all learn, the more that we can teach others. We can all learn from those around us. You are never done learning. The better that these compilations are, the more revenues that they'll generate and the more revenues that InterviewGirl.com brings in from the compilations and projects that it produces, the more people we can help (more misery can be eliminated). For these reasons, as Interview Girl, I need to: learn more, earn more, and then give more. This is what I strive to achieve.

> "If a man empties his purse into his head no one can take it away from him. An investment in knowledge always pays the best interest."
>
> —Benjamin Franklin (1706-1790)

InterviewGirl.com = A movement

InterviewGirl.com is a movement to get everyone to join in and be willing to eliminate some of the world's misery in some way. A movement is a group of people pursuing a common cause. Movements are characterized by discontent, vision, and action. For good or for evil, movements change the world. To better understand movements, Steve Addison's characteristics that describe movements are helpful. Addison, a life-long student of movements that renew and expand the Christian faith describes that Jesus founded a missionary movement that now spans the globe. His followers are called to continue his mission in the power of the Holy Spirit. From biblical, historical, and contemporary case studies, Addison identifies five recurring characteristics of dynamic missionary movements.[49] These characteristics are: a white-hot faith, commitment to a cause, contagious relationships, rapid mobilization, and adaptive methods.

There are a myriad of movements where people have the philosophy that if everybody joins in to help, then a difference can be made. Often times, these movements strive to get everyone to do their "little" part to make a big difference all together. One of these movements is a movement of kindness that Conari Press discusses in *Random Acts of Kindness*,

"Kindness is what we do, person to person, moment to moment. It is about being who we truly are. Its power is not only easily accessible to anyone who cares to use it, but it also can never be diminished; it expands with every action. It has the ability to utterly transform another person's life through the simplest of actions. It has the capacity to return us to the very core of our humanity. Kindness can and does open hearts, erase boundaries, and change lives."[50]

Conari Press' *Random Acts of Kindness* is about getting a lot of people to perform little acts of kindness. If everyone were to be kind, then the world would be a happier place. *Whole Foods* wants to inspire communities to build sustainable food systems that are equitable and ecologically sound, creating a just world, one food-secure community at a time. *Whole Foods* has their "One Dime at a Time" program. It provides an incentive to customers to eliminate single-use plastic bags and develop stronger communities all at the same time. At the register, customers have the option to receive a 10 cent per bag refund as cash back off their receipt or they can choose to donate it to that month's selected charity organization. Kiva is an organization with the slogan, "Changing the world one loan at a time." With $25, you can become a *Kiva* lender and watch your money transform a life. The money is not a gift. Clients repay their loan on a monthly basis. In fact, *Kiva* partners have an incredible repayment rate of over 99 percent. Once repayment is complete, lenders can either keep their money or redistribute it to another entrepreneur.

All of these movements were an initiative to get each of us to do something small and from everyone contributing a little something, all of us *together* would be able to make a big difference in our world. One act of kindness at a time will transform the world into a more pleasant place, one dime at a time will make our planet more ecologically sound, and one loan at time will transform the life of someone in an area that needs the loan. Each and every one of us doing a little something can lead to all of our "small" individual actions together becoming extensive changes in our world.

Piece by piece—slicing away MISERY

Misery exists in this world. People in some parts of the world live in contradistinction to other parts of the world. InterviewGirl. com's main undertaking is to get everyone to join in and do their part by committing to slicing off a piece of the misery in this world. Each of us can do something small and together we can all make a difference. In the context of InterviewGirl.com, sharing a story or supporting the Interview Girl Foundation are two small actions that one person could take. You may read this and think that there are seven billion people on earth, how does what I do even matter? To quote the words of Rabbi Dov Greenberg, "We are no more than a wave in the sea of humanity, a grain of sand on the surface of infinity."[51] How then can you and I make a difference? I once heard a story about a boy who was picking up starfish. A youth was picking up starfish stranded by the retreating tide and throwing them back into the sea to save them. A man went up to him and asked, "This beach goes on for miles, and there are thousands of starfish. Your efforts are futile, it doesn't make a difference!" The boy looked at the starfish in his hand and threw it into the water, "To this one," he said, "it makes all the difference."

Changing Our Thinking

"A new type of thinking is essential if mankind is to survive and move toward higher levels."

—Albert Einstein

Problems like: AIDS, poverty and human trafficking seem like such discouraging problems that we get lost in where we should begin in trying to break them down. How can we change the situation of a problem such as a single parent who has AIDS and also has six children and no income? How can we make it better? How can a child with an illness who has no family to take care of him/her receive medication? It seems overwhelming, but if you break a problem down into smaller parts and steps, solutions can be found. The Interview Girl Foundation was created so that we could identify a problem and then tackle that individual problem piece by piece.

Analysis is the breaking down of a problem into smaller easier to solve problems. Exactly how this is done determines the strength of your analysis. According to Jack Harich, the lead systems engineer and sustainologist at *Thwink.org*, more than anything else, an analytical approach is the use of an appropriate process to break a problem down into the smaller pieces necessary to solve it. Each piece becomes a smaller and easier problem to solve. Problem solving is puzzle solving. Each smaller problem is a smaller piece of the puzzle to find and solve. Putting the pieces of the puzzle together involves understanding the relevant parts of the system. Once all the key pieces are found and understood, the puzzle as a whole "snaps" together, sometimes in a final flash of insight.[52] Appropriate is a key word in the above definition. If your problem solving process doesn't fit the problem at hand, you can execute the process to the highest quality possible and still not solve the problem. This is the reason most people fail to solve difficult problems. They're using an inappropriate approach without realizing it. The process doesn't fit the problem. No matter where you look, unless you're using an appropriate analytical approach you will never find enough pieces of the puzzle to solve a difficult problem. Even the most brilliant and heroic effort will not solve a problem if you're using a problem solving process that doesn't fit the problem.

> "The difficulty lies not so much in developing new ideas as in escaping from old ones."
> —John Maynard Keynes

Thwink points out that lack of a process that fits the problem is why the alchemists failed to turn lead into gold. It's also why so many people and organizations, as well as entire social movements, are failing to turn opportunities into successes. Ironically, as I was just about to finish this InterviewGirl.com book, I came across *Thwink*. I had just spent the past year thinking about how to break down the larger problem of orphans suffering from HIV and having no access to medication into smaller solutions that could slowly help the overall larger problem. *Thwink* articulated how I viewed the AIDS problem. It was a large issue, so in order to begin to tackle the issue, the Interview Girl Foundation had to break down the big, overwhelming problem and begin by helping individuals. The fundamental premise of *Thwink. org* is that only an analytical approach can solve difficult social problems. Analytical means the use of analysis to solve problems. Analysis is breaking a problem down into smaller problems so they can be solved individually. Good analysis uses a process to direct the analysis. A process is a repeatable series of steps to achieve a goal.[53] For a process to work, it must fit the problem and be used correctly. That's why an analytical approach is the use of an appropriate process to break a problem down into the elements necessary to solve it. Each element becomes a smaller and easier problem to solve.

Morgan Jones, former CIA analyst and considered to be the master of analysis, breaks down exactly what structuring one's analysis means in the *Thinker's Toolkit*. The word analysis means separating a problem into its constituent elements. He concludes that doing so reduces complex issues to their simplest terms. Jones speaks about the importance of considering alternatives,

> "If we are to solve problems, from those confined to a single individual to those affecting whole nations, we must learn how to identify and break out of restrictive mindsets and give full, serious consideration to alternative solutions. We must learn how to deal with the compulsions of the human mind that, by defeating objective analysis, close the mind to alternatives."[54]

He concludes that failure to consider alternatives fully is the most common cause of flawed or incomplete analysis.

Thwink consists of a small band of innovators out to change the way modern activism works. They believe that root cause analysis is necessary to solve difficult social problems. They are also convinced that deep, correct root cause analysis of insanely difficult social problems like sustainability is possible. *Thwink* sees that solving the sustainability problem is not a matter of doing the same things better, but rather it's a matter of doing something different, radically different. They urge that once common good activists start using the same problem solving tools that business and science have long been using, they will be able to make strides so great they will astonish themselves. *Thwink* describes their method as: "If you know where the bull's-eye is, your solutions can't miss. The bull's-eye is the root causes, which are found by root cause analysis." Jack Harich pronounces that certain tools have long been applied to all sorts of difficult technical problems, but they have seldom been deeply applied to difficult social problems. He urges us, "Thwink about it" and then poses the questions: How many activists talk in terms of root causes, process improvement, and understanding the structure of a problem in terms of its key feedback loops? He believes that not enough activists think this way. The world's problem solvers are failing to solve problems like global environmental sustainability and the corporate dominance problem because they are pushing on low instead of high leverage points. Harich explains,

> "Activists are presently running blind. They're like a blind bull stumbling around in a china shop. They can't see the difference between what resolves root causes and what does not due to reliance on an instinctual problem solving process rather than an analytical one. If activists would switch to an analytical approach that fits the problem, as science did back in the 17th century when it adopted the Scientific Method, they would be able to correctly analyze difficult problems and find the high leverage points necessary to solve them."[55]

In *Cracking Creativity*, Michael Michalko sets forth that when you break out of your established patterns and ignore the conventional wisdom, you'll discover that there are many solutions.[56]

InterviewGirl.com and the Interview Girl Foundation's quest to begin a movement that works toward eliminating misery in our world starts as each of us change our thinking. The majority of people see a situation like the AIDS epidemic in Africa as impossible. This is the first problem. We cannot see it this way. The solution is closer than we think and the problem is not impossible. We can't think that it'll always be that way, but rather, we need to alter our thinking and think that if we change certain little things, they'll make a big difference in the lives of those struggling with AIDS in Africa.

> "The most destructive force you and I have—and the most constructive—is our own unconscious emotional and thinking and feeling state."
>
> —Ernest Holmes

> "Whether you think you can, or you think you can't—you're right."
>
> —Henry Ford

InterviewGirl.com hopes to spread the message that we can all contribute to slicing off a piece of the misery within this world.

Reverse Engineering What InterviewGirl. com Hopes To Accomplish

InterviewGirl.com shares stories because as it shares stories we are working to alleviate misery in the world (remembering the world is a cake analogy, it is slice by slice, piece by piece that we are eliminating different miseries that exist). The objective of the Interview Girl Foundation is to eliminate misery throughout the world. Obviously, this is a broad mission and explicit projects through the Interview Girl Foundation need to focus on specific miseries that exist. The Interview Girl Foundation had to decide

BECAUSE THE MEDICINE RAN OUT

where to begin in its efforts to eliminate misery that exists throughout the globe.

In his article, *How to Achieve Your Goals Through Reverse Engineering*, Mark Hayward defines reverse engineering as, "The process of discovering the technological principles of a device, object or system through analysis of its structure, function and operation. It often involves taking something apart and analyzing its workings in detail."[57] As Amara's story was the catalyst for this entire InterviewGirl.com movement, the work that the Interview Girl Foundation aspired to do in helping to eliminate miseries that exist in the world needed to begin with the foundation assisting sick individuals without access to medicine. Helping AIDS victims who do have access to medicine in Africa were the first individuals experiencing a misery who the Interview Girl Foundation wanted to help. The Interview Girl Foundation needed to reverse engineer its end goal in Africa.

The Interview Girl Foundation created a project, *Operation A^2*. *Operation A^2* came up with a plan to eliminate misery that exists within one country in Africa. From that country, *Operation A^2* broke that down even further and zeroed in on a region. From that region, it chose a village and within that village, *Operation A^2* would help a *person*. By starting with helping a single person, then we will help another person and then another and eventually our results will multiply to helping people throughout the village, then maybe the Interview Girl Foundation's *Operation A^2's* efforts to eliminate misery will multiply to the point where we help another village and in time perhaps our efforts will multiply to the point where we help people throughout the country, so our goal will go back to where it started: the country level.

At IntervierwGirl.com, when we say that we want to slice off a piece of the misery in the world, we can do that by reaching out to help *individuals* and then person to person we can see a ripple effect throughout the world. This type of effect has happened before and it can happen again. We help someone and then they help someone else. In *Self-Health Revolution*, Michael Zenn discusses spreading the message to get healthy, "Perhaps it starts with one person who tells another person; they grow into a few, a few becomes a group, a group becomes a crowd, a crowd becomes a mass, and a mass gives birth to a movement, a movement turns into a revolution."[58] Historically, the American Revolution began in just the way that Zenn describes. It started as a group of people that eventually gave birth to a movement. The American Revolution started because the colonists were upset about the concept of "no taxation without representation," but soon worked its way to realize that the colonists' basic rights were at stake. Yes, the colonies were taxed unfairly by the British, they were also not represented in the Parliament, and the British Crown also denied the colonists the basic rights of a British citizen. The Americans finally saw that what they wanted was a free democracy, not just less taxation and more representation in Parliament. The demand for no taxation without representation soon became a symbol of democracy for many. What starts with one person telling another person something has the capacity to grow into a larger movement.

The underpinning behind the Interview Girl Foundation's philosophy is that by helping an individual person, a ripple effect can spread from this initial effort. This is an age old principle that history has brought to light umpteen times. Person to person is indeed the only way that the world can be changed. Many of the greatest fundamental changes that have taken place in any society throughout human history started with a grass-root effort.[59] The Jewish tradition of Chanukah reflects this idea of "person to person." If you notice a house with candles burning in the window, chances are that it's a Jewish family celebrating Chanukah, the Jewish festival of lights. Rabbi Dov Greenberg explains, "The Chanukah candles shine their radiance into the street. Our task is to bring light, morality and holiness not only inside our own homes, but also outward into the world." Rabbi Dov Greenberg continues that Chanukah has something simple but quite significant to say. We repair the world in small steps, light by light, act by act, day by day. God asks us to do what we can, when we can. Each act mends a fracture of the world.[60] By starting with helping an individual person, the Interview Girl Foundation hopes to reach its ultimate preponderant goal, which is to one day grow into a relief effort that has affected an entire continent and beyond.

> "Never doubt that a small group of thoughtful, committed citizens can change the world; indeed, it's the only thing that ever has."
>
> —Margaret Mead

Humanity as a whole is transformed as each of us reach out to assist individual people. By each of us pledging to slice off one piece of the misery that individuals in this world undergo, we can transform humanity (as we each "take a slice of the cake"). Large scale changes start with small steps. A considerable issue such as poverty is eradicated when we reach out and begin to deal with the comprehensive problem on an individual basis (person to person). As the Interview Girl Foundation starts by helping one person, this will eventually turn into an effort that is helping members of an entire community. One by one, becomes many with time and momentum, and as the Interview Girl Foundation helps people throughout that community, well, in time, the foundation will help numerous people living throughout an entire country. By my being in contact with the director of several different orphanages in Africa, the small profits from InterviewGirl.com's initial project *Operation A²—Aiding AIDS* can help individual orphans without access to medicine at these orphanages. We will start by helping one orphan at a time. As the profits grow, we'll reach farther and help more orphans. InterviewGirl.com's ultimate goal is that the changes that the Interview Girl Foundation helps individuals to make will hopefully transcend to others. The Interview Girl Foundation will aid in slicing off a piece of the misery that someone is experiencing. In time, hopefully that individual will help someone else who too is experiencing misery. When the person who the Interview Girl Foundation helps then helps someone else, that person has surpassed their dire situation.

"Only a life lived for others is a life worthwhile."

—Albert Einstein

The Interview Girl Foundation's *OperationA2—Aiding AIDS* was created to help to slice off a piece of the misery (AIDS) within Africa. You'll read more about the Interview Girl Foundation in Chapter twelve and the good that *OperationA2—Aiding AIDS* plans to achieve. Person by person, story by story, humanity can become better as individuals' miseries are eliminated. InterviewGirl.com was instituted in order to help people by eliminating miseries that people endure. Ultimately, InterviewGirl.com will help individuals who are experiencing certain miseries through the unequivocal virtue that we gain from stories.

It all came together

"Act as if what you do makes a difference. It does."

—William James

My love for interviewing began with my initial two projects as a graduate student in History. I started collecting stories from people who were exiled from the now ex-Yugoslavia after World War Two (present day Slovenia and Croatia) as well as collecting stories from World War Two veterans who were still alive. Out of my experience interviewing for my studies, my interview aims then grew to a project that I called *Travel Girl*. As Travel Girl, it was my goal to document and share all of my exciting travels with people as well as the stories about people whom I met and interviewed while I was traveling. *Travel Girl* had a brief stint on the web, but I knew that *Travel Girl* was not completely what I was trying to achieve. From all of these experiences, InterviewGirl. com emerged.

From collecting WWII stories to collecting stories from the exiles from the region of Venezia Giulia (what used to be Yugoslavia),

InterviewGirl.com has now expanded to me interviewing people and collecting stories about successful diets, nutrition guidelines, Vietnam veterans, Iraqi war veterans, people suffering from eating disorders, firefighters, teachers, politicians, immigrants, prison in-mates, homeless individuals, refugees, doctors, charities, travel experiences, and countless other stories. There is no end to the list of stories InterviewGirl.com is collecting. You can learn more about InterviewGirl.com's current projects in Chapter 15. I have now collected stories in the following categories from individuals around the world and the stories that I continue to collect are not limited to these categories. I welcome each and every story that anyone wants to share.

Categories Collecting STORIES at InterviewGirl.com:

Africa Stories	Homeless Stories	Leukemia Stories	Poverty Stories	Websites I Cannot Live Without
Beach Body Coaches	Hope (Stories)	Life In Prison	Productivity Tips	Weight Loss Programs and Specialists
Beauty Secrets	Hospital Stories	Living During a War and/or People Who Grew up during Wartime	Reading a Book Changed My Life	Weight Loss Success Stories
Being a Writer	Illness Stories	Major League Baseball	Refugees	Who is your Hero/Mentor? Why?
Bloggers	Immigration Stories	Medical School	September 11, 2001 (Stories)	World War Two Stories
Bodybuilding	In the line of Duty (Stories from Firefighters/ Policemen)	Model Stories	Service	Government, Politics and Politicians (Stories)

College Stories	Individuals With Developmental Disabilities	NLP	The Story of My Life—Advice from Elderly	Law School (Stories)
Eating Disorders	Japan Crisis 2011	Nonprofit Doctors	Teachers	Personal Trainer Stories
Engagement Stories	Iraq War Stories	Online Stories	Travel Stories	Wealth/ Created a Fortune/ Millionaires
Entrepreneurs	Italian Vacation Stories	Overcoming Overeating	Untold Stories from the ER	Vietnam Stories
Goals	People who have started amazing Organizations and/or Foundations	Making a Difference	Miracle Stories	Any Story You Have To Share

From collecting these valuable stories that people have to share, InterviewGirl.com's inclusive goal of eliminating peoples' miseries (and we'll do that by reaching out person to person) will eventually be achieved.

Share A Story Today!

Interview Girl's Early Years

Little kids are always asked, "What do you want to be when you grow up?" Ever since I can remember, I always wanted to be a Pediatric Oncologist because when I was younger I met a little boy at a baseball game who ended up dying of leukemia. It was difficult for me to understand why this boy died. In thinking about a career, I always wanted to be able to, as I thought at the time, "save a boy like him." Why was I so affected by this boy's death when I was younger? Looking back now, I understand that it is because his story stayed with me as the years passed. As a child, I did not just learn a fact that a person died from my parents, but I knew someone. I had memories of playing games with him at a certain park, so when I learned about his death, his story remained with me.

As it turns out, I am one of those girls who becomes queasy around blood. Despite this monumental obstacle, I still entertained the idea, "Can I be a doctor?" for many years. Well as you might guess, I'm not a doctor. The fact that I am not a doctor and I cannot physically help heal sick children has always been in the back of my mind. I constantly think, "How can I help those with disease, sickness, and/or major problems?" Then there was a time when I wanted to become a Psychologist or a Social Worker. Again, my thought process was that I could help people work through their problems. I know that it sounds so general, but I have always wanted to help others somehow. When I filled out those career questionnaires, "helping people" always proved to be my strength. The question that I face is: how can I, this twenty-something high school teacher with a bunch of graduate degrees in the Humanities possibly help alleviate some of the major unjustness in this world?

This is how I can help. I can donate the proceeds from this project and you can help me in my mission by sharing your story. InterviewGirl.com is a project where stories will be collected in various categories and then the stories will be put together as a compilation of stories. The stories collected and interviews completed through InterviewGirl.com will be disseminated in various ways. I have always loved storytelling and I admired and could never get enough of a good story. This project really combines two of my greatest passions: helping others and telling / reading stories. We will go into further detail about all of InterviewGirl. com's projects later, but besides compilations, sometimes sharing just one story by itself or having one speaker is also a part of InterviewGirl.com's mission. Compilations are InterviewGirl.

com's major focus, but there are many ways that we can raise money for those who are experiencing a form of misery. As Interview Girl, it is my goal to share stories that make an impression on people and/or stories from which everyone can learn.

I have been teaching the past few years and yes I love my job, the kids, the school, my colleagues, but part of me has always had regret that I could not take on the endeavor of medical school due to the minor detail that I faint when I see blood! Now it makes sense, I was meant to do this ... INTERVIEW and SHARE what I learn from the interviews. When I graduated high school, I was voted easiest to talk to. I love interviewing people and learning about others. Since I work full-time now, I usually do my interviews for InterviewGirl.com after work. After a long day of work, I enjoy every minute of my interviews. When I am speaking with a 90 year old veteran from the Second World War and he tears up as he says, "I saw the most beautiful woman I had ever seen in my entire life." A few moments later in the interview, he revealed that he was speaking about the first time that he ever saw his wife. As I left that particular interview, I learned from the WWII veteran that after 90 years of life experience, when it's all said and done, love is what matters in this story called life. His other half is what matters most to him. She meant more to him than anything else in the world. These are powerful life lessons.

When I was in Ghana, Africa, I asked the founder and director of the orphanage, Edem Richard why he decided to start an orphanage for children with no parents (children suffering from HIV/AIDS and children who were rescued from human trafficking). He explained to me, "It was a necessity." AIDS is such a problem in Africa that Edem felt compelled to do something to make changes to the calamitous situation starting right in his own community in Kpando, Ghana. As I interviewed individuals, such as Edem, I was able to see what lengths people go to in order to make a difference in this world and this matters and it is inspiring. Edem was an everyday citizen in Ghana who saw a need for an orphanage. He saw a problem and then he did something about it.

This is a story that is enlivening. The orphanage that is housing 30 plus African orphans that Edem started runs on donations. What Edem did to get the orphanage started and what people are doing to keep it running is stimulating and inspirational. When people hear a story like this, it inspires them to be better. People need to learn stories like this. The chief happening at InterviewGirl.com is to learn stories like these and then to share them with the world. The world is filled with stories and as Interview Girl, I want to hear them and then bring the stories to you.

Long before InterviewGirl.com was even a concrete idea in my head, questioning people, talking with people, trying to learn everything that I could from everyone whom I met is intrinsically part of who I am. In fact, many people who know me have at one point or another become annoyed at times because I ask so many questions. Being inquisitive is part of who I am. I am someone who believes that you learn something from everyone with whom you have the privilege of coming into contact. Through my experiences in graduate school, I came to understand and love interviewing people. The thing is that I keep meeting amazing people in my life who inspire me to aspire to achieve more in various distinctive areas. I am fortunate because there are countless people in my life who constantly influence me in a way that make me want to become a better version of myself. From interviewing people and from reading peoples' stories, I have learned that we must have the mentality that if they did it, so can I. I also believe that there is always something that we can do to make a difference in this world.

As I completed my graduate degrees, with these experiences, I ingratiated myself with a love for reading and learning. As valuable and enriching as my formal education has been and it truly has been a privilege to have had the opportunities to study in the places where I have, I firmly believe that we learn exceedingly through others. Reading, categorizing information and taking notes are another part of my fiber. When people are asked, what do you genuinely love to do? One of my answers is always: read.

InterviewGirl.com is a place for people to share their stories and then we'll disseminate these stories with the world so that other people can be inspired from these stories. When others share their stories and their experiences with us, we grow and glean insights from hearing peoples' stories. As I interviewed World War Two vets for one of InterviewGirl.com's compilation projects, numerous gentlemen shared that they believe that it is from others that we learn an appreciable amount in this world.

Interview Girl's Emergence

I love to travel and I have spent the last decade traveling whenever I could. Through all of my travel, I became filled with stories. Actually, as I told you already, InterviewGirl.com started as *Travel Girl* and then morphed into InterviewGirl.com. *Travel Girl* was a vehicle to share all of my stories from traveling the globe. Being a teacher and single in my twenties allowed me to travel every single summer. Through traveling, I met and came into contact with matchless individuals and experienced a sundry of different scenarios from these pleasant people with whom I was fortunate enough to cross paths. I spent the summers in my twenties traveling and from those experiences; I always came home thinking, "Man, that is a marvelous story that people need to hear." In all of the places that I traveled to—I became filled with unexpected stories. One of the over-arching lessons that graduate school and all of my experiences of traveling to unique places has taught me is that we are constantly learning from others. Yes, you learn both good and bad elements, but you learn a great extent from other people.

For years, I have considered myself to be a Renaissance Soul. I could never assuredly figure out what it was that I wanted to do. I was perpetually signing up for new classes and activities, but I couldn't find the one thing that I genuinely and unmistakably felt was my calling. Do I want to be a teacher, a journalist, a writer, a psychologist, a PhD candidate, become a social entrepreneur, own a business, take people to Italy, start a travel agency, write a screen play, do something with fitness, get a degree in geriatrics, study philanthropy, and my career ideas could continue, but you get the idea. My ideas were always going back and forth. I just kept signing up for class after class. I would finish one degree and then start my next advanced degree in a different area. Then one day, it hit me. I wanted to interview people and then share those stories to help others grow as they learned new perspectives. I decided that we could change the world one story at a time and I never looked back.

Finally it makes sense. I am so passionate about InterviewGirl. com's mission that I look forward to coming home from my full-time job and working on InterviewGirl.com. I unceasingly look forward to doing interviews and working on putting together a new compilation for InterviewGirl.com. For example, if I am running errands, cooking dinner, or chatting with my friends; I cannot wait to get back to this work. I know this is it. InterviewGirl.com and the Interview Girl Foundation just came to me. Do you know how hard it is to find the domain name that you want on the internet in the 21st century? Well with InterviewGirl.com, I thought of the name and then I checked for InterviewGirl.com and sure enough, it was there. There was no InterviewGirl.com before I created this idea. This doesn't happen a lot in this day and age where millions of people own internet domains.

I always admired immensely those people who can tell great stories. I always thought, "What a gift!" I would strive to be like those individuals that I met who had the capacity to tell a fascinating story. I had to figure out a way to bring all of my passions together in a way that could help people. Somehow I wanted to use my passions and from this help to eliminate some of the misery that exists in this world.

InterviewGirl.com is in actuality all of my life experiences coming together. InterviewGirl.com is my way to try and reach people around the globe, so that InterviewGirl.com can put together some interesting, inspirational, useful, and entertaining compilations of stories. A story can be powerful, efficacious, impressive, influential, mighty, omnipotent, dynamic, compelling, dominant, competent, effectual, paramount, energetic, and potent. From the perspective that one gains from a story, a story can change his/her world. As learning Amara's story while on my trip to Africa altered my world, it is my hope that the stories that you read that have been collected and put together by InterviewGirl. com will transpose valuable insights into your world.

Everywhere I went—there seemed to be another great story

"If a person gives you his time, he can give you no more precious gift."

—Frank Tyger

The greatest gift that you can give an individual is your time. You are in a hurry. You are tired. You don't feel like being social, but there is that person there who seems lonely and wants to talk. Have you ever been in that situation? I have. Every single time, when I wanted to be selfish and just go home, but I stayed a few moments longer to listen to someone, from those moments came unforgettable stories. The people that I encountered during those moments shared insights with me that made me think and take one thing or another under consideration that I had never previously thought to do. I had an ah hah moment. I heard stories that forced me to ruminate issues that I would not otherwise think about and stories that people don't always hear and most importantly I learned a unique perspective. In giving time to someone who was reaching out to me, he/she actually gave something emphatically rewarding back to me. I believe this is an example of the "Pay It Forward" concept. I put someone ahead of myself. I was tired and I wanted to go home, but I could tell that someone needed to talk for a few minutes, so I put a smile on my face and gave this person my attention and time. Many times from these moments came incredible stories.

One of InterviewGirl.com's projects is stories from homeless people. This project emerged because I have made it a point that whenever a homeless person asks me for money, I agree to give him/her $5, if he/she will speak with me and answer my questions. (I explain to the homeless person this InterviewGirl.com idea.) When I was skeptical about speaking with a homeless person because random thoughts were going through my head like, "he may hurt me," but I had a conversation with him, anyway, from those conversations came ineffaceable stories. The homeless person's story helped me to understand what it must be like to live without a home.

Prior to the IPhone, I used to carry around with me my little flip video camera everywhere that I went. Years ago, when I discovered the "flip camera," I thought that it was the most amazing contraption. I was elated about the idea of a pocket sized video camera. People around me used to tease me about what seemed like my pointless video taking obsession. My thinking was that you never knew when a good story would emerge.

As I said, InterviewGirl.com started out as *Travel Girl* and a few other early ideas. It was what I took away from my experience in Africa and from the subsequent research and stories that I compiled that all my ideas came together and InterviewGirl.com was born. I knew that I had a collection of stories from my own traveling experiences, but I also knew that others had a plethora of other stories to share, as well. We can learn from those around us. There are an abounding amount of stories out there that need to be shared. Everyone has a story and a message. We learn from others and there is always something that we can do to make a difference in this world. These two thoughts are the pillars that InterviewGirl.com is built around. At InterviewGirl.com, we want to help others and share stories with the world. We believe that we can learn from others and change the world while doing this.

People are shaped and affected by those with whom they spend their time or by stories that people tell to them. For example, Leonardo Da Vinci met and worked with Niccolo Machiavelli, the Italian political theorist. Some believe that Leonardo Da Vinci instructed Machiavelli to the concept of applied science. Machiavelli then combined what he learned from Leonardo Da Vinci with his own insights about politics into a new political and social order.[61]

With hopefulness, optimism, faith, courage, and anticipation, InterviewGirl.com and the Interview Girl Foundation have come up with a plan to try and change some of the statistics that I shared with you in the beginning of the book. These statistics are further expounded upon in Chapter 19. Writing books and collecting stories was always something that I wanted to do, but now I am motivated to act on this idea of mine. Just as I was introduced to stories that affected me in a way that I will never ever be the same when I was in Africa, InterviewGirl.com hopes to introduce you to many interesting and unknown stories – stories that you'll find fascinating and stories that you'll find useful. Whenever I meet someone or someone is telling me something, I am thinking of the InterviewGirl.com project to which I can add the new information. Compiling, collecting, recording, and researching information and resources is how I focus a considerable amount of my time. The various projects at InterviewGirl.com are what I have in mind as I bring together this information.

Meeting someone like Edem in Ghana through my travel was such an inspiration and an experience from which I gleaned an infinite wisdom. Edem challenged my perspective about the world. Meeting recovering alcoholics who poured their hearts out and shared with me what finally made them come around and stop drinking helped me to understand about hard times. Stories like these that people shared with me affected me because they taught me invaluable lessons. Traveling to Africa was the catalyst, the experience where InterviewGirl.com was born, but the traveling that I did in my twenties was also filled with story and after story from astounding people that influenced me and ultimately affected my life in a way that I would not disregard just because the time came and went.

InterviewGirl.com will bring the world well researched, well organized, useful information and resources along with astonishing stories. These stories and information will serve individuals who need advice and expertise and the profits from these stories will serve those in this world who are experiencing some form of misery, like orphan children in Kpando, Ghana. All of the effort behind InterviewGirl.com is so that hopefully someone like Amara will have access to medication that is very much needed. The energies behind this project are to do what we can to eliminate miseries that exist. I wholeheartedly believe that one story at a time, the world can be changed.

> "Those who bring sunshine into the lives of others cannot keep it from themselves."
>
> —James M. Barrie

From Questions to forming a Nonprofit: The Interview Girl Foundation

InterviewGirl.com is an international project for the enhancement of listening to and learning new stories and with that purpose we will help those less fortunate than ourselves in this world. Questions are a central tenant of my work as Interview Girl. I ask people questions to bring the world more knowledge and advice about things that they wonder. Interviewgirl.com aspires to get everyone to ask the question: What can I do to help eliminate someone else's misery within this world?

The Interview Girl Foundation is a nonprofit organization dedicated to getting every individual in the world to join in and do their part in helping to eliminate some of the misery that exists within this world. As individuals partake in InterviewGirl.

com, they can contribute to slicing off a piece of the misery in the world. InterviewGirl.com's projects are completed with the objective that distributing the project will help to eliminate the misery that someone somewhere experiences. People all around the world experience misery. The Interview Girl Foundation strives to build programs to help eliminate misery where it exists in different areas of the world (project by project). The Interview Girl Foundation believes that human dignity is a fundamental right for all. When the misery that someone lives with is eliminated, he/she then experiences dignity. People's lives change when they are treated with dignity.

Eliminating misery is a broad thing to achieve because many parts of our world are plagued with misery. "Eliminating misery" had to be narrowed down. The Interview Girl Foundation had to decide which ill (individuals living in poverty, children who are victims of child trafficking, or people suffering from AIDS), its debut project would help. The Interview Girl Foundation creates projects to target *different* miseries that people experience, but given my time in Africa and the affect Amara's story had upon me, the orphan's misery (those who were ill with no medicine) were the first individuals whom I wanted to help. Helping the AIDS crisis (specifically orphans affected by this pandemic) seemed like a good place to start with helping to eliminate misery that people experience within this world. As mentioned before, the Interview Girl Foundation's project: *Operation A²* was the first project that our foundation created. Project *Operation A²* is aimed at raising money to get AIDS orphans medicine. This is the first step: getting medicine for AIDS victims. As explained in Chapter 12, there is a whole series of steps in the plan to help lessen the misery of the AIDS epidemic in Africa. The Interview Girl Foundation creates projects to zero in on specific problems. Projects like *Operation A²* are created through the Interview Girl Foundation. This is the beautiful part about the Interview Girl Foundation, whom we are helping, the misery we are hoping to eliminate can always change and we can help multitudinous, diverse needs through our efforts.

Giving and helping were my initial intentions, but as my research unfolded about poverty, not only was giving as much as possible the Interview Girl Foundation's focus, but more importantly, I wanted to make sure that what the Interview Girl Foundation gave to "eliminate miseries" was spent on policies and programs that worked. I wanted the Interview Girl Foundation's efforts to "eliminate miseries" to succeed. The Interview Girl Foundation needed to spend money to eliminate miseries effectively. Through careful and diligent research there was no reason that the Interview Girl Foundation could not set up a sound program that delivered results. Enough has been completed and tracked about humanitarian aid that by analyzing the empirical evidence of what has been done, our nonprofit organization has evidence that cites what would be the best way to go about "aiding" the people with AIDS (*Operation A²*).

Through a careful analysis of humanitarian undertakings and modeling what worked best and what did not would allow the Interview Girl Foundation to set up a successful program to help people suffering from HIV/AIDS. Tremendous strides have been made in development thanks to the eight Millennium Development Goals (MDGs)—which range from halving extreme poverty rates to halting the spread of HIV/AIDS and providing universal primary education, all by the target date of 2015. These goals form a blueprint agreed to by all the world's countries and all the world's leading development institutions. They have galvanized unprecedented efforts to meet the needs of the worlds poorest. Through my research, I learned about amazing organizations that are making strides in a positive direction in Africa and I wanted to continue this relief and follow the lead of people achieving visible progress in the lives of people who experience difficulties. Organizations like Catholic Relief Services, CARE, Nelson Mandela Foundation, DATA, William Jefferson Clinton Foundation, the Global Fund to Fight AIDS, UN AIDS, AVERT, Missionaries of Africa and the World Health Organization were such a positive inspiration and proof that we could help. I was impressed and inspired by the work of all of the aforementioned organizations. I studied Catholic Relief Services most closely and I learned what they were doing to help people throughout the world. The Interview Girl Foundation completes this same type of life changing work in different areas that needed help in this world.

The Interview Girl Foundation did not need to guesstimate what may work best when it came to "aiding" those living in poverty or those suffering from AIDS. From the data and trials that are available from research organizations such as *Innovations for Poverty Action* (IPA) and the *Abdul Latif Jameel Poverty Action Lab* (J-PAL), we have a better understanding of what works and what does not. Thanks to the efforts of institutions like these and the UN and its partners for building a better world, there is data available about what development efforts are the most efficient. From pertinacious and conscientious research, health care management, nonprofit finance, organizational development, fund raising management, conflict management, and human resource management all began to make more sense. I created the Interview Girl Foundation knowing that it would implement a program that would deliver results by modeling the best practices from all the organizations that it studies.

> "Desire is the starting point of all achievement, not a hope, not a wish, but a keen pulsating desire which transcends everything."
>
> —Napoleon Hill

Since InterviewGirl.com collects stories and profits from sharing these stories are used to eliminate someone's misery, it was necessary to figure out how the Interview Girl Foundation could *best eliminate* someone's misery. The first step in this cause to find the solutions to eliminate anyone's misery began with my ability to ask the right questions. *Operation A²* desires to assist orphans who have HIV/AIDS and no access to medication. I decided to reverse engineer the problems that the literature illuminated about AIDS in Africa: too many impoverished people, too little infrastructure, and lack of consistent medical care in remote areas. I started from the end results that we hoped to see and made my way forward, just as Dan urged me to do that evening in Tampa. I thought, yes, there are impoverished people, but the question that needed to be asked was: *What can we do to help people not to be impoverished?* This question was followed by: *What can we do to bring more infrastructure to Africa?* and *how can we bring consistent medical care to remote areas?* As I stated already, as the Interview Girl Foundation began to ask questions, a new part of the research revealed itself. People were "aiding" the Africans as the nonprofit I was founding hoped to do, but what could we do differently? Was the aid working? Would giving money be enough? Dambisa Moyo's *Dead Aid* and William Easterly's *The White Man's Burden* unveil how more problems are created when billions of dollars are given to places that lack the capacity to spend the money effectively. New questions arose and the scope of *Operation A²* through the Interview Girl Foundation was to give meaningful aid and to permanently change things and eliminate miseries in Africa rather than to temporarily mediate a problem by sending some money.

The Interview Girl Foundation which is newly off the ground, initiated our work here: by asking the correct questions. The Interview Girl Foundation launched *Operation A²: Aiding AIDS* to begin eliminating misery that exists for orphans with HIV/AIDS in Africa. I knew that together organizations and individuals around the world could make a difference if everyone chipped in to help eliminate someone else's misery. This is the cornerstone of InterviewGirl.com: getting everyone to join in and help to eliminate some of the misery that happens in this world. The Interview Girl Foundation has its work cut out, but we started by asking meticulous questions and from starting there, we were able to put together a plan of what it was that we wanted to achieve— the difference that the Interview Girl Foundation wanted to make.

An Experience that Lasts a Lifetime

Many times in our lives we experience things and for that moment or for the first few months after the experience, we are still affected. As I stated, I have done a great deal of traveling in my twenties. My experience has been that you go to a new place and for some time after the experience you are still thinking of it, but after a few months, you are back to your normal routine and the lovely people whom you met while traveling are now thoughts of the past. My experience in Ghana was different. Still to this day, I lay there at night and I can't fall sleep as I picture the orphans and the poverty in Africa (poverty that I saw and poverty that I became well versed about due to the stories that I read). I'll be watching a movie with my friends and my mind is totally drifting and picturing the orphans. I vividly remember Donkor wanting to play tag with me. I am driving in my car and Asantuwa and Ebeneezer's faces will pop into my mind. I am walking into my graduate seminar and "Because The Medicines Ran Out" runs through my mind and I am reminded that benevolent Amara died because she did not have access to life saving medication.

This book began by discussing my trip to Africa and the subsequent research (following my trip) on global issues that upset me because they do not seem fair. The point of this movement is to make those unfair realities better for people. The proceeds from the first compilations of stories produced from InterviewGirl.com are for those children who are ill and experience the misery of no access to medication. It has been difficult to sum up InterviewGirl.com and how and why this project commenced. The best way for me to go about doing that was to share Amara's story. By understanding her story, you can better understand the purpose and scope of InterviewGirl.com. The orphans in Africa are the first of many people whose miseries I hope to help to alleviate. I have included the disheartening statistics about poverty, AIDS, and child trafficking in Chapter 19.[62]

InterviewGirl.com making the World a Better Place—By Helping One Person at a Time Through Collecting One Story at a Time

The profits from initial projects produced through InterviewGirl.com are to help lessen the misery of orphans dealing with the hardships of HIV/AIDS in Africa (*Operation A²*), but playing a role and eliminating misery in this world when we can is the larger goal of the Interview Girl Foundation. InterviewGirl. com gives you the chance to help those in this world who are experiencing misery. By sharing a story on InterviewGirl.com, you can help to give those suffering with AIDS hope (*Operation A²*). The details about how InterviewGirl.com will help others are explained in Chapter 9 and Chapter 12. Orphans suffering from AIDS is an area where the initial proceeds from projects completed at InterviewGirl.com go (*Operation A²*), but from there we will expand to help alleviate other miseries. We have the possibility to help countless people. Maybe an orphan in Africa isn't the first cause that you would like to help. In time, the charities, organizations, people whom the Interview Girl Foundation can help are endless. With each compilation that is made and/or project that InterviewGirl.com sponsors, the proceeds can go toward helping new people: people who are sick, people who lost their jobs, remarkable charities, people who need help when disaster strikes, children with leukemia, people who are homeless, children who are starving, refugees without a home, people suffering from malaria, etc. You name it and there is the possibility of helping individuals experiencing assorted forms of misery.

Profits from projects completed at InterviewGirl.com are used for those in this world who need help (those experiencing a form of misery). The mission of InterviewGirl.com is to get each and every one of us to join in and assist in eliminating some of the misery that people experience in this world. The other part of InterviewGirl.com's undertaking is to *share stories* and by doing this to help the millions of people struggling with various issues and/or who are looking for advice in certain areas. The helpful compilations that are put together at InterviewGirl.com will support people seeking advice and/or knowledge in diverse areas. When you share a story through InterviewGirl.com, people benefit in two ways from the story that you share (How you help people in two ways by sharing your story is covered in more detail in Chapter 9).

CHAPTER FOUR

Individuals Who Inspire Interview Girl

People who enliven my Interview Girl spirit

Have you ever been on a trip that has changed your life? Have you ever met someone and your life was never the same after meeting that individual? Have you ever taken a course that altered the course of your own life? In Michael Gelb's *How to Think Like Leonardo DaVinci*, he proposes the question, "What life experience most profoundly impacted your life?" The first time I read his book, numerous life experiences came to mind, but after the summer I spent in Ghana, there was an experience that stood out. Volunteering at an orphanage in Kpando was a life altering experience for me. It was my time in Ghana, Africa that stirred me to do *something*. That something emerged into creating this InterviewGirl.com movement. Interviewing people and hearing their stories is the fortitude of InterviewGirl.com.

Throughout my life, I have been inspired by the work of individuals like Edem, James Orbinski, Esther Duflo, Jacqueline Novogratz, Mother Teresa, Father Gassis, former Pope John Paul II, former Pope Benedict XVI, Kofi Annan, Jack Harich, my friend, Sara, my sister and my Mom. There are countless other individuals who have encouraged me throughout my life, but I'll stop the list here because naming everyone who has inspired me will be another book in itself. The stories that I know about the lives of these people, those I know personally and those about whom I read, each story tugs at my heartstrings in a particular way. In their own unique way, they each instigate the work that I complete as Interview Girl.

Edem

To begin, I'll never forget when I was in Africa and Edem explained to me that he felt that it was a "necessity" to build a Children's Home because so many in his community were orphans because their parents died of AIDS. I was struck by Edem's use of the word *necessity*. Nobody was paying Edem. He saw a need in his community, so he started a movement to help those children without parents. I was inspired by Edem's constant efforts to do what he could to try and raise donations for the orphans. Edem came from a well off family and he was taken care of, but he saw that people in his community were suffering from the hardships of AIDS, so he made it his mission to try and help these children who were left with no parents. Edem took action to help others.

Dr. James Orbinski

Dr. James Orbinski is one of my mentors because he serves as a model of a compassionate doctor. As a former member and president of Doctors Without Borders, also known as MSF, he has served in some of the world's most chaotic places, like Somalia, the refugee camps of Afghanistan and Rwanda, both before and during the genocide. I am moved by Orbinski's desire to do good as a doctor as well as by his efforts in International Relations.

Dr. James Orbinski is the director of the Africa Initiative and senior adviser to the Vice President of Programs at CIGI. He is also CIGI Chair in Global Health at the Balsillie School of International Affairs. Orbinski is a globally recognized humanitarian practitioner and advocate, as well as a leading scholar in global health. After extensive field experience with Médecins Sans Frontières / Doctors Without Borders (MSF), he was elected MSF's international president from 1998 to 2001. In 1999, he launched MSF's Access to Essential Medicines Campaign and in that same year, accepted the Nobel Peace Prize on behalf of MSF for its pioneering approach to medical humanitarianism, particularly for its approach to witnessing. Orbinski worked as MSF's Head of Mission in Goma, Zaire in 1996-1997, during the refugee crisis. He was MSF's Head of Mission in Kigali during the 1994 Rwandan genocide and MSF's medical co-coordinator in Jalalabad, Afghanistan during the winter of 1994. He was MSF's medical co-coordinator in Baidoa, Somalia during the civil war and famine of 1992–1993. Orbinski's first MSF mission was in Peru in 1992. For his medical humanitarian leadership in Rwanda during the 1994 genocide, he was awarded the Meritorious Service Cross, Canada's highest civilian award.

I am in awe of Orbinski's intellectual accolades and his contributions to the field of medicine, but Orbinski's response to what he saw in Rwanda has particular resonance with me. In 1994 in Rwanda, he acted and spoke, while an entire world stood by without helping. He remained as a doctor while the violence continued more around the hospitals. He was one of the last doctors left in Kigali. He made a choice. His choice was to stay and save what lives he could, to relieve what suffering he could. To use his words, "it was that simple, and that hard."[63] He did not leave until the genocide ended. During the 100-day period from April to July 1994, one million men, women and children—including 85 per cent of all Tutsis in Rwanda—were murdered, and another half-million people (including moderate Hutus) were injured, by Hutu extremists. Orbinski entered Rwanda in mid-May, at a time when almost everyone else had fled (including UN agencies, aid organizations, and the U.S. Marines). Orbinski served as MSF's head of mission during the Rwandan Genocide. Orbinski called the Rwandan Genocide, "the most transformative moment in my life." After experiencing the genocide, Dr. Orbinski decided to do what he could within International relations in order to make the world that he saw in Rwanda that troubled him better. The actions that Orbinski took in Rwanda helping people who were suffering during the genocide and the actions that he has since taken to make the world a better place are what infuse me with hope that the actions that I take matter.

An Imperfect Offering is a memoir Orbinski wrote about his experiences in *Doctors Without Borders*. *An Imperfect Offering* is one of those books that I read that honestly changed my life. Orbinski's words about his experiences as a humanitarian doctor have a place within my heart. In his book, he described his question as, "How am I to be, how are we to be in relation to the suffering of others?" In his gentle, thoughtful tone, he elaborated on this concept,

> "To enter into what draws you, what calls you, is to live your question ... I have always been fascinated with science, particularly with the methodology of science, and what this means in terms of action—what you can do with what you know. My questions have really come out of these loves and I've been drawn to what is classically defined as humanitarian medicine, humanitarian work."

In an interview Dr. Orbinski completed with Stacey Gibson for the *University of Toronto* magazine, he explained,

> "It's not about creating the perfect future. It is about responding to another human being who is suffering in a very particular way, and responding to them in a very particular way. With the expectation that—that is the starting point of what we are as human beings."

Orbinski's call to act is what I find indeterminately inspirational. He is someone who saw the worst of the worst and he chose to respond. As Orbinski himself put it, "It's a choice." We all have a choice in our lives. We can choose to stand by, ignore, or we can take concrete actions and try to create a world with less misery. People like Dr. James Orbinski move me to make the right choices. Dr. Orbinski's actions disclose that humanitarianism is about responding to another human being who is suffering in a very particular way. The point of creating InterviewGirl.com and the Interview Girl Foundation and writing this book is so that we can respond to peoples' miseries in our world.

> "What I've experienced is that I can't know the future. I can't know if anything that I do will change what happens tomorrow. I can't know with certainty, but what I do know is if I do nothing, nothing will change."
> —Dr. James Orbinski

Esther Duflo

Esther Duflo is an internationally renowned economist whose research has helped change the way governments and aid organizations address global poverty. Her revolutionary work applying randomized trials to determine which social policies actually work best to relieve poverty has led to numerous accolades. Most recently she was named one of the "Top 100 Global Thinkers" for 2012 by *Foreign Policy* magazine. As with Dr. Orbinski, Duflo's intellect impresses me, but as Dean Karlan, professor of Economics at Yale University and a colleague to Duflo affirms, "She's an absolute rock star. She's a great example of the new wave of development economists—people who are really bright and dedicated to theory, but are driven by improving the world around them." Duflo's work in the field inspires me because it's imbued with the message that "taking action" is what changes the world. Instead of endlessly debating ideology, Duflo believes in tracking empirical evidence. The method she embraces is a scientific one, employing randomized trials, with one group of patients getting the economic "treatment," the other a placebo. As with Edem and Dr. Orbinski, I am inspired by economist, Esther Duflo because her work is also about activism. She is working to make changes for those living in poverty and she is doing it in a way that uses rigorous scientific trials to make sure that her work leads to actual changes and more than good intentions for people experiencing poverty.

Jacqueline Novogratz

Jacqueline Novogratz is the founder and CEO of Acumen Fund, a non-profit global venture fund that uses entrepreneurial approaches to solve the problems of poverty. Acumen Fund aims to create a world beyond poverty by investing in social enterprises, emerging leaders, and breakthrough ideas. Under Novogratz's leadership, Acumen Fund has invested more than $80 million in 70 companies in South Asia and Africa, all focused on delivering affordable health care, water, housing and energy to the poor. These companies have created and supported more than 57,000 jobs, leveraged an additional $360 million, and reached over 90 million lives. In December 2011, Acumen Fund and Novogratz were on the cover of Forbes magazine as part of their feature on social innovation. Prior to Acumen Fund, Novogratz founded and directed The Philanthropy Workshop and The Next Generation Leadership programs at the Rockefeller Foundation. She also founded Duterimbere, a micro-finance institution in Rwanda. She began her career in international banking with Chase Manhattan Bank.

It was Novogratz's entrepreneurial approaches to solve the problems of poverty that first drew me to her work, but as I read about her and learned about all that she was doing, not only was I on the same page that she was about how to eliminate poverty (sustainable changes that stay with people after the donor leaves), but I was touched by the stories that she shared to help us better comprehend her work. Stories like the ones that she shared about Jane, Sister Mary Theophane, and John Gardner represent how people in Novogratz's life affected the person who she became.

In *The Blue Sweater*, a memoir about her work, Novogratz shares stories about who impacted her in her life beginning from an early age. The people who Novogratz met and spent time with gave me an understanding of why she did the things that she did throughout her career and life. Novogratz's first-grade teacher, Sister Mary Theophane once told her that "to whom much is given, much is expected." Novogratz credits the compassion of West Point, N.Y. and the nuns who taught her, particularly, Sister Mary Theophane, as having helped her decide that she "was going to live out loud."

Novogratz elucidated that while she was getting her MBA at Stanford, professors give a preview of their upcoming classes to aid students in course selection. At one session, a tall, graceful elderly man in a gray suit and a fedora stood up to speak. Novogratz described that it was impossible not to listen to what he had to say. After the session, she went to find Professor Emeritus John Gardner in his office and asked him if he ever had time to talk about some of the issues that he raised earlier in his speech. From that meeting, Novogratz didn't stop talking with Gardner until he died over a decade later. She learned that he had been secretary of health, education, and welfare under Lyndon Johnson. After resigning from the Johnson administration as one of the most powerful government officials in the country, he founded a grassroots citizens' organization, Common Cause, at age 56. Novogratz remarked, "John Gardner understood what self-renewal was all about—he lived it." Novogratz's account of what she learned from Gardner struck a chord with me. Her friendship with John Gardner, a professor emeritus who mentored her until his death at age 89 in 2002 was a heartening story.

While working in the developing world, she encountered Jane in a Nairobi slum and learned that Jane was a former prostitute.

Novogratz's story about Jane is propelling because she shares how Jane's dreams of escaping poverty, of becoming a doctor and of getting married were fulfilled in an unexpected way.

As these stories present, Jane's dignity, the advice from Sister Mary Theophane and the professor's wisdom affected Jacquelyn Novogratz in her life. Jane, the woman who Novogratz met in the Nairobi slum, represents hope, Sister Mary Theophane gave Novogratz inspiration to go onto to do meaningful work such as starting Acumen Fund, and John Gardner trained Novogratz to be a better listener. What Novogratz gleaned from her encounters with Jane, Sister Mary Theophane and John Gardner are ideas that are ingratiated in InterviewGirl.com.[64] At the core of the Interview Girl Foundation is the belief in the importance of listening to others. We, ourselves grow when we listen to other people. What starts with our listening to people leads to us eventually having the compassion to go on and assist others. As we listen to stories, we cultivate diverse perspectives. Novogratz learned many things from John Gardner, but above all, she learned to listen from Gardner. Novogratz's story about her friendship with Gardner had such an influence on me because I understand what it is like to become friends with someone older than you and to treasure your friendship with him/her. Over and over, Gardner revealed the value of listening to Novogratz. As a philanthropist, this was an immensely useful skill for Novogratz to learn. One of the bearings that InterviewGirl.com brings to the world is that this movement aids people in learning to listen and as individuals become better listeners, the world then becomes a better place.

Mother Teresa

I find Mother Teresa's work inspiring because she righteously embodies what it means to help someone. She devoted herself to helping others. Mother Teresa stands out as one of the greatest humanitarians of the twentieth century because of her indefatigable commitment to aiding those most in need. As one humanitarian doctor reflects, "Humanitarianism doesn't exist in a vacuum, it operates in a dirty reality, and that forces you to struggle with your principles." She combined profound empathy and a fervent commitment to her cause with incredible organizational and managerial skills that allowed her to develop a vast and effective international organization of missionaries to help impoverished citizens all across the globe. She was passionate about the work that she did. Despite the enormous scale of her charitable activities and the millions of lives she touched, to her dying day she held only the most humble conception of her own achievements. In summing up her life, Mother Teresa said, "By blood, I am Albanian. By citizenship, an Indian. By faith, I am a Catholic nun. As to my calling, I belong to the world. As to my heart, I belong entirely to the Heart of Jesus."[65] What motivates me the most about Mother Teresa's life is her humility alongside her pledge to help those in the world who lived in profound misery.

Bishop Macram Gassis

Bishop Macram Gassis is the Catholic bishop of El Obeid, which includes Darfur, and is less than 2 percent Catholic. After decades of fighting for independence from the north, southern Sudan seceded on July 9, 2011, becoming the Republic of South Sudan. In January 2011, nearly 99 percent of the region's voters had approved a split from northern Sudan in an internationally backed referendum. One of the least developed countries in the world, South Sudan nonetheless contains most of the oil that has fueled Sudan's growth over the past decade. The South's departure did not put an end to conflicts. There were many unresolved issues, and Sudan and South Sudan soon began disagreeing bitterly over how to demarcate the border and share oil profits. (The conundrum of the two Sudans is that both countries are extremely dependent on oil, but while the export pipelines run through the north, the bulk of the crude oil lies in the landlocked south).

Bishop Macram Max Gassis of the El Obeid Diocese, which includes the Nuba Mountains and Abyei in South Sudan, has worked tirelessly for decades to protect the God-given rights of all people to live in peace and security. Until his exile, Bishop Gassis played a unique role as the only Sudanese Bishop who was also a native Arabic speaker (the language of the North Sudanese government). This enabled him to serve as the liaison between the Bishops' Conference and the government and gave him distinctive insight into the danger posed by the Sudanese government to its own people. From Kenya Bishop Gassis organized relief for residents of southern Sudan (including parts of what is now the new nation of South Sudan) and the Nuba Mountains terrorized by war—areas that other relief agencies were unable to reach due to an embargo imposed by the Sudanese government. He secretly flew urgently needed food, medical supplies, and aid workers to the region always under threat of attack from government forces. The Bishop himself has been attacked on pastoral visits to the area, where he has sought to provide support to Catholics and non-Catholics alike.

He has created greater international awareness of the catastrophe in South Sudan by testifying to foreign governments, the United Nations Human Rights Commission, other non-governmental agencies, the media, and other Bishops on the atrocities committed in South Sudan. Kathryn Jean Lopez imparts, "American politicians give speeches on "dialogue" with Islam. In the Nuba Mountains of Sudan, Macram Gassis does it. And he does it through action: Life-endangering charity and clarity." For decades Bishop Gassis' work to protect the God-given rights of all people to live in peace and security makes him another one of my mentors. The Sudanese government created dangerous situations for its people and Bishop Gassis took actions to make life better for the citizens living in these situations.

Former Pope John Paul II

In 1978, John Paul made history by becoming the first non-Italian pope in more than four hundred years. As the leader of the Catholic Church, he traveled the world, visiting more than 100 countries to spread his message of faith and peace. A vocal advocate for human rights, John Paul often spoke out about suffering in the world. He held strong positions on many topics, including his opposition to capital punishment. A charismatic figure, John Paul used his influence to bring about political change and is credited with the fall of communism in his native Poland. I admire former Pope John Paul II for umpteen reasons, but I find his avocation for human rights particularly inspirational.

Former Pope Benedict XVI

Another individual who has inspired me is former Pope Benedict XVI. I am most moved by Benedict XVI's writings. As a historical scholar, I appreciate Benedict XVI's erudition. The pope's scholarly writings will continue to influence future generations. This is the beauty of writing things down; generations after an individual is gone, their thoughts and ideas remain. As Hermann Hesse wrote, "Without words, without writing and without books there would be no history, there could be no concept of humanity." Benedict's writings will bring light to people as readers slowly think them through. Michael Novak refers to Benedict as the quiet Pope, the scholar. Novak writes,

> "Benedict may carry in his mind and soul more erudition about more eras of history and more cultures and languages than all but a handful of others on earth. But in his writings on the life of Christ—the latest being on the infancy of Jesus—he writes for you and me, not the experts. For them, the solidity of his work speaks for itself. Benedict himself wrote beautifully

about love. A certain form of love is the inner fire of
God—Deus Caritas Est."

What Benedict stands for and the scholarly genius behind Benedict
XVI's quiet presence is inspirational to me.

Kofi Annan

Another person who I came to admire from the first decade
of the 21st century is Kofi Annan, the seventh Secretary-General
of the United Nations. He was originally from Ghana and he
served as Secretary-General from 1997 to 2006. At Mr. Annan's
initiative, UN peacekeeping was strengthened in ways that enabled
the United Nations to cope with a rapid rise in the number of
operations and personnel. It was also at Mr. Annan's urging that,
in 2005, Member States established two new intergovernmental
bodies: the Peace building Commission and the Human Rights
Council. Mr. Annan likewise played a central role in the creation
of the Global Fund to fight AIDS, Tuberculosis and Malaria, the
adoption of the UN's first-ever counter-terrorism strategy, and
the acceptance by Member States of the "responsibility to protect"
people from genocide, war crimes, ethnic cleansing and crimes
against humanity. His "Global Compact" initiative, launched in
1999, has become the world's largest effort to promote corporate
social responsibility.

Mr. Annan undertook wide-ranging diplomatic initiatives. In
1998, he helped to ease the transition to civilian rule in Nigeria.
Also that year, he visited Iraq in an effort to resolve an impasse
between that country and the Security Council over compliance
with resolutions involving weapons inspections and other
matters—an effort that helped to avoid an outbreak of hostilities,
which was imminent at that time. In 1999, he was deeply involved
in the process by which Timor-Leste gained independence from
Indonesia. He was responsible for certifying Israel's withdrawal

from Lebanon in 2000, and in 2006, his efforts contributed to securing a cessation of hostilities between Israel and Hezbollah. Also in 2006, he mediated a settlement of the dispute between Cameroon and Nigeria over the Bakassi peninsula through implementation of the judgment of the International Court of Justice. His efforts to strengthen the United Nation's management, coherence and accountability involved major investments in training and technology, the introduction of a new whistle-blower policy and financial disclosure requirements, and steps aimed at improving coordination at the country level.

I respect Kofi Annan's salient role within diplomatic initiatives within International Reactions when he was Secretary General of the United Nations. Most of all, I consider Kofi Annan to be an inspirational figure because he urged member states of the United Nations to accept the "responsibility to protect" people from genocide, war crimes, ethnic cleansing and crimes against humanity as well as his central role in the creation of the Global Fund to fight AIDS, Tuberculosis and Malaria. Calling the HIV/AIDS epidemic his "personal priority", Mr. Annan issued a "Call to Action" in April, 2001, proposing the establishment of a Global AIDS and Health Fund, which has since received some $ 1.5 billion in pledges and contributions. People who have AIDS or people experiencing genocide, war crimes, ethnic cleansing and other crimes against humanity are all people who live in misery. Kofi Annan took initiatives to combat these cruelties that humans face. Holding a stately position such as Secretary-General of the United Nations is impressive, but I find Mr. Annan's concern for humanity enlivening.

Jack Harich

Jack Harich is a *Thwink.org* systems engineer. Harich's desire to help others and his new plan to bring about some changes in environmentalism are encouraging. Harich expresses that when he was younger, "I just felt the need to help others. This deep drive may also be related to learning the Golden Rule: "Do unto others as you would have them do unto you."" He also attributes this to possibly coming from his dad, who helped his sons learn how to build things. Harich elaborates,

> "That was light years ago. In 2001 my passion evolved into a more ambitious one: helping to solve the global sustainability problem. That problem is so big and so impossibly difficult that the only way to have more than a 1% chance of success is to take a completely different approach. The heart of this is to first develop a new set of tools, the ones needed to crack the problem wide open. Only then, after we have the right tools in our hands, can we take the second step. This would be applying the tools to solve the problem. It's a matter of ready, aim, fire, instead of the more popular ready, fire. The aiming step is analysis. Deep, correct analysis of difficult problems requires reams of analysis done with the right tools. There is no other way."

What Harich describes about analysis is valid. I admire Harich for his passion to help others and for his belief that deep, correct analysis of difficult problems requires quantities of analysis done with the right tools. Harich unveils that just because a problem is large in size, we shouldn't shy away from trying to ameliorate this problem. Individuals like Harich invigorate me to believe that *Operation A²'s* aims to aid the AIDS crisis will make a difference. The AIDS epidemic is an immense problem, but with asking tough questions coupled with correct analysis, the problem can make progress.

People I Know Personally Who Have Inspired the Interview Girl Spirit

"Dimmi con chi vai e ti diro' chi sei" is an Italian proverb that means: Tell me who you go with and I'll tell you who you are. We are all shaped and defined by those whom we come into contact with in this world and by the time that we spend with others. The individuals mentioned thus far are people whose stories I read in books. The stories about the above individuals decidedly resonated with me to the point that they stayed with me. Through the pages of books filled with words that when those words came together were stories that I could not forget because Edem, James Orbinski, Esther Duflo, Jacqueline Novogratz, Mother Teresa, Father Gassis, former Pope John Paul II, former Pope Benedict XVI, Kofi Annan, and Jack Harich all made the world a better place. The world does not just transform. The world becomes better where misery exists when people take actions. Peoples' actions change the world. That's why I revere everyone mentioned so far. They all acted and through their actions they helped others.

People whom I personally know have greatly affected my role as Interview Girl and what I hope InterviewGirl.com can bring to the world. I'll start with my friend, Sara. I met Sara when I was a freshman at Saint Mary's College. She had the most pleasant disposition. I lived with Sara when I studied abroad in Rome.

She always put others before herself. Sara is someone who truly does not judge others and I think this is commendable. We are all human and we all condemn and judge, but not Sara. InterviewGirl. com will spread positivity. Sure there are bad things happening in the world, but I want InterviewGirl.com to spread positivity. There are many inspiring and uplifting stories. These are the stories we should share. Sara's humility and positive spirit are qualities that I hope permeate this InterviewGirl.com movement.

I have always marveled at my sister's wonderful personality as well as her independence. She does not rely on anyone else to get things done. She, herself does what it is that she needs to do. She always has. This is important for the Interview Girl community to learn. We cannot wait for others. We need to act. Each of us needs to take actions. My sister taught me the value of steady state improvements over time. She does what she needs to do when she should. More than many people I know, she represents this lesson well. She exudes the virtue of diligence. From those working at the Interview Girl Foundation, to everyone living in this world, if we would all apply diligence to what we do, the world would be a better place.

The greatest compliment anyone can ever give me is, "you are just like your Mom." This always has been and will continue to be the best compliment that I've been given. I remember when I was in an interview for my very first job, the gentleman interviewing me asked, "who is your mentor?" and I replied before he could even finish the question, "my Mom." My mother is my ultimate mentor. She is someone whom I continually strive to be like. As children, we are shaped and defined by our parents. I am grateful for all that my Mom taught me, but above all, she taught me about love and sacrifice because she has selflessly sacrificed for our family her entire life. She instilled within me one of this movement's founding pillars: there is always hope. It is especially during the difficult times that I can't forget this. What I want people to take away from InterviewGirl.com is that there is always hope—Always. We must believe that hope will prevail in this world. Misery exists in this world, but there is hope that we can help to do something to lessen the misery for those living in it in this world.

> "But there's a story behind everything. How a picture got on a wall. How a scar got on your face. Sometimes the stories are simple, and sometimes they are hard and heartbreaking. But behind all your stories is always your mother's story, because hers is where yours begin."
> —Mitch Albom, *For One More Day*

Before elaborating further on InterviewGirl.com's strategies, I felt compelled to introduce you to stories that I delight in—stories about people whom I respect and admire. Stories shape and define us all. Although we do not always recognize how they do, when you look into "the whys and the how" behind peoples' decisions, you come across stories that have influenced people along the way. The stories of individuals like Edem, Dr. James Orbinski, Esther Duflo, Jacqueline Novogratz, Mother Teresa, Father Gassis, John Paul II, Benedict XVI, Kofi Annan, Jack Harich, my friend, Sara, my sister and my Mother have a special place in my heart. The work that each of them are doing in our world is moving and encouraging. These individuals and countless others inspire me that by doing something, we can make a difference in this world. One of InterviewGirl.com's founding and guiding pillars is: the more stories you hear, they become a part of you. Often times, once a story enters your heart and your world, you cannot go back. You have to live according to the new story that resides inside you. Stories motivate us to act. I admire the individuals mentioned in this Chapter because I heard and read stories about them, or in the case of the ones close to me, I know their personal stories because I lived some of it. A part of each of these stories and countless others throughout the world all come together in InterviewGirl. com's mission and purpose.

CHAPTER FIVE

The Birth of an Idea

"We keep moving forward, opening new doors, and doing new things, because we're curious, and curiosity keeps leading us down new paths."

—Walt Disney

What is behind an idea?

Charlie Rose once asked Bruce Springsteen, "When do you write?" His reply, "When I have an idea." Any dynamic force or paramount commodity in this world started with an idea. InterviewGirl.com is no different. As an inquiring student, I always asked people questions and in the process, I learned some unmitigated and memorable stories. Story after story seemed as if they just came to me. As my love and passion for collecting stories grew, InterviewGirl.com developed during this process. I wonder if InterviewGirl.com will actually work. There are times when I am doubtful, yet I have never given up hope because I am fascinated with learning about good ideas. Things that are now considered to be stupendous, revolutionary ideas took time to catch on. When those ideas first came about, they were not seen that way. From studying how history's greatest ideas emerged, I've learned that you need to stick with an idea and not give up on it—even if your initial successes are not fruitful.

I wondered what the stories were behind those ideas that we consider to be invaluable ideas? I was intrigued by the stories that I came across. Dr. Jonas Salk did not come up with the cure for polio in his lab. Salk was working on a cure for polio in a dark basement in Pittsburg. He was not getting results there. He went to Italy and while he was walking around in a monastery, he experienced different ideas, including one that led to the polio vaccine.[66] Dino Zaharakis was 11 years old when he did not like the stand that his Dad built for their IPad. He wanted to build a better stand for his new IPad. He came up with a device that he called dzdock. His Dad helped him create a prototype and set up a website to market it. They founded a company to produce them, and from Dino's desire to build a better stand, a new business was born.[67] Paul McCartney of the Beatles woke up one morning with a melody fully developed in his head. He thought that perhaps he had heard it somewhere, but when he thought about it, he could not figure out any other song like it. He worked on lyrics and gave it a title, "Yesterday." As you know, it went on to become one of the most recorded songs in history.[68] Philo Farnsworth envisioned the first electronic television while plowing a field.[69] J.K. Rowling was on a train pondering the plot of a novel for adults when the idea of a child wizard came to her.[70] The Hubble telescope failed and embarrassed NASA. James Crocker was a NASA engineer. In the shower, Crocker was contemplating the Hubble disaster. He looked at the shower head, which could be adjusted to the user's height. In this moment, he made the connection between the shower head and the Hubble problem and invented the idea of placing corrective mirrors on automated arms that could reach inside the telescope and adjust to the correct position.[71] The stories behind how some of history's greatest ideas came to be each have their own unique story, but there are some similar traits that we recognize when we look at where it is that good ideas come from.

Many ideas coming together

Ideas happen when a combination of things come together for an individual. In *Making Ideas Happen*, Scott Belsky argues, "Ideas don't happen because they are great – or by accident. The misconception that great ideas inevitably lead to success has prevailed for too long."[72] David Murray holds that ideas are an amalgam of other peoples' ideas coming together in your new idea in *Borrowing Brilliance*. Murray suggests what the material in his book will do for people. He writes,

> "Ideas give birth to one another. Using this metaphor, your subconscious mind becomes the womb in which new ideas are created. You'll learn how to give birth to them by teaching your subconscious to define, borrow, and combine and so you'll feed it with problems, borrowed ideas, and metaphorical combinations. Then you'll incubate your idea and let your subconscious form a more coherent solution. I'll teach you to use your judgment of this new solution as the mechanism by which to drive the evolution of the idea, in the same way that the fight for survival drove the evolution of organic species."[73]

Murray's description of how he would coach people to get ideas seemed accurate as I reflected on the emergence of InterviewGirl. com. InterviewGirl.com became a reality with many of my ideas coming together. In the next few pages, we will look at some phenomenal ideas that have emerged in this world and transcended over time. We have all heard the story about Facebook and the movie, *The Social Network* has popularized the story about the founder of the site. Facebook is an important idea to speak about because it was an idea that changed the world as we once knew it. Sharing information with one another, sharing content over the internet is now a part of everyday life because of Facebook. Facebook promotes the sharing of ideas between people. InterviewGirl.com is based on sharing stories. Through InterviewGirl.com, people can share stories in specific categories. The story behind Facebook authenticates this notion about ideas giving birth to one another. As you learn the story about how Facebook came to be, you observe that Facebook was a series of events and little attributes that came together before Facebook became the hugely popular social networking site that it has become.

The Birth of an Idea: The Story of Facebook

Mark Zuckerberg is the co-founder and chief executive of Facebook, the world's largest social network, with more than 800 million active users around the world, and roughly 200 million in the United States, or two-thirds of the population. Facebook, born in Mr. Zuckerberg's Harvard dorm room in 2004, has grown from being a quirky site for college students into a popular platform that is used to sell cars and movies, win over voters in presidential elections and organize protest movements. It offers advertisers a global platform, with the exception of China, where Facebook does not operate.[74] One example of the types of change that Facebook has led to include the story of how Facebook played a key role in the various democratic uprisings over the past couple of years. In 2011, during the Arab Spring, it allowed protesters in Egypt to communicate with each other and the world during weeks of demonstrations that led to the ouster of autocratic President Hosni Mubarak.[75] As the Arab world erupted in revolution, a new generation used the internet and social media to try to overthrow their hated leaders. How we communicate with one another, how we invite people to events, how we keep in contact with individuals, and the list never ceases to end—all of these happenings were altered with the internet start-up known as Facebook in 2004.

Facebook emerged with several ideas coming together. Mark Zuckerberg wrote Facemash, the predecessor to Facebook, on

October 28, 2003, while attending Harvard as a sophomore. The site was quickly forwarded to several campus group list-servers, but was shut down a few days later by the Harvard administration. Zuckerberg expanded on this initial project that semester by creating a social study tool to help his classmates study for an art history final, by uploading 500 Augustan images to a website, with one image per page along with a comment section. He opened the site up to his classmates, and people started sharing their notes. The following semester, Zuckerberg began writing code for a new website in January 2004. He was inspired, he said, by an editorial in *The Harvard Crimson* about the Facemash incident. On February 4, 2004, Zuckerberg launched "Thefacebook", originally located at thefacebook.com. Just six days after the site launched, three Harvard seniors, Cameron Winklevoss, Tyler Winklevoss, and Divya Narendra, accused Zuckerberg of intentionally misleading them into believing he would help them build a social network called HarvardConnection.com, while he was instead using their ideas to build a competing product.[76] There was some controversy surrounding who gets the credit for the original idea of Facebook.

This controversy surrounding the birth of Facebook illuminates my point here about ideas. Ideas develop as many thoughts and others ideas come together. There has been no other way. People get ideas from interacting with one another. Peoples' ideas materialize as they expand on other peoples' ideas. New ideas begin for people as they look at things in their current world and expand and add to these particularities and characteristics that surround them. For example, when you read something new, often times something from that reading will connect with something else you have read or with what someone said to you previously. Ideas happen as we make different connections between materials. In the book, *Imagine: How Creativity Works*, Jonathan Lehrer sheds light on connections as he writes,

> "The brain is just an endless knot of connections. And a creative thought is simply ... a network

that's connecting itself in a new way. Sometimes it's triggered by a misreading of an old novel. Sometimes it's triggered by a random thought walking down the street, or bumping into someone in the bathroom of the studio. There are all sorts of ways seemingly old ideas can get reassembled in a new way."[77]

Like Scott Belsky and David Murray, Jonathan Lehrer contends that ideas happen when networks of information in our brains connect themselves in a new way. Arthur Koestler famously termed "bisociation"—the crucial ability to link the seemingly unlinkable. Psychologist, Dean Keith Simonton suggests that geniuses are geniuses because they form more novel combinations than the merely talented.[78] Many who have studied the art and practice of creativity urge that linking things together is the defining characteristic of the creative mind.

Ideas Give Birth to Other Ideas

"The best way to have a good idea is to have a lot of ideas."

—Dr. Linus Pauling

In *The Idea Hunter*, Bill Fischer and Andy Boynton establish that if you believe that ideas are everywhere, then you'll start finding them in droves. Fischer and Boynton go on to explain how Jack Welch brought this spirit to General Electric in the 1980's. Prior to that point, the creation of novel ideas had to take place within the boundaries of an organization. Welch arrived on the scene and set out a new vision that he originally called integrated diversity. The approach came to be known as boundarylessness. Boundarylessness made heroes out of people who recognized and developed a good idea, not just those who came up with one. Leaders were encouraged to share the credit with their teams rather than take full credit themselves.[79] Many good ideas come from individuals who emulate valuable ideas that are already being used by others or ideas that have been used in the past. People then have to implement those ideas into their own particular setting or circumstance. Bill Fischer and Andy Boynton inform, "Innovation is fueled by diversity. And part of a diverse game plan is to take ideas in one setting and use them in a very different one."[80] Thomas Edison gives the advice, "Make it a habit to keep on the lookout for novel and interesting ideas that others have used successfully. Your idea needs to be original only in its adaptation to the problem you are working on." It is still a mystery as to who invented the wheel and when the wheel was invented. According to archaeologists, it was probably invented around 8,000 B.C. in Asia. The oldest wheel known however, was discovered in Mesopotamia and probably dates back to 3,500 B.C. In *Borrowing Brilliance*, David Murray establishes how the wheel was an idea that was built upon throughout history. "An idea forms over time the way an organic species forms. An idea is a living thing, a descendant of the thing it is derived from, the way a rock evolved into the wheel, the wheel into a chariot, and the chariot into the automobile. Ideas give birth to one another."[81] The wheel is probably the most important mechanical invention of all time. Nearly every machine built since the beginning of the Industrial Revolution involves a single, basic principle embodied in one of mankind's truly significant inventions (the wheel). It's hard to imagine any mechanized system that would be possible without the wheel or the idea of a symmetrical component moving in a circular motion on an axis. From tiny watch gears to automobiles, jet engines and computer disk drives, the principle is the same. The original wheel evolved into many brilliant inventions throughout the years. The origins of contemporary Western thought can be traced back to the golden age of ancient Greece when Greek thinkers laid the foundations for modern Western politics, philosophy, science, and law. Their approach was to pursue rational inquiry through adversarial discussion. They decided that the best way to evaluate one set of ideas was by testing it against another set of ideas. In Politics, the result was democracy.[82] Michael Michalko's research found that one of the paradoxes of creativity is that in order to think originally, we must familiarize ourselves with the ideas of others.[83] New ideas emerge when someone breaks down his/her thoughts and compares his/her thoughts with the thoughts of others. All ideas are a combination of many forces coming together and/or parts of other peoples' ideas that are combined with one's own thoughts.

Ideas Emerge: Dan Pallotta's Story and Amy Tan's Advice

"Ideas are like rabbits. You get a couple and learn how to handle them, and pretty soon you have a dozen."
—John Steinbeck

Dan Pallotta is the founder of Pallotta TeamWorks, which invented the multiday AIDSRides and Breast Cancer 3-Days. He is the president of Advertising for Humanity and the author of *Uncharitable: How Restraints on Nonprofits Undermine Their Potential.* In 1999 someone very close to Dan committed suicide. It was from this heartrending situation that an idea came to Dan for a suicide prevention event called, "Out of the Darkness." "Out of the Darkness" has now raised millions for the cause. Dan clarifies, "That idea would never have come to us sitting in our conference room at Pallotta TeamWorks trying to force an event into being. It came from a confluence of tragedy and emotion and timing. And, as a result, it was authentic, not a contrivance."[84] Compilations and projects produced at InterviewGirl.com give people the opportunity to learn about and read about events, people and stories that they have not been exposed to previously. When you are brought out of your comfort zone and into a new situation or when life presents you with some unknowns, often times it is in these burdensome situations that people ascertain new ideas. In a

YouTube video giving advice on Niche ideas, uploaded from user, katiemariepatton, the woman giving advice in the video advises that if one needs an idea, they should go to the library.[85] When you read something and you learn something, it is then that you think of other good ideas because you begin to connect what you read to your own personal life experiences.

Creativity is often discussed as we detect where it is that ideas come from. Author, Amy Tan speaks about the importance of focus. In discussing how she gets her ideas, she clarifies that once she identifies the question, she then sees examples of that question all over the place. She describes that she gets hints everywhere once she has questions that she is seeking. At the celebrated TED conference, Tan poignantly enlightens, "It seems like it's happening all the time. You think its coincidence. You think serendipity, but it may also be explained that now you have a focus. You are noticing it more often." When you know what you are looking for, it becomes easier to have ideas. You begin to notice the cues that are everywhere just as Amy Tan informs us. In *Snap, Seizing Your Aha Moments*, Katherine Ramsland points out,

> "As we develop a defined or vigilant awareness, we notice more things. We become more attuned to the immediate world. Small details take on more meaning. What turns one thing rather than another from background into figure is the attention we pay—the significance we attribute to it. We become more mindful as a habit. We look and we see. The habit of focus keeps us awake and alert."[86]

As Tan and Ramsland explicate, when you know what you are looking for, it becomes easier to have ideas. Jim Rohn, the personal development expert, remarks that you make your life better with ideas. He urges people to keep a journal and document their ideas. In Michael Michalko's *Cracking Creativity*, he gives the reader nine strategies to think like a creative genius, in strategy three

(Thinking Fluently), he argues, "We think of a creative genius as a mysterious person who spontaneously creates ideas out of the blue. This is not so. This is not how a creative genius gets ideas. He or she gets ideas by working hard and incorporating deliberate thinking practices."[87] When individuals have focus and direction, it is then that ideas "come to" people.

> "Discovery is seeing what everybody else has seen, and thinking what nobody else has thought."
> —Albert Szent-Gyorgyi

Ideas Emerge from Leonardo Da Vinci to Michelangelo's *David*

You get the idea—all things that we consider resplendent in our world started with an idea. That great idea was formed as hints, clues, and relevant information all came together. Ideas don't happen in isolation. Scott Belsky believes that "the forces of community are invaluable and readily available. You must embrace opportunities to broadcast and then refine your ideas through the energy of those around you."[88] What and who one comes into contact with shapes one's ideas. The truth is that oodles of the world's greatest ideas have emerged over time. These about-face ideas that once they come to fruition alter our lives as we once knew them came to the individuals who originally thought of them a little bit at a time. Take for example the founder of Wal-Mart, Sam Walton. Mr. Walton explains,

> "Somehow over the years, folks have gotten the impression that Walmart was something I dreamed up out of the blue as a middle-aged man. It's true that I was forty-four when we opened our first Walmart in 1962, but the store was really an outgrowth of everything we'd been doing since Newport—another case of me being

unable to leave well enough alone, another experiment. And like most other over-night successes, it was about 20 years in the making."[89]

Jonathan Harris is a storyteller and Internet anthropologist. Harris told Scott Belsky that ideas aggregate over time and they pop up one day when you are in the shower. He continued to describe the second phase as deciding that you are going to pursue this given thing. Once you've decided, it's a different mind-set from that point forward.[90] It is important to act on the ideas that you have. As with Sam Walton, David Murray, Scott Belsky, Jack Foster, Jonathon Leher; Jonathan Harris too believes that ideas emerge over time.

I have been fascinated with where ideas come from and the creative process. William James describes the creative process as "a seething cauldron of ideas, where everything is fizzling and bobbing about in a state of bewildering activity." Dr. Richard Restak, a Clinical Professor of Neurology at The George Washington University School of Medicine and Health Sciences believes that creativity isn't a mysterious gift, but rather it is a natural human ability. In *The Prepared Mind of a Leader*, Bill Welter and Jean Egmon teach, "while creativity is complex, our imagination is based on human capabilities and experiences each of us already has had and just need to practice reassembling in new ways." There is a lot of wisdom in motivational speaker, Charlie 'Tremendous' Jones' words, "You'll be the same in five years as you are today, except for the people you meet and the books you read." The books in my library on ideas and creativity have quadrupled in the past year. Jonah Lehrer's *Imagine: How Creativity Works* is a book about how people connect everyday things to unexpected things. It is the story of how we imagine. According to Lehrer,

"Creativity should not be seen as something otherworldly. It shouldn't be thought of as a process reserved for artists and inventors and other creative types. The human mind, after all, has the creative impulse built into its operating system, hard-wired into its most essential programming code. At any given moment, the brain is automatically forming new associations, continually connecting an everyday x to an unexpected y."[91]

George Lois states that creativity is discovering ideas rather than "creating" them and John Cleese defined it as "a way of operating" rather than a mystical talent. The more people whom you speak with, the more books that you read, the more classes that you take, and ultimately, the more that you experience in life—this is what allows one to better make connections and as we continually make connections, this is how distinguished ideas emerge.

Leonardo Da Vinci, considered by many to be the greatest genius of all time, believed that to gain knowledge about the form of problems, you begin by learning how to restructure it in many ways. As Dean Keith Simonton characterizes that geniuses are geniuses because they form more novel combinations than the merely talented, Leonardo Da Vinci looked at problems from diverse perspectives and then was able to answer the problems different than most people.[92] What Da Vinci means by learning how to restructure problems in many ways is that he felt that the first way that he looked at a problem was too biased toward his usual way of seeing things. He would restructure his problem by looking at it from one perspective and move on to another perspective and then another. From each perspective, his understanding would become stronger and he would better understand the problem. Leonardo Da Vinci called this thinking strategy saper vedere (knowing how to see). It is necessary to look at things from a different perspective. When one looks at something differently, this is often when ideas materialize.

Looking at something from a diverse perspective allows one to see something that he/she could not otherwise see. Michael Michalko explains that Phillip Reiss, Chester Carlson, Fred Smith,

Charles Duell, and Robert Millikan all had ideas, but because people around them were focusing their attention in the wrong areas, their ideas never came to fruition. Phillip Reiss invented a machine that could transmit music in 1861. He was most likely a few days away from inventing the telephone. Communication experts persuaded him there was no market for this device because the telegraph was good enough. Chester Carlson invented xerography in 1938. Every major corporation scoffed at his idea and turned him down. They believed that since carbon paper was cheap and in abundance, no one would buy an expensive copier. Fred Smith was a student at Yale when he came up with the concept of Federal Express, a national overnight delivery service. The U.S. Postal Service, UPS, predicted his enterprise would fail. People thought that based on their experience in the industry, no one would pay more for speed and reliability. In 1899, Charles Duell, the director of the U.S. Patent Office suggested that the government close the office because everything that could be invented was invented. In 1923, Robert Millikan, winner of the Nobel Prize said that there was absolutely no likelihood that man could harness the power of the atom.

Someone's good idea is often times when an individual has the same information as everyone else, but that individual sees "something" different. It is all about perspective, which is ironic because InterviewGirl.com was founded to share new perspectives with the world. According to Michael Michalko, "geniuses have the ability to connect the unconnected by forcing relationships that enable them to see things to which others are blind."[93] Samuel Morse's story is a good example of an individual connecting the unconnected. Morse could not figure out how to produce a signal strong enough to be received coast to coast. While he saw horses being exchanged at a relay station, he forced a connection between relay stations for horses and strong signals. He then figured out that the solution was to give the traveling signal periodic boosts of power.[94] Obtaining good ideas comes from an individual's ability to make new combinations as well as their ability to connect the unconnected. Genius transpires when one finds a new perspective on a problem by restructuring it in some way.[95]

Michelangelo, the great Renaissance painter, sculptor, architect, poet, and engineer, is another individual whom we can learn from about getting ideas. Michelangelo teaches us that we need to have a plan. Scholars have described that Michelangelo had amazing vision because he saw art where others only saw rock. He is quoted as saying, "In every block of marble I see a statue as plain as though it stood before me, shaped and perfect in attitude and action. I have only to hew away the rough walls that imprison the lovely apparition to reveal it to the other eyes as mine see it." Michelangelo chiseled away at the *David*, his masterpiece each day. He saw what it was that he wanted to do before it was done. "Every block of stone has a statue inside it and it is the task of the sculptor to discover it," Michelangelo said. He saw *David*, he saw the *Pieta*, and he saw Moses. I knew that I wanted to write, I knew that I loved listening to stories, I knew how compelling stories could be, and I knew that there were too many people experiencing misery in this world. InterviewGirl.com was a concrete idea in my head. Now it was a matter of taking action and making the idea a reality. I made a list, organized the list into a plan, and before you knew it, InterviewGirl.com was born and this book was being written.

> "Many great ideas go unexecuted, and many great executioners are without ideas. One without the other is worthless."
>
> —Tim Blixseth

InterviewGirl.com is Born

> "In the long run, men hit only what they aim at."
> —Henry David Thoreau

My point is that I had an idea. Actually I had several ideas and from these ideas eventually came InterviewGirl.com. I always have ideas. I have words, thoughts, and ideas jotted down in numerous notebooks as well on scrap paper all over the place. After my trip to Africa all of these ideas came together and InterviewGirl.com was officially born. As Amy Tan described creativity, as "focus" came to my "InterviewGirl.com" idea, there now seemed to be an organization and purpose to my "compiling" habit. All of these notes, ideas, and stories that I had been jotting down for years now had a specific scope to serve. There were times when I questioned my pointless note taking habit. I would always take notes as I read books, I would jot down family memories that I did not want to forget, I would take notes during the homily at mass and the list could go on. I had all of these stories that I had heard and collected through the years. I could not decide what book to write. As I said, InterviewGirl.com started as *Travel Girl*, then it was meant to be a voice for those who cannot be heard to share their stories, then it was a World War Two stories compilation, then it was a compilation of stories about exiles from Venezia Giulia after World War Two, but it has morphed into many other areas, as well.

Interview Girl.com had been brewing. Writing stories, reading, learning, traveling, and interviewing people— these things are a natural part of who I am. They are unequivocally part of what makes me—me. Rather than constantly beating myself up for not being a doctor or a scientist who can cure the AIDS disease, I decided to use the talents that God gave me to make a difference in the lives of others. After volunteering in Africa and learning Amara's story, it all came together and InterviewGirl.com came to fruition. I had a vision, a plan to achieve that vision, and the tenacity to do the work to make the vision a reality. My reason for wanting to make InterviewGirl.com a reality is because of the misery that many people in this world experience. InterviewGirl. com is a way to help alleviate some of that misery. InterviewGirl. com collects stories and then brings all of these stories together in order to introduce people to new ideas. As Interview Girl,

I believe that everyone whom I meet has a story to share. As I traveled the past few summers, there were stories everywhere that I went. The stories came from the enthralling individuals that I met along my journeys of travel. Projects produced at InterviewGirl. com are filled with stories about different people who have been interviewed. InterviewGirl.com then shares these stories with the world.

George Mandler is a leading researcher in the problems of consciousness. When you keep a historical record of your ideas and problems, you initiate a phenomenon that George Mandler calls mind popping. Mind popping is when a solution or idea seems to appear, after a period of incubation, out of nowhere.[96] The founder of Walmart said that his idea was a long time in the making. I agree with this. I feel the same way about InterviewGirl. com. Sam Walton explains,

> "They thought Walmart was just another one of Sam Walton's crazy ideas. It was totally unproven at the time, but it was really what we were doing all along: experimenting, trying to do something different, educating ourselves as to what was going on in the retail industry and trying to stay ahead of those trends."[97]

Experimenting and trying new things allowed Sam Walton to create his new store. The same goes for Thomas Edison and many other legendary creators that have lived throughout history. Thomas Edison had the brilliant idea that he did because of the environment he created. The profound and knowledgeable ideas did not just come to him, but rather his practices fostered the development of his ideas. As Michael Gelb and Sarah Caldicott write, "Edison's charismatic optimism, passionate curiosity, love of learning, storytelling, and appreciation for the diverse talents of his staff all contributed to the creation of an unprecedented culture of innovation."[98] Edison continually worked at innovation.

His scintillating ideas did not just pop into his head out of the blue.

> "To accomplish great things, we must not only act, but also dream; not only plan, but also believe."
>
> —Anatole France

The Power of a Story

When David Choe told ABC News that with the godlike amount of money that he would have from the stock going public, "Where I could actually change the world," as I read that phrase, it was as if it jumped off the page. I finally got it. In order to make real changes in this world, to help terminate a misery that exists, I had to develop something useful for individuals, something that people would want because my creation would serve them in some capacity. Once I developed or created something that people would appreciate because it did in fact serve them or solve problems that they experience, I would be able to generate revenue. Every great invention, every medical breakthrough, every advance of humankind began with passion: a passion for change, for making the world a better place, for contributing, and/or for making a difference.

> "The most powerful weapon on Earth is the human soul on fire."
>
> —Ferdinand Foch

I passionately believe that stories have the power to reshape a person's world. I also knew that stories sell. Take for example, *Harry Potter*. *Harry Potter* is a series about a bespectacled boy-wizard with a tragic past and a potentially heroic future that began in 1997 with "Harry Potter and the Sorcerer's Stone." *Harry Potter* has become one of the most successful book publishing sensations of all time, credited with turning millions of young people into avid readers. J.K. Rowling, the author, created multi-layered plots with a lively cast of characters performing an array of magical feats against the overarching theme of good versus evil. The seven-book series (one volume for each of Harry's years at the Hogwarts School of Witchcraft and Wizardry) was finished in 2007, when "Harry Potter and the Deathly Hallows," the final installment, was released. This final volume became the fastest-selling book in history, with more than 11 million copies sold during the first 24 hours in three markets alone. All seven "Harry Potter" books smashed sales records, selling 450 million copies worldwide, and have been translated into 70 languages. As a result, Ms. Rowling, a single mother when she started writing the series, is now one of the richest women in Britain.[99] People are drawn to the stories of the "Harry Potter" books.

The Hunger Games trilogy is another example of a story that moved many people. In August of 2012, *The Hunger Games* "put life into the stagnant home entertainment market," as fans snatched up 3.8 million DVDs and Blu-ray discs in the title's first two days on sale in the U.S. and Canada. That was more than either of the last two "Twilight" films. In February of 2012, "The Twilight Saga: Breaking Dawn, Part 1" sold 3.2 million DVDs and Blu-rays on its first weekend, while "Eclipse" debuted to 2.7 million units in December 2010.[100] The satisfying stories of *Harry Potter* and *The Hunger Games* make people want to find out more and hear how the stories finish. We live in a world where facts are easy to come by. Facts and specifics are now ubiquitous and through a Google search, information is right at our finger tips. Daniel Pink believes that what begins to matter more is the ability to place these facts in context and to deliver them with emotional impact. Stories have dynamism that can touch people's lives. People love stories. I knew that there was the possibility to help people through the use of stories. Although it took some time for InterviewGirl.com and the Interview Girl Foundation to emerge, I recognized that there was something special that existed in stories, something magical. Science fiction author, David Brin shares, "storytelling is the only absolutely verified form of magic. Magic is the creation of subjective realities in other people's heads."[101] Using stories was a way for me to contribute to defeating a misery such as Amara not having access to medication.

"Books are a uniquely portable magic."
—Stephen King

A Catalyst

"Problems are the previous addresses of new ideas."
—Dan Zadra

The ideas were there, but it was when I sat there one night watching videos that I took of the children whom I met in Africa, when I looked at these videos a little closer, it was then in that moment, that I took concrete actions and acted on my ideas. That is another important point about ideas. You can have the most amazing idea in the world, but if you don't take actions toward making that idea a reality, it will not become an actualization. In *How to Get Ideas*, Jack Foster describes that most people get an idea, they tell some people about it, the people all say, "wow, that's great," and then they go onto something else and never do anything more about the idea they told people about. Foster continues, "The truth is: There is no difference between a.) having an idea and not doing anything with it and b.) not having an idea at all."[102]

"Even if you're on the right track, you'll get run over if you just sit there."
—Will Rogers

What is it that makes people finally accomplish something or take necessary action? Often times, a "catalyst" is what makes someone do something and/or propels an individual to take a necessary step in order to achieve something. There are many examples of a catalyst, a certain event, and/or a moment that forces people to finally do something. Sometimes people can be catalysts. A catalyst is often a person whose talk, enthusiasm, or energy causes others to be more friendly, enthusiastic, or energetic or that precipitates an event or change.

One common phenomenon in our society is when someone hits "Rock Bottom," it is then that they triumph over failure. Steve Jobs was fired from his own company; Nelson Mandela spent 27 years in prison; and Abraham Lincoln failed in business, had a nervous breakdown, and was defeated in eight elections. Jobs, Mandela, and Lincoln all faced adversity, yet they went on to achieve extraordinary success. Nelson Mandela spent 27 years in prison before becoming the first President of South Africa to be elected in a fully representative democratic election. During his time in jail, he kept a scrap of paper in his cell that contained the words of a poem by William Ernest Henley, entitled "Invictus." It ends with the famous lines, "I am the master of my fate: I am the captain of my soul."[103] Donald Latumahina discusses bouncing back after difficulties in his blog, *The Power of Hitting Rock Bottom*. A female responded to Latumahina's blog, where he discussed how to take advantage of hitting Rock Bottom,

> "I can really relate to this post. After my brother died 8 years ago, I was devastated. However, from his death, my husband and I took a look at the direction our lives were heading and decided that none of us knows how long we have on this planet, so we were going to make the best of the time we have. We completely changed our focus and made the decision that we were going to live each day as a special day. Looking back now, my brother's illness was the catalyst to the life we have now. Some good has come from something so tragic and sad."[104]

This woman was devastated after her brother's passing, but she used this as a catalyst to live her life differently from there on out. When difficult life situations arise, there are those people who find a way to work around these less than ideal circumstances and then they go onto accomplish the unthinkable. The story of Liu Wei exhibits how a boy took on a challenge that many saw as intractable. Liu Wei was a ten year old in China when he was playing hide-and-seek. After he came into contact with a high-voltage wire, he received a severe electric shock. In order to save him, his arms were amputated. This situation was particularly heart-breaking for Liu Wei because it was his dream to become an accomplished pianist. A lot of people would just give up on the dream of becoming a pianist after such a traumatic loss, but Wei learned to use his feet to accomplish basic piano skills. Even with losing his arms, Liu Wei did not give up on his dream to be an accomplished pianist. Not only did he master playing the piano with his toes, but he also became a prodigy. He was twenty-three when he entered *China's Got Talent* and won the contest.[105] Liu Wei embraced his struggle of losing his arms and despite the obstacle, he decided to pursue his goal and become a pianist. Often times a catalyst makes someone do something. The catalyst could be an adversity as it was in Liu Wei's case or it can be a particular moment, an emotional reaction to something, a spark that occurs after meeting someone, or many other instances that ignite a person to take action and do something.

Bill Drayton is the founder of *Ashoka*. *Ashoka* was founded in 1980. The organization helped originate the concept of social entrepreneurship, working outside of the government and business sectors to find sustainable solutions for societal needs. *Ashoka* fosters citizen-led innovation focused on social change. Drayton discloses,

> "In 1962, when I was 19, I visited India. With introductions from people involved in the U.S. civil rights movement, I was able to visit with several of

the leading Gandhians there. The hundred-to-one difference in average per capita income between America and India at the time was a stark reality for the people who became my friends there. Action was essential, and given the magnitude of the problem, it had to be significant. But as a college sophomore, I had little wealth or power. I knew that finding an approach with maximum leverage was critical."[106]

Drayton was affected by the difference in per capita income between America and India. As he, himself said, "Action was essential." Drayton met people affected with a misery and he was determined to do something to help change this misery for the people experiencing this misery. What Drayton saw in India became a catalyst for him to take action.

As I sat there that fall evening, when looking a little closer at the videos that I had taken with my flip camera in Africa a few months before, I noticed something in the videos of the children that I never saw before. Asantuwa, a little orphan girl who is HIV positive, seemed so sad. I was mad at myself for not spending more time with her. I missed the children and I was upset that I could not do more to help them. I wished that I had more money to send them to make sure that they all had access to medicine, if it was needed. I was inspired to make a difference (to change the fact that kids like Amara do not have access to medicine), yet I felt like I was just sitting across the world not doing a thing. I leaned back in my chair, I noticed piles of books on the floor surrounding my desk. There sat the stacks of books about AIDS, Africa, human trafficking, ideas, creativity, development economics and poverty. As my back pushed the mesh back of my chair even further back, my eyes glanced from the floor where the books were scattered to my computer screen. Asantuwa's melancholy look was frozen on my computer screen. My eyes moved from my computer to the wall above my computer desk. I looked at the cork board mounted on the wall above my desk. There inhabited the $10 Ghana cedis bill that I pinned in the middle of the cork board and the name **AMARA** written on a note card. I never did get a chance to take a picture of Amara, but I would never forget her soft smile and gentle tone, "Auntie Victoria, please explain geology to me ...." Awhile back I had pinned the Ghana cedis money and Amara's name to my cork board to remind myself ... that sweet girl died because "the medicines ran out" to put things into perspective for me when my life got "stressful" at home. I gazed at the picture of Asantuwa frozen on my computer screen. As I looked up a little from the computer screen, I saw the Ghana cedis pinned to my cork board next to Amara's name. In the time that it took my eyes balls to move from *A* to *A* in Amara's name, I opened up a blank word document and I found myself typing, "InterviewGirl. com—Changing the World One Story at a Time." InterviewGirl. com had been born.

> "True compassion is more than flinging a coin to a beggar; it comes to see that an edifice which produces beggars needs restructuring."
>
> —Martin Luther King Jr.

CHAPTER SIX

Who Doesn't Love a Story?

Who doesn't love a story?

A GOOD STORY CAN:

- shake you by the roots
- make you rethink old truths
- paste large questions in the sky
- inspire you to reach for what you cannot

The Power of a Story

"A life without stories would be no life at all."
—from Alexander McCall Smith's, *In the Company of Cheerful Ladies*

Who doesn't love a good story? Your favorite teacher is the one who tells the best stories. Your favorite uncle is the one who makes you laugh with his exaggerated stories. For all the Catholics out there who attend weekly mass, the homilies that resonate with you and that you remember are when the Priest shares a powerful story during the homily. On a cold Sunday in January, I just made it in time for noon mass. You know your Saturday night was eventful when you can barely make noon mass. I couldn't tell you one line from the actual Gospel that day. I was there in the pew. I heard the Gospel, but I can't remember the details. I do remember how the Priest started the homily, though. He told us a story about how he was attending a basketball game and at half time, there were performers called the transformers. He then explained their performance in detail. His personal story about attending that basketball game led to the main point of his homily. The Gospel that particular day told the story about how Jesus turned water into wine and how this was a miraculous transformation. I remembered the points that the priest made about transformation and the questions that he posed to us about what we could transform in our own lives because of the story that he shared. How many times have you become engrossed with a good story? It probably happens more than you even realize. How many times have you stayed up late reading a novel that you couldn't put down, or watching a movie that you couldn't turn off? How many times have you pushed yourself harder after hearing the story of someone else's success, or changed your opinion after reading a convincing article in a magazine or newspaper? Stories have a powerful effect upon people.

Every movie that you love is a story that is told to you through the medium of video. We all love stories and stories help us, guide us, enrich us, and make us understand on a deeper level. When you get together with old friends, you all sit around and tell those great stories that have emerged through the years of your friendship and everyone roars with laughter. The most dynamic public speakers are the ones who grab their audience's attention through the story that they are sharing. Online marketing experts encourage individuals to get people to follow them in whatever endeavor they are undertaking online by sharing their story with the audience.

The best teachers and professors are the ones who use analogies and tell stories to make the curriculum come alive. The curriculum becomes more than just facts and dates, but it becomes ideas and themes that the students will remember for many years to come. In a history course, if a teacher just spits out facts and those facts don't make any sense, you don't understand the curriculum and it is boring, but if you have a teacher who has done some research and knows some heart-stirring stories to plug in along with the historical details and bring all the pieces together, well then you become interested. Take a US History class, for example.

Many people know that Harry Truman was President of the USA at the end of WWII, but do they know the story behind how Truman became President of the USA? Do they know what Harry Truman was doing twenty years before he was destined to be President of the USA? In 1922, Truman was 38 and he had gone bankrupt in the clothing business. He said to his wife, "I can't die like this. I know that I was born to do something more." She told him that she believed in him. Twenty-three years later in 1945, that same man was President of the United States of America. When a story like this is inserted into the U.S. history curriculum, history class becomes more enjoyable and a lesson is learned. Many times in life, people have to overcome adversity before they can succeed at something.

Anytime I mention Harry Truman, I cannot help but think of Jimmy, one of the World War Two vets whom I befriended and what Jim taught me about Mr. Truman. Jim told me a story about a sign on the President's desk when I asked Jim a question about whether he liked FDR or Truman more since he was alive through both presidential regimes. Jim painted a picture of Truman's office for me as he described that a sign "The Buck Stops Here" was on President Truman's desk in his White House office. Through a story behind the story, Jim narrated that the sign was made in the Federal Reformatory at El Reno, Oklahoma. Fred M. Canfil, then United States Marshal for the Western District of Missouri and a friend of Mr. Truman, saw a similar sign while visiting the Reformatory and asked the Warden if a sign like it could be made for President Truman. The sign was made and mailed to the President on October 2, 1945. I cannot forget Jimmy, a 96 year old WWII vet whom I befriended in completing my WWII interviews, slamming his palm down on the table, smirking while saying, "The Buck Stops Here," as he told me a story about President Truman, so that I could better understand Truman's presidential regime. History is filled with many untold interesting and intriguing stories. If history is made up of fascinating stories, then so too is life. Sharing stories is the premise behind InterviewGirl.com. The Interview Girl Foundation, the non-profit organization that is part of InterviewGirl.com is centered around people sharing stories. InterviewGirl.com's mission is to collect peoples' stories and then to share them with you.

> "Story is a round space in which the ear and the tongue, together, create the magic."
>
> —*Personal Writing Book*

Human beings wish to listen to stories. There wouldn't be life on planet Earth without stories. The influence of an admirable story can motivate people to do more than you would imagine. Through the years I've heard phrases like: the power of a good story can move mountains. As Dr. Hannah B. Harvey, an award-winning professor, an internationally recognized performer, and a nationally known professional storyteller characterizes, "The gift of storytelling may be one of life's most powerful—and envied—skills. A story well told can make us laugh, weep, swell with pride, or rise with indignation."[107] In an interview with the managing director of the Wharton Interactive Media Initiative, Peter Guber explains that in the past 40 years of his career, "in virtually every part of storytelling, from writing books and speaking and teaching and being a newscaster and being a talk show host for 533 interviews and making thousands of movies and television shows—is that we are all wired as storytellers." He believes that the amazing thing is we're all born as storytellers and story-listeners and somehow we don't venerate its value.

I believe that InterviewGirl.com will succeed in becoming an effort that can make a difference in this world because there are an indefinite numbers of stories that need to be shared. As I was deciding how to contribute to humanity, how to serve, and the idea that a story can profoundly affect someone was the major principal around which I wanted to create an organization. Hearing a powerful story can alter one's life. The power of a story became the backbone of InterviewGirl.com. Hearing the right story at the right time can change someone's reality. In Amanda Low's Blog entry, *After Sandy Hook, I've Changed My Mind on Gun Control*, she describes that after learning the story of the tragic events at the elementary school in Connecticut, she changed her mind about gun control.[108] She felt one way for a long time, but a lugubrious story was able to diversify her view point. For many Christians, often times it is in hearing a certain Bible passage that from that point forward something in their reality is then altered.[109] There are countless accounts of individuals who found their "faith," found "Jesus," were "saved," etc. after it was that they heard a story from the Bible or they started to read the Bible. These individuals then converted to Christianity because those stories from the Bible resonated with them. Certain stories make history more interesting. Certain stories make us understand events differently. Hearing a story allows people to look at their circumstances from a new perspective.

> "After nourishment, shelter and companionship, *stories* are the thing we need most in the world."
>
> —Philip Pullman

In today's modern world, stories are an intrinsic part of our societies and cultures. Movies, books, music, news media, religions, architecture and painting, you name it, and the influence of storytelling is exhibited in all aspects of our life. Stories define our values, desires, and dreams. They also define our prejudices and hatreds. In Robert McKee's *Story*, he asks us to imagine all the stories that happen in one global day, "the pages of prose turned, plays performed, films screened, the unending stream of television comedy and drama, twenty-four hour print and broadcast news, bedtime tales told to children, barroom bragging, and back-fence Internet gossip." Humankind has an insatiable appetite for stories. McKee continues "story is not only our most prolific art form but rivals all activities—work, play, eating, and exercise—for our waking hours. We tell and take stories as much as we sleep—and even then we dream." McKee asks us, "Why? Why is so much of our life spent inside stories?" As critic Kenneth Burke tells us, "Stories are equipment for living."[110] Stories do help people to live their lives. Take for example, the "Boy Who Cried Wolf" story. Many of us learned the lesson that you cannot pretend something happened if it actually did not because then when the "real" scenario hits, no one will believe you, from this very story. When civilizations throughout history have fallen, the only things that survive in those civilizations are the art and the stories that were written down or the stories that were shared orally that were then passed onto the next generation via word of mouth. It is believed by most historians and psychologists that storytelling defines and binds our humanity. Humans are perhaps the only animals that create and tell stories. The stories that comprise the compilations that are produced at InterviewGirl.com will help individuals in their lives. By people sharing their stories, we can all learn immeasurable lessons and ideas.

Science proves the power of stories

"Humans are not ideally set up to understand logic; they are ideally set up to understand stories."
—Roger C. Schank, Cognitive Scientist

Scientific research unveils that stories stimulate the brain and even change how we act in life. Neuroscientists validate that there is increased activity in the brain when humans hear and tell stories. Leo Widrich, the co-founder of *Buffer*, a smarter way to share on Twitter and Facebook, tells *Lifehacker* that individuals' brains become more active when they tell stories. When people learn facts, a certain part in the brain gets activated. Scientists call this Broca's area and Wernicke's area. Overall, learning facts and pieces of information hits the language processing parts in the brain, where individuals decode words into meaning. Nothing else happens in the brain when someone decodes words into meaning. When an individual is told a story, things change dramatically. Not only are the language processing parts in someone's brain activated, but any other area in one's brain that he/she would use when experiencing the events of the story are also activated. A story can put one's whole brain to work.[111]

Certain stories have undoubtedly helped us shape our current thinking and way of life. When we tell these stories to others, our stories can have the same effect on the people listening to our stories that our stories had on us. Uri Hasson, a professor from Princeton together with a team of scientists conducted a study that monitored peoples' brain activity while stories were shared. Hasson and his team had a woman tell a story while in an MRI scanner. Functional MRI scans detect brain activity by monitoring blood flow; when a brain region is active it needs more blood to provide oxygen and nutrients. The active regions light up on a computer screen. The team of scientists recorded the woman's story on a computer and monitored her brain activity as she spoke. She did this twice, once in English and once in Russian; she was fluent in both languages. Hasson's study illuminates that the brain of the person telling a story and the brain of the person listening to it can synchronize. Hasson gives the example,

"When the woman spoke English, the volunteers understood her story, and their brains synchronized.

When she had activity in her insular, an emotional brain region, the listeners did too. When her frontal cortex lit up, so did theirs. By simply telling a story, the woman could plant ideas, thoughts and emotions into the listeners' brains."

The experiments from neuroscientists like Uri Hasson showcase that a story can make someone feel as if he/ she experienced the same thing as the storyteller. If someone tells people about how delicious certain foods were, their sensory cortex lights up or if they tell them a story about motion, their motor cortex gets active. Cognitive Neuroscientist Michael Gazzaniga suspects that narrative coherence helps us to navigate the world. He believes that narratives help people to know where they are coming from and where they are headed. He holds that narrative coherence tells people where to place their trust and why. One reason we may love fiction, he says, is that it enables us to find our bearings in possible future realities, or to make better sense of our own past experiences. He shares, "What stories give us, in the end, is reassurance. And as childish as it may seem, that sense of security—that coherent sense of self—is essential to our survival."[112] Joshua Gowin (PhD) cites how the team of scientists at Princeton, led by Uri Hasson that conducted the study about how peoples' brains sync up when they tell stories, may also explain another phenomenon of story-telling. What he terms as, story-stealing,

"Do you have a friend that you can tell one of your stories to, and then two weeks later the friend tells you the same story, except now it happened to them? Perhaps, by telling them, you transferred the story to their brain. They felt as if they were there, if only vicariously through you. Take it as a tribute to your gift as a good storyteller."[113]

When someone hears a story, it is as if the individual is living that story. Any of us who have enjoyed a story that someone told us may have felt this tendency. Now science also substantiates that the people who are listening to one's story and the individual sharing the story experience the same effect.

Science evidences that sharing stories bring people together. Stories bring meaning and understanding to what is happening in people's lives. Jill Bolte Taylor, author of the *New York Times* bestselling memoir *My Stroke of Insight: A Brain Scientist's Personal Journey* also describes how stories help people to make sense of the world around them. Her research about the left brain's ability finds that,

> "One of the most prominent characteristics of our left brain is its ability to weave stories. This storyteller portion of our left mind's language center; is specifically designed to make sense of the world outside of us, based on minimal amounts of information. It functions, by taking whatever details it has to work with, and then weaves them together in the form of a story."[114]

Dr. Jill Bolte Taylor's personal story is particularly interesting because she is a Harvard-trained and published neuroanatomist who experienced a severe hemorrhage in the left hemisphere of her brain in 1996. On the afternoon of this rare form of stroke (AVM), she could not walk, talk, read, write, or recall any of her life. It took eight years for Dr. Taylor to completely recover all of her functions and thinking ability. Her training as a neuroanatomist and her personal experience of a stroke have led her to draw the conclusion that our brains take information from the world around us and then weave that information to form stories.

We all enjoy a good story, whether it's a novel, a movie, or just something one of our friends is explaining to us. If you look back to your own experience as a student, you probably remember that classes were boring when the teacher seemed as if he/she just randomly explained a bunch of facts, but you loved it when you had a teacher who told memorable stories. According to *Psychology Today*, telling stories is the best way to teach, persuade, and even understand ourselves. There is no doubt that we can all relate to feeling much more engaged when we hear a narrative about events. An article in the *New York Times* on Neuroscience and Fiction reaffirms,

> "Indeed, in one respect novels go beyond simulating reality to give readers an experience unavailable off the page: the opportunity to enter fully into other people's thoughts and feelings ... Individuals who frequently read fiction seem to be better able to understand other people, empathize with them and see the world from their perspective."[115]

Neuroscience supports the value of fiction and the value of stories. When we hear a story, it is as if we lived that story.

History's Story Lovers

After learning about how neuroscience proved that storytelling activated certain parts of the brain, I was curious to study illustrious historical individuals and see what connections I could find about those individuals (those people who "make it into" the History books, as they say) and storytelling. Three historical figures in particular attracted my attention as I researched about people throughout history that enjoyed sharing stories. Leonardo Da Vinci, Thomas Edison, and Abraham Lincoln all loved storytelling. On top of the paintings, sketches and inventions, Leonardo Da Vinci crafted fables. Leonardo is not generally remembered as a storyteller, but he wrote many fables. Some scholars consider his fables to be in a similar category as those of Aesop. Fables are very short, but involve complicated ideas. Below is a sample of Leonardo Da Vinci's fable, *The Tongue & the Teeth*:

The Tongue & the Teeth

Once upon a time there was a boy who had a bad habit of talking more than was necessary.

"What a tongue!" sighed the teeth one day. "It is never still, never quiet!"

"What are you grumbling about?" replied the tongue arrogantly. "You teeth are only slaves, and your job is merely to chew whatever I decide. We have nothing in common, and I shall not allow you to meddle in my affairs."

So the boy went on chattering, very impertinently sometimes, and his tongue was happy, learning new words every day.

But one day, when the boy did some damage, and then allowed his tongue to tell a big lie, the teeth obeyed the heart, sprang together and bit the tongue.

From that day onward the tongue became timid and prudent, and thought twice before speaking.

To learn that Leonardo Da Vinci was an author, storyteller and debating partner affirmed my belief that history's "greats" appreciate the power within stories. Leonardo's stories spread quickly and each became modified as it was passed from person to person. Several different versions now exist of Da Vinci's fables. To this day, Da Vinci's fables are told in the Tuscan countryside.[116]

In *Innovate like Edison*, Michael Gelb and Sarah Caldicott unfold that Edison once confessed his enjoyment of storytelling to a reporter when he boasted, "I was very fond of stories and had a choice lot ... with which I could usually throw a man into convulsions." They articulate that Edison loved to share tales and deliver each story with a poker face. Edison's stories "even had his devout Methodist mother-in-law cheering." Gelb and Caldicott along with many other historians illuminate that Edison retained his boyish love of funny stories and pranks throughout his whole life.[117] When looking at all of the practices in Thomas Edison's life that make him as successful as he was, his love of storytelling cannot be denied. His optimism, curiosity, and his insatiable quench to learn all contribute to his innovations, but his love for stories is there too.

Abraham Lincoln has been called America's Greatest Storyteller. Lincoln was born in a Kentucky log cabin in 1809, his surroundings "being squalid, his chances for advancement were apparently hopeless, but he proved otherwise. He was a keen politician, profound statesman, shrewd diplomatist, a thorough judge of men and he possessed of an intuitive knowledge of affairs."[118] His *Emancipation Proclamation* freed more than four million slaves. He was the first Chief Executive to be assassinated. Lincoln's story is one that is stirring because without school education, he rose to power through hard work and by proving that he was the best candidate for the job. Many aspects of Lincoln's story are captivating, but we will focus on his love of storytelling. In *Team of Rivals*, historian and biographer Doris Kearns Goodwin, suggests, "Lincoln became an extraordinary orator and storyteller as a result of a Herculean act of self-creation." Goodwin is one among the many scholars who consider Lincoln to be America's greatest storytelling leader.

Lincoln was in a childhood environment that allowed him to learn storytelling. His family lived on the frontier at a time of great migration. At that time, adventurers, peddlers, and pioneers making their way West would stop over at farms in the Eastern states where Lincoln spent his early years. At all hours of the day, they would do what people did back then to entertain themselves. They would swap stories. Lincoln's father, Thomas, was "a born storyteller," according to Goodwin, with "a quick wit, a talent for mimicry, and an uncanny memory for exceptional stories." Goodwin describes how Lincoln, as early as age six or seven, would stand on a tree stump and entertain the other children, emulating the adult storytellers, but he would share the tale in his own words, and in his own style. Like his father, young Lincoln found that he, too, could grab and hold a crowd. "He had discovered," Goodwin writes, "the pride and pleasure an attentive audience could bestow." Still a child, he was already on the path to becoming the Lincoln of history. He was, Goodwin asserts, "already conscious of his power."

Abraham Lincoln used his skill of storytelling throughout his life, including when he was President of the United States. George Templeton Strong, New York lawyer and philanthropist, wrote in his diary at length about a meeting between Strong, President Lincoln, and Henry Ward Bellows, a Unitarian minister and president of the United States Sanitary Commission. Strong wrote in his diary about the meeting and included a Lincoln story in dialect. He wrote this story in a way as if it captured the president's diction. The President "told us a lot of stories," Strong reported. In response to a discussion about the pressure from abolitionists for the president to take action against slavery, Lincoln told the following story:

> "Wa-al that reminds me of a party of Methodist parsons that was traveling in Illinois when I was a boy, and had a branch to cross that was pretty bad—ugly to cross, ye know, because the waters was up. And they got considerin' and discussin' how they should git across it, and they talked about it for two hours, and one on 'em thought they had ought to cross one way when they got there, and another way, and they got quarrellin' about it, till at last an old brother put in, and he says, says he, 'Brethren, this here talk ain't no use. I never cross a river until I come to it."

Strong then concludes, "It was a characteristic Lincoln moment. He deflected the question of what he would do about slavery; he used the story as a device to explain his policy; in a display of folksy wisdom, he got his listeners to laugh."

There is no doubt that Lincoln loved to tell stories. Many people who met with him commented on his endless supply of anecdotes and jokes. Lincoln's stories served as much more than idle entertainment. As McClure tells us in *Lincoln's Yarns and Stories*, one might even argue that, by providing a needed outlet for the president and offering colloquial wisdom about matters of policy, they helped the Union win the war. Ralph Waldo Emerson, Walt Whitman, Count Adam Gurowski, and George S. Boutwell all commented on Lincoln's storytelling ability. Ralph Waldo Emerson enjoyed Lincoln's stories. He once commented, "When he has made his remark, he looks up at you with a great satisfaction, and shows all his white teeth, and laughs." Walt Whitman saw Lincoln's storytelling ability different than Emerson did. Whitman thought it was "a weapon which he employed with great skill." Count Adam Gurowski, a Polish exile who worked in the State Department, also observed, "In the midst of the most stirring and exciting—nay, death-giving—news, Mr. Lincoln has always a story to tell." Former Secretary of the United States Treasury, George S. Boutwell predicted about our now famous storytelling President, "Mr. Lincoln's wit and mirth will give him a passport to the thoughts and hearts of millions who would take no interest in the sterner and more practical parts of his character."[119]

Leonardo Da Vinci, Thomas Edison, and Abraham Lincoln all loved reading stories and telling stories. Is it a coincidence that these individuals who all loved to hear and tell stories have inimitably, each in their own way, influenced history or does their love of storytelling speak to the so called magic in stories? Stories help people to become all that they dream of becoming.

> "There have been great societies that did not use the wheel, but there have been no societies that did not tell stories."
>
> —Ursula K. Le Guin

Stories from Religion to School

"Stories are equipment for living."

—Kenneth Burke

Stories are undeniably equipment for living. Stories are central to the world's major religious institutions. The scriptures of our transcendent religions take the form of parable and story, instructing and inspiring us to reach a morally superior level. The Holy Books of the major world religions tell the stories of the origins of those religions. The Bible is made up of different stories that comprise the story of Christianity. In a Catholic mass, for example, it is the idea that Catholics tell their story before they come to the table. The readings and the Gospel are the stories and the Eucharist is the meal. In Judaism, the Torah tells the story of much of world history as it unfolded in a theater called Israel and it tells the story of the Jewish people.

In Hinduism, we find many stories in the Hindu scriptures. The oldest form of Hindu scriptures, Veda, means wisdom or knowledge, and contains hymns, prayers and ritual texts composed during a period of a thousand years. The Upanishads are a collection of secret teachings including mystical ideas about man and the universe. The word, Brahman, comes into focus within this group, which is the basis of reality, and atman, which is the self or soul. Next is the Ramayana, which is one of two major tales of India. The work consists of 24,000 couplets based on the life of Rama, a righteous king who was an incarnation of the God Vishnu. The Mahabharata is the second epic and is the story of the deeds of the Aryan clans. It is composed of 100,000 verses written over an 800 year period. Contained within this work is a classic called the Bhagavad Gita, or the "Song of the Blessed Lord." It is one of the most sacred books of the Hindus and the most read of all Indian works in the entire world. The story is centered on man's duty, which, if carried out, will bring nothing but sorrow. The significance of this story is based on Hindu belief of bhatki, (devotion to a particular god as a means of salvation). These two stories have become ideals for the people of India in terms of moral and social behavior. The Puranas are an important source for the understanding of Hinduism, and include legends of gods, goddesses, demons, and ancestors describing pilgrimages and rituals to demonstrate the importance of bhakti, caste and dharma (basic principles of the cosmos or an ancient sage in Hindu mythology worshipped as a god by some lower castes).[120]

Religions are centered around stories. Christianity, Judaism, and Hinduism exhibit how stories are central to each religion. The followers of the world's major religions develop their belief in the religion from the stories that are a part of these religions.

Story-time is part of elementary school classes across America. When I was studying to be a teacher and I had to complete classroom observations, I spent some time observing in elementary school classes. The teacher reading aloud to the students was a captivating scene. The students would eagerly sit around their teacher in silence as she read, listening in awe to the story that the teacher was reading. With every page that the teacher turned, the students inched closer to the teacher. It was as if the closer they became, the quicker that they could then hear and find out what would happen next within the story. The "read-aloud" was an enchanting part of the school day for the children. Jessica, an elementary school teacher in Chicago shares, "the magic that happens when the students gather around me for story time is hard to put into words. Seeing the students' eyes as they hear the stories is so very rewarding." My sister, an elementary school teacher, shared with me how she taught her class the story of Roanoke and the following day, a little boy came up to her and said, "I was dreaming about what happened to the people at Roanoke." The boy became so engaged in the breadth of the story that his teacher taught him about Roanoke that he went home wondering about the story to the extent that the story made its way into his dreams. Article after article for parents states the importance of reading to your children and how reading aloud to your children is one of the greatest gifts that you can give to them. In the afterword of *Character is Destiny*, John McCain gives the advice,

> "Shared stories help to strengthen the bonds between generations. Through stories we impart the wisdom of our experience and pass along our values when we read aloud to the children in our lives. We also create shared moments and memories that last a lifetime. Reading aloud to a child has the critical benefit of helping to lay down the building blocks necessary for them to learn to read on their own. Listening to stories helps children build vocabulary, improve their reading skills and succeed more readily in school. Being read to is an important step on the road to becoming a good reader and one of the best ways to ensure a lifelong love of literature and reading."

John McCain shares some earnest advice. All children love when stories are read to them.

Storytelling is central in society and this shines through in innumerable ways as we look at the breakdown of our world. From everyday life, to school, to religion, we communicate with each other by the means of stories. InterviewGirl.com's nonprofit organization, the Interview Girl Foundation is working to bring AIDS victims medication through its project *Operation A²*. The story about how Oxford University scholar William D. Hamilton, a prominent scholar in the field of evolutionary biology and Michael Worobey, a young Rhodes scholar from Canada formed an unlikely partnership and the tale about how the two went to Africa to research HIV's birth was shared in *Tinderbox: How the West Spanked the AIDS epidemic and how the world can finally overcome it.* As we learned earlier, sadly, Hamilton died while on this journey to discover science that could potentially change the direction of the fight against AIDS. There is another thought-provoking aspect to this story that Craig Timberg and Daniel

Halperin share in *Tinderbox* that relates to InterviewGirl.com. In looking at Michael Worobey and his work as a scientist trying to discover more about HIV, Worobey uses a "story" in his work. Worobey believes that all living things carry DNA that dictate how they grow and change and that also, when analyzed with the right tools, tell the "story" of their evolution. Worobey's research is centered around collecting stories about individuals' evolution to eventually find HIV's birth. At InterviewGirl.com, stories are used in order to purchase medicine for AIDS victims and it is DNA that tells the story about how HIV began in humans in the first place. Worobey's use of a story in his work and InterviewGirl.com's use of a story is a "story" coming full circle since InterviewGirl.com is using the stories that we collect in order to help AIDS victims in Africa with *Operation A²* as Worobey too used a "story" in his research about HIV in Africa. Albeit, it may be a stretch, but all of this research about good ideas, creativity, and connections, I could not help but make this connection about the use of a story in Worobey's scientific work and the how the Interview Girl Foundation plans to use stories to make a difference in the world.

History of Storytelling

"The universe is made of stories, not atoms."
—Muriel Rukeyser

Storytelling history is ancient. The power of a good story has a few thousand years of history behind it. Stories are as old as humankind. Humans have told stories since the days when humans lived in caves. Telling stories has been one of our most fundamental communication methods for over 27,000 years. Since the first cave paintings were discovered, people have been sharing stories with one another. As Tom Kelley and Jonathan Littman explain, "Storytellers have captivated the attention of their fellow humans for as long as there have been evening fires to tell tales around."[121]The oral storytelling tradition is as old as language itself. Traditionally, oral stories have been handed over from generation to generation. Nobody knows when the first story was actually told. Some historians believe that the first stories were shared in caves. We do know that as families grouped with other families and formed clans, the storyteller, who was good at telling heroic events or other important events of the tribe, began to reach a position of respect and power. People found the person telling the stories interesting and began to listen to him. The priest, the judge and the ruler were perhaps the earliest to use this art effectively in the history of storytelling. Storytelling days were considered important. Before man learned to write, he had to rely on his memory to learn anything. In order to do this, he had to be a good listener. A good storyteller was always respected. He could easily find an audience that was willing to learn every exciting bit of information in his stories. These stories were also shared with others in distant lands, when people traveled. The stories traveled with them. It went the other way too, when people returned home, they brought with them exciting new tales of exotic places and people.[122]

Cave paintings going back 25,000 years or more dramatically portray the story of the great Paleolithic hunts undertaken by our earliest ancestors. Storytelling history is primordial because stories helped people to share information long ago, before we had a written language and the internet. Moving past the Paleolithic Age in the history of civilization, from the ancient Maya to the ancient Egyptians, stories recovered years later instruct us today about these early people. By this time in history, now people were beginning to use written marks to communicate stories. Individual marks written on the Mayan pyramids and marks that were left on the tombs of the Pharaohs from ancient Egypt tell a symbolic story of those cultures as well as how the view of our place in the universe has evolved over time.[123]

The *Epic of Gilgamesh* to the company of Apple

The *Epic of Gilgamesh* is perhaps the oldest written story on Earth and the oldest surviving tale in the history of storytelling. It comes to us from Ancient Sumeria and was originally written on 12 clay tablets in cuneiform script. It is about the deeds of a famous Sumerian king, King of Uruk and it recounts the adventures of the historical king. Other early known records in the origin of storytelling can be found in Ancient Egypt, when the sons of Cheops entertained their father with stories. To jump ahead in the history of human civilization, throughout Celtic Europe, the reciters of poetry were highly esteemed for their disciplined talent of maintaining and passing on the stories of tribes and clans.

Let's return for a moment to what we've already mentioned about what neuroscience proves stories do to our brains and how stories are central to the world's religions. If you look back 10,000 years ago, traditions were passed down orally. Family members told each other stories. There was no education except teaching young people how to memorize stories. Cognitive research has shown that the human brain organizes stories very efficiently. That's why stories about characters and people are easy to remember. There are many reasons why we relate and respond to stories. We're often drawn to narratives. From the story of Jesus to Shakespeare, this cannot be denied. Look at the power of Christianity, the story Jesus has impacted billions of people for thousands of years. Jesus' followers told stories about Jesus and people used these stories as their teachings. Jesus understood the power of story as illustrated in the numerous parables recorded in the New Testament.

In the sixteenth century, Shakespeare used his storytelling craft to bring history into literature. Shakespeare remains a global bestseller today. Modern companies also represent the power of stories. Apple's former CEO Steve Jobs is known to be the greatest CEO storyteller in the world. It's not an accident that Apple became the most valuable company in the world due to the fact that Jobs captivated hundreds of millions of people with what's possible and what could be done with Apple's products. Moving onto Hollywood, although we all notice the fancy special-effects of Hollywood movies, what we find thrilling is actually found in the stories behind the box-office bestsellers today. George Lucas' epic films have grossed a figure that is approaching $10 billion. For over 25 years, filmmaker Ken Burns has been producing films. Burns is one of the first documentary film makers that comes to mind when people think of documentaries. Why is it that Burns produces such remarkable films? Ken Burns is a historian, a researcher, and a documentarian, but above all, he is a gifted storyteller. In *The Ten Faces of Innovation*, Tom Kelley and Jonathan Littman point out, "Stories persuade in a way that facts, reports, and market trends seldom do, because stories make an emotional connection."[124] Being a gifted storyteller has its advantages and is illuminated through figures like Jesus, Steve Jobs, and Ken Burns. A well-crafted narrative can keep the people, values, and life lessons that someone holds dear alive and give an individual the power to influence their children, their employees, and others. The foundation of our human existence, the essence of who we are as a species, is contingent on story.

> "Facts don't persuade, feelings do. And stories are the best way to get at those feelings."
>
> —Tom Asacker

Storytelling and Business

In the world today, there is a growing interest in the art of storytelling among today's business leaders. The reason is because as we have learned, we as human beings have been communicating with each other through storytelling since the days when humans lived in caves and sat around campfires exchanging tales. The purpose of why businesses use stories today is different from why individuals used stories back when people were hunting and gathering. Storytelling is an ancient form of sharing, but it's receiving modern-day attention as one of the best ways that businesses and individuals can communicate their ideas. One of the first business lessons in the modern world is that companies should not share all the details; instead they ought to create an experience for their customers. Businesses use storytelling to achieve a practical business outcome with individuals, teams, a client or a large audience. Businesses are using the purposeful use of narrative to achieve a practical outcome.

Some of the world's leading thinkers: John Seely Brown, Steve Denning, Katalina Groh, and Larry Prusak all noted the importance of the role of storytelling in the world and explained why storytelling would become a key ingredient in managing communications, education, training and innovation in the 21st Century. As these thinkers warned us what would happen in the first years of the 21st century, it did end up happening. Organizational storytelling is movement to make organizations aware of the stories that exist within their walls. Steve Denning is the world leader in organizational storytelling. In *A Whole New Mind*, Daniel Pink tells us the story about Steve Denning and how he was moved to a department known as knowledge management at World Bank. From this move, Denning discovered that an organization's knowledge is contained in its stories.

John Seely Brown is the Independent Co-Chairman of the Deloitte's Center for the Edge and a visiting scholar and advisor to the Provost at University of Southern California. Previously, he was the Chief Scientist of Xerox Corporation and the director of its Palo Alto Research Center (PARC)—a position he held for nearly two decades. Brown provides a scientist's perspective about storytelling. Brown describes how we are constructing knowledge all the time, in conversation, through narrative. He specifies, "We are personalizing it that way, we are constructing it, for ourselves. This is a very powerful metaphor."[125]Cognitive scientists have shown that stories can change the way we think, act, and feel and we can all relate to how a certain story made us feel in our own lives. Leaders in any field can use the power of a good story to influence and motivate their teams to reach new goals. Stories can inspire everything from understanding to action. Stories can create legends that an entire workplace culture can build upon (as happened with the company, Apple). Stories have the power to break down barriers and turn a bad situation into a good one. Stories can capture our imaginations and make things real in a way that facts cannot. Stories can be powerful leadership tools. Great leaders know this, and many top CEO's of business today use stories to elucidate points and sell their ideas. Businesses throughout the world draw upon great stories that they've heard or read. They use these stories to better get across hard truths and to spread their message to people. Businesses and brands connect to people's hearts by the stories they tell. Many of the Internet gurus discuss that people buy stories. In describing organizational storytelling, Daniel Pink breaks down how businesses distinguish their goods and services in the market place from the stories that they tell about their products.

The momentum of the organizational storytelling movement proves that people buy stories. We see it throughout society. The purpose of InterviewGirl.com is to distribute stories that people want to hear and to then generate revenues from these stories. The revenues will then make a difference in the lives of others (eliminate someone's misery). The people who read the stories that InterviewGirl.com shares will also benefit. People cultivate new perspectives when they hear and learn new stories. You should share a story on InterviewGirl.com and your story can become a part of one of our compilations or projects. By sharing your story, you're helping others in two ways. These ways are described in detail in Chapter Nine. InterviewGirl.com collects, compiles, and shares stories. Our undertaking (InterviewGirl.com) puts together information and shares stories with you.

There is a magic in stories that isn't seen elsewhere

"Storytelling is the only absolutely verified form of magic. Magic is the creation of subjective realities in other people's heads."

—David Brin, Science Fiction Author

The history of storytelling reveals that stories came in different varieties throughout human history. Myths, legends of all kinds, fairy tales, trickster stories, fables, ghost tales, hero stories, and epic adventures, these stories were told and then retold throughout societies. These stories were passed down from generation to generation. The stories that were shared reflect the wisdom and knowledge of early people. In early human history, stories were often used to explain important but often confusing events and disasters in nature at those early times. For example, stories explained: fire, storms, thunder, floods, tidal waves, and lightening. It was common for people to believe in the stories of gods, which bound them to a common heritage and beliefs. Sharing stories has been a part of humanity since the beginning of time. From looking at the history of storytelling to what we now understand about storytelling from neuroscience, it is apparent that humans have a hard-wired ability for learning through stories. Stories are how we record both the monumental events of life and the small, everyday moments. The oral storytelling tradition is as old as language itself. Throughout history, stories have primarily existed in the verbal realm, preserving and passing knowledge across generations before they were captured in print. This was true of the ancient epics, and it's true today.

Your family's history, your company's history, the stories you tell that define and shape your identity are all stored in your mind and shared through your actions and words. The power of storytelling goes back to the beginning of time. It is an age old art that has shaped humanity as we know it. Stories are just as much a part of our lives in this modern world as they were a part of humans' lives in early human history. People's Facebook pages are essentially a platform for them to tell and share stories about their life. The same goes for an individual's Instagram page. He/she shares stories about his/her life with his/her followers through pictures. In today's world, with the internet, distribution of people's ideas has become free. Now InterviewGirl.com has the power to share people's stories with the entire connected planet from one computer. Technology has enhanced InterviewGirl.com's mission. This is important in InterviewGirl.com's story. From a computer with an internet connection in Chicago, InterviewGirl. com can collect stories from all over the globe.

Why did I choose to use stories as the force behind InterviewGirl.com and our goal to change the world by eliminating miseries that exist? Well it is pretty simple, to be human is to have a story and we think of our lives as a story. Story is the structure that gives meaning and order to our lives. Stories are how we convey our deepest emotions and talk about those things that we value the most. It is through the stories we tell that we are most able to portray the fullest array of human emotion. Stories affect people in many respects. They appeal to our reason and intellect by providing evidence and information to strengthen arguments and help us make informed decisions. Emotionally, they bond us to others who share the same story and give us a sense of belonging and community. Finally, they are the connection to a long forgotten past. We do not always realize it, but that past is the rich source of the images and symbols that unconsciously motivate our behavior today.[126]

In Chapter One, you learned that more than 1,000,000 children worldwide will become victims of child trafficking this year, 1.2 million children in Sub-Saharan Africa alone die of AIDS every year, 25,000 people die every day of hunger-related causes, and 34 million people worldwide are living with HIV and almost 70% of them live in sub-Saharan Africa. After you turned the page, the details of those harsh statistics most likely left your mind, but you probably still remember Amara's story and my reoccurring dream about how "the medicines ran out." A good story has the power to instigate a myriad of reactions. What I learned about Amara was this "story" that many people weren't aware of. Or more accurately, not that they weren't aware that orphans sometimes die of HIV/AIDS, but the problem most likely seemed far removed from their everyday life. I wanted to share my "Kpando story" with the world. I knew that many others had stories that they too could share with the world. We have all had those times in life when you hear a story and you are inspired to make a change.

Through the stories that InterviewGirl.com shares, we hope that people are stirred to change and become better in whatever capacity they are seeking to thrive. By the virtue of the stories that InterviewGirl.com shares, hopefully people will be compelled to somehow make a difference and decide to help eliminate some of the misery in this world. Also, from a historical perspective, if we don't document these stories, they'll become forgotten. Everyone wants their story told. As Hamlet is dying, his last request to Horatio is that his story be told. Hamlet's death is a powerful scene because within this scene, he articulates the wish in all of us: to have our story told. Storytelling enables us not only to tell stories, but also to tell our story. There is magic in hearing a splendid story and that is InterviewGirl.com's mission—to capture and share spellbinding stories. From sharing stories with one another, we can all learn and grow in infinite ways. Spreading stories to help people enrich their own lives and spreading stories to eliminate miseries that some experience is why InterviewGirl.com was founded.

CHAPTER SEVEN

Learning from Stories

The Power to Learn from Stories: Become a Student

"Stories are medicine. They have such power; they do not require that we do, be, act anything—we need only listen."
—Clarisa Pinkola Estes

Learning is one of the vital elements that is part of InterviewGirl.com. Our compilations and projects are produced so that people have the opportunity to **learn** and continually advance. We should all constantly strive to be a better version of ourselves. There is always more to learn no matter who you are. In *The Art of Exceptional Living,* Jim Rohn describes that you can get along without some meals, but can't get along without some ideas, examples and inspiration. He expounds, "There's a bible phrase that says humans cannot live on bread alone or food alone. It says the next most important thing to bread is words. Words nourish the mind. Words nourish the soul. Humans have to have food and words to be healthy and prosperous. Make sure you have a good diet of words every day." He then poses the question, "Why not call good books and cassettes tapping the treasure of ideas?"

Rohn encourages us to continue learning throughout our lives. Throughout *The Art of Exceptional Living*, Rohn reminds us that it is who we become in our lives that matters. Through continual learning, meeting new people, hearing their stories, and gaining different perspectives, we regularly enhance our lives.

"Knowledge is power."

—Francis Bacon

Julie Burstein delivered a powerful lecture at the TED conference, *4 Lessons in Creativity*. She points out that the best way to learn about anything is through stories. Similarly, scientist, John Seely Brown shares,

> "Even a scientist (such as I) must admit that knowledge cannot be captured via a formula or equation. It calls for new intellectual constructs and the challenge of background assumptions. And it is enriched by events, objects, people, or situations—such as storytelling, documents, knowledge artists, and communities of practice—that provide us with different perspectives and lenses through which to view the world."[127]

Brown deciphers that the knowledge that people glean in their lives comes from individuals interacting with one another and it comes from individuals hearing stories.

One of the best ways for authors to provide evidence to support their arguments within their work is through sharing stories. By articulating and sharing stories, Malcolm Gladwell makes the claims that he does in *Outliers*. In *Outliers*, he asks the question: what makes high-achievers different? His answer is that we pay too much attention to what successful people are like, and too little attention to where they come from (their culture, their family, their generation, and the particular experiences of their upbringing). In *Outliers*, Gladwell takes the reader on an intellectual journey through the world of "outliers." The reader meets the best and the brightest, the most famous and the most successful in certain fields as Gladwell shares stories about these individuals. Through stories he explains the secrets of software billionaires, what it takes to be a great soccer player, why Asians are good at math, and what made the Beatles the great rock band that they were. For example, Mr. Gladwell shares stories about Chris Langan, who has a genius-level IQ of 195 and who came from a poor, dysfunctional family and J. Robert Oppenheimer, who was a child with a similar IQ to Chris Langan's but whose wealthy, privileged childhood helped give him more of an advantage to get what he wanted out of the world. Through stories about Chris Langan and J. Robert Oppenheimer, Gladwell proves his theory that talent alone is not enough to ensure success that opportunity, hard work, timing and luck play important roles as well.[128] It is through sharing stories that Gladwell makes the assertions that he does in his book.

When Buffer co-founder Leo Widrich started to market his product through stories instead of benefits and bullet points, the number of sign-ups shot up considerably. Widrich challenges us that the next time we struggle with "getting people on board with our projects and ideas, to simply tell them a story, where the outcome is that doing what you had in mind is the best thing to do." Just as Princeton researcher Hasson's experiments authenticate that storytelling is the only way to plant ideas into other people's minds, Leo Widrich's experience with Buffer is also an example that solidifies the scientific claim that our brains become more active when we tell stories.[129]

To return to Bill Drayton, the man who pioneered the field of social entrepreneurship, Drayton believes that the best way for people to understand the field of social entrepreneurship is through stories. While a student at Harvard College, Balliol College in Oxford University and Yale Law School, he launched a number of organizations, including Harvard's Ashoka Table, an interdisciplinary weekly forum in the social sciences, and Yale Legislative Services. From 1981 to 1985, while working part-time at McKinsey, Drayton founded both *Ashoka* and *Save EPA*, the predecessor to Environmental Safety. After receiving a MacArthur Fellowship in 1984, he was able to devote himself fully to *Ashoka*. *Ashoka* is an organization that was created to collaborate with change makers in a team of teams' model that addresses the fluidity of a rapidly evolving society. It can be difficult to understand the field of social entrepreneurship. As Drayton describes *Ashoka*, he maintains, "People understand this field by anecdote rather than theory." Hearing a story is the best way to understand what exactly a social entrepreneur does. The job of a social entrepreneur is to recognize when a part of society is stuck and to provide new ways to get it unstuck. To say a social entrepreneur helps to get society unstuck may be confusing, but as one learns Dr. Maria Montessori's story, who a social entrepreneur is begins to make more sense.

Maria Montessori applied to the University of Rome's medical program, but she was rejected. She took additional courses to better prepare her for entrance to the medical school and she eventually made it in. When she graduated from medical school in 1896, she was among Italy's first female physicians. Maria Montessori's early medical practice focused on psychiatry. She also developed an interest in education, attending classes on pedagogy and immersing herself in educational theory. Her studies led her to observe and then question the dominant methods of teaching children with intellectual and developmental disabilities.

The opportunity to improve on these methods came in 1900, when she was appointed co-director of a new training institute for special education teachers. Maria approached the task scientifically, carefully observing and experimenting to learn which teaching methods worked best. Many of the children made unexpected gains. The program was declared a success.

In 1907 Maria accepted a new challenge to open a childcare center in a poor inner-city district. This became the first Casa dei Bambini, a quality learning environment for young children. The youngsters were unruly at first, but soon showed great interest in working with puzzles, learning to prepare meals, and manipulating materials that held lessons in math. She observed how they absorbed knowledge from their surroundings, essentially teaching themselves.

Utilizing scientific observation and experience gained from her earlier work with young children, Maria designed learning materials and a classroom environment that fostered the children's natural desire to learn. News of the school's success soon spread through Italy and by 1910 Montessori schools were acclaimed worldwide.

In the years following, and for the rest of her life, Maria dedicated herself to advancing her child-centered approach to education. She lectured widely, wrote articles and books, and developed a program to prepare teachers in the Montessori Method. Through her efforts and the work of her followers, Montessori education was adopted worldwide. Maria Montessori pioneered a child-centered approach to education and she made it her life's work to carry out spreading this mission.

Stories help us to understand the field of social entrepreneurship. Maria Montessori's story allows us to understand who a social entrepreneur is. By appreciating what Montessori did throughout her life, we can better apprehend who a social entrepreneur is. Montessori made it her life's work to teach the world that the child-centered approach to education was the best way that students learn. Her work opened the vista of modern educational theories in our world today.

Social entrepreneurship is the essence of why the Interview Girl Foundation was created. Helping to create social entrepreneurs is how the Interview Girl Foundation hopes to contribute toward helping those less fortunate in the world. The profits from projects produced at InterviewGirl.com are contributed toward innovative solutions to society's most pressing social problems. There is not one cause as to why the Interview Girl Foundation was solely created, but rather the Interview Girl Foundation aids organizations and individuals who are coming up with solutions to change society for the better. As Drayton asserted, the best way to understand why *Ashoka* was created was to hear a story about the organization. Stories too are the best way to depict what the Interview Girl Foundation is achieving. As the Interview Girl Foundation eliminates miseries in the world, InterviewGirl.com will share stories detailing what is being done to eliminate these miseries.

A Lesson from the Greeks

"If a man empties his purse into his head no one can take it away from him. An investment in knowledge always pays the best interest."
—Benjamin Franklin (1706-1790)

Humans learn from those around them. Without even realizing it, we acquire knowledge from other people all the time. As we bring "focus" to amassing knowledge from those around us, we have the capacity to learn even more. From the perspective of a girl who was a student from the time I was three in *La Petite Early Learning Academy* all the way until my upper twenties, becoming a student is beneficial. I was even a graduate student during my first year of high school teaching. I have been in school for a long time. Being a student allows one to understand that there is always more to learn. Become a student in your life and look at and study the people in this world who have done what it is that you want to do and learn from them. We all need to have the mentality, if someone else did something, I, too can do this. Many of the "expert gurus," as they are called, preach this notion of modeling and becoming like those whom we admire. They encourage us to study those who have done what it is that we want to do. In her motivational talks, Chalene Johnson often says, "anything anyone else has done, you can do it too." Brendon Burchard speaks about how he studied "best practice" when he was developing his online brands that are now multi-million dollar brands. Children emulate their parents and those around them. They model the behaviors that they see.

> "Preach the Gospel always; if necessary, use words."
> —Attributed to St. Francis of Assisi

As we observe different illustrious individuals throughout History who chose to learn from those around them, we can appreciate the value in this idea of "becoming a student." Going back to Ancient Greece, there is the famous example of Plato, who modeled after his teacher, Socrates. Athenian Socrates is best remembered for his use of critical reasoning, by his unwavering commitment to truth, and through the vivid example of his own life. He set the standard for all subsequent Western philosophy. Our best sources of information about Socrates's philosophical views are the early dialogues of his student Plato, who attempted to provide a faithful picture of the methods and teachings of his master.

In Ancient Greece, Aristotle also authenticates the power of being a student. Aristotle was a student of Plato. Aristotle is immensely important in ancient Greek philosophy, making contributions to logic, metaphysics, mathematics, physics, biology, botany, ethics, politics, agriculture, medicine, dance and theater. As the father of the field of logic, he was the first to develop a formalized system for reasoning. Aristotle observed that the validity of any argument can be determined by its structure rather than its content. A classic example of a valid argument is his syllogism: All men are mortal; Socrates is a man; therefore, Socrates is mortal. Given the structure of this argument, as long as the premises are true, then the conclusion is also guaranteed to be true. Aristotle's brand of logic dominated this area of thought until the rise of modern propositional logic and predicates logic 2000 years later. Aristotle's emphasis on good reasoning combined with his belief in the scientific method forms the backdrop for most of his work. For example, in his work in ethics and politics, Aristotle identifies the highest good with intellectual virtue; that is, a moral person is one who cultivates certain virtues based on reasoning. In his work on psychology and the soul, Aristotle distinguishes sense perception from reason, which unifies and interprets the sense perceptions and is the source of all knowledge.

Although, Socrates, Plato, and Aristotle all lived over 2,000 years ago, contributions that they made to society still affect our modern world. Plato and Aristotle each learned from their predecessor and their mentorship with their teacher set the basis for what they would then continue to do. We can learn from those around us and use what we learn to make our own discoveries as Plato and Aristotle did. For example, Aristotle is famous for rejecting Plato's theory of forms. You can learn from people around you as you add to, distinguish from, and/or combine your knowledge with the knowledge that you acquire from those individuals from whom you are learning.

"Necessity... the mother of invention."

—Plato

"All the gold which is under or upon the earth is not enough to give in exchange for virtue."

—Plato

"We are what we repeatedly do. Excellence, then, is not an act, but a habit."

—Aristotle

"It is the mark of an educated mind to be able to entertain a thought without accepting it."

—Aristotle

Learning from Others

"Ubuntu"—the only way for me to be human is for you to reflect my humanity back at me.

InterviewGirl.com's compilations and projects share tips, advice, stories, resources, and scholarship to help people understand and uncover different perspectives about the world. From stories that people share, people can assimilate, absorb, and comprehend information and ideas. The stories that people share will help others. There are countless stories out there that we must share. Having the right knowledge can make a tremendous difference within someone's life. People may not yet have done something or achieved something because they are missing the know-how. There are numerous examples that we could talk about here, but one example could be in the domain of weight loss. Maybe someone is overweight because he/she isn't equipped with the right knowledge about how to successfully lose weight. Sometimes even just learning a few new pieces of knowledge and tweaking a few habits in one's life can revolutionize a person's health. One of many projects being completed at InterviewGirl.com is collecting stories from people who have lost weight. InterviewGirl. com's *Weight Loss Advice and Tips* compilations will help to arm individuals with the knowledge that they need to help them lose weight. Having the right knowledge and know-how can make all the difference. InterviewGirl.com hopes to give individuals this edge. Learning from others is the linchpin of InterviewGirl.com. Getting people to share stories will allow everyone to learn from one another.

Returning to John Seely Brown (a scientist who shares his perspective on storytelling), he expounds his theory of knowledge by highlighting the importance of our interactions with others. Brown gives his own take on Descartes' famous statement, "I think therefore I am." Brown declares that rather than, "I think therefore

I am," "we participate and therefore we are," has influenced him. He explains that we come into existence; we come into being through participation with others. Essentially, understanding is basically socially constructed with others. Brown articulates that psychoanalysis has a lot to do with object relation theory, in terms of how identity gets formed. It is in participation with others that we come into a sense of self.

Brown's statement, "we participate and therefore we are" made me think of the African proverb, "I am because we are; we are because I am." This African proverb has the beautiful message that we exist in community with a multiplicity of voices, and we thrive because we share the responsibility for that community with others. *I Am Because We Are* is a film describing the journey that Madonna embarks on, exploring the lives of children who have been orphaned by AIDS, and have suffered more than one can sometimes imagine. *I Am Because We Are* is set in Malawi, Africa. Madonna leads us through many heart-wrenching stories that ultimately remind us how interconnected we are. I did not see this film until about three weeks before this book was about to be finished, but as I watched the film, Madonna's own personal discoveries from Malawi were similar to how I have felt since I returned from Africa and began my research on some of the miseries that exist in our world. Amara's story and the subsequent research that I have since completed has led to personal discoveries that I have made. From what Madonna witnesses in Malawi, she too makes personal discoveries. The film introduces us to disturbing things that exist in Malawi's culture, but ultimately the film is meant to challenge us and call us to action. Founding InterviewGirl.com, starting the Interview Girl Foundation, and writing this book were my way of doing just that: I am taking action and I hope that as people learn about InterviewGirl.com, they too will be called to action.

> "Humankind has not woven the web of life. We are but
> one thread within it. Whatever we do to the web, we do

to ourselves. All things are bound together. All things connect."

—Chief Seattle

Chris Abani was imprisoned three times by the Nigerian government. Abani introduced me to the concept of *ubuntu*: "the only way for me to be human is for you to reflect my humanity back at me." There is no way for us to be human without other people. As Abani writes, whether in his novels, *GraceLand* and *The Virgin of Flames* or in his poems, he tells the stories of people: people standing up to soldiers in Nigeria, people being compassionate when it was least expected, and ultimately stories of people being human and reclaiming their humanity. It is funny how things come together and connect as you obtain knowledge. Similar to Abani, Dr. James Orbinski held that humanitarianism is about individual human beings reaching out to other human beings. In the case of MSF, this is done by individuals completing one medical act at a time. Dr. Orbinski became one of my mentors as I learned about humanitarian action in the twenty-first century. I first read an *Imperfect Offering* after I checked it out at the library. It was a book that moved me so much that I had to order it for my personal library. I ordered the book from Amazon.com. My copy of an *Imperfect Offering* is another example of how interconnected we all are. The copy that was sent to me was signed by James Orbinski himself. Dr. Orbinski's career in MSF and subsequent role in international relations since his time as a doctor for *Doctors Without Borders* was inspiring to me and perhaps inspiring isn't even the right word, beyond inspiring, the stories that I read about Orbinksi motivated me. Motivation is defined as the process that initiates, guides and maintains goal-oriented behaviors. Motivation is what causes us to act. It was several divergent elements coming together for me, but one of those pieces being my awareness of individuals like Dr. James Orbinski that made me go from feeling sad when I learned about certain realities in the world to taking concrete actions and actually trying to do something to change those realities. Chris Abani reminds us that, "the world is never saved in giant messianic acts but in simple accumulation of gentle invisible little everyday acts of compassion." I ripped out the cover page that had a dedication to another individual from my copy of *An Imperfect Offering* that I ordered online. I added the signed cover page to the cork board above my desk where I pinned the note card with Amara's name written on it and the $10 Ghana cedis bill. The addition of the signed dedication from Dr. Orbinski to my cork board would remind me that in order to change anything, it was necessary to *act*.

"The simplest answer is to act."

—Unknown

Why Compilations?

The idea of grouping alike things together, grouping things by categories and lists that feature similar subjects, and highlighting commonalities are some of the best ways that humans learn information. Remember how you always had to make Venn Diagrams to help you organize the information that you read when you were in school?

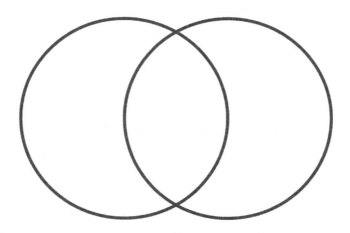

People in our society are drawn to compilations. Think about it. *People Magazine* always has cover stories that say: the 100 prettiest, hottest, richest, (and many other groupings) people. *Extra* and the *Biography Channel* constantly feature the Top 100, Top 50, etc. of different categories from sexy to beautiful to hot to talented. In the *Simple-ology* course that Mark Joyner offers on blogging, he gives advice on how to write a successful blog. He teaches the aspiring blogger about the importance of making lists. He describes how individuals are drawn to lists because diverse information is presented all together.

On-line support groups have grown to be a popular entity in American life. Examples of this include all of the people who interact with different Facebook communities and people who religiously motivate and check in with one another on Instagram. Pinterest is a pin board-style social photo sharing website that allows users to create and manage theme-based image collections such as events, interests, hobbies and more. Users can browse other pin boards for inspiration, "re-pin" images to their own collections and/or "like" photos. Pinterest's mission is to "connect everyone in the world through the "things" they find interesting" via a global platform of inspiration and idea sharing. Pinterest allows its users to share "pins" on both Twitter and Facebook, which allows users to share and interact with a broad community. Founded by Ben Silbermann, of West Des Moines, Iowa, the site is managed by Cold Brew Labs and funded by a small group of entrepreneurs and inventors. It is one of the "fastest growing social services in the world."[130]Pinterest is the idea of taking a bunch of similar items and then grouping them into categories. The use of hashtags (#) as people make posts on Pinterest, Facebook, Twitter, Instagram, and other social media hubs allow people to see all the posts associated with a particular category (the word that the hashtag is). The use of hashtags in social media again demonstrates how when we group things by categories, we can acquire more of an awareness from the information. At InterviewGirl.com, it is our hope that if one reads a story from a compilation, he/she will better relate to the other stories that are part of that compilation of stories.

Michael Gazzaniga, the cognitive neuroscientist who is a pioneer in the study of hemispheric (left vs. right brain) specialization describes the left hemisphere function in the brain as organizing our memories into plausible stories as "the Interpreter." In *Your Storytelling Brain*, Jason Gots explains,

> "Gazzaniga suspects that narrative coherence helps us to navigate the world—to know where we're coming from and where we're headed. It tells us where to place our trust and why. One reason we may love fiction, he says, is that it enables us to find our bearings in possible future realities, or to make better sense of our own past experiences. What stories give us, in the end, is reassurance. And as childish as it may seem, that sense of security—that coherent sense of self—is essential to our survival."[131]

As Gazzaniga's research in neuroscience illustrates, when people read stories within a compilation or they read a story that relates to their own personal story, they are reassured when they discover that other people's reactions (other people's stories) have similarities with their own story. This helps people to work through their own feelings and thoughts as they think, "good, it's not only me who experiences *xyz*."

As Interview Girl, it is my purpose to speak with many different people and then to identify commonalities in all interviews. With most compilations that are put together at InterviewGirl.com, similarities will be culled out from the various interviews. People love lists, anthologies and compilations. Individuals' attraction toward "grouping" content is evident in Facebook groups, in Pinterest, and in the lists created by many publications. Bloggers include lists in their blog entries as they break content down for the public because people enjoy lists and other "compilations" of content. Perhaps the reason that the general public enjoys reading lists and groupings of advice and opinions all together is because it comforts people to think, "It's not only me. You struggle with this too." The public likes to read compilations. At InterviewGirl. com, we recognize that there are commonalities in the stories that people share, but each story is unique in its own way too.

Compilations Share More Than One Story

Another reason why there will be an exposition of different stories that are collected and then put together in the compilations produced at InterviewGirl.com is because it is important to not just tell one story. Our lives, our cultures, are composed of many overlapping stories. To use the words of novelist Chimamanda Adichie, "The single story creates stereotypes, and the problem with stereotypes is not that they are untrue, but that they are incomplete. They make one story become the only story." In an efficacious talk Chimamanda Adichie delivered at TED, she tells the story of how she found her authentic cultural voice and warns us that if we hear only a single story about another person or country, we risk a critical misunderstanding. We need to engage with all stories. InterviewGirl.com's providing compilations is a way to protect against the single story. For example, some of the statistics presented in Chapter 19 may give the idea that Africa is a continent full of catastrophes. There are people who are living in misery in Africa and we as humans should want to do something to help eliminate that misery—this is why InterviewGirl.com was created, but there are other stories that are not about devastation. Amara's story is *one* story in Africa. Throughout Africa, there are other stories that have different endings than Amara's story. I don't want Amara's story to portray the African continent in one way. An orphan dying of AIDS is one reality in Africa, but there are also other realities.

There are stories about people who have created successful businesses. In Kenya, Ory Okollh, 23 helped found Ushahidi, a web platform that allows people worldwide to report news from their cell phones or computers. Their reports are immediately uploaded to an online interactive map so people can get instant updates.

Ushahidi, which means "testimony" in Swahili, has changed the game in real-time tracking of emergency events via cyberspace.[132] According to *Economist* magazine, six of the world's 10 fastest-growing economies from 2001 to 2010 were in Africa. They include: Ethiopia, Mozambique, Tanzania, Democratic Republic of the Congo, Ghana, Zambia, and Nigeria. Experts purport that Africa's economic growth is impressive, but we need to remember that these countries have a smaller base from which to grow. For example, Ethiopia's GDP in 2011 was $95 billion, compared to the U.S. GDP of $15 trillion. Two major factors are driving Africa's growth: 1.) A burst of international investment and 2.) The rise of entrepreneurs, many of them women.[133] Africa's economic growth is another story that exists in Africa.

There are stories of misery within Africa and the purpose of the Interview Girl Foundation is to eliminate these miseries, but there are also stories of hope, transformation, and progress. All these stories need to be told and shared. One story cannot represent a country or a group of people. Chimamanda Adichie recognizes that there are other stories besides stories of misery and despair within Africa. She authenticates that people have resilience and that people thrive despite the government. As Chimamanda Adichie shares, it "create stereotypes" when people make blanket assumptions and statements regarding geographical areas or groups of people. Often times what happens in society is that based on one story that individuals learn about a geographical place in the media, this one story then becomes a representation of an entire community. This happens with religious groups, as well. Africa consists of 54 countries where over 1,000 languages are used and 797 million people live. One story cannot represent Africa. The Western notion that Africans are helpless and they need "the white folk to save them" is not the case nor is it a solution to eliminating miseries that exist in Africa or anywhere in the world. One story or image should not represent large groups of people. We all have different stories. Chimamanda Adichie divulges that there is not a single story as she expresses,

"Stories matter. Many stories matter. Stories have been used to disposes and malign, but stories can also be used to empower and humanize. Stories can break the dignity of a person or they can be used to repair that broken dignity. There is never a single story about a single place. When we reject the single story, we regain a kind of paradise."

Adichie's artful and adroit explanation about the importance of all stories reminds us why it is important to continually grasp different perspectives. InterviewGirl.com will do just this. By interviewing numerous individuals and hearing their stories, we can help to prevent against "stereotyping" entire countries. InterviewGirl.com will collect stories to present different perspectives and to protect against "the single story."

How Stories Play a Role in Today's World

My notebooks filled with handwritten notes that I've taken for years about anything and everything, knowledge that I've gleaned from the books that I've read, my life experiences, and my research all imparted the dynamism of a transcendent story and the importance of learning. How could these two principle ideas at the heart of InterviewGirl.com be turned into a movement that made money to help others who were experiencing misery? This is the question that I have grappled with over the past two years. It's hard to get people to donate money, but what if we could get them to donate stories? What if people could share a story with InterviewGirl.com and then we put all these stories together for people to read or hear? What if people whom society wants to hear from agreed to have an interview with InterviewGirl.com?

We live in an information age. Content is gold. It's always helpful to look at History to see how the world has come to be the way that it is. In the case of InterviewGirl.com, it was necessary to look at how we arrived at this age where information is now readily available through the internet. George Friedman describes the history of the world from 1900 to 2000 in *The Next Decade* as he asks the reader to imagine the world in each twenty year time period. In the early 1900's, Europe ruled the Eastern Hemisphere. Most of the world was either directly or indirectly controlled from a European capital. There were no wars and Europeans were enjoying prosperity. By the summer of 1920, Europe had been torn apart by World War One. At the end of the war, Europe needed to be rebuilt and the Austro-Hungarian, Russian, German, and Ottoman Empires were gone and millions had died in the war. By the summer of 1940, Germany reemerged, conquered France and dominated Europe. At the end of World War Two, Germany was defeated. By 1960, Europe was occupied. It was split down the middle between the United States and the Soviet Union. The European empires were collapsing, and the USA and Soviet Union were competing over who would dominate. By 1980, to contain the Soviet Union, the United States formed an alliance with Maoist China. By 2000, the Soviet Union had completely collapsed. China was still communist in name but had become capitalist in practice. NATO had advanced into Eastern Europe and even into the former Soviet Union. The world was prosperous and peaceful, but then September 11, 2001 happened and the world changed yet again. As Friedman suggests,

> "There is no magic twenty-year cycle; there is no simplistic force governing this pattern. It is simply that the things that appear to be so permanent and dominant at any given moment in history can change with stunning rapidity. Eras come and go. In international relations, the way the world looks right now is not at all how it will look in twenty years."[134]

Similar to Friedman, Daniel Pink does a good job of looking at the world to see how it has come to be the way that it is in *A Whole New Mind*. He explains economic evolution by using a screenplay metaphor. In his metaphor, economic steps are the acts in a movie and the members of society are the actors in this story. The first act was the Agricultural Age. The central player was the farmer. Work was defined by the hard labor of planting and harvesting the field. The second act began in the nineteenth century and is called the Industrial Age. The primary actor in this age was the factory worker. The worker worked the machines and work was defined by long hours and repetitive tasks. The third act began in the twentieth century and is the Information Age. This act is dominated by the knowledge of workers. The worker gathered and disseminated information, and work was defined by the management of facts and figures. Pink expresses that most of us are children of the information age.[135] The next act is the Conceptual Age. The main characters now are the creator and the empathizer. Pink declares that we've progressed from a society of farmers to a society of factory workers to a society of knowledge workers and now we are progressing yet again to a society of creators and empathizers, of pattern recognizers and meaning makers.[136] InterviewGirl.com will provide content that will help people who read the compilations and books that InterviewGirl.com puts together. As people learn new information through stories, it is through this information that possibilities then begin to happen for individuals. The more information that you learn and the more that you experience, you begin to make connections. The time that we now live in, technology releases endless possibilities for humans and it opens many doors for us. As Daniel Pink proposes, "in the Conceptual Age, we must awaken the power of the narrative."[137]

> "Eventually everything connects—people, ideas, objects. The quality of the connections is the key to quality per se."
>
> —Charles Eames

Compilations and products produced at InterviewGirl.com will bring the world information and stories and it is then up to people who hear the stories and obtain the knowledge to create and aggrandize this information from there. As we have learned, all great ideas are a series of connections coming together. Tim

Berners-Lee's story is no different. Berners-Lee first proposed a project that would eventually become the World Wide Web. While working at CERN in 1989, Berners-Lee came up with an idea for managing information using a network of interconnected computers that created a web of resources available to all. Berners-Lee saw the right way to bring two tools together so the World Wide Web was established. As Berners-Lee puts it, "The Web arose as an answer to an open challenge, through the swirling together of influences, ideas, realizations from many sides, until, by the wondrous offices of the human mind, a new concept jelled."[138] He continues, "I happened to come along with time, and the right interest and inclination, after hypertext and the Internet had come of age. The task left to me was to marry them together." Projects produced at InterviewGirl.com will expose people to new stories and information. InterviewGirl.com's mission is promoting the power of the narrative, which is crucial in the day and age in which we live. Susan Conley, author of *The Foremost Good Fortune*, in explaining why she is grateful to authors who write stories, shares, "When there is this magical alchemy of this living writer teaching there is the potential for transformation. Lives can be changed by storytelling." I knew that lives could be transformed when people heard certain stories. I had to take this notion and create a movement to begin to try and eliminate miseries that exist in our world.

How Can Sharing Stories Possibly Change the World?

"Learn from yesterday, live for today, hope for tomorrow. The important thing is not to stop questioning."
—Albert Einstein

Incredible innovations and accomplishments begin when individuals ask the correct questions. The idea (InterviewGirl.com) was there, now it was a matter of time. The questions were brewing. What had to be done to get InterviewGirl.com going? Walking through a busy mall, waiting in line to get into a bar, standing in line at lunch, sitting in my graduate seminar, or standing in line at airport security, as I was surrounded by amenities and luxuries of the place where I lived, I thought, if one book could generate revenues, what if I could create numerous books that were filled with exceptional and edifying stories? What if I shared interviews with people in a medium other than a book? The possibilities to get someone like Amara medication began to fill my mind. The profits from stories collected at InterviewGirl.com would assist people and the stories themselves would help other people too.

Stories:

Certain stories are indescribable and ineffable because often times the individual sharing the story has an amaranthine passion for the subject or person that he/she is describing in the story. We all have different talents and gifts. We all have a passion for divergent things. InterviewGirl.com allows people to share their own unique and particular passions. In many of InterviewGirl.com's projects, people share their passions along with others who have the same passions. When others then read these stories about someone's passion, they will become inspired by the passion (story) of the person sharing the story.

Proceeds/Profits:

The proceeds/profits from the compilations of stories that come from projects at InterviewGirl.com are for helping others (for example, helping someone like Amara get access to medication). As InterviewGirl.com developed, I understood that my intention was in the right place with "wanting to eliminate misery" within our world, but the idea of just "giving" charity was not all I envisioned, yet initially, I didn't know what more to do. The debate about aid and charity and how often times even though an intention is in the right place, the aid that someone sends can cause more harm than good is a reoccurring theme within this book. However this being said, the Good Samaritan effect does exist and research supports the virtuous cycle of private charity, so I knew the Interview Girl Foundation's goal of helping to eliminate miseries was possible. Our efforts can and do make a difference in the lives of others.[139] I knew that I could raise a bunch of money and help various causes and I knew that although there would be flaws within the charitable effort, it was still a noble thing to do and would make some sort of difference, but how could the Interview Girl Foundation actually help social problems on a large scale? This is where the restlessness came in and although I was excited about my plans to create a program to eliminate misery, I wondered if this effort could actually make the world a better place. Through books I read, stories I heard, and the research I completed, I became fascinated with individuals who were social entrepreneurs. *Ashoka* defines a social entrepreneur as,

> "Just as entrepreneurs change the face of business, social entrepreneurs act as the change agents for society, seizing opportunities others miss and improving systems, inventing new approaches, and creating solutions to change society for the better. While a business entrepreneur might create entirely new industries, a social entrepreneur comes up with new solutions to social problems and then implements them on a large scale."

In *How to Change the World*, David Bornstein defines social entrepreneurs as people who "identify resources where people only see problems. They view the villagers as the solution, not the passive beneficiary. They begin with the assumption of competence and unleash resources in the communities they're serving."[140] Everything I read about social entrepreneurs seemed to discuss individuals. I wondered how to make the Interview Girl Foundation a team of these individuals or even how to bring social entrepreneurs from around the world together because if we did that, results would be accelerated by selecting entrepreneurial teams (rather than single entrepreneurs). Organizing training multiple teams would be a more efficient way to create large scale change. As this question became the focal point as the Interview Girl Foundation was being created, how our foundation would use profits to make meaningful change began to form.

There are three components to the Interview Girl Foundation's purpose:

1) The Interview Girl Foundation devises projects that offer solutions to social problems that go beyond immediate "band-aid" solutions.
2) The Interview Girl Foundation contributes to organizations and individuals who are pursuing innovative ideas. These organizations also have a strategy about the action needed in order to make the ideas happen.
3) The Interview Girl Foundation works to find ways to help make collaboration across organizations and industries happen.

I understood that for the Interview Girl Foundation or any organization to succeed at problem-solving in society committed collaboration was the key. No person or organization could do it alone. InterviewGirl.com is a vehicle to spread the good news about organizations throughout the world that are making a difference and the Interview Girl Foundation helps to bring these organizations into contact with one another. Long-term goals for the Interview Girl Foundation are to invest in those nonprofits and organizations doing innovative work. The Interview Girl Foundation creates its own projects targeted at eliminating misery, but its larger focus is on collaborating with social entrepreneurs who *already* created successful projects. When people in the world who are making a difference partner together, the process of creating meaningful change is expedited. Once a certain organization has successfully implemented programs in one place, then the Interview Girl Foundation can join forces with that organization and bring that organization into contact with other organizations and help all the organizations to work together to also be successful in more difficult locations. The Interview Girl Foundation would help to establish implementation plans that are successful. Next the Interview Girl Foundation would help to develop qualified teams who could carry out the replication plans in communities in need. Behind the Interview Girl Foundation is a strong commitment to share information and to collaborate. The Interview Girl Foundation concentrates on bringing successful social entrepreneurs into contact with one another because as these social entrepreneurs work as teams rather than individuals, more can be accomplished.

Although the Interview Girl Foundation has these grander plans about how to bring about large scale changes in society, we will start where we can and that is with helping a person who needs our help. So, we go back to the basics. The Interview Girl Foundation and InterviewGirl.com were created to eliminate misery. Through the Interview Girl Foundation, we will help who we can, with what we have, to start. The compilation royalties from projects completed at InterviewGirl.com are used to help someone who is living in misery. The thing is that really what isn't very much for most us is a huge help to someone in this world, like the orphans in Africa, for example. In Chapter nine, what a dollar can buy for someone in Africa is discussed.[141] The initial profits from products produced at InterviewGirl.com go toward *Operation A²*, a project directed toward helping orphans suffering from HIV/AIDS. Profits contributed to *Operation A²* will be used for medicine and other life-changing tools and resources to help eliminate the miseries of people in the developing world. As time goes on, the Interview Girl Foundation will move onto to help other people experiencing other miseries, as well.[142] The acumen as to why I started InterviewGirl.com was to eliminate the misery that someone within this world was experiencing. Even if the compilations of stories that InterviewGirl.com puts together don't generate abounding profits, any little contributions that we can give to the orphans or any other individual who is experiencing some form of misery will help. Sharing a story won't take much of your time and/or making a small donation won't make a large dent in your bank account. Although *Operation A²* is beginning small, the transcendence of what we ultimately hope to achieve is behind each small action taken in our early efforts. Each story that is shared and/or donation that is made may seem like a small effort, but when all of the small exertions come together, one day InterviewGirl.com will reach the movement level that it aspires to reach.

One By One: Everyone Sharing a Story Can Make a Difference

"I expect to pass through life but once. If therefore, there be any kindness I can show, or any good thing I can do to any fellow being, let me do it now, and not defer or neglect it, as I shall not pass this way again."
—William Penn

The small things that we can do make a difference in the lives of others and if everyone does something small, these seemingly small acts add up to change the less than ideal circumstances and make them better. This is one of the life lessons discussed in Chapter 14. InterviewGirl.com is working to get everyone to share a story. Remember when you were a little kid and you were taught to share with others? Mother Teresa is thought to be one of the world's foremost experts on poverty. When a reporter asked Mother Teresa why there is poverty in the world, she answered that the reason that we have poverty is because we are not willing to share. By sharing your story, life experience, advice, expertise, or insight, whatever it is that you can contribute to one of our compilations, you will be helping to make this world a better place. InterviewGirl.com is a place to share stories, insight, and advice.

InterviewGirl.com will be able to distribute incredible content with the world as you share your stories.

We have all heard that we improve as human beings as we read great literature. The importance of reading is not a secret. For years as a lover of books, I felt illuminated by the stories that I read. These stories not only enlivened me, but they provided me with a sense of instruction when I needed inculcation. Novels, stories and dramas can help us understand the complexities of life. Growing up I loved to read. I found the stories from literature entertaining. The stories were inside of books that I could not put down, but more than that, I now realize that as I read book after book, I gained a sense of empathy as I learned the stories of:

- Atticus Finch in Harper Lee's *To Kill a Mockingbird*,

- Mr. Darcy and Elizabeth Bennet in Jane Austen's *Pride and Prejudice,*

- Holden Caulfield in J.D. Salinger's *Catcher in the Rye,*

- Lolita in Vladimir Nabokov's *Lolita,*

- Holly Golightly in Truman Capote's *Breakfast at Tiffany's,*

- The Little Prince in Antoine de Saint-Exupery's *The Little Prince,*

- Santiago in Ernest Hemingway's *The Old Man and the Sea,*

- Hana in Michael Ondaatje's *The English Patient,*

- Florentino Ariza in Gabriel Garcia Marquez's *Love in the Time of Cholera,*

- Charlie Marlow in Joseph Conrad's *Heart of Darkness,*

- and of course Jay Gatsby in F. Scott Fitzgerald's *The Great Gatsby.*

The benefits of reading great literature have long been affirmed by university studies and by taking a deeper look at how successful individuals spend their time, reading timeless literature is always one of the activities where people spend their time. It is the stories about each of the characters mentioned above that make those books timeless classics. The stories of the characters in those books carry with them influential lessons. I always knew that there was this power, this magic to stories. I just never could quite articulate this. For many years, my articulation of this concept was, "I really like to read."

Neuroscience confirms that the brain does not make much of a distinction between reading about an experience and encountering it in real life. Studies in Neuroscience reveal that in each case, the same neurological regions are stimulated. When I learned that now brain science proves this claim that I had about there being "power in stories" to be true, I was delighted and from this feeling of elation, my aspiration as to what InterviewGirl.com could grow into blossomed. David Brin defines magic as "the creation of subjective realities in other people's heads." There is no way to try and get someone to feel exactly what you are feeling. The closest we can come to achieving that as human beings is by telling someone a story. "Changing the world one story at a time" isn't just a catchy phrase for InterviewGirl.com. It is the mission of InterviewGirl.com and the expectation of the Interview Girl Foundation is that as the stories come into InterviewGirl.com, we will reach out and help to eliminate the misery that someone in the world experiences. Through projects that are completed using "stories" that are collected one story at a time at InterviewGirl.com, the Interview Girl Foundation will assist one person at a time from the profits that come from InterviewGirl.com's projects. By beginning with helping one individual, in time, the Interview Girl Foundation will be a part of creating new solutions to change society for the better.

CHAPTER EIGHT

Why is Interview Girl qualified to Interview?

Where my experience with interviewing began—My MA in History and Life Long Research Project

Much of my work at InterviewGirl.com consists of my going out to interview people. As it is taking some time for the public to become aware of the InterviewGirl.com website, InterviewGirl.com's projects began with my reaching out to people and asking them to share their stories with me rather than people sending me their stories through InterviewGirl.com. I have completed hundreds of interviews up to this point in order to bring some meaningful and noteworthy stories to you. As touched upon in the previous chapters, there was a succession of events that led up to the birth of InterviewGirl.com.

Going back even further than discussed already (*Travel Girl*), when I was a sophomore in college, I studied abroad on the Saint Mary's College Rome Program. My Mom's family is from Italy, but I never really understood her family's history. I knew that my Mom was born in Novara, but her family is from a town called Fiume, which is today Rijeka in Croatia. While I was studying abroad in college, one weekend, I went to visit my Mom's uncle who lived in Genoa. At the time, my Italian wasn't great, so I had to piece together what my great uncle was telling me. I managed to pick up some of what he was saying and then he showed me some old black and white photographs as he told me a story about why my mother's family immigrated to the USA. Through beautifully sounding Italian words and characteristically Italian hand gestures, my benevolent uncle explained to me why Fiume was no longer an Italian town and why it was now in Croatia. My uncle's revealing this story to me in Italian, adds to the impact that the story had on me. The same stories that people explain to me in Italian, when I try to write about them in English, I feel as if something gets lost in translation. I was intrigued by what my Uncle shared with me and from this meeting; I began to further research my Mom's family history, which inspired what eventually became the topic for my MA in European History years later.

I am a high school teacher and a graduate student. I work full time as a teacher and I attend graduate school in the evenings. It was through my Master's degree in European History that I received a stockpile of experience with interviewing. Specifically, it was through completing my Thesis for my MA in History that I obtained experience with interviewing people. I interviewed exiles from Italy who were displaced after the Second World War. In 2008, I seriously began interviewing exiles for my Thesis, but I have been captivated by this part of Italy's history for years now. Long before I began my Thesis, I read all that I could about the town (Fiume) my Mom's family was from—a town that was introduced to me through my great uncle Angelo's story. That weekend I decided to go meet some of my mother's family, I learned a story that would intensely shape the next decade of my life. A story that my uncle shared with me in Italian at a time when I had only one year of Italian classes under my belt led to my forming questions and these questions eventually turned into a graduate level research project that took me on a journey throughout the world (USA, Italy, the Balkans, Canada, and Australia) to find the answers (the stories I was after). Similar to how Amara's story influenced this InterviewGirl.com project, the story surrounding my mom's family history that my great uncle shared with me formed what I would choose to study in graduate school (European History and Italian).

The map of Europe was altered after the Second World War. Part of Italy became part of Yugoslavia after World War Two. What happened to the exiles who left this land when the boundaries changed after WWII was the topic that I researched for my Thesis that I had to complete for MA in European History. After the Second World War, the world had to rebuild. Arthur James Balfour was the Prime Minister of England 1902–1905 and he wrote the Balfour Declaration stating official British approval of Zionism. As Balfour has said, "Statesmen of all countries are beginning to discover that the labors and difficulties of peace are almost as arduous and require almost as great qualities as those which are demanded for the conduct of a successful war." For my Thesis, I researched the effects of Europe's political, economic and cultural borders shifting after World War Two. I wanted to incorporate first hand stories into this research since people were still living that lived through the border changes that happened after World War Two. In order to complete my Thesis, I completed many interviews with exiles that used to live in the former Yugoslavia. I went to great lengths to get into contact with these exiles. I traveled to Canada, the Balkans, throughout Italy, throughout the USA, Slovenia, and Croatia. I also did phone interviews with exiles that are currently living in Argentina, South America, and Australia. (By the way, I did all these interviews in Italian (because it was a hobby of mine to continue learning Italian in my twenties)). This detail is important in InterviewGirl.com's emergence. I figured, if I traveled to Italy and to the Balkans to learn all these stories from people who don't speak a word of English for my graduate Thesis, I would be able to collect stories through Interview Girl.com in order to make a difference in the world.

Little by little, like a detective, I discovered the story of the exiles' experiences (those who left the former Yugoslavia) after

WWII. It was as if the story came together to make sense for me. First in learning Italian, then in studying History, and finally through talking with numerous exiles who left their land that used to be Italy, but became Yugoslavia after World War Two, I understood this historical story. It was like putting the pieces of a puzzle together and what unfolded is what I consider to be an untold story from Italy's history. The interesting part that I learned is that even other Italians weren't aware of this story. When I was in Italy over the summers and I would ask Italians living in Italy about my research, they didn't know what I was talking about. I found this untold story that was missing from the history books fascinating. I decided to make a documentary film about Venezia Giulia (the geographical area that I was studying for my Thesis) after World War Two. This documentary was shot by using my little flip video camera as I traveled around Italy and the Balkans completing these interviews and before I purchased my flip camera, the interviews were completed as I took notes by hand in a notebook as I spoke with the exiles. I have journals upon journals filled with notes from various interviews.

Somewhere along the way, I decided that I did not only want to share the stories of the exiles, those who left the land along Italy's Adriatic coast after World War Two, but I was also riveted to hear the stories from those who stayed. That was what brought me to the Balkans during the summers of 2011 and 2012. I heard the perspective of individuals who lived in what was Italy before World War Two started, but now they are citizens living in Slovenia and Croatia. I heard the stories of those who stayed in what became Yugoslavia after WWII. I put the documentary together by explaining: Here are the stories that I learned on my journey through the world to meet those that once lived in Venezia Giulia (the border zone along Italy's Adriatic Coast). The documentary begins by explaining that in meeting the exiles as well as the people who did not flee, I learned the following stories ... and then I present the stories of both groups. Those Italians who were uprooted after World War Two were the first group of individuals that I interviewed to learn their stories. These stories then became my first compilation of interviewees and the first stories that I was determined to capture and then share.

It Wasn't Easy

"It's Hard to Beat a Person that Never Gives Up"
—Babe Ruth

It should be noted that when I first started this research about the partition of land after World War Two along Italy's Adriatic coast, the stories weren't there. I constantly would hear, "They are all dead. You are too late." But, the thing was that I knew that people with these stories were still alive. I did not give up. I persevered and I eventually found "the story" that I was looking for. "Vittoria, they are dead and those who are living, they are all too old. They don't want to speak with you." I heard this response over and over. At times, I thought that I was too late. Then I would remember my Uncle Nino (my mother's brother) and how vividly he answered my questions. I knew there were others out there around his age who would remember too. I did not give up even when my attempts to set up interviews failed. I kept at it and in due course, through, of all things, using social media and the internet, I finally began to find leads. Eventually, I was in contact with hundreds of exiles as well as the descendants from those who were exiled from the land that used to be at one time Italy, then was Yugoslavia after World War Two, and presently is Slovenia and Croatia. An interview project that I was told by person after person would not work because "those people are now old" became an actualization in my research that I was sedulously working on day in and day out to hear people's stories.

From the interviews that I completed for my Thesis I learned what I set out to learn: the point of view from the Istrian, Fiuman and Dalmatian exiles after World War Two and the point of view of individuals who never left their land after the war and what their life is now like living in Croatia and Slovenia. I set out to answer the questions: What happens when borders change at the end of a war and land that was once one country becomes another country? How do people define ethnicity and identity? Do these notions move beyond the country who is holding political power? From the exiles I learned the stories that I was hoping to learn, but I also learned a great deal more. I learned life lessons that I'll always remember and I'll never, ever be the same after learning these lessons. The exiles taught me a plethora of knowledge and wisdom, but above all, I learned that in the face of adversity, one must continue on in life. People cannot give up. My MA in History and even before I was ever a graduate student, my Life Long Research Project (to learn the stories of the exiles) inspired InterviewGirl.com. I thought, "If I did this with the Fiuman, Istrian, and Dalmatian exiles who were quite elderly and did not communicate in English, I can do this with other areas too."[143]

Once my Thesis was turned in, I began collecting stories from all over the nation about World War Two from those still living today who were alive during the war years. I have interviewed many people in their 80's and 90's all throughout the Chicago land area, but I have also done phone interviews and interviews using the web camera on my computer with people throughout the world for my World War Two stories project. Interviewing people who lived during the Second World War and veterans who served during the war was an experience that profoundly affected me as an individual. The stories that men and women from the WWII generation shared with me changed the way that I would see the world. I gained an immeasurable perspective from having the privilege and honor to speak with these individuals. I had umpteen ideas in my head about what I could do with all of these interviews. My passion for interviewing started with collecting stories from exiles who left what used to be Yugoslavia after WWII, then in collecting stories from people who live in Croatia and Slovenia who at one time lived in Italy. Moving on from Italy's border, for my next project, I began to interview WWII vets and/ or anyone alive during the Second World War to hear their stories and eventually my continued enthusiasm to interview grew into InterviewGirl.com.

I believe that I am qualified to interview because as a graduate student I studied how to complete an ethical interview and the techniques to use when interviewing. I put this knowledge to practice as I interviewed exiles in order to complete my Thesis for my MA in History and then when I interviewed people who were alive during WWII. In just a few years that I worked on these projects, I interviewed hundreds of individuals. Many of these individuals were often hard to get a hold of because they were elderly. One day it hit me. What if I could apply "interviewing" to learn all sorts of remarkable stories and then sell these stories to raise money for the orphans in Africa or any group of people who need help (who experience misery). I wanted to use stories to eliminate miseries in our world. This is exactly what I am doing with InterviewGirl.com. I am learning stories associated with the various compilations that have been started and once the compilations are complete, I'll share these stories with the world. What I experienced from interviewing the exiles who left Venezia Giulia, from interviewing those living in present day Slovenia and Croatia who also lived there when the land was part of Italy, and from interviewing the individuals who experienced WWII—was what I now wanted to accomplish with InterviewGirl.com in a wide array of topics.

I had a purpose and a vision that was unyielding. My trip to Africa broadened my horizons—especially learning Amara's story. Comparatively speaking, in all of the time I've been on this Earth, I spent, but a glimpse of time with Amara, but meeting her offered me a glance that allowed me to see a reality diverse from my own. As Cesare Pavese put into words, "We do not remember days, we remember moments." Edem uttering, "Because the medicines ran out" and Amara querying about *how mountains are formed, what causes drought* and *if indeed aluminum is harder than gold?*

are moments etched in my mind and in addition, those moments will always have a special place in my heart. Amara impels me to do something that will make a difference in this world and to get others to help me make this difference. It became my vision that what would begin with individuals sharing stories through InterviewGirl.com could lead to people authentically engendering changes that need to be made in this world. By sharing stories, we can all help to eliminate some of the misery that exists here on earth. Through stories, we can bring millions of people like Amara *hope*.

World War Two Project

I completed interviews with the Istrian, Fiuman, and Dalmatian exiles and the WWII vets with insistence to get them done as fast as I could. I felt as if I was up against the clock. Time was against me. The clock was ticking. The race had begun. I had to finish all these interviews *before it was too late*. I read somewhere that the WWII vets were dying at a rate of 800 a day. There was an urgency to get out there, to contact nursing homes, to contact VFW posts and American Legion posts, to make calls, to make fliers, to get into contact with the World War Two generation and capture their stories before they passed on. I was determined to hear the "stories" of the WWII Vets before they were gone. This pressure of knowing that the vets were dying off forced me to get out there and interview. No matter how tired I was, no matter how long of a day I had, I went, I completed my interviews, and boy am I glad that I did.

It became this astounding experience that I believe profoundly helped to shape the person that I am. As with everyone with whom you have the privilege of coming into contact, you grow and you learn something. I was forever touched by meeting the individuals that I was lucky enough to meet from the World War Two generation. The World War two stories compilation was originally intended to be about war stories, but as I completed these interviews, I learned more than just stories about war. I learned about life. I learned about death. I began to reflect on mortality. I understood that this life ends. It was hard to one week have an interview with someone and three weeks later to learn that he/she passed away. I literally had some interviews with people on their death beds. From this experience of speaking with the WWII generation, I was changed for the better. I couldn't go back. The truth is that I have way more interviews than I need to produce the compilation, but I keep doing more interviews because I love the elderly and all that they teach me. Conversing with the elderly made me yearn from a place deep inside me to want to become better in a myriad of ways. To use the words of Matthew Kelly, who in my opinion explains it best, we all need to become a better version of ourselves.[144] My conversations with the WWII generation made me want to do just that. I wanted to become better. I wanted to seize each day because time doesn't last forever. I wanted to live a life in accordance with correct priorities. Interviewing the elderly taught me considerable lessons. Often times in life when you are working, well it feels like work. This—the interviews, meeting the WWII vets, it never gets old.

I learned that at the end of your life, many people have the same questions and the same regrets. I thought that speaking with a World War Two veteran would teach me that nothing in life could be worse than war, and yes it was difficult for the vets to speak about war and again and again I heard that war is terrible. There is no other way to describe it. However, I heard stories beyond the horrors of war. When an 86 year old, who served in the Pacific six decades ago, declares that nothing is worse than seeing the love of your life sick and ill and seeing her deteriorate and get worse day after day, as a tear runs down his cheek, you reflect on relationships and life. These lessons, these stories stick with you. You understand about love in a new way. As I learned life lessons from the veterans, I knew that I could learn life lessons from the elderly. This in turn, became another compilation of stories at InterviewGirl.com.

A 95 year old, World War Two veteran (John) lives in a nursing home in Illinois. John and I met in a common room in the nursing home where he resides for his interview. When I walked in and saw him sitting there, I literally felt as if I was having a personal meeting with Santa Claus. John had a welcoming presence about him that began with his gigantic smile that radiated from his face. One cannot help but notice John's sweet smile and of course his characteristic long white beard. John had one of those smiles that makes our world a better place. From his stories detailing the greatest World Series baseball games ever played to his synopsis of every President's administration from Herbert Hoover to Barack Obama, as John talked, I was spellbound. I learned more in the two hours that I spent with John that day than I did in reading fifty secondary sources telling me about those Presidents.

At the completion of our interview, he wanted to show me some pictures, so he had to wheel himself in his wheel chair to his room at the other end of the nursing home to show me these pictures. We made our way through the halls of the nursing home passing nurses, aides, janitors, and John's friends who were parked in their wheel chairs against the wall throughout the hall, all the while moving at what seemed like a snail's pace. John's jovial and good-natured character came out as he acknowledged and said hello to every person whom we passed. John used his right hand to turn the right wheel on his wheel chair and slowly inch himself forward—one turn of the wheel, on the wheel chair at a time. Sitting in wheel chairs at the end of the hall, were some ladies who were evidently very ill. They could not even hold their own heads up. "I like to call it the point of no return," John said as he pointed to the sickly women at the end of the hall. I looked up to see the women drooling from the mouth, arched completely over making them look like they were hanging over the chair, rather than sitting in it. The women looked completely out of it. John then pointed to the end of the hall and expressed, "you see what I mean, the point of no return?" John's notation here made me aware that our time here on Earth is limited. We need to be grateful for our health because those ladies with their heads sagging at the end of the hall, they did not have their health and well ..... it showed.

As a student of history, I wanted to speak with people who actually lived through an event (in this case: WWII) and ask them questions about what they experienced. I knew in even 10 years from now, I would not have the opportunity to do that with people because everyone who experienced WWII would be dead. From every WWII interview that I completed, not only did I learn the interesting war stories that I set out to learn, but I always learned other fascinating stories, separate from the war, from these people's lives. Most of the veterans were eager to tell me about their granddaughter's latest degree or activity or their grandson's new job. What medals they received while in duty were mentioned only from a direct question proposed by me, but I have video after video filled with people telling me stories about their children and grandchildren. Interview after interview turned into a discussion about the veterans' families and just how proud they were of their family and how much their family meant to them. In my World War Two Stories project, yes I heard my WWII Stories that I set out to learn, but I also learned other stories and lessons along the way. The value of time was one of the most important lessons that the WWII generation taught me. When two months after I interviewed a vet, he passed on, well this taught me the value of time. Our time here on Earth is indeed limited. We cannot take this for granted. There is a time limit on our lives. We should each try to seize each day to the fullest. You cannot always say tomorrow. Some things must be done today.

> "One day you will wake up and there won't be any more time to do the things you've always wanted. Do it now."
> —Paolo Coelho

> "Make every day your masterpiece."
> —John Wooden

"Carpe Diem."

To this day, I continue to complete interviews with the WWII generation. Collecting *WWII stories* is a project in progress at InterviewGirl.com. I spend part of my daily commutes to school making phone calls to nursing homes, VFW's, and American Legion posts asking if there is any interest from their residents/ members to share their stories. Along the way of collecting WWII stories, a new project developed, I have interviewed several 100 year olds (or older). A new compilation project emerged for InterviewGirl. com. This project is called *Conversing with the Centenarians.* I have enough stories for both the WWII stories compilation and the stories from the 100 year olds, but I continue to make the calls to organizations looking for more stories. I continue to go to these interviews. I do this because the stories that the WWII generation shared with me are compelling and people who were alive during WWII are still living, so while I have the opportunity to speak with these people, I go and I listen intently to their stories. I cannot wait to share their influential stories with you in the near future.

Continual Lessons from Interviewing

Having the opportunity to speak with someone at the end of their life was and continues to be a gift to me and one that I will treasure. I did not finish these interviews all that long ago and I have received several phone calls since my interviews from the children of the WWII vets asking me if they could have a copy of the interview that I completed with their father because he has now passed away. Linda, the daughter of Al DeVries called me when she came across a flier about my WWII stories project as she was cleaning out her father's belongings. She asked if her father ever met with me. I told her that he had. We were talking and I offered to send her a copy of her Dad's interview. She told me that her Dad went on Honor Flight and she started to choke up when she was reading the honor flight description to me, "Bring the vets to the memorial to honor them." Some things in life are greater than money. I'm sure Linda would not have accepted all the money in the world in place of a copy of her Dad's interview. His story is now captured. It is now timeless. If we do not hear stories and then document them, they can become forgotten. Documenting someone's story gives that individual the gift of immortality. Linda's father served in the Second World War. She had not even heard some of his stories. Giving her that copy of her father's interview genuinely was a gift. Al DeVries explained aspects of the war that I had read about in the history books over and over, but as he went into detail about the events, through his personal narrative, history came alive and I understood better than I ever had the course of events he lived through that I had read about various times before I ever met him. His story made me understand the history in a new way. His story made me feel as if I too lived it.

> "We're all made of stories. When they finally put us underground, the stories are what will go on. Not forever, perhaps, but for a time. It's a kind of immortality, I suppose, bounded by limits, it's true, but then so's everything."
>
> —Charles de Lint

I did not realize just how difficult it would be to learn about the passing of the vets, sometimes just shortly after my conversations with them. I mean I knew that I was rushing to do the interviews because the people were so elderly, but to one day have a fluid conversation with them and then to find out that they are gone was difficult for me and continues to be difficult for me. As I began uploading the videos that I had of the interviews, I would pause the interviews at certain spots as they were playing. I sat there in front of my computer and I stared at the individual frozen on my computer screen who had shared his story with me.

I pondered how I could possibly give justice to this gentleman? How could I share his powerful story with the world in a way where the world would understand what he lived through? I now had this monumental task ahead of me.

My documentary about Fiume and the exiles (the topic for my Thesis for my MA in European History) really should be the first project that I publish, but instead I found myself founding and creating InterviewGirl.com. I had to get this idea going (InterviewGirl.com) before I completed the WWII Stories compilation book or the Fiume documentary. I knew orphans like Amara were dying each day because "the medicines ran out." I wanted to start eliminating miseries like this as soon as possible. Stories from the exiles who left Italy's Adriatic Coast after World War Two and stories from the World War Two veterans are two compilations of stories that will be coming to you soon from InterviewGirl.com. I struggle with trusting myself to share the stories from individuals who lived through WWII because I wonder if I can ever even begin to successfully convey the significance of someone's fascinating story, but I cannot think of a better reason to take on this immense task than to use these beautiful stories that I've had the privilege of hearing from the WWII generation to make the world a better place by eliminating misery.

CHAPTER NINE

InterviewGirl.com HELPS people in TWO ways

InterviewGirl.com: A *Movement* to make a Difference in the World

"The best way to find yourself is to lose yourself in the service of others."

—*Mahatma Gandhi*

Although InterviewGirl.com started out as what I thought would be a charity, it is more than that, it is a *movement* to make a difference in the world. Profits that come from the products produced at InterviewGirl.com are used to help "slice off" a piece of the misery that exists in today's world (returning to the "world is a cake" analogy). My trip to Africa was the catalyst that started InterviewGirl.com, but even before that trip, I have always wanted to help make life better for those living in poverty. The fact that of the 1.8 billion children in developing countries, 600 million of them live on less than $1 (U.S.) a day is unacceptable.[145] I remember seeing a picture of a child that my parents sponsored when I was a little girl. My parents would send money each month to help support this child. I thought that was an honorable thing to do. Since I've returned from Africa, I continually think, "Is there something that I can do to make so and so's misery a little better?" I don't always even know who the "so and so" is, but the thought that 25,000 people die every day of hunger-related causes makes me want to take action. As I throw away the food that we didn't eat from our refrigerator each week, I think, "Is there a way or a system to get this food to people who need it?" I find myself more cognizant of things that I may not have used to notice.

I know that action needs to be focused and start somewhere. InterviewGirl.com's mission to slice off a piece of the misery in this world inaugurates with the Interview Girl Foundation's project, *Operation A²* that targets those suffering from AIDS without access to medication in Africa. As time passes, with each new compilation of stories or project that InterviewGirl.com is working on, a new area (misery) will be targeted. At the beginning of each project that InterviewGirl.com produces, it will state where proceeds from that particular project are going to go. We will work to eliminate the miseries that different individuals experience. Each project is dedicated to eliminating a different misery. InterviewGirl. com was created in order to make a difference in this world. If I could invent a new product or create an entertainment item that would generate money, I would. However, my gifts are writing and storytelling. I can write and I can tell stories. God blessed me with a mind, a heart, fingers to type, ears to listen empathetically and for this reason, I put together these interesting compilations and from selling them, I hope to make a difference in this world and to "slice off" a piece of the misery that someone is facing. YOU can help make a difference in this world. Sharing a story through InterviewGirl.com is such a marvelous way to try and help others. It won't even cost you any money.

Have you found yourself thinking, I want to help people. I want to do something. What can I do to make a difference? If I had money, I would be more than willingly to donate to those who need help. InterviewGirl.com is different from ordinary charities because it is not a charity where you have to give money (SAY

WHAT?!?! I don't have to give money!). In order to help people through InterviewGirl.com, you just need to share a story and the beautiful part is that we all have different stories to share based on our own distinctive life experiences. That being said, for some, you may prefer to just give money rather than to take the time to submit a story. You can donate money if you are someone who is beyond busy or if you are someone who is fiscally well off. In fact, for some people, the ability to write a check is their greatest gift. Deep down most of want to help others by donating money to our favorite charities, but then everyday life kicks in and we can barely afford our own lives, let alone donate to charity. With InterviewGirl.com, you don't have to donate your money. All you need to do is share a story. The purpose of InterviewGirl. com is to collect stories and then to share them. You never know whom your story can touch. Maybe you don't have a lot of money to donate. Who does? But, what event, story, tragedy, and issue have you dealt with in your life? What's your passion? Share your experiences. We can all benefit from learning your story. Helping others (eliminating misery) is InterviewGirl.com's greatest mission, but collecting stories and then sharing these stories is a part of how InterviewGirl.com plans to carry out this mission. InterviewGirl.com is a *movement* to get everyone to do their part in helping to eliminate some of misery that exists in the world. In eliminating miseries that people experience, the Interview Girl Foundation strives to help people get back on their feet. We are helping to eliminate misery, but we are also starting a *movement* to give people the tools that they need to keep the changes going once the funds from the Interview Girl Foundation are gone. Poverty is eliminated when things are changed permanently for the next generation. This is the end objective as the Interview Girl Foundation works to eliminate misery in this world. In time, people will not need aid or charity from the Interview Girl Foundation, but rather they'll be able to help themselves. When someone who the Interview Girl Foundation helps then helps someone else, the cycle that the Interview Girl Foundation began is complete.

Developing the Interview Girl Foundation
to reach beyond Good Intentions

Initially as my ideas were forming, InterviewGirl.com and the Interview Girl Foundation were to be a charitable effort. However I knew that there are some loopholes in charity. In speaking about her time in Africa in the *Blue Sweater*, Jacqueline Novogratz expresses, "I saw some of the worst that good intentions, traditional charity, and aid can produce: failed programs that left people in the same or worse conditions."[146] Although now I am more conscious of the loopholes that exist in charity, still now, I believe in the power of charitable efforts to create change. Charity is defined as: generous actions or donations to aid the poor, ill, or helpless and/or something given to a person or persons in need. I believe in the effectiveness of benefaction. Resonant throughout my life, starting from a place deep inside me, within my heart, I feel that it is a moral imperative to help lessen the suffering of fellow humans who are enduring difficulty. This being said, I also understood that my intention was in the right place, but I wanted to make sure that the Interview Girl Foundation had more than good intentions as it began its work to eliminate miseries throughout the world.

I voraciously read about both sides that comprise the donor aid issue. Some people argue that aid actually prevents countries from developing and they think that it should be stopped. The loopholes that existed and failed charitable efforts seemed to exist largely in the realm of large government to government aid packages. Others purport that aid makes a difference to the lives of the poorest people around the world. It is a vital way to help to lift millions of people out of poverty. Advocates for donor aid believe that when it comes to why aid works, it comes down to that with healthy and educated people, poor countries can develop their economies and stand on their own two feet. Proponents of aid suggest that thanks to money from rich country donors, in the last few years we have seen: 1.4 million extra HIV positive people on life saving antiretroviral drugs and 40 million children who never would have learned to read and write are now getting an education. They credit that aid has helped to make these things happen. Promoters of aid trust that if aid is given correctly, aid can help to reduce corruption. The money can be spent in a way that empowers people in developing countries to speak up, tell their governments what they need and hold them accountable for how aid money is spent.

The Interview Girl Foundation is a private nonprofit organization, so I was interested in the *positive* changes that charities could help create for individuals in their lives. Literature reveals that private charities do in fact achieve a world of good. In Chapter seven, we learned that the Good Samaritan effect does exist and the help that many charitable organizations provide to people throughout the world validates this virtuous cycle of private charity. According to Dr. J. Harvard Maridal, a research fellow and policy analyst focusing on the issues of human happiness, prosperity, and well-being, "regulation and bureaucracy of centrally administered government programs can impede help from getting to those-in-need, but alternatively, private charity not only leads to more effective and humane help, charitable exchange is beneficial for the receiver and the giver."[147] Ultimately, Dr. Maridal authenticates that our charitable efforts can and do make a difference in the lives of others. Doug Bandow, an analyst from the Cato Institute (a public policy research organization) shares,

> "Fighting the poverty that inevitably results is certainly a worthy endeavor. Unfortunately, however, experience demonstrates that while abundant government spending might alleviate some material poverty, it will simultaneously encourage other material poverty. An alternative strategy is to start with private aid. One reason is that compulsory compassion is an oxymoron: One does not demonstrate generosity by taxing other people. Another reason is more pragmatic. Private

groups can effectively speak to the whole person, addressing spiritual needs and behavioral problems, for instance, and insisting on personal reform. Government, through initiatives such as workfare, can offer only a pale imitation of such private efforts."[148]

Private aid efforts have the potential to help people who need the assistance. The task ahead of me as I created the Interview Girl Foundation was to make sure that our programs had more than good intentions and actually made an effective difference in the lives of those who were living in misery. The problem that many people see with alms-giving is that it is just a temporary solution to the misery that one faces.

The Interview Girl Foundation is working to avoid some of the ambiguities of traditional charity that the world has seen. Although there are loopholes in aid, the Interview Girl Foundation strongly believes in helping someone in need (someone experiencing misery). This is why the foundation has been set up to start where we can with what we have, but behind the Interview Girl Foundation's plan to start by assisting one orphan in one country is our foundation's guiding larger vision (to be a part of creating innovative solutions to some of society's most pressing social problems). The Interview Girl Foundation had to begin its efforts in one village, within one country, where it looked at the needs of one orphan and assisted him/her, but these initial efforts start what the foundation hopes to implement on a large scale.

The Interview Girl Foundation is continually working to become better by finding ways to challenge the status quo and help people to make meaningful changes in their lives not just temporary solutions with handing out "aid" in a particular moment, but then when the next moment arrives, our foundation would not be present. We would start where we could and give what was needed, but understanding the miseries of those whom we were helping was crucial because people know their own needs and desires. By listening to those actually experiencing the misery was the best way to be able to help get rid of it. The world undoubtedly faces grand challenges in Global Health. The Interview Girl Foundation would like to do its part in helping to make these challenges better. One of InterviewGirl.com's underlying principles is that everyone should do something in order to eliminate some of the misery that exists in this world. As people throughout the world all strive to do something (take "their slice" of the cake), these grand challenges in Global Health can become better.

That Bigger Plan: Becoming a Social Entrepreneur

As I created InterviewGirl.com and the Interview Girl Foundation, helping others was the idea behind the project. The whole point of all of this is to help others, serve people experiencing miseries in some capacity. It is my way to try and make the world a better place. From researching the debate regarding foreign aid, what was behind my intention to "help" shifted. I could not just raise money, hope that this was doing "good" and stop there. Rather, the effectiveness of the revenues that were collected (how they were making a difference) was of utmost importance as InterviewGirl.com and the Interview Girl Foundation came to be. Along my journey to founding InterviewGirl.com, I explored what social entrepreneurs were doing throughout the world and as I did this, I knew what the preponderant focus of the Interview Girl Foundation would be. Yes, the foundation was created to eliminate misery in areas of the world where it existed, but the Interview Girl Foundation would not only send money to an area in need, but beyond these initial steps that are necessary to eliminate a misery that exists, the foundation would play a role in helping to create solutions to some of society's problems. According to *Ashoka: Innovators for the Public*, social entrepreneurs are individuals with innovative solutions to society's most pressing social problems. They are ambitious and persistent, tackling major social issues and offering new ideas for wide-scale change. Rather than leaving societal needs to the government or business sectors, social entrepreneurs find what is not working and solve the problem by changing the system, spreading the solution, and persuading entire societies to take new leaps. Social entrepreneurs often seem to be possessed by their ideas, committing their lives to changing the direction of their field. They are both visionaries and ultimate realists, concerned with the practical implementation of their vision above all else. Just as entrepreneurs change the face of business, social entrepreneurs act as the change agents for society, seizing opportunities others miss and improving systems, inventing new approaches, and creating solutions to change society for the better. While a business entrepreneur might create entirely new industries, a social entrepreneur comes up with new solutions to social problems and then implements them on a large scale.[149]

Charitable giving would be one aspect of what the Interview Girl Foundation does, but our plans reached beyond this. I added become a social entrepreneur to my list of life goals. My quest to become a social entrepreneur began as I created InterviewGirl. com and the Interview Girl Foundation. I needed to become a social entrepreneur and I needed to connect and collaborate with other social entrepreneurs throughout the globe who were making a difference and as I did this, the changes that the Interview Girl Foundation was hoping to make within society would reach beyond band-aid, temporary solutions. As I listed the characteristics of social entrepreneurs, I wondered if I was one or if I could become one? I looked at InterviewGirl.com and the Interview Girl Foundation and wondered if they met the criteria to change the world. On a basic level, my contribution to society was the stories that I collected as Interview Girl and creating the Interview Girl Foundation is how I planned to generate revenues to help develop innovative solutions to society's most pressing social problems. InterviewGirl.com is different than ordinary charities because 1.) People do not have to just donate money, but they can "donate" their story and 2.) InterviewGirl.com is a movement to change the world (eliminate some of the misery that exists) and we will do just this—one story at a time.

You help people in *two* ways when you participate in InterviewGirl.com

By participating in InterviewGirl.com, you can *help* people in two ways:

1) The royalties from InterviewGirl.com's projects help people who need the assistance (someone who is living in misery).
2) When a person reads the stories that are shared in projects produced at InterviewGirl.com, those stories will make an impression on that individual.

By sharing a story or donating to the Interview Girl Foundation you are then helping people in two ways. You are helping the people who read the stories and you are helping the people living in misery. Individuals living in misery will benefit from InterviewGirl.com sharing the stories.

People benefit when they read stories. Take our compilation of *WWII Stories*, for example. One story in the compilation of WWII Stories shares with you the perspective of a couple who lived in Nazi Germany while the Nazis were in power, but they weren't Nazis themselves. You gain tremendous perspective from hearing what they have to say and at the same time, you hear one heck of a story. Two projects being completed at InterviewGirl. com include our *WWII Stories* project as well as the *Life Lessons from the Elderly* project. I have visited hundreds of nursing homes and collected stories from elderly people living in those nursing homes. When I ask them to share "what lessons do they have for the younger generations?" the lessons that they have to share are worthwhile and meaningful. The more people whom I reach out to, I am constantly reminded that everyone truly does have a story to share. When people read/hear other people's stories, they thrive as their own perspectives deepen and they have the ability to make more connections from hearing the stories.

In the compilations that are produced at InterviewGirl.com, lessons collected from people around the world are coupled with stories from history and various stories featured in magazines and books. Each project, each compilation has a theme and research has been completed to highlight that theme. Through InterviewGirl.com's website, people have contacted me and asked to start a particular category or to feature their story solo. Also, through some of InterviewGirl.com's undertakings interviews are shared via the internet and social media, so people can glean valuable insights from the extraordinary people whom I have interviewed. InterviewGirl.com produces books and lectures too, not just compilations, but in all of InteviewGirl.com's products, astounding stories are shared.

First Way to Help People by Participating in InterviewGirl.com

"As you grow older, you will discover you have two hands: one for helping yourself, the others for helping others."

—Audrey Hepburn

When you share a story on InterviewGirl.com, first, you will help the person who reads your story once the compilation is published because reading your story will be therapeutic for those going through what you went through and/or are going through. For example, if you are an individual who had an eating disorder and now you have overcome that eating disorder, your story can be a source of inspiration for the many others who are struggling with the very eating disorder that you once struggled with in your life. By people sharing their stories, they will help others as others read the stories and learn from and relate to the stories. As Clarisa Pinkola Estes pointedly shares, "Stories are medicine. They have such power; they do not require that we do, be, act anything—we only listen." As one starts to complete research about storytelling, over and over again, one reads that humans are born for stories and stories affirm who we are. Mr. Rogers carried a quote in his wallet that said, "There isn't anyone you couldn't learn to love once you heard their story." Storytelling deepens our understanding of who we are as human beings. We all want affirmations that our lives have meaning. Connecting through stories is one of the greatest ways that humans have to affirm their life's meaning. Stories cross the barriers of time. We relate to past, present, and future stories. Stories allow us to experience the similarities between ourselves and others.

Have you ever read a book, an article, heard the greatest piece of advice that transformed your life from that point forward? That happens often in society. Sure, maybe certain stories shared in certain compilations won't be life altering, but that goes for anything in life. Not every history class that you take is your favorite class. Not every exercise DVD that you try allows you to reach your goal weight. The thing is that you never know what will resonate with an individual and what can even change a life or turn a life around. You never know what element or detail that is stated or the piece of advice, story, or words of encouragement that are shared can help someone in their life. In any article, book, or speech, there may be fifty tips that people have shared that people have heard, but then there will be that one tip that someone shares that is new and transforms the way that one does things from there on out. A good example that I can think of is about a push-up. I interviewed a personal trainer and she shared that before she was a personal trainer, she had been doing push-ups for years when one day a trainer at a gym corrected the form of her push-up. She explains that as she started to do push-ups correctly, within days, her arms and shoulders started looking more toned.[150]

The expertise and helpful advice given to her transformed her workouts and it was such a little change. From that little change, her journey to becoming a personal trainer began. Have you ever had an experience where you changed one little thing and it made all the difference in your life from there on out? Knowledge, tips, tricks, anecdotes and advice make a difference in how we do things. Going from having a "flip" phone to a "SMART" phone is one of those changes that can alter your experiences. Having an internet connection on your SMART Phone—this is a change that makes your life easier. With the internet connection on your phone, now when you need a phone number or directions, it's all just a click away. Many of the individuals interviewed for InterviewGirl.com's compilations comprised of stories about weight loss shared how they changed or tweaked one or two small habits and this then revolutionized their lives. After changing just a few things that they did daily, weight loss became much simpler. Manifold duties in life seem complicated. With the right knowledge and direction, these complicated tasks become simpler. Albert Einstein once said, "If you can't explain it simply, you don't understand it well enough."

> "Knowledge is power. Information is liberating. Education is the premise of progress, in every society, in every family."
>
> —Kofi Annan

> "Knowledge is power."
>
> —Francis Bacon

> "None of us is as smart as all of us."
> —Eric Schmidt, *University of Pennsylvania Commencement Address*, 2009

BJ Fogg, author of *Persuasive Technology*, directs research and design at Stanford University's Persuasive Technology Lab. In this lab, individuals create insight into how computing products—from websites to mobile phone apps—can be designed to change people's behaviors. Fogg's research demonstrates that the key to lasting change does not lie in planning big, monumental changes, but in thinking really, really small. Fogg describes how when you create tiny habits, you can change your behavior and your life forever. He gives the analogy that if you plant a tiny seed in the right spot, it'll grow without coaxing. Fogg teaches people to look at what they want to change and then to break that down into tiny behaviors. He maintains that the key is to put these tiny behaviors in the right spot. The right spot is after something you are already doing and then to allow the new, tiny behavior to grow. He argues that the beauty in this process is that you don't have to draw much on willpower, rather you plan out what you want to happen and then let the natural process emerge.[151]

"Little by little, a little becomes A LOT."
—Tanzanian proverb

Whatever demons or issues you are struggling with or whatever big goal that you hope to achieve, most likely you aren't as far from achieving this as you believe that you are. The correct knowledge and ideas that you accumulate can have a tremendous impact on helping you to do what it is that you want to do or to help you stop doing something. When you don't know the next step to take, information can point you in the right direction. What you read in life in general and what you read within InterviewGirl.com's compilations has the potential to change your life. It will happen when you least expect it. Our compilations are chock-full of content. People will be able to retrieve very useful material from the compilations produced at InterviewGirl.com. This is the first way to help people at InterviewGirl.com: to share valuable tips, knowledge and life experiences that others can benefit from learning from you.

"Books change our lives."
—Matthew Kelly

Learning from Others

"We don't know a millionth of one percent about anything."

—Thomas Edison

The Pygmalion Effect is where you get what you expect. It turns out that lucky people expect the best. They are certain that their future is going to be full of good fortune and these expectations become self-fulfilling prophecies. Ask around and you'll find that "lucky" and "unlucky" people have astoundingly different expectations. How do you get to the point where you expect the best? You get there through knowledge. There are no secrets. If someone else did something, you too can do it. Harry Truman uttered, "In reading the lives of great men, I found that the first victory they won was over themselves .... self-discipline with all of them came first." Truman, who was the 33rd President of the United States, studied those habits of successful people. In emulating successful individuals and learning from them, he made himself better. You too can learn from others.

The first way that InterviewGirl.com will help others is through the books, compilations, videos, audios, and speeches that come from InterviewGirl.com. Our compilations are well researched with information included from articles, books, blogs, you name it and we referenced it, as well as personal interviews. The stories that go to print and the topics that books are written about will help people, but they'll do more than that, they'll inspire them. InterviewGirl.com will also sponsor speakers and talks where illustrious individuals will have the opportunity to come speak to groups and the fees that people pay to hear these speakers will be donated to those who are experiencing a form of suffering. The possibilities are endless. I have many ideas germinating as to how we can make money for those less fortunate (experiencing misery). The main idea behind InterviewGirl.com stems from the idea of sharing stories and knowledge with others. Again, the aim here is two-fold:

1) People who hear the speaker or people who read the stories will become enriched and "become a better version of themselves."[152]
2) The profits from InterviewGirl.com's projects will be used to help to eliminate someone's misery.

What if you could read a book that had interviews where many of the best time management experts all shared their secrets together in one book? Or what if you could read a book that shared advice from interviews completed with 25 of the top personal trainers in the nation all together? What about a book that has interviews compiled from 30 different millionaires where their stories are told and their secrets to wealth are revealed? What if you had stories like these compiled all together? It would have an unbelievable influence on you. You would take away some key ideas and themes that you saw emerge in interview after interview or traits that made certain interviews distinctly different. The work of InterviewGirl.com is to highlight commonalities and themes that emerge again and again in all the interviews. These are all projects that I am currently working on. It takes quite a bit of effort to get people to donate their precious time to do an interview with me, a twenty-something girl who is looking to generate some money to make changes in the world by eliminating some of the misery that exists, but the compilations that are started through InterviewGirl.com are going to be worth reading.

"All men by nature desire knowledge."
—Aristotle (384 BC-322 BC), *Metaphysics*

You never know what piece of advice or knowledge might change your life. Sometimes people are in the right place at the right time and they meet someone or they hear something that will influence them from that point forward. A little piece of advice given to Isaac Newton from his Cambridge tutor proved to heavily influence Newton throughout his life. In the 17th century, students were encouraged to keep a large "commonplace book" in which they recorded all their notes and acquired knowledge. Newton's Cambridge tutor gave him the advice to instead start a set of small notebooks, each dedicated to a specific subject—theology, mathematics, chemistry, and philosophy. Newton took his tutor's advice. Newton's method of inquiry was to pose a question, study and analyze all the evidence, and record his deductions in his notebooks. In their blog, The *Art of Manliness*, Brett and Kate McCay point out that Newton had an obsession for organizing and categorizing information, and he would typically lay out his notebooks by listing the subjects he wished to study throughout the notebook and then entering notes under the headings as he learned and gathered new knowledge. He would also start in on both ends of the notebook at once, covering different subjects on each end and numbering the front half with Roman numerals and the end half with Arabic numerals. He would then return later to fill in the blank middle section with a different subject.[153] The advice given to Newton from his tutor about keeping small, separate notebooks for each subject was integral in Newton's later success. Isaac Newton is one of the names that people think of when they are asked to list historical geniuses. As with Leonardo DaVinci, Charles Darwin and Thomas Edison, Newton's note taking is credited as one of the life habits that helped him to discover and do all that he did. Advice that he was given early on by his tutor influenced habits that Newton developed. These habits aided Newton in his future successes.

Jonas Salk developed the vaccine that eradicated polio. Salk assembled men and women from very different domains to interact during his group sessions. He did this because he believed that by interacting with different individuals, it would help him to bring out new ideas that couldn't arise from the minds of individuals who were from the same domain. When you come into contact with different individuals with different expertise, your horizons expand. The discovery of DNA's structure came about because people from different disciplines collaborated. James Watson (microbiologist), Maurice Wilkins (X-ray crystallographer), Francis Crick (physicist), and Linus Pauling (chemist) discovered DNA's structure when they all worked together.[154] Content shared in products produced at InterviewGirl.com will expose you to fields that are not your expertise. You flourish as an individual, cultivate confidence, develop new habits, and rise above your demons as you learn advice and knowledge. As you grow, you continually become a better version of yourself and as you do this … you can transform your life.

"Wisdom is like fire. People take it from others."
—Hema (DRC) African proverb

History Students write Historiographical essays

As a lifelong learner (literally I was in school from age 3 until my upper twenties), I understand the power of knowledge through inquiry. It was in completing my BA in undergrad (4 years) and 3 different Masters Degrees (6 years) in grad school that I honed the ability of how to research. I have an MA in Language and Literacy, an MA in Italian, and an MA in History. The compilations from InterviewGirl.com are well researched. An amalgamation of different resources are used, experts in various fields are interviewed, and the compilations feature interviews from people all around the world who have shared their stories through InterviewGirl.com.

I mastered the technique of writing a historiographical essay while I completed my MA in History. Historiographical essays are written by advanced history students. Historiography is a trait that is signature to the historian and is a craft of its own. A historiographical essay compares the work of many historians. A history student reads and analyzes each historian's research and then reports what it was that a particular historian argues. First a history student explains what it is that a particular source is arguing then a history student comes up with a thesis and draws his/her conclusion from all that he/she read and analyzed. The methodology for a historiographical essay can be very different than that used when writing regular research papers. First, it is important to note that the term "historiography" refers to the actual process of writing about history. In a historiographical paper, the student is not supposed to simply examine what happened during a specific period in time, but rather the student should discuss how historians have interpreted specific events, people or trends of the past and must then explore the major debates and arguments that arose among professional historians. A regular history of the Holocaust, for example, could explore the nature of German anti-Semitism and concentration camps in Europe, but a historiographical approach would take a look at how other historians explored this topic in their books and articles, and highlight major differences of opinion, or specific schools of thought. When writing a historiographical essay, one's research is based largely on secondary sources, that is to say, the works of other historians.

At InterviewGirl.com, we Learn More, Earn More, Give More

Why am I going on about a historiographical essay? You need to understand what a historiographical essay is so that you can understand the approach that is used as I put together compilations at InterviewGirl.com. I wrote numerous historiographical essays and research papers during my years as a graduate History student. The training that I received in my years as a history student will be implemented into projects produced at InterviewGirl. com. There is an element of scholarship that is applied to all compilations from InterviewGirl.com. As a graduate student in history, I analyzed how different historians explored topics in their books and articles and compared each historian's take on specific topics. This same approach is applied to all interviews submitted on InterviewGirl.com. Commonalities that emerge in interviews will be culled out for InterviewGirl.com's readers. People will learn from products produced at InterviewGirl.com because a historiographical approach has been applied to curating the interviews. The approach in which content is shared through our various projects is designed to bring people information in the best possible way. The first way to help people by participating in InterviewGirl.com is to help people with the stories (CONTENT) that people share. You will help others when you share your story on InterviewGirl.com. InterviewGirl.com shares valuable content and knowledge. You can learn something and grow in one way or another and your life will be enriched from all products produced at InterviewGirl.com.

Projects in Progress

Take for example InterviewGirl.com's compilations featuring weight loss stories, dieting stories, and/ or stories about eating disorders (3 separate projects). The diet industry is a multibillion dollar industry. There are slathers of diet books out there. The public is inundated with information available regarding the topic of losing weight. Some people may be confused as where to even begin when it comes to wanting to lose weight. Most people buy a diet book or choose a particular diet to follow because they heard that it worked for someone else or a friend of theirs had tremendous success on the diet. They figure if the diet worked for their friend then it should work for them too. Or, people discover diets through an internet search, by coming across a diet presented in a magazine ad, or from an infomercial that promises to make them lose weight. It seems like many of the diet books and diet ads start with something like, "Have you tried every diet book out there just to learn that you lost weight and then gained it all back?"

I set out to do InterviewGirl.com's *Weight Loss Stories* project with the hope that I would be the scholar to decipher which diet it was that truly worked. I would do this by applying a historiographical approach to the science of dieting. I began this project about weight loss for InterviewGirl.com by gathering data about various diets, interviewing people who are experts in the diet industry, and comparing and contrasting what authors found in their research about dieting. My end goal in this project was to report to you the secret, the answer to how to lose weight and keep it off. As the research for this compilation for InterviewGirl.com unfolded, I discovered that there is not one answer to this question. However, I did observe that commonalities emerged from various interviews that I completed and commonalities emerged from all the diet books that I studied. I found useful strategies and ideas about weight loss. Certain truths surfaced time and time again and those ideas that surfaced in book after book or in interview after interview were the ones that seemed valid and weight loss "truths" worth sharing. My research was also filled with hearing many stories about people's trials and tribulations with their weight. These stories that I heard bring tremendous insight into this question, *How to lose weight and keep it off?* that so many people struggle with in their lives. The *Weight Loss Stories* compilation book begins with common themes, weight loss advice, trends that are reported by nurses, doctors, personal trainers, and finally what successful dieters themselves have to say.

In another compilation (project) from InterviewGirl.com, diets are reviewed and presented. In the *Diets* compilation, diets are reviewed, the key points of that diet are laid out, particular "key elements" (what makes that diet unique from the 400 others) are shared, and then, the end of the book brings together common lessons that come from all the diets. In my investigation for InterviewGirl.com's *Diet* compilation, in my reading, researching, analyzing, learning about over 400 diets, I learned not only that there are some universal lessons that we can apply to dieting, but also some lessons that we can apply to life. When I applied the historiographical approach to my research on dieting for InterviewGirl.com's compilation projects about weight loss, "dieting" began to make more sense.

As I interviewed people for both the *weight loss* stories and *diet tips* compilations, I quickly realized that everybody has different ideas and tips, but commonalities emerge. This is one of the specialties at InterviewGirl.com. The craft of historiography is applied to all compilations put together at InterviewGirl. com. Commonalities that come up again and again in interviews are highlighted within the compilation of stories. My years as both a student and teacher of history influence all projects at InterviewGirl.com. Applying historiography to all the interviews that I complete makes products produced at InterviewGirl.com different from other people who complete interviews.

The skill of historiography is about recognizing patterns and similarities in history. Patterns are a powerful source of creativity and can lead to breakthrough thinking and results. The importance of recognizing patterns is comprehended in the game of chess. In the game of chess, the difference between a Grand master and a mere expert is not in skill or intelligence, but in the ability to recognize patterns, and in turn can beat the expert consistently in game after game.[155] Compilations about diversified subjects are created at InterviewGirl.com. People will recognize patterns as they are reading and/or hearing stories from InterviewGirl. com. As people read the different stories within one compilation produced at InterviewGirl.com and as they read stories from other compilations about other subjects, individuals will benefit. Noticing patterns will support people in their creativity and other skills. It seemed so natural for me to apply this skill to the interviews completed at InterviewGirl.com since I had trained to research, interview and write for all those years in graduate school. Taking a historiographical approach to our work at InterviewGirl.com is unique to the organization and it allows individuals to assimilate information from the compilations produced by InterviewGirl. com into their lives. This is the first way to "help" an individual when you share a story on InterviewGirl.com: our compilations and projects will help people with the content, advice, tips, and information shared within our projects.

Graduation

As I sat in the audience of graduation for my third Master's degree, I remember the key note speaker, Van Vlahakis recounted, "Now, use that degree to change the world." That is exactly what I wanted to do. Van Vlahakis is the owner and the chief executive officer of *Earth Friendly Products*. He brings more than 43 years of management expertise to the chemical manufacturing industry. He is the epitome of the American dream. He was an immigrant from Crete, Greece and came to the USA with twenty dollars in his pocket. He was determined to pursue a successful career in business. After earning a degree in Chemistry from Roosevelt University, Vlahakis secured employment at Armor Dial and Simonize Company. In 1967, after working in the janitorial services industry for eleven years, Vlahakis recognized the need for more effective cleaning products and made the courageous move to start his own business in his garage, Venus Laboratories. Due to Vlahakis' innovative formulas and patents, Venus Laboratories quickly moved out of his garage and into the public eye. In 1978, Vlahakis created the formula for Pet Stain & Odor Remover as well as the famous Nature's Miracle line. In 1989, Vlahakis' concern to provide non-toxic cleaning products to the public caused him to create an Eco-friendly household and commercial cleaning products line—Earth Friendly Products. Today, Vlahakis' award winning products are sold at retailers all around the world including, Walmart, Costco, Sam's Club, Whole Foods, Trader Joe's and other fine retails worldwide.[156]

In Mr. Vlahakis' graduation speech, he explicated that in order to put our education to use, we would have to reach out to others. He encouraged us to focus on making a positive impact as he highlighted how service to the community was important. He urged us to travel to other countries and to learn about other cultures that exist on our planet. He insisted that we must go beyond Chicago and beyond the United States because "really education just begins when you leave the classroom." He concluded with encouraging us to go forth and do great things and to make our lives count for something meaningful. The reason I can tell you about the speech made at my commencement ceremony is because I have notes that I jotted down in the booklet handed to each of the graduates at the ceremony. I remember the guy sitting next to me laughing as he whispered to me, "this is graduation, why are you taking notes?" Like I said, long before InterviewGirl.com ever existed, it has been inherent in my nature to observe, record, learn, and share what I have learned with others. I was taking notes at graduation because Mr. Vlahakis speech had valuable content and I did not want to forget the knowledge that he was imparting to us.

As a graduate student in History, I just spent years perfecting the craft of historiography. Now it is time to apply this craft to interviews, compilations, and projects produced at InterviewGirl. com. The first way that InterviewGirl.com will "help" the world is through the knowledge and stories that are shared in projects created at InterviewGirl.com.

Learning Something Changes Things

When it comes to mastering tasks and circumstances, learning something, acquiring knowledge, learning how to do something faster, adding in a missing step, or hearing some extra advice can all make a tremendous difference for people. People who read, watch, or hear products and projects produced at InterviewGirl. com will acquire knowledge (the advantage of knowing) from

InterviewGirl.com's products (books, compilations, audios, speeches, panels of people answering questions, and interviews shared). The projects produced at InterviewGirl.com will provide an individual with essential knowledge and with that knowledge and know-how, there is the potential for someone's world to change. Opportunities will arise, one's confidence will rise, and he/she will become unstoppable.

We can always learn—even in those things that one is familiar with, there is room for additional proficiency. In *What I Learned Today*, Erica O' Grady discloses that if you walk 20 minutes in any direction-everything changes. She explains that she has tested this theory on the cobbled streets of Paris, across the Danube in Budapest, in the Seattle neighborhood of Ballard, and on the boardwalks of Venice Beach—each and every time she has stumbled on an adventure. She continued that she tested this theory in her own backyard, "There is nothing more unfamiliar than the familiar. I think sometimes we forget that you don't have to travel across oceans or continents to find adventure. Sometimes 20 minutes in any direction can change everything."[157] O' Grady's example of how an environment changes as we walk establishes how things continually change and as individuals comprehend new realities, their world can be altered. Even in subjects that people are well versed in, there are always more insights to learn.

> "The more I live, the more I learn. The more I learn, the more I realize, the less I know."
>
> —Michel Legrand

We have all heard stories about how after someone read a quote, met someone, read a book, took a course, and other opportunities when people came into contact with information, from that point forward, a metamorphosis happened in someone's life. Quotes have resonated with individuals and often times an individual will make that particular quote their personal mantra from there on out. There are people who read a book and it is after reading that book that an individual's life is transformed. Examples about how one nugget of knowledge or know-how altered one's reality are multitudinous. My Mom tells the story of how she was in Dr. Trovato's Italian literature class at Northwestern University and she viewed Italian literature as well as life in general different after this class. This teacher taught this class in such a way that it profoundly affected my Mom's life. My Mom explains it as:

When I was taking a course on the Divine Comedy for the third time at age 33 after being married with three children and in the midst of two aging and ailing parents, I was truly beginning to understand what Dante was saying in the greatest epic poem of all time, the Divina Commedia. My father would soon have a stroke that would paralyze him on the right side and my mother was in the middle stages of Alzheimer's. It was at this crossroad of my life that I was in Dr. Trovato's class.

This time in my life would become for me a reflection of the Good News of Christ. My class was every Wednesday night and even though my dear father had just had his stroke and hospitalized, I felt the need to attend this class even more for my survival. I was working full-time teaching Italian as a high school teacher, raising three children with my dear husband, taking a grad class on Dante, taking care of my Mamma with Alzheimer's on the weekends and suddenly having to contend with my dear Papa's debilitating stroke. People would often tell me to join a support group, but my support or life line came from my faith, my family, and from the hopeful messages that I was receiving from Dr. Mastrobuono's Dante Studies class (which initially came from Dr. Trovato, my most favorite professor from Northwestern, my alma mater for my MA in Italian). The love I experienced through my Catholic faith, my Italian family, and my study of Dante spelled out one, incontrovertible form and definition of love that was called CARITAS! All these types of love were inextricably linked. The more I would imitate Christ's love for us, the more I would become who I was meant to be. Through this beautiful lesson of what love really is, I found peace, joy, and HOPE in my life. Through my studies of Italian literature as an MA graduate student at Northwestern with Dr. Trovato and through my biblical studies as a catechist at my Catholic church, I clearly began to understand how Faith and Reason go hand in hand. The love I was going to have to give and continue to give in my life that would cause me to have an internal conversion was God's sacrificial love or "Caritas". I was going to have to place others before my own needs and wants.

My esteemed professors of the Divine Comedy reached me in a very personal, intellectual, and spiritual way that spoke to me in a very intimate way at that very challenging and difficult time in my life. I truly was becoming an adult capable of unremitting compassion (caritas) and generous humanity at this time confronting the mortality of my parents as well as anticipating my own. This work of sublime poetry from the 13th century was more relevant to me than any modern writing had ever been. It demonstrated that the human condition never changes and that morality never changes because at the core we are born to love and be loved as God so loved the world that He gave his only Son so that we may be saved and have life both here on this earthly kingdom of God and well as eternal life in heaven after we die.

"Caritas" is what I so beautifully not just learned and understood but experienced so deeply in my mind, heart, and soul. I truly learned how to love sacrificially and charitably. I experienced my parents' love all my life and my husband's and children's love through our marital covenant, but it was not until I experienced the suffering of my parents that I truly learned how to love. Through great literature and through magnanimous professors who

could explain and exemplify spiritual love so beautifully and coherently to me was I finally able to understand as well as verbalize what love is.

I wish I could have more eloquently told my two esteemed professors how much their teachings of Dante meant to me, saving me in all senses of the word, changing me forever, and to this day, continuing to give me HOPE in a world that wants to give us despair.

Dr. Trovato's son sums up so beautifully what his father was to him and to students like me,

"Yes, my dad was many things to many people, and to me he was a moral beacon—a guide by which it could look into the darkness and see the light shining bright and continuously pointing in the right direction. Today his light shines bright on the horizon. It is there for all of the people he touched throughout his life. It is there for us."

I heard Dr. Trovato give one of his last lectures on Dante in the twilight of his life and soon after he died in 2009, but his teachings on Dante and anecdotal stories of his own life will always nourish my heart, mind, and soul. He will always be one of the greatest mentors and most loving human beings I have ever known. How privileged and blessed was I to have had Dr. Trovato as my Italian Professor. He was a beacon of God's light that emanated from his face, from his teachings, and from his deeds as a good and humble human being. He lived what he taught and what he taught was beautiful, good, and true. What I pieced together was Scripture, Faith, Reason, and Familial Love in a masterful literary work whose central theme of "Caritas" would change me forever.

Someone else who truly enlightened me on Dante was Pope Benedict XVI. Herewith attached is a preface he wrote for his encyclical, Deus Caritas Est. It says so eloquently what I have intuited from my experiences of Caritas (God is Love) through my sufferings and joys that came and continue to come through loving others as Christ loves us. Perfectly! I can only love perfectly by loving Christ and loving others as I love Him. In this way we can love God, know Him, and serve Him by serving our fellow man, especially the poor, the disenfranchised, and the persecuted in our world. In this way we are truly free, at peace, and in harmony with God's plan for us.

I cannot possibly put into a few pages all of my spiritual and philosophical thoughts, insights, messages, and discoveries that profoundly affected me from my study of Dante with Dr. Trovato and Dr. Mastrobuono. I would also like to say that my vast appreciation for my Dante studies could not have matured without the maturation of my faith and Scripture.

In the following preface of Pope Benedict's Encyclical, Deus Caritas Est (God Is Love), he begins to speak of Dante in his encyclical on the theme of Love in a way that expresses in words so perfectly what I know or have intuited so perfectly in my heart. I would encourage everyone to read this preface and encyclical to begin the reading of the Divine Comedy. I encourage you because the vision and comprehension of "Caritas" will transform you as it transformed me. I was able to see God's luminous face and God's charitable heart through this long journey of faith and Dante studies.

"The strength of "Caritas" depends on the strength of faith of all its members and collaborators. The spectacle of suffering man touches our heart. But charitable commitment has a meaning that goes well beyond mere philanthropy. God himself pushes us in our interior to alleviate misery. In this way, in a word, we take him to the suffering world. The more we take him consciously and clearly as gift, the more effectively will our love change the world and awaken hope, a hope that goes beyond death."

The Italian literature class my Mother took at Northwestern University transformed her life. My Mom learned "Caritas" from Dr. Trovato's course about Dante.

In the chapter, "The Three Percenters," from *The Code*, Chalene Johnson explains that her life was altered when she left Brian Tracy's seminar in 1998 and he challenged the audience to work from a list that was related to their goals. Mr. Tracy spoke of creating goals and daily tasks. He explained the discipline it required and how most people, even after hearing him that day, would leave and never fully apply these simple principals. Johnson took that as a challenge. She was enlightened when she heard that less than 1% to 3% of people consistently maintain daily lists in order to keep themselves on task. Johnson reveals,

> "It grabbed my attention like a slap in the face. I had just stumbled upon the ultimate equalizer, and it had been there all along. Suddenly I realized the power within my reach. I now believed that everything on my master list of goals was actually possible; I would have to change some of my habits, but the rewards were too great not to do it! All I needed was to "refine" my list making it to be consistent with my goals."[158]

Hearing Brian Tracy speak at the seminar that evening altered Johnson's life from that point forward. Something snapped, connections were made. Chalene Johnson is the founder and CEO of the former company Powder Blue Productions, the fitness and lifestyle company that produced Turbo Wear, Turbo Kick, PiYo and Hip Hop Hustle.

Nicholas Kristof and Sheryl WuDunn's narration of a story about Anne Gilhuly in *Half the Sky* is another example of how someone read something and what she learned in the article motivated her to take action. Ian Fisher wrote an article in the *New York Times* about Edna, an African woman and her dream of building a hospital in Somaliland. Anne Gilhuly, a recently retired English teacher from Greenwich High School in a wealthy suburb in Connecticut read the article that Fisher wrote about Edna's audacious dream. Anne had no particular interest in Africa or maternal health, but the article about Edna's desire to build a hospital in Somaliland moved Anne Gilhuly. Anne's friend, Tara Holbrook also read the article and they spoke about it on the phone.

In the late 1990's, Somaliland won a civil war and had broken off from Somalia. Edna retired from the World Health Organization in 1997. She told the Somaliland government that she was going to sell her Mercedes and take the proceeds, as well as her savings and pension, to build a hospital. Officials from the government felt that Edna's vision was noble, but too ambitious for Somaliland. When the hospital was mostly built but still did not have a roof, Edna's money ran out. The UN and other donors were sympathetic, but they refused to provide the rest of the money needed. This is when Ian Fisher wrote an article in the *New York Times* about Edna and Anne Gilhuly and Tara Holbrook read the article.

After Anne and Tara became aware of Edna's story and what she hoped to do from Ian Fisher's article in the *New York Times*, a whole set of actions were set into motion for Anne and Tara, including, contacting Edna, speaking with former American ambassador Robert Oakley, contacting a group of people in Minnesota who also read the article and had an interest in helping, and applying for tax-exempt status for *Friends of Edna's Hospital*, a support organization that the Minnesota group started. Ian Fisher's article from the *New York Times* spurred Anne Gilhuly's interest and then help in Edna's mission to build a hospital in Somaliland.[159]

Jim Rohn, one of the founders of the personal development industry, credits his friendship with Mr. Shoaff as a life changing experience. The questions that Mr. Shoaff posed to Rohn made him think and continually challenged him to become better. Mr. Shoaff was Rohn's original mentor. He was his mentor over a five-year period of time before he died at age 49. He taught Jim Rohn some "extraordinarily simple things," as Rohn put it. He coached that "life puts some of the more valuable things on the high shelf so that you can't get to them until you qualify." One of the ways that Jim Rohn urges people to reach the high shelf is, "if you want the things on the high shelf, you must stand on the books you read. With every book you read, you get to stand a little higher." One of the greatest lessons that Rohn learned from Mr. Shoaff that forever had an impact on him was, "Success is something you attract by the person you become." Rohn declared that phrase changed his life. Jim Rohn then taught many others that success is not to be pursued, but to be attracted by the person you become. He taught people to put their energy into becoming "a better you, the best you." The advice that Jim Rohn learned from Mr. Shoaff had a profound effect on Rohn's life.

What you learn can recalibrate your own life. Through obtaining knowledge, interaction with others, advice from others and learning people's stories, my Mom, Chalene Johnson, Anne Gilhuly, and Jim Rohn all experienced moments where from what they learned, a transformation happened and their lives were changed.

Right, like a STORY can Change the World?

It can. One by one: stories matter. Think of that story that you tell to your friends that makes them laugh and submit that story to InterviewGirl.com. By you doing that you'll make someone laugh when they read your story in a compilation and by you contributing your story, you'll help the compilation to be filled with stories. The first way that YOU can help others through InterviewGirl.com is through the stories that you share with the world. You never know how your story will touch someone's life. By sharing your knowledge, you are helping people. Your insights are valuable and you don't know what an individual can glean from hearing about your experiences. Visit InterviewGirl.com and check out our projects. Questions are posed as you click on each project. Read through them. If there are some questions that you can answer, submit a story, or sign up for an interview.

Second Way of Helping: Proceeds from InterviewGirl.com's Projects will be used to help those in need (Eliminate Miseries)

The second way that you'll help others when you participate in InterviewGirl.com is from the profits that are made when the compilations and other products that are produced sell. The profits InterviewGirl.com generates are used to eliminate misery that exists in the world. The initial profits from InterviewGirl. com's compilations are for the Interview Girl Foundation's *Operation A²*. *Operation A²* is a project dedicated to eliminate the miseries that orphans who have HIV/AIDS in Kpando, Ghana experience.[160] As time goes on, the Interview Girl Foundation will continue to reach out and help all sorts of people and groups. The orphans in Ghana suffering from AIDS are where we will begin to eliminate miseries and we will move to eliminate the miseries of many different groups as the Interview Girl Foundation expands. In order to accomplish anything, you have to start somewhere, so children in Africa without families to take care of them are whom we will first try and help through *Operation A²*.

The profits that come from the first two projects released from Interview Girl.com (*WWII Stories* and *Stories from Venezia Giulia—Italy's Adriatic Coast after WWII*) will be donated to helping orphans with AIDS living in Ghana, Africa (*Operation A²*). These first two products that will be released from InterviewGirl.com (stories about WWII and Italy's Adriatic Coast) are labors of love. They were my first proactive interview projects that eventually led to this movement (InterviewGirl.com) to make the world a better place through sharing stories. InterviewGirl.com also has other philanthropic ideas that the Interview Girl Foundation will organize and sponsor, such as having speakers come and participate in a panel. Revenues generated from InterviewGirl. com's efforts will be donated to help people who are experiencing a form of suffering. Putting together "compilations" of stories is what InterviewGirl.com is currently working to complete.

Operation A² begins in Ghana, but the Interview Girl Foundation has plans to make a difference throughout the world, so after Ghana, *Operation A²* will move on to other parts of Africa to continue helping orphans without access to medication all throughout Africa. *Operation A²'s* focus is to raise money for education and medicine. Specifically, we are raising money to guarantee sick orphan children the medicine that they need. Many of the orphanages in Africa run solely on donations. We will be donating our profits from the compilations to make sure that children in these orphanages have access to medication and education. However, there is more to *Operation A²* than just handing out the money. Monitoring how the donations effect positive change is a part of the Interview Girl Foundation's work. *Operation A²* is the Interview Girl Foundation's current project that has been set up to alleviate the misery of individuals as the project is dedicated to working to help orphans with AIDS.

> "If I have the belief that I can do it, I shall surely acquire the capacity to do it even if I may not have it at the beginning."
>
> —Mahatma Gandhi

Besides projects and initiatives started at the Interview Girl Foundation (like *Operation A²*), our foundation also plans to partner with charities and organizations whose work is already leading to changes that have erased miseries for people. The Interview Girl Foundation will donate our proceeds to these various causes, as well as partner with the organizations to further bring about large-scale social innovation. One of InterviewGirl. com's compilations: *People Making a Difference in this World* is a compilation about charities, non-profit organizations, individuals, and groups who are striving to make the planet a better place. In completing this compilation, I researched many organizations that already do dynamic and innovative work for those less fortunate in the world. *Stand for Africa* is an organization that was created to help children who have been orphaned by parents with HIV/AIDS. The Mission of *Stand for Africa* is to turn ignorance into awareness; indifference into compassion; and despair into hope. *Stand for Africa* explains that in America a dollar can: sit on your dresser as change, get lost in the bottom of your purse, buy a pack of gum, buy an inexpensive cup of coffee, buy a cheap toy in a dollar store, and buy a small box of french fries, but in Africa, a dollar can pay for a doctor's visit, purchase a Malaria cure for three people, feed one child three meals for a day, buy a pair of pants, a shirt and some underpants for a small child, and buy enough water for a family of three to drink for a week. When you share a story on InterviewGirl.com to be compiled within one of our compilations and then we sell that compilation and the proceeds go to one of the Interview Girl Foundation's projects such as *Operation A²*, your contribution is truly helping someone.

The Interview Girl Foundation has a specific action plan in place in order to help those less fortunate. InterviewGirl.com's initial profits are going toward *Operation A²*. *Operation A²* will help orphans who don't have access to medication in Africa. *Operation A²* is discussed in further detail in Chapter 12. After first hearing Amara's story and other stories that introduced me to a legion of miseries throughout the world, I felt as if I saw that there was this great need for help, but I couldn't figure out how to help. Until it dawned on me, I can write and I can interview, and with those skills, I hope to make a difference in the lives of others. Knowing that a dollar in Africa can pay for a doctor's visit, prevent Malaria in three people, feed one child three meals for a day, buy clothes for a small child, or buy enough water for a family of three to drink for a week, I knew that any sort of effort that I could generate to help the orphans would help alleviate someone's misery somewhere. The intent of InterviewGirl.com is to collect stories, to put these stories into compilations with other stories, and then to use the profits from these stories to help others. One story at a time, person by person, compilation by compilation, a difference can be made in this world. One story at a time, InterviewGirl.com will erase the misery that someone experiences.

There Needed to be More to *Operation A²* than Donating

I was affected by Amara's story. On an emotional level, this story became a part of me. Her story led to my interest in Africa and development economics. According to Paul M. Lubeck from Merrill College, in the 1990's and into the 21st century, the world experienced an unprecedented crisis in sub-Saharan Africa. The depth and duration of economic decline, coupled with ecological degradation, political paralysis, and institutional decay, created an unprecedented crisis in sub-Saharan Africa. Explanations for the multiple crises of African development focus on debates regarding the necessity of market-oriented economic policies, the capacity of African states to manage either development or reform and the way in which African institutions reproduce societies that are resistant either to state-centered development or to market forces.[161] *Operation A²* was in its creation stage amidst my introduction to the debate about the effectiveness of giving aid for global challenges like health, food security, climate change, and humanitarian assistance.

There is no doubt that selling compilations compiled with interviews that I've completed is helpful to those who read the compilations, but was giving away the profits from these compilations actually helpful to AIDS victims? My research to create an effective project (what would become *Operation A²*) that aided the "AIDS" crisis is where the Interview Girl Foundation began its work. Figuring out the right questions and the "how" about *Operation A²* was a venture in itself that turned into a journey of discovery for me. There needed to be more to the Interview Girl Foundation's plan to "aid" AIDS victims other than just raising money. *How* could this money best be used?

According to Dambisa Moyo, every day, about a billion people go hungry in the world. Nearly a third of these, 300 million people, live in sub-Saharan Africa. Yet 60 per cent of the world's unfilled arable land is also in Africa. Moyo suggests that theoretically, these statements suggest three things: first, that Africa should be able to feed itself; second, that Africa should be a net supplier of food to the rest of the world; and third, that we are dealing with a structural problem, such as market failure.[162] People who believe that aid does not work argue that despite these well-known facts, a culture of foreign aid dependency has led to a situation where African governments lose the incentive to implement necessary policy reforms that would remedy these problems. Africa has received over $1 trillion dollars in international aid over the past 50 years, intended for health care, education, infrastructure and agriculture, among other things. The opponents of aid believe that unfortunately, despite good intentions, much of it has been ineffective in combating poverty and spurring economic growth in a sustained way, which it was meant to do. This is because most aid is given without effective conditions attached, but also because of the negative impact aid can have on an economy. It's important to differentiate between the different types of aid. The opponents of aid discuss that the aid given directly to African governments has proved to be problematic. A government needs to be able to implement reforms to address problems that a nation is facing. No amount of foreign aid will ever be able to fix this age old maxim about successful societies (that governments need to answer the citizens' concerns).

The challengers to foreign aid allow us to see warnings that we should look to avoid, but the proponents for aid also point out the positives that come from foreign aid. Those supporters behind the effectiveness of aid believe that when it comes to reducing poverty and disease, aiding to eliminate these miseries is necessary. They understand that yes studies site the failed attempts of charity, but they remind us to also remember that voluntary charity has been shown to help the poor. J. Harvard Maridal describes perfectly what governments should do,

> "The more the government intervenes in the charitable sector, the more voluntary charity declines. Governments should instead work to increase economic freedom to spur the type of voluntary charity that makes the poor—and the societies in which they live—better off."[163]

A nonprofit organization such as the Interview Girl Foundation can make changes in our world and more importantly do "good" beyond intentions. The Interview Girl Foundation is this type of voluntary charity Maridal describes that makes the poor and the societies in which they live better off. With *Operation A²'s* aspirations, worthy progress can be achieved. Another part of the argument from those who do not believe that aid helps is that when a foreigner steps in and gives aid, it makes it seem like Africans are helpless and need help. When it comes to how to do good (eliminate someone's misery) beyond good intentions, the best way to help someone living in poverty or someone suffering from AIDS who lives in poverty is to increase the range of alternatives to help people and empower them to improve their communities. I think Paddy Ashdown, a former UN high representative for Bosnia and Herzegovina describes aid well,

> "Aid isn't perfect but neither are governments or people. Our moral stand on foreign aid is the right one for vulnerable children, for the global economy and for shaping the type of world we want to live in. Yet in a world that is growing increasingly turbulent, increasingly interconnected and increasingly violent, helping others to break out of the cycle of poverty,

disease and hopelessness is not only morally right, it is also in our own enlightened self-interest."[164]

The debate concerning foreign aid can continue, but it is important to recognize the strong arguments from both sides of the debate. As Abhijit Banerjee and Ester Duflo argue in *Poor Economics*, both sides to the aid debate have an element of truth, but it's not the whole truth. The question is not whether aid works, but what works? We need to make sure that the money that is spent "to eliminate miseries" is being spent on the right policies. This is where *Operation A^2* is focusing and doing our research. We want to make sure that we are providing medicine to AIDS victims and that those victims have a way to continue to get the medicine when *Operation A^2* is no longer there.

I came to the conclusion that AIDS victims needed medication, but more importantly they needed a vehicle to continue to get medication after the profits made from the compilations ran out. More than raising lots of money to solely provide medication, the new objective of the Interview Girl Foundation became to come up with ways to get people to learn how to provide for themselves and not just depend on aid or hand-outs. InterviewGirl.com was created to eliminate miseries. Those miseries can exist anywhere in the world. We will work to eliminate those miseries. As Paddy Ashdown enlightened, there are things that we should do to help vulnerable children in society. The Interview Girl Foundation can continue to help those defenseless people. For now, *Operation A^2* has begun its work to help to eliminate the misery that orphans who have AIDS experience.

Project: C^2: Committed Collaboration

Operation A^2 is the first project that the Interview Girl Foundation created, but the Interview Girl Foundation's larger focus is to be a part of creating innovative solutions to some of society's most pressing social problems. *Operation A²* focuses on the societal problem of AIDS. *C²: Committed Collaboration* is an ongoing exploit through the Interview Girl Foundation that concentrates on helping to foster committed collaboration among the world's social entrepreneurs who develop bold and innovative new solutions to social and environmental issues. InterviewGirl. com collects stories about people and organizations. Our website and products are for the purpose of spreading content and ideas. By continually being aware of what social entrepreneurs throughout the globe are doing, we will spread this message so that the public becomes aware of these inspirational stories. The guiding principle behind the Interview Girl Foundation is to foster the development for collaboration across organizations and industries. The Interview Girl Foundation is working to develop undertakings to allow this to be able to happen (*C²: Committed Collaboration*).

We live in an age where information is readily available. There are models out there working to eliminate miseries that exist. The Interview Girl Foundation concentrates on getting people to replicate those models. InterviewGirl.com will spread the news about foundations, philanthropists, social investors, and infrastructure organizations and the Interview Girl Foundation will work to bring about collaboration among diverse organizations and fields because as they work together more can be achieved. Just like how some of history's greatest innovations have happened when brilliant minds from distinctive fields came together, the Interview Girl Foundation knows that to "change the world" as we eliminate certain miseries, it would take collaboration across fields. *Project C²* at the Interview Girl Foundation is working to bring people into contact with one another.

One Story at a Time, We'll Change the World

"No one can do everything, but everyone can do something and if everyone does something, then together we can change the world."

—Author Unknown

If you were to submit a story to InterviewGirl.com today or if you were to buy one of our compilations or products, the profits from the compilations will be benefiting those orphan children who are experiencing miseries (*Operation A²*), but the actual story that you share will be helping someone too. People develop as they read inspiring stories. Everybody has a story to share and we can all grow as individuals from hearing these stories. When someone learns helpful advice, it can change one's life. There is an abundance to learn and there is always someone from whom we can learn. Hearing stories never gets old. By participating in this project, you can help people in **two** ways. By sharing your story, you are helping those who are going through exactly what you went through and/or someone who needs your advice. You are also helping another group of specific people whom the profits from the compilations will target. Share a story today because by YOU doing this you will help others in two ways.

"One must always be careful of books and what is inside them, for words have the power to change us."

—Cassandra Clare

You will help someone when you share a story, but you'll also benefit when you read InterviewGirl.com's compilations. InterviewGirl.com's various compilations will give you the tools, the training, and/or the motivation that you need in different areas of your life. People must not think that whatever little thing that they could do is not going to make a difference anyway. Even little efforts can make a big difference. Every act counts, no matter how small! You can share your stories with InterviewGirl.com and together ... one story at a time ... we can make a difference in this world. Each of us has a story to tell. What is yours? Visit InterviewGirl.com and share your story.

"It's the little details that are vital. Little things make big things happen."

—John Wooden

"The human tendency to regard little things as important has produced very many great things."

—Georg C. Lichtenberg

"I try to do the right thing at the right time. They may just be little things, but usually they make the difference between winning and losing."

—Kareem Abdul-Jabbar

"Whatever you do will be insignificant, but it is very important that you do it."

—Mahatma Gandhi

CHAPTER TEN

Why Do This? What's in it for me? Why YOU Should Participate in InterviewGirl.com.

Helping Others: Doing Good for Others does Good for You

I hope that you would like to share a story just to share a story, but just in case helping others isn't a strong enough motivator to get you to share a story, the truth is that in helping others, you actually help yourself and you become happier.

Technology and science are advancing every day. Science is continually developing innovative ways to understand the world and the human beings who inhabit it. Disciplines like biology, philosophy, epidemiology, evolutionary science, genetics, psychology, computer science, and medicine have all met each other in the field of neuroscience. More and more, neuroscientists are demonstrating that "the brain is behavior."[165] Neuroscientists are finding it difficult to not look at both the brain and behavior together. Happiness is a hot topic in modern psychology. Daniel Gilbert, Malcolm Gladwell, Sonja Lyubomirsky, Daniel Pink, Martin Seligman, Jonathan Haidt, and the list goes on, have all contributed to the scholarship on the subject. It is now clear by the standards of social science that happiness is not just defined by worldly success. Human beings are one of the most social animals on our planet. Scientific research elucidates that people's social relationships are what matter most when it comes to happiness. Nature has designed us to experience happiness when we are connected to others. We are happiest when our social connections are strongest. When humans' social connections are lost, people feel devastated. At the conclusion of *This Emotional Life*, the host of the show, Daniel Gilbert, a social scientist from Harvard University, determines that it is our social relationships that most determine happiness. In arriving at this conclusion, many of the things that make humans happy are studied throughout the film.

Helping others was one of the phenomenons that helps people become happy themselves. It makes sense that when you do something nice for someone, you too feel better, but now scientific evidence shows that lending a hand and helping others leads to your own happiness. In an article, "Do Good, Feel Good" from *MSN Health & Fitness*, Lisa Farino reveals that new research suggests there may be a biochemical explanation for the positive emotions associated with doing good. She explains that while evolution may have primed us to feel good from giving, it may not be the only reason helping others makes us feel better. Since depression, anxiety, and stress involve a high degree of focus on the self, focusing on the needs of others literally helps shift our thinking.[166] In a recent study published in the *Proceedings of the National Academy of Science*, participants' brains were monitored by MRI scans while they made decisions about donating part of their research payment to charitable organizations. When participants chose to donate money, the brain's mesolimbic system was activated, the same part of the brain that is activated in response to monetary rewards, sex, and other positive stimuli. Choosing to donate also activated the brain's subgenual area, the part of the brain that produces feel-good chemicals, like oxytocin, that promote social bonding. Studies in modern Neuroscience validate that people who reach out to others make themselves feel good in the process, as well. In his reflection, "What Makes Us Happy,"

Mario Paredes elucidates, "To find happiness, we must love and serve others, especially the most needy."

> "I am only one, but I am one. I cannot do everything, but I can do something. And I will not let what I cannot do interfere with what I can do."
> —Edward Everett Hale

As Interview Girl must and always does, I will use a story to illustrate this insightful point. Austin Michelle Cloyd, the daughter of Bryan Cloyd, professor of accounting and information systems at Virginia Tech, and Renee Cloyd died in the shootings at Virginia Tech University in 2007. Austin was killed in a shooting rampage that killed 33 people. One of the emergency response workers that responded to the deadly killings, who was one of the people trying to identify bodies communicated that one of the hardest parts was to hear cell phones going off over and over and knowing that loving families were on the other side not getting any answers. Austin's father, Bryan Cloyd, confirms, "That's what that day was like, a day of horror and hopelessness," calling his daughter's phone and not receiving any response. In detailing the experience, Mr. and Mrs. Cloyd disclose that their initial emotions surrounding their daughter's death was as if they had the life sucked out of them. They felt like they had no sense of direction and no idea how to get past that moment. Mr. and Mrs. Cloyd asked themselves what was next? Mrs. Cloyd felt like she had to let the world know who Austin was. She did not want her just to be a dead person. Mrs. Cloyd describes her now deceased daughter, "Austin was a vital person who was making an impact. She volunteered in Appalachia as a high school student." Since Austin's passing, Mr. and Mrs. Cloyd now volunteer there. They drive college students several hundred miles to repair homes in impoverished communities in rural Appalachia. Mr. and Mrs. Cloyd hope by connecting themselves to their daughter's cause, they can connect with the people who connected with their daughter. It turns out as they are doing this work, they are moving their own lives forward.

By volunteering in Appalachia and helping others, it soothes their own grieving process. Mr. Cloyd declares,

> "All the people who we meet out here and work with on their homes, they all have a story. A lot of times that story involves a tragedy or something that happened to one's family. Learning these people's stories has allowed me to see that everyone has pain. This has helped to put our grief into perspective."

Mrs. Cloyd shares that she thinks that a lot of people do not have the confidence of being loved, "I have that to be able to give to others." Mrs. Cloyd and her husband go on trips like this with these students because she believes that if she can give this confidence that people need to one person, and then that person gives it to someone else, then the chain continues. She points out, "I can no longer give it to Austin, but I can give it to others."

Austin Michelle Cloyd lived life boldly. She sought out new experiences and embraced those she felt passionate about. She was not afraid of failing because she knew that, even in failure, she would learn from the experience. Her favorite quote was, "No one can do everything, but everyone can do something. And if everyone does something, then together we can change the world." Austin Cloyd's story is important because it is an example of how by her parents volunteering and helping others in Appalachia, they are actually helping themselves to deal with what must be one of life's greatest challenges: the loss of a child. What is particularly inspiring about Austin Cloyd's story is that her favorite quote ("No one can do everything, but everyone can do something. And if everyone does something, then together we can change the world") is the crux of what InterviewGirl.com and the Interview Girl Foundation are based upon. The purpose of InterviewGirl. com is to help people understand that when we all do something small, then together we can change the world. As Austin Michelle Cloyd went to Appalachia every year to take part in making the world a better place, we can all also do our part in striving to make the world better in the small actions that we each take.

In *How Helping Others Can Reduce Stress and Increase Happiness*, Elizabeth Scott writes, "Many people find volunteering time, money or castoffs as a way to give life meaning." The examples could continue to ascertain the links that exist between "helping" and "happiness." I am confident that many of your own personal life examples lead to this claim about "helping others helps yourself," but now scientific research from the fields of psychology and medicine confirm this, as well. In Todd Beeler's *The Seven Hidden Secrets of Motivation*, he suggests that the biggest problem facing you right now is not lack of money, not lack of talent and not lack of information, but the biggest problem facing you right now in your motivation is that you don't have a bigger problem facing you and that the biggest challenge facing you is that you don't have a bigger challenge facing you. Beeler goes onto reference Abraham Maslow's *Motivation and Personality* to describe self-actualized people. Maslow believes these individuals are not concerned about themselves. According to Maslow, self-actualized individuals have some mission in life, some task to fulfill, some problem outside themselves. These people live in the widest possible frame of reference. This impression of being above small things, having a larger horizon, a wider breath of vision is of the utmost social and interpersonal importance to self-actualized individuals. It seems to impart a sort of serenity and makes life easier. In his piece on motivation, Beeler shares that the best way to motivate yourself is to help other people. It's just one more reason to try and get you to participate in InterviewGirl.com, when you help someone else, you help yourself. Robert M. Sherfield writes, "Study after study on altruism, giving, and volunteerism suggests that the people who are more involved in these activities report an increased quality of life for themselves. In giving, the gifts are returned tenfold."[167]

If you were to share a story on InterviewGirl.com, imagine how you would feel if you heard feedback through the comment forum on InterviewGirl.com that someone turned their life around because of a story that you shared. Helping others does lead to your own happiness. Think about a time in your life when you saved the day for someone and he/she was beyond grateful. How did that make you feel? There's a famous Chinese proverb:

If you want happiness for an hour, take a nap.
If you want happiness for a day, go fishing.
If you want happiness for a month, get married.
If you want happiness for a year, inherit a fortune.
If you want happiness for a lifetime, help somebody else.

Pay It Forward

"The greatest good you can do for another is not just to share your riches but to reveal to him his own."
—Benjamin Disraeli

"Paying It Forward" is another underlying principle surrounding the InterviewGirl.com movement. In sharing your story, you'll be "Paying It Forward" and helping others to overcome something that you once struggled to overcome. As you disseminate your knowledge out into the world, you "pay it forward." *Pay It Forward* is a beautiful book that was made into a movie. When I read *Pay It Forward*, I was exhilarated. It is the story of how a boy who believes in the goodness of human nature sets out to change the world. Trevor McKinney, a twelve-year-old boy in a small California town accepts the challenge that his teacher gives his class: a chance to earn extra credit by coming up with a plan to change the world for the better—and to put that plan into action. Trevor chooses three people for whom he will do a favor, and then when those people thank him and ask how they might pay him back, he will tell them that instead of paying him back, they should each "Pay It Forward" by choosing three people for whom they can do favors, and in turn telling those people to "Pay It Forward." The 12 year old boy tries to create a human chain letter of kindness and good will. In general, when you share your story with others and in sharing your story with InterviewGirl.com, you: "Pay It Forward."

To return to *This Emotional Life*, Daniel Gilbert asks, "Can we transmit happiness to others?" He enlightens us that evidence suggests that happiness is as contagious as the common cold. Gilbert happily reports that science proves that if someone does good for one person and then that individual goes on and does good for another person, happiness can be passed along from person to person and it can travel further and faster than any of us realize. Science evidences that people can transfer happiness to fellow humans. InterviewGirl.com is a project where people are sharing stories person to person and the Interview Girl Foundation is striving to eliminate a person's misery by reaching out and helping one person at a time. Science substantiates that happiness can be transmitted from person to person. InterviewGirl.com's activities pass along goodness from person to person as we all share stories and from sharing these stories, we can help to eliminate someone's misery in the process.

> "In helping others, we shall help ourselves, for whatever good we give out completes the circle and comes back to us."
>
> —Flora Edwards

Creativity leads to healing

If you choose to share a story on InterviewGirl.com, sharing your story will be therapeutic for you. Laura Oliver, who holds a Master of Fine Arts Degree in Creative Writing and Literature from Bennington College, argues that one of the best solaces for emotional wounds is creativity. She clarifies that creativity is different from staying busy. Doing something creative, whether it is writing, drawing, composing lyrics, changing your hairstyle, planting a garden, thinking of a great gift, or redecorating a room, connects you to yourself and a power greater than yourself.[168] If you are struggling with something, if you have experienced something difficult in your life, when you share your story through InterviewGirl.com, this experience will help you to rise above the adversity that you are facing. By sharing your story in an oral interview, by writing down your story or by having someone video tape you sharing your story as you explain your story orally, your creative juices will begin flowing because you are participating in a project. You are doing this (sharing your story) for a cause that is greater than yourself and this will help you to overcome whatever issue that you are dealing with. You are helping others by sharing your story, but really you are also helping yourself. What I considerably love about InterviewGirl.com and the Interview Girl Foundation is that you help others in two ways and you help yourself as you participate in this project.

Consider Some Recent Research: Help Others

- Students who performed five acts of kindness a day increased their happiness.

- Providing emotional support to others significantly decreased the harmful health effects of certain kinds of stress among older people.

- People who donated money to charity got a boost in a feel-good part of the brain, as revealed in brain imaging research.

You can share your story with InterviewGirl.com by:

1) Writing your story and submitting it via the U.S. postal mail to InterviewGirl.com's headquarters or by uploading your type written story onto InterviewGirl.com.
2) Over the phone in an interview with someone from InterviewGirl.com.
3) Through submitting a video of you telling your story.
4) Through an in-person interview where you tell your story to Interview Girl or a staff member from InterviewGirl.com.
5) Through an on-line interview where we use the web camera and you complete an interview (Skype, FaceTime, Google Hang Out, etc.).

Share Your Story Through Writing

"The pen is mightier than the sword."

One of the options to share your story is to write it out or type it out and then to submit it to InterviewGirl.com. Writing can be a therapeutic exercise. You'll be helping someone else when they read the story that you have shared, but you will also be helping yourself in the process of sharing your story as you write your story. People believe that taking a pen to paper can be just as good as medication or a therapist's couch. Writing can help people heal spiritually and emotionally. It is well known that when people take a pen to paper and put their goals on paper in writing, it is much more likely for one's goals to come to fruition.

The book, *Asthma Free in 21 Days* describes a study that was conducted with asthma patients at the State University of New York at Stony Brook, School of Medicine. The study participants wrote about their most stressful experiences. The control group wrote about their daily activities. Forty-seven percent of the patients who wrote about their challenging life experiences showed improvement in lung function that wasn't related to medication or other factors. Twenty-four percent of the control group showed improvement, as well. Both of the groups improved their lung function through writing. Research by psychologist James Pennebaker has shown that people who used writing to make sense of their traumatic life experiences had the long-lasting effect of feeling happier and less anxious. Half of the group members wrote about a difficult or traumatic event in their lives. The other half of the group, the control group, was asked to write about their day or to describe their living environment. A year later, he examined the subject's medical records. The people who wrote about their difficult experiences were healthier than the others. Pennebaker expounds that it was the meaning-making that mattered. The people who showed increased insight into their difficult situation stayed healthier than those who simply wrote about their daily routine.[170] Writing down your story is one medium to share your story through InterviewGirl.com. Not only will your story be helping the two groups that InterviewGirl.com aims to help 1.) those who are reading the compilation and 2.) those people living in some sort of misery whom the Interview Girl Foundation is trying to help, but when you write your story, you will also be helping yourself to heal. Research has proven that writing has healing power. If you choose the writing option to share your story, this is a therapeutic undertaking for you.

"Thoughts disentangle themselves passing over the lips and through pencil tips."

—Anonymous

"What writing does is bring you back to the natural state of mind, the wilderness of your mind where there are no refined rows of gladiolas."

—Natalie Goldberg

"Putting pen to paper lights more fire than matches ever will."

—Malcolm Forbes

Speaking /Sharing leads to healing

Think about it, people go to a psychiatrist and they talk about their problems. By orally sharing your story in an interview (or even by writing out your story), you will feel better after you converse with someone and/or let your feelings out. Talking with someone about your problems will allow you to overcome your problems and help you to get through them. By completing an interview with Interview Girl, you'll be telling your story and talking about your life experiences. Even just completing the interview is an ameliorative endeavor for those of you who are sharing difficult life experiences. *Voice of Warriors* is a nonprofit organization where volunteers donate their time to educate the public at events such as conferences and media appearances on the after effects of living with life after war. In February 2012, VOW Talk Radio had an episode about the power of sharing your story and how it can lead to healing. In VOW's blog entry, *Dealing with Life After Combat— Sharing leads to healing*, Beth Pennington writes,

> "How do you deal with life after combat? Whether you are a veteran or a family member of one who has served, it's likely that your life and the lives of your family members have changed. Things simply can't be the same once combat has become a part of the family history.
>
> Many of us keep everything bottled up inside. We don't know who to trust, who will listen, who will understand, and who will care. We are afraid of the repercussions if we speak out and we do everything we can to avoid the stigma associated with problems

that arise with combat injuries such as traumatic brain injury and post-traumatic stress.

Maybe you open up to a friend. Maybe you see a counselor. Maybe you write a blog or maybe you are a part of a social networking community. Chances are you have found that talking about your struggles with others who understand is a huge help to surviving the difficulties your family now faces in life after combat."[171]

Coming home after experiencing a war is not something I can even begin to comprehend. The frame of reference that I have comes from the stories that I have heard from hundreds of WWII vets. Time after time, the difficulty of adjusting to life after war was conveyed to me as I asked them about "after" the war during our interviews. It must be extremely difficult for returning veterans to deal with all of these emotions. Living through a war, witnessing a war, and serving as a soldier in a war or other difficult experiences cannot be easy to handle. Research reveals that when an individual shares those experiences that he/she experienced with others, it can lead to healing for the individual who underwent the traumatic experience. Again, as with sharing your story with the public by writing your story, the same goes for sharing your story orally, you will help others when you share your story in one form or another at InterviewGirl.com, but in you sharing your story, it will also help you.

Sharing Your Story through Video

Through my travels throughout the world the past few summers, I carried around a little flip video camera and I tried to capture as much of my experiences on the video camera as possible. After several months when I would return home and see the videos, I would remember everything as it was. Images I had forgotten would come back to me when I saw the videos. Taking video made it all so real. When I saw the videos of the orphans that I had taken in Africa and I saw the children's' faces in these videos, it was one of the catalysts that actually made me take "action" steps to somehow do something to change the world in some way by getting rid of some of the misery that people experience. Watching the videos that I took with my flip camera undoubtedly played a part in the start of this project, InterviewGirl.com.

With the internet and web cameras, completing interviews has become easier than ever. Your stories can come alive if you video tape yourself sharing your story. In Jim Rohn's *The Art of Exceptional Living*, he encourages people to take pictures, to capture all that they can. Technology has advanced considerably since *The Art of Exceptional Living* was released, but as Rohn urges us, it is important to capture our life's memories through pictures and videos. There is a video upload option at InterviewGirl.com. You can submit the video of you sharing your story there or you can sign up for an interview on InterviewGirl.com and we can have a video interview over Skype. Heck, you can even take a video of you sharing your story with your IPhone and then text the video to InterviewGirl.com's phone number.

Money doesn't make you happy

When will people learn? Money doesn't make you happy. There are plenty of people with millions and millions of dollars and those people are the cover story about drug over-dose, divorce, and other tragic life situations. From the scientists who now study happiness we have discovered that it is when people use money in a proactive way, this is what makes them happy—not the actual money itself. The reason being is because as we get more and more "stuff," it becomes harder to supersede the happiness we felt when we first started getting materialistic things. Money doesn't make you happy. It should not take scientific findings for us to understand this, but science too verifies that the money itself will not make an individual happier.

The two keys that legitimately bring about happiness for you are the quality of your social relationships with other people and your sense of purpose, which is how and why you are serving others in this world. Ironically, rather than the "me, me, me" tendency that we often see in modern society, the happiest people on the planet are those individuals who serve others. Putting somebody ahead of yourself fosters true happiness. In *The Seven Hidden Secrets of Motivation*, Todd Beeler describes that most people are depressed because they don't have a real problem. He urges people to get out there and do volunteer work, to volunteer in a homeless shelter, or to volunteer to work in a hospital with sick children. He pronounces that when people see the real problems of others, their own problems are brought into perspective. Beeler believes that one of the main reasons that people in the U.S.A. have so much depression and anxiety is because they don't have a bigger problem to worry about. The fact of the matter is that when you put someone ahead of yourself, unbelievable things happen; you get past your own problem and see a bigger picture. This is the core message at the center of Christianity. You need to put others before yourself. Other famous ideas that at the core teach that putting someone ahead of you will ultimately lead to your own happiness, whereas just focusing on yourself will in fact depress you, include: Maslow's five-stage hierarchy, Sir Isaac Newton's Third law, Mother Theresa's example of love-centered service, Buddha's wisdom that "everything is everything" and the Golden Rule. These are all perspectives that encourage human beings to look beyond themselves. People who have a mission greater than themselves are the happiest individuals in this world.

Alcoholics Anonymous is successful in helping people to overcome alcoholism because part of their program focuses on interaction with others. Why does someone become an alcoholic or why does a person develop any type of addiction or malady?

Well there are various reasons and hereditary is one of them, but unhappiness and depression are reasons why people often turn to drug overdose or alcoholism. Why does AA, Alcoholics Anonymous help people to recover? One of the reasons that AA is successful in aiding recovery is because individuals are interacting with others. At AA meetings, a person meets people and in some cases, people have sponsors. Studies have shown that individuals who have sponsors have a better chance of staying sober. When someone sponsors someone else, not only does the person he/she is helping get better, but the sponsor gets better too. In 2006 psychologist Rudolf H. Moos of the Department of Veterans Affairs and Stanford University and Bernice S. Moos published results from a 16-year study of problem drinkers who had tried to quit on their own or who had sought help from AA, professional therapists or, in some cases, both. Of those who attended at least 27 weeks of AA meetings during the first year, 67 percent were abstinent at the 16-year follow-up, compared with 34 percent of those who did not participate in AA. Of the subjects who got therapy for the same time period, 56 percent were abstinent versus 39 percent of those who did not see a therapist—an indication that seeing a professional is also beneficial. When an individual interacts with someone else, each person helps one another. One of the reasons that Alcoholics Anonymous helps alcoholics is because people suffering from alcoholism interact with others at the meetings and people develop a rapport with their sponsors through the program. Alcoholics cultivate interpersonal relationships with others when they join AA. The relationships that they develop help individuals to overcome alcoholism. People become happier as they reach out to others. Sharing a story through InterviewGirl.com is a way to reach out to others. Consider working with InterviewGirl.com and share a story today.

Still not convinced?

The "Pay It Forward" concept doesn't quite do it for you. You want to know what you are going to get in return for taking the time to share a story or sign up for an interview with InterviewGirl. com. In Ancient Babylonia, *The Code of Hammurabi* was the law and it was based on the principle of retaliation, "an eye for an eye." A person's punishment was what it was that he/she did to someone else. Some of you may need something more than the part of InterviewGirl.com's mission that by sharing your story, you have the ability to help countless others. For those of you who are thinking, "what's in it for me?," although your story will affect numerous others as you share it, we will publish your name, contact information, a synopsis of your business or organization, your book title, website, and other important information, so your business/ organization can get exposure in the compilation or project that it is a part of. InterviewGirl.com is another avenue to spread the word about your product, website, or business. InterviewGirl.com's compilations and projects will be exposure for all.

Helping others makes you less hungry

For those of you trying to lose weight and perhaps you plan to order one of InterviewGirl.com's compilations on dieting, weight loss, nutrition, fitness, and other health related areas, I encourage you to share a story because if for no other reason, who doesn't want to be thinner? According to a Gallup News Service Poll, 6 in 10 Americans want to lose weight.[172] One of the biggest reasons that many people cannot lose weight is because people are unconsciously not happy about a certain area in their lives, so often times, they eat and continue to keep on eating to try and make up for this missing feeling. When you do something for someone other than yourself, you become happier and healthier. It baffles my mind that more weight loss gurus don't focus on this aspect: serving others. Everything in life becomes easier and falls into place when you are happier. Serving others, interacting with other people, and doing things for people other than yourself allows you to become happier. As you become happier, everything, even losing weight becomes easier.

> "We are all broken and wounded in this world. Some choose to grow strong at the broken places."
> —Harold J Duarte-Bernhardt

There are people in this world who need help. In different ways, we all experience misery in our lives. As Emilio Estevez articulates, "We are all wonderful, beautiful wrecks. That's what connects us—that we're all broken, all beautifully imperfect." Your story, message, or advice can help somebody with a misery that he/she experiences. This concept of you having the capacity to help others should motivate you to share a story on InterviewGirl.com. This component—putting others before yourself and reaching out and helping someone else is missing from a lot of self-help books. Stories from many philanthropists and others who have served make clear that the people who the philanthropists were serving gave something back to the philanthropists. The people receiving the aid helped the philanthropists just as much as the philanthropists helped them. Testimonials from those who have served as well as scientific research establishes that when you do in fact help someone, you actually help yourself.

Pay It Forward: Share a Story

> "Nobody can do everything, but everyone can do something."
> —Author Unknown

Finding Forester is a story about a boy who was pushed by his teacher to be his best. Sometimes with a little bit of positive influence, progressive changes can be made in people. We can all help someone else to achieve their fullest potential. Your story or anecdote can be what someone else needs to hear. So please join InterviewGirl.com and share a story because your story and insight from the story is advice and it can transform a life. The irony of it all is people want more and more—a bigger house, a better car, a more expensive vacation, and yet what authentically brings happiness to someone is when he/she puts another person before himself/herself. If you share a story on InterviewGirl.com, a ripple effect will be put in place and many people throughout this world will be served in exuberant ways. It's true. Each of us can do a little something and in the small things that we all do, big changes can be made. Through all of us sharing our stories, miseries that exist in this world can be eliminated.

> "I am only one, but still I am one. I cannot do everything, but still I can do something; and because I cannot do everything, I will not refuse to do the something that I can do."

CHAPTER ELEVEN

Using Technology to our Advantage

InterviewGirl.com will work because it is the 21ˢᵀ Century

> "The Wright Brothers created the single greatest
> cultural force since the invention of writing. The
> airplane became the first World Wide Web, bringing
> people, languages, ideas, and values together."
> —Bill Gates

The technology that exists in the world today is what will allow InterviewGirl.com to become a movement that will help to eliminate misery in this world. With technology the world has become smaller. According to the *Merriam-Webster* dictionary, Globalization is

> "The process by which the experience of everyday life,
> marked by the diffusion of commodities and ideas, is
> becoming standardized around the world. Factors that
> have contributed to globalization include increasingly
> sophisticated communications and transportation
> technologies and services, mass migration and the
> movement of peoples, a level of economic activity that

has outgrown national markets through industrial combinations and commercial groupings that cross national frontiers and international agreements that reduce the cost of doing business in foreign countries."

We can get into contact with people around the globe from sitting in front of our computer screen in our own home. The technology available today as well as social media tools will help InterviewGirl.com to spread its mission throughout the world. We need to use this technology to our advantage at InterviewGirl. com. Until InterviewGirl.com made its debut on the web, I had gone after every single story that I have heard in one of my interviews. I contacted individuals, I traveled to see them, and I asked specific questions to the people who I interviewed. Through InterviewGirl.com, I have been able to open up the spectrum in the sense that people can now submit stories on their own. I will still continue to proactively go after certain stories, but hopefully the InterviewGirl.com website and on-line community will continue to bring in stories.

> "We have an opportunity for everyone in the world to have access to the entire world's information. This has never before been possible. Why is ubiquitous information so profound? It's a tremendous equalizer. Information is power."
>
> —Eric Schmidt, *University of Pennsylvania Commencement Address*, 2009

Why is Social Media Powerful?

The internet and technology today make it so that we can reach more people without having to get on a plane and meet each person face to face. Facebook now has 1 billion users. That means that 1 in 7 people on the planet have a Facebook account.

From film and media to medicine, Social Media has changed the way that we do business, leveled the playing field, and ultimately altered the way that we communicate. Raiyan Laksemana explains how social media helped him to find a job in film and media in his native Indonesia. He details, "Before social media, learning from the best was like trying to fly from Earth to Mars. Everybody is milking everyone else by commoditizing connections. With social media, anyone is just a few pages away." Laksamana explains that the more leveled playing field of social media is enabling him to not only find jobs for himself, but to also create jobs for others. "In Indonesia, we were clueless as to how to create jobs in the film and media industry. All of the major companies and studios were taking the profits and setting barbaric pricing. What we found is that Indonesia has tens of millions of mobile Internet users and our mobile growth is actually ranked 8th in the world." Laksamana took that information, and then created a marketing and regulatory platform for the smaller, independent producers. The hope is that in doing this it would allow the money to go back to where it needs to go, rather than to those who are not directly involved in the creation of content. "If this works as we have planned, it will trigger a thriving, egalitarian media ecosystem in Indonesia and it's all thanks to social networking. The system of learning and the opening of a new market would not have been possible without it."[173] As Social Media opened doors for Raiyan Laksemana, it has done the same for many others throughout the world as well. In her blog, doctor, Natasha Burgert, unravels that Social Media for her is about: 1.) Being part of the health social media and blogging community has given her a connection and an outlet. It allows her to express herself as a physician and a mom, creating a "professional diary" of her life. 2.) She has met amazing people with big ideas and bigger hearts, who inspire and challenge her daily. 3.) She has seen a glimpse of how big an effect a group of vocal health writers can have; how active advocates can act to correct falsehoods and incorrect reporting. She is a part of a movement; a way that health care is changing. 4.) She unexpectedly found how one purpose could be defined, in such a short amount of time.[174] Social Media helped Dr. Burgert to attain more in her profession as a doctor. From film makers like Raiyan Laksemana to doctors like Natasha Burgert, social media is used by all and when used effectively, social media can enhance one's cause or purpose.

Statistics about Social Media

Over 50% of the world's population is under 30. Out of those under 30, 96% of them have joined a social network. Facebook tops Google for weekly traffic in the USA. 1 out of 8 couples in the US met via social media. It took radio 38 years to reach 50 million users. It took TV 13 years to reach 50 million users, internet 4 years to reach 50 million users and the IPod 3 years to reach 50 million users. Facebook added over 200 million users in less than a year. IPod application downloads hit 1 billion in 9 months. If Facebook were a country it would be the world's 3rd largest (China, India, Facebook, United States, Indonesia, Brazil, Pakistan, Bangladesh). A United States Department of Education study revealed that online students out performed those receiving face-to-face instruction. 80% of companies use social media for recruitment. YouTube is the second largest search engine in the world.[175] Half of the one billion registered Facebook users use it every day. Research from *The Social Habit* indicates that in the sample surveyed, 80% of Americans between 12 and 24 have a Facebook account. It is difficult to think of any brand in history that has had that kind of market penetration.[176] Even in the elementary schools, technology is an important part of the curriculum. Coder Dojo is a new global movement that is teaching elementary school children how to create software and apps. Technology, the computer, social media, and the internet permeate throughout our lives. Social media is a powerful tool. For example, businesses around the world are using social media to their advantage. Social media is one of the multifarious tools that exist in today's world that will aid InterviewGirl.com in its mission to make the world a better place through human beings sharing stories with one another.

Social Media is Changing the World

Social media has had a tremendous impact on businesses and will continue to in the future. Melanie Notkin, founder of SavvyAuntie.com describes that in the summer of 2007 she discovered Twitter through a blog post by Jeremiah Owyang,

> "It was the perfect "Peoria" testing ground as a marketer. As I was developing SavvyAuntie.com, I was able to leverage my innate curiosity and ask my new Twitter friends about the role they play as aunts or as moms who rely on the aunts in their kids' lives. It really helped me build a better online destination. Over time, I met true pioneers in this new media such as @ScottMonty @AaronStrout @ChrisBrogan @GaryVee @Zappos and of course @BrianSolis who taught me so much on how to connect and inspire my audience."[177]

By the time she launched SavvyAuntie.com in July 2008, the support from the Twitter community was so strong, "SavvyAuntie" was the most Tweeted word that day. Melanie Notkin's story is one of millions about people who have spread their message via the World Wide Web and/or by using Social Media platforms. In a 2012 Social Media Marketing Industry Report, Michael Stelzner reports that even with a minimal time investment, the vast majority of marketers (85%) indicated their social media efforts increased exposure for their business. He also notes that nearly all marketers who have been employing social media marketing for a year or longer report it generates exposure for their business. A significant 95% of those conducting social media activities for more than 3 years agree, as opposed to 73% of those who have been doing it for 6 months or less.[178] Even just two decades ago, to start a business, you had to actually make something. You needed assets, funding and some way to tap into the traditional business infrastructure. With social media and the internet, those business barriers have been destroyed. Inspiration and creativity is seen in many businesses on the internet today. One of the most amazing results of the advent of the internet and social media becoming a part of everyday life for citizens throughout the world is that with an internet connection, boundless possibilities present themselves for people.

Who owns a business is no longer just an inevitable result of your family's economic conditions or the university you attended. In human history, first civilization encountered the agricultural revolution, then the industrial revolution, now, we are living through the digital revolution, which refers to the radical reshaping and restructuring of society caused by digital technology. Some experts who report about technology and social media believe that social media is the biggest shift in society since the Industrial Revolution. There are many reasons why experts feel this way, but one of the major reasons is that social media allows businesses to now have equal footing if they have a high speed internet connection.

The power of a story and how it can affect people is the heart of the idea responsible for InterviewGirl.com. All of the statistics that I just shared about Twitter, Facebook, and YouTube (and I could continue with sharing the staggering statistics) are interesting and prove that the internet and social media should be used in movements and ideas today, but as student of history, I am always interested in International Affairs and the Arab Spring was the final convincing catalyst in how important technology would be in InterviewGirl.com's undertaking. Very recently, we can see the power of Social Media in the Middle East.

The Arab Spring of 2011 has already changed the region and the world. Ordinary people have lost their fear and the perception that once existed. Ordinary people in Tunisia and Egypt no longer think that their rulers are invincible. This mind-set is now gone. In Tunisia in 2011, four weeks of protests, fueled by Facebook and other social media networks, concluded with the unthinkable: Zine el Abidine Ben Ali, president for the past 23 years, fleeing the country.

Even after the collapse of Ben Ali's dictatorship, many people believed that Egypt would be a different matter. The 30-year-old, U.S.-backed rule of Hosni Mubarek was thought to be too ruthless for protests to succeed in creating real change. However, millions in Tahrir Square and across Egypt were determined that they should be allowed to make the choices that others around the world had made for themselves. After 18 days of protests, Hosni Mubarek was gone. All across the country, crowds erupted in celebration.

Revolutions have happened throughout history. Revolutions happen when people want to bring about a change. Various factors contributed to the revolutions in Tunisia and Egypt, but undoubtedly Social Media played a role in the people's involvement in toppling the regimes of both Zine el Abidine Ben Ali and Hosni Mubarek. Did social media (Facebook and Twitter) cause the revolution in Tunisia and Egypt? Although it did not cause the revolutions directly, these tools did speed up the process by helping to organize the revolutionaries, transmit their message to the world as well as incite international support.

All of the components of InterviewGirl.com come together: the power of story, the need to help people (eliminate the misery that some experience), and living in the age of technology that we do. The new media devices that are a part of everyday life in the 21st century are also about stories. If we think about what Facebook really is or what Twitter is, it is a combination of stories. People love to create stories. Platforms like Twitter, Instagram, and Facebook are a combination of sharing stories while we participate in a community—something bigger than ourselves. InterviewGirl.com is a new social media site, but this time stories, advice, and content are being shared for the *purpose* of helping others (eliminating misery). If you share a story on InterviewGirl. com, you'll be contributing to the movement to slice away some of the misery within this world. The proceeds from the content that we put together and then share with the world at InterviewGirl. com will help others.

Let's look at an example from InterviewGirl.com. One of the current projects at InterviewGirl.com is a compilation of stories from those who spent time in Iraq—any soldier who has a story from the Iraq War, also called Second Persian Gulf War (2003-2011). What if 40 soldiers who were in Iraq submit and share their stories about their experiences in Iraq (even if they just share a few reflections and memories)? The stories that those individuals share are then put all together by our team of experts at InterviewGirl. com. The compilation of stories from the Iraq War would sell. The release of the compilation of stories about the Iraq War would allow the public to find out more about people's firsthand accounts and experiences as they read the compilation of stories about Iraq. The profits that come from selling these stories would then be used to help people in this world who are suffering from some sort of misery. One example of the Interview Girl Foundation helping to eliminate misery may be to start a project geared toward providing medication for someone who is suffering from malaria. If InterviewGirl.com were to sell 40,000 compilations at $8.00 each, we could raise $320,000. That would allow us to provide medication to 960,000 children who are suffering from malaria. InterviewGirl.com has the potential to help eliminate many peoples' miseries and as we do this InterviewGirl.com's compilations and projects will educate, touch, and help countless others in the process.

InterviewGirl.com is steadily going to change the world one story at a time. We need to create a movement. Sharing a story, advice, or idea on InterviewGirl.com can easily be completed in the world today. When an individual shares a story, he/she'll be helping to slice off a piece of the misery in this world. Please visit InterviewGirl.com and share a story.

You can share your story with InterviewGirl.com by:

1) Writing your story and submitting it via the U.S. postal mail to InterviewGirl.com's headquarters or by uploading your type written story onto InterviewGirl.com.

2) Over the phone in an interview with someone from InterviewGirl.com.

3) Through submitting a video of you telling your story.

4) Through an in-person interview where you tell your story to Interview Girl or a staff member from InterviewGirl. com.

5) Through an on-line interview where we use the web camera and you complete an interview.

Applying Advanced Technology to International Development and Global Health

In an article, *Top 6 Technologies That Are Revolutionizing How We Socially Connect*, Alice Yoo throws light upon where, how and why we are socially connecting online. Yoo shares that one of the sites with the most influence right now on the internet is *Reddit*. The user-generated news link site has recently garnered reams of attention. In 2012, *Reddit* had more than 37 billion page views and 400 million unique visitors. More than its incredible numbers, *Reddit* employs incredible power as people from all walks of life visit the site to share and read some highly personal and often inspiring stories.[179] A platform such as *Reddit* confirms the underlying belief behind InterviewGirl.com: we are all interested in stories.

As technology has transformed the world in how we interact, do business, communicate, and learn information; technology too can transform the fields of International Development and Global Health.

The stories about Erica Kochi, Christopher Fabian, and Dr. Joel Selanikio represent how by harnessing the power of technology, International Development and Global Health are making strides forward. The Interview Girl Foundation is working to eliminate miseries in these areas, so we can appreciate how these individuals are using technology to impact International Development and Global Health.

More than half of the six million births each year in Nigeria are not recorded. Without a birth certificate, a child is much less likely to get educated, be vaccinated or receive health services. Two young UNICEF staffers, Erica Kochi and Christopher Fabian, made registering a birth as easy as sending a text. They've employed similar methods to prevent early deaths as well, creating systems to track the distribution of some 63 million insecticide-treated mosquito bed nets to stop the spread of malaria. Erica Kochi and Christopher Fabian are using technology and accessible, intuitive interfaces to quickly transform the face of humanitarian aid and international development. The world benefits from the efforts of Kochi and Fabian.[180] What is remarkable about the story of Kochi and Fabian is that they are employing simple actions to help make monumental changes to make a major difference in society. The Interview Girl Foundation seeks to be a part of creating innovative solutions to society's most pressing social problems. One way for our foundation to aid in these kinds of solutions is to bring people together who are making a difference through their work (*Project: C²: Committed Collaboration*). The Interview Girl Foundation hopes to partner with individuals like Kochi and Fabian.

Collecting global health data was an imperfect science. Workers walked through villages to knock on doors and ask questions, wrote the answers on paper forms, then input the data into computers, and from this information that was collected, countries would make huge decisions. Dr. Joel Selanikio has concentrated on collecting health data throughout the past decade. He began with the Palm Pilot and Hotmail, and now he is moving into the cloud. Dr. Joel Selanikio is the CEO of *DataDyne*, a social business working in fields such as international development and global health. Selanikio started to experiment with electronic data capture back when the Palm Pilot was cutting edge technology. In the years since then, he has helped to experiment with the growing potential and availability of technology and the growing ubiquity of the cloud. Combining the two has led to systems such as Magpi mobile data collection software. Previously known as "EpiSurveyor," the service now has over 20,000 users in more than 170 countries. Dr. Joel Selanikio helped to make collecting global health data a more organized science. Dr. Joel Selanikio's actions make an exceptional difference in the lives of those experiencing misery. His contributions to improve collecting global health data also make an impact toward the overall forward development in the fields of International Development and Global Health.

As people throughout the world are, we need to use technology to our advantage at InterviewGirl.com and the Interview Girl Foundation. We need to utilize technology to benefit our mission: to help eliminate miseries throughout the world as we spread stories throughout the world. The Interview Girl Foundation can use advances in technology within International Development while our teams are out in the field (throughout the world) trying to eliminate misery that exists. As the Interview Girl Foundation capitalizes on the benefits of technology in today's society as it completes its work, thanks to technology, stories too will be collected faster through InterviewGirl.com.

Expediting the Interview Process

I will continue to travel and hear stories from people around the world, but let's use this 21st century technology that is at our fingertips to our advantage. I cannot travel the world to interview everyone, but I can have phone interviews as well as video interviews with a web camera at a much faster rate than having to do in-person interviews. Having to do person to person interviews as I did with the Italian exiles that left what was Yugoslavia after WWII and as I did with my World War Two Stories project will take a long time due to me having to travel to each location and meet each and every person. However, if we use this technology and people submit their stories through InterviewGirl.com and I am completing interviews with individuals via the computer, then we can collect stories at a much faster rate. Don't get me wrong, I am still open to person to person interviews, but to get more stories collected and the compilations published at a faster rate, we should proactively employ the technology available today.

If we use the internet and web camera to do interviews, we can eliminate travel time and as Interview Girl, I will be able to accomplish my mission at a faster rate. I plan to collect stories through interviews at an accelerated rate by collecting stories through InterviewGirl.com. As I make the shift from person to person interviews to video web conferencing using the internet, I think of the historical example of the difference in production time of automobiles when automobiles were put together in the assembly line for the first time. Henry Ford is the father of automotive mass production, but Ransom E. Old is the father of the automotive assembly line. In order to keep up with the increasing demand for those novel contraptions, horseless carriages, Ransom E. Old created the assembly line in 1901. The new approach to putting together automobiles enabled him to more than quadruple his factory's output, from 425 cars in 1901 to 2,500 in 1902. Many people think that it was Henry Ford who invented the assembly line. What Ford did was improve upon Old's idea by installing conveyor belts. Installing conveyor belts cut the time of manufacturing a Model T from a day and a half to a mere ninety minutes.[181]

InterviewGirl.com will utilize the advanced and innovative technology available in order to fulfill its mission to gather stories and complete interviews with people from around the world. By my having the ability to complete interviews through webinars, web cameras, phone calls, and so on, I will be able to get into contact with more individuals. Say you want to share a story, but you don't have time to type it out.

No problem. Sign up for a phone interview or an interview through the internet and web camera. We will block a half hour from your day and do this. Heck, you could even do this interview with InterviewGirl.com from your cell phone while commuting in your car!

We are all diverse individuals with assorted insight to share in divergent areas. There are many categories on the website (InterviewGirl.com). InterviewGirl.com is welcoming and collecting stories from *everyone*. I understand that we cannot all meet in person, but I sincerely hope to meet you in the virtual world via the World Wide Web. Drop me a line on InterviewGirl.com and share your story, your advice, your experience ... YOUR contribution to InterviewGirl.com today.

CHAPTER TWELVE

Who Benefits from this Nonprofit Organization?

If The World Were a Cake

"One person can make a difference and everyone should try."

—John F. Kennedy

We covered how to share a story and why you should share a story as well as the advanced technology at our finger tips that will allow millions to submit stories to InterviewGirl.com. Now we delve into *who* we will be helping. *Eliminating misery* is the reason why InterviewGirl.com and the Interview Girl Foundation were established. At InterviewGirl.com, we hope to make the Earth a better place by eliminating miseries that people experience.

It can be overwhelming with where to begin when you want to make a difference because the world is such a big entity. We feel as if we are such a tiny part of the larger world, so often times the idea of us "making a difference" better lends itself to being an ideological construct. Misery is everywhere. The Interview Girl Foundation had to decide where to begin with our quest to help people. What problem should we begin with: AIDS, poverty, hunger, malaria, pneumonia, disease, illness, sadness, loneliness, homelessness, war, famine, and this list could most definitely continue. The Interview Girl Foundation hopes to help all of these people, but we have to start somewhere. One of the consummate historical lessons that one can learn from studying the most successful individuals who have lived throughout human history is about the power of "focus." You need to decide what it is that you want to do and then work to achieve that endeavor. Deciding what you want and focusing on that result is the starting point of achieving anything. Once you know exactly what it is that you hope to accomplish, you need to break that outcome down into small steps. As the ancient Chinese proverb enlightens, "A journey of a thousand miles begins with a single step." In *21 Great Ways to Improve Your Productivity*, Brian Tracy gives examples of considerable goals that people break down into smaller tasks to eventually achieve the overall substantial goal. His examples include: people losing weight by eating a little less and exercising a little more each day and people becoming wealthy by saving their money a little bit at a time. As the famous saying goes, "Rome wasn't built in a day." Anything admirable and sensational that is accomplished takes time and dedication and is completed a little at a time. That is the only way. Anthony Trollope, a prolific novel writer who also revolutionized the British postal system, held, "A small daily task, if it be really daily, will beat the labors of a spasmodic Hercules."

The Interview Girl Foundation had to focus on what it was that it wanted to achieve (which was providing children like Amara with medicine that they did not have access to). However, "providing medicine" was an "immediate" response, as they say, a "band-aid solution" to the bigger AIDS crisis. In the broader picture, the ultimate purpose of the Interview Girl Foundation through InterviewGirl.com is to eliminate misery that exists in the world and we will do this by working to bring about social change in places where misery exists. The Interview Girl Foundation works to develop networks of people who can bring about change (*Project: C²: Committed Collaboration*).

The Interview Girl Foundation is one nonprofit organization that I started because I met a girl who died because she did not have any medicine. The point of founding this organization is to prevent miseries from happening like the one Amara experienced, but in order for large-scale social change to take place in the world, it would require more than the isolated intervention of individual organizations like the Interview Girl Foundation. Coming in and passing out medication will ameliorate the issue for a time, but as soon as the program providing the medication goes away, the "misery" returns. In order to identify and solve social problems on a large scale, it requires broad cross-sector coordination, not just one organization working in isolation. In an article for the *Stanford Social Innovation Review*, John Kania and Mark Kramer challenge, "What might social change look like if funders, nonprofits, government officials, civic leaders, and business executives embraced collective impact?"[182] In order to eliminate a misery such as the AIDS epidemic, human trafficking, or poverty, large-scale social change has to happen. This type of change happens when many areas of society come together to solve problems. *Project: C²: Committed Collaboration* is a venture through the Interview Girl Foundation that plugs away at bringing nonprofit organizations, government officials, funders, civic leaders, and businesses together in order to make a collective impact when addressing social issues. History's most influential ideas emerged when an individual combined two or more disparate ideas. Ideas that have transcended a particular time period and influenced future generations happened when people from different disciplines came together and combined together their expertise. As we have witnessed within history's first-rate ideas that have emerged, in order to help create social change, people around the world developing innovations and making a difference would need to collaborate. InterviewGirl.com shares stories from people around the world. In the same way, through *Project: C²: Committed Collaboration*, the Interview Girl Foundation reaches out to social entrepreneurs and effective change makers throughout the world and encourages the best practices from all these individuals and organizations to be brought together in order to address social issues facing the world.

Although the Interview Girl Foundation's vision is to help bring about large-scale social change in society, the Interview Girl Foundation begins its aspirations to change the world by eliminating a single individual's misery. To one day achieve this grand vision, the foundation will help one person, then move onto another individual and eliminate his/her misery and continue this process. Many people are ill, suffering, starving, dying, experiencing natural disasters, famine, war, disease and experiencing other difficult gravities. The list of difficulties and mayhems that individuals live with is never ending. Whom we are helping is always changing and each compilation of stories or project completed at InterviewGirl.com helps a different group of people. Whom the proceeds from each project completed at InterviewGirl.com benefit are stated in the beginning of each compilation that is produced at InterviewGirl.com. It is clear that the Interview Girl Foundation was created to help people. As time goes on, we will reach out to help many different people (eliminate different miseries).

Little by Little

InterviewGirl.com collects a few stories at a time and from the earnings that come from distributing the stories, the Interview Girl Foundation reaches out and eliminates an individual's misery. This idea of "little by little" guides InterviewGirl.com. Yes, the Interview Girl Foundation yearns to help bring about large-scale social change in society, but in order to get to that point, starting small and helping individuals would eventually lead to a movement that could actually change the world. In *More Than Good Intentions*, Karlan and Appel emphasize, "Addressing world poverty is a dynamic, complex problem. But we won't solve it if we see it only as that. We need to see individuals. Individuals with different capabilities and different needs."[183] The Interview Girl Foundation through Interviewgirl.com hopes to make a difference by helping a few individuals at a time. As time goes on, this effort will multiply. When we help a few people week after week, month after month and year after year, those few suddenly become many. The best way to understand InterviewGirl.com's plan to eliminate misery is through the analogy: *If the world were a cake.* The analogy is simplistic, but it embodies the Interview Girl Foundation's plan and undertaking. If the world were a cake, each and every one of us is responsible to take a slice of the cake. At InterviewGirl.com, we believe that everyone can help to "slice" off a piece of the misery in this world. If we slice a cake into pieces and everyone takes a piece, eventually the cake is gone. Piece by piece, we can eliminate misery and transform humanity. Each of us can "take a slice of the cake" by sharing a story on InterviewGirl.com, spreading the word about InterviewGirl.com or making a donation to the Interview Girl Foundation. InterviewGirl.com will transform humanity because of our aspiration to get everyone to join in and slice off a piece of the misery in this world.

> "No matter how big and tough a problem may be, get rid of confusion by taking one little step toward a solution. Do something."
>
> —George F. Nordenholt

Underlying beliefs behind InterviewGirl. com and the Interview Girl Foundation:

- *Stories* have the power to change lives

- Each and every one of us can do something to make a difference. We will make a difference in the world, *one by one* (one person at a time, one act at a time)

- PAY IT FORWARD

- By working toward our desired outcome, *little by little*, it will be achieved

Where to Start

"There are a thousand hacking at the branches of evil to one who is striking at the root."
—Henry David Thoreau, *Walden*, 1854

To return to the Interview Girl Foundation's first question, with all of the people in this world experiencing misery, where do we start with the enterprise of beginning to eliminate some of this misery? Imagining our world to be a cake, the Interview Girl Foundation has to make a slice somewhere to begin. The first geographical place where we will make a slice into the cake is in Africa. It was what I saw and experienced in Africa (learning Amara's story) that made InterviewGirl.com come to fruition, therefore AIDS, hunger, and child trafficking are the miseries that the Interview Girl Foundation's *Operation A²* is fighting to eliminate. Of course these are extensive problems that will take many efforts from all different angles to eliminate, but by striving to make the life of a single orphan better, by reaching out to help one orphan at a time; these larger issues plaguing the continent can make progress in time. Making the life of an orphan better is the goal that was in mind as *Aiding Africa: Operation A²* began its research and came up with its plan to help the orphans. Fifty years ago, U.S. President John F. Kennedy declared that, "By defining our goal more clearly, by making it seem more manageable and less remote, we can help all people to see it, to draw hope from it, and to move irresistibly toward it." To narrow the focus of *Operation A²* even further, the project specifically aimed at helping orphans who had AIDS and did not have access to medicine. The project would provide medication to orphans with AIDS. To eliminate a large misery that many people are dealing with such as people with AIDS not having access to medication, we reverse engineered this goal *(how could we get AIDS victims medicine?)* and essentially brought laser focus to what it was that we wanted to achieve. In trying to solve the misery of AIDS in Africa, a country needed to be chosen, a region within that country, a town within that region, an orphanage within that town, and an orphan in that home. *Operation A²* would begin to eliminate misery by starting with helping *one* orphan. Reaching out to a single orphan and providing him/her with medication and education was the only way to begin to deal with these bigger, ponderous issues within Africa.

> "Addressing world poverty is a dynamic, complex problem. But we won't solve it if we see it only as that. We need to see individuals. Individuals with different capabilities and different needs."
> —Dean Karlan and Jacob Appel

The Interview Girl Foundation's *Operation A²* set out to begin to erase the misery of people with HIV/AIDS within Africa not having access to medication. At my graduation ceremony, Mr. Van Vlahakis reminded us that the biggest challenges are often solved by simple solutions. Reverse engineering what we wanted *Aiding Africa: Operation A²* to achieve in Africa was crucial in developing a plan to eliminate the miseries that we were hoping to eliminate. The poverty that exists in Africa and all the people who suffer from AIDS is not caused by one factor, but rather by an amalgamation of causes coming together. Reverse engineering *Operation A²'s* objectives in Africa allowed us to see that in wanting to eliminate a misery such as the spreading of AIDS, this could not be done without looking at poverty, for example. Jacqueline Novogratz, CEO of Acumen Fund, explains that when it comes to the complexity of poverty, income is only one variable of many that we should examine because really it's a condition about choice and lack of freedom. Complexity is the perfect word for the conundrum that is faced for tasks such as wanting to eliminate HIV/AIDS or eliminating poverty. A cookie cutter, perfect plan was what I envisioned as I set up the Interview Girl Foundation's *Operation A²*, but I learned that poverty, AIDS, human trafficking, and other miseries are complex and many areas in a society need to be taken into consideration. As Appel and Karlan propose in their research about erasing global poverty, to attack a problem like AIDS, it had to go back to the individual. *Operation A²* wanted to help alleviate the misery of children suffering from AIDS. This was a problem in Africa in general, but before *Operation A²* looked at the problem at the country level, it needed to focus on what had to be done in order to help a single orphan. With our starting to help 1 orphan with AIDS in Ghana, *Operation A²* began its work in eliminating this misery. According to the most recent UN data, there were approximately 160,000 orphans because of AIDS in Ghana.[184] As we helped one orphan, then another, then another, and so on, over time the misery would become less and less. As InterviewGirl.com collects one story at a time, the Interview Girl Foundation eliminates the misery that people who have AIDS (and no medication) experience by helping one orphan at a time. As *Operation A²* took off, I thought that getting medication to those suffering from AIDS was the key and this was what I made the main focus of the Interview Girl Foundation's *Operation A²*. As I researched AIDS, Africa, and what non-profit organizations are currently doing in Africa, what has worked and what has not, I learned that just "giving aid" and/or "giving charity" was not enough, but rather I wanted the Interview Girl Foundation to know where the aid was going and if in fact, the aid that our nonprofit organization gave—was in fact "aiding."

In the early stages of *Operation A²'s* research, I kept hearing that giving aid makes things worse. This worried me. Would I unintentionally be contributing to the problem? I once heard the analogy about the image of a cracked bowl. We can fill it a thousand times, spend a lifetime trying and in the end, it would still be empty. If we fix the crack, then the bowl gets filled. I wanted to fix the crack, not just keep refilling the bowl. As I began to come up with a plan to make *Operation A²* a reality (a way to actually assist orphans with AIDS), I listed all of my questions. Tina Seelig, author of *inGenius: A Crash Course on Creativity* explains that the way that a person asks the question determines the type of answers he/she will get. She teaches that the questions that one asks will determine the frame into which the answers will fall. If a person doesn't ask the questions in a thoughtful way, he/she won't get really interesting answers. She gives the example of the Copernican Revolution and how it came about by reframing the question: what if the sun is the center of the solar system? Asking the question this way then opened up the entire study of astronomy. Listing the questions that I had about development aid was important because from here what I was trying to understand would make more sense.

Economists Dambisia Moyo and Jeffrey Sachs lead the debate in development economics about whether or not aid actually helps. This argument is largely about whether or not to stop sending money to African governments. The aid that Moyo discusses in her book *Dead Aid* is the billion dollar government to government aid packages. The first question for *Operation A²* was what exactly is aid? Aid (also known as Overseas Development Assistance or ODA) is the assistance governments, non-government organizations (examples: World Vision, Red Cross, Caritas), businesses, and individuals of one country give to the people of another country to help reduce poverty and achieve sustainable development. Next I needed to look at: What kinds of aid are there? I learned that there are three types of aid. The first type of aid is humanitarian aid. This is aid that goes toward a tsunami, hurricane, or other natural disaster. As Moyo pointed out, there is a moral imperative as human beings part of global community to act when emergencies occur. The second type of aid is aid where people will send their money to support a girl to go to school in Africa, for example. This type of aid is known as charitable intervention. Some economists find charitable intervention to be band-aid solutions to the problem of poverty because this type of aid will never make economies grow at requisite levels of growth where a meaningful dent in poverty can be made. The third type of aid is those billion dollar government to government aid packages that many African governments receive. Moyo conjectures that it is this type of aid that is part of the problem. She outlines how aid has failed to deliver on its original promises. To elucidate this point, it is necessary to go back sixty years. The 1950's and 1960's were a time when many African countries were coming out of colonialism. One of the prominent economists of the time, Stout identified that savings lead to investment and investment then leads to growth. Policy makers wanted to use aid which would lead to investment which they then thought would lead to growth. They believed that countries would experience growth in their economies which would then lead to the alleviation of poverty. Africa has received over one trillion dollars of aid over last 60 years, yet, poverty is more entrenched now than before. 60 years ago, 10% of Africans lived on a dollar a day. Now over 70% of Africans live on a dollar a day.[185] What Dambisia Moyo evinces made sense, but I also understood Jeffrey Sachs as he justified that impoverished countries, with impoverished governments, can't solve these problems on their own. After differentiating about various kinds of aid, my next question was: Is there a different way for the Interview Girl Foundation to provide aid other than traditional charity? In the meantime, I thought a band-aid solution is a better solution than no solution at all and watching someone like Amara die because she did not have access to medicine.

It is interesting how world's collide. Connections are powerful and take meaning as we notice them. For example, an individual gets an idea because of the continual connections that are made in his/her mind. This same phenomenon materializes as people read and learn information. The more that you read, as authors reference the work of other people, often times, you have read the work of the individual to whom the author is referring. Psychologist Pamela Rutledge explains, "We perceive and remember something based on how it fits with other things. One way the brain sorts things is by metaphors." It is interesting to note that Paul Collier was Dambisia Moyo's PhD supervisor. Collier wrote *The Bottom Billion*. *The Bottom Billion* was another book that helped me to understand poverty as I set out to make sense of it this last year. When it comes to aid, Moyo holds that a finite transparent exit strategy is needed. She gives the examples that aid intervention such as the Green revolution in India and the Marshal Plan worked because they were short, sharp, and finite. When aid does not have a deadline, governments don't see that they have to find alternate ways to finance economic development. From the literature, I understood why the government to government aid packages could be problematic. However when it came to charitable intervention, I knew *Operation A^2* could help to eliminate miseries. It made sense that charitable intervention was seen as a band-aid solution to the problem of poverty because it will never make economies grow at requisite levels of growth and eventually make a meaningful dent in poverty. It became a big part of *Operation A^2's* plan to provide medication to someone who had AIDS, but it was also part of the plan to make sure that a plan was in place to make sure that he/she could have a way to provide medication for himself/herself when *Operation A^2* was gone. As within any society in the world, an efficient government and sustainable economy are needed in any country for people to legitimately be lifted out of poverty. I understand this part of the debate, but in the meantime, providing someone who is sick with medication seemed necessary. As Moyo exemplifies when she describes humanitarian aid (disasters, etc.), when something happens, it's a moral imperative to help that person.

Everyone can help to slice off a piece of the misery in this world. What slice will you take?

Going back to the larger plan

"Like slavery and apartheid, poverty is not natural. It is man-made and it can be overcome and eradicated by the actions of human beings."

—Nelson Mandela

Scientist, Helen Epstein discusses how you cannot cure AIDS just by discovering a vaccination. She argues how underlying causes and problems surrounding the disease must be addressed. In Epstein's *The Invisible Cure*, she tells the story about how in the early 1990's, she was working in Kampala at the Uganda Cancer

Institute. After some time in Africa, she realized just how hard it was to make an AIDS vaccine. In Uganda, she befriended a local zoologist who was studying a plant mixture that had been used for centuries by Ethiopian peasants to cure a variety of ills. He suggested that Epstein try the mixture to determine if it was true if it could cure yeast infections of the skin, such as athlete's foot or ringworm. Epstein thought that this was not a cure for AIDS, but since many AIDS patients suffer from yeast infections, it could be a start. Ringworm is extremely common in Ugandan children, so families in the Kampala suburb started to come see Dr. Epstein. One morning when she was out of town, her landlord awoke to the sound of murmuring and clanking metal. A crowd gathered at his front gate. The visitors told him that they had heard there was a lady in the house who had special medicine for sick children. At the time, when Epstein heard what happened, she was relieved to have not been there. In *The Invisible Cure*, she reflects, "Now, looking back, I am sorry I wasn't. What I should have done was write something for international newspapers about the sorry state of health services in Uganda."

Helen Epstein went on to attend Graduate School in England in public health trying to find a cure for AIDS. In looking back on her time in Kampala, she continues,

> "Only later did I realize the opportunity I had missed. Back then I was still subject to magic-bullet thinking— the idea that serious public health problems could be addressed without considering their social and political causes. The Ugandans seemed to know better, but their message was lost on me."

Epstein concludes that the only cure to help AIDS victims is to take everything into consideration, to break down the social and political causes of people's situations. In her Epilogue, she depicts how the continent of Africa struggles to cope with many scourges, including winner-take-all economic development, political corruption, civil conflict and AIDS. She chronicles how some of these cults like the Lord's Resistance Army are destructive, but she then concludes, "But some cults are positive. They start with ideas that get people talking and they develop into social movements that change things for the better. Until we find the magic bullet, this is the only cure." Helen Epstein is a scientist who has devoted her life to curing AIDS and she advocates that yes, the science is important, but positive social movements are the key to moving forward in Africa as we try to help those suffering from AIDS.

Quickly, I realized that *Operation A²* needed more to its plan than just providing medication to orphans because what would happen if *Operation A²* could no longer provide medication to these orphans? Generating positive social movements that bring about permanent change (rather than band-aid solutions) for the victims of AIDS, hunger, and child trafficking is the overall goal for the Interview Girl Foundation in Africa and the initiatives *Operation A²* is working toward. Reaching the "movement" level that affects an entire community will begin with the Interview Girl Foundation helping a single individual. In order for the Interview Girl Foundation to improve the life of one orphan, the larger context of what was happening in Africa needed to be examined. It seemed reciprocal, *Operation A²* needed to consider the needs of a single individual at the same time it had to mull over the grander issues taking place within the continent. In examining the background and circumstances as to why HIV was spreading in Africa, it is clear that one contrivance is not the cause of AIDS spreading in Africa, but rather many issues are tangled together and it is the jumble of all of these issues that leads to the HIV virus spreading within the continent. The problems in Africa seem to overlap one another. Can helping people with AIDS be addressed without looking at why poverty exists? In trying to figure out why so many people suffer from malaria, can this question be addressed without looking at why people don't have access to safe water and sanitation? There is a connection between human trafficking and AIDS. Often times the victims of human trafficking are children who have been orphaned because their parents died of AIDS. The connections endlessly continue on. So, yes the Interview Girl Foundation's *Operation A²'s* mission is to help orphans who are suffering from AIDS, but in order to do this, a multifaceted plan is needed. In my research, it became clear that just "giving money" to someone like Amara would not be enough to "erase this misery." It was necessary to discover the underlying causes and issues as to why there were so many people who had AIDS. The complexities of problems like AIDS do not have "single bullet or magic bullet solutions," as many authors refer to the solutions that are tried to alleviate the AIDS epidemic as. Rather than rush into a big fundraiser, raise a bunch of money and send that money off, *Operation A²* needed to find out what works best when it comes to the tasks of eradicating poverty and offering care to AIDS patients.

Not just honing in on HIV, but conducting research about poverty in general is where *Operation A²* concentrated its work in its initial stages. Doing empirical research and looking at what has worked and what has not in organizations' past efforts to eliminate poverty was one of the primary tasks for *Operation A²*. "Giving aid" (providing medication) was a starting point, but it would not be enough to stop here because what would the citizens do when funds from *Operation A²* ran out? Dean Karlan and Jacob Appel embolden, "To make a difference in the fight against poverty, we need more than good intentions, more than what sounds good, and more than what looks good anecdotally. The answer isn't always what we want it to be, and frankly that does not matter. We need to think clearly, ask tough questions, and set up objective processes for learning the answers."[186] Let's look at the following analogy that *Thwink.org* shares: The first thing a good doctor does is find the symptoms of the illness. The second is find the root causes, which requires examination and testing. Only after the root causes are found does the doctor prescribe a treatment. If the diagnosis is correct, the treatment will usually work. If the diagnosis is wrong, the treatment will usually fail and will often make the problem worse. If this basic process works for the science of medicine, it can work for sustainability. We just need to fine tune the process so that it fits the problem.[187]

Providing medication to children who have AIDS and no access to medication seemed like a necessary first step. If someone was sick, we should try and help him/her to get better, but analyzing how to remove someone from the situation of poverty and how someone can sustain himself/herself were vital for the Interview Foundation to explore, as well. How would people get medication when the Interview Girl Foundation was no longer providing medication? As I built the Interview Girl Foundation, this became as important as a question as how could *Operation A²* raise money for AIDS victims (without access to medication) in the first place? Anne Hunsaker Hawkins, a humanities professor at the Penn State College of Medicine, spent several years observing the staff and patients at a pediatric AIDS clinic in southern Ohio. She discloses that HIV infection in America is both a real disease and a symbol of larger and even darker realities: drug abuse, sexual irresponsibility, prostitution, and patterns of child abuse or neglect that are associated with most cases or perinatally acquired HIV infection.[188] As Hawkins describes HIV in America, the disease cannot be looked at without taking into consideration other realities surrounding it. This same lesson needed to be applied to Africa. The larger context of what was causing the orphan aid crisis needed to be investigated.

It was in the framework of understanding the debate in the field of economics over whether or not aid helps individuals in the fight to end poverty that I created *Operation A²*. I had taken note after note detailing how some people argue that aid is crucial and others argue that when someone gives someone else aid, it prevents people from discovering their own geniuses. According to George Friedman in *The Next Decade,*

"The system of international aid that now dominates so much of African public life cannot possibly have any lasting impact, because it does not address the fundamental problem of the irrationality of African borders. At best it can ameliorate some local problems. At worst it can become a system that enhances corruption among birth recipitants and donors."[189]

While in his blog post, *Aid Ironies*, Jeffrey Sachs praises the effectiveness of foreign aid,

"Nine million children die each year of extreme poverty and disease conditions which are almost all preventable or treatable or both. Impoverished countries, with impoverished governments, can't solve these problems on their own. Yet with help they can. The Global Fund to Fight AIDS, TB, and Malaria, and the Global Alliance on Vaccines and Immunizations are both saving lives by the millions, and at remarkably low cost. Goldman Sachs gives out more in annual bonuses to its workers than the entire rich world gives to the Global Fund each year to help save the lives of poor children. And when Goldman Sachs got into financial trouble it got bailed-out by the U.S. Government."[190]

I came to understand that there is validity in both arguments. As we have seen economist, Ester Duflo and others doing in their work, we too needed to change our questions. The question isn't whether or not aid works, but what works? The Interview Girl Foundation creates programs based on what it is that successful organizations and individuals already do efficaciously in order to bring about changes that lead to a better world. The Interview Girl Foundation's *Aiding Africa (Operation A²)* is our first project and the victims of HIV are the first people whose misery we hope to eliminate. The purpose of the project: *Aiding Africa (Operation A²)* is to help those suffering with AIDS with no access to medication to eventually be able to help themselves to obtain access to medicine. The key to "eliminating a misery" like "no access to medication" is to help to provide health care and education and by doing this, it will lead to victims of AIDS being able to take care of themselves once the assets from *Operation A²* are gone.

One of the underlying questions behind the Interview Girl Foundation's aspirations in Africa through *Operation A²* is: what can be done to allow people living in poverty to no longer have to depend on traditional aid? Aid (providing medicine) cannot be given forever, so another solution was needed. As George Friedman conveys, "the aid itself will not solve Africa's problems, but it might ameliorate some of them, at least for a time. It is possible that it will do some harm, as many aid programs have had unintended and negative consequences."[191] Wanting to help the AIDS crisis was my intention as I founded InterviewGirl.com, but as Karlan and Appel urge, "more than good intentions were needed." I wanted to make sure that whatever money is spent, whoever spends the money, that it's spent on the right policies that will help to alleviate the misery of someone with AIDS that has no access to medication. The individual who at one point had no access to medicine needs to be able to provide himself/herself with medication in time. How could the Interview Girl Foundation build a framework of social and economic supports to foster the development of not only providing medicine to someone initially, but beyond that helping to create systems that ensured someone would have the necessary means to be able to provide for himself/herself when *Operation A²* went away? The solutions seemed to be to find a way to bring affordable clean water, housing, health care, and education to people living in poverty because if individuals have these necessities, they can then provide for themselves and their families. The Interview Girl Foundation is working to create programs that develop systems that bring access to clean water, housing, health care, and education to people living in poverty.

I find the debate about donor aid interesting and I see the points that both sides are making, but I knew a real problem existed, so I wanted to figure out what exactly it was that was "harmful" about aid that the literature spoke of and then begin to come up with a solution. Every time I saw Amara's name on the board above my computer, I was reminded that "the medicines ran out." The debate that exists is important and needed, but I needed to get medication to sick orphans. This was my first task. In my quest to create *Operation A²* as I explored charities and non-profits, I also uncovered that a virtuous cycle of private charity exists. Everything I believed about humanitarianism as well as what I understood about the good that charities can do confirmed my belief in "the good Samaritan effect." Humanitarianism, aid, development economics, poverty, all the questions, all the theories, all the data, it was difficult not to get bogged down. Really to me it was more simple: someone like Amara died because she did not have access to medication. My focal question became: what could I do to help alleviate that misery? And of course I deeply wanted more than good intentions, I wanted more than a band-aid solution, but I knew that getting someone like her medication was the first key to eliminating this misery. Figuring out how to keep the medication coming and a way for an individual to get himself/herself medication were steps two and three in the grandiose plan, but as with any life endeavor, you need to start somewhere and that place for *Operation A2* is to get an orphan without access to medication, the medication that he/she needs.

Breakdown of what the money will be used for in *Operation A²*

I had to design what *Operation A²'s* relief efforts would entail. I researched long and hard trying to figure out exactly how much money is needed to educate a child, provide HIV medication to an orphan, provide malaria medication, build a well, and other necessary steps that need to be taken in order to help someone in poverty reach sustainability. Depending upon where a child lives within Africa, the figure changes. I wasn't exactly sure how

Operation A² would provide medication on a large scale to orphans. As Novogratz shares in an interview with the *PTPI Blog*, "You don't have to change the world all at once. But if you see something you do want to change, don't wait until you have all of the right facts and all of the money. Just start. Start with a small step and then let the work teach you. But do it. Especially if the idea scares you."[192] I reached out to various contacts that I have made in different regions of Africa over the past year. From sending e-mails, writing letters, and even making phone calls, I began collaborating with those people in organizations already making a difference in the lives of others. From contacting people whom I met when I was in Africa (people who are running organizations in Africa), to making different contacts with social entrepreneurs to contacting other charity and NGO organizations in Africa, the Interview Girl Foundation was able to target specific areas of need (misery). The Interview Girl Foundation aspires to help individuals one by one, then community by community, individuals throughout an entire country, and eventually individuals throughout the continent. *Operation A²'s* efforts launch in one orphanage in one country where we help a single orphan and as the Interview Girl Foundation grows, we will help another orphan, and then another, and so on and so forth, until we then branch out to other orphanages in Ghana and after that we'll move on to other countries. The Interview Girl Foundation strives to assist in bringing about large-scale social change in society and understands that the only way to do this is through broad cross-sector coordination that *Project: C²: Committed Collaboration* aims to foster, but in working toward achieving our ultimate vision, *Operation A²* initiated its work with a plan of reaching out to individuals.

One of the key themes in this book is that throughout the history of human civilization, anyone who has accomplished something noteworthy, invented something, and/or overcome an obstacle, that person looked at their problem and then asked the correct questions. Coming up with good questions is an integral part of my work as Interview Girl. Eliminating someone like

Amara's misery began with the Interview Girl Foundation forming the right questions. Creating *Operation A²* started with a series of questions. In Dean Karlan and Jacob Appel's book about how to make our aid dollars more effective, they urge us, "to think clearly, ask tough questions, and set up objective processes for learning the answers."[193] This seemingly complicated, what at times seems helpless situation in Africa (AIDS crisis) can make progress and has made tremendous progress within the last decade compared to where the problem was at in the 1990's. The Interview Girl Foundation wants to continue this positive progress and keep the momentum going. Although we have seen progress that we should be proud of within the last decade, it is normal to feel as if AIDS is still a behemoth problem in Africa.[194] This may be true, but we cannot give up hope. Beginning with providing AIDS victims medicine, changes can be made. People have the attitude that providing AIDS relief cannot be done because of the extent of the problem. Yes, we are looking at a reality of 34 million worldwide are living with HIV and almost 70% of them are in sub-Saharan Africa, but this misery can improve beginning with us asking the right questions about how to turn those statistics around.

Obviously, as it turns out, I wasn't the first person to think of this: eliminating the misery someone with AIDS experiences. Governments, charities, organizations, and NGO's were already working to help people suffering from AIDS. Now the question left for me was: Was what these organizations were doing to eliminate the misery of people who had HIV/AIDS working? In last decade, powerful new medications have made it possible for people infected with HIV to live long healthy lives. These medications are part of what is Antiretroviral Therapy. At first, medicine was only available in wealthy countries. In poorer countries, only 7 out of every 100 people who needed medicine could get medicine. In 2003, despite the availability of antiretroviral therapy, very few people with HIV/AIDS were receiving treatment for HIV in the poorer parts of the world. The situation was regarded as a serious health and human rights crisis. In light of this, former

President George W. Bush made a commitment to substantially increase US support for addressing HIV and AIDS worldwide. The U.S.A set out to change this health crisis with the President's Emergency Plan for AIDS Relief (PEPFAR). It made money available to provide money and HIV care to poor people in developing countries. Catholic Relief Services and their partners created a program called AIDS Relief. The goal of this program is to provide treatment to as many people as possible as quickly as possible. The Interview Girl Foundation studied Catholic Relief Services' AIDS Relief programs as well as the work of many other organizations helping to eliminate the threat of AIDS in Africa.

Operation A^2 is modeled after the best practices from programs like Catholic Relief Services, CARE, the Nelson Mandela Foundation, DATA, the William Jefferson Clinton Foundation, the Global Fund to Fight AIDS, UN AIDS, AVERT, Missionaries of Africa and the World Health Organization. All of these organizations are making tremendous strides in the fight against AIDS in Africa. The Interview Girl Foundation researched the statistics about what these organizations have already achieved and the systems that these organizations use, so that we could provide efficient help based on modeling systems that were successful in helping to alleviate the AIDS crisis. The Interview Girl Foundation desired to set up a program, *Operation A^2*, emulating those programs that have been productive, but beyond that, the Interview Girl Foundation's ultimate vision is to bring together all of these organizations that are helping problems in order to make a collective impact for social change (*Project: C^2: Committed Collaboration*).

Through the stories that I learned about people affected by AIDS and people working to better the AIDS crisis, *Operation A^2* was designed. As I learned stories from the people who have worked for NGO's and other start-ups and as I uncovered stories from individuals who have spent time with people who have AIDS in different parts of the world, *Operation A^2* became an actualization. Reading about these organizations already completing meaningful work in the field, interviewing the leaders behind these organizations, and in learning stories about people who have AIDS is what will allow *Operation A²* to do the work that we hope it can do. Karlan and Appel argue that the most obvious and ubiquitous figures that charities and development programs advertise – dollars spent, people enrolled – are only signposts. If we don't understand how these things lead to the welfare of recipients, we are losing sight of what matters – helping people make real improvements in their lives.[195] From comprehending the stories of people suffering from AIDS and the stories of those who have worked directly with individuals who have AIDS, *Operation A²* was able to develop its questions. Below are some of the questions that I've developed for the Interview Girl Foundation to look at as we begin to tackle AIDS and poverty in Africa with *Operation A²*. The questions are in the Problems part of the chart:

Problem	Solution
There are not enough doctors and nurses who know how to treat HIV.	The Interview Girl Foundation would like to start programs to help medical providers become experts.
It is difficult to deliver the medicine to people in villages in remote areas.	To allow this to happen, the Interview Girl Foundation needs to build strong supply chains.
Rural villages are too far from hospitals and sick people cannot get there.	The Interview Girl Foundation needs to help hospitals to centralize as well as to create satellite clinics.

"Changing the World" starts when an individual or a group of people ask the right questions. That's what I do as Interview Girl, I ask people questions. *Operation A²'s* vision is nothing less than the transformation of AIDS orphans from hopeless, suffering victims into productive members of their community with an exciting vision for a greater community. Jacqueline Novogratz, the founder of Acumen Fund, formed a friendship with John Gardner while she was a student at Stanford completing her MBA. In one of her many conversations with John Gardner, he told her, "Think about community. People need to feel responsible to one another. Otherwise, we will breed successful individuals who don't feel connected enough to the greater society."[196] As *Operation A²* aids orphans and helps them to overcome their illness, they will then grow up to be productive members of their communities. That is the overall goal of *Operation A²*, yes initially, it provides medicine to someone who is ill, but with this medication an individual can go to school and become trained in some way that ultimately gives back to the community. The Interview Girl Foundation believes that anyone anywhere can help to change these little lives by someone sharing a story on InterviewGirl.com or making a donation to the Interview Girl Foundation. *Operation A²* wants to provide medicine to people infected with HIV/AIDS because from here, many changes can be made. Our mission is to help the children in Africa, starting with the ones in Kpando, Ghana who are dealing with the hardships of HIV/AIDS. By the Interview Girl Foundation focusing on medicine and education, we can help orphans with AIDS to be able to overcome their illness. What begins with someone who is ill receiving medicine, with medication, he/she can then become a productive member of his/her community rather than a suffering victim. Funds that come from *Operation A²—Aiding AIDS* will be contributed toward the efforts explained below.

Pay It Forward: *Operation A²—Aiding AIDS*

"Money is not for getting things, money is about changing things."

—Suzanne Evans

Aiding Africa (Operation A²) is a project that the Interview Girl Foundation started in Africa. How it works:

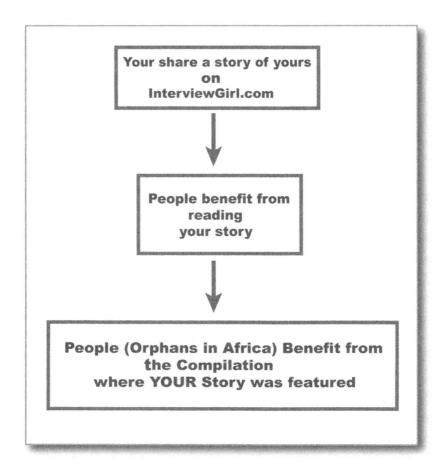

The above diagram depicts *paying it forward*. A story that you share on InterviewGirl.com helps to get our compilations and projects to generate revenues. These revenues contribute to the Interview Girl Foundation's *Operation A²—Aiding AIDS*. From donations given to the foundation and from profits from InterviewGirl.com's products, the Interview Girl Foundation plays a role in helping those who are experiencing assorted forms of misery.

Part One: Medicine

Operation A²'s first task is to distribute medication to sick individuals without access to medication. If someone like Amara does not have access to medication, it is her fundamental human right to have access to medication. If someone is ill and the sickness that he/she has is treatable, society needs to work to come up with ways to provide that individual with medication. The first part of *Operation A²'s* plan is to get sick people medication. There are other parts to the plan, but getting an ill person medication is step one. Dr. Jeffrey D. Sachs is the Director of The Earth Institute, Professor of Sustainable Development, and Professor of Health Policy and Management at Columbia University. He is Special Advisor to United Nations Secretary-General Ban Ki-moon on the Millennium Development Goals, having held the same position under former UN Secretary-General Kofi Annan. He is Director of the UN Sustainable Development Solutions Network. Sachs discloses his ideas about how to help the AIDS crisis in Africa as he describes that this is a chance for people to get together and solve problems that are already having terrible daily consequences for hundreds of millions of people who "we do not see, they are voiceless, they are off the radar screen, but they are suffering from the inaction of a world that promised to help but that has not yet moved to help."[197]Sachs gives the example of a woman who is poor and dying of something that we know is treatable, but she does not have money. He urges,

> "We have to say that humans actually deserve this as a right. Disease coming from ecology causes poverty, poverty causes disease. It goes around in a vicious circle. And by helping the poor to get access to the things that they need to be healthy in medicines, in preventative techniques, this is the way to break the vicious circle of poverty to disease to poverty to disease from poverty

to disease that holds so many hundreds of millions of people in that trap of extreme poverty in Africa."[198]

By providing medication to someone with AIDS, *Operation A²* plays a role in helping to break this vicious cycle described by Dr. Jeffrey Sachs. Once the sick individual has medicine and is well, then he/she can do those things that are necessary for him/her to be able to support himself/herself (attend school, hold a job, etc.).

In the developing world, ninety percent of all death and suffering occurs from infectious diseases.[199] InterviewGirl.com and the Interview Girl Foundation believe that humans who experience misery and suffering have to the right to experience life without this suffering. InterviewGirl.com as a project is trying to do just this: eliminate people's suffering from the profits that come from the stories that we share. One of the core beliefs and underpinnings of the InterviewGirl.com movement is that people's lives change when they are treated with dignity. The Interview Girl Foundation was created to make this vicious cycle (poverty to disease, disease to poverty) that exists better. The Interview Girl Foundation can provide basic medical services for people living in poverty.

Operation A² needs to provide lifelong ARV treatments, but it also needs to treat individuals with Tuberculosis (TB), for example. Tuberculosis (TB) is the number one killer of people living with HIV/ AIDS; due to weakened immune systems, they are much more likely to develop the disease. Unfortunately, diagnosing TB in people with HIV is difficult and the lack of effective diagnostic tools means many people go undiagnosed. Drug-resistant forms of TB (DR-TB) are even more difficult to diagnose and treat. The drugs to treat DR-TB can have intolerable side effects that make it difficult for patients to continue taking them, and some TB drugs can also interact with HIV medicines, therefore, they cannot be taken at the same time. Integrating HIV and TB care is critical to lessening the burden on people infected with both HIV and TB, and ensuring they stay on treatment.

After experiencing seeing patients die because they did not have access to medicine when he was out in the field, Dr. James Orbinski describes the goals for *Doctors Without Borders* in *An Imperfect Offering,* "As doctors we witness our patients dying from diseases like AIDS, TB and sleeping sickness because life-saving medicines were too expensive, and sometimes not available at all. The fight for access to essential medicines would be MSF's next challenge." Dr. Orbinski shares a story about a girl in the border zone between Cambodia and Thailand that emphasizes how difficult it is when medicine is not available for sick patients. HIV/AIDS was rampant in this border zone especially among the girls who worked the bars and brothels. Dr. Orbinski met this girl as she lay in her bed covered in skin sores. She had a fever and asked Orbinski to help her. She was dying of AIDS. Orbinski expounds that antiretroviral, or ARV drugs had converted AIDS into a disease as treatable as diabetes. Antiretroviral, or ARV drugs had been developed with largely publicly funded research, and the rights to them had then been sold to the pharmaceutical industry. The lifelong ARV treatments were now patented, and the monopoly allowed the companies to charge whatever they wanted. Orbinski explains that the average cost of the patented drugs was $15,000 a year in 1998.[200] A friend of the girl in the bed dying from AIDS heard about the new ARV drugs and said in broken English, "She no more good for bar. No medicine for her. Impossible. But we still see her." Orbinski then makes plain, "Her friend was right. There wasn't a hope in hell that we could offer this young girl anything more than comfort."[201]

Operation A² works to make sure that people like that young girl dying in that bed have access to medication. That story took place in 1998, since then considerable progress has been made and the Interview Girl Foundation wants to help continue this progress. At the beginning of the 21st century, very few people in the developing world had access to HIV treatment. This was in large part because of the very high prices of antiretroviral drugs (ARVs) and the international patents that stopped them from being manufactured at cheaper prices. However, in 2001 drug manufacturers in developing countries began to produce generic drugs under special terms in international trade law. In sub-Saharan Africa, countries including Kenya and South Africa passed bills that made it legal for them to purchase generic drugs from abroad. The vast reduction in price made possible by the manufacturing of generic drugs meant that expansion of treatment of HIV/AIDS on a global scale was possible.

In 2003, the World Health Organization (WHO) launched the ambitious target of reaching 3 million people in low- and middle-income countries with ARVs by 2005. It was not intended as a final objective, but as a stepping stone to universal access. Though the target was not attained until 2007, this was a success in a number of ways. Treatment was vastly expanded with coverage tripling from 400,000 people in December 2003 to 1.3 million in December 2005. This included an eight-fold increase in sub-Saharan Africa. In recent years, considerable energy and money have been spent trying to achieve universal access to treatment for HIV and AIDS. This was part of a wider objective to provide universal access to treatment, care and prevention by 2010. Most countries aspiring to expand treatment access set themselves a goal of providing antiretroviral treatment to around 80 percent of those in need. Considering the relative success of the 3 by 5 target, the international community set another target in 2006 that aimed for universal access to HIV treatment, prevention and care by 2010. However, by the time of WHO's 2008 universal access report, the heads of UNAIDS, UNICEF and WHO conceded that most countries would not meet the 2010 targets of 80 percent of those in need receiving treatment. Although the 2010 target was not met, with current global treatment coverage at 54 percent, the goal of universal access to HIV treatment remains an important one for low- and middle-income countries around the world, with a new target of universal access by 2015 agreed in 2010. In 2011, the international community recommitted to the goal of universal access. This time, countries committed to achieving universal access by 2015. The goal of universal access is also part of the Millennium Development Goal (MDG) which includes the goal of halting and beginning to reverse the spread of HIV/AIDS by 2015. As of 2000, there were still no official donor-supported programs to enable poor Africans to receive antiretroviral treatment for AIDS. Thanks in large part to the agenda-setting power of the MDGs, donor programs to fight AIDS began to be implemented, and more than six million Africans now receive antiretroviral treatment supported by official donor programs.[202]

Getting AIDS victims' medication is an integral component of *Operation A²*. In congruence with the Millennium Development Goal (MDG) which includes the goal of halting and beginning to reverse the spread of HIV/AIDS by 2015, *Operation A²* is doing its part to help the world see these goals come to fruition. *Operation A²* is taking our "slice of the cake" in trying to alleviate the misery of HIV/AIDS, but the Interview Girl Foundation stays the course and recognizes that its ultimate vision (*Project: C²: Committed Collaboration*) is to be a part of bringing organizations together in order to make a collective impact because this is what will lead to social change: universal access to medication. Providing medicine to orphans with AIDS is a crucial part of *Operation A²'s* plan, but making sure trained health care providers are present is another necessary step. The Interview Girl Foundation examined: what can be done to improve life expectancy within Africa in general? When it came to answering this question, training the health care providers was an area where *Operation A²* could focus its work. Research has indicated that the life expectancy of the population in rural areas in Africa has been shortened by the effect of three deadly diseases: HIV/AIDS, Tuberculosis, and Malaria. We strive to help improve the health situation at the grassroots level by running workshops for Health Care Providers to give preventative, promotional, rehabilitative and curative treatment to the grassroots people in the region where *Operation A²* is doing its work. This can be done by evaluating the local health situations, by relevant audiovisual awareness campaigns, and information and study sessions. Getting trained Health Care Providers into rural areas is another procedure in *Operation A²'s* course of action.

More than Providing just Medicine ... but Providing *Care*

Sub-Saharan Africa has 24% of the global disease burden, yet it has 3% of the world's health workers.[203] When I researched what this *really* means, it means that doctors and nurses simply do not have the time to take care of patients. A concrete example of this is what takes place in an overcrowded health clinic. In an overcrowded clinic, a nurse might see 50 to 100 a patients a day. That leaves the nurse just minutes with each patient that she sees. Within a matter of minutes that nurse has to complete many tasks regarding a patient who may have HIV. A nurse has to counsel for the HIV test, perform the HIV test, explain the results, dispense a single dose of nevirapine, explain how to take the drug, discuss instant feeding options, reinforce exclusive instant feeding, tell the patient to come back to the clinic in a year, perform the infant HIV test at 12 months and then explain the results. Another angle of *Operation A²* emerged as stories such as the example above had a profound effect on me. *Operation A²* needed to provide better ways of providing care to sick patients. People go to health clinics in Africa for care. Just giving someone a drug isn't enough. Medicine does not equal medical care. Certain knowledge that we obtain challenges us and shapes our understanding of the world. "Medicine does not equal medical care" was one of those eye opening phrases that helped me to better grasp an understanding of the AIDS crisis. Doctors and nurses don't have the time or skill to tell people what to do in ways that they understand with the shortage of health care workers that exist. Scientific studies show that patients who don't feel cared about by their doctors have longer recovery rates and poorer immune function. No longer was just providing medicine *Operation A²'s* focus, but now *Operation A²* concentrates on what it can do in order to provide medicine to sick patients as well as what it can do to in order to bring in more health care workers.

Providing medicine and providing medical care were both needed to assist those suffering with HIV/AIDS. Both of these aspects became the focal point of *Operation A²*. A new literary genre known as pathography: the personal narrative concerning illness, treatment and sometimes death, helped me understand that when trying to "aid" someone with a disease, we need to focus on the individual's needs, not just "the disease." Anne Hunsaker Hawkins' *Reconstructing Illness* conveys that there is a tendency in contemporary medical practice to focus primarily not on the needs of the individual who is sick, but on the condition that we call disease. *Reconstructing Illness* presents numerous case studies and demonstrates that "only when we hear both the doctor's and the patient's voice will we have a medicine that is truly human."[204] I knew that *Operation A²* needed to provide better ways of providing care to sick patients and somehow individuals who were not doctors also had to become involved in providing this care.

In all of the eye opening stories that I learned about the shortage of health care workers in Africa, Dr. Mitchell Besser provides a good answer to this dilemma. He moved to Cape Town in January 2000, joining the University of Cape Town's Department of Obstetrics and Gynecology. Dr. Besser recognized the need for services that would provide education and psychosocial support to pregnant and recently delivered women who were battling with an HIV diagnosis, allowing them to make healthy choices for themselves and their babies. This recognition was the founding principle behind *mothers2mothers*. Dr. Besser started *mothers2mothers* at Groote Schuur Hospital in Cape Town in 2001. He identified South Africa's HIV-positive mothers as a valuable, underutilized resource for strengthening public health care systems in the fight for the prevention of mother-to-child transmission of HIV. Dr. Besser's *mothers2mothers* has been successful in Cape Town and it has developed from this single support-group in Cape Town to a multinational organization employing over 1000 HIV-positive mothers who work in over 400 sites in 7 countries.

Providing medicine was only *one* part of the solution (Part One: (Medicine)) behind *Operation A²*, but it was by no means the only area that *Operation A²* needed to address. In order to "eliminate the misery of those with no access to medicine," *Operation A²* also needed to build programs that helped to train health care providers. *Operation A²* creates programs that take place at the grassroots level. *Operation A²* runs workshops where Health Care Providers are trained to give preventative, promotional, rehabilitative and curative treatment to the grassroots people in the region. A part of *Operation A²'s* strategy is to train Health Care Providers properly, but training Health Care Providers also includes training everyday people. By teaching citizens who inhabit the region (for example, family members) how to care for a sick patient, then the people in the region can provide the care that HIV/AIDS patients need. The plan behind *Operation A²'s* program consists of providing medication to sick patients (AIDS victims) as well as providing training to Health Care Providers. *Operation A²* can help to mitigate miseries orphans with HIV/AIDS experience as it assists in providing medication and medical care. Both (medicine and medical care) are needed.

InterviewGirl.com's prominent focus is to hear people's stories. Interestingly, *Operation A²* formed as I learned stories about individuals who were living through the AIDS pandemic in Africa. These stories enlightened me about what it was that needed to be done in order to lessen the misery of the AIDS pandemic. Learning people's stories helped me to see the "needs" that existed in communities and where *Operation A²* should focus its efforts. All the statistics made much more sense when I read or heard people's personal stories about the dilemmas that they faced. It was as if the stories instructed me about what steps needed to be taken. I understood more clearly what needs were not being met for those at the heart of the AIDS pandemic as I heard individuals' stories. It was through hearing these stories that I finally began to digest just how to create a more effective *Operation A²*. At the same time, the stories that I learned about individuals who were already making a difference in the AIDS pandemic through their philanthropic efforts inspired me and made me firmly believe *Operation A²* could and would achieve a world of good through our programs. I also imagined what the world would be like if highly structured collaborative efforts took place across governments, NGOs, multilateral organizations, universities, and companies around the world. The stories about what each of the individual organizations was doing to help lessen miseries across the globe imbued me with hope that through large-scale collaborations between all of these groups, substantial impact on a large-scale social problem, such as AIDS, could be achieved.

Part Two: Education

"Education is the most powerful tool you can use to change the world."

—Nelson Mandela

Orphans without access to medication experience misery and this is why I chose to create *Operation A²*. In order to address this misery, we need to challenge practices that currently shape health care and education in regions that are the home to numerous orphans. Part one of *Operation A²* targets medicine and part two of *Operation A²* is about education. The first steps in *Operation A²'s* plan to achieve this goal (eliminate the misery of orphans without access to medication) are to provide the sick children with medication as well as treatment and medical care. Sending the children to school is the next part of the puzzle. As Nelson Mandela's powerful words remind us, with education we can change the world. Education has long been identified as a key tool in shaping future generations. Both community advocates and policy makers look to educational programs to provide the best anti-poverty mechanisms that under-served communities can utilize.

Throughout Africa, millions of children are out of school because of lack of government support and infrastructure. When a girl doesn't attend school, she is more likely to become affected with HIV and then to die. According to the United Nations, the fastest way to eliminate worldwide poverty is to educate girls. Illiteracy rates are inordinately high: for all of sub-Saharan Africa above 15 years of age, 49% of females and 32 percent of males. The parents of many children in Africa only have a fifth grade education. Or else, at age 12, many children's parents have died; so a 12 year old is left to cater for his/her three little siblings. Often times the most educated person in these African villages where the children live only made it up to high school. Families live on less than two dollars a day.[205] There is no public assistance. This is the story about hundreds of thousands of children in Africa who are stuck in this cycle of poverty. Education is the tool that will allow the poor communities in Africa to overcome poverty. When a child is educated, their future is altered.

Successful development programs indicate that the only way to break the cycle of poverty and ensure the prosperity and self-determination of the African people is to invest in resources that provide access to quality education for kids. *Operation A²* was created with the intention to help AIDS orphans and impoverished youths to break the cycle of poverty in rural communities, through the creation of educational and sustainable development opportunities. *Operation A²* is an effort to create tangible, sustainable solutions to meet the needs of hundreds of orphans in the village of Kpando, Ghana and after *Operation A²* has aided the orphans (with no access to medicine) in Kpando, we will move onto different villages in Ghana and then throughout Africa. Profits from InterviewGirl.com's projects will aid in the development of education by helping to provide finances to pay for school fees, lunch fees, teachers, resources, desks, buildings, and other necessary elements that make education possible.

I remember sitting in a classroom and seeing a quote by Woody Allen written on a poster hanging on the wall, "Eighty percent of success is showing up." In 2007, a Standford professor gave his students an assignment to build a Facebook application and get people to use it. Some applications became so popular that students made good money out of them. Some even turned into companies. The students at Stanford showed up to class and did their assignment because they had to.[206] In the same way, the orphans need to get to school. They need to *show up*. If they are there (school), they too will rise to the challenge and education will markedly benefit them. Funding and finances make education possible. The Interview Girl Foundation will help to provide money for school fees, lunch fees, teacher salaries, resources, teacher training, desks, buildings, and other necessary elements that make education possible. Funding and grants can initially assist in providing education, but overtime, individuals need to have a means to pay their own school fees. Besides helping orphans to initially get into school, beyond that, the Interview Girl Foundation's programs strive to give individuals the tools that they need in order to be able to assist in providing their own education as time passes.

Part Three: Infrastructure

Ultimately, the Interview Girl Foundation's *Operation A^2* is a project created in order to help the AIDS crisis in Africa. My notebooks came to be filled with multitudinous questions as I researched to create an *Operation A^2* that would provide "more than good intentions" to the world. As important as it is to see each individual we are trying to help (each orphan), at the same time, referring back to what is happening within a "country" where an orphan lives or even the "continent" of Africa in general, allows *Operation A^2* to create a more successful program. Researching to create *Operation A^2* was a journey in itself as I continually attained augmented information. One thing that I understood is that Africa's infrastructure needed to be strengthened. As mentioned before, Africa is a continent made up of 54 countries and each country has its own story, but across the continent infrastructure could be strengthened.

When I was in Africa, I learned that when an adolescent girl has her period she would miss an entire week of school. In certain areas, there is no plumbing and there are no toilets. I am trying to explain this as properly as possible, but basically people pea all over the streets, anywhere that they can. The girl would stay home from school because there was nowhere to place the "blood" that came from her period. In Kpando, women wore long dresses. When they needed to urinate, they would go off toward a corner and spread their legs and pea while standing or squatting. An infrastructure system was lacking. In an article from the Economist from the summer of 2011, *A road to somewhere: What do Africans need most— aid or infrastructure?* Dar Es Salaam and Nairobi write,

> "Whether it is taking vegetables to market, getting water from a tap or turning on the lights, almost everything is slower, less reliable or more expensive in Africa than it needs to be. The African Development Bank (AfDB), which finances big investments on the continent, says that a shortage of roads, housing, water, sanitation and electricity reduces sub-Saharan Africa's output by about 40%. There is no controversy in saying that shoddy infrastructure is holding the continent back."[207]

Questions such as: *Can infrastructure be created? How is infrastructure created? How does infrastructure develop? Are there things that outside organizations can do to aid in developing infrastructure in a country?* lined my notebooks. Could *Operation A²* help bring infrastructure to Africa? If Africa had better infrastructure, would there be less diseases there?

Infrastructure is defined to include the main networks that underpin the economy—air transport, information and communication technologies, irrigation, ports, power, railways, roads, sanitation and water. The Interview Girl Foundation creates projects to aid in developing Africa's infrastructure. Many Africans live in remote parts of the country with no services and no running water. More than 1 in 8 people in the world don't have access to safe drinking water. 1 out of every 5 deaths under the age of 5 worldwide is due to a water-related disease. Nearly 80% of illness in developing countries is linked to poor water and sanitation conditions. Infrastructure brings water. The statistics about poor water sanitation as well as people's stories chronicling what is like to live with poor water sanitation are evidence to this misery that exists due to poor infrastructure. Infrastructure is needed. The Interview Girl Foundation has identified this as a problem. There are things that can be done to help alleviate the misery of poor water and sanitation conditions in Africa. The ideas are flowing as to what can be done. The Interview Girl Foundation works to advance systematic solutions to major social problems, but we always begin where we can. Initial, small steps like organizing trips of students and/or volunteers to go to Africa and help build roads, help build toilets, and the like are a starting spot to making a difference.

> "Every great dream begins with a dreamer. Always remember, you have within you the strength, the patience, and the passion to reach for the stars to change the world."
>
> —Harriet Tubman

The overall endeavor at InterviewGirl.com is to eliminate people's miseries. *Operation A²* is only **ONE** project at the Interview Girl Foundation. Different projects are and will be created through the Interview Girl Foundation in order to target diverse miseries that exist in our world. For example, through the Interview Girl Foundation, we strive to: relieve the AIDS victims from the misery of not having access to medication, aid the children dying because they are starving to death or dying from preventable diseases because they live in poverty, and to assist the victims of child tracking. The Interview Girl Foundation invests in projects to build Africa's infrastructure because as Africa's infrastructure improves, miseries that exist for all the individuals mentioned as well as countless others improve. The Interview Girl Foundation is doing its part (taking its slice of the cake) as it begins to eliminate some of the misery plaguing this world through *Operation A²*. All along, the Interview Girl Foundation's long-term guiding vital vision (to bring organizations across the world together in order to make a collective impact for social change (*Project: C²: Committed Collaboration*) guides its every step.

> "All our dreams can come true, if we have the courage
> to pursue them."
>
> —Walt Disney

CHAPTER THIRTEEN

Changing the Course of History for the Next Generation (Helping ONE person ... Surveying it ALL)

Operation A²: A Step Further than Medicine

Operation A²'s initial vision to help get medication to orphans without access to medication (in honor of Amara) developed considerably over time. Simply just passing out medicine was not a comprehensive solution to the problem. Although medicine would "help" the HIV/AIDS victim, we needed to think about how a patient would continue to get medicine throughout his/her life. *Operation A²* nor any other charitable intervention can last forever. The most effective development programs strive to mitigate the causes and impact of HIV and AIDS; to promote food security among rural households; to economically empower vulnerable groups and young people, and to promote democracy, human rights and good governance. *Operation A²* had its laser focus: to help orphans without access to medication, but it was important for the Interview Girl Foundation to understand how all these social issues connect in order to better target the focus (AIDS) of *Operation A².* Effective overall development programs needed to be studied in order for the Interview Girl Foundation to build a successful *Operation A²*. The AIDS epidemic does not make sense without looking at poverty, food security, vulnerable groups, democracy, human rights, and good governance.

Operation A²'s initial goal was to provide medicine to orphans who have HIV/AIDS with no access to medication, but *Operation A²'s* vision grew. *Operation A²* strives to be a part of creating an HIV/AIDS and poverty free society where every person is valued and treated equally before the law. Bono, the lead singer of U2, one of the most popular and influential rock bands of the last 30 years, is a figure admired both within and outside of the music industry. Bono is also a humanitarian and crusader for the world's poor. Bono updated the world about the news on poverty in 2012. He reveals that the biggest disease is not a disease, but it is corruption. As chapter eleven discusses, technology is changing the world and technology can aid in a country's ability to overcome corruption. Corruption within a country's government is one of the bigger underlying challenges behind problems like HIV/AIDS, poverty, disease, child trafficking and hunger. The Interview Girl Foundation attempts to play a role in making these challenges that people experience better. InterviewGirl.com is a movement because movements lead to transformations in our society. Goals part of *Operation A²* include providing education and medication to orphans with AIDS, but positive social movements where citizens demand that their governments answer, this is what transforms how people living in poverty change their lives. Creating projects and programs that help people to overcome miseries is important because as these "miseries" for people became better, these overall larger issues plaguing some parts of the world then improve. As Bono shares, "It's called transparency—open data sets. Technology is turbo charging this. It's harder to hide bad things. For example, in Uganda people want to know how their money is being spent."[208] There is not one fail proof plan to solving any social issue that society faces, but even as programs like *Operation A²* spread this news about technology, citizens living in misery are more apt to come up with ways to get their governments to answer.

Microfinance

Developing what the Interview Girl Foundation would come to be has changed and developed and is still developing. I set out on a quest to found this nonprofit organization with the intention of writing a plan that someone would be able to follow steps A,B,C,D,E, etc. and if he/she did that, then his/her problem could be solved. In the beginning, I wanted to arrive at the destination. The destination that I yearned to get to was the creation of a relief plan that would work (a plan to help someone with HIV/ AIDS who lives in poverty). I wanted to create a blueprint that could be applied to each situation where people experience a certain misery. Along my journey to create the Interview Girl Foundation, I discovered the world of microfinance. From reading about successful development programs to reading the stories of individuals who overcame poverty, it became clear that microfinance has been revolutionary in the developing world. Microfinance is a term for the practice of providing financial services, such as micro credit, micro savings or micro insurance to poor or disadvantaged individuals. By helping them to accumulate usable large sums of money, this expands their choices and reduces the risks they face. Microfinance consists of making small loans of usually less than $200 to individuals to establish or expand a small, self-sustaining business. For example, a woman may borrow $200 to buy chickens, so she can sell eggs. As the chickens multiply, she will have more eggs to sell. Soon she can sell the chickens. Each expansion pulls her further from the devastation of poverty. Today, microfinance plays a major role in the development of many African nations. Its impact is substantial enough to have warranted acknowledgment by the United Nations which declared 2005, "The international year of microfinance," reminding people that millions worldwide benefit from microfinance activities. I knew that the Interview Girl Foundation needed to tap into microfinance in order to target some of the bigger issues that surrounded *Operation A²'s* targeted focus (AIDS). One program (*Loan Lending*) that came to be part of the Interview Girl Foundation creates projects that empower small businesses. The goal of this program is to provide a "start" and financing that will enable small businesses to expand. *Loan Lending* helps to provide employment and in doing so can contribute to national development. This project also involves providing the important training and support to ensure that these businesses succeed.

Although microfinance has helped many African countries to develop, it isn't the "magic bullet" solution to ending poverty either. We need to remember that there is not just one solution that will fix the AIDS crisis, hunger, poverty, child trafficking, or any other global, social, political, economic or environmental issue that affects people on a large scale. There is not one formula with steps X, Y, Z to follow that will solve any of these social problems. As much as I hoped microfinance would and could be a solution to solving poverty, it was just that. It was a solution for certain people in certain places, but microfinance was not the secret weapon to the development crisis in developing countries. Despite the complex elements that are part of understanding AIDS, poverty, development economics, and microfinance, the solution that the Interview Girl Foundation needed to implement in its programs was much simpler. We needed to listen. We needed to listen to who it was that we wanted to help. A founding pillar of InterviewGirl.com is that *listening to stories* has the power to transform one's life. The Interview Girl Foundation and its programs would continually change based on the communities that they served. *Loan Lending* is one program available through the Interview Girl Foundation for people interested in a microfinance loan. This program would not be thrown at individuals; rather it was available for those who it could serve. Setting up a plan to do away with misery that exists for people starts with the Interview Girl Foundation listening to the people who were experiencing a type of misery that the foundation wanted to help eliminate. The Interview Girl Foundation listening to those they hoped to help parallels InterviewGirl.com's mission to listen to stories from people around the world.

Operation A² came to be based on the philosophy that community-led initiatives are an effective way of addressing the social challenges of HIV/AIDS in a sustainable way at the community level. The Interview Girl Foundation's *Operation A²* creates programs that are run by local staff and volunteers who consult regularly with the communities who the project has been set up to help in order to ensure that *Operation A²* is responding to needs in the community. By collaborating with people in a particular community and listening to their needs, *Operation A²* can help people accordingly. *Operation A²* would not just enter a community and throw our plan on people, rather we needed to listen to what it was that the individuals needed and we would help to create specific systems for tailored needs. This type of philanthropy causes sustainability and progress. Creating a blanket plan and expecting it to work for everyone would not be more than a good intention. An analogy can be made to public education. Not every program or intervention will work for every teacher and every class. Each class of students has diverse needs and strategies that work and that vary from teacher to teacher and school to school.

Although *Operation A²* was created to help ORPHANS—our programs reach beyond orphans

Operation A²'s main goal is to get treatment to victims suffering from AIDS, but *Operation A²* understands that making sure a person can continue to receive medication is as vital as providing him/her with medication. After the Interview Girl Foundation initially gets the AIDS victims started on the treatment, the goal is for the patient to then support himself/herself through his/her business or other community job. In the case of the orphans, they would be well enough to attend school and then in time the job would come. In the case of the adults who we are helping, the Interview Girl Foundation might help the AIDS victims establish their own sustainable business while being treated. Although the intention of *Operation A²* is to provide medicine to orphans who have AIDS and no access to medicine, in order to really do that on a scale that would "erase" the misery that exists, *Operation A²* needed to focus on the AIDS pandemic in Africa beyond the orphans. Orphans who are suffering from AIDS with no access to medication is the first "misery" being targeted to eliminate, but programs through the Interview Girl Foundation such as our *Loan Lending* program are created for adults. By *Operation A²* helping adults, this can prevent children from even becoming orphans in the first place. Through *Loan Lending*, the Interview Girl Foundation helps the adults establish a business. For example, the person might receive chickens, goats, pigs, cows or other animals. By getting these animals, the person is getting nourished and providing food to his/her family. He/She can then sell eggs and chickens to a local market and earn money from this. In the process, he/she is becoming a successful businessman/woman through selling his animals. Not only are the individuals and the individual's family benefiting, but all of his neighbors benefit too. By giving the individual the skills he/she needs to become self-sufficient, he/she is setting up a foundation to be able to care for himself/herself. *Loan Lending* works toward creating entrepreneurs and/or people who hold other service positions within the community. The individual, the family, the neighborhood, the community, the city, the country, and the world benefit from the AIDS patients becoming self-sufficient entrepreneurs and/or people who hold service positions (jobs) within the community. When an AIDS patient receives medicine, parents survive and children go to school and learn vital skills. They return to their villages as leaders. This is how the cycle of poverty is broken.

As a student of history, if we look at any successful civilization on this Earth, one of the most important things in any type of community is to have a form of an economy. Customary for my role as Interview Girl and the creation of the programs I was working on, questions suffused my notebooks as the Interview Girl Foundation created its *Loan Lending* program: Do a thriving economy and health care correlate? Why is *Operation A²* concerned about creating entrepreneurs? Shouldn't *Operation A²* just concentrate on getting antiretroviral medication to AIDS patients? How can a nonprofit organization help a country's economic development? A look back in the history of human civilization is always the precise place to start when trying to solve any current problem. A thriving economy is an integral part of any successful civilization. The Indus Valley Civilization and the Aztecs were two early civilizations that flourished and both civilizations had successful economies. Looking back to the early Indus Valley Civilization, beginning sometime around 2300 BC, this civilization developed in two major city areas along the river valleys of the Indus, Ravi, and Sutlej, just beneath the Himalayan Mountains in modern Pakistan and Northeast India. Aside from the subsistence of agriculture and hunting, the Indus people supported themselves by trading goods. Through trade, the Indus Civilization expanded its culture, coming into regular contacts with faraway lands. The early Aztec economy consisted of a type of barter system as this was a pre-capitalist society. Minor purchases were made with cacao beans imported from lowlands. In the marketplaces, a small rabbit might have been worth 30 beans, an egg cost 3 beans while larger purchases of cloth could range from 65 to 300 cacao beans. A prosperous economy is an integral part of any successful civilization, such as the Indus Valley Civilization and the Aztecs.

Traditional economies refer to countries which have their economy based on the basic economic activities of hunting and gathering or farming. A traditional economy is basically an economic system where resources are allocated by inheritance, a strong social network is there, and the economy is based on indigenous technology and methods. Many African countries use agriculture as their main basis for growing food and for jobs. Of Africa's 54 countries, well over half of them still use traditional ways of gathering and producing food even now in the year 2013. Even if *Operation A²'s* main purpose is to help AIDS victims by providing medication, the ambition to get Africa's economy stronger cannot be overlooked. To verily help eliminate the misery of "no medication" for people, the community's economy cannot be forgotten. Africa's economy can develop when jobs are created and entrepreneurial opportunities emerge for citizens. *Operation A²* needed more than a plan to provide medication to AIDS victims, but it also needed to focus on stimulating economic growth within communities in the remote parts of Africa in the poorest regions. Without individuals learning to support themselves in their communities, moving away from poverty could not happen permanently. Without stimulating economic growth in a country's economy, people will not enduringly be removed from poverty. For this reason, *Operation A²* could not just focus on getting medicine to orphans with AIDS. Providing medication was a necessary first step, but making sure that orphans have access to an education as well as helping adults start businesses is what will allow the adults and one day, the orphans to be able to provide medication for themselves. When an orphan can provide himself/herself with medication, then in the future, he/she can provide for his/her family.

The Interview Girl Foundation created a program (*Loan Lending*) to improve the livelihoods of people living with HIV/AIDS in the local community. *Loan Lending* set up a revolving loan fund, which provides soft loans at zero percent interest. The loans will enable people to set up small income generation activities, such as selling fruit and vegetables, cows, pigs, or other items. By helping someone set up a way to generate income, he/she can then strengthen his/her income and boost self-esteem. Helping people generate an income will also help people living with HIV/AIDS have greater access to food security, improve their general health, and to provide greater support to their families. Loans are repayable within 12 months, so that the fund can continue to help others in need of a helping hand. All loan recipients will receive training on setting up small businesses. For example, borrowers will be provided with a simple cashbook and support from *Loan Lending* to complete it.

Operation A² and *Loan Lending* are programs through the Interview Girl Foundation that were created in order to help with miseries that exist in the world. There is a caveat before we go any further. Our programs *Operation A²* and *Loan Lending* listen to members in a community because if programs through the Interview Girl Foundation are what they envision is best for them, then the Interview Girl Foundation is there to help, but our programs should not be obligatory for anyone. *Operation A²* and *Loan Lending* present individuals with options. All of this discussion about getting economies to grow at requisite levels, we cannot forget that development must enrich human lives, not just increase national production. Development must increase people's choices. These choices extend to all spheres of life, including, health, education, political freedom, social participation, cultural enrichment, and a healthy environment. Development initiatives should not just be about increasing incomes. The purpose of the Interview Girl Foundation is to eliminate misery that exists in the world. As Amartya Sen, the Nobel-laureate champion of democratic development for the world's poor, explains in *The taste of true freedom*, "Therefore, it is vital to search for a new development model which enhances human lives, not marginalize it and which treats economy and technology as tool, not as end."[209] In *The Blue Sweater*, Jacelyn Novogratz delineates, "poverty is about lack of choice." Similarly, former PM of India, Atal Bihari Vajpayee characterizes poverty as a,

> "State of deprivation which has multiple dimensions. Trying to measure it in terms of income alone is grossly inadequate. The poor are in fact deprived of capabilities which may originate from several sources: personal, social and political. It can only be measured using some multidimensional approach, exemplified by

say the multidimensional poverty index. Sustainable poverty removal efforts involve following a human development approach to build the capabilities of the poor."[210]

InterviewGirl.com and the Interview Girl Foundation were created to spread stories and by doing this to eliminate miseries in the world. The Interview Girl Foundation's aspiration is not just to make the economy grow in an area where misery subsides, but to enrich human lives by helping to eliminate a misery that exists. This is the underpinning and backbone of our movement. Projects sponsored through the Interview Girl Foundation seek to eliminate misery that individuals experience in order to make their lives better because every human being on the planet deserves to be treated with dignity. A guiding principle behind the InterviewGirl.com movement is that people's lives change when they are treated with dignity. The purpose of our programs are to eliminate miseries individuals live with because this brings people the dignity that they deserve.

Operation A²: Creating a Ripple Effect

The coming together of *Operation A²* unfolded through the research I completed, stories I heard, statistics I learned, and interviews I conducted. *Operation A²* developed as I heard people's stories. I constructed the framework of solutions that would guide *Operation A²*: part one (medicine) and part two (education). Providing medicine and medical care are ways to help children who have HIV/AIDS and providing education to children is a way to take children out of the cycle of poverty. As I realized the solutions needed, *Operation A²* focused on the question: how do we set up schools and hospitals in Africa? Funds are needed to get medication and the resources for education to communities *Operation A²* serves in Africa. To help orphans suffering from

AIDS, the locus of *Operation A²* also points to areas beyond the disease. Providing children with the necessary medication to treat the disease is vital, but *Operation A²* has programs in place in order to help the adults, as well. To get to the root of an issue such as poverty, multiple solutions are needed. The goals of the Interview Girl Foundation's programs are not to create dependence, but rather to provide resources and tools to people that allow them to provide for themselves and their families. With the tools made available to individuals, they can succeed in becoming self-sufficient citizens as well as entrepreneurs. A cycle is the best way to view the Interview Girl Foundation's work. This cycle (a chain of goodness) all starts with providing medicine to AIDS victims. From the parents surviving and not getting sick, children don't have to become orphans and the parents are well enough to work to be able to sustain their families. Or when an orphan with AIDS receives treatment, he/she is well enough to attend school, and then one day he/she will be able to support his/her own family. The ripple effect is in place from there.

Humanitarians best serve the world when they inspire an individual. My journey through narratives and stories about individuals living with HIV/AIDS, individuals living in poverty, organizations making the world a better place, and how philanthropists are changing our world exposed this lesson. Individuals do not want to be taken care of. Individuals need to be given the opportunity to fulfill their own potential. Many aid projects create dependence and history has shown, this actually helps no one in the long run. The Interview Girl Foundation teaches people skills that they need and empowers them to create their own destiny. I was now a long way from the initial notes in my notebook when I first came back from volunteering that summer. *Operation A²* isn't a program that gives people money so that when the money runs out, they'll go back to square one. *Operation A²* is an effort that helps people beyond what looks good in theory. All projects at the Interview Girl Foundation are interested in providing resources to individuals so that people can use these resources to help eliminate the miseries around them. When people are given the skills and tools that they need, they can better their lives. Once they have these tools, it is up to them to make changes.

Far-removed from my initial "plan" to complete a list of necessary steps in order to "save" people, *Operation A²* developed into a development program that helps to provide HIV/AIDS victims the treatment that they need. Once the victims have their treatment, they'll be able to pursue their dreams and complete an education, become an entrepreneur, or serve the community in some other capacity. *Operation A²* will have a ripple effect because citizens will follow one another's lead and become self-sufficient members of their community. When someone sees a neighbor or friend thriving thanks to medicine, most likely he/ she will want to experience that same positive affect. Creating a ripple effect within African communities where individuals are taking care of themselves and their families is just as important as providing the necessary medication to HIV/AIDS victims. *Operation A²— Aiding AIDS's* initial efforts are targeted at raising money to ensure that citizens suffering from HIV/AIDS in Africa will be treated because from this first step, each developing step can then take place.

> "Tell me and I forget, teach me and I may remember, involve me and I learn."
>
> —Benjamin Franklin

The Interview Girl Foundation's programs help to develop the infrastructure, support, and education that will help communities to grow and develop. The people living in a community run the projects that our resources and tools help to get started. As scholarship on international aid and development in developing countries reveals, the key is not to just keep giving foreign aid to people, but we need to help them become entrepreneurs or be able to sustain themselves in some way by providing a framework with resources. Only when people can sustain themselves can the cycle of poverty end. The profits from projects completed at InterviewGirl.com help the Interview Girl Foundation to develop programs that assist an individual in being able to support himself/herself. As the proverb says, "Give a man a fish and you feed him for a day. Teach a man to fish and you feed him for a lifetime." Giving an individual the tools, knowledge, and resources that he/she needs is the key to break the cycle of poverty, but it is important to remember that the same exact plan with prescribed steps cannot be applied to each individual. Dean Karlan and Jacob Appel argue that the teach-a-man-to-fish approach has been around for decades. They give the analogy,

> "For natural-born fishermen, it can work. But the problem is that some people are bad at baiting the hooks; some can't cast worth a damn; some have arthritis and can't grip the reel to haul in a catch; and some don't live near a river with enough fish in it. Some people think fishing is just plain boring. Come dinner, all these folks are out of luck. They can't eat rods and reels and lessons about casting."[211]

In reality, every individual situation is different. This is what is unique about *Operation A²'s* humanitarian efforts, we will individually help people. Providing medicine and education are the tools that we will use, but individuals will drive their own future. At the Interview Girl Foundation, we need to listen to what it is that people need in the communities where we are trying to eliminate miseries. People in their own communities have needs. We cannot expect to dictate what these are. As Dean Karlan and Jacob Appel expose as they broke apart the "teach a man to fish analogy," we cannot assume anything. The Interview Girl Foundation cannot assume what individuals need. *Operation A²* aids individuals on an individual basis. Everyone has different needs. There cannot be one blanket plan that is prescribed to all.

This will not work. Rather individuals have to be targeted and their specific needs met.

The Interview Girl Foundation's overall objective is to be a part of fostering collaborative efforts that have the potential to achieve substantial impact on a large scale social problem (*Project C2: Committed Collaboration*), but in order to one day attain large scale reach, the Interview Girl Foundation's efforts to eliminate miseries needed to start with assisting individuals. How the Interview Girl Foundation helps people (teaching or providing tools and resources) is varied based on the individual being served. Anyone living in misery has needs that need to be met. This is why the most meaningful task for the Interview Girl Foundation is to *listen* to who is living in the misery. As we listen to them, it is only then that we can begin to assist in doing away with the misery. InterviewGirl.com *listens* to people's stories and the Interview Girl Foundation *listens* to those who it hopes to help because by listening to each other's stories, in this act, the world becomes a better place.

The backbone behind the InterviewGirl.com movement is that people's lives change when they are treated with dignity. As one hears someone else's story, they are treating that person with dignity. The Interview Girl Foundation's *Operation A²* had to begin its work by helping individuals, but to genuinely change the world (eradicate miseries like people with HIV/AIDS having no access to medicine, people living on less than \$2 a day, and human trafficking seizing to exist), partnerships between nonprofit organizations, NGO's, governments academic institutions, and businesses that each specialize in different areas had to take place. As all of these entities collaborate, large scale social problems would no longer be large scale problems. Until *C²: Committed Collaboration* takes off and the collaboration is in full swing, the Interview Girl Foundation reaches out to individuals and provides tools and resources to help someone eliminate a misery he/she is facing.

"Give a man a fish and you feed him for a day. Teach a
man to fish and you feed him for a lifetime."

—Chinese Proverb

Changing the Course of History for the Next Generation

"The issue of poverty is not a statistical issue. It is a
human issue."

—James Wolfensohn

One of the leading lessons from the history of human
civilization is that there is always hope within any situation, no
matter how dismal at first the situation may seem. The ambition
of the Interview Girl Foundation's *Operation A²—Aiding AIDS* is
pretty simple: we want to restore hope to those suffering with
AIDS. AIDS is seen as a fatal disease. Getting people suffering
from AIDS treatment is essential because if they have their health,
they can go about living their lives. After treatment, the person
who was once someone suffering from a fatal disease is now an
individual who can become an entrepreneur and/or person who
holds a job in his/her community. The person's work can allow
him/her to sustain himself/herself. The sense of pride that the
person has spreads throughout the community. Once he/she felt
helpless and lost. His/her hope is restored. It will inspire others
to want to experience the same transformation that he/ she has.
He/she transcends what once was a fatal disease and an impossible
situation to becoming a leader and teacher to an entire community.
By becoming an entrepreneur and/or person in a service position,
it gives the individual dignity. In *The Blue Sweater*, Jacelyn
Novagratz explains,

"Once I let go of the idea of being Mother Superior
trying to save the masses and instead found the joy of
building systems that really do allow people to change

their own lives, then I could be much more myself and challenge people to reach higher. What I learned is people live up and down to the expectations others place on them. That was incredibly liberating to me."

The Interview Girl Foundation believes that human dignity is a fundamental right for all. As we help to eliminate miseries, people experience the dignity that they deserve. People's lives change when they are treated with dignity. When an individual has a means to make an income, he/she can survive. Children can go to school. They won't end up in a situation like where their parents came from. This changes the course of history for the next generation (medicine and education). This is how the cycle of poverty is broken. The Interview Girl Foundation's *Operation A²—Aiding AIDS* will do its part in helping to slice off a piece of the misery in Africa as we provide medicine to one AIDS victim at a time. What starts with people becoming healthy leads to creating communities where people are working and/or becoming entrepreneurs. By beginning with our mission to get medicine to one orphan suffering from AIDS, from helping to eliminate that one orphan's misery, a process for change begins. From helping one person, the context of the whole situation becomes better. The cycle that we hope to see broken starts with getting medicine to an orphan and after one orphan receives medicine, then we move onto the next and then the next. Just like this book was written one word at a time, *Operation A²—Aiding AIDS* will provide treatment that will lead to lasting change one person at a time.

A Little Bit Makes a Big Difference

"Little by little, a little becomes a lot."

—Tanzanian proverb

Starting with helping a single individual or if someone were to donate a few dollars, from those humble beginnings, as time passes, capacious changes can be made. Rev. Felix Osasona, M.S.P., the development director for *Missionary Society of St. Paul* illuminates this philosophy. In 2011, the *Society of St. Paul* had a campaign to help the children in Malawi. Rev. Felix Osasona contacted people all over the world and he explained that there was an emergency in Malawi. He let them know that if emergency aid didn't reach the African country as soon as possible, more than 4 million people would starve to death, mostly children and with this emergency in Malawi, every minute, three children would die. *Missionary Society of St. Paul* launched a campaign to help the starving victims and only asked for people's nickels and pennies. Rev. Felix Osasona explained that it's pennies a day to save a child's life. Osasona urged, "With only $15.00, we can save ten children for two weeks. That's pennies a day to save a child's life." A little bit from you can make a difference in someone else's life. The *Society of St. Paul's* campaign to help the children in Malawi emblematizes how our pennies and dimes can save lives.[212]

More than One Solution

The Interview Girl Foundation helps the orphans to deal with this illness that has fallen upon them. Having HIV/AIDS cannot be seen as an impossible situation, but rather the orphans need to see that they can rise above this impossible situation. Helping the orphans to realize that there are ways to deal with their illness and there are ways to generate an income allows them to understand that the difficult situation can be overcome. By treating HIV/AIDS and figuring out a way for someone to make a living, well this changes the course of history for the next generation. The Interview Girl Foundation's pursuit is to develop programs that assist in changing the course of history for the next generation. The cycle of poverty is broken when someone escapes this deadly cycle. People make changes in their lives and in doing this, they make things better for the next generation. It is crucial for the orphans to understand what to do in order to control the disease (HIV/AIDS), so they do not get deathly ill.

With its focus on eliminating the misery of HIV/AIDS, part of *Operation A²'s* mission is to help people to overcome poverty because if people no longer live in poverty, living with HIV/AIDS is more manageable. *Operation A²'s* focus on helping people to have access to an education and means to become entrepreneurs is because economic freedom is one of the strongest tools available to fight poverty and is responsible for the greatest advances in reducing poverty over the last century. The economic growth created by increased economic freedom reduces poverty by giving more opportunities to workers and helping them avoid the poverty trap. With economic growth, absolute poverty levels are reduced, as is inequality, as relative poverty levels tend to decline as well. In the past two decades, we have seen poorer nations dismantle command-and-control methods and give markets greater latitude. As Steve Chapman instructs, "Economic growth, not redistribution, has been the surest cure for poverty, and economic freedom has been the key that unlocked the riddle of economic growth."[213] For these reasons, providing medication and immediate solutions were needed, but exceeding the immediate solutions, how people would contribute to their country's economy could not be overlooked in the creation of the Interview Girl Foundation. Tiziana Dearing, the former CEO of Boston Rising, a start-up fund and grant making organization that supports individuals, families, and communities as they chart their own paths out of poverty, instructs, "in order to break the inter-generational poverty cycle, we must invest in individual choice and control."[214]Atal Bihari Vajpayee (Former PM, India) advises, "Poverty is multidimensional. It extends beyond money incomes to education, health care, political participation and advancement of one's own culture and social organization." Richard McGill Murphy writes, "Many of today's leading social entrepreneurs have created organizations that are neither businesses nor charities, but rather hybrid entities that generate revenue in pursuit of social goals."[215] The Interview Girl Foundation is one of these. The Interview Girl Foundation believes that an organization cannot just approach one solution. John Gardner told Jacelyn Novogratz in one of their coveted conversations, "Philanthropists should find innovations that release the energies of people."[216] When looking at the misery that we are hoping to eliminate in Africa, more than one solution is needed which is why programs through the Interview Girl Foundation target poverty, AIDS, socio-economic systems, and more. Providing Antiretroviral Therapy to AIDS victims is one step in *Operation A²'s* plan to aid in eliminating this misery.

Person to Person

The economic theories behind growth within an economy, studies about poverty alleviation, microfinance strategies, and social entrepreneurship all are part of complicated systematic solutions that are needed to make changes in communities where people live with miseries like poverty and HIV/AIDS. The Interview Girl Foundation's plan on a more basic level is much simpler: Every person should share a story on InterviewGirl.com because as everyone does this, we can use these stories to generate revenues for our mission: to eliminate miseries that exist in our world. InterviewGirl.com's ambition is to get everyone to join in and share a story. As it is the objective to get all individuals involved in IntervewGirl.com, the Interview Girl Foundation is also completing its mission within Africa *person by person*. We will reach out to individuals one at a time and in time there is the possibility for changes throughout entire communities to happen. Hope is given to those suffering with AIDS as *Operation A²—Aiding AIDS* implements its person by person approach and provides medication to one individual at a time. Society cannot look at

AIDS as a fatal disease and an impossible situation, but rather we need to see an individual with AIDS as a situation where we can restore hope. We need to help the victims with AIDS survive and help them to obtain a means of income. By bringing AIDS victims treatment, it gives them so much hope and self-worth.

The Interview Girl Foundation hopes to slice off a piece of the misery in Africa by helping the Africans to have improved health care, education, and small businesses supported and run by locals within the community. In improving the health care, education, and local businesses in Africa, Africans suffering from HIV/AIDS are given hope that they can overcome their deadly illness. Too many people say that the cycle of poverty cannot be broken. It can. With a little pointing in the right direction (help from others), it can be broken. When certain miseries are eliminated, people can begin to make changes in their world. At the Interview Girl Foundation, it is our philosophy to help individuals start a process, but then the people will live their lives by sustaining themselves in their community. There is no magic way to cure ills such as poverty or AIDS. The Interview Girl Foundation believes that by providing life-altering products and services to people, they can then change their own lives. This is how the cycle of poverty is broken: Eliminating someone's misery—one person at a time. InterviewGirl.com's mission is to learn more, earn more, and then give more and because of the Interview Girl Foundation's work, a movement in order to eliminate the misery that someone suffering from AIDS lives with was set into motion. The Interview Girl Foundation's projects exhibit what can be done to bring about real change in Africa for people living in misery dealing with poverty or AIDS.

> "If you are successful, it is because somewhere, sometime, someone gave you a life or an idea that started you in the right direction. Remember also that you are indebted to life until you help some less fortunate person, just as you were helped."
>
> —Melinda Gates

InterviewGirl.com in the Future

"To the world you may just be one person, but it takes only one person to make a difference in the world …"

—Anonymous

It was paramount for *Operation A²* to develop a plan that would bring about results. The Interview Girl Foundation does not have the perfect solution to a misery such as all the people suffering from AIDS, but we have ideas and we will keep trying these designs one by one. In each idea that we try, we are hoping to help and make a difference in someone's life. All the questions that I was coming up with surrounding extreme poverty and the AIDS dilemma, the research I completed concerning the debate that existed: Does foreign aid work?, and my relentlessly digging to hear peoples' stories were all vital in shaping the Interview Girl Foundation as it formed. The Interview Girl Foundation is not a business or a charity, but it is an organization that combines aspects of both. The Interview Girl Foundation endeavors to achieve social good where misery exists. It completes altruistic efforts as if it was a private charity while generating revenue in pursuit of making the world a better place. Our programs are based on well researched strategies. We have a long term plan and solution in place. However, the Interview Girl Foundation's programs are willing to concede to any shortcomings in our ideas and our programs will continually be willing to change the game "plan" as life unfolds. Our ideas and their implementation will change based on needs that people have. For example, as new innovations and technologies become a part of society, best practices to bring about social change will emerge. The Interview Girl Foundation will change how it does things based on what develops in society as the years pass. There isn't one solution to dealing with social problems that exist in a society. There is not one answer to solving the AIDS crisis and the dilemma of poverty. Microfinance would not be the magic solution for the Interview Girl Foundation, but rather one useful tool that some people somewhere can utilize. The world is comprised of different communities of people who come from diverse cultures. The needs of a group of people together with their environment creates a culture that exists in a community. This is why unique societies emerged in ancient Greece and ancient Mesopotamia, for example. The Greeks and the Sumerians had different cultural practices that sustained them. People need solutions to specific miseries that they experience in their particular community. We cannot forget this. The Interview Girl Foundation cannot expect to show up and dictate anything, rather we can assist by providing necessary assistance, programs, and tools.

> "Whenever I see people doing something the way it's always been done, the way it's 'supposed' to be done, following the same old trends, well, that's just a big red flag to me to go look somewhere else."
>
> —Mark Cuban

The Interview Girl Foundation understands that indeed we need more than good intentions. We plan to achieve more than good intentions, but as Dean Karlan and Jacob Appel argue, we may fail, but we will learn from our mistakes and then we will get up again. Just like Albert Einstein and Thomas Edison did each time that they failed. The Interview Girl Foundation will take each failure as a lesson to do better next time. Each new project at the Interview Girl Foundation will test new theories and hopefully lasting strides can be made and if not, someone will have learned from our mistakes. Someone else will pick up where we left off and do better. We will try, fail, and then try again and in the process hopefully make a difference. We will continually work to eliminate someone's misery when we see that it exists. The Interview Girl Foundation knows that there is always hope to change things and get rid of miseries that someone out there lives with in their life.

I spent the past year steeped in research trying to come up with a plan that would not be flawed so that the Interview Girl

Foundation would and could be a nonprofit with more than good intentions. I realize that in our efforts to eliminate misery, not everything will work perfectly and that's okay because someone will pick up where we left off and do better. They will add on to our initial idea and over time hopefully miseries can be eliminated. In an interview with John H. Ostdick from *Success* magazine, Jacqueline Novogratz explains to him regarding her work at Acumen, "For it's all part of a grand plan, even if the original playbook got tossed thousands of miles ago."[217] The plan is always going to change. The Interview Girl Foundation needs to be open to this. In reflecting on her experiences, Novogratz makes known, "I learned that micro enterprise is an important part of the solution, but it is not the only part. I also learned that traditional charity alone can't solve the problems of poverty." *Operation A²* has asked good questions and has a mission to eliminate misery by reaching out to help one person at a time. We hope that what we do will make a lasting difference, but we know for sure that each and every story that we collect and share through InterviewGirl. com has the capacity to touch someone's life. As the Interview Girl Foundation works to eliminate the misery that an orphan with AIDS has, InterviewGirl.com will share stories because we are certain that stories benefit us all.

> "If you want to succeed, you should strike out on new paths, rather than travel the worn paths of accepted success."
>
> —John Rockefeller

> "Done is better than perfect."
>
> —Mark Zuckerberg

A part of InterviewGirl.com's future plans are not just to print stories, but to share stories through the internet, pod casts, TV, and video. Reading a story is extremely valuable, but something special happens when one hears a story. Think back to the story about Abraham Lincoln and his love for storytelling. Louis P. Masur remarks,

> "Even where, as with Strong's account, we can verify a story or joke as being told by Lincoln, we are handicapped by being able only to read it, not hear it. A visitor once remarked that Lincoln's stories seemed dull in print, "unless you could give also the dry chuckle with which they are accompanied, and the gleam in the speaker's eye, as, with the action habitual to him, he rubs his hand down the side.""[218]

Hearing people share stories resonates with individuals. The oral storytelling tradition has power in it. Many stories will also circulate as the public visually sees and audibly hears interviews completed by InterviewGirl.com through various technological mediums.

Essentially, InterviewGirl.com hopes to begin conversations between individuals. A physicist, David Bohm completed research on the lives of Einstein, Heisenberg, Pauli, and Bohr. He drew the conclusion that their incredible breakthroughs took place through simple, open, and honest conversation.[219] The importance of dialogue can be traced back to Socrates from ancient Greece. In Greek the word dialogue means talking through. The Greeks believed that the key to establishing dialogue is to exchange ideas without trying to change the other person's mind. The basic rules of dialogue for the Greeks were "Don't argue," Don't interrupt," and "Listen carefully."[220] As InterviewGirl.com releases stories and projects that it puts together and as people read and listen to other peoples' stories, conversations can begin as people are introduced to new perspectives about the world. Just by individuals beginning to have conversations with one another and authentically listening to one another, the world can become a better place.

Your Action Plan

"The artist is not a special person; every person is a special kind of artist."

—Michael Michalko

There are a lot of programs out there that are working to make the world a better place, but misery still exists, so we need to keep working to eliminate these miseries. The world needs to do something to help those living in misery. One of InterviewGirl. com's compilations is a project about people completing service through organizations and charities throughout the world. Please check out this project to see what social entrepreneurs, volunteers, and philanthropists are completing through non-profit organizations that exist in our world.[221] If you have a topic or an idea that you believe needs help, we can help you to collect information on this topic, put together a compilation of stories, sell the compilations and then we can give the cause the profits that come from this endeavor. *Operation A²—Aiding AIDS* is one project through the Interview Girl Foundation. *Operation A²* is a program that can make a difference in the world by working to make the life of orphans with HIV/AIDS better. More than we need to create more programs to eliminate various miseries, we need to identify and recognize those programs throughout the world that are working effectively to bring about change. We need all of these notable efforts to collaborate together. The Interview Girl Foundation is working to help bring social entrepreneurs from across organizations throughout the world together (*Project: C²: Committed Collaboration*).

A large part of Chapter twelve and thirteen were dedicated to describing the Interview Girl Foundation's *Operation A²— Aiding AIDS*. The initial profits from the initial compilations will be helping the victims of HIV (and in order to help HIV victims, *Operation A²* is targeting problematic issues in Africa, in general), but as time progresses, the possibilities of whom the

Interview Girl Foundation can help are endless. The Interview Girl Foundation is not just a program to help the orphans who need help in Africa, but the foundation was created to eliminate misery in this world. It is not just a charity that sends money hoping it will achieve some good. In his book about humanitarian doctors, Dan Bartolotti writes, "The world of aid is dominated by big institutional actors who can lose sight of individual suffering." *Doctors Without Borders* has the term "sans frontiers" because you have to be willing to cross a border to attend to suffering. The Interview Girl Foundation agrees with *Doctors Without Borders* when it comes to helping individuals who are suffering. This foundation believes that solutions to social issues come from well thought out questions that address the underlying causes of these issues. The Interview Girl Foundation was created to help people who experience misery, but to do this in a way where solutions are well researched and designed to make a difference. Ultimately, the Interview Girl Foundation is a non-profit organization that combines the best qualities that charities, private foundations, and businesses have to offer.

No matter how bad you have it. Someone has it worse. What can you do today to make someone's misery better? InterviewGirl. com's mission is to get everyone to slice off a piece of misery in this world. Orphans suffering from AIDS and victims of human trafficking are whom we started to help through *Operation A^2*, but the Interview Girl Foundation's altruistic efforts won't end here. Going back to the "world is a cake" analogy, one slice at a time, we'll proceed to help different people. I would like to interview all sorts of interesting individuals from whom people cannot wait to hear, and then I want to donate the profits from selling these valuable interviews to help slice off a piece of the misery in this world. However, our profits will not be donated just to be donated, but they will be used for projects that bring about social good based on what evidence establishes actually does the greatest good.

Sometimes in life, you meet a particular person, in a particular spot. Your path crosses their path and then your life is never the same. We never know whom we will meet and how they will affect us. I could have gone anywhere last summer, but I went to Africa. My brief rendezvous with Amara as well as the other children in Kpando transformed me. The stories that I came home with changed my life because I felt compelled to make a difference after meeting the orphans at the Children's Home. My plan to make this difference is through sharing stories. If you share a story with me and pass on the word about InterviewGirl.com, one story at a time, we will slice off a piece of misery in this world. Anything that needs to be accomplished in our lives begins with a plan. Your action plan: Go to www.InterviewGirl.com, read through our projects, choose one, and share a story. You may also click other and tell us your story and we will start a new project. Or you can go to www.InterviewGirl.com and click on the Interview Girl Foundation's *Operation A²—Aiding AIDS* and make a donation. By you sharing your story, we move toward the inestimable progress that we hope to make. The "Pay It Forward" effect is in full swing.

"Let us not love with words or tongue but with actions and in truth."

—1 John 3:18

CHAPTER FOURTEEN

Lessons from Interview Girl

Lessons from Interview Girl as a History student

"There is no history of mankind, there are only many histories of all kinds of aspects of human life."

—Karl Popper

The Interview Girl Foundation is sedulously working to relieve misery in this world. From people suffering from AIDS, victims of human trafficking, and all those whose lives are shortened by the poverty cycle, the foundation creates projects to help eliminate these miseries. Looking at all the problems that certain people in the world are facing, it may seem overwhelming with where to begin slicing away at the misery. As you delve into the problems that the orphans in Africa are experiencing, you may think that it's impossible to undo injustices such as poverty, AIDS, or human trafficking. That kind of thinking isn't going to get us anywhere! Throughout human civilization, we have witnessed numerous people who have changed the course of history and influenced their sphere of living by their charisma, hard work, strong faith, intelligence and talent to name a few traits. Through geographical expansion, art and entertainment, science and technology, literature, politics, statesmanship or games and sports, these individuals have created history by their work. Great explorers like Vasco Da Gama and Columbus discovered new lands. Alexander the Great almost conquered the whole world. Geniuses like Aristotle, Leonardo Da Vinci, and Albert Einstein expanded the horizon of knowledge by introducing the public to new thoughts and inventions.

As both a student of History and a History teacher, I have been studying the history of the world. "What are the greatest lessons that we can learn from studying the most well-known individuals throughout World History?" is the question that I have been cogitating the last few years. The greatest and most successful people throughout human history have common traits. You too can learn these traits. It is part of InterviewGirl.com's mission to produce compilations and books that help you to learn and to become a better version of yourself. As Interview Girl, I have taken the greatest lessons from all of History and coupled this information with the stories and information that people share with me during the interviews that I have been completing. Together the stories that I've collected from the people who I've studied within History along with the people who I've interviewed, will allow you to learn some new lessons and to hear some stupendous stories.

As a student of History, I learned some of life's transcendent lessons. Ultimately, I learned that throughout history, there were ordinary people who did extraordinary things. This is an important lesson for you to remember. The most exceptional feats and deeds of civilization as we know it today were completed by ordinary people who did extraordinary things. Most people think there are a few extraordinary people who have lived throughout human history, but really when you dig a little deeper, you learn that throughout human history, ordinary people do extraordinary things. Below are stories about ordinary people who did extraordinary things in the history of our humanity.

Guess Who? You will find the answers on the next page:

1) 27 publishers rejected his first book. This man became legend through his children's books.

2) This man gave up a medical career. His Father told him, "You care for nothing but shooting, dogs and rat catching." He later became the father of modern biology.

3) This boy handled the violin awkwardly. His teacher called him "hopeless as a composer," while he was completely deaf; he wrote five of his greatest symphonies.

4) Disneyland was rejected by the city of Anaheim. This man was bankrupt several times. He famously has said, "All our dreams can come true, if we have the courage to pursue them."

5) She lost her hearing and vision at age 18 months. She was an author and humanitarian.

6) He was thrown from a horse and broke two ribs. Two days later he broke a world record.

7) His Aunt Mimi said that he would never make a living playing guitar.

8) He was kicked out of school for asking too many questions.

9) A single mother on welfare who decided to picked up a pen and paper and write a story.

10) At age 10, the only word he knew in English was "shoe."

11) He flew over 200 different types of aircraft, but is known for a single step.

12) He wanted to go into business making watches.

13) Born to migrants, his motto was, "Si, se peude." "Yes, it can be done."

14) He sold his Volkswagen to build 50 circuit boards.

15) He didn't talk until the age of 3.

16) Started a movie company with $750. He went on to win 32 Oscars.

17) She sat in the front of the bus.

18) He was denied an appointment to Annapolis.

BECAUSE THE MEDICINE RAN OUT

19) Waived the director's fee in exchange for licensing rights.
20) Critics said that she lacked focus and skills.
21) He missed the final shot in his High School Championship game.
22) She was the only women in the race.
23) Dropped out of Harvard to work on a little business idea.
24) She found her life's calling at age 12. [222]

1) Dr. Seuss
2) Charles Darwin
3) Ludwig van Beethoven
4) Walt Disney
5) Helen Keller
6) Chuck Yeager, Test Pilot
7) John Lenin, Musician, composer
8) Thomas Edison, inventor
9) J.K. Rowling
10) Jerry Yang, Co-founder of Yahoo
11) Neil Armstrong, astronaut
12) Henry Ford, auto maker
13) Cesar Chavez, activist
14) Steve Jobs, CEO Apple Computer
15) Einstein, scientist ($E = mc^2$)
16) Walt Disney, Animator / Film Maker
17) Rosa Parks, Civil Rights Leader
18) Dwight Eisenhower, Supreme Allied Commander
19) George Lucas, Film maker / billionaire
20) Michelle Kwan, 5 world championships
21) John Wooden, 10 NCAA Titles
22) Danica Patrick, Indy Driver
23) Bill Gates, CEO Microsoft, Humanitarian
24) Mother Teresa, Nun, Humanitarian

One of the prominent lessons that I learned as a history student is that ordinary people do extraordinary things. As a student of history, I started out with the goal to study: what common traits do the most successful people who have lived and walked this Earth throughout the history of human civilization have in common? The traits that stuck out were hard work, determination, perseverance, and effort. My research informed me that indeed history isn't filled with a few extraordinary people, but rather a few ordinary people in societies throughout civilization have decided to do extraordinary things or those people had extraordinary tenacity and work ethic. Most people have the perception that certain people are born with supernatural traits. The truth is that it is ordinary people who do extraordinary things in their lives. Success in anything has one fundamental aspect: effort. Usually perseverance, hard work, dedication, and commitment lead to these individuals' accomplishments.

As a student many years ago, I remember my first history textbook and wondering why certain names were in bold letters. I wondered how the textbook authors decided who gets their name in bold. Florence Nightingale is a name that is in bold in every history book. As a high school student, I remember thinking that she was this extraordinary person and she must have been way different than me. She must have been a genius because her concerns for sanitation, military health and hospital planning established practices which are still in existence today. As I read, as I learned about her life, as I came to understand Nightingale's story, it turns out that she wrote letters — hundreds of letters. What is even more interesting about Nightingale's story is she not only wrote letters, but she was bedridden and she still did all this revolutionary work and founded modern nursing in the process.

During the 1840's, low moral standards were associated with nursing. Mr. Nightingale would not allow his daughter, Florence to work as a nurse in Salisbury Hospital like she wanted to. Nightingale was finally permitted to accept an unpaid position as superintendent of the Institution for the Care of Sick Gentlewomen in London. She gained a reputation for an excellent administrator. In the fall of 1854, England went to war (Crimea) with Russia. Around this time in history, war journalism was happening and the English public began to hear about wounded soldiers in the Crimean campaign being left to die without basic medical attention. In October of 1854, Sidney Herbert, secretary of war, sent Nightingale a letter asking her if she would take charge of nursing in the military hospitals in Scutari, a district of Istanbul. From Herbert's correspondence, she was able to help British soldiers during the Crimean War. Nightingale arrived in

Scutari in November and she found the military hospitals not to be functioning. The barracks and general hospitals contained almost 2,400 sick and wounded soldiers. The basic surgical and medical supplies were unavailable. The soldiers laid in filthy clothes. The hospital barracks were infested with rats and fleas. Cholera, typhus, and dysentery were endemic. Deaths were not being properly recorded. Nightingale reorganized the military hospitals in Scutari.

Nightingale suffered from Crimean fever during the war. She suffered from frequent fainting fits, physical exhaustion, and remained bedridden for the rest of her life. From her sofa, she wrote many letters and memos and she greeted countless visitors. She did not recover from the fever she suffered in her thirties. For five and a half decades until her death in 1910, she was often too weak to stand, yet she authored an estimated 12,000 letters, 200 books, reports, and monographs. Nightingale established standards for sanitation and hospital management that still affect the world. Nightingale's 1860 book *Notes on Nursing: What it is and What it is not?* is still assigned to nursing students today. Nightingale preferred working behind the scenes to get laws changed. She began the process that transformed nursing into a modern profession. Florence Nightingale wasn't born extraordinary. Nor was anyone else who will be presented in this chapter. She was an ordinary female who did extraordinary things because she had the tenacity to do the work. She saw a problem first hand: thousands of men were dying because of lack of order, cleanliness, and adequate supplies in the hospitals in Scutari. Nightingale did not just complain about this problem, but she took actions to play a part in fixing it.

Many people believe that they don't have what it takes to make a difference in the world. They believe only people like Mahatma Gandhi, Mother Theresa, Thomas Edison, Albert Einstein, Bill Gates, and the likes, are capable of making a difference. The truth is, every one of us is put in this world to contribute and make a difference to the world in our own inimitable way. It need not be anything out of the world. It just needs to be something you do with the intention of "doing good," paying it forward, or serving others. This is central to InterviewGirl.com's philosophy. If everyone does a small something, sizeable changes can be made over time. Each and every one of us can make a difference in the world. Historical scholarship enlightened me that history is filled with some miraculous and remarkable stories and when those stories are told, history comes alive. We can all learn valuable life lessons from these stories. Being a student of history has taught me some valuable lessons. I hope that you will find the following historical lessons and stories (listed below) as fascinating as I did. Just learning how the following people used a notebook will get you thinking.

Lesson One: Write it Down

Write it down. Write what? Write down your thoughts, your to-do's, your goals, your memories, your ideas, this list can go on. This is one of the greatest lessons that I learned as a student of history. People who are considered to be history's greatest creators all used notebooks. Maria Popova, the writer behind *Brain Pickings*, a highly influential and addictive curation of the best content from the web and beyond, writes that "the to-do list might be the secret to willpower, and it is certainly an essential tool of creativity, as anyone from Leonardo da Vinci to John Lennon can attest." Let's look at some of history's note takers.

Mark Twain kept 40-50 pocket notebooks for over four decades of his life. He often began one before embarking on a trip. He filled the notebooks with observations of people he met, thoughts on religion and politics, drawings and sketches of what he saw on his travels, potential plots for books, and even ideas for inventions (he filed 3 patents during his lifetime). Many of his entries consist of the short, witty, pithy sentences he is famous for. He felt that if he did not write such things down as they came to his mind he would quickly forget them. He would also record in his notebooks what had happened that day, such as what he had eaten and who he had seen.

I remember hearing that while working on a draft for *Stars Wars*, director George Lucas confined himself for 8 hours a day in his writing room. It was interesting to learn that he also carried a pocket notebook with him at all times so he could write down ideas, words, and plot angles on the go. Names like Jawa and Wookie began as quick scribbles in Lucas' notebook. Like Twain, George Lucas too carried around a notebook.

Isaac Newton began his habit of keeping a notebook as a boy. He would write out lists of words and recipes for things like colored dyes. When he arrived at Cambridge as an undergraduate, students were encouraged to keep a large commonplace book in which they recorded all their notes and acquired knowledge. As you learned earlier, Newton took his Cambridge tutor's advice and started a set of small notebooks, each dedicated to a specific subject—theology, mathematics, chemistry, and philosophy. Newton's method of inquiry was to pose a question, study and analyze all the evidence, and record his deductions in his notebooks. Newton had an obsession for organizing and categorizing information. According to Brett and Kate McKay, he would typically lay out his notebooks by listing the subjects he wished to study throughout the book and then entering notes under the headings as he learned and gathered new knowledge. He would also start in on both ends of the notebook at once, covering different subjects on each end and numbering the front half with Roman numerals and the end half with Arabic numerals. He would then return later to fill in the blank middle section with a different subject.[223] Of all of the people throughout history who have used notebooks, Newton's use of the notebook was particularly intriguing for me because of his obsession for organizing and categorizing information. Organizing and categorizing information is a substantial part of the work completed at InterviewGirl.com.

John D. Rockefeller had a passion for detailed bookkeeping. He loved to meticulously study his record books and journals. He was constantly trying to figure out ways to make his business more efficient; he was never satisfied with the status quo. Rockefeller took his notebook on tours of his refineries and processing plants. He carefully observed the plants as he made notes of ways things could be improved. He always followed up on these ideas.

Thomas Alva Edison is one of America's most famous inventors and another individual who wrote a great deal of his thoughts and ideas down. Everything Edison invented was written down in excellent detail in 3,500 notebooks. These notebooks included laboratory records, early drafts of patent applications, letters, photos of models, and other memorabilia. Historians were able to trace the invention process from the first thought of an idea jotted down in his notebook, through the experiments, and ending with a finished mass-produced product.

In 1978 eight historians wanted to look at all of Edison's notebooks, sketches, and drawings. These historians were the first people to look at the documents since Edison died. They were told there were over a million pages of documents. The historians thought it would take about 10 years to put the papers on microfilm and in a book. Their plan is known as the "Edison Papers Project." As the historians began work on the project, they discovered that the dusty stacks of papers were a mess. Many hadn't been touched since Edison's death. The historians went from building to building, room to room, drawer to drawer. It took more than a year just to find all the papers. They found four to five million pages in the paper collection. Needless to say it took much longer than 10 years.

Many of Thomas Edison's greatest ideas only emerged after he had made hundreds of drawings and cartoons. General Electric has a collection of Edison's sketches and doodles that he made about the electric light bulb. Most of them are undecipherable, but the important thing to remember is that each of them had meaning for Edison and moved his thinking along closer and closer to his discoveries.[224]

Martha Graham created her own dance vocabulary with simple drawings and sketches. Her notebooks are full of drawings and sketches of her ideas and thoughts, which enabled her to conceptualize them without using words. Martha Graham is considered to be a genius in modern dance.[225]

Keeping a notebook, writing things down is a definite commonality that shines through as we study history's "greats," those individuals who we remember years later. Writing is often used as a healing tool. In looking at people struggling with eating disorders, obsessive compulsive disorder and other addictions, writing has been proven to be one of the best therapies. People always have success with writing things down. For this reason, journaling is an integral component that is part of many diets for those who are struggling with their weight. This same concept goes for people who have financial problems. When people are struggling with money, they're asked to jot down each and every time that they spend money. As Susan Love describes, "The pen is mightier than the sword when it comes to hacking your way out of a jungle of problems."[226] From losing weight to psychological problems, keeping a diary and recording thoughts has helped millions of people in overcoming their issues.

How a to-do list can make people more productive and the effectiveness of check-lists are widely discussed within success literature. In one of his bestsellers, Dr. Atul Gawande shows what the simple idea of the checklist reveals about the complexity of our lives and how we can deal with it. Knowledge and facts are omnipresent in the world today. The know-how is there for us within society, yet avoidable failures continue to plague us in many organized activities. Avoidable failures happen in health care, government, law, and the financial industry. In Checklist Manifesto, Dr. Gawande argues that the reason is simple: the volume and complexity of knowledge today has exceeded our ability as individuals to properly deliver it to people—consistently, correctly, safely. We train longer, specialize more, use ever-advancing technologies, and still we fail. Gawande makes a compelling argument that we can do better, using the simplest of methods: the checklist. Through the stories that he shares from the operating room table to how pilots fly planes, he reveals what checklists can do and how they could bring about striking improvements in a variety of fields, from medicine and disaster recovery to professions and businesses of all kinds. The insights that Gawande purports are making a difference. Already, a simple surgical checklist from the World Health Organization designed by the ideas described in Gawande's book has been adopted in more than twenty countries as a standard for care and has been heralded as "the biggest clinical invention in thirty years."[227] In *Checklist Manifesto*, Dr. Gawande argues that the complexities of technology in the 21st century may be best handled by the simplest solution like a checklist. Keeping track of what you are doing through writing, such as using a check list simplifies even the most complex of tasks such as surgery.

One lesson that you can immediately take away from Interview Girl as a History student is to "write it down." Write down your to do's, your thoughts, your goals, your finances, your grocery list, your memories, really the list of what you can write down could be enduring, but just write it down. There is something magical that happens when that pen hits the paper. You'll heap great rewards if you begin keeping notebooks. And yes in the 21st century, you can take your notes on your smart phone, tablet or IPad. There are many applications in our modern society that make "writing it down" convenient for us. As Interview Girl, I have numerous notebooks. I am always making observations. I am always asking questions. This role just seems logical for me. It sincerely fits me. Analyzing the notebooks and sketchbooks of some of history's greatest creators, we see that these famous people took copious notes. They kept notebooks. You should too. There are certain trends with certain people in history that cannot be denied. As all the individuals discussed above did as well as Leonardo DaVinci, Charles Darwin, and Einstein, you too should write it down.

Lesson Two: Ask the Right Questions

"If birds can glide for long periods of time, then... why can't I?"

—Orville Wright

As a historical figure, Socrates teaches us about the importance of questioning. Going back to Ancient Greece, Socrates and his pupils understood that the root of education and understanding goes back to questioning. Socrates was a Greek philosopher who is considered to be one of the greatest and most important philosophers who ever lived. The interesting thing is that he left no writings at all. Most of what we know about his life and work comes from the writings of his disciples, Plato and Xenophon. Socrates engaged in the questioning of his students in an unending search for truth. He sought to get to the foundations of his students' and colleagues' views by asking continual questions until a contradiction was exposed, thus proving the fallacy of the initial assumption. This became known as the Socratic Method, and may be Socrates' most enduring contribution to philosophy. Socratic seminars are used in advanced university courses throughout the world today.

"Understanding a question is half an answer."

—Socrates

Thomas Alva Edison is one of America's most famous inventors and another inquisitive individual about everything surrounding him. Edison saw huge change take place in his lifetime and the fascinating part is that he was responsible for making many of those changes occur. His inventions created and contributed to modern night lights, movies, telephones, records and CDs. Edison is most famous for his development of the first electric light bulb. When Edison was born, electricity had not been developed. By the time he died, entire cities were lit by electricity. Much of the credit for electricity goes to Edison. Edison truly was a genius. How is it that Edison did all that he did? He asked the right questions. He was a very curious child who asked a lot of questions. The story behind Edison's initial schooling is that he began school in Port Huron, Michigan when he was seven. His teacher considered "Thomas to be a dull student who asked too many questions." It is believed that math was Edison's least favorite subject. When the teacher told his mother that Thomas couldn't learn, Edison's mom became angry at the teacher's strict ways. She took her son out of school and decided to home-school him. Edison was a home-schooled, self-educated person. Edison understood that education was his own responsibility. He learned to be persistent, he learned reading was very important, he learned from watching others, he learned that science is fun, and he learned that education is something that lasts your whole life.

Edison hung around railroad yards, newspaper offices, and machine shops. He worked in a jewelry shop and at telegraph offices. He worked with clockwork, printing equipment, and different telegraphy instruments. He studied and experimented with these tools during his spare time. He became an expert on the telegraph. The more he learned about telegraphy, the more he wanted to learn. He took apart equipment and reassembled it until he understood how it worked. He experimented with ways to make it better. Ultimately, when he did not understand things, he asked questions. He constantly questioned and with these questions came brilliant inventions like: the light bulb and phonograph. His inventions deeply affected the shaping of modern society. Some people say he single-handedly invented the 20th century. Edison's nature to question things undoubtedly contributed to his genius discoveries.

It was also in Charles Darwin's nature to question things. As Darwin once remarked to C. Lyell, "Looking back, I think it was more difficult to see what the problems were than to solve them." In *Borrowing Brilliance*, David Murray gives the example that when Darwin said that it was more difficult to see the problems than it was to solve them, Darwin was referring to understanding that there are many problems woven together and in order to alleviate one problem, you must address another problem.[228] Ultimately, you solve problems by asking the correct questions. Darwin was aware of the problems with problems. Darwin did not just think of a problem in isolation, but rather he "understood their entire hierarchy."[229] To return to lesson one for a moment (keep a notebook and write things down), we know that Darwin continually asked questions because Darwin's notebooks survive today and they are filled with pages of questions and problem definitions.

Albert Einstein is another individual who emulates the importance of questioning. When Einstein thought about a problem, he always found it necessary to formulate his subject in as many different ways as possible. He was once asked what he would do if he knew that a huge comet would hit and totally destroy the earth in one hour. Einstein said that he would spend fifty-five minutes figuring out how to formulate the question and five minutes solving it.[230]

Thwink.org is dedicated to solving the sustainability problem with root cause analysis. *Thwink.org* describes Modern Activism as:

1. "Ready—Define the problem.
2. Aim—Analyze the problem with Root Cause Analysis.
3. Fire—Develop and implement solutions that can't miss."[231]

Thwink.org believes that "solving the sustainability problem is not a matter of doing the same things better, but it's a matter of doing something different—radically different." The thinkers behind *Thwink.org* purport that countless solutions to the environmental sustainability problem have been tried over the last forty years. While there have been some small successes, the overall problem has not been solved. They explain that the global ecological footprint is at 50% overshoot and rising, with no credible solution in sight. Individuals from *Thwink.org* view popular solutions as not able to resolve root causes underlying the environmental sustainability problem. They site how root cause analysis has worked well for business problems. The founders of *Thwink.org* challenge the public with asking, "Why can't it work for large-scale social system problems like sustainability? All problems arise from their root causes." The Modern Activism that *Thwink.org* describes begins with people defining the problems. Defining the problems correctly starts with people asking on the button questions. When the right questions are asked, then root cause analysis can take place and then solutions can be implemented.

In your life, ask questions. Seek to learn new things. Don't focus on why something is not happening. Instead focus on how to make something else happen. Question, question, and question some more. Asking questions is another important lesson that I can share with you from Interview Girl as a History student.[232]

"Wisdom begins with Wonder."

—Socrates

"We were lucky enough to grow up in an environment where there was always much encouragement to children to pursue intellectual interests; to investigate whatever aroused curiosity."

—Orville Wright

Lesson Three: Continual, Unrelenting Effort Often Produces Dramatic Results

"No. Don't give up hope just yet. It's the last thing to go. When you have lost hope, you have lost everything. And when you think all is lost, when all is dire and bleak, there is always hope."

—Pittacus Lore, *I Am Number Four*

To put it very simply: being able to stick with it is often times the trick between those who succeed and those who do not. This is a trait that many people who "we remember in history" have in common. A business friend once asked Edison about the secret to his success. Edison replied, "Genius is hard work, stick-to-itiveness, and common sense." However, Edison's "common sense" was very uncommon. More patents were issued to Edison than have been issued to any other single person in U.S. history: 1,093. Edison continually put effort into his endeavors.[233]

When I was on the high school track team, to get us pumped up at the beginning of the season, the coach presented the word *tenacity* to our team and explained what it meant. Tenacity means persistence, perseverance, steadfastness, what it takes, resolve, obstinacy, backbone, application, intransigence, pertinacity, and resoluteness. The coach of my track team was trying to make the point that as athletes we needed to have persistence and no matter how hard the practices got, we could not give up and we had to persist. We needed to imagine achieving the end result of what we wanted to achieve at the end of our season during the hard times mid-season.

Thomas Edison, Johannes Kepler, Albert Einstein, Sir Isaac Newton, and Linus Pauling are some historical figures who are all known for their tenacity. In interviewing the elderly in nursing homes for various InterviewGirl.com projects, when I would ask couples who were married for 40, 50, 60, or even 70 years what their secret was to a successful marriage, they would attribute their 40, 50, 60, or 70 year marriages to "sticking it out through the difficult times." Continual, unrelenting effort often produces dramatic results is another life lesson that I learned as a History student and a lesson that I learned as Interview Girl that will bring you far in your life.

Here are some other historical examples that prove into order to get unprecedented results, you need to put in effort day after day after day. Andrew Wiles worked for seven years before he proved Pierre de Fermat's Last Theorem. For centuries this was a proof that eluded thousands of mathematicians. Richard Gatling spent four years working on a machine gun before he succeeded. Nikola Tesla, the inventor of alternating current, regularly worked from ten in the morning straight through until five the next morning, seven days a week.[234] Having perseverance and sticking to something is a trait that many times in life makes one person succeed over any other. This is an important lesson that should not be forgotten. Many of the individuals presented throughout this chapter have the remarkable stories that they do because they never gave up on what it was that they wanted to achieve.

> "We wrote to a number of the best known automobile manufacturers in an endeavor to secure a motor for the new machine. Not receiving favorable answers from any of these we proceeded to design a motor of our own."
> —Orville Wright

The story of the Wright brothers illustrates an unrelenting tenacity and a will not to give up. For thousands of year's human flight was just a dream. It was considered the very definition of the impossible, but two young men set the impossible as their goal and forever changed the world. It was not smooth sailing for the Wright brothers. They built seven flying machines and crashed each more than once. Frustration and disappointment seemed more overwhelming after each attempt, yet they never stopped believing. George W. Melville, the chief engineer of the US Navy said, "Wings .... If God had intended that man should fly, he would have given him wings."[235] This was the common belief as the Wright brothers pursued their dream of flying a plane. A flying toy, a gift from their father, sparked a lifelong interest for the brothers. They worked in a bicycle shop, but they pursued flight as a hobby. Along the way, the hobby became a passion that relentlessly drove them to try new things, to challenge conventional wisdom, and to continually strive harder and reach further.

After each failure, they rebuilt and modified their efforts, continually applying what they had learned. Like very great success, manned flight was the result of false starts, detours and dead ends. Through the disappointments and doubts, determined perseverance and an unwavering belief in their dream led them on. In December 1903 a *New York Times* editorial questioned the intelligence of the Wright Brothers who were trying to invent a machine, heavier than air that would fly. "It simply defies the laws of physics," the editorial wrote. One week later, at Kitty Hawk, the Wright Brothers took their famous flight. On Dec. 17, 1903, in spite of dangerous gusts of wind and below freezing temperatures, they took a desperate gamble. If they wanted to be home by Christmas, they had to put their belief in the impossible into action. At 10:35 am, in a flight lasting only 12 seconds and covering just 120 feet, they did what men and women had only dreamed of doing for centuries .... They flew. They kept trying even after this. On the fourth attempt the plane landed 852 feet and 59 seconds from its starting point, snapping a support but otherwise undamaged. They achieved the impossible.

A monument in honor of their "first flight," erected on November 19, 1932, reads, "In commemoration of the conquest of the air by the brothers Wilbur and Orville Wright. Conceived by genius, achieved by dauntless resolution and unconquerable faith." As Jay Coulter suggests, "Like the Wright Brothers, it's time to dream the impossible, to set your goals with dauntless resolution, to put into action an unconquerable faith to achieve the impossible. When you do, you'll discover that maybe God does intend that men should fly!"[236]

The story of Wilbur and Orville Wright reveals how continual, unrelenting effort can produce dramatic results. The Wright Brothers never gave up on their desire to invent a machine that would fly. They persisted in the face of adversity. Even when everyone around them questioned their idea—they kept working on their dream. History has proven time and time again that continual, unrelenting effort often produces dramatic results. This is another one of history's greatest lessons.

"The difference between a successful person and others is not a lack of strength, not a lack of knowledge, but rather a lack of will."
—Vince Lombardi

"Rise and rise again until lambs become lions."
—Robin Hood

"It is possible to fly without motors, but not without knowledge and skill."
—Wilbur Wright

"Do not let yourself be forced into doing anything before you are ready."
—Wilbur Wright

Lesson Four: Never Give Up

"Never let your head hang down. Never give up or sit down and grieve. Find another way."
—Satchel Paige

Perhaps it's just another way to say that continual, unrelenting effort often produces dramatic results, but never giving up is another one of the greatest lessons that history teaches us. Sir Ernest Shackleton's expedition to the Antarctic with his crew of 28 men teaches us to never give up. The mission of Shackleton and his crew on their expedition was to cross the Antarctic on foot. At this time, that was something that was never done before.

Five months into the expedition their ship, the Endurance, became stuck in the heavy ice flows near Antarctica. It was not uncommon for ships to get stuck periodically in the ice flows and Shackleton believed that the ice would eventually recede and free the ship. His focus was on the expedition and he did not lose sight of what it was that he wanted to do. However, over the next three weeks the ship solidly became frozen in the ice. Attempts to free the ship were futile. At the end of February, 1915, the crew prepared the ship to become their camp for the remainder of winter. At this point, Shackleton abandoned his primary goal for the expedition and turned his focus toward returning to England. His expedition had become a rescue mission.

By October, eight months after being stuck, the pressure created by the ice finally took its toll on the Endurance. The ship began to come apart and sink; making it uninhabitable. The order to abandon ship was given and the entire crew began to salvage as many supplies as they could. They took the sled dogs, food, gear and three lifeboats and moved their camp to the ice flow next to their sinking ship.

At this point, the temperatures were brutal. The temperatures were around -15 degrees F on average. For the next five months, the expedition camped on the ice flow surviving on what little food they had left. In April, the ice flow that they were camped on began to break apart. Shackleton ordered the crew to take only essential supplies and board the life boats. They fled the disintegrating ice flow and traveled seven days by sea to Elephant Island. Elephant Island was a barren place to be stranded; made up mostly of rock covered snow with temperatures reaching -20°F.

For the next nine months, under Shackleton's leadership, the broken expedition remained on the island. Ultimately, Shackleton knew that their survival depended upon his ability to reach an outpost that was more than 800 miles across the most treacherous ocean seas in the world. Shackleton was determined to save his crew. Along with five crew members, Shackleton set out to make the journey. The odds of making it were 1 in 100. Nautical scholars consider this journey by lifeboat to be one of the greatest nautical accomplishments in maritime history. Shackleton successfully made it to the outpost and returned to Elephant Island with a rescue party four months later.

On August 30, 1916 after 22 months of being stranded on a barren rock in subzero temperatures, the crew of the Endurance was rescued. All twenty eight crew members survived the ordeal. Many of those crew members credit the strong faith that their leader had and his willingness to not give up as the reason why they survived. The odds were against Shackleton, but he never gave up. He eventually returned his crew to safety.[237] Shackleton's story is an example of someone who never gave up because he was determined to get his crew to safety.

"Adversity introduces a man to himself."
—Author Unknown

Abraham Lincoln is another historical figure who could be the epitome of the important historical lesson to "never give up." Some historians say that no U.S. president suffered more hardship than Abraham Lincoln because of his eight election failures and the civil war. Despite the challenges that Lincoln faced, throughout his presidency, he remained steadfast and committed to his beliefs and aims for the nation. Lincoln is quoted saying that if by the end of his term, "I have lost every other friend on earth, I shall at least have one friend left, and that friend shall be down inside of me." Abraham Lincoln did not give up during the difficult times. When people are asked to rate the four most influential or the "top" 4 U.S. Presidents, Abraham Lincoln continually ends up on that list.

Even if you do not know much about French impressionist art, you have most likely heard of Vincent Van Gogh. Vincent Van Gogh is also an historical example of someone who did not give up even though it seemed like he was not succeeding. Van Gogh only sold one painting in his lifetime and it was sold to a friend. Despite the fact that his paintings were not selling, he kept painting and finished over 800 pieces. Many people in our modern society admire Van Gough and want to buy his work and his most expensive painting is valued at $142.7 million.[238] Sir Ernest Shackleton, Abraham Lincoln, and Vincent Van Gogh never gave up on what it was that they wanted to achieve. You shouldn't give up either.

We should remember the importance of persistence in politics. Most appropriate given *Operation A²'s* cause (one that seems impractical at times): to provide medication to all orphans with HIV/AIDS living in poverty. As historian Hugh Thomas reminds us, "Persistence is the most important quality in politics. It was possessed in heroic quantity by Wilberforce."[239] William Wilberforce was an English member of parliament and social reformer who was very influential in the abolition of the slave trade and eventually slavery itself in the British empire.[240] Throughout the course of Wilberforce's plan to end the practice of slavery, he did not give up and continued to work toward this target, even though at times, his intentions seemed like they could never possibly come to fruition.

> "And human will is the strongest force ever created. There are those born to succeed and those who are determined to succeed. The former fall into it, and the latter pursue it all costs. They won't be denied. Nothing daunts them."
>
> —Sherrilyn Kenyon, *Invincible*

Lesson Five: It Has Happened Before and It Can Happen Again

History has proven time and time again that what starts with one individual can spread to many. As J. Michael Zenn declares, "Perhaps it starts with one person who tells another person; they grow into a few, a few becomes a group, a group becomes a crowd, a crowd becomes a mass, and a mass gives birth to a movement, a movement turns into a revolution." History teaches us that revolutions often happen when one person or a small group of people do something. This concept of "one person taking action can lead to boundless results" is one of the founding beliefs behind InterviewGirl.com as an organization. At InterviewGirl.com, it's our philosophy that each of us sharing a story can help us to create a movement to make the world a place with less misery. All of us can help to change the world as we reach out to eliminate the misery of one individual at a time through the Interview Girl Foundation.

History has exposed that the actions of a single individual, in time, can lead to starting a revolution. Below are some of those individuals:

- Twelve Jewish fishermen and a lowly carpenter turned the world upside down in one generation: *Jesus Christ*

- A French nineteen year old peasant girl once bravely raised a flag and repelled the armies of England, reclaiming her homeland for all time: *Joan of Arc*

- An Indian broke the bonds of English tyranny and freed his people from the most powerful nation of that era: *Gandhi*

- A housekeeper refused to give up her seat on a bus and sparked a movement that has brought freedom and equality to millions of people: *Rosa Parks* [241]

If it has happened before, it can happen again. Beyond question one person can make a difference in this world. We are reminded of how what starts with a few people taking actions can lend itself to becoming a larger movement with the story about a town in Poland during the 1980's.

Poland, 1982: Want to make a political statement? Take your television for a walk.

In an article, *10 Everyday Acts of Resistance That Changed the World*, Steve Crawshaw and John Jackson describe what Václav Havel called "the power of the powerless." They give examples of how regular people, from Denmark to Liberia, have stood up to power and won. The story that they share about citizens in Swidnik expresses how what starts with a small group can turn into a movement. What started in one town in Poland in the 1980's eventually spread to other towns and cities. The rise of Solidarity, a popular movement created in August 1980 by striking workers in the shipyards of Gdansk and across Poland, caused panic in the region that had ruled the country since the Second World War. On December 13, 1981, the Communist authorities put tanks on the streets to stop Solidarity once and for all. Hundreds were arrested; dozens were killed.

Despite the tanks and arrests, Poles organized protests against the ban on Solidarity, including a boycott of what they believed was the fiction-filled television news. You may be thinking that a boycott of the TV news could not by itself embarrass the government. Who could tell how many were obeying the boycott call? In a small town, Swidnik in eastern Poland, they found a way. Every evening, the inhabitants went on a walk. The streets would fill with Swidnikians, who walked and talked during the half-hour evening news. Before going out, some placed their switched-off television set in the window, facing onto the street. Others went a step further. They placed their disconnected set in a stroller or a builder's wheelbarrow, and took the television itself for a nightly outing. "If resistance is done by underground activists, it's not you or me," one Solidarity supporter later noted. "But if you see your neighbors taking their TV for a walk, it makes you feel part of something. An aim of dictatorship is to make you feel isolated. Swidnik broke the isolation and built confidence." The TV-goes-for-a-walk tactics spread to other towns and cities. The walkers irritated the government, however the authorities felt powerless to retaliate. Going for a walk was not, after all, an official crime under the criminal code. Eventually, the curfew was brought forward from 10 p.m. to 7 p.m., thus forcing Swidnikians to stay at home during the 7:30 news, or risk being arrested or shot. The citizens of Swidnik responded by going for a walk during the earlier edition of the news at 5 p.m. instead.[242] One group of people, even when it is a small group of people can start to change things within society. The citizens of Swidnik confirm that what a small group of individuals does can make a big difference. The group's actions have the power to motivate other people to join the group.

Movements Grow

History has proven time and time again that what starts with one individual can spread to many people as time passes. A very recent example of this is what happened with the Arab spring of 2011. As Steve Crawshaw and John Jackson write about Egypt and Tunisia,

> "Victories like this, born of small acts toward monumental change, are not new. Throughout history both recent and distant, ordinary people have found innovative and inspiring ways to challenge violent regimes and confront abuses of power: bringing down dictators, changing unjust laws, or simply giving individuals a renewed sense of their own humanity in the face of those who deny it."[243]

The citizens of Egypt and Tunisia played a role in changing the governments that were in place there.

Compassion International grew from the desire of one man to help children in need. Everett Swanson was moved by the plight of Korean orphans in the early 1950's. He went on to establish a program through which caring people could sponsor needy Korean children for a few dollars a month. In turn, those children would be provided benefits including food and clothing as needed, education, shelter, and health care. In 1952, that one man, Mr. Swanson released 35 children from poverty. By 1962, 35 children had become 10,000. By 1977, the number grew to 25,000. By 1998, the number grew to 250,000. In 2003, there were 500,000 sponsored children and 1,000, 000 children were sponsored in 2009. Everett Swanson authenticates that a movement that one person starts can turn into a movement that many people follow. Swanson's program was the basis for what became Compassion International (CI). CI's work has since expanded to 22 countries, including the United States, providing life-changing benefits for needy children with or without families.[244]

Catholic Relief Services celebrated its 70th anniversary in 2013. Catholic Relief Services has done some prodigious humanitarian work throughout the world. Childhood deaths in the developing world have been cut by 1/3 since 1990. Catholic Relief Services provides common immunizations to protect against common diseases like polio and measles and they save 3 million lives each year. Thanks to Catholic Relief Services, 15 million more children went to school in the last decade. Catholic Relief Services grew out of one church's goal to aid people. One church's mission has turned into today Catholic Relief Services having helped to save millions of lives.

All of the stories shared here highlight how small acts that people do make a big difference. History validates that small acts compiled together can in fact lead to monumental change. This lesson is particularly inspiring because InterviewGirl.com is based on the idea of the power of one. At the heart of InterviewGirl.com is the idea that the power of **one** story that is shared authentically can make a difference and the idea that by reaching out and helping to eliminate even **one** individual's misery, the Interview Girl Foundation will make a difference in this world.

Lesson Six: Overcoming Failure

"Many of life's failures are men who did not realize how close they were to success when they gave up."
—Thomas Edison

Through reading historical text books and primary source documents, history students come to understand the stories about individuals who have incomparably influenced our world. By learning these individuals' stories, we uncover the code to life's paramount lessons. One tried and true historical lesson that spans the ages is that one must fail in order to succeed. Individuals need to overcome failure and use this experience to then move forward in their lives. We have all been in History class. Certain people have their names in bold in the history book. A friend once asked me, "What is it that allows someone to be the person who get their name in bold in the history book? I mean millions of people live in a society, yet only a few names make their way into the standard history textbook." That was one of those exceptional questions that gets one thinking. In my estimation, someone gets their name in bold because the individual contributes to humanity in a way that outlasts his/her own lifetime. We learn about the feats and extraordinary accomplishments of these individuals, but if you "delve" a bit deeper, as a History student, I learned that before success for many of these individuals often times comes failure. This is a valuable lesson from history that we can all review.

> "Success is going from failure to failure without losing your enthusiasm."
>
> —Winston Churchill

History's "greats" often overcame adversity in their lives before they were successful. If I were to ask you, who is the best pitcher of all time? People who follow the game of baseball may respond Cy Young. Cy Young is considered by many to be the best pitcher of all time. He is credited with this lofty ideal because he won 511 victories. Do you know that he also lost 315 games? Swimmer Mark Spitz thought that he had failed. He thought that he would win five gold medals at the Olympics in Mexico City. He won only two then, but four years later he won seven. Babe Ruth struck out 1,330 times, but he hit 714 home runs. Before Cervantes wrote *Don Quixote*, the man had held several government jobs and failed at all of them. He served time in prison. He injured his left hand in the war. He owed money on several debts. Finally, he picked up a pen and wrote *Don Quixote*, which has proved to be a timeless classic. Robert Frost is the greatest of all American poets. He was a failure for some twenty years. He was 39 before he ever sold a volume of poetry. Today he is considered to be one of the finest writers that has ever lived. His poems have been published in 22 languages. He won the Pulitzer Prize for poetry four times. He had more honorary degrees granted to him probably more than any other man of letters and Congress named him an American Poet Laureate. Many of us know why Babe Ruth and Robert Frost are remembered in history, but delving further into their stories reveals that before success came failure. Today the name Albert Einstein is synonymous with genius. Albert Einstein too overcame adversity. Einstein did not speak until he was four and did not read until he was seven, causing his teachers and parents to think that he was mentally handicapped, slow and anti-social. Eventually, he was expelled from school. He was refused admittance to the Zurich Polytechnic School. Historians describe that he had a slower start than many of his childhood peers. Despite this slow start, he eventually caught up pretty well. The lives of Cy Young, Mark Spitz, Cervantes, Robert Frost, Babe Ruth and Albert Einstein imbue to us a valuable life lesson. All of these people who "have their names in bold in the history book" teach us that you cannot quit when you fail, but you must persevere and push forward.

"There is no failure except in no longer trying."

—Elbert Hubbard

The stories of many famous authors authenticate how these authors failed as writers before they eventually succeeded. John Grisham's first book *A Time to Kill* took three years to write. The book was rejected 28 times until he got one yes for a 5,000 copy print. Grisham has now sold over 250 million total copies of his books. Stephen King's first book *Carrie* was rejected 30 times and he threw it in the trash. His wife retrieved it out of the trash and encouraged him to resubmit it. The rest is history. He has sold more than 350 million copies of his books.[245] When Seth Godin started, he received 900 rejection letters in the mail from book publishers. Godin is now the author of 17 books that have been bestsellers around the world and have been translated into more than 35 languages. He writes about the post-industrial revolution, the way ideas spread, marketing, quitting, leadership and most of all, changing everything. Some of his books include: *Linchpin*, *Tribes*, *The Dip* and *Purple Cow*. In an interview with Ryan Essmaker, Godin shares, "I think "creativity" is better described as failing repeatedly until you get something right."[246]

The lesson of overcoming failure is also edified through some of history's greatest innovations. Apple's iPad is an example of a product that was created out of an initial failure. The iPad wasn't the first tablet like device Apple created. The Newton was Apple's first try at a tablet, the only device that made it from concept to a real product. The Newton was not successful in the market. One of the first things Steve Jobs did after he returned to Apple was get rid of the Newton. We cannot be afraid to admit failure. Jobs stopped a product/ project that was not delivering results (the Newton). This is all part of the process. In life we must learn from our mistakes and be sure to build on the experiences that we learned along the way.[247]

Retired U.S. Navy Rear Admiral Robert Shumaker was shot down in 1965 and spent eight years as a POW in North Vietnam. Back in 1965, when Shumaker was a lieutenant commander during the war in Vietnam, he became the second American aviator to be shot down and captured by the North Vietnamese. He was held in several prisons, including the infamous "Hanoi Hilton," where he was beaten, tortured and spent long periods in solitary confinement. Shumaker was released in 1973. After his release, he went on to earn a doctorate in electrical engineering. The now-retired Navy rear admiral has been awarded military honors that include the Distinguished Service Medal, two Silver Stars and Purple Hearts, and the Distinguished Flying Cross. Shumaker endured eight years of captivity and torture in North Vietnam. After the adverse experience of spending those years in a POW camp, he used the adversity to go on and do other remarkable things in his life.

It is interesting to note that in a study completed by Dr. Dennis Charney, a Professor of Psychiatry at Mt. Sinai School of Medicine, Bob Shumaker and many others were asked if they could eliminate the POW experience from their life, would they? Shumaker and others all said that they would not because they learned things; they learned tools that proved to be useful in their lives that they could not learn in any other way. Bob Shumaker's story teaches us that inside each of us is the capacity to overcome the most horrific of stresses in our life and even ultimately learn, strive and grow from these stresses. Shumaker's story is another example of an individual who overcame adversity.

> "Ever tried. Ever failed. No matter. Try Again. Fail again. Fail better."
>
> —Samuel Beckett

Overcoming failure is one of InterviewGirl.com's topics for stories that we are collecting for a compilation of stories. Speaking with individuals and learning what lengths they'll go to in order to overcome adversity has been beyond inspirational. General George Patton has remarked, "I don't measure a man's success by how high he climbs, but by how high he bounces back when he hits obstacles." Any story, any historical individual who has obtained something that "wows" you, as you dig deeper into the background of this story, you learn that their story, their success was not a story without obstacles and adversity. We cannot forget that for every brilliant idea that Thomas Edison had, he had many that never came to fruition. Just a few examples were shared in this section, but volumes upon volumes could be written on this topic.

> "Failure is merely a speed bump on road to success. I can accept failure, but I can't accept not trying."
>
> —Michael Jordan

Lesson Seven: Hard Work

Thomas Edison once famously stated, "Genius is 1 percent inspiration and 99 percent perspiration." There is no substitute for hard work. This is an age old adage. We've heard it time and time again, but there is such truth in this statement. There are no real secrets to success. Success in anything has one fundamental aspect: effort. To achieve exponential results requires additional effort and then even more effort after that. One needs to take action. Action needs to be taken with commitment. When extra effort is applied, exponential results come about. Sometimes in life that little extra determination will get you to go beyond the original results that you were hoping to obtain.[248] As the saying goes, "Hard work beats talent when talent does not work hard." On an athletic level, it is clear. There are plenty of "gifted" athletes that never excel because they rely on their natural ability to get them through the game or competition. Examples of this take place with players in middle school, high school and/ or in professional athletics. It is always sad to see money and fame ruin a great athlete's career. When it comes to academics, "hard work beats talent when talent does not work hard" is also true. Some students refuse to study because they think that they don't need to because they can get by with not studying. Many stories circulate about kids who struggled through school and ended up very successful in life. Sometimes challenges individuals face make them far more prepared for the real world. Working hard pays off in life.

In *Cracking Creativity: The Secrets of Creative Genius*, as Michael Michalko explains how the minds of geniuses work, he writes, "a distinguishing characteristic of genius is immense productivity."[249] It turns out that geniuses produce a lot of material. They produce a large quantity of work and in the process, a masterpiece is then created. In order for an individual to be immensely productive, he must work a lot. He must work continually. Thomas Edison held 1,093 patents. Bach wrote a cantata every week. Mozart produced more than six hundred pieces of music. Einstein published 248 other papers in addition to his famous paper on relativity, and T.S. Eliot had numerous drafts of "The Waste Land."[250] Another way of looking at producing a massive quantity of work as the above individuals did is that in order to do that someone must work hard day in and day out. As Michalko brilliantly points out, "a distinguishing characteristic of genius is immense productivity." Ultimately, an individual is productive by working hard.

Lesson Eight: Time is the Greatest Gift

How you spend your time determines how you live your life. Everyone on Earth has 86,400 seconds each day. In *First Thing Every Morning*, Lewis Timberlake expounds that time, "carries over no balances and allows no overdrafts. You can't hoard it, save it, store it, loan it or invest it. You can only use it—time." To produce greatness in anything, someone must invest time in their endeavor. The earlier you start something, the better the outcome will be. If you start saving for retirement in your twenties compared to your fifties, you'll amass more money. The earlier a child learns a language, learns to play an instrument, or begins a sport, the easier it is for the child to pick up that language, instrument or sport. Time unequivocally is the most dignified gift to all of us.

Muhammad Yunus' story is particularly motivating given the Interview Girl Foundation's desires (to eliminate miseries that exist in the world (such as poverty)). Yunus' story exposes how even with the most outstanding idea time is needed in order for an idea to catch on and spread. Muhammad Yunus is a social entrepreneur. Yunus is credited with spreading the idea of micro-credit as a strategy to overcome poverty. He challenged banking theory by showing how to systematically extend collateral-free loans on a cost-effective basis to poor villagers. Yunus did this on a scale that garnered worldwide attention. The Grameen Bank has 7.1 million borrowers throughout 77,000 villages. Keeping track of delivering and recovering all those loans is quite a job. Grameen Bank did not amass millions of borrowers overnight. It took time for Grameen Bank to become a success. It took almost a decade just for the basics in the Grameen Bank's system to come into place. As David Bornstein writes, "there were plenty of missteps and corrections along the way." Micro-credit as a strategy has been revolutionary in mechanisms introduced to overcome poverty. Yunus' Grameen Bank grew to be a success story, but he invested a lot of time in his ideas before he or the world saw them come to fruition.

The Interview Girl Foundation invests in programs that aid social entrepreneurs themselves and more importantly in programs that bring social entrepreneurs from around the globe into contact with one another (C^2: *Committed Collaboration*). Muhammad Yunus and his Grameen Bank idea is an example of the type of program that the Interview Girl Foundation is eager to help succeed in order to eliminate miseries that exist in our world.

Here are six terrific truths about time:

- **First:** Nobody can manage time. But you can manage those things that take up your time.

- **Second:** Time is expensive. As a matter of fact, 80 percent of our day is spent on those things or those people that only bring us two percent of our results.

- **Third:** Time is perishable. It cannot be saved for later use.

- **Fourth:** Time is measurable. Everybody has the same amount of time...pauper or king. It is not how much time you have; it is how much you use.

- **Fifth:** Time is irreplaceable. We never make back time once it is gone.

- **Sixth:** Time is a priority. You have enough time for anything in the world, so long as it ranks high enough among your priorities.[251]

Lesson Nine: Believe in Yourself

"All things are possible to him who believes."

—Mark 9:23

In Lesson Six, we learned about "Overcoming Failure," through the stories about Stephen King and John Grisham, among others. King and Grisham's stories emblematize the many authors who were rejected, but later in their lives, they became best-selling authors. King and Grisham started out receiving rejection letter after rejection letter from publishing companies. Like King and Grisham, Walt Whitman couldn't find anyone to publish *Leaves of Grass*, so he published it himself. E.E. Cummings couldn't find anyone to publish *No Thanks*, so she published it herself. The same story goes for: Mark Twain's *Huckleberry Finn*, Irma Rombauer's *The Joy of Cooking*, and Richard Bolles' *What Color is your Parachute?* George Bernard Shaw wrote for twenty years before he ever sold a thing. All of these individuals believed in themselves and their stories even when book publishers did not.

Marion Donovan invented the disposable diaper. She tried for many years to sell her invention to established manufactures. No one wanted it. She ended up starting her own company. Steve Jobs and Steve Wozniak asked Atari and Hewlett-Packard to fund their projects. Both Atari and Hewlett-Packard said no, so they decided to make Apple computers themselves.[252] To return to the Wright Brothers for a moment, Orville Wright did not have a pilot's license. Understanding that Orville Wright did not have a pilot's license conveys the idea that Orville Wright and his brother Wilbur did not need permission to change the world. They did not need someone else's permission, what they needed was creativity, passion, and persistence. They had an abundance of all three. As someone who loves to travel, I am exceedingly grateful that they possessed these qualities. Also, we should remember that their idea was not widely embraced at first. This did not stop them. Their idea had never been done. That inspired them rather than turning them away from their idea. Their idea was risky. They believed in it anyway. Their idea failed many times, but they knew that it could succeed. The Wright Brothers did not have permission to fly. After all, Orville Wright did not have a pilot's license. They did not need permission from others because they believed in themselves. They wanted to fly and committed to making it happen. People need to believe in themselves. Sometimes in life, you have to do things yourself. Achieving accomplishments that someone dreams of begins when he/she first believes in himself/herself.

> "The only thing that stands between a person and what they want in life is the will to try it and the faith to believe it possible."
>
> —Rich Devos

Lesson Ten: Rome wasn't built in a day

You have probably heard someone say, "Rome wasn't built in a day." This is referring to the idea that Rome was a mighty empire at one time and today Rome is the capital of Italy. Rome began in the 9th Century BC as a little Italian village. Legend has it that two brothers, Romulus and Remus, decided to build a city together. It is said that after an argument, Romulus killed his brother, Remus, and named the city Rome, after himself. Romulus focused on building a town, then a city, and the vision was then carried on generation after generation becoming one of the most famous cities ever to have existed in human history. Romulus began by building a town and over time, that town became the vast civilization that dominated the Mediterranean region for centuries to come. The town that Romulus built became a dynasty that would one day become the Roman Empire.

Beginning in the eighth century B.C., Ancient Rome grew from a small town on central Italy's Tiber River into an empire that at its peak encompassed most of continental Europe, Britain, much of western Asia, northern Africa and the Mediterranean islands. It is important for us to remember that this growth did not happen all at once. Among the many legacies of Roman dominance are the widespread use of the Romance languages (Italian, French, Spanish, Portuguese and Romanian) derived from Latin, the modern Western alphabet and calendar and the emergence of Christianity as a major world religion. After 450 years as a republic, Rome became an empire in the wake of Julius Caesar's rise and fall in the first century B.C. The long and triumphant reign of its first emperor, Augustus, began a golden age of peace and prosperity; by contrast, the empire's decline and fall by the fifth century A.D. was one of the most dramatic collapses in the history of human civilization.[253] Even after the fall of the Roman Empire, although it took time, Rome re-emerged during the Middle Ages and Rome is still the capital of Italy today. Rome is continually on *Forbes'* list of the top twenty most visited cities in the world. "Rome wasn't built in a day" is a meaningful lesson for us to understand as students of history.

Anything that you want to accomplish in life should be broken down into smaller parts. By taking a large goal and breaking into yearly tasks to achieve, monthly tasks to achieve, weekly tasks to achieve, and daily tasks to achieve, that goal will one day come to fruition. By doing a few small things each day, significant goals are eventually reached. The best goal setting programs in the world all teach that you need to break your goal down into smaller achievable outcomes and then you need to work at your goal each and every day by completing daily tasks and action steps. Think of those daily tasks toward your goal as "pieces from a cake." You get rid of an entire cake by taking one slice from the cake at a time: piece by piece.

Taking our larger goal (eliminating misery) and breaking that into smaller tasks (depending upon the misery we are targeting, the tasks vary) is one of the foundational ideas behind InterviewGirl. com. "Imagine the world to be a cake" is InterviewGirl.com's philosophy about how we can help to stop suffering in the world. We believe that everyone can help to slice off a piece of the misery in this world. The Interview Girl Foundation was created to help people and our work will begin with helping people in one location. As time goes on, we will reach out to many different people who experience various miseries. Our ambition at InterviewGirl.com is to get everyone to join in and slice off a piece of misery in this world. Behind our ideology is the premise that as we target a misery that exists and go after that misery, piece by piece, this is how we can eliminate miseries that exist on our planet and transform humanity. As if we were to slice a cake into pieces and everyone takes a piece, eventually the cake is gone. The Interview Girl Foundation's *Operation A²* will not be able to eliminate all orphans' misery in Africa in a few months or in a year, but overtime as stories are shared and revenues are generated, changes can be made—miseries can be eliminated.

Lesson Eleven: They Said It Couldn't Be Done ... Achieving The Impossible

Stories about Pope John Paul II and Wilma Glodean Rudolph.

Pope John Paul II

During the cold war years, people felt as if there was nothing that they could do in order to defeat communism. Pope John Paul II encouraged people to see otherwise. During World War One, the huge Russian Empire fell to Communist rule. By the end of World War Two, half of Europe was also under communist regimes and enslaved behind "the iron curtain." Totalitarian communism is a system in which the state claimed ownership of all or most physical property (factories, farms, houses). The state also held a monopoly on intellectual life. No one was allowed to own a private business and no one was allowed to express belief in any philosophy besides Marxism. Totalitarian communism was in place throughout Eastern Europe. For the next half-century, people lived in a world dominated by two Superpowers (USA and Soviet Union). People were in fear that another World War could break out. This did not happen because both sides used nuclear weapons as a threat. Both sides had the capacity to inflict mass destruction upon the other. As glim as things looked at one point, surprisingly fast, the Iron Curtain was lifted and the Cold War came to an end. During 1989 and 1990, the Berlin Wall came down, borders opened, and free elections banished Communist regimes everywhere in Eastern Europe. In late 1991 the Soviet Union itself dissolved into its component republics. The pope played a role that contributed to the defeat of totalitarian communism. The church, first in Poland and then elsewhere, broke the monopolies that communist regimes had over physical property and intellectual life because it offered people a safe place to meet and intellectually it offered them an alternative way of thinking about the world. Pope John Paul expressed his faith publicly, openly, and with many cultural and historical references. This was impactful in countries whose regimes tried to control both culture and history, along with everything else.

One of the other ways that John Paul helped to bring down communism is because of his unusual ability to get people out on the streets. He was able to get people out on the streets because of his charisma, celebrity, and faith. As Natan Sharansky and others have written, communist regimes achieved their greatest successes when they were able to fragment people, keep them apart and keep them afraid. When the pope first visited Poland in 1979, he was greeted not by a handful of little old ladies, as the country's leaders predicted, but by millions of people of all ages.[254] Anne Applebaum annotates that her husband, 16 years old at the time, remembers climbing a tree on the outskirts of an airfield near Gniezno where the pope was saying Mass and seeing an endless crowd, "three kilometers in every direction." The leaders and the police that were part of the regime were nowhere visible. "There were so many of us, and so few of them." On the Pope's visit to Poland, the pope kept repeating, "Don't be afraid."

Solidarity, the first mass anticommunist political movement was organized in Poland a year later. Pope John Paul's visit the year before was influential in this movement's taking off. After Solidarity's rise in Poland, other countries like Hungary and East Germany began to organize themselves against communism. John Paul showed that communism could be stood up to. He showed the people that they did not need to be scared of the alarming communist regimes. The story about Pope John Paul's influence in defeating communism because of his effect on people is an example of overcoming something when people did not think that it was possible. It wasn't a coincidence that "civil society" began to organize itself in other communist countries as well not long after Pope John Paul's visit to Poland. If it could happen in Poland, it could happen in other places. The Pope showed the world that the most important things could be said in public no matter what political regime was in power.

Wilma Glodean Rudolph

Wilma Glodean Rudolph became the first American woman to win three gold medals in a single Olympics. She did this at the 1960 Rome Olympics. Her story prior to arriving at the Olympics in 1960 is inspiring and proves that things can be done even when the odds are against us.

On June 23, 1940, Wilma Glodean Rudolph was born prematurely and weighed only 4.5 pounds. Wilma was the 20th of 22 children in the Rudolph family. Her family was African American living in a time of segregation. The local hospital was for whites only. Mrs. Rudolph was forced to care for Wilma herself. Wilma had polio. Her left leg and foot were becoming deformed. The doctors told Wilma's Mom that she would never walk and she would have to wear steal braces on her leg. Mrs. Rudolph refused to accept this diagnosis. She set out to find a cure. She found out that Wilma could receive treatment in Nashville. For the next two years she drove Wilma 50 miles each way to get physical therapy. Wilma's family was very supportive of her. Everyone worked with her to get better. At age 12, she could walk normally without the assistance of her crutches. At this point, she decided to become an athlete. At the 1960 Rome Olympics, Wilma became the first American woman to win three gold medals in a single Olympics. The little girl that could hardly walk without the assistance of crutches and braces overcame her challenges and won three Olympic gold medals.[255]

> "My Mother taught me very early to believe I could achieve any accomplishment I wanted to. The first was to walk without braces."
>
> —Wilma Rudolf

Lesson 12: Seize Opportunities Others Miss

Many social entrepreneurs seize opportunities that the rest of the world misses. From those individuals taking these opportunities, they then create innovative solutions to society's most pressing social problems. In the United States, Susan B. Anthony fought for Women's Rights, including the right to control property and helped the USA to see the adoption of the 19th amendment. John Muir is a naturalist and conservationist. He established the National Park System and helped found The Sierra Club. In India, Vinoba Bhave is the founder and leader of the Land Gift Movement. He caused the redistribution of more than 7,000,000 acres of land to aid India's untouchables and landless. In Italy, Dr. Maria Montessori developed the Montessori approach to early childhood education. In Great Britain, Florence Nightingale is the founder of modern nursing. She established the first school for nurses and fought to improve hospital conditions. In France, Jean Monnet is responsible for the reconstruction of the French economy following World War II, including the establishment of the European Coal and Steel Community (ECSC). The ECSC and the European Common Market were direct precursors of the European Union. Susan B. Anthony, John Muir, Vinoba Bhave, Dr. Maria Montessori, Florence Nightingale, and Jean Monnet all seized opportunities that other people missed. From these individuals seizing opportunities when they arose, they were then able to intercede in creating solutions to social problems plaguing society in each of their countries.[256]

Lesson Thirteen: Have Faith

Rev. Father Peter Mary Rookey imbues the salience of having faith

In the fall of 2012, I visited International Compassion Ministry in Olympia Fields, Illinois. I contacted Fr. Rookey's office about interviewing Fr. Rookey about his experiences in World War Two as well as his life experiences as a Catholic priest for a project that I was working on for InterviewGirl.com. I thought that I was there to interview Father Rookey, but it turns out that the office scheduled me to be there for a prayer session with him. I decided to use this opportunity to pray for a little baby whom I know who would need a kidney transplant later that year. I entered the International Compassion Ministry office and I had to wait in the waiting room until our prayer session with Father Rookey would begin.

I remember a reverent woman leading the seven of us sitting in the waiting room of International Compassion Ministry through the rosary. "Our Father, who art in heaven, hallowed be thy name..." While each person kneaded worn beads between thumb and forefinger, the group prayed aloud, "Hail Mary, full of grace, the Lord is with thee..." By the conclusion of the last prayer on the last rosary bead, I was so excited for Father Rookey to come out. As a group, we awaited the appearance of Rev. Peter Mary Rookey, OSM, known to his followers as the healing priest. As we were praying and waiting for Father Rookey to arrive, everyone there seemed to be filled with hope that in whatever they were praying for, a miracle could be achieved with the support of this faithful priest.

Although I thought that I was there to interview him that day, being able to pray with Father Rookey was such a blessing and I am grateful that it worked out the way that it did. In just a few months, I would spend a long afternoon with Father Rookey and after my initial interview with him in his office at the Servants of Mary in Chicago; I would also be able to interview him again during several follow-up visits with him. There are so many aspects to Father Rookey's story that instruct the importance of faith, but we will begin with an experience from his childhood. He and one of his eight brothers had been hanging out on the streets of Superior, Wisconsin looking for failed fireworks on a July 4th in the early 1920s. "We were lucky to find a pretty good-sized firecracker that hadn't exploded," Rookey explained. Rookey and his brother tried to light the short fuse while young Peter held it close, blowing on the firecracker to fan the flame. "I was blinded when the firecracker went off that far from my eyes," Rookey declared, holding his hands 8 inches from his face to show me. After testing Rookey's sight when his final bandages were removed, the family doctor announced that Peter would never see again. The doctor explained that medical science could do nothing to restore his vision. Rookey's mother, Johanna McGarry Rookey, refused to accept the doctor's hopeless prognosis. "She led the family in prayer every evening, saying that if we prayed for a miracle the Lord would provide one," Rookey pronounced. Each evening Johanna, husband Anthony Daniel Rookey and their 13 children gathered in the family's living room in fervent prayer. Within a year, his sight was restored. "It truly was the first miracle I'd ever witnessed. It was then I decided I wanted to become a priest," he smiled. He entered the Service (the Order of Servants of Mary, hence the middle name he took on his ordination) seminary on Chicago's West Side as a teenager in 1930.

Fr. Peter Mary Rookey, O.S.M is known as the healing priest. He received Christ's gift of healing in 1948. Since then, thousands of healings have been reported worldwide. Witness letters, some with medical consensus, have been submitted to the International Compassion Ministry. When asked about the healings, Fr. Rookey justifies them as, "I just do what He told us to do and the people are delivered and healed. We are answering the last command of Jesus,... 'They shall lay their hands upon the sick, and they shall recover' (Mk. 16:18)." Rookey's mother never lost her faith that her son would regain his sight through the power of prayer. The Rookey family was told that young Rookey would never see again, but his family had faith that he would see again. They continued to pray as a family for Rookey's recovery. Using his faith, Rookey has gone onto to help many others use their faith in difficult times. His faithful servitude has allowed many to witness miracles.

Not long after that interview with Father Rookey, I was fortunate enough to spend a full day with Father Rookey. I had a private mass with Father Rookey at the Servants of Mary on Jackson Boulevard in Chicago. After mass, Father Rookey came over for lunch at my parent's house. At the end of the day, after the commute back to Chicago from the suburbs, I had to escort him up to his room. I pushed him in his wheel chair through the halls of the seminary. His room was pretty barren. I reflected on the sacrifices that this man made so that he could give his time in prayer to Christ to pray for the healing of so many others. It just so happened that when I was bringing Father Rookey back to his room (finishing this interview) that Sunday evening, many other Americans were watching the Super Bowl. I received a text from a friend, "I can't believe you are missing our Super Bowl party." I smiled and thought, "This moment is far better than any Super Bowl party would ever be." As Interview Girl, there are times when it is necessary for me to miss something or to get up early or to stay up late, but it's all worth it. What an incredible opportunity it was for me to spend yet another day with Father Rookey. It was one of those days that I would never forget. Here I was with this man who lived through the Great Depression, World War Two and all the usual historical events that I asked people his age about. But beyond that, here was this man who had helped to heal thousands of people and brought so many individuals back to the gift of their faith. I walked back out to my car that cold January night. Inside my flip video camera was yet another power story: the story of Father Rookey. This was a story that the world needed to hear. There were many life lessons that Father Rookey taught me through my visits with him, but above all, he taught me about the importance of having faith.

> "We all have weaknesses that affect our body, mind, and spirit. But it is our will to overcome them that decides how we live. With men this is impossible; but with God all things are possible."
>
> —Fr. Peter Mary Rookey, O.S.M.

Lesson Fourteen: A Little Bit Makes a Big Difference

> "Great things are not done by impulse, but by a series of small things brought together."
>
> —Vincent Van Gogh

It's that little bit, the little extra that often makes the biggest difference. It's that tiny extra effort that separates the good from the great. Water temperature proves this concept best. Raising the temperature of water by one extra degree means the difference between something that is simply very hot and something that generates enough force to power a machine. At 211 degrees, water is hot. At 212 degrees, it boils and with boiling water, comes steam, and steam can power a locomotive.[257] Singularities that seem very small can actually make a huge difference in an overall outcome.

Investing a small amount of your time into an endeavor, little by little, makes a big difference over time. It is those people who exercise a little each and every day who then see changes within their physiques. A little bit of time spent exercising day after day after day pays off. According to a study reported in *Time magazine*, even small amounts of exercise can improve heart health. The U.S. Department of Health and Human Services recommends adults get 2 hours and 30 minutes (150 minutes) of moderate activity every week. The study concluded that those who manage to work in the recommended 150 minutes of exercise a week had a 14% lower risk of heart disease than those who did not exercise at all. When they compared the group who got the recommended exercise to those who only got 75 minutes of exercise, they found the less-exercised participants still had a 14% lower heart disease risk. That's just three 25-minute brisk walks a week. Even just a little bit of exercise goes a long way.

"Pay Yourself First" is a phrase commonly used in personal finance and retirement planning literature that means to automatically route your specified savings contribution from each paycheck at the time it is received. The savings contributions are automatically routed from each paycheck to your investment account, so this process is said to be "paying yourself first;" in other words, paying yourself before you begin paying your monthly living expenses and making discretionary purchases. When you "pay yourself first" check after check, this little bit of money from each pay check adds up to be a sizeable amount as the years pass.

Does a little bit make a big difference? Just ask the silver medalist track runner at the Olympics the difference in his/her 100 yard sprint time from the gold medalist's time? In one of Anthony Robbins' inspirational talks, he describes how the tiniest changes yield massive results. One of the interesting stories that Anthony Robbins shares to illustrate this point is about a plastic surgeon that is at the top of his craft. The surgeon explained to Robbins what it takes to make someone beautiful. He told Robbins that the difference between someone who is gorgeous and average is if the space between the top part of one's lips and their nose is the same size as one's eyes. If this space is the same size, then the individual is gorgeous. If it's one millimeter more, you have an average face. The surgeon makes one to two millimeter changes in his patients and his patients then look like a different person. Robbins goes onto to explain that when people make little shifts in how they do things, this can lead to magnificent results and major changes in time.

Atul Gawande is a surgeon, writer, and public health researcher. He practices general and endocrine surgery at Brigham and Women's Hospital in Boston. He is also Professor of Surgery at Harvard Medical School and a Professor in the Department of Health Policy and Management at the Harvard School of Public Health. In *Better, a surgeon's notes on performance*, Atul Gawande examines three core requirements for success in medicine: diligence, to do right, and ingenuity. In describing diligence, Gawande writes, "People underestimate the importance of diligence as a virtue. No doubt this has something to do with how supremely mundane it seems." Gawande shares a story from one of his first years as a doctor about his senior resident and how he went back to check on a patient one more time that morning and because he did that, because he checked on her once more, she survived. Gawande reflects, "It is this little act that I have often thought about since. It was a small thing, a tiny act of conscientiousness. He had seen something about her that worried him." To further set forth the importance of diligence, Gawande describes how Rotary

International pledged a quarter of a billion dollars to eradicate polio from the world. UNICEF agreed to organize the worldwide production and distribution of the vaccine, and the USA made the campaigns one of CDC's core initiatives, supplying both expertise and considerable funding. He points out "the campaign has averted an estimated five million cases of paralytic polio thus far." Wrapping up the discussion about the ideal of eradicating polio from the globe, Gawande closes with,

> "Beneath the ideal is the gruelingly unglamorous and uncertain work. If the eradication of polio is our monument, it is a monument to the perfection of performance—to showing what can be achieved by diligent attention to detail coupled with great ambition."

When we look at preeminent undertakings, such as the eradication of polio, paying attention to the littlest details in any endeavor is what allows the grandeur accomplishments to eventually take place.

Little acts that we choose to do can make a prodigious difference in someone's life. You never know what compliment that you give someone, smile that you share, or kind action that you take can authentically affect the person with whom you are sharing the little act. Often times these "little acts" take very little effort on the doers' part, yet they tremendously impact someone in a positive way. I heard a story about a baker in New York whose small, kind acts really affected individuals in a genuine way. The baker would give his extra bread to the homeless and this little gesture on the baker's part was what spurred a homeless man to then turn his life around from that point forward. The homeless man was so touched by the baker's kind heart that he wanted to be able to share compassionate acts, like the baker had, one day in his own life, too. The man knew that in order to do that, he first had to be able to take care of himself. A baker giving his extra bread to the homeless was a small gesture on the baker's part that momentously affected how the rest of the homeless man's life would unfold.

Little acts of kindness, small gestures, and just very slight actions or tasks often considerably affect people. This is InterviewGirl. com's mission: one story at a time, we'll change the world. We will. If you believe something, then you'll achieve it. What's the difference between a dreamer and goal achiever? The goal achiever takes small steps each day to make that dream come true. The small things that we all do steadily make an exceptional difference as time passes. In the framework of InterviewGirl.com, the small act of sharing a story will allow us to make an immense difference in the lives of others. One story at time, misery will be eliminated.

> "If you think you're too small to have an impact, try going to bed with a mosquito in the room."
> —Dame Anita Roddick, British businesswoman,
> humanitarian, founder of *The Body Shop*

Lesson Fifteen: Stepping Up and Doing the Right Thing ... Even When Everyone Around You Is Not

> "In matters of style, swim with the current; in matters of principle, stand like a rock."
> —Thomas Jefferson

Denmark, 1943: A nation conspires to save the lives of 7,000 Jews

The Holocaust was the systematic, bureaucratic, state-sponsored persecution and murder of approximately six million Jewish individuals by the Nazi regime and its collaborators. "Holocaust" is a word of Greek origin meaning "sacrifice by fire."

Most likely you have heard some of the horror stories from the holocaust, but amidst the despair, there are stories of hope and survival and stories that reveal to us what lengths some individuals went to in order to save other individuals' lives.

In September 1943, the Nazis prepared for the deportation of all Danish Jews to concentration camps where death would follow. Georg Duckwitz, a German diplomat with a conscience, deliberately leaked the plans for the roundup. Gathering the Jews was due to begin on Rosh Hashanah, the Jewish New Year. Thanks to the information from Duckwitz, the Danes swung into action. Teachers told students to go home and pack their things. Friends and strangers both provided alternative accommodations, so that nobody would be at home when the Nazis came knocking on the door at the registered addresses of Jewish families. Adults and children checked into hospitals under false names and made up nonexistent ailments. Others appeared at chapels, as if to attend a funeral. The mourners then traveled out of Copenhagen, as part of a huge funeral procession. Families were transported to remote beaches, where boats picked them up at night and took them to safety. Others arranged escapes in broad daylight. In Copenhagen, families stepped into canal boats that advertised "Harbor Tours." These special harbor tours avoided traditional sights, delivering their passengers to waiting fishing boats instead. Families hid in the hulls, or were covered by tarpaulins, herrings, and straw, and were ferried to neutral Sweden to wait out the war in safety. As a result of Duckwitz stepping up and doing the right thing and as a result of Danish solidarity, 99 percent of Denmark's 7,000 Jews survived. What started with one man doing the right thing led to thousands of lives being saved.

The Story of Nonna Bannister

Nonna Bannister carried a secret almost to her Tennessee grave: the diaries she kept as a young girl experiencing the horrors of the Holocaust. The *Secret Holocaust Diaries* is a book about a girl who was taken from Russia to Germany to work in a labor camp during WWII. Nonna's writings tell the remarkable tale of how a Russian girl, born into a family with wealth and privileges, was exposed to the concentration camps and learned the value of human life and the importance of forgiveness.

In August of 1942, Anna (Nonna's mother) and Nonna had to leave Russia. They boarded a train headed for Kassel, Germany. They were packed into cattle cars with other women in order to go work in Germany. In her diary, Nonna writes, "We are packed like sardines in a can into the cattle cars of the train."[258] The train passed through Poland on its way to Germany. At one of the stops in Poland, a young Jewish woman tried to save her baby by tossing her into Anna's arms. In her diary, Nonna shares,

> "Mama and I had placed ourselves closer to the open door of our train car, hoping to get some fresh air. Suddenly there was a young girl running alongside our car—no one knew where she had come from. She had a look of terror in her eyes, and she had her arms around a small bundle. Her black hair was blowing in the wind, and she was so thin that you could see her bones protruding from her neck and her shoulders. She hurled her bundle at Mama, and before any of us realized what happened, Mama stood there holding a bundle in her hands—and we heard a baby cry! The young woman was still running alongside our train car. She yelled out, "Please, oh please save my baby—please give her a Russian name!""[259]

Anna's mother wanted to save this baby and give it a Russian name as the desperate Jewish mother pleaded from alongside the train. However, Dunja, another woman told the SS about the baby, "It's a baby Jew—the Jewish woman threw it into our car at the last stop." After hearing this, the SS guards then killed the baby.

Nonna's mother wept in shock after the baby was killed. Anna was trying to do the right thing in trying to save the baby from the SS.

In February 1943, the Germans transferred Anna and Nonna to work in a hospital that had been built for the prisoners of war and people from the labor camps. The hospital was for people of all nationalities. It was built like barracks and was adjacent to the Catholic hospital at Marienkrankenhaus, Germany. Nonna explains in her diary, "When we arrived at the hospital, two Catholic nuns came out to greet us and were joined by the priest. They were so friendly and so kind that Mama and I were a little bit in awe! The nuns directed us up to the fifth floor of the Catholic hospital and assigned a room for us to live in."[260] As the translator's note reveals, the Catholic hospital must have seemed like paradise to Nonna and Anna. They had been sleeping on mattress less boards at the camps, and here they had real, clean beds. They also enjoyed good healthy food instead of stale bread and watery cabbage soup. Though they were still technically prisoners, the nuns and priests treated Anna and Nonna like valued coworkers. As Nonna writes in her diary, "Mama and I were very happy that such good luck had come our way, and we were treated like family members by the priests and the nuns." The nuns gave Nonna the German name Lena Schulz to hide her identity. In reflecting on her diary entries, Nonna expresses, "We felt a great deal of security with the Catholic nuns and priests taking care of us and shielding us from the unrelenting terror that the Nazis had unleashed against so many innocent people." The translator's note in *Secret Holocaust Diaries* adds, "Nonna believed that the Catholic nuns at Marienkrankenhaus saved her life. She later credited them with hiding her from her enemies and protecting her from danger."[261]

In September 1943, the Gestapo sent Anna a letter telling her to report to the Gestapo headquarters for some document verification. Anna reported as she had to and after that day, Nonna's mother never came back. Nonna had no idea what happened to her mother. Four weeks after her mother disappeared, Nonna received a card of notification from the Gestapo that her mother was a prisoner. The card had been mailed from the Concentration Camp Ravensbruck, located in Furstenberg. Nonna writes in her diary, "The postcard was very official, and it was mailed in October 1943. The card had my mother's prisoner number on the front—her number was 23893. These numbers were tattooed on the prisoners' arms, so there was no way out for her now that she was a marked woman." Records show that 132,000 women entered Ravensbruck between 1939 and 1945. 50,000 women died there. Nazis enacted slave labor, inflicting strict rules and grave punishment, even death. The Soviets liberated Ravensbruck in April 1945. Given the Nazis' knowledge of the Jewish baby incident, Anna surely suffered severely at Ravensbruck. The nuns cared for Nonna after her mother was sent to the concentration camp. The nuns arranged for Nonna to attend a parochial school to complete her high school education.

The nuns who were part of the Catholic order running the hospital in Germany went against the grains of the time and treated Anna and Nonna with dignity and respect even though Anna and Nonna weren't Germans and the nuns were instructed to treat Russians such as Anna and Nonna as prisoners. The nuns changed Nonna's name in order to protect her and once Anna was taken away by the Gestapo, the nuns took it upon themselves to look after Nonna, an adolescent at that time.

As Duckwitz stepped up and did the right thing in Denmark in 1943, Nonna Bannister's story is another story from the Holocaust that represents people who did the right thing even when others around them were not. Anna did the right thing as she tried to save the baby before someone snitched about what she was attempting to do and the Catholic nuns did the right thing in all that they did to take care of Nonna. Sometimes it's necessary to step up and do what's right even when everyone around you is not. Of all the times in history to represent this lesson about: stepping up and doing the right even when everyone around you is not, individuals that went against the tendencies of the day and age during the Holocaust, helped to save lives.

Abby Johnson

This next story will be seen as controversial as everyone has different views about abortion, but this is a story about a woman who stood up and made a change from her current circumstances when she realized that morally she did not agree with the company for whom she worked.

Abby Johnson has always had a fierce determination to help women in need. It was this desire that both led Abby to a career with Planned Parenthood, our nation's largest abortion provider, and caused her to flee the organization and become an outspoken advocate for the pro-life movement.

During her eight years with Planned Parenthood, Abby quickly rose in the organization's ranks and became a clinic director. She was increasingly disturbed by what she witnessed. Abortion was a product Planned Parenthood was selling, not an unfortunate necessity that they fought to decrease. Still, Abby loved the women that entered her clinic and her fellow workers. Despite a growing unrest within her, she stayed on and strove to serve women in crisis.

All of that changed on September 26, 2009 when Abby was asked to assist with an ultrasound-guided abortion. She watched in horror as a 13 week baby fought, and ultimately lost, its life at the hand of the abortionist. At that moment, the full realization of what abortion was and what she had dedicated her life to hit Abby. From there, a dramatic transformation took place. Desperate and confused, Abby sought help from a local pro-life group. She swore that she would begin to advocate for life in the womb and expose abortion for what it truly is.

Planned Parenthood did not ignore Abby's exodus. They are fully aware that the workers who leave are their greatest threat. Instantly, they took action to silence Abby with a gag order and took her to court. The lawsuit was decided in Abby's favor and thrown out of court.

The media was, and continues to be, intensely interested in Abby's story as well as her continued efforts to advocate for the unborn and help clinic workers escape the abortion industry. She is a frequently requested guest on Fox News and a variety of other shows and the author of the nationally best-selling book, *Unplanned*, which chronicles both her experiences within Planned Parenthood and her dramatic exit.[262] Everyone in the organization where Abby worked saw abortion one way. Just because Abby's views differed from the group, this did not stop her from standing up for what she believed in.

The stories about Georg Duckwitz, Nonna Bannister, and Abby Johnson all symbolize people who did the right things when others around them were not. Just because everyone is doing something doesn't make it right. What can you do differently in your life than those around you?

> "Whenever you find yourself on the side of the majority, it's time to pause and reflect."
>
> —Mark Twain

> "Right is right even if no one is doing it; wrong is wrong even if everyone is doing it."
>
> —Augustine of Hippo

Lesson Sixteen: Putting Things Together

> "To make knowledge productive, we will have to learn to see both forest and tree. We will have to learn to connect."
>
> —Peter F. Drucker

Sometimes hearing a story or learning something new will present you with supplementary facts and/or pieces of information that you weren't aware of previously. This new information will connect with other things that you have heard and learned in the past. As you put things and ideas together, connections are made in your mind. As these connections are made, often times, new ideas are created or a new enduring understanding is reached. How you see something is altered after things are put together in a new way. As the work of Thomas Kuhn about paradigms teaches, it is from the intersection of ideas that true breakthroughs and new developments then occur. Similarly, Michael Michalko affirms, "Yes associations and imaginative connections are essential elements of creativity; they distinguish ideas that are truly original and innovative from those that are logical, but inconsequential." [263]Correspondingly, Stephen Jay Gould concurs that connections between the seemingly unconnected are the secret of genius.

Learning to make connections is important for students, thinkers, innovators, and for overall achievement. Thomas Edison's experience at the railroad tracks is a story about things coming together. While selling newspapers along the railroad, something happened that changed Thomas Edison's life. Edison saved the life of a station official's child. The child fell onto the tracks of an oncoming train. The boy's father thanked Edison by teaching him how to use the telegraph. Edison used scrap metal to build a telegraph set and practiced the Morse code. From Edison's encounter with the boy's father, he then used the knowledge that he learned from the boy's father in his own innovations. Edison put together ideas and knowledge that the boy's father shared with him and then implemented that information within his own inventions.

The AC motor came to fruition as Nikola Tesla made a connection between two conditions. Nikola Tesla forced a connection between the setting sun and a motor that made the AC motor possible by having the motor's magnetic field rotate inside the motor just as the sun rotates around the earth.

The story behind the creation of the cell phone also emblematizes connections coming together for the cell phone's creator. Martin Cooper put unrelated things together and in time the first personal cell phone was created. While working for Motorola, Martin Cooper created the first personal cell phone. One day, Cooper was watching *Star Trek* on television. *Star Trek* gave its characters all a manner of impossible items, from teleportation systems to spacecraft that zipped through the universe with ease. Cooper watched Captain Kirk flip open his handheld communicator and give an order to one of his crew. Suddenly, Cooper sat up. He'd seen it many times, and yet now he really noticed. That was what he wanted—a portable device one could carry around in a pocket or purse, flip open, and talk to whomever one wanted, no matter where he/she was.[264] You never know when things will "come together" for an individual and a new idea will emerge. Inventions throughout history have stories about "light bulb moments" for people when things came together for them, when those individuals made a connection to something else. Martin Cooper gives people the advice to, "think of new ideas, new ways of doing things, to day dream. But an inventor needs a foundation of science or engineering, of education to make these dreams come true. An inventor needs imagination and practical knowledge."[265] In Dr. Jacob Bronowksi's, *The Ascent of Man*, he expresses that a genius is a person who has two great ideas. The work of the genius arises from the person's ability to get them to fit together.[266]

Leonardo da Vinci's genius was the ability to see the process of the results rather than the results of the process.[267] Leonardo da Vinci continually made connections. These connections that he repeatedly made are what make us recognize him as the genius that he was. Leonardo da Vinci believed that once you listed a set of distinctions, you could generate new possibilities by combining them in various ways, or fill in the holes and missing links by anticipating features that have not yet been encountered. Combining key elements for the purpose of constructing something new was a cornerstone of his genius.[268] For example, he forced a relationship between the sound of a bell and a stone hitting water.

This enabled him to make the connection that sound travels in waves.

Putting things together is necessary and important as we create inventions, innovations, and make discoveries. I'll never forget InterviewGirl.com's light bulb moment. As I was checking out at *Whole Foods* and I saw the sign, "one dime at a time," suddenly I thought, "one story at a time." Walking out of *Whole Foods* that day was a crucial moment in the formation of InterviewGirl.com. I made a connection in my mind and heart that even with one dime changes could be made in the world. I built InterviewGirl.com and the Interview Girl Foundation from the clear connection that happened that day as I read "one dime at a time" and focused on how Amara's story affected me. Connections between a variety of aspects that I had encountered in my life came together and I decided that I wanted to do my part to somehow make a difference to make the world a better place.

Lesson 17: Read

Lynn Butler understands that, "reading is a window to the world." Educators are instructed that reading opens a window to the world for their students. Reading is a foundational skill for learning, personal growth, and enjoyment. As a lifelong learning skill, reading goes beyond decoding and comprehension to interpretation and development of new understandings. Reading is to the mind what exercise is to the body. By reading, people can travel to places outside of their day-to-day environment. They can share in the lives of others, still living or long dead, who they may never meet. People can learn how to do new things even when they don't have a teacher nearby to teach them. Of course nobody can forget the famous line from *Good Will Hunting* when Matt Damon's character, Will retorts, "You wasted $150,000 on an education you coulda got for $1.50 in late fees at the public library." In this memorable scene, Damon's character is making the point that by reading you become highly self-educated. Before Ray Bradbury passed on, he shared that he never went to college, instead, he went to the library all day, three times a week, until he got married at 27. Until he died, he regularly organized fundraisers for libraries.

> "You will be the same person in five years as you are today except for the people you meet and the books you read."
>
> —Charles "Tremendous" Jones

Charlie "Tremendous" Jones passionately promoted the reading of books. Jones was an entertaining humorist, and he passed along his messages with a brand of humor that endears him to audiences and makes his messages memorable. His ability to quote and reference varied literature was an impressive testament to his own commitment to reading. Jones did a lot more than simply read. He advocated sharing books and the messages they offer, and he certainly practiced what he preached. Leader Network interviewed Jones in 2006. Jones shared,

> "The heart of my life is books. My favorite saying is: You are the same today you'll be in five years except for two things: the people you meet and the books you read. In every turning point and crisis of my life, there's always been a book that helped me think and see more clearly and keep laughing and keep looking up and keep my mouth shut. I would never tell anybody I ever had a problem, so everybody always thought I was on top of the world, and yet I was just like everybody else with problems coming out of my ears. Now, when people come to my office, they come to talk to me. Instead of conversing with me like they think they are going to do, I get them reading. I pick out some great books and have each person read three or four sentences. I just received another email from a person

recounting how his life was changed by learning the power of reading together—rather than talking. I just can't get over the power of a little book—sometimes only 30 or 40 pages—that literally turns and shapes an entire lifetime. Yet most people say, "I don't read." My heart aches for those people since I remember when I didn't read because I was so ignorant. In my case, I was always blessed because I was ashamed of my ignorance; most people are proud to be ignorant."

After an interview Scott Giambalvo had with Charlie "Tremendous" Jones, Giambalvo reveals,

"A walk through his offices (and private library) told me what kind of man Charlie Jones is. A man that reads. Almost every room had cases and cases of books lining the walls. His private collection includes the only known complete set of Oswald Chambers's hardcover's, over 270 volumes on Lincoln alone, 85 on Washington, and countless others on Lee, Jackson, Livingston, Huston, Patton, Churchill and many more. His collection is truly tremendous."

Charlie "Tremendous" Jones told Giambalvo,

"Reading builds your mind and expands your thinking. In a world where the average American reads one to two books a year, if you read just one book a month you'll be ahead of the pack tenfold. Remember though, that you have to think about what you read. Apply it to your life and realize how it could impact your own experiences. Learn from it. Finally, share it. Knowledge is nothing if it is not given away freely. If you give because you have, you'll develop a greater capacity to give."[269]

Jones' advice about sharing what you learn is alongside InterviewGirl.com's mission to share our stories because as we do that, we are "paying it forward" to others as we impart our knowledge and ideas.

Let us not forget the advice to become a genius that someone who is considered by many to be the greatest genius of all time once gave. Albert Einstein advised, "If you want your children to be brilliant, read them fairy tales. If you want them to be geniuses, read them more fairy tales." Thomas Edison also loved to read and Edison's parents loved to read. They read to him works of good literature and history. They had many books that young Edison eagerly devoured. Before he was 12, he had read works by Dickens, Shakespeare, Edward Gibbon's *Fall of the Roman Empire and Decline*, and more. Reading opens doors for individuals, teaches people things, and exposes people to new notions. There is power in stories. Reading changes lives. One of the reasons InterviewGirl.com is collecting stories is so that people can read them. Again, interesting how it all comes together. Charlie "Tremendous" Jones purports that knowledge is nothing if it is not given away freely. Sharing stories is central to our work at InterviewGirl.com. We want knowledge to be disseminated through sharing stories.

Below you will find what some people throughout history have had to say about reading:

"To add a library to a house is to give that house a soul."

—Cicero

"A room without a book is like a body without a soul."
—Marcus Tullius Cicero

"Children's books are written for upbringing...but upbringing is a great thing; it decides the fate of the human being."

—Vissarion Grigor'evich Belinskii

"Reading is to the mind what exercise is to the body."

—Richard Steele

"When I step into this library, I cannot understand why I ever step out of it."

—Marie de Sevigne

"The library is not a shrine for the worship of books. It is not a temple where literary incense must be burned or where one's devotion to the bound book is expressed in ritual. A library, to modify the famous metaphor of Socrates, should be the delivery room for the birth of ideas—a place where history comes to life."

—Norman Cousins

"The best of my education has come from the public library... my tuition fee is a bus fare and once in a while, five cents a day for an overdue book. You don't need to know very much to start with, if you know the way to the public library."

—Lesley Conger

"Books are the treasured wealth of the world and the fit inheritance of generations and nations."

—Henry David Thoreau

"Once you learn to read, you will be forever free."

—Frederick Douglass

"The medicine chest of the soul."
   —Inscription over the door of the *Library at Thebes*

"Nutrimentum spiritus. (Food for the soul)"
                    —Inscribed over a German library

"Information is the currency of democracy."
                              —Thomas Jefferson

"With one day's reading a man may have the key in his hands."
                                    —Ezra Pound

"If over others you would leap, then in a book you must seek."
                              —Chinese proverb

"A library is where people, One frequently finds, Lower their voices And raise their minds."
                              —Richard Armour

"I cannot live without books."
                              —Thomas Jefferson

"There is not such a cradle of democracy upon the earth as the free public library, this republic of letters, where neither rank, office, nor wealth receives the slightest consideration."
                              —Andrew Carnegie

"A book is like a garden carried in the pocket."
                              —Chinese Proverb

"Reading is a basic tool in the living of a good life."
—Mortimer J. Adler

"Books are the quietest and most constant of friends: they are the most accessible and wisest of counselors, and the most patient of teachers."
—Charles W. Eliot

"The more that you read, the more things you will know. The more that you learn, the more places you'll go."
—Dr. Seuss

"Words are the voice of the heart."
—Confucius

"Books to the ceiling, Books to the sky, My pile of books is a mile high. How I love them! How I need them! I'll have a long beard by the time I read them."
—Arnold Lobel

"At the moment that we persuade a child, any child, to cross that threshold, that magic threshold into a library, we change their lives forever, for the better."
—Unknown

"Until I feared I would lose it, I never loved to read. One does not love breathing."
—Harper Lee, *To Kill a Mockingbird*

"I read because one life isn't enough."
—Richard Peck

"What a school thinks about its library is a measure of what it thinks about education."
—Harold Howe, *former U.S. Commissioner of Education*

"If we didn't have libraries, many people thirsty for knowledge would dehydrate."
—Megan Jo Tetrick

"The closest thing you will find to an orderly universe is a good library."
—Ashleigh Brilliant

"Reading is a means of thinking with another person's mind; it forces you to stretch your own."
—Charles Scribner, Jr.

"So please, oh PLEASE, we beg, we pray, Go throw your TV set away, And in its place you can install A lovely bookshelf on the wall."
—Roald Dahl, *Charlie and the Chocolate Factory*

"A library is thought in cold storage."
—Herbert Samuel

"He who has a garden and a library wants for nothing."
—Cicero

"A library is a fuelling station for your mind."
—Steve Leveen

"Books fall open, you fall in."
—David McCord

"I find that a great part of the information I have was acquired by looking something up and finding something else on the way."

—Franklin P. Adams

"A library is not a luxury but one of the necessities of life."

—Henry Ward Beecher

"Libraries enable the past to talk to the future."

—Edward Cornish

"Reading is a window to the world!"

—Lynn Butler

"I have always imagined that Paradise will be a kind of library."

—Jorge Luis Borges

"Knowledge is Power."

—Francois Bacon

"We must be the change we wish to see in the world."

—Mahatma Gandhi

"Outside of a dog, a book is man's best friend. Inside a dog, it's too dark to read."

—Groucho Marx

"It was as though I had been dying of thirst and the librarian had handed me a five gallon bucket of water. I drank and drank. The only reason I am here and not in prison is because of that woman. I was a loser, but she showed me the power of reading."

—Gary Paulsen

"When I discovered libraries, it was like having Christmas every day."

—Jean Fritz

"I have lived a thousand lives lost within the pages of a book."

—Robert Cormier

"Give me a room whose every nook is dedicated to a book."

—Frank Dempster Sherman

"In a library we are surrounded by many hundreds of dear friends."

—Ralph Waldo Emerson

"I go into my library, and all history unrolls before me. I breathe the morning air of the world while the scent of Eden's roses yet lingered in it, while it vibrated only to the world's first brood of nightingales, and to the laugh of Eve. I see the pyramids building; I hear the shoutings of the armies of Alexander."

—Alexander Smith, *Books and Gardens*

"The love of learning, the sequestered nooks, and all the sweet serenity of books."

—Henry Wadsworth Longfellow

"Knowledge is of two kinds: that which we know and
..."

—Samuel Johnson

"Knowledge is free at the library. Just bring your own
container."

—Unknown

"Reading is to the mind what exercise is to the body."
—Richard Steele

"Reading is a discount ticket to everywhere."
—Mary Schmich

Lesson Eighteen: Perfect Is the Enemy of Good

Perfect is the enemy of good is an aphorism or proverb meaning
that insisting on perfection often results in no improvement at all.
The phrase is commonly attributed to Voltaire whose moral poem,
La Bégueule, starts, "Dans ses écrits, un sàge Italien, Dit que le
mieux est l'ennemi du bien" (In his writings, a wise Italian says that
the best is the enemy of the good). Aristotle, Confucius and other
classical philosophers all warned against extremism in general in
their writings. In the early 1900's, an Italian economist by the name
of Vilfredo Pareto created a mathematical formula describing the
unequal distribution of wealth he observed and measured in his
country. Pareto observed that roughly twenty percent of the people
controlled or owned eighty percent of the wealth. In the late 1940s,
Dr. Joseph M. Juran, a Quality Management pioneer, attributed
the 80/20 Rule to Pareto, calling it Pareto's Principle. The Pareto
Principle or 80/20 rule explains "Perfect is the enemy of good"
numerically. You can apply the 80/20 Rule to almost anything,
from the science of management to the sciences of the physical

world around us. For example, 20 percent of a company's inventory on hand occupies 80 percent of the company's warehouse space. Similarly, 80 percent of its inventory line items (Stock Keeping Units) come from 20 percent of the company's vendors. At the same time, it's likely that 80 percent of their revenues will be the result of sales made by 20 percent of their sales staff. And 20 percent of the company's workers will cause 80 percent of its problems, while another 20 percent of its personnel will deliver 80 percent of the company's entire production. The formula appears to work in both directions.[270]

"Progress Not Perfection"

A lesson that I've learned as a student of history is that perfect can be the enemy of good. When people take things to extremes, often times this can backfire. You don't have to attain perfection. Sometimes if we do not reach perfection, then we want to give up. Exercising moderation seems to be the key to a balanced life. In various areas in one's life, another way to view moderation is by understanding that sometimes striving to be good every day is better than being absolutely perfect every once in a while. A very simple example, but keeping up with tidying up your home every day makes more sense than to let it go until it is a disaster and then to clean it so well that it looks immaculate for a day or two, but after those initial days then again you let it go until it is an unorganized mess.

"A small daily task, if it be really daily, will beat the labours of a spasmodic Hercules."

—Anthony Trollope

Lesson 19: The Power of Habit

"We are what we repeatedly do. Excellence, then, is not an act, but a habit."

—Aristotle

Aristotle aforesaid, "We are what we repeatedly do. Excellence, then, is not an act, but a habit." Those practices that we do over and over determine outcomes in our lives. Reputable individuals that have lived throughout human civilization all made good habits a part of their daily lives. Habits are about repeating a behavior. Parallel parking, gambling, exercising, brushing your teeth and every other habit-forming activity all follow the same behavioral and neurological patterns, says New York Times business writer Charles Duhigg. His new book *The Power of Habit* explores the science behind why we do what we do—and how companies are now working to use our habit formations to sell and market products to us.[271]

Developing new habits and/or breaking old ones is often difficult for individuals. Some people argue that one cannot break an old habit, but one can develop new habits. BJ Fogg directs the Persuasive Tech Lab at Stanford University. He has examined the question: how do humans trigger a behavior that is a habit for them. It hit BJ Fogg that he needed to make it really simple. He wanted to incorporate a tiny change into his day (like one tiny sip of water or one push up and so on). People create tiny habits where there are routines already set up. His research indicates that tiny habits work out really well. Fogg discovered that the secret was to incorporate a new habit by adding it in after an existing behavior. He teaches that if you use an existing behavior and you put a new behavior after, then the triggers are your existing behaviors. He says that you don't need to set alarms, but you need to establish what will come after. He urges us to start practicing tiny habits. Fogg teaches that one's existing behavior becomes anchor for the new behavior.[272]

When we incorporate habits that are beneficial to us into our daily lives, our lives change. History shows that people with successful habits then have successful lives. What's great about living today is that new science enlightens us that habits aren't destiny. As Charles Duhigg shows in *The Power of Habit*, by harnessing this new science, we can transform our businesses, our communities, and our lives. Now we can achieve success by focusing on the patterns that shape every aspect of our lives. We all have the power to transform our habits. Science shows practices that can be used to help people transform their habits.[273] This is powerful because as we transform our habits, our lives change. The things we do daily, over and over determine what our future looks like. An undeniable lesson from history is that we are what we repeatedly do. We are our habits.

Lesson Twenty: Take Action

"Action is the foundational key to all success."
—Pablo Picasso

You can have all the knowledge in the world, you can have the best intentions, and you can have a first-rate plan in place, but unless you act, what it is that you want to do will not happen. The biggest reason why one's dream doesn't come to fruition is lack of action. Newton's first law of Motion states, "A body in motion remains in motion unless it is acted on by an external force. If the body is at rest it remains at rest." Once you get started it is easier to stay in motion, but the most difficult part is that first movement. The first action is usually the hardest part. Little by little, one's actions will gather momentum, and before you know it, he/she will have achieved his/her goals. Goals that are never achieved can often be traced directly back to Pablo Picasso's famous quote, "Action is the foundational key to all success."

When Edem explained to me that day that Amara died, I was heartbroken. It was an abhorrence to learn that a sweet, young girl with a lot of potential died because there wasn't enough medicine. I was bothered by what happened, yet, initially, I didn't know what to do. I knew that if I did nothing, then nothing would change, but if I did something, even something small, then maybe I could contribute to making the problem better. Taking the initiative to learn about the AIDS pandemic in Africa was the first action step that I took. InterviewGirl.com's journey to becoming a reality started as I attempted to learn more about poverty, AIDS, and child trafficking. Through my enlightenment about these social issues, I became even more infuriated with some of the misery that is part of our world. I consider education to be a virtue because education opens doors for people. Beyond doubt knowledge puts aspirations within reach for individuals. If someone knows something, this knowledge spurs him/her to take action. For example, the knowledge of medicine creates cures for diseases and helps doctors to save patients. Whereas, lack of knowledge can keep doors shut. The less someone knows, the less of an impact he/she can make on the world and the more he/she is held back. Everything individuals learn is a door to something (even if it is learning something little, it makes a difference). What people know is what gets them around in our complicated world. Education is a virtue because the more that we know, the easier it becomes to take action because it's hard to just stand by when we fully understand miseries happening around us.

As I attained more knowledge about these miseries (poverty, AIDS, and child trafficking) and above all as I learned the stories of the people who live in these miseries, I was deeply affected. The only thing left for me to do was to act, so that's what I did. I took small action steps day after day and I continue to take steps each day to spread the word about InterviewGirl.com, the Interview Girl Foundation, and this book. Taking action is one of History's greatest lessons. You need to act. Without taking action nothing will happen. Even when you take small actions, these can make a substantial difference as the days pass.

"Education is the key to unlock the golden door of freedom."

—George Washington Carver

"Words are mere bubbles of water, deeds are drops of gold."

"Talk does not cook rice."

—Chinese Proverb

Lesson 21: Service

"Only a life lived in the service to others is worth living."

—Albert Einstein, German-Swiss-U.S. scientist

Of all of the prevailing lessons that we learn as we study history, the lesson that the best use of our time is time that is spent serving others is unparalleled. We need to learn to ask, how can we serve those around us. Late Holy Father, John Paul II conveys that the purpose of a Catholic university is to prepare a student to, "learn to think rigorously, so as to act rightly and to serve humanity better." Pope John Paul II's words always stuck with me as I was in school. I thought all of this schooling, all of this studying was to somehow serve humanity. I created InterviewGirl.com to serve people in two ways. One of the most profound messages embodied in the teachings of Jesus, Gandhi, and Mother Teresa is in the call to serve others. Jesus, Gandhi and Mother Teresa challenge us to consider, who our work is serving? As Eileen Barker, a mediator based in San Rafael, CA, studies Gandhi, she challenges us to reflect upon: Are we offering our services to those in the community who most need them? Are there ways we can contribute to those whose problems are often unseen and whose voices are often unheard?[274] Rather than view the poor as separate from ourselves, Jesus, Gandhi and Mother Teresa challenge us to see our oneness with the poorest among us. Jesus, Gandhi and Mother Teresa beckon us to serve the poorest and weakest, and in so doing, serve ourselves. One of the problems plaguing the world is that 1 billion people live in poverty. Below is a story about how one man's actions started a movement to eradicate poverty.

A Priest's Call to Service Helps Lead a Movement to Eradicate Poverty

Joseph Wresinski was born to immigrant parents in a poor neighborhood in Angers, France. He grew up in a family which suffered from poverty and social exclusion. In 1946, he was ordained as a priest and served in industrial and rural parishes where, right from the beginning, he related to the most deprived families. In 1956, Father Joseph Wresinski was assigned by his bishop to be a chaplain to 250 families placed in an emergency housing camp in Noisy-le-Grand, near Paris. The families lived in huts erected in a muddy field. Wresinski explains his years in Noisy-le-Grand as, "The families in that camp have inspired everything I have undertaken for their liberation. They took hold of me, they lived within me, they carried me forward, and they pushed me to found the Movement with them." In 1957, Father Joseph and the families of the camp founded the first association which was later to become ATD Fourth World. They replaced soup kitchens and the distribution of old clothes with a library, a kindergarten and a chapel. Joined by the first few volunteers, he soon created a research institute on extreme poverty which brought together researchers from different countries and disciplines. Since it started, the development of ATD Fourth World has been inspired by Father Joseph's own experience as a child in a poverty-stricken family and by his daily contacts with very poor families and members of the ATD Fourth World Movement's Volunteer Corps.

Father Joseph's firm purpose was to unite all sections of society around the very poorest. He succeeded in gaining recognition of the poor as partners in society. On October 17th, 1987, in the presence of 100,000 people from every social background and continent, Father Joseph unveiled a commemorative stone in the Trocadero Human Rights Plaza in Paris. On this marble his call is engraved: "Wherever men and women are condemned to live in poverty, human rights are violated. To come together to ensure that these rights be respected is our solemn duty." Since then the commemorative stone has become a rallying point for people from all walks of life. They gather to bear witness to the very poorest people in the world and to make a personal commitment to join forces with them in abolishing poverty and social exclusion. October 17th was declared "International Day for the Eradication of Poverty" by the United Nations in 1992. In several countries, on the 17th of each month, people gather for a short commemoration in honor of people who suffer from extreme poverty, and to renew their commitment to them.[275]

From Father Joseph Wresinski's service to the 250 families placed in an emergency housing camp in 1956, a movement to end poverty grew out of this service. Many around the world are now working to eradicate poverty. Nelson Mandela issued a rallying cry to make poverty history in front of over 22,000 people in Trafalgar Square as he famously stated, "Like slavery and apartheid, poverty is not natural. It is man-made and it can be overcome and eradicated by the actions of human beings." Father Joseph Wresinski's actions started a movement to eradicate poverty. His call to eradicate poverty was born from his years of service in the emergency housing camp.

The most eminent lesson that all the years of history teach us: Helping others, the capacity to serve is what matters most and this lesson is the bedrock of InterviewGirl.com's movement.

Below is what a few other distinguished individuals throughout human civilization have to say about service:

"He who wished to secure the good of others, has already secured his own."

—Confucius

"Imagine what a harmonious world it could be if every single person, both young and old, shared a little of what he is good at doing."

—Quincy Jones

"We cannot all see alike, but we can all do good."

—P.T. Barnum

"When you help someone up a hill, you find yourself closer to the top."

—Brownie Wise

"An essential part of a happy, healthy life is being of service to others."

—Sue Pattom Thoele

"You have not lived a perfect day, even though you have earned your money, unless you have done something for someone who will never be able to repay you."

—Ruth Smeltzer

"Caring is a reflex. Someone slips, your arm goes out. A car is in the ditch, you join others and push ... You live, you help."

—Ram Dass

"Make the world better."

—Lucy Stone

"You can start out with nothing and end up with everything if you are willing to serve by sowing your service as a seed."

—Bill Winston

"May I never get too busy in my own affairs that I fail to respond to the needs of others with kindness and compassion."

—Thomas Jefferson

"How wonderful it is that nobody need wait a single moment before starting to improve the world."

—Anne Frank

"I don't know what your destiny will be, but one thing I know: the only ones among you who will be really happy are those who will have sought and found how to serve."

—Albert Schweitzer (1875-1965) *German theologian, philosopher, and physician*

"The more a man takes the needs of others on his own heart, the more he must take his own heart to God. You are not here merely to make a living. You are here in order to enable the world to live more amply, with greater vision, with a finer spirit of hope and achievement. You are here to enrich the world, and you impoverish yourself if you forget the errand."

—Woodrow T. Wilson (1856-1924) *Twenty-eighth President of the USA*

"If you can't feed a hundred people, then feed just one."

—Mother Teresa (1910-1997) *Albanian-born missionary*

"I was hungry and you gave me food."

—(Matthew 25:25)

Lessons from Interview Girl as a History Student

Within the books and primary sources that History students spend considerable hours interpreting, a history student is introduced to multitudinous memorable stories that impart some unforgettable lessons. Illustrious individuals from History fascinate generation after generation. There are certain people who we read about years later because as we say, they "changed the world." What can we learn from these individuals? Studying the "Greats" from History and their feats are another aspect of the work that is done at InterviewGirl.com. Compilations are made out of all of the stories that I hear in interviews, but I also read, study, compile, and then put together compilations and projects for you about people and events from history. At InterviewGirl. com, we know that there are ceaseless concepts for you to learn and it is our hope that you'll both learn as well as glean ideas from all of our compilations and projects that are put together. All projects produced at InterviewGirl.com are created because from "paying it forward" as we share stories, we have the opportunity to reduce some of the misery that exists in our world.

A Few More Lessons: Lessons from Interview Girl as Travel Girl

"Tourists see. Travelers seek."

I have been able to travel during my summers for the past decade starting in college and then after college. I ascertained immeasurable lessons from the experiences of traveling the world in my twenties. Meeting people in cultures diverse than my own proved to be rife with lessons that I would not forget because I gained a different perspective each time that I traveled to a new place or I met a new person. The unique perspectives that I was able to reap through traveling made me think if I am only one person and I have heard so many stupefying stories from my travels alone, imagine the stories that I could hear if I were to ask other people to share their travel experiences? I knew that there had to be millions of other stories out there from people who traveled, as well. TravelGirl.com was an initial idea that I created to collect and share travel stories with the world. Obviously, *TravelGirl* morphed into InterviewGirl.com. Now *Travel Stories* are one category and project at InterviewGirl.com. The purpose of InterviewGirl.com's *Travel Stories* is to share those life lessons that I learned from my own travel experiences as well as to get others who have traveled to different parts of the world and have disparate experiences to share their stories. InterviewGirl.com's compilation filled with travel stories has some spectacular stories to share.

> "Fairy Tales always have a happy ending. 'That depends ... on whether you are Rumpelstiltskin or the Queen.'"
> —Jane Yolen, *Briar Rose*

In *Briar Rose*, Jane Yolen instructs that we all have discrepant perspectives. The paramount lesson that I procured as "Travel Girl" has to be perspective. InterviewGirl.com collects stories and disseminates these stories because as we do this, people are heralded with variant perspectives. Depending upon your perspective, you'll see things differently in this world. Take the situation below, for example. It is the same story, but people view the story with different lenses.

"He's giving us a worksheet again! Ughhh! I can't believe it!" Nicole says to Kelly as they sit next to each other in Chemistry class. "I know! He never teaches us a thing!" Kelly responds to her lab partner. The kids in this Chemistry class see their instructor, Mr. Levine as lazy. What they don't know ....

"I'm sorry, Mr. Levine, Henry's levels are down yet again," the nurse explains to Mr. Levine that evening after school. George Levine puts his head down and shakes it back and forth. Mr. Levine was at the hospital, where he slept every night because his son was dying of leukemia. He would leave work, the high school every single day and go to the hospital to watch and spend time with his dying son. Mr. Levine was hoping and praying that his 10 year old son would get better.

If Nicole and Kelly, the two Chemistry students saw Mr. Levine's reality outside the chemistry classroom maybe their perspective about him being lazy would change? One becomes enriched in a myriad of ways from traveling, but being introduced to new perspectives from your travels is inimitable. As one travels, he/she is introduced to new ideas about culture, perspective, power, religion, and overall ways of life. InterviewGirl.com's "Travel Girl" compilation (*Travel Stories*) will present you with many perspectives from around the world. People have traveled all over the world and submitted some of their best travel stories to InterviewGirl.com.

"We can complain because rose bushes have thorns, or rejoice because thorn bushes have roses."

—Abraham Lincoln

I came to appreciate "perspective" during my time as "Travel Girl." Learning that people have different perspectives based on what is that they have experienced in their lives is a valuable lesson that humbles us when we understand that it is a colossal world out there abounding with many perspectives besides our own. We all see things divergently. Each of us has a different lens through which we see the world. The subculture and situation that we come from determines the diverse lens from which we view our surroundings.

As my own trip to Africa was the catalyst to start InterviewGirl.com, a few stories from Ghana will best depict what I mean by this notion of perspective. In the village where I stayed in Kpando,

Ghana, there is no running water and there is no electricity. You shower with one bucket of water that you fetch from a well. You then poor that water over your head as you are standing behind this wall made of stones. You are out in the middle of nature essentially. It's you, the air, the hardly sturdy blockade that's made of stones to hide you from others seeing you, and your bucket of water.

Well maybe out of habit, maybe out of tiredness, I had not slept in days, and even though I did not have running water and a shower head over my head as we do here in America, I put a lot of shampoo in my hair. I began to poor the water from the bucket on my head to rinse out the shampoo. Soon enough the water ran out and I had shampoo in my eyes. So there I stood, reaching for my towel that was hanging over the stone blockade with one eye squinted open because I still had shampoo in my eyes and in my hair. As I reached for my towel, with one eye partly open, vaguely out of the corner of my eye—I saw that now behind the stone wall, there sat me in "my shower space," an empty knocked over bucket, and a goat. When I began the "shower" (which would take place with a bucket of water), it started out as naked me, a bucket filled with water and the area behind the stones. Now just moments into the shower, it was naked me with soap filled eyes, an empty bucket and a goat all in the tiny space behind the stones.

The second that it registered that a goat was only a few inches away from me, I grabbed that towel as fast as I could and sprinted out of the shower area. I mean sprinting. Mind you I was undressed for the shower so I was only partly covered up by my towel as I was sprinting through the communal yard that connects the little huts that my neighbors lived in. One of the neighbors, Xavier saw me running and began to comfort me from afar as he shouted, "it's ok." My response to this sweet man trying to calm down the crazy, screaming American girl in the middle of this rural village, "no, it's not ok that there is a goat in my shower! It is not okay!"

Like I said, it's all about perspective, to me an American girl who grew up in suburbia with running water and electricity and no animals, opening your eyes and finding a goat next to you is one of the scariest things that I remember in my entire life. To a native Ghanaian in the village of Kpando, a goat that comes near you is no big deal. Perspective. It's all about where you come from, what you are used to, and the environment where you live. What lens do you see the world with and why? More importantly try and understand why it is that some people see things the way that they do. From their perspective, how they view a situation, may just make sense.

The transcendent lesson that I learned as Travel Girl is to try and keep another's perspective in mind. By changing our perspective, it allows us to alter the way that we see particular elements in our shared world. Russell Kirk popularized the term "moral imagination." Although, we should remember that Edmund Burke first defined "moral imagination" in his *Reflections on the Revolution in France*. Russell Kirk defines "moral imagination" as,

"A uniquely human ability to conceive of fellow humanity as moral beings and as persons, not as objects whose value rests in utility or usefulness. It is a process by which a self "creates" metaphor from images recorded by the senses and stored in memory, which are then occupied to find and suppose moral correspondences in experience. An intuitive ability to perceive ethical truths and abiding law in the midst of chaotic experience, the moral imagination should be an aspiration to a proper ordering of the soul and, consequently, of the commonwealth. In this conception, to be a citizen is not to be an autonomous individual; it is a status given by a born existence into a world of relations to others. To be fully human is to embrace the duties and obligations toward a purpose of security and endurance for, first and foremost, the family and the local community. Success is measured by the development of character, not the fleeting emotions of status."[276]

Percy Shelley writes, "To be greatly good, a man must imagine clearly, he must see himself and the world through the eyes of another." Moral imagination is when we try to see the world as someone else would. Hearing and learning stories is the best way to embark on strengthening our moral imagination.

One's reality is shifted with a little bit of perspective. In an interview with a veteran from World War Two, I asked the vet what he believed to be a lesson that was beyond compare that he learned from serving in the Pacific during the war. He shook his head carefully, looking down at the table as reflected on the question. Moments of silence passed before he shared, "there is more to the world besides my neighborhood. This is the greatest of all lessons that WWII taught me." Through the stories that are collected at InterviewGirl.com, we hope to bring you new, distinctive, and different perspectives from around the world. Recognizing our perspectives, how we see the world, is salient because the way that we see the world determines how we live our lives.

"There are no facts, only interpretations."

—Friedrich Nietzsche

"Man, to be greatly good, must imagine intensely and comprehensively; he must put himself in the place of another and many others; the pains and pleasures of his species must become his own. The great instrument of moral good is the imagination."

—Percy Bysshe Shelley

414

Lessons from Interview Girl as INTERVIEW GIRL: Become a Student

"Wisdom is Wealth."

—Swahili (African Proverb)

Interview Girl as a History student and Interview Girl as Travel Girl emerged from my enchantment with learning about the world and others who inhabit our planet. My love affair with being a student and learning new stories, entities, material, configurations, and circumstances created my role as Interview Girl in the first place. Anything that you want to learn how to do, someone else has already done. You need to learn from those who have done what it is that you want to achieve. Anything that you want to do, you can learn from someone who has already accomplished what it is that you would like to do. Beyond question, reading allows you to self-teach yourself just about anything. Today with technology and the internet, it is easier than ever to spread knowledge and information to others. Early on I learned the expediency that speaking with others would bring people in their lives. There is a profuseness that one learns through other people. That's the whole basis for InterviewGirl.com. In interviewing people, people would share their wondrous stories with me and then I would share these stories with the world.

You must believe that no one is smarter than you, no one is more talented than you. You can learn whatever it is that you desire to learn. InterviewGirl.com is a vehicle to get you there. You have the capabilities and resources to be educated in any area you choose. Don't waste this gift. Learn, learn, learn! Never stop learning. Compilations and projects produced at Interviewgirl.com will help you to learn what it is that you want to learn. All of InterviewGirl. com's products and resources are produced to help you learn, grow, and view the world in a different manner. The profits from these products will then help to eliminate an individual's misery. As discussed in Chapter 12 and Chapter 13, in order to eliminate misery that an orphan with HIV/AIDS experiences, providing education is an integral part of the plan because people having access to an education is one of the keys to eradicating poverty. As *Operation A²* provides education to orphans without access to medication, through the stories that it shares, InterviewGirl.com also dispenses education to people throughout the world

"Try to learn something about everything and everything about something."

—Thomas Huxley

"Nobody is born wise."

—African proverb

Wrap Up of the Consummate Lessons from Human History

"The difference between school and life? In school, you're taught a lesson and then given a test. In life, you're given a test that teaches you a lesson."

—Tom Bodett

As Interview Girl as a Historian and as Interview Girl as Travel Girl, I gleaned lessons that helped me to understand the world and my place within it better. To sum up, the lessons that I learned as a History student are that in order to be successful, you need to apply unrelenting effort. You need to: write down your ideas, ask the right questions, and never give up. You need to remember that continual, unrelenting effort often produces dramatic results, it's happened before and it can happen again, overcoming failure is a stepping stone to great things, hard work pays off, you have to believe in yourself, Rome wasn't built in a day, just because someone says something cannot be done doesn't mean that it can't, a little bit makes a big difference, to do the right thing, you need to continually make connections between things in your life, to read, don't become obsessed with being perfect, the course of your life is determined by your habits, remember to take actions, serving others is the best use of your time, your perspective makes all the difference and to never stop being a student.

History informs us that it is ordinary people who do extraordinary things in their lives. It isn't that a few people are born lucky. This is one of the exalted secrets edified in the stories that comprise the history of our global world. Stories instruct us about what to do because as we realize that throughout human civilization, it has been ordinary people who have changed the world, this gives us the motivation, courage, tenacity, and the will to take action as people from the realm of history have done before us time and time again. Often times, those individuals who "changed the world" saw a need in their community and then rose to the challenge. You and I can help to make the world a better place as all the individuals discussed throughout this book have done.

As we learn content in school, we are taught lessons and then given a test. In life, you're given a test that teaches you a lesson. The compilations produced at InterviewGirl.com will continue to share these invaluable lessons with you. What lesson can you share with InterviewGirl.com and what lessons can InterviewGirl.com share with you? InterviewGirl.com's compilations and projects will introduce you to some venerable stories, but they will also impart life lessons that stick with you as you go on in your life. Just like those classes in school where long after you forgot the content, you remembered a story or a lesson from the "content" that was part of the school curriculum. As Mark Turner explains in *The Literary Mind*, "Rational capacities depend on it. It is our chief means of looking into the future, of predicting, of planning, and of explaining ... Most of our experiences, our knowledge and our thinking is organized as stories."[277] To return to lessons about history content (Harry Truman) in a social studies class, by now, maybe you forgot the years of Truman's presidency that were mentioned earlier in the book, but you probably remember that he overcame adversity. You recall this because you remember the story about him talking to his wife about how he believed that he was destined to do something greater when he was broke 20 years before he became President. How President Truman overcame adversity is something that you can conjure up because you learned this engaging anecdote about Truman in a story.

As Daniel Pink concludes in his chapter on "Story" in *A Whole New Mind*,

> "We are our stories. We compress years of experience, thought, and emotion into a few compact narratives that we convey to others and tell to ourselves ... Story represents a pathway to understanding that doesn't run through the left side of the brain."[278]

Pink then describes the popular scrap booking movement as well as the popularity of genealogy as millions search the Web to piece together their family histories. He concludes, "What these efforts reveal is a hunger for what stories can provide—context enriched by emotion, a deeper understanding of how we fit in and why that matters. We must listen to each other's stories and we must remember that we are each the authors of our own lives."[279] InterviewGirl.com hopes to engage the world in listening to one another's stories. Projects created at InterviewGirl.com are alive with the aforementioned lessons along with varied other lessons. At InterviewGirl.com, we will: learn more, earn more, and by doing this, we will then give more to people who are experiencing a form of misery. InterviewGirl.com's plan where each action affects the next is all put into place through the medium of sharing stories.

"We owe it to each other to tell stories."

—Neil Gaiman

CHAPTER FIFTEEN

Compilations and Projects Currently in Progress at InterviewGirl.com

The point of this part of the book is to give you a taste of some of the compilations that are currently in progress. As Interview Girl, I have been hard at work documenting the stories of various people in order to share their stories with you. As we have discussed, you can learn an assemblage of material from others. People have gone through exactly what you are going through. By hearing their stories, you acquire insight and inspiration to overcome what you want to overcome because after all, people before you have successfully overcome obstacles and accomplished their desires. What if you could read a book with advice from people who have successfully started businesses around the world? Or what if you are in school and you are contemplating attending medical school someday, but you are not sure about what to expect? InterviewGirl. com is working on a compilation of stories from medical students. Have you ever wondered what it was like on September 11th for those directly affected? Are you curious about what it was like to be a U.S. soldier in Iraq? Have you wondered what it's like to be homeless? These topics along with a myriad of others are compilations underway at InterviewGirl.com. Interviews from people on various subjects are being compiled to bring the world stories about all of these subjects. Here are a few samples from some of the upcoming compilations underway at InterviewGirl. com:

Africa Stories	Homeless Stories	Leukemia Stories	Poverty Stories	Websites I Cannot Live Without
Beach Body Coaches	Hope (Stories)	Life In Prison	Productivity Tips	Weight Loss Programs and Specialists
Beauty Secrets	Hospital Stories	Living During a War and/or People Who Grew up during Wartime	Reading a Book Changed My Life	Weight Loss Success Stories
Being a Writer	Illness Stories	Major League Baseball	Refugees	Who is your Hero/Mentor? Why?
Bloggers	Immigration Stories	Medical School	September 11, 2001 (Stories)	World War Two Stories
Bodybuilding	In the line of Duty (Stories from Firefighters/ Policemen)	Model Stories	Service	Government, Politics and Politicians (Stories)
College Stories	Individuals With Developmental Disabilities	NLP	The Story of My Life—Advice from Elderly	Law School (Stories)
Eating Disorders	Japan Crisis 2011	Nonprofit Doctors	Teachers	Personal Trainer Stories
Engagement Stories	Iraq War Stories	Online Stories	Travel Stories	Wealth/ Created a Fortune/ Millionaires
Entrepreneurs	Italian Vacation Stories	Overcoming Overeating	Untold Stories from the ER	Vietnam Stories

Goals	People who have started amazing Organizations and/or Foundations	Making a Difference	Miracle Stories	Any Story You Have To Share

Untold Stories from World War Two

The WWII Stories compilation is one of InterviewGirl.com's first projects to be released. Speaking with the men and women who were alive during World War Two was an influential experience for me that was filled with some stories that need to be shared. I spoke with these World War Two vets late in their lives, most of them were in their eighties and nineties. I collected stories from those living during the era including housewives, clerks, nurses, lieutenants, generals, soldiers, marines, pilots, navy seals, prisoners of war, and exiles. I have interviewed over 500 World War Two vets. A sample story is below:

Living in Nazi Germany

Elvin and Ester, Residents of Nazi Germany who were not members of the Nazi Party

Elvin and Ester are a married couple who currently (2011) reside in a retirement community in Chicago. They lived in Nazi Germany during World War Two, but they weren't Nazis. On a cold December day, I visited a delightful retirement community. The Christmas spirit permeated throughout the retirement home. The activities director told me that I would be meeting first with a couple who was from Germany.

I sat in the communal room and waited for the couple to arrive. After a few minutes, they walked in hand and in hand—an adorable sight. They took their seats and after introductions, we began. I asked Elvin and Ester to explain their experiences and memories from World War Two.

When It Began

The thin elderly gentleman, Elvin begins,

"The 1st of September 1939. That was the day the war started. Families quickly responded to the war. When my mother came home on that day, she told me that I could no longer eat as much bread as I wanted to eat. This was the first impression I had of WWII."

Ester, his wife chimes in,

"I remember that day like it was yesterday. I was 13 too. From the beginning, we saw it coming that life would be much more difficult. For example, my family owned a store and they, "the Nazis" closed our store quite a few times because we had Christian services there. The first of September was my brother's birthday. He was supposed to come home that day."

Her brother was completing his mandatory two years of military service after college. With her head down as her voice became softer, she reluctantly explains, "He never came home. He was later on killed in the war." Wanting to change the subject from her brother's death, Ester recounts,

"There was glorious music all over. People thought that, the world was ours. We marched into Poland. We were only allowed to listen to one radio station. My father had ways to get us other stations, though, so we got the truth, but other people, they didn't know any better. It rubbed us so wrong—the whole era. We didn't understand what everyone was celebrating. We didn't understand why they would play this music. I remember my father said, "It is now—the time of the Devil coming.""

After quoting her Father, Ester pauses and then finishes with, "And it was."

Wartime

As Elvin and Ester's experiences in Nazi Germany unveil, the difficulties of living during wartime was a theme, a commonality that emerged in interview after interview from people who lived in European countries while World War Two was happening. Elvin describes that,

"Everything got scarce. You can get used to eating less. Instead of having two slices of bread, you can have one slice, but I remember everything became less."

After describing the conditions in Germany, Elvin recalls,

"The danger was how would the war continue? The war was part of other European countries besides Germany. Poland and Austria became a part of the war too."

It seemed important for Elvin that I understand the hardships that Hitler brought to Austria and Poland as well. He continued,

"There were other countries that were taken over. Austria was occupied by Hitler before the war and people in Austria were told that they had to speak the

German language. The Austrian leader had to tell the people that they were conquered by Germany."

Elvin pauses and then he explains an example to me,

"The next morning people would wake up in Austria and they would learn about the new German military borders."

His wife now chimes in as she makes a smile that indicates that the word that she is about to say will not make any sense, but she says, "Hitler called it freed, you know?" Ester goes onto describe how Germany was bombed by Britain. Pointing toward her husband, Ester pronounces,

"His family was bombed out four times. Elvin was pulled from school and called to the army when he was 18, but that was near the end of the war."

As the bombing from England came up, Elvin begins to tell me a story from his life years later here in America that reminded him of the bombing. He begins,

"I had a strange experience. We went to Georgia. Georgia had a beautiful state park. You can use your RV there and park overnight. When we got into the gate of the state park, I couldn't believe that there was an American bomber, a huge airplane at the park."

Someone at the park told him that the huge plane was a B-17. Elvin responded to this individual,

"Oh no, I saw B-17's that flew over our city for one or two hours and destroyed about a quarter of the city by dropping their bombs. One hundred B-17's flew over our city for 1 to 2 hours and destroyed ¼ of the city for by dropping their bombs. I know what a B-17 is!"

Elvin was sure that he would never forget what a B-17 was because of his scary experience of being bombed during the war. He continues to shake his head as he repeats, "I know what a B-17 is." Ester then further describes wartime Germany. She declares,

"There was darkness all over. For years we were used to that: darkness. There were no street lights for years. The government kept it dark so that the enemies wouldn't discover a city. We had very little lighting. At my home, we had thick blankets by the windows so that no shimmer of light would get through. For years this went on. There was a curfew that was very early. All cars were taken away from people. There were no cars. We all had bicycles, except for people from the government, some of them had cars."

She pauses, contemplating just how to explain her thoughts,

"It looked like the young people were for it, but the older people, especially Christians, saw the danger in it all."

She shakes her head,

"We still know all the verses from the songs honoring Hitler from those days. We had to sing the songs two times a week. Music was a big plus for Hitler. It is how Hitler won the young people. If you didn't show up to Hitler's Youth, then the guards would come visit your parent's home. If you missed a couple practices, then the guards would come to your home and check up on you. We were constantly under surveillance. There was no voting, nothing like that. After school, we had to

425

practice marching with Hitler's Youth. We marched and we sang. Even back then, I remember thinking how wrong some of the songs were."

At this point, she begins to sing a part of one of the songs,

"Today we are rulers of Germany, tomorrow the whole world is ours. Today we are rulers of Germany; tomorrow the whole world is ours."

Ester continues to describe her experiences as a girl in school in Nazi Germany,

"My homeroom teacher for five years was a complete Nazis. He hated the Christians. It was a difficult time in school."

To further elaborate on her homeroom teacher, she adds,

"There was a big movie house. Every young person had to go to the movie house on Sunday. On Monday in school, Dr. Gold would ask, "Who did not go to the information meeting on Sunday?" When we were not there, he asked us, "Why didn't you go?" He then gave us long-term papers to write."

Freedom is the Greatest Gift of All

Ester made it clear that her father was anti-Nazi,

"My Father told our neighbor that this war was really unnecessary. My father thought that he knew the neighbor really well and yet they came for my father. Our neighbor told the authorities about my father. Luckily, we were able to get away. We left Germany with a refugee train. We did not have anything, but it did not matter that we left everything behind because we were going to freedom. If they take everything else from us again, I can handle it. I just could not handle not to live in freedom anymore. That is the greatest thing of all the other good things we have in America. It was not until I was 22 that I was able to know what freedom was. In my twenties, my family came here in America."

Living in America is a gift to Ester because she understands what it is like to live without freedom. Speaking with Elvin and Ester, residents of Nazi Germany who were not members of the Nazi Party and learning about the curfew, no street lights for years, the music, and the only radio station that they could listen to exemplified the censorship that existed in Germany during the 1940's. Their clear memories of events that took place nearly 60 years ago epitomizes just how much living in Nazi Germany affected their lives. Those of us, who have lived in a country where we have freedom of speech, press and religion our entire lives, we are very fortunate and by hearing Elvin and Ester's story, we are introduced to a new perspective. We understand that these are freedoms that should not be taken for granted. Ester made a powerful statement when she described that freedom is the greatest privilege that we have as American citizens. She experienced what it is like to live without freedom, so freedom unequivocally was a value that mattered immensely to her.

Ester and Elvin who lived during Nazi Germany expound what it was like to live in a regime where the government controlled all aspects of one's life. For another project for InteriewGirl.com, I interviewed a young man in his late twenties. He was doing missionary work in China. I asked this gentleman if he felt the presence of communism in China? He responded,

"Yeah, definitely in the mental state and government policies. Economically it is a free market, but even then the government can control your business. People have

427

no sense of individual worth here. You're just a part of the machine and your worth is in if you play your part. If not, your family shuns you. Yeah that's hard for me. I try and convince the Chinese here that they have beautiful minds."

It is interesting to note that Ester and Elvin described similar policies in Nazi Germany as the young man whom I interviewed recently who now lives in China.

The stories that comprise InterviewGirl.com's *WWII Stories* compilation were collected from 2008—2014. The people who shared these stories were many years removed from WWII. InterviewGirl.com's *WWII Stories* project is a collection of stories about peoples' experiences in WWII, but it is also a collection of stories from elderly people, speaking near the end of their lives, and they share some valuable life lessons. The people who lived through the Second World War share some thought-provoking contrasts between life then and life now. Hearing the stories of the individuals who lived through WWII causes us to reflect and think about our own life. Many of the people interviewed made it clear that at the end of your life, it's the relationships in your life that matter most. This was a theme that was shared time and time again from the elderly. The relationships someone has with others are what are most important to the individuals when they are looking back on their lives through the years. When you hear the WWII vets' stories and their insights, it forces you to think: how are the relationships in my life? How much their spouses, children and grandchildren meant to them recurrently emerged. One of InterviewGirl.com's first projects that will be released is a compilation of stories from individuals who were alive during World War Two. Elvin and Ester's experiences in Nazi Germany are one of many stories that will be shared in this project at InterviewGirl.com.

Love Stories

A few of the compilations that we are working on at InterviewGirl.com include a collection of stories about how gentlemen proposed to their ladies, a compilation chalk full of wedding planning advice from brides who have been through planning a wedding, and a compilation filled with good, old fashioned love stories.

Who doesn't love a good proposal to marriage story? Even in just the early stages of InterviewGirl.com being live on the internet, *Love Stories* has proven to be a popular category. Girls from around the country have shared their engagement stories. This compilation filled with engagement stories is going to remind us all that courtliness still exists. Guys who are thinking of popping the question soon, you won't want to miss this compilation from InterviewGirl.com. You can get some great ideas! Why re-invent the wheel? A second grade teacher shared that after she began wearing her engagement ring to school, one of her students, pointed at her one day as he noticed the ring on her finger, he excitedly said, "Ms. Javsky is proposed!" She explained, "It was the cutest thing, instead of saying "engaged," he said, "proposed.""

A Walk Along the Beach

The following story is from a gal who asked to remain anonymous. It is totally fine if you choose to remain anonymous in any of InterviewGirl.com's projects. The girl shares that she and her boyfriend were in Florida for a wedding. The day after the wedding, they were taking a walk along the beach. She bent down at one point and she picked up a stick. She said that she asked her boyfriend to write their names in the sand. He agreed. She was looking toward the ocean and when she turned back, she noticed that he wrote, "will you marrie me?" She said that her immediate response was that she laughed because she noticed the spelling error, but then she replied, "Yes, baby I will!" After hugging him, she then corrected his spelling mistake. *A Walk Along the Beach* is one of many romantic proposal stories that InterviewGirl.com has collected from people.

Sharing a Story Helps People in Two Ways

Serving other people is why InterviewGirl.com was started. Interviewgirl.com is collecting stories and advice about weddings and planning weddings. As with all projects at InterviewGirl.com, the people reading the compilation of stories and the people who submit the stories are both served in the process. What bride doesn't miss the wedding planning process after her big day? Many brides share that is can be difficult to spend so much time and energy planning a wedding and then all of a sudden the detailed-oriented planning process is all over. Well, if the bride were to share her experience from planning her own wedding with InterviewGirl. com, she is helping a female who is now planning her wedding with the advice and knowledge that she imparts, but she is also helping herself to slowly wean herself off of the wedding planning frenzy and bring closure to the wedding planning process as she shares her story to serve others who are now going through the wedding planning process.

Below are some of the other compilations that InterviewGirl.com has started:

Living with Alcoholism

For this compilation, stories from those suffering from alcoholism are shared. I have interviewed people who enrolled themselves in AA. Also, I have read many publications and many of the stories printed from various AA groups throughout the world. Alcoholics have been interviewed. Some have successfully overcome their vices. Others have not. Below is a story from a man who sobered up.

The story shared below first appeared in *High and Dry*, the newsletter of Seattle Alcoholics Anonymous, in February 2000. The man in the story Floyd now lives in Silverdale, Washington.

Prison was a tough teacher

If we ever need a poster boy for the miracle of Alcoholics Anonymous, my nominee is Floyd C. of Redmond. Floyd has been sober since June 15, 1956, when he reluctantly got into the AA program in a California prison forestry camp in Oak Glen. "I worked in the kitchen scrubbin´ floors and serving and all that sort of thing. I was still psycho. I was still nuts. I still gave ´em a hell of a hard time for a long time. But I ended up as secretary of the group." Here's what life was like for Floyd before that: As a kid in Oregon, I skipped school for three days. I was declared incorrigible and put in the Oregon State Reformatory for five years. I stayed there till I was 16. That was one of the toughest reform schools in the United States. They would put a steel boot on you, lock it on, and make you work in the fields. They had these long straps and they'd whip you if you ran away. Then you'd get put in a hole in the ground, sort of like a manhole. There was a mattress and a jug of water and a pot, and it was pitch dark. I went 30 days at a time down there. "They'd make you go to church on Sunday, hallelujah type of church, but I raised so much hell. There couldn't be a God if I was being treated the way I was. So every Sunday, instead of me going to church with all the other kids, they'd lock me in solitary confinement. I didn't mind, though. I was never allowed to be alone excepting solitary confinement, and I liked that." That was only the beginning. Floyd drifted down to California and went to prison twice, the first time for burglary and the second time for robbery. In between, he bummed around the country. "My whole life was mixed up. I ran into a fella I'd been in reform school with, and we came up to Seattle together. I got into heroin for a little while. We were boosters, you know, shoplifters, and the police told us to get out of town or they'd kill us. I was in my 20s then. They caught me down on Jackson Street, took my money, took my knife and broke it, and then gut-punched me till I couldn't see straight. That was going on all over the United States at that time.

"So I left town as quick as I could, hitchhiking. In Montana, I stayed in a bush three days and started to kick [the habit]. I made it back to the road and a guy picked me up and bought me a bottle of wine. That helped a lot. But I didn't know how to get drugs anywhere but in Seattle, so I went East to Philadelphia, sobered up and went to work.

"I stayed for over a year in the early '50s, ran a restaurant there, and then I got drunk. The police took me home the first time 'cause, you know, we used to give them free food. The second time, I woke up in Washington, D.C. with the boss's car and all the receipts for that night. So I kept goin'. A couple weeks later, I was in Miami, Florida, sleeping in the park, completely broke. And the police told me to get out of there, so I went to New Orleans. I really went down at that point.

I slept in a car in a used car lot, and made a little money robbing church boxes.

432

"That ended when the police told me they had a road gang they could put me on if they saw me around town anymore. So I hitchhiked out to Los Angeles. It took a long time 'cause people'd smell me and kick me out of their cars. Most of the way, I rode on the back of cattle trucks and in pickups.

"When I got there, I was almost dead. But I remembered an old buddy in Portland who had told me about Central Avenue. I worked my way down there, and my Higher Power must have been working for me 'cause I ran into this one buddy. He took me to an empty house they all called The Pit. We had cold water and gas, was all. They undressed me and put me in a tub of cold water that damn near killed me. They had to change the water about three times, I was so filthy. One of 'em took my clothes and threw 'em in an alley about three blocks away. They didn't want 'em any closer. "Well, they nursed me back to health, and I felt I really owed 'em somethin' for saving my life. I did some petty thieving around there, until I got hold of a double barreled, sawed-off 12-gauge shotgun. Me and a buddy got hold of an old car and went down to Culver City. I held up a bar there, but unbeknownst to me, Red, who was waiting in the car, was suckin' on a bottle to keep up his courage. We went down the road a couple of blocks and he turned against a 'no left turn' sign with a couple of cops watching across the street. I told him to step on it, but when the cop yelled to pull over, he did and we were on our way back to jail.

"I'd been drinkin' steady every day for four years, and the Lincoln Park jail wouldn't give me even an aspirin to calm me down. I went insane. When I woke up three months later, I was in San Quentin again, in the psych ward. I stayed in one cell there, 8 by 5. I was nuts. I cussed the toilet. I thought the warden was shootin′ sparks up to make me gag. I thought I was on Death Row. When they came in to take me to the doctor, I fought ′em every time, so they'd come in with a mattress, get me up against the wall, then down on the floor and choke me till I passed out and they could get the straps on me.

"I did some hard time, San Quentin, Folsom, Chino. The first time I was in San Quentin, I killed a couple of guys with a baseball bat who tried to molest me. Those guys had a knife on me. I was only 21. They deserved it. I wasn't prosecuted. They didn't do that in those days. Instead, they sent me to Folsom."

Amazingly, Floyd was released to the forestry camp at Oak Glen. "I was still nutty as hell. The other inmates were afraid of me. Even after I found Alcoholics Anonymous, I gave the jailers a hard time for a long time. But after I became secretary of the group in there, the Parole Board noticed a radical change in me and let me out after five years where I would usually have got 10.

"You had to have a job to get parole. My family had dropped me completely. I wrote probably a hundred letters, and never got one back. It was the Salvation Army that sponsored me so I could get out. I think the world of them.

"Back in L.A., I moved into a halfway house called New Horizons. It was while I was there that I met Bill W. on two different occasions. Bill would spend the evening, no, the night talking to us guys. I wasn't too impressed till the second time he came and remembered my name and everything I'd said before. He gave me a silver dollar, flipped it over to me and told me I could make a couple of phone calls or get a couple of drinks with it, my choice. I still have that silver dollar. I'll probably leave it to my son someday. Bill signed my

Big Book, too. The first edition that had a red cover, but I lost it."

Floyd married shortly after leaving prison. "She was an addict, pure and simple. She wasn't an alcoholic, but she'd go to meetings with me and they'd kick her out. A friend of ours who was an alcoholic invited six of us over to his house, and out of that meeting came Narcotics Anonymous. That was about 1960.

"NA won't ever be as big as AA. Drug addicts are not the same as alcoholics, and most don't live that long anyway."

The couple moved briefly to Joplin, Missouri "'modern' in a rental ad meant it had an inside toilet"' and then came to Seattle, where they were active both in Alcoholics Anonymous and in starting Narcotics Anonymous programs. "My wife and I were talking in all the schools and churches, mainly about pot. That was in the 70s. We started a methadone program, and helped start Sea-Dru-Nar. The only thing I didn't like about SeaDru-Nar was the attack therapy I thought a better approach was love and understanding."

Tragically, his wife was hit by a drunk driver and suffered brain damage. She became addicted to drugs again and two years later died of an overdose.

Floyd clung to his sobriety through all these events, helping to start Hilltop, now the Alano Club of the Eastside. It is there and the 23rd & Cherry Fellowship that he attends most of his meetings. He used to be a regular at the old Fremont Hall in Fremont, too.

'I used to get into a fight a year. At the old Fremont, where I went for a long time, guys were crowding across the table punchin' each other till I made an announcement that the next guy that turns on somebody would have to fight me. And you know, it stopped.

"We had problems with bikers there. One of 'em came up to me with a chain one time, and I threw him down the stairs. He took the door off. Then we went across the street and had a talk with those bikers about yelling at our girls. They never bothered them again.

"I still go to seven or eight meetings a week. I have been to well over 20,000 in my lifetime. For the first 20 years I was in the program, I went to at least one or two meetings a day, and on the weekends I'd go to three or four a day. AA was my life. That's all I did.

"My health is good; I'm still working at the plumbing trade that I first learned in reform school."

It took a lot of years, but Floyd finally came to believe in God. "I had a Higher Power, but I didn't believe in God. Then one day, a guy said to me, 'It's easy as hell. God is love.' so after 25 years in AA, I finally had my awakening. And I had more help from a fantastic lady who told me, 'Just remember one thing. Floyd is no big deal.' once I accepted that, my whole life changed. And you know, now I do not have a bad day."[280]

Stories from Online Businesses

In this compilation, many individuals who successfully started on-line businesses are featured.

Stories from the Best Bloggers

In this compilation of stories, people who write blogs who have over 100,000 followers and subscribers have been interviewed. They share their secrets, inspirations, and advice on how to write as well as manage a successful blog. Featured within this compilation of stories are some of the most inspirational Blog posts from the internet.

What the Politicians have to Say

This particular project underway at InterviewGirl.com started when I sent letters asking elected officials or people who work in government offices to share their stories. I sent letters to: various senators, individuals holding statewide offices, congressional representatives, people on various boards and commissions, people holding regional positions within the government and so on. This project has morphed into many stories being shared, such as, stories from people who ran for office, but then lost. People who served in office, but are no longer serving and people who have volunteered in political offices also share their stories. When this project was started the idea was to get people from the political realm to share their stories. Notable stories have been shared so far and we hope to receive many more stories.

Time Management Secrets

"Lost time is never found again."

—Proverb

Time is our greatest asset. For this compilation of stories, I reached out to many of the time management and success gurus, as they are called, and asked them to share their secrets and short cuts about time management.

How I made it in Hollywood

Actors and actresses have been contacted and asked to share their stories about how they made it in Hollywood.

Making Peace with Vietnam

Vietnam War veterans have been interviewed for this compilation of stories. Very similar to how InterviewGirl.com's compilations about *World War Two* stories and *Korean War* stories are being put together; this project is sharing the memories and stories from those who served in Vietnam.

Becoming an Author

In this compilation, the stories about the lives of numerous best-selling authors are revealed. The common practices and rituals that these authors have in common with one another when it comes to being a successful writer are highlighted. The idea for this compilation was to get authors to share their tips and tricks of the trade.

Voices Of Those Who Cannot Be Heard

As you know InterviewGirl.com started out as a vehicle to voice voices of those who are not always heard in our world. I have gone to great lengths to secure interviews with prison inmates, people living with disabilities, elderly living in nursing homes, people hospitalized for eating disorders and many others. All of these individuals have a unique perspective to share.

When you speak with someone who has been in prison for many years, it forces you to see the world through another lens. To hear what life is like from the perspective of someone who knows what the walls inside a jail are like is eye opening. In interviewing prison-in-mates, I have found that the in-mates' stories range from individuals who are remorseful and wish to be a different person to those who are bitter and seem as if they still have not repented for what it is that they did wrong.

Anonymity matters to many of these individuals and for that reason InterviewGirl.com respects the privacy of individuals in its compilations, projects, books, speeches, and interviews. A person's preference when it comes to authorship of the story always comes first. If someone chooses to remain anonymous, his/her wish is respected. We adhere to your instructions as to what information can be disclosed with all stories that are submitted to InterviewGirl.com. Projects put together under *Voices Of Those Who Cannot Be Heard* are all filled with interesting stories from people that we do not often hear about within society. Projects like this are completed because one of InterviewGirl.com's overall intentions is to help people learn about different perspectives that exist in the world.

Finding Fitness

In this inspirational compilation of stories, you'll find the stories about hundreds of individuals who found fitness and as they found fitness, it transformed their entire life. Celebrities, famous "fitness" personalities, and many others have all shared insights that are featured in this excellent compilation. From YouTube "fitness" gurus, to Beach Body coaches, to nutritionists, to personal trainers, you name it and they have been interviewed. InterviewGirl.com interviewed these individuals in order to share their expertise and bring you this compilation filled with advice and stories.

The Stories Behind The DIETS

There are millions of "diets" out there. I set out to do InterviewGirl.com's project on dieting with the hope that I would be the scholar to decipher which diet it was that veritably worked. I started to gather "stories" about dieting. My plan was to gather data, interview doctors, nutritionists, and dietitians, read books written about various diets, compare/contrast what all these authors found in their research about dieting, and from this process, I wanted to then uncover the diets that worked.

What emerged is a product from InterviewGirl.com: *Dieting Debunked*. In *Dieting Debunked*, first, over 50 diets are compared and contrasted. I review each diet, sum up the major ideas about that diet, and pick out particular "key elements" (what makes that diet unique and different from the others). Parallels and differences from the diets reviewed are highlighted in *Dieting Debunked*. Then, the end of the book brings together lessons that we can learn from each of the diets presented throughout the analysis. I had originally intended to bring out the lessons that we can apply to dieting (eat less, move more, stop drinking pop, watch your portion sizes, etc.), but through the research and interviews that are being completed for this project, I am learning not only the lessons to a successful diet, but I have discerned lessons that we can all apply to our lives. In reading, researching, analyzing, and learning about 50 different diets, I learned not only that there are some universal lessons that we can apply to dieting, but also some lessons that we can apply to our lives that will make us more balanced in our lives.

Dieting Debunked reviews all these diet books and then gives the readers the best advice from each book. Basically, this project sums up advice from all of these diet books combined. Unfortunately, there is no one answer to the weight loss game. There is no magic pill or sure fire diet secret. It was my goal when I set out to write this book to find the diet secret that worked best. When people see a trim person, they often think, "What's that person's secret?" Chances are he/she eats healthy, he/she exercises, and he/ she leads a balanced life.

The historiographical approach is applied to this compilation. Commonalties in the diets are highlighted for you. What works to achieve weight loss is pointed out. Common themes that are seen in diet after diet are established. In this compilation, hundreds of diet books, diet websites, and diet and nutrition articles are presented. *Dieting Debunked* provides hundreds of resources all together. This will help you to locate the specific information that you are looking for as you attempt to debunk dieting.

Stories from Doctors and Nurses

This category started as I sat in the hospital waiting for various family and friends of mine to give birth to their babies. I am not someone who can sit for very long, so I would wander throughout the hospital while we were waiting for the babies to be born. By this point, I was carrying little InterviewGirl.com business cards that I created around with me. As I walked the halls of the hospital, I passed doctors and nurses. The ones that offered me a friendly smile, although feeling uncomfortable, as they say, "I gave it a try," as I handed them one of my InterviewGirl.com business cards while quickly explaining the idea behind InterviewGirl.com. I asked if they could share stories or advice about what it is like being a doctor. Some looked at me as if I was crazy, but others warmly responded and we set up an interview right then and there.

I have met with several doctors and other doctors/nurses have emailed me some riveting stories and advice about the profession. This compilation has been divided into two parts. The first part is advice for medical students and the second part is stories from the field. How doctors are serving us and what it is like working in a hospital, ER, volunteer situation, and in the medical field, in general are shared within this compilation.

Collecting College Stories

Pretty much anyone who has attended college and is now in the "real" world has been in a situation where he/she has told people a story from his/her college days. People orally sharing their stories has been the most popular way for individuals to share stories about when they were in college. If you have a funny story from college that makes people laugh or if you have some sort of other story pertaining to your college years, please consider sharing your story with www.InterviewGirl.com.

Life Lessons from the Elderly

I love each and every interview that I partake in, but interviewing the elderly has captured a special place in my heart. I will never forget what I gleaned these past four years from interviewing many people ages 75 and up. I genuinely gained *Wisdom from the Wise* as I set out to do this compilation.

In completing this compilation, I continually went to different nursing homes and elderly persons' facilities and asked the elderly to share their life advice. I was on a quest to find out: What do people with 80 plus years of experience of living on this planet have to say? I heard some stupendous advice and stories as I interviewed the elderly.

The elderly are a group of people who fall under the *Voices That Are Not Always Heard* category. These are the types of stories InterviewGirl.com strives to share with the world. A certain connotation goes along with how we view old people living in nursing homes. The elderly are just that—elderly, but they are filled with stories to share and they want to share their stories. We can all learn from what the elderly have to contribute.

An opportunity to volunteer to help interview has emerged from this particular compilation project. As the elderly share their stories and advice, the content that they share helps the people who read the compilation of stories. The people interviewing the elderly are also helping the elderly because elderly tend to get lonely. This act of interviewing the elderly (sitting down and having a conversation with them) is a service to the elderly. Once again, InterviewGirl.com helps people in profuse ways: 1.) The content that the elderly share helps people as they read compilation projects produced at InterviewGirl.com, 2.) the people interviewing the elderly provide a service to the elderly, and 3.) the proceeds from the *Life Lessons from the Elderly* project help to eliminate misery in our world.

Charities in Africa

What are nonprofit organizations, NGO's, countries, and charities doing in Africa? Charities serving in Africa and people completing missionary work warm my heart because I knew these charities and individuals helped people like sweet Amara. In developing a plan about what exactly the Interview Girl Foundation would achieve in Africa, the debate that I discovered in development economics about the issue of donor aid led me to find out more about charities and what they are currently doing in the world. I researched hundreds of charities and their effectiveness as I designed *Operation A²*.

Charities in Africa is one compilation underway at InterviewGirl.com, but InterviewGirl.com has projects and compilations that list hundreds of charities (all over the world— not just Africa). InterviewGirl.com's projects that feature charities and people making a difference in the world list and explain numerous organizations. These organizations making a difference are featured all together for you in the InterviewGirl.com project. You can read about these charities and hear about all the good that is being done through them in projects produced at InterviewGirl.com. InterviewGirl.com loves sharing and spreading stories about benevolent, kind-hearted, and philanthropic individuals and organizations who are achieving good in our world. Spreading the word about inspiring people who are making a difference is part of InterviewGirl.com's mission. These kinds of stories need to be shared with the world.

Humanitarian Hope

Humanitarian Hope details philanthropic endeavors undertaken by people throughout the world. Chronicling philanthropic undertakings has been fascinating to research. It is indefinitely inspiring to learn how many people are trying to good in this world. This compilation has been one of my favorite to put together. Numerous projects at InterviewGirl.com promote charities, ideas, and entities striving to make the planet better. The purpose of the *Humanitarian Hope* compilation is to expose organizations that exist and to spread the word about them and their purposes. Founders of nonprofit organizations have been interviewed and asked how the organizations were started, what the organizations do, where the profits go, and so on. Essentially, this compilation reveals the progress that is being made throughout the world to eliminate various miseries that exist.

The purpose of *Project: C²: Committed Collaboration* through the Interview Girl Foundation is to be a part of creating innovative solutions to some of society's most pressing social problems. The Interview Girl Foundation's ongoing exploit to assist in fostering committed collaboration among the world's social entrepreneurs who have develop bold and innovative new solutions to social and environmental issues is what drives *C²: Committed Collaboration*. As compilations such as this one (*Humanitarian Hope*) are put together, the Interview Girl Foundation becomes more aware of the efforts underway to make the world a better place. As the Interview Girl Foundation becomes aware of these efforts, it then allows the foundation to connect and network with organizations throughout the world. In truth, to make the world a better place, we all need to collaborate together. The Interview Girl Foundation nor any sole foundation can cause social change, but when diverse sectors of society, governments, NGO's, and private institutions work together, it is then that social issues begin to change for the better. *Project: C²: Committed Collaboration* yearns to bring together people and organizations who are already working to make the world a better place. As these individuals collaborate, miseries can be attacked from manifold angles. People working together is what creates innovative new solutions to social and environmental issues.

Stories Through Audio

InterviewGirl.com shares many of its compilations, programs, stories, and interviews that are completed in various audio formats. Many interviews that have been completed are now in the process of being uploaded onto our YouTube channel, uploaded to our Podcast, made available in mp3 form for downloading, and added into our programs that come with an audio component. Sharing InterviewGirl.com's work in audio programs is essential because of the benefits associated with hearing a story and because of how many people enjoy hearing a story orally. As discussed previously, a well told story is one of the key components that determines how a story affects people. InterviewGirl.com is working to make stories that are shared available for you in various audio formats.

Summary

InterviewGirl.com has already collected some amazing stories and our projects to bring you these stories are in progress. InterviewGirl.com is also teeming with further projects that I could not yet mention in this book. Until I get the "okay" from those who I plan to interview, I didn't want to release those projects quite yet. What I can tell you is that there are various compilations "in progress" where I am contacting illustrious individuals for interviews. Part of InterviewGirl.com's mission is asking people to share their stories on their own, but I'm also still proactively seeking out individuals asking them to share their stories. People who the world would both benefit and enjoy hearing from are being contacted about completing interviews with InterviewGirl. com.

InterviewGirl.com will not only feature stories that people share, but important information from articles, scholarly journals, books, newspaper articles, etc. will also be added into the various compilations. My training as a graduate student taught me how to research and a multitude of InterviewGirl.com's compilations will feature personal stories coupled with scholarship and research. People are alive with infinite stories and information that other people would enjoy learning. It is the goal of InterviewGirl.com to hear these stories and then to put this information into organized and easy to read compilations.

A whole slew of different categories from which to choose to share your story are available on InterviewGirl.com. People can read through these variegated topics and then decide which story they would enjoy sharing. Chances are that InterviewGirl.com has a compilation in a category that your story would fall under and if we don't, we'll start a new category. If you have suggestions about projects to start, please let us know the topics at InterviewGirl. com. As time goes on, we can add countless other topics. Of course, as mentioned already in this book, anonymous entries are accepted at InterviewGirl.com, as well. InterviewGirl.com started collecting stories in categories in areas where I could get people to complete interviews. In the last year, the project has grown and it has the potential to flourish even more as time passes. InterviewGirl.com is working to collect stories from multifold categories because it's a diverse world comprised of individuals with assorted interests. I am so excited about the direction of the InterviewGirl.com movement. Some of the stories that have been collected are without a doubt transformative. Some make you laugh. Others make you cry. Incredible compilations filled with bounteous stories are coming soon from InterviewGirl.com.

If you are interested in being an interviewer for InterviewGirl. com, please apply on the website. InterviewGirl.com collects a sundry of stories because our projects present many stories all together. The compilations will feature hundreds of resources all together for readers or listeners of InterviewGirl.com's projects. When you purchase a compilation from InterviewGirl.com, you get an "all in one" guide with many resources already pulled all together.

InterviewGirl.com gives your organization or business a chance to get exposure. For example, we are featuring charities and businesses from around the world in our *businesses, on-line businesses* and *charities* compilation projects. People's websites, Facebook pages, and Twitter accounts will be featured in these projects. If you own a business or run a charity, sharing a story or information about your business or charity with InterviewGirl. com gives your organization publicity.

Check out InterviewGirl.com on the internet and you will be able to see all the magnificent projects (latest compilations) that we have started. I bet there is a category that you can contribute to and if not, submit your story in the other option. We all have a message, a story to share, and what you have to say will resonate with someone somewhere.

InterviewGirl.com concentrates on collecting stories and making compilations, but solo projects, books, speeches, lectures, talks, etc. are all also sponsored by InterviewGirl.com. This chapter presented a very small sample of some of the compilations that are currently in progress. Please go to www. InterviewGirl. com and check out the compilations underway. If someone whom you know can share a story, please pass along InterviewGirl.com's project information. When you visit InterviewGirl.com, you will be able to see all of our current projects.

CHAPTER SIXTEEN

Questions about Interview Girl, InterviewGirl. com, and the Interview Girl Foundation

In this chapter, you will find some common questions that people have about Interview Girl, InterviewGirl.com, and the Interview Girl Foundation.

If I donate to the Interview Girl Foundation, will I see where the profits have gone?

Yes, there is a "what we've done section" on our website to see how the proceeds from the projects at InterviewGirl.com have helped people (eliminated miseries). Also, all contributors to the Interview Girl Foundation will receive a bi-annual newsletter about what the Interview Girl Foundation is doing throughout the world.

What if I have an amazing story to share, but I don't want my name published?

Don't worry; if you do not want your name used, by all means, we won't use your name. A lot of people go through an experience and it's really hard or they would never admit to that experience. No problem, you can remain anonymous. Submit an entry without your name. If you ask to NOT use your name, we will honor and respect this request.

Is my story worthy?

Maybe you checked out InteriewGirl.com and you saw a category, but you think that your story is not worthy. For example, maybe you think, "Yea, I lost weight. So what, so have hundreds of other Americans. People don't need my advice or they don't want to hear my story." Your story is needed! It is. Someone will benefit from hearing about your experiences. Also, by adding your story to the compilation, it can add to the other stories and all the stories together will complement one another. There is not a story that is not worthy. InterviewGirl.com collects and appreciates *all* stories.

Will all stories submitted be published in a compilation project?

Unfortunately, we cannot publish all stories, but on the website, archives have been set up and all stories submitted will be posted there.

CHAPTER SEVENTEEN

Conclusion: Part One: There is always Hope

"Try not to become a man of success but rather to become a man of value."

—Einstein

Will It Work?

"Do not wait to strike till the iron is hot; but make it hot by striking."

—William B. Sprague

This may be a pipe dream and the amount of people that I am hoping to get to share stories will fall short, but I thought, if I don't put myself out there, we will never know and every time I see a picture of Taycutay or Asantuwa or any orphan whom I met in Africa, I realize that it's worth putting myself out there as I attempt to spread this idea. Dr. James Orbinski describes that you understand circumstances in a very different way when you have a friend who is part of those circumstances. When you meet individuals and they become more than statistics on a page, you go from wishing circumstances were different to taking concrete actions in order to change those circumstances. After seeing all that he saw serving as a doctor for *Doctors Without Borders* during the Rwanda genocide, people ask Dr. Orbinski how he copes. He says that you will not see him looking in a self-help book. He believes that you need to actually engage the world in which you live. He maintains that you need to engage the world that causes you to feel a certain way. As Dr. Orbinski espouses, InterviewGirl. com is a way for me to become engaged in the world in which I live. Spreading the idea that we can all do something to eliminate some of the misery that exists in our world is the best way that I can commence to engage this world.

Sometimes I doubt my InterviewGirl.com idea, but, then I remember that they told Albert Einstein that he was "mentally slow, unsociable, and adrift forever in foolish dreams." I reread the story about how before Albert Einstein won the Nobel Prize in Physics in 1921, he did not speak until age four and did not read until age seven. I have been turned down for many interviews that I strived to get. These moments get me down, but then I recall that Michael Jordan was told, "Boy, who you kidding? You can't slam no ball!" and he was cut from his high school basketball team. As we all know, in 1992, Jordan played in the summer Olympics with the original Dream Team and he went onto to win 6 World Championships. Many people consider Michael Jordan to be the best basketball player that ever lived.

> "I've failed over and over and over again in my life and that is why I succeed."
>
> —Michael Jordan

One of the scrolling images that flashes across my computer screen when the computer goes into sleep mode is an airplane because it hints to me that man was told that he would never be able to fly long distances through the air in a machine, yet look at all the places that I've traveled to in an airplane. In the late 1800's, Simon Newcomb, a prominent astronomer and the head of the U. S. Naval Observatory observed, "... no possible combination of known substances, known forms of machinery, and known forms of force, can be united in a practical machine by which man shall fly long distances through the air." Orville and Wilbur Wright accomplished what they were told they could not do. In December of 1903, Orville Wright took the Flyer for a 12-second, sustained flight. This was the first successful, powered, piloted flight in history. Right before that 12-second, sustained flight took place, the Wright brothers made two other attempts to fly their machine, one of which resulted in a minor crash. Before the successful 12-seconds, they failed. Without the Wright brother's invention, Charles Lindbergh and Amelia Earhart would not have made their solo trans-Atlantic flights until much later. Aircraft would not have been as effective in the world wars, and jet and rocket engines would have been developed later as well. The Wright Flyer is also the precursor to the space shuttle. The Wright brothers made powered flight possible and many other accomplishments developed from what they made possible. Initially they were told that they would never be able to fly a machine through the air.[281]

Human history edifies that people attain what was at one time "impossible." Maybe just maybe, one story at a time, we can make the world a better place. You can be negative about my desideratum and doubt that I can do any good anyway or you can share a story, spread the word about InterviewGirl.com, or purchase one of InterviewGirl.com's compilations. In life, we all have choices. Please choose to be positive and support InterviewGirl.com's humanitarian efforts. I once heard that the difference between successful people and those who fail is that success people do those things that failures don't want to do. As Interview Girl, as I embark on this endeavor to be successful at collecting enough riveting stories that they sell at a rate that will help to change the world, I am asking you to share your story with me. For the past eight years, I have been "after" stories. I have been enthusiastically seeking out people asking them to share their various stories with me and now I am asking you to do the same. In this way, one story at a time, we'll change the world. With every story that is collected and disseminated, we can erase someone's misery.

I have chosen to take my passions and to create InterviewGirl. com. Through hearing stories and then sharing these stories, the world can be changed. It won't happen overnight, but slowly we can slice away some of the misery that exists in our world and that's why InterviewGirl.com was created—to make this world a better place. A man who honorably played a vital role in 20th century history, the late Pope John Paul II once said, "Learn to think rigorously, so as to act rightly and to serve humanity better." I was in school for a long time. I want to put that schooling to good use. I now know what I am meant to do. I am here to serve the world and make it a better place by doing what I love most: learning, meeting new people, sharing stories and writing.

Do A Little Something

One of the matchless historical lessons that stands the test of time is that anything that is accomplished in life is done a little bit at a time.[282] As individuals lose weight, accumulate wealth, and write a book—by working on those tasks a little bit at a time, people make a difference in this world and in the lives of others in the same way: *little by little*. If we look at any of the feats in human history, grander things and accomplishments from humans on this Earth, these achievements were accomplished by individuals completing small tasks on a daily basis. That is exactly how anything gets done. The Interview Girl Foundation strives to makes small improvements in the lives of others by reaching out to one person and then the next and then the next and so on. As John Wooden declares,

> "When you improve a little each day, eventually big things occur ... Not tomorrow, not the next day, but eventually a big gain is made. Don't look for the big, quick improvement. Seek the small improvement one

day at a time. That's the only way it happens—and when it happens, it lasts."

Compilation by compilation, project by project, InterviewGirl. com will help to eliminate the misery that a few people are experiencing and as time goes on those few will become many. The Interview Girl Foundation will donate the proceeds from a particular compilation of stories that InterviewGirl.com publishes to a group of people undergoing a certain misery or to a specific person. Story by story, person by person, profit by profit, together we have the opportunity to shave off a piece of misery in today's world and although I love a great story for a great story, I cannot think of a better reason to want to write and share stories: to help and serve others—to eliminate misery.

I have always believed that you could do anything if you put your mind to it and that a positive attitude and a willingness to make a difference go a long way. We cannot, we must not think that "my story" or "my little donation" will not matter anyway. It can make a difference and it does. In anything in life, every little bit counts. As Gary Ryan Blair articulates in *Everything Counts*, "Everything you say; every thought you entertain; and everything you do has a direction, which serves as an advance or a retreat in respect to your pursuit of excellence. Everything—regardless of size or intent—has bottom-line consequences; therefore everything counts. This is the golden rule of excellence."[283] The little actions that we each take to eliminate someone's misery will make the world a better place. Share a story today. By you taking the time to share a story with me, I will take your story and share it with the world and one compilation at a time, we will begin to slice off a piece of the misery in today's world, starting by helping the children dealing with the hardships of HIV/AIDS in Africa (*Operation A²*).

"You don't have to have much before you give, for the little you have can make a difference in the life of others."
—Edem, Founder of *Children's Home* in Kpando

The small steps and actions that we take can make a difference. Even what may seem like very small actions can compound and eventually lead to mind-boggling changes. In order to sincerely make a difference in our world, we need to get *everyone* to do something. If everyone does something, then together we can all make a difference.

"It is the greatest of all mistakes to do nothing because you can only do little—do what you can."
—Sydney Smith

Serving Others

"How far that little candle throws his beams! So shines a good deed in a naughty world."
—William Shakespeare, *Merchant of Venice*

We all have distinctive and different stories, talents, advice, and experiences to share. According to educator, writer, and speaker Leo Buscaglia, "You want to be the most educated, the most brilliant, the most exciting, the most versatile, the most creative individual in the world, because then you can give it away; and the only reason you have anything, is to give it away." By an individual sharing his/her knowledge and stories, he/she is contributing to humanity. Robert M. Sherfield states,

"Service to others is about giving something that no other human on earth could possibly give -you! It is about finding what is rare and divine in your soul that you would like to share with the world. Service to others is about digging deep into the caverns of your abilities, your talents, and your personality and finding the gift that you want to share with humanity."

You want to become the best version of yourself because when you are, you can serve others most advantageously. Wanting to help and serve others is one the core ideas responsible for InterviewGirl. com. As we serve others, we are eliminating some of the misery that exists in the world.

Profits from products produced at InterviewGirl.com are used to help others (eliminate miseries), hence why service and helping others are root ideas in InterviewGirl.com's movement. Service and helping others are different than trying to force our help on someone or trying to "rescue" anyone. As it is said, "Do unto others as they would have you do unto them." When helping an individual disenfranchises that individual, service has taken a wrong turn. In *The Blue Sweater*, Jacqueline Novogratz tells a story about how she joined a nonprofit microfinance organization for women based in New York City. Novogratz was placed in Africa through this organization. She was an ambassador to African women with an office at the African Development Bank. Her job was to help local country organizations across West Africa get started. The African Development Bank sent Novogratz to attend a conference. Novogratz shares, "The African women made it clear in a public way that I was neither wanted nor needed as an ambassador in West Africa." A woman from Cote d'Ivoire snapped at Novogratz, "We have women who can and should staff that office and help us build the West Africa region. I don't understand why anyone thinks we should have a young girl who is not even African!"[284] Novogratz reveals that she did not know how to confront their fears head-on, but she knew that she had been hired to jump-start the actual work because a West African office still had not been built. Novogratz's experience at the African Development Bank is a good example of people becoming annoyed when they feel as if someone was sent to "save" them. "Do unto others as they would have you do unto them" is a central part of *Operation A²'s* initiative to provide medication and education to those who have AIDS. Concepts like "third world countries," "saving," and "rescuing" are not part of the Interview Girl Foundation' philosophy. Dr. Orbinski explains, "I dismissed the phrase Third World Development with all of its in egalitarian and paternalistic overtones. It implies that we have reached some sort of Utopian ideal ....where we are "first" and the rest of the world is struggling to reach the same place."[285]

We need to see the world as a nation of humanity. We are all part of the human story. Dr. Paul Edward Farmer is an American anthropologist and physician who is best known for his humanitarian work providing health care for people. Dr. Farmer describes caring for others—visiting them in their homes, helping them fill prescriptions, washing their dishes, etc. Dr. Farmer suggests that doctors, nurses, and community health workers should be accompagnateurs (a word adopted from Haitian Creole) to their patients. To Farmer, accompaniment is different from aid. "Aid" connotes a short-term, one-way encounter: one person helps, and another is helped. Accompaniment seeks to abandon the temporal and directional nature of aid; it implies an open-ended commitment to another, a partnership in the deepest sense of the word. As Dr. Farmer encourages, we need to be "accompagnateurs" to those experiencing misery. The Interview Girl Foundation believes in asking the people who are experiencing a misery what their needs are and "aiding" from there. The Interview Girl Foundation understands that showing up with a plan with already made decisions that do not take into account the specific people experiencing miseries will not help people. People at the Interview Girl Foundation can learn as much from the people whose misery we are working to eliminate as those individuals can learn from us at the Interview Girl Foundation.

> "Treat people as they want to be and you help them become what they are capable of being."
> —Johann Wolfgang von Goethe

We all have stories to share. It has been said everyone is broken in their own way. Even if one person experiences a "misery" that someone else doesn't, well that other person experiences some form of misery in their own way. We are all people, and people screw up every day. I'm reminded of the story from the Bible where the people wanted to stone a woman to death for cheating on her husband. Jesus' response was, "He who is without sin should cast the first stone." I guess when we judge someone else; it makes us feel better about ourselves and makes us forget about our idiosyncrasies. Every government, every group, every charity, every church, no matter the denomination, is made up of people who are broken. We want to remember that we are all broken in our own ways, so if there is way to eliminate someone's misery, maybe one of our own idiosyncrasies will get better in time. "Helping" an individual can often times be misconstrued as one's culture/way of life being perpetrated on someone else. In Jacqueline Novogratz's story about the African Development Bank, she maintains that the Africans "neither wanted nor needed saving." Her description is accurate when she states that it is not healthy for anyone to feel that they should save someone else. *Operation A²* is not about "saving" in any way, shape or form. The Interview Girl Foundation is about understanding one another. Misery can be eliminated when we try to understand one another. It's reciprocal. Becoming empathetic is important because you want to learn about life from someone else's point of view. Nobody should have to live in misery and the Interview Girl Foundation strives to prevent anyone anywhere from living in misery.

"Everyone has the power for greatness, not for fame, because greatness is determined by service."

—Dr. Martin Luther King Jr.

Through a Story, I Changed ... which Led to Collecting Stories

"You never know all the good, a simple story can do."
—Interview Girl

Everyone has had those moments in life where you are never, ever the same after the moment. I'll never forget that day when Edem said, "Because the medicines ran out." When I think of that moment, I can still feel the hot, African sun beating down, permeating through the vehicle's window as I sat squeezed between my suitcases in the van heading back to Accra from Kpando. I still vividly see Edem's piercing, wide open brown eyes looking into mine and then looking down just before he softly shared the news. That moment was a catalyst that sparked me to want to make a change. Learning about Amara's death taught me about empathy. I wanted to become a better person—a person that could help others or someone who could make a difference in this world. As we all have, I had heard the concept of "making a difference" many times, but this time I was inspired to take meaningful actions and actually make a difference for those less fortunate somehow. InterviewGirl.com developed from the perspectives that I captured about the world while I was in Africa. When I came home, I could not stop researching, reading, and learning about some of the world's greatest miseries. That was not enough though (the knowledge), the research made me understand these miseries better, but I wanted to do something more. I found myself coming up with a plan to alleviate some of them—starting with helping people experiencing the misery of AIDS in Africa.

After learning the stories of many orphans suffering from AIDS, it dawned on me that medicine, science, and technology were all needed to help AIDS victims, but on a more basic level, I felt that it was necessary to look at people without AIDS and ask ourselves, "what could we do?" Of course I knew that people could give money to nonprofits such as the Interview Girl Foundation, but before money, science, or medicine, we needed to begin somewhere else. Ultimately, I came to the conclusion that more people needed empathy, myself included. Humanity would better be able to serve victims of AIDS, victims of human trafficking, or the world's poorest people if we all became more empathetic. A major step toward our goal to eliminate these larger problems within sectors of society commences as individuals throughout the world cultivate their sense of empathy, compassion, and concern. Service and humanity begin with empathy. As InterviewGirl.com was created "service and humanity begin with empathy" was what guided me as the idea unfolded. What is done at InterviewGirl. com: collecting and sharing stories, helps people to become more empathetic.

We all need to see each other in order to bring out the full potential in others. People need to have their specialness reflected back in the eyes of others in order to see it themselves. When we empower others, we can collectively come together to bring our best selves forward in order to solve the world's biggest problems. There is power in empathy. Let's just say for a second that I made enough money to distribute antiretroviral medication to everyone in the world who needed the medication. This wouldn't be enough to cure the AIDS pandemic. The lengths that people have gone to in order to help others in this world are inspiring. Why then are so many miseries left when many organizations and groups have assisted others through the years? Multiplied reasons contribute to why miseries exist, but when a misery exists, there are people who are not being treated with dignity. You are familiar with the Interview Girl Foundation's crucial first step: analyzing the scenarios when giving foreign aid ended up a failed attempt. My investigation into the foreign aid debate led to our understanding that an efficient government and sustainable economy are needed in any society, in any country for people to be lifted out of poverty in a way that would last. In an article, "Toward the end of poverty," from the *Economist*, Jon Berkeley suggests,

"The MDGs may have helped marginally, by creating a yardstick for measuring progress, and by focusing minds on the evil of poverty. Most of the credit, however, must go to capitalism and free trade, for they enable economies to grow—and it was growth, principally, that has eased destitution."

Toward the end of the 20th century poverty rates went down largely because developing-country growth accelerated, from an average annual rate of 4.3% in 1960-2000 to 6% in 2000-2010. Around two-thirds of poverty reduction within a country comes from growth. Greater equality also helps, contributing the other third. A 1% increase in incomes in the most unequal countries produces a mere 0.6% reduction in poverty; in the most equal countries, it yields a 4.3% cut.[286] Economists express that China is responsible for three-quarters of the achievement mentioned above,

"Its economy has been growing so fast that, even though inequality is rising fast, extreme poverty is disappearing. China pulled 680 million people out of misery in 1981-2010, and reduced its extreme-poverty rate from 84% in 1980 to 10% now."[287]

As Jon Berkeley concludes,

"It will be harder to take a billion more people out of extreme poverty in the next 20 years than it was to take almost a billion out in the past 20. Poorer governance in India and Africa, the next two targets, means that China's experience is unlikely to be swiftly replicated there."

Efficient governments that answer to citizens where free markets and free trade prosper lead to people being lifted from poverty.

Capitalism and free trade enable economies to grow—I understand this part of the foreign aid debate and the problems that people see with charities, but in the meantime, providing someone who is sick with medication seemed necessary. Certain programs through the Interview Girl Foundation focus on getting countries' economies to grow because as this happens, there is less poverty. Providing sick orphans with medication was the first part of *Operation A²'s* plan and the Interview Girl Foundation has programs that target long term sustainability rather than band-aid solutions, but in the interim, projects produced at InterviewGirl. com would allow all of us to learn more stories and by people hearing stories, we gain responsiveness, empathy, and compassion. As much as the Interview Girl Foundation has plans to provide aid and medication to people who are ill, with monetary means alone, the Interview Girl Foundation nor any other foundation can eradicate AIDS. Money is not enough. Aid is not enough. Even if a country's economy grew at the necessary levels, this still would not be enough to eliminate miseries like AIDS, poverty, or human trafficking. Donna Hicks, PhD is an associate at the Weatherhead Center for International Affairs at Harvard University. She is the author of *Dignity: The Essential Role It Plays in Resolving Conflict.* As she put it, "There is no such thing as democracy without dignity, or can there be authentic peace if people are suffering indignities?"[288] Human's desire for dignity resides deep within people, defining our common humanity. Hicks writes, "If our capacity for indignity is our lowest common denominator, then our yearning for dignity is our highest." Human interaction is centered around people being treated with dignity. InterviewGirl. com is a vehicle that helps to promote treating others with dignity.

When people begin to alter their thinking and ultimately they learn to listen more carefully, they then begin to hear the needs of humanity. When we become more empathetic, we can begin to understand more fully how our hands can be the hands that can change a human life. I believe that when you do this—gain empathy, you have made a difference in the world. InterviewGirl.

com comes into play because one way for us to become more empathetic is for us to understand that the world is filled with stories and as we learn these stories, we ourselves become enriched because our perspective about the world in which we live develops. A man in Afghanistan once said to James Orbinski, "No scars, no story, no life." Dr. Orbinski then articulates,

> "Sometimes, the best story is in the space between the words—a space that is a window onto a different way of seeing. And when there are no easy answers, stories are all we have."

Stories help us to understand the people and larger world around us. Hearing a fact or knowing a misery exists is one thing, but when someone acquires another individual's story, a new way of understanding is achieved. Stories help us to become better versions of ourselves because we become more empathetic. Robert M. Sherfield explains empathy beautifully,

> "Empathy is when you put yourself in the lives of others. It is when you truly understand their pain, joy, fears, and actions on an internal level. Empathy at its highest level is when you are involved enough to know what other people need and how you can help them with their needs. Most of the time, people with the greatest empathy are those who know how to listen to what is spoken and to what is not spoken."[289]

All humans want to be seen, to be heard, and to have a way to respond to our needs. This is the essence of empathy and this is why people becoming more empathetic is at the core of this movement. Even with the medicine, the economics, and the money, without people wanting to learn about the miseries of others, an integral component of what will allow us to make the world a better place is missing. As Donna Hicks articulates democracies do not exist without dignity. Efficient governments that answer to citizens where free markets and free trade prosper lead to less poverty. Efficient governments are shaped when governments treat their citizens with dignity. People are treated with dignity when other people are willing to listen to them. InterviewGirl. com encourages people to *listen* to others.

> "Nobody made a greater mistake than he who did nothing because he could only do a little."
>
> —Edmund Burke

In *An Imperfect Offering*, after James Orbinski recounted his service in Rwanda for *Doctors Without Borders*, he explained that he returned to McMaster University with research questions about AIDS and other diseases. He articulated that what he had seen in Rwanda had raised questions not simply about failed vaccination strategies and inadequate clinical case definitions. He now had moral and political questions about who gets what, about why some get more than others, and most importantly, who decides. Orbinski submitted his required reports as well as a series of reflections once he returned to Canada. In his reflections, he told stories about what he had seen. He finished with his account about how he changed in his time in Rwanda. He ended with,

> "It may seem naively idealistic, but I know that as long as we can imagine a better tomorrow, we can work toward a better tomorrow. Such idealism has seeded the world with some of its greatest accomplishments and social institutions. I can change my own life and practices to make these ideals live in what I do in my life today."[290]

I once heard someone explain the difference between a revolutionary and a saint. The person said that a revolutionary tries to change the world around him/her whereas a saint changes things he/she does in his/ her own world knowing very well that the outside world surrounding him/her may not change. We can all do something to eliminate some of the miseries that exist. No one individual, no one organization, no one NGO, no one country, and no one person single-handedly can change the world, but we can all do something. Each of us can change our own world and do positive things. Worrying about the opulence of problems in our world and how they seem impossible to tackle because they are so large won't accomplish much. We need to take actions. As an individual, what can each of us do? In the context of InterviewGirl.com, we can all share a story. As Dr. James Orbinski impeccably articulates, "Ideas can be a profound force, more powerful than militaries or economies. Their power is rooted not in weapons or money but in people acting in concert."[291] InterviewGirl.com is an idea to make the world a better place as we all listen to more stories and as we do this, we can eliminate miseries that exist too.

> "Vision without action is a daydream. Action without vision is a nightmare."
>
> —Japanese Proverb

Changing the World starts with our Questions

Different perspectives and ideas are shared in the compilations and projects that we produce at InterviewGirl.com. People learn to become better listeners through the stories that InterviewGirl.com shares. The Interview Girl Foundation has plans that are filled with statistics about bed nets, antiretroviral medication, high-quality medical equipment and how to deliver world-class medical care in rural areas. The science is important and funds are needed to provide medication to AIDS patients, but as much as the Interview Girl Foundation's desideratum is to generate revenues for medicine and other scientific contrivances, research without heart or concern for humanity can lead to our worst nightmares. InterviewGirl.com's mission and purpose is as important as the Interview Girl Foundation's plans to generate revenues for "the medicine" that will be distributed to orphans suffering from HIV/ AIDS. InterviewGirl.com aims to "make a difference" in this world by spreading the messages:

1) The *little* things that we *all* do can make a *big* difference
2) We should all do what we can to eliminate the misery of someone else (serve others)

and

3) We should all strive to become more empathetic.

Science needs to create antiretroviral medication, money is needed to purchase this medication, foundations are needed to distribute this medication to people who are ill, and a plan is needed to help people to be able to sustain themselves when the nonprofit organizations leave, but apart from all of this, humanity's capacity to yearn to understand another's point of view is what will allow the world to change. The cynosure of InterviewGirl.com is to get people to hear the points of view of others.

"We are changing the world" is a slogan that has been part of campaigns throughout history. As Dr. Orbinski always reminds us in *An Imperfect Offering,* he went back to his questions. He continually looked at questions that guided him. Questions like: "Why does one child die of diarrhea in Africa while another in Canada survives this apparently innocuous illness?" The questions that individuals ask are what lay the foundation for progress, change, and movement forward. "Changing the world one story at a time" is the slogan behind InterviewGirl.com. As with the other concepts I pondered this past year, I wondered and thought: How does one actually change the world? As with any endeavor, looking to the past and what was done and then after examining the past, determining what could be done differently in the future is where I began when I set out to answer, "How does one actually change the world?" To start, the question: *What are those events within History that are actually considered to have changed the world?* guided me. I made a list of significant historical events. In one of my notebooks, *how does one actually change the world?* was written at the top of a page. Underneath my heading, I jotted down the names: Ashoka, Martin Luther King Jr., Thomas Clarkson, William Wilberforce, Florence Nightingale, Mother Teresa, Gandhi, and Rachel Carson. Each of these individuals faced a huge injustice and complex problem that existed in the world in which they were living. Under the list of names, I wrote the question, how did these people actually *engage* the world in which they were living?

In United States History, racial discrimination seemed like a complex problem entrenched in the South's history. Most people alive during the Civil Rights era most likely felt like there was nothing that they could do about a problem like racial discrimination. However, Martin Luther King Jr., Rosa Parks, and the Freedom Riders changed the course of the times. In other parts of the world, during different time periods, Thomas Clarkson and William Wilberforce managed to lead a campaign for the end of slavery in Great Britain. Gandhi successfully fought discrimination and political oppression on two continents using only nonviolent means. Rachel Carson started the environmental movement after she published the book, *Silent Spring* in 1962. The challenge for InterviewGirl.com is to make the world aware that miseries do exist and we can all contribute to ending these miseries. To begin eliminating miseries, *Operation A²* was created as I tried to figure out a way to provide orphans living in poverty with medication. Of course, I felt like trying to make a dent in the AIDS epidemic was an overwhelming problem and my intent to sell stories to help it seemed like a long shot, but I knew that racial discrimination was also a complex problem in the South's history, yet through the actions of people like Martin Luther King Jr., the incontrollable problem of racial discrimination became less of a problem. As much as the AIDS dilemma is a huge problem plaguing our modern world, writing out the question, *how have people in history changed the world?* and arriving at the stories of those who have played a role in changing the world in which they lived because they engaged the world in a particular way helped motivate me to take the shot—even though it's a long one.

Thomas Clarkson

Stories from History indicate that ordinary individuals helped society to overcome immoral historical injustices that have existed. Signature to InterviewGirl.com's mission is the power of a story and the story of Thomas Clarkson depicts how a student who discovered the inhumanities of slavery helped to abolish the Transatlantic Slave Trade—something that the average person in Clarkson's time thought that they could not regulate. Most of us remember that William Wilberforce is one of the leading figures in the abolitionist movement. Thomas Clarkson is another noteworthy individual in the story behind the abolition movement. Clarkson worked to abolish the Transatlantic Slave Trade and slavery itself.

To go back to the 1800's, slavery existed in British territories. It did not even exist in Great Britain itself. For the average British family of the 1800's, slavery was something that existed, but since it happened in places other than Britain, it was not something that most people paid any attention to. Many of the miseries that exist in today's world may not happen in "our" world that we experience each day (our subculture), but they are still miseries that humans experience. 2.5 billion people do not have access to a toilet.[292] Every year, 1.5 million people die from hunger, including 16,000 children (that's one child every five seconds) [293] and in 2012 alone, 1.6 million people died from AIDS.[294] These are not realties that I come into direct contact with on a daily basis in my life in Chicago (other than when I turn the pages of the books that describe these problems), but these miseries exist throughout the world. Just because I do not physically see them happening does not mean that they do not happen. Thomas Clarkson was a leading campaigner against slavery and the slave trade in Great

Britain. He was born in Wisbech, Cambridgeshire, England in 1760. Clarkson's strong antislavery stance was formed when he was a student at the University of Cambridge.

Clarkson began questioning the inhumanities of slavery and the slave trade as he gathered materials for an essay contest which set out to answer the question, "Is it lawful to make slaves of others against their will?" Clarkson determined a person cannot be considered property against their will, "as all were originally free: as nature made every man's body and mind his own; it is evident that no just man can be consigned to slavery, without his own consent."[295] After learning about the injustices of slavery while writing his paper, Thomas Clarkson further researched slavery. He traveled to ports throughout the United Kingdom and gathered evidence to help raise awareness and build a case against the slave trade. In an effort to gather hard facts about the Slave Trade, Clarkson took many risks as he visited many ports and went aboard the trading vessels. One of the first African trading ships Clarkson visited was called *The Lively*. It was not a slave ship, but its cargo had a powerful impact upon Clarkson. The ship was full of beautiful and exotic goods: carved ivory and woven cloth, along with produce such as beeswax, palm oil and peppers. Clarkson could see the craftsmanship and skill that would have been required to produce many of the items and the idea that their creators could be enslaved was horrifying to him. Clarkson bought samples from the ship and started a collection that he added to over the years. The collection that he kept in a large box included crops, spices, raw materials, and other intricate goods. Clarkson also made a drawing of a slave ship's hold, which depicts how slaves were packed tightly for the Middle Passage.

Clarkson participated in many abolition societies. In 1787, he helped found the Committee for the Abolition of the Slave Trade also called Society for the Abolition of the Slave Trade. He contributed to this committee by gathering information from ports during his travels. He noticed how pictures and artifacts were able to influence public opinion, more than words alone, and quickly realized that the contents that he had been collecting might reinforce the message of his anti-slavery lectures. He used the contents to demonstrate the skill of Africans and the possibilities that existed for an alternative humane trading system. The box filled with evidence became an important part of his public meetings. Some historians say that Clarkson was one of the first to provide an early example of a visual aid in a lecture. Clarkson along with a former slave, Olaudah Equiano traveled 35,000 miles on horseback and they lectured all over Britain. In 1792, 300,000 people boycotted sugar from the West Indies. More people than were eligible to vote in British elections signed a petition against slavery that same year. In 1823, Clarkson joined forces with William Wilberforce to campaign for the end of slavery. Wilberforce presented Clarkson's picture of the Middle Passage and other artifacts from Clarkson's travels to Parliament to draw attention to the inhumanities of the slave trade. Together they served as vice presidents for the Anti-Slavery Society also called Society for the Mitigation and Gradual Abolition of Slavery throughout the British Dominions. Ten years later in 1833, slavery was abolished in the United Kingdom with the Slavery Abolition Act. Clarkson then worked toward emancipation in the United States until his death in 1846.

Clarkson was instrumental in defeating slavery in Great Britain because he explained to the English exactly what conditions were like on slave ships and plantations. When people in Great Britain actually reflected upon what it meant to pack human beings into the hold of the ship, it was then that citizens turned against slavery. To the average individual alive during the 1800's, slavery was a part of life and the thought of eradicating it sounded like a noble thing to do, but how could that actually happen? Sure people felt bad when they learned about what happened in British territories, but most individuals thought along the lines of, "could the average person do anything to end this injustice?" As Nicholas D. Kristof and Sheryl WuDunn write in *Half the Sky: Turning Oppression into Opportunity for Women Worldwide*, in the time when Clarkson lived, "abolitionists were seen as idealistic moralizers who didn't appreciate economics or understand geopolitical complexities such as the threat from France."[296] Thomas Clarkson is admirable because he took his inquisitiveness as a student into the field to ask further questions and obtain evidence. Clarkson made it his mission to explain to the English exactly what conditions were like on slave ships and plantations. He told the British public stories about what he had seen and learned about slavery. When people saw Clarkson's artifacts and heard his stories from his travels, public opinion slowly began to change. Clarkson's use of stories in his campaign to end slavery is yet another example of the power in a story.

Clarkson's story as a student who asked questions unequivocally emanates one of the distinguished lessons that I learned as Interview Girl as a History student: indeed ordinary people do extraordinary things. Clarkson was a student who asked questions. He sought to answer those questions by going out and obtaining peoples' stories. When people in the British public comprehended the stories of the slaves, their opinions about slavery then began to change. Clarkson's actions greatly influenced the campaign for the end of slavery. Problems that exist in our world seem so vast, miseries that exist seem too big, too overwhelming, too intractable, but there are steps that we can take and things that we can do to make a difference. Clarkson's story was one of many that influenced the direction of the Interview Girl Foundation. I read about Socrates, Aristotle, Martin Luther King Jr., Mother Teresa, Gandhi, Nelson Mandela, James Orbinski, Pope John Paul II, St. Therese of Liseaux, Father Moreau, Maria Montessori, Florence Nightingale, Ashoka, Giuseppe Moscati, Jean Monnet, Thomas Jefferson, Abraham Lincoln, Lech Walesa, Sir Thomas More, Joan of Arc, and countless others. I discussed their stories with anyone who was willing to listen. I wanted the stories of these individuals to guide the Interview Girl Foundation's moral understanding of how to best bring about social change in our projects and programs that we would create in order to eliminate misery. These individuals took actions that played a role in shaping the world in which they lived. In every free moment that I had, I immersed myself with the stories about what social entrepreneurs throughout history did and what social entrepreneurs throughout the world are doing today. Engaging, questioning, and digging further into these stories was as if it was a guide for me to follow. The direction of the Interview Girl Foundation formed and shaped from my exposure to aspects from all these peoples' stories.

"The best way out is always through."

—Robert Frost

Since I first began researching to make InterviewGirl.com come to fruition, my knowledge about social initiatives and social action has developed. I've become versed with prevalent stories from various disciplines. The material I was learning continued to make connections to other parts of the research that I had already learned. When I would watch a TED talk, something would be mentioned and there would be a correlation with something from a book that I read. For example, Ester Duflo's work connected with Dambasia Moyo's work. Dr. Helen Epstein and Dr. James Orbinski had similar reflections about AIDS. The connections were there. There was no doubt. In studying the history of the world, it could not be denied that ordinary people's actions lead to major changes in human civilization. The power within stories and ideas was inarguable. Evidence, stories, and anecdotes that proved that it was possible to change the world one story at a time were coming through in various books, speeches, articles, scholarship and everything that I was reading. It was there. This idea: InterviewGirl.com was coming full circle.

Mind and Heart

"I am because we are …. I am not defined without you."

—Mathews A.P. Chikoanda

As humans, we are all connected. We need to begin to see our place in the world within the larger context. In *Moral Imagination*, Mark Johnson defines "moral imagination" as, "an ability to imaginatively discern various possibilities for acting in a given situation and to envision the potential help and harm that are likely to result from a given action."[297] Moral imagination is when you try to put yourself in another person's shoes. The concept of "Moral Imagination" is important to InterviewGirl.com because as you read anybody's story, you exercise "moral imagination." In several of her TED talks, Jacqueline Novogratz speaks about "Moral Imagination." Moral Imagination is when we can see past ourselves and our plans and our aspirations and not just live for our own feelings and our own ideals, but for others around us and before us, and way into the future. We are often so short sighted. As Novogratz annotates, part of "moral imagination" is to think about others and future generations and this may be the most difficult challenge that humans face. InterviewGirl.com was created to help all of us exercise our moral imagination. The best exercise to strengthen one's moral imagination is to read, listen to, and hear stories about others and from the stories for us to acquire a genuine desire to become involved in the world. How can we understand people across the world? How can we relate to people from cultures that are different from our own culture? How do we know if we are authentically helping someone? Gandhi urges us,

> "Whenever you are in doubt, or when the self becomes too much with you, apply the following test. Recall the face of the poorest and the weakest person whom you have seen, and ask yourself if the next step you contemplate is going to be of any use to that person."[298]

The best way to help anyone is when the person providing a service uses their mind together with their heart. In *The Blue Sweater*, Novogratz shares a moving story about how she visited Phnom Penh, Cambodia in 1994 and met a Buddhist monk, Maha

Ghosananda. Ghosananda was reviving the tradition of Dhammayietra, a nationwide pilgrimage across the country, including parts that were covered in land mines. Initially Novogratz was having difficulty getting Ghosananda to explain what he was doing. She wanted the world to understand the peace marches. After some time passed in silence, Ghosananda communicated to Novogratz,

"If you move through the world only with your intellect, then you walk on only one leg. If you move through the world only with your compassion, then you walk on only one leg. But if you move through the world with both intellect and compassion, then you have wisdom."[299]

Of course back in the 1800's, the founder of the Congregation of Holy Cross, Blessed Basil Moreau believed and taught that teachers had to be concerned with the education of the whole person—with the head as well as the heart. In 1821, Moreau was ordained a priest for the diocese, later becoming a seminary professor teaching philosophy and theology, while enthusiastically continuing his pastoral duties. By 1835, Moreau had organized a group of young and energetic "auxiliary priests" whose mission was to travel the diocese, assisting in educational and spiritual growth programs at parishes. In Father Moreau's view, teachers had to be concerned with the education of the whole person—with the head as well as the heart.[300] In our lives, we should all make decisions with our mind as well as with our heart. The Interview Girl Foundation creates, develops, and then implements programs to eliminate miseries as it uses its mind and its heart.

"*We shall always place education side by side with instruction;* **the mind will not be cultivated at the expense of the heart**. *While we prepare useful citizens for*

474

society, we shall likewise do our utmost to prepare citizens for heaven."

—Father Basil Moreau, Founder of *Holy Cross*—(Moreau, *Circular Letter 36*)

As many notes as I took, stories I read, and statistics that seemed to loom in my face, no matter how innovative the science or revolutionary the economic theory, I knew that generating revenues to purchase medication will alleviate an aid's victim's pain, but I felt that just passing out medication isn't enough. It wouldn't be enough to change the world. *Operation A²* has its plan to distribute this medication, but the power behind a story is what will indubitably make InterviewGirl.com work. It's important for you to share your story and to want to hear someone else's story because as you do that, you learn to listen, you become empathetic, you read other stories, you gain perspective, and you want to serve (help others) and as each of us genuinely want to find out about those around us, humanity changes. Without moral audacity and commitment to humanity, monetary donations and technical virtuosity won't solve the problems that plague many. Just giving aid, although a generous, virtuous and noble gesture, a further step was needed. Distributing medication as well as a plan to help people to be able to sustain themselves after the Interview Girl Foundation left where it was helping was crucial in the Interview Girl Foundation's plan to intervene in the AIDS crisis, but also integral in this organization's mission was for every one of us who is a part of humanity to ask: what could we each do better in order to understand individuals who also inhabit our world?

As Helen Epstein conveys about the AIDS crisis, there is no magic cure. Cutting edge research together with heart and concern for humanity drive InterviewGirl.com. That is why collecting and distributing stories is central to InterviewGirl.com's plan to help eliminate peoples' miseries. By collecting and distributing stories, InterviewGirl.com will make its mark on the world. As you read a story and you learn someone's reality, you become filled with empathy and as we all gain more empathy, we become more inclined to help others and when everyone has the view point and capacity to complete their "little service," larger issues plaguing our society will start to subside.

From the beginning of time, the power of a story has been passed from generation to generation. For over 27,000 years, since the first cave paintings were discovered, telling stories has been one of our most fundamental communication methods. Our generation is no different. We too love stories. Reporter Janine di Giovanni has been to the worst places on Earth to bring back stories from Bosnia, Sierra Leone and most recently Syria. Janine di Giovanni gave a powerful talk on what she saw in war and as she concluded, she said, "All I can do is hope that if you remember anything from what I have shared with you today, you can remember the story of Sarajevo or the story of Rwanda, then I've done my job." As di Giovanni articulates, she is there to shed light in some of the darkest corners of the world and she is able to do this through telling stories about those places. Throughout humanity, we all live in different cultures, we all live in very different circumstances, and we all have our own stories. InterviewGirl.com was formed because from this act of sharing stories, a misery that someone in this world is experiencing can be jettisoned.

> "We cannot live only for ourselves. A thousand fibers connect us with our fellow men; and among those fibers, as sympathetic threads, our actions run as causes, and they come back to us as effects."
>
> —Herman Melville

One Final Lesson from Interview Girl ... Hope

"When I despair, I remember that all through history the way of truth and love has always won. There have been tyrants and murderers and for a time they seem invincible but in the end, they always fall—think of it, always."

—Mahatma Gandhi

There are miseries throughout the world and we are working to eliminate these miseries, but undeniably amidst the misery, there are also stories of hope. My time in Ghana introduced me to a story and my research introduced me to an assemblage of other stories. It is important to remember that there is not just one story to define a problem. Death and despair is one story when learning about the AIDS crisis, but there are also other stories about innovation and survival. In order to overcome the crisis, strides have been made in a positive direction. These hopeful stories exist too. As I created the Interview Girl Foundation, my initial desire was to introduce people to disheartening statistics and to get the message across that we had to do something to help those less fortunate, and there are miseries out there throughout the world, but somewhere along the way, I learned that it's more important for us to see the stories of hope that are woven in with the misery that is present. I witnessed hope in the fight against HIV/AIDS in advances in technology, in philanthropic endeavors, in courageous doctors from organizations like *Doctors Without Borders*, in missionaries' selfless deeds and in the overall Global effort to do something to stop the spread of AIDS. I learned that relief was still needed when it came to the AIDS crisis, but I also saw the inspiring and unbelievable things that people throughout the world were doing to help eliminate this misery.

Anne Hunsaker Hawkins tells six inspirational stories about children living with HIV and the remarkable people who care for them in *A Small, Good Thing*. The powerful stories that she shares about one HIV clinic in one part of the world are a testament to the power of human kindness and what she calls "ordinary goodness." Hawkins writes,

"For such systematic cultural ills we have yet no cure. But in the tiny microism of a single pediatric clinic and the community it serves we can see the forces of ordinary goodness that rally to help children with HIV and their families."[301]

In the time that Hawkins spent at the AIDS clinic, she learned about all the contemporary systematic cultural ills and why the AIDS dilemma was present within the community, but she also couldn't help but notice the human goodness and kindness that existed amongst the despair in that particular pediatric clinic for AIDS patients.

To return to Jacqueline Novogratz, who founded and leads Acumen Fund, a nonprofit that takes a businesslike approach to improving the lives of the poor. Novogratz describes how she saw hope in one of the poorest zones within Kenya,

"As we were walking thru the Mathare Valley in Kenya, it was literally impossible not to step in the raw sewage and the garbage outside the little homes, but at the same it was also impossible not to see the human vitality, the aspiration and the ambition of the people who lived there."

She goes on to tell a moving story about an encounter in a Nairobi slum with Jane, a former prostitute, whose dreams of escaping poverty, of becoming a doctor and of getting married were fulfilled in an unexpected way. Jacqueline Novogratz was amidst poverty, garbage, and death, and while these miseries existed in the Mathare Valley, Novogratz also witnessed "the human vitality, the aspiration and the ambition of the people who lived there."

In *Showing Up For Life*, Bill Gates Senior expatiates about the loss of a child on the other side of the world. He renders, "We want to protect ourselves from the pain of knowing how truly tragic it is. It may be natural to turn away, but if we do, the hope that sometimes resides next to the pain may escape us." He then asks us to look at some numbers and challenges us that we may be able to feel a sense of hope about what might be done to change them. He shares,

> "Even in developed countries, the poor die five to ten years before the rich. In the last 25 years, the number of people in Sub-Saharan Africa living on less than a dollar a day has almost doubled. Every thirty seconds a child somewhere in the world dies of malaria. The hope that resides beside that last statistic is this: Some scientists are now working on a malaria vaccine to prevent the disease, while others are investigating better treatments for those who already have it. I know we can change these numbers. In fact, I've seen dedicated people all over the world changing them. We can and we will conquer these problems when, instead of turning away, we learn to embrace them as our own."

Even with a dire statistic like "every 30 seconds a child dies from malaria," the hope is that many individuals are donating their time and talents to help rid the world of malaria. Thanks to the actions of these individuals, people who experience the misery of malaria have hope.

In the "Introduction" of *Unthinkable: Who Survives When Disaster Strikes and Why*, Amanda Ripley writes, "Writing a book about disasters may sound voyeuristic or dark, and there are times when it was. But the truth is, I was mesmerized by this subject because it gave me hope."[302] Ripley researched and covered tragedies and amidst the sorrow, like Hawkins, Novogratz, and Gates, she too found hope. The lengths that people involved in the disasters went to in order to help their fellow men inspired Ripley. In the thick of these challenging times, the luminosity of hope radiated from the people who put themselves in danger in order to aid a fellow human being.

In *Poor Economics*, Abhijit Banerjee and Ester Duflo analyze what the poor are able to achieve and where and for what reason they need a push in order to overcome poverty. The book examines the larger questions: Are there ways for the poor to improve their lives and what is preventing them from being able to do these things? Banerjee and Duflo construe that we are dealing with big, intractable problems, but there is a lot of hope. *Poor Economics* makes clear why hope is vital and knowledge critical and why we have to keep on trying even when the challenge looks overwhelming. Ultimately, Banerjee and Duflo decipher that success isn't always as far away as it looks. Despite the colossal problem of world poverty, Abhijit Banerjee and Ester Duflo contend that there is hope to lessen the poverty that exists.

> "Hope not only meets despair in equal measure, it drowns it."
>
> —Dr. Maskalyk

To further characterize hope, let's again return to my mentor when it comes to being a compassionate doctor, Dr. James Orbinski. Orbinski lived unspeakable horror as he lived through the Rwanda genocide. To use his words,

> "Literally running red with blood, in the face of a million people murdered, massacred in mass graves across the country, in the face of the egregious political malfeasance and political failure that meant that there was no military intervention to stop the genocide, that fundamentally altered my world view. And it wasn't an intellectual experience, you know, it's not something that you read about. It's something that I lived."[303]

Confronted by this appalling abhorrence, Orbinski also writes about some miraculous moments. For instance, a woman who had been terribly mutilated showed him remarkable courage. Orbinksi describes how she basically tried to calm him. The woman was one of 600 casualties, one particular day who were laid out on the streets outside the hospital. There were so many people that day who were brought to the hospital because of gunshot injuries, machete injuries, land mine injuries and other injuries. This woman had had both of her ears cut off. She had both of her breasts cut off. Her Achilles tendons had been cut and she had a carefully cut pattern of slashes laid into her face. Orbinski put his experience with her into words,

> "I remember trying to look after her and give her a few sutures to stop the major bleeding, and then I would have to move onto the next patient, and the next patient and the next patient. And I remember looking at her and suddenly it wasn't simply—I wasn't simply as a technician, as a medical technician, a person providing sutures, four life threatening sutures, but I suddenly saw that to inflict this kind of injury you have to really think about it. And you had to really enjoy delivering that kind of suffering to that woman. I remember looking at her and suddenly just being overwhelmed by what she had experienced. And I turned and I vomited and it was the only time during the genocide that I vomited. And she immediately understood what was happening to me, and she reached out and she touched my arm, very gently, and she said in Kenyan Rwanda, shaw. Shaw is a Rwandan word meaning my friend, and umada is a Rwandan word meaning courage. Have courage, find your courage. And that's what she said to me."[304]

Orbinski's experience with this Rwandan woman who was lying in the middle of the road suffering in the most profound way and yet she responded to his dissonance, to his disruption, to what he was feeling displays hope amongst the wretchedness of the times. He then sutured a few of her arteries, the ones that were bleeding significantly and were they not sutured, she would have died. After he had finished there were many more cuts that needed to be closed, but she could see there were many more patients. Nurses were calling him for the next patient, and the next patient and the next patient, and she told him to go. Speaking Rwandan, she said, "go." Orbinski explains that she knew exactly what he was experiencing and what he was feeling. She told him to go, to go onto the next patient. Orbinski reflects, "I think in many ways that story encapsulates the beauty if you will of what we can be as human beings even in the most egregious of circumstances."[305]

As Orbinski was surrounded by suffering and death, the lambency of human goodness shined through in the most profound way as the suffering woman told him, "have courage, find your courage." In telling the story about the woman's pain, Orbinski reminds, "We must not forget what we can be as human beings." We can choose to be good. Camus' *The Plague,* a novel about a plague epidemic in the large Algerian city of Oran, captures this exact feeling. As Camus' narrator in *The Plague* observes, "what we learn in a time of pestilence is that there are more things to admire in men than to despise." Even in the times of despair, there are always those individuals who exude qualities for us to admire. Anytime there is a tragedy, there are always stories of hope and stories about what lengths people went to in order to help other people. We cannot forget these stories. We need these stories to motivate us and see us through the demanding times.

> "It is often in the darkest skies that we see the brightest stars."
>
> —Richard Evans

Reporter Janine Di Giovanni has been to some of the most unfavorable places on Earth to bring back stories from war zones. In *Madness Visible,* she tells stories of human moments within large conflicts and explores that shocking transition when a familiar city street becomes a bombed-out battleground. When Di Giovanni explains what she saw in war, she rationalizes that she sees incredibly heroic people doing what it is that they have to do. She unfolds that this is pretty much why she does what she does,

> "Sadly there will always be wars. I am deluding myself if I think as a writer I can stop them. I can't stop a war. I'm not a UN conflict resolution worker. All I am is a witness. My role is to bring a voice to people who are voiceless—To shine a light in the darkest corners of the world. This is what I try and do. My métier is to bear witness. That is the crux. The heart of the matter."

Di Giovanni's stories about the brave acts of courage that she has seen amidst war and how she witnesses heroism amongst the difficult times brings truth to what Camus' *Plague* taught us: there are many acts of courage and bravery to admire during hard times. Di Giovanni, who has reported some of the most abysmal acts that have happened in our world, draws the same conclusion as Camus' *Plague*. Fred Rogers, the host of the TV program *Mr. Rogers' Neighborhood* once said, "When I was a boy and I would see scary things in the news, my mother would say to me, "Look for the helpers. You will always find people who are helping."" There will always be trying times, but among iniquitous people that are around, virtuous and worthy individuals are there too. A classic example of this is in J.R.R. Tolkien's *The Two Towers*, when Sam says to Frodo,

> "I know. It's all wrong. By rights we shouldn't even be here. But we are. It's like in the great stories, Mr. Frodo. The ones that really mattered. Full of darkness and danger, they were. And sometimes you didn't want to know the end. Because how could the end be happy? How could the world go back to the way it was when so much bad had happened? But in the end, it's only a passing thing, this shadow. Even darkness must pass. A new day will come. And when the sun shines, it will shine out the clearer. Those were the stories that stayed

with you. That meant something, even if you were too small to understand why. But I think, Mr. Frodo, I do understand. I know now. Folk in those stories had lots of chances of turning back, only they didn't. They kept going. Because they were holding on to something."

Mr. Frodo then asks Sam, "What are we holding onto, Sam?" and Sam responds, "That there's some good in this world, Mr. Frodo... and it's worth fighting for." As Sam holds, there is good in this world. We should do what we can to bring out the good.

One of the finest examples of hope that I can think of is when someone is ill and people keep praying for a recovery (they do not give up hope) and then the individual recovers. In *Love, Medicine, and Miracles*, in discussing therapy, Bernie Siegel, M.D. explains that the therapy itself isn't necessarily useful, but people heal doing something they believe in, something that gives them hope.[306] Hope is important in the medical healing process. If a patient gives up hope, even with advanced medicine, recovery is much more difficult. A little boy whom I know is an exemplification of the importance of holding onto hope during the trying times of an illness. A few months into his mother's pregnancy, she did not have any amniotic fluid, so the doctors knew that something was wrong with the baby's kidneys. Doctors were not even sure if the baby would survive. Many doctors kept commenting on how there was "no medical explanation" for this or for that as the baby pulled through time and time again. His loving parents and grandparents prayed, prayed, and continued to pray. They never gave up hope. This baby's story can be considered a miracle. His story is a paragon about the power of "mind" and "heart" combined. The strong faith and belief that that the family of the boy had that he would get well united together with the sagacity of modern medicine allowed a child with very little function in his kidneys to resume a normal life after his kidney transplant. There were times when medical science pointed toward this child not surviving, but he did. No matter how dismal the diagnosis, the parents and family never gave up hope on this beautiful child.

The Indo—European root of the word hope means that there will be a change in direction. Things will start to go in a different way. My Mom taught me that there is always hope. Whatever we were discussing, whatever the situation, no matter how bad things seemed to become, my Mom always contended that there was hope. I first started collecting stories, anecdotes and quotes about hope because it was a theme that my Mom loved. I even bought the domain, www.lasperanza.com (Italian for Hope). I thought that my Mom could do something with this idea that she believed in and loved. La Speranza (Hope) was my Mom's life theme. She is an Italian teacher and centers her classes around the lessons of hope that are embodied in Italian literature and culture. I wanted her to be able to do something with this beautiful concept that she loved. I came across many unbelievable stories dealing with hope as I compiled stories that had to do with hope for my Mom. One of the most valuable life lessons that my Mom enlightened me to understand is that there will be bad times, times of despair, times when we are down, times when things don't go our way, but no matter what—there is always *hope*.

> "In the course of history, there comes a time when humanity is called to shift to a new level of consciousness, to reach a higher moral ground. A time when we have to shed our fear and give hope to each other. That time is now."
>
> —From Wangari Maathai's *Nobel Lecture*,
> delivered in Oslo (December, 2004)

The overwhelming statistics regarding the AIDS crisis that I learned were an impetus to found InterviewGirl.com (19 million people had already died of the AIDS disease, nearly 3 million more were dying every year, and thirty-three million were infected with the virus). However, as I immersed myself with stories from all ends of the AIDS dilemma, I also discovered that there was much to be hopeful about. The initial statistics no longer seemed impossible to overcome. I saw hope in "aiding" the AIDS victims because since 1995, antiretroviral treatment has added 14 million life years in low- and middle-income countries, including 9 million in sub-Saharan Africa. Also, according to the UNAIDS Global Report, "A far greater number of lives will be saved if universal access is reached globally."

Bono, the lead singer of *U2*, uses his celebrity to fight for social justice worldwide: to end hunger, poverty and disease, especially in Africa. Bono reminds us that Nelson Mandela asked us to be that great generation that overcomes the most extreme offense to humanity, extreme poverty. In looking at the strides made in the fight to overcome poverty in the 21st century, Bono too reports that, "there is hope." He divulges that facts are what tell humans what is working and not working. He believes that there is hope to overcome poverty, disease, and hunger because individuals have fought for, innovated for, and campaigned for the progress forward that has been made in the last twenty years.

The facts vivify humanity's hope to overcome poverty, disease, and hunger. Since 2000: 8 million more aids patients are getting lifesaving antiretroviral drugs, child mortality is down by 2.65 million a year, and the number of people living in extreme poverty has declined from 43% of world's population in 1990 to 33% in 2000 to 21% of the world's population in 2010. Bono happily shares that the number of people living in extreme poverty has been halved since 1990. He points out if you live on less than $1.25 a day, this "isn't just data, this is everything, this rapid transition is a root out of despair and into hope. If the trajectory continues, the amount of people living on less than $1.25 will get to zero." Bono reminds, "This is great news. We need to keep the momentum going." 21% of the world's population living in extreme poverty is still too high. 21% of the world's population still is unnecessarily losing their lives, so there is still work to do. We know the obstacles in our way right now and we should work to overcome them. Bono warns that inertia is how we may stop this momentum that has been started, "Momentum it's how we can bend the arch of history down toward zero." He concludes, "Once you have this image in your brain, you can't erase it. It's transformational. We are here to try and infect you with this. Be contagious, spread it, share it, pass it on, and you will join us and countless others in the fight to end poverty." The Interview Girl Foundation is playing a role in keeping the momentum that Bono discusses going. InterviewGirl.com will share science, facts, and emotions in the stories that it shares. Much progress has been made since 1990 in the fight to overcome extreme poverty. The progress that civilization has witnessed thus far provides so much hope for humanity.

To draw this lesson about hope to its conclusion, it seems appropriate for us to focus on the AIDS dilemma. Given Amara's story that ignited the birth of InterviewGirl.com and *Operation A²*'s crusade to help orphans who have AIDS, what AIDS teaches us about hope is the perfect culmination to this compelling lesson. In *Tinderbox: How the West Spanked the AIDS epidemic and how the world can finally overcome it*, Craig Timberg and Daniel Halperin identify hope in the fight against AIDS, "The epidemic is a story of lost opportunity, of unforeseen consequences, and of (mostly) good intentions gone awry. And yet, we also share a battered but persistent hope: The epidemic has depended on human action for its birth and spread, and so too could human action finally overcome it."[307] Craig Timberg and Daniel Halperin take notice of the hope that exists in the fight to transcend the AIDS epidemic. The stories in *Tinderbox* bring forth a dynamism that impels us to ask: What actions could we, as humans take to overcome the epidemic? Undeniably hope lie ahead for *Operation A²* and its ambition to aid in overcoming the miseries like the one that sweet Amara once lived with at the Children's Home. The only thing left for me to do was to act. I had the knowledge, I heard peoples' stories, now as my fortune cookie from that Chinese restaurant months earlier advised me to do: the only thing left to do was *to act*. My way "to act" was to set up a movement that collected stories and to then use these stories to eliminate misery.

There is always hope. No matter how debauched a situation becomes, hope remains. This is a lesson that my Mom and an incredible little boy that I am lucky enough to know taught me. This is also an age old historical lesson that has stood the test of time. Hope will prevail. We must never forget this. As dark as it gets, when you dig further, hope can be found. As Anne Hunsaker Hawkins, Jacqueline Novogratz, Bill Gates Senior, Amanda Ripley, Abhijit Banerjee, Ester Duflo, James Orbinski, Albert Camus, Sam from J.R.R. Tolkien's *The Two Towers*, Janine di Giovanni, Bono, Craig Timberg and Daniel Halperin all describe, no matter what one experiences, there is always hope.

> "The ideals which have lighted my way and gave me courage to face life cheerfully have been kindness, beauty and truth."
>
> —Albert Einstein

Unimaginable stories of hope surfaced as I completed research for my MA in European History. Part of my research illuminated the ills of communism and yes, I heard those stories, but I also learned what lengths people went to in order to overcome adversity while under communism. As I was researching about AIDS in Africa and I learned godawful statistic after godawful statistic, I also could not help, but come across beautiful stories of hope. As Hawkins describes in *A Small, Good Thing,* there is ordinary goodness all around us. As much misery as there is that exists in our world, we cannot discredit the countless stories that are a testament to the power of human kindness and ordinary goodness. By each and every one of us doing little things to eliminate miseries, we can all make a meaningful difference in this world. When Dr. James Orbinski was awarded the Nobel Peace Prize, in his speech, he elucidates,

> "Despite grand debates on world order, the act of humanitarianism comes down to one thing: individual human beings reaching out to their counterparts who find themselves in the most difficult circumstances. One bandage at a time, one suture at a time, one vaccination

at a time. And, uniquely for Médecins Sans Frontières, working in around 80 countries, over 20 of which are in conflict, telling the world what they have seen. All this in the hope that the cycles of violence and destruction will not continue endlessly."[308]

InterviewGirl.com was created to share stories in the name of Humanitarianism and Philanthropy. The definition of Philanthropy is love for humankind. It is derived from the Greek words "philos," which means loving and "anthropos," which means humankind. The purpose of Philanthropy is to improve the wellbeing of humankind by preventing and solving social problems. Philanthropy arises out of Love. We can show our Love for humankind by translating it into action. It has been said that the human spirit is a powerful motivator. As humans, we cannot deny our shared humanity. When we understand what it means that our fellow brothers and sisters exist in misery, this can reach us on a visceral level and we will not stop until we change the status quo (erase those miseries). Humanitarianism is about individual human beings reaching out to assist other human beings who live in adverse circumstances. In the case of MSF, this is done by individuals completing one medical act at a time. At InterviewGirl.com, human beings reach out to other human beings as individuals share one story at a time. By each of us doing something, we can eliminate innumerable miseries. When we as humans *act*, we have the ability to be greater than ourselves. At InterviewGirl.com, our love of humankind is shown through the stories that we share. We touch the lives of those around us as we share our stories with other human beings.

"Hope is the thing with feathers
That perches in the soul,
And sings the tune—without the words,
And never stops at all."
—Emily Dickinson

"Hope is a waking dream."
—Aristotle

CHAPTER EIGHTEEN

Conclusion Part Two: Together, One Story at a Time, We Can Change the World

Learning to Listen

"The most important thing to do is really listen."
—Itzhak Perlman

Where does hope begin? It derives from each of us becoming a more giving person and we do that by cultivating our sense of empathy. We begin this movement of human beings reaching out to other human beings (helping to eliminate misery that exists in the world) as we each strive to become more empathetic. Giving is most appreciated when you give what is truly needed, not what you think is needed. Dr. Ernesto Sirolli, a noted authority in the field of sustainable economic development, articulates this beautifully in a speech (*Want to help someone? Shut up and listen!*) that he gave at the TED conference in 2012. Sirolli wrote *Ripples from the Zambezi: Passion, Entrepreneurship and the Rebirth of Local Economies*. He started doing aid work in Africa in the 1970's and quickly realized changes that he wanted to make within aid work. In 1985, he pioneered Esperance, a small rural community in Western Australia, a unique economic development approach based on harnessing the passion, determination, intelligence, and resourcefulness of the local people. The striking results of "The Esperance Experience" have prompted more than 250 communities around the world to adopt responsive, person-centered approaches to local economic development similar to the Enterprise Facilitation model pioneered in Esperance. Sirolli contends that helping others begins when people are willing to listen to other people (when those wanting to help listen to those whom they are helping).

Similarly, in *The Invisible Cure*, Helen Epstein entrancingly expresses the importance of listening when it comes to trying to solve a public health crisis as she explains that she should have listened to the people of Uganda instead of going to graduate school in England as she did when she was there trying to find a cure for AIDS. Epstein argues that there are solutions to the AIDS crisis, and some of the most effective ones may be simpler than many people assume. Understanding what is precisely needed can come from learning to listen with an empathetic ear.

Dr. James Orbinski reveals how listening to what Jose Venturelli, "a heavyset, gregarious man with a warmth and seriousness of purpose,"[309]said when he was in medical school resonated with Orbinski throughout his life. Jose Venturelli was a Chilean doctor and a refugee to Canada. Orbinski had many teaching sessions with him, but one in particular stayed with Orbinski throughout the years. Venturelli showed the class slide after slide of bruises, broken bones, shattered feet, and electrical burns to genitals. The teacher described to the class the betrayal, the human failure that torture is. Orbinski remembers Venturelli emphatically saying, "We can do this to each other, or we can decide not to. It is a choice."[310] Orbinski thoughtfully listened to Venturelli while in medical school. When out in the field as a doctor and he saw horrendous human catastrophes, Orbinski pondered what he had listened to years earlier and chose to act to try and make those cataclysms better.

"My parents taught me how to listen to everybody before I made up my own mind. When you listen, you learn. You absorb like a sponge—and your life becomes so much better than when you are just trying to be listened to all the time."

—Steven Spielberg

John Gardner was Jacqueline Novogratz's mentor. According to Novogratz, Gardner was a man of "tremendous accomplishment, integrity, and humility. Throughout his life, John focused not on his career but on how he could position himself to serve others in the world." Gardner once gave Novogratz advice to focus on being interested rather than interesting. Novogratz reflected, "Fifteen years later, I understand his wisdom: a focus on being interested in others is the very foundation for a life of meaning and purpose. John frequently reminded me to commit to something bigger than myself."[311] How do we put Gardner's sage advice to Jacqueline Novogratz into practice? You become interested in others by listening to them. Before starting the Philanthropy Workshop at the Rockefeller Foundation, Novogratz made it a point to speak with Gardner. The Philanthropy Workshop was created to help philanthropists learn how they could best serve others. Gardner articulated,

"The one thing for you to teach is that the most important skill needed is listening. If philanthropists don't first listen, they will never be able to address issues fully because they will not understand them. Second, philanthropists should focus on supporting others to do what they already do well rather than running programs themselves."

Novogratz went on to create her workshop and she and other philanthropists came together to discuss a commitment to learning and to giving strategically. What Gardner communicated to Novogratz became invaluable for her to acquire as she undertook philanthropic endeavors throughout her career. The most important skill needed for philanthropists hoping to make a difference in this world is listening.

"The fool speaks, the wise man listens."

—Ethiopian proverb

Alberto Cairo leads the International Red Cross orthopedic rehabilitation work in Afghanistan. He has spent the past two decades in this war-ravaged nation helping an estimated 100,000 Afghan landmine and accident victims learn to find the strength within themselves to not only walk, but also to hope, again. In a country where the disabled are generally given pity but no rights, Cairo found a way through micro-loans, positive discrimination schemes and home schooling to give tens of thousands of disabled Afghans a job and a sense of dignity and pride. Alberto Cairo discloses, "There is always a better way to do things. I have learned a lot from these people. This way of working. This way of thinking. All we have to do is listen to the people that we are supposed to assist. To make them part of the decision making process and then of course to adapt."[312] Like Ernesto Sirolli and John Gardner, Alberto Cairo encourages us to listen to the people whom we are trying to assist. By learning to listen more carefully, we can hear the needs of humanity. The world today focuses on *telling*. Think about it, social media in our world is about telling people around us about us. I am encouraging you to *listen*. As Interview Girl ... I LISTEN. InterviewGirl.com is a listening ministry. As we become better listeners, a shift in thought happens and a genuine want for change emerges. We will understand more fully how to eliminate anyone's misery when we concentrate on learning to listen. We can embark on our ambition to change the world as we each become a better listener.

This begins as we all share our stories and welcome with open arms hearing other people's stories. One story at a time—we can make the world a better place. I remember as a child I would "go play" with other kids in my class at school. I would go to their homes or they would come to mine. I remember vividly the day that my parents made me go play with this girl in my class who was different than all of my other friends. None of the girls in my class seemed to like this one girl because she came from a dissimilar culture than all of us. My parents making me do this—this act of spending time with someone "different" than me, was an exercise in shaping whom I became. My perspective expanded that day. I became more empathetic. I understood that the world was filled with diverse individuals. People from different backgrounds than mine also coexisted in this world and I needed to respect them. Not only did I need to respect this girl, but I also needed to want to find out about her culture and who she was. Dr. Maskalyk is a humanitarian doctor who worked in Sudan. He believes that people are hungry to be brought closer to the world, even its hard parts. Dr. Maskalyk describes that he writes about Sudan because "that which separates action from inaction is the same thing that separates my friends from Sudan. It is not indifference. It is distance. May it fall away." As we hear the stories of others, we understand the world better. Through ingesting people's stories, the distance that sometimes separates us begins to fade away.

> "Empathy is seeing with the eyes of another, listening with the ears of another, and feeling with the heart of another."
>
> —Alfred Adler

The Interview Girl Foundation had its plans, but despite the science, despite development economics, the work that the Interview Girl Foundation wanted to do had to begin with our staff wanting to *listen* to whom it was that we wanted to help. We would listen to the stories of the people experiencing the misery of AIDS first hand and after we did this, then we could begin to help them—to eliminate their miseries.

> "We cannot live only for ourselves. A thousand fibers connect us with our fellow men; and among those fibers,

as sympathetic threads, our actions run as causes, and
they come back to us as effects."

—Herman Melville

"When you start to develop your powers of empathy
and imagination, the whole world opens up to you."

—Susan Sarandon

We Are All Connected

"Get ready! Ideas move very quickly when their time
comes."

—Carolyn Heilburn

From reading stories about people living in heart-rending
miseries, to learning accurate statistics surrounding these miseries,
to understanding about the different types of humanitarian aid,
to being introduced to the field of development economics, to
recognizing what has worked to make positive changes for people
experiencing misery, to noting what has not been successful in
overcoming poverty, to delving deeper into social problems like the
spread of AIDS, the list about how my knowledge was extended
as I researched an area that I developed an insatiable curiosity
for could go on, but I just kept thinking that knowledge wasn't
enough. I needed to put this knowledge to use in a way that served
others. As David Bornstein declares, "the existence of knowledge
and the widespread application of knowledge are very different
things."[313] The cork board above my keyboard has amassed a few
items since the start of this book. As I look up to the cork board,
I see Amara's name (which makes me remember her angelic face),
a $10 Ghana Cedis bill, Father Rookey's prayer card (the healing
priest I was fortunate enough to meet), a picture of our new Pope,
the autographed title page from *An Imperfect Offering*, and an

495

e-mail my Mom sent to contacts that she knew in Italy years ago as I embarked on my first journey to hear peoples' stories that summer I went to Italy and the Balkans to speak with those who used to live along Italy's Adriatic coast.

I sit here at my computer desk and I see the top of my word document that says: InterviewGirl.com book. As I look up, I see Amara's name written on the note card pinned to my cork board above my desk. I begin to reflect on everything that happened to arrive at this point (writing the conclusion of this book). I know that writing the conclusion of this book is in actuality just the beginning of an important mission to attempt to eliminate some miseries that exist in this world. I remember setting up the InterviewGirl.com website, sending out hundreds of flyers asking people to participate in this ambition to try and make the world a better place by agreeing to complete an interview, and of course typing out this book one word and time. I now know by heart the stories about individuals and what lengths they went to in order to start organizations that are now making a difference in the world. Their stories motivated me. As I wrap up this book, the first of many of InterviewGirl.com's compilations and projects, I reflect on all that happened to lead me to this point and I eagerly look to the future with anticipation about how the Interview Girl Foundation can help those in this world experiencing miseries.

We have all experienced meeting those individuals who have a great effect on our lives. In the interviews I've completed thus far, I remember all those with whom I spoke and I appropriately know I may never speak with most of them again. Many of the World War Two vets whom I was lucky enough to interview have now passed away. I remember their glances. Their looks. Their smiles. And of course their stories. There is an ancient Chinese proverb that says, "An invisible thread connects those who are destined to meet, regardless of time, place, and circumstance. The thread may stretch or tangle. But it will never break." I felt connected to these individuals because they shared their story with me. To me, because of the stories that I was fortunate enough to hear, World War Two

496

was no longer a war discussed in a history book, but a time when fascinating people like Jim, Bob, Tim, Eda, Franco, Lino, Chris, Katie, Mae, Guido, Bill, Reinhold and countless others lived, loved, served, worked, overcame adversity, and survived the war.[314] Sure there was over a 70 year age difference between "la gente giuliana" and the WWII vets and myself, but their stories, these would always be a part of me. My life was vastly different from the people who told me their stories about their lives when they were a little younger than my age during the WWII years, but as the ancient Chinese proverb reveals, I was destined to meet these individuals and now that I heard their stories – part of my heart would always belong to the WWII generation. Through listening to their stories, these individuals became my friends. Although most of them I never spoke with again after our interview, I would not forget what they shared with me.

Final Thought

My research that I have not yet finished on Fiume and Italy's Adriatic coast stares at me each and every day as I see numerous hard drives filled with interviews from "la gente giuliana" scattered throughout my office, and although I am enthusiastic about creating a finished product from the research I began years ago about the exiles, the current state of the world (the knowledge that I gleaned from InterviewGirl.com's research) and all the miseries that exist were not something I could requisitely look beyond. I expressly kept thinking that it had to be changed—all these miseries could not exist (poverty, hunger, poor sanitation, AIDS, human trafficking, etc.). Story after story about what some people face throughout the world was now a part of my world. Knowing that there was something that I could do to help the AIDS victims was what drove me to write a minimum of an hour a day no matter what. All the writing instructional books urged to fit in writing no matter what, so that's what I have attempted to do this past year.

James Orbinski was friends with a Catholic monk named Benedict. As Orbinski described his friendship with Brother Benedict, I was reminded of the friendships that I had cultivated through interviewing the last few years. Orbinski would go see Benedict at the Oka monastery just outside of Montreal. They would go on walks through the forest around the monastery. As Orbinski describes his first walk with Benedict, "Benedict listened more carefully than I had ever been listened to before." Orbinski unravels how he was preoccupied by questions about suffering, the struggle to escape it or the living of lives in it. Orbinski tried to explain to Benedict how confused he was by what we were capable of, by the pain we inflicted on one another. Benedict then told him, "There is no escape, James. There is only what you do." Orbinski reveals that this was the beginning of his learning how to live in the world. At this point, Orbinski was not certain what he would do, but when he spoke with Benedict, he felt like his unanswered questions were relaxed. James Orbinski and Benedict helped one another. In another moving scene from *An Imperfect Offering*, Orbinski went to see his monk friend after some time in medical school and experience in the hospital. He told his confidant about the first patient that he witnessed die. Benedict listened to Orbinski carefully and as they walked through the forest, he warned young James of becoming a user of what he knew as he uttered, "The knowledge is one thing. Who you are and what you do with it is quite another."[315] This advice that Benedict shared with Orbinski helped him to be open to the question of "how to be as a doctor," and ultimately eventually in his non-direct way, help Orbinski to choose what he chose to do: join MSF.

What led me to spend a year reading about what causes poverty and what we can do to alleviate extreme poverty? Why was I so focused on helping AIDS victims? Why was I fortunate enough to do the traveling that I had? What made me make time to do the research that I did? A nun who greatly affected Jacqueline Novogratz when she was younger shared with her, "To whom much is given, much is expected." I had all this knowledge. The question was now what to do with it? My desire to share stories—stories of those voices who aren't always heard became an aspiration to me. The idea of a story and having to share it and pass it on was continually on my mind. So many of the WWII vets shared thoughts with me along the lines of, "You should know..... People don't understand." I wanted to capture memories and stories before it was too late for the WWII generation. Benedict's profound words spoke to me: "The knowledge is one thing. Who you are and what you do with it is quite another." This InterviewGirl.com project is a way for me to share my knowledge while attempting to get everyone to join in and help to alleviate some of the world's miseries.

"Knowing is not enough; we must apply. Willing is not enough; we must do."
—Johann Wolfgang von Goethe

Describing the purpose of the Interview Girl Foundation succinctly is to help eliminate peoples' miseries. "Eliminating miseries" was distinctly chosen to describe the Interview Girl Foundation's work. Projects created through the Interview Girl Foundation target different areas, different miseries in the world. The emergence of the Interview Girl Foundation's *Operation A^2* developed over the past year. Originally, I wanted to raise money to provide medicine for someone like Amara. I dreamed of raising money for medicine that HIV/AIDS victims needed, but the Interview Girl Foundation grew into a quest to rid the planet of poverty and to make sure that the antiretrovirals that Interview Girl Foundation provided were not just a band aid solution to someone's misery. Organizations throughout the world achieving positive social change partnering with other organizations doing the same thing will allow "changing the world" to happen. The Interview Girl Foundation's all-embracing mission (C^2: *Committed Collaboration*) is to play a role in helping to make this happen in our world. People need to be given a chance to fulfill their own potential. Aid projects have demonstrated that even when the best intentions are in place, too many projects create dependence that helps no one in the long run. The Interview Girl Foundation believes in the people whom we are hoping to serve.

Operation A²'s plan is not perfect. I kept wanting to tweak the plan, to do more development research. Finally it hit me. I could no longer tweak. I had to get the ball rolling. I am sure that there are loop holes in the Interview Girl Foundation's *Operation A²*, but it's a start. The Interview Girl Foundation begins its work by providing medication to orphans who do not have access to medication. Predominantly, the foundation will continue to ask questions, just like Amara enquiringly did in Kpando that summer. She had an insatiable inquisitiveness to understand and learn from that outdated book about an obscure subject. Amara was our impetus; I knew that it was *Operation A²'s* questions that would determine its reach. From the work that the Interview Girl Foundation completes, we will reflect, ask tough questions, and set up an objective process for learning the answers. As all time-honored historical lessons exhibit, greatness in any endeavor originates from asking the right questions. The Interview Girl Foundation will develop its questions as we work. Its questions will be developed from listening to who it is that is experiencing the misery.

> "Experience is what you get when you don't get what you want."
>
> —Dan Stanford

I became inspired as I read stories about individuals who worked in organizations and exhilarated by the stories about the individuals whose lives were changed because of the good that an organization did. I was enlivened from learning the stories behind Acumen Fund, UNICEF, Kiva, Catholic Relief Services, Save the Children, Rotary Foundation, St. Jude's Children's Research Hospital, Special Olympics, Ashoka, Mercy Corps, Habitat for Humanity, Lions Clubs International Foundation, World Vision, Council on Foreign Relations, Bill and Melinda Gates Foundation,

Water Partners International, Wounded Warrior Project and so many others. The difference that these projects were making in other people's lives mattered. People needed to hear their stories and limitless other stories. The ultimate goal that Jacelyn Novogratz has for Acumen is to help create a world in which every human being on the planet has access to basic, affordable services, so that they have a choice of freedom. In the late 1990's, Doctors Without Borders started a campaign to bring people throughout the world access to essential medicines. The Interview Girl Foundation is joining Acumen, Doctors Without Borders, and countless other organizations doing proactive work to play a role in helping to eliminate miseries that exist in this world. Maybe the Interview Girl Foundation's *Operation A²* does not have a perfect solution to guarantee AIDS orphans medication for life, but we are striving to help a problem that I saw firsthand. What humanitarian reason or crisis the profits from our organization are used for will continually shift, but hearing peoples' stories and sharing these would remain the crux of InterviewGirl.com and hearing and sharing stories was the belief on which this movement was founded.

Because We Can

Why do I take all the time to complete these interviews? Because I can and because these interviews make a difference. Why try and raise money to help eliminate the miseries that AIDS orphans experience? Because we can. We can complete one undertaking at a time and through our efforts miseries can be eliminated. The Interview Girl Foundation provides medicine to one orphan at a time and we are able to do this because InterviewGirl.com is collecting one story at a time.

As I sat in my office reading the fancy intellectual debates about foreign aid, I would look up from the books and see Amara's name peering at me from my cork board and I knew that even if the Interview Girl Foundation did not have the perfect plan to undo some of the grave injustices that exist, it would always be working toward a better, more efficient plan. Any large project has a multifaceted plan. Step one in the Interview Girl Foundation's *Operation A²'s* program is providing medication to someone who is sick. Bambelela is a South African spiritual hymn. Bambelela is a Zulu word meaning "Hold on" or "Never Give Up." Miseries like AIDS victims not having access to medication, individuals being trapped within poverty, people who are victims of human trafficking, a child not having the means to attend school, and many other miseries plague the world. We cannot give up on helping these miseries because they are immense in scope. Historians generally look to Hippocrates as the founder of medicine as a rational science. Before Hippocrates, medicine was seen as magic and superstition. Hippocrates said, "Where there is love for mankind, there is love for the art of healing." We can help to heal those living in miseries. InterviewGirl.com continues to collect and share stories and while InterviewGirl.com continues to share stories, the Interview Girl Foundation will not back down on its mission to help to eliminate these miseries that exist. One of the ministers from Sudan's government said to Doctor James Orbinski, "you MSF fellows and ladies. Why do you do it?" Orbinski immediately replied to him, "Because we can." So, I ask you all, why should we care to want to help eliminate misery (the misery of someone you don't even know)? My answer to you is: Because we can.

"Life is trying things to see if they work."

—Ray Bradbury

Back to the Basics

"A #2 pencil and a dream can take you anywhere."

—Joyce Meyer

From what started with one person taking a pen to paper and writing out questions, lists, plans, and ideas, the world has been altered countless times in history. The Interview Girl Foundation goes back to the basics as it attempts to come up with solutions to miseries that exist in the world. The basic task of asking the right questions is the foundation behind the Interview Girl Foundation's aspirations and imaginings about a better world. The stories about Muhammad Yunus and Bill Drayton personify how even though both individuals created organizations that reformed existing conditions, Yunus and Drayton both began with the basics as they completed their revolutionary work.

Muhammad Yunus' solution to world poverty is simple and it goes back to the basics. It is founded on the belief that credit is a fundamental human right. His solution is to lend poor people money on terms that are suitable to them, to teach the poor a few sound financial principles, and from doing this, they will then help themselves. In 1983, Muhammad Yunus formed the Grameen Bank, meaning "village bank" founded on principles of trust and solidarity. In *Banker To the Poor*, Yunus imparts, "We were convinced that the bank should be built on human trust, not on meaningless paper contracts."[316] The Grameen Bank is a bank devoted to providing the poorest of Bangladesh with minuscule loans. In Bangladesh today, Grameen has 2,564 branches, with 19,800 staff serving 8.29 million borrowers in 81,367 villages. On any working day Grameen collects an average of $1.5 million in weekly installments. Of the borrowers, 97% are women and over 97% of the loans are paid back, a recovery rate higher than any other banking system. Grameen methods are applied in projects in 58 countries, including the US, Canada, France, The Netherlands and Norway.

Yunus' idea was born in 1976 when he loaned $27 from his own pocket to forty-two people living in a tiny village. These micro-entrepreneurs only needed enough credit to purchase the raw materials for their trade. Yunus' small loan helped them break the cycle of poverty for good. Yunus realized that access to even a small amount of credit can transform the lives of the poorest citizens of the world. The process to Grameen Bank became a reality as he and his student volunteers went out into the communities and spoke with the poor people themselves. The amount of poor people in Bangladesh at the time was overwhelming, but Yunus returned to the basics to begin to attempt to solve this crisis. He spoke with individual people about what micro-lending could do for them. There was no other way to get the Grameen Bank started other than person to person interaction. Yunus and the student volunteers who helped him had to be persistent. They had to work for a long time at achieving their ideal before it became a reality. After starting with the basic effort of spreading the idea by one individual telling another one, in time, Grameen Bank eventually became a reality.

Another specific example of how Yunus used inherent everyday skills to build this micro-credit program is seen in an instance when he was in the process of setting up the Grameen Bank. When he ran into some difficulty with the repayment mechanism, his solution started with a notebook. Borrowers claimed they had paid their daily installment, and the pan seller said they had not. Yunus decided to then keep it as simple as possible. He articulates, "Arguments were unending, I knew we had to simplify the procedure. So I bought a notebook, and on the left I wrote each borrower's name. In the center I made three columns showing amounts paid per installment and the date."[317] Using his notebook, Yunus devised a way to keep track of borrowers and if they paid their daily installment. Writing things down as a log in a notebook is an exercise where one returns to the basics. The simple act of logging the amounts paid per installment aided Yunus in the development of the Grameen Bank.

Today, more than 250 institutions in nearly 100 countries operate micro-credit programs based on the Grameen methodology, placing Grameen at the forefront of a world movement toward eradicating poverty through micro-lending. To come up with a solution to world poverty, Yunus went back to the basics. His

Grameen Bank idea is founded on the belief that credit is a fundamental human right. What makes this idea so brilliant is that it is simple: lend poor people money on terms that are suitable to them, teach them a few sound financial principles, and they will help themselves. Yunus started with the "basics" and twenty-three years after he established Grameen Bank, he won the Nobel Prize for Peace for his work in eradicating poverty.

Bill Drayton is the founder and CEO of *Ashoka: Innovators for the Public*, which now has about 3,000 social entrepreneurs in the field all over the world. Drayton is credited with creating and building the field of social entrepreneurship. The inspiring aspect of Drayton's story was what he had to do in the beginning in order to build *Ashoka*. Analogous to Yunus, he too began with the "basics."

Drayton has worked as a lawyer, management consultant, and a government administrator, but over the past twenty five years, his main preoccupation has been traveling around the world looking for individuals who are working to bring about systematic social change. Along the way, he's had thousands of detailed conversations with these people and has kept track (with little notebooks and a microcassette recorder) of things they are doing that work and things that don't.[318]

To get *Ashoka* going, Drayton asked some colleagues whom he believed possessed the values and skills that would contribute to a strong institution to join his endeavor. During their Christmas vacations in 1978 and 1979, Drayton and his colleagues took exploratory trips to India, Indonesia, and Venezuela to figure out how to design a program to spot social entrepreneurs when they were still relatively unknown and predict the ones most likely to achieve major impact in the decades ahead.

Over a two-week period, Drayton and his team would meet with 60 or 70 people. They would go see someone for breakfast, two during the morning, someone for lunch, someone for afternoon tea, and then someone for dinner. Drayton explains,

"We were systematic about it. We would go and see anyone who had a reputation for doing something innovative for the public good. And we kept asking questions: Who in your field, as a private citizen, has caused a major change that you really respond to? How does it work? Is it new? Where do we find this person? Then we'd go and see that person and ask the same questions and get more names. We'd turn each name into a 3x5 card, and as the weeks went by, we'd begin to get multiple cards on people. At the end we had mapped out who was doing what in different fields."[319]

By 1981, Drayton had collected hundreds of three-by-five cards, and *Ashoka* was ready to hold its first selection panel.[320] Bill Drayton went on interview after interview and he filled out note cards about what he would hear from people. An undoubtedly simple act: asking people questions and keeping track of their answers is how Drayton began to build *Ashoka*. It was a simple act that went back to the basics, but Drayton was tenacious. He has had conversations with thousands of people. Also, he asked the *right* questions. He would methodically go to his interviews and then document what he learned each time. Both Yunus and Drayton stayed the course as they continued to complete the *basic* tasks that they started completing when they began their ideas. Not giving up and continuing to complete these basic tasks was what brought them eventual success.

Interview Girl asks questions. That is what I do. I question. From the questions that I ask people, they then share fascinating stories and anecdotes with me. It is from the questions that individuals ask that change eventually occurs. The world begins to change as we ask questions. The Interview Girl Foundation asks questions: Is it possible to eradicate poverty? Can we extend health care to every corner of the world? Can human trafficking be stopped? Can we reverse the spread of HIV/AIDS? Can we make sure that every child in every country receives a good education? Although positive answers to the above questions may seem beyond reach today, we can change the world as we ask these questions, ask what has been done to achieve these visions so far and ask what still needs to be completed in order to fully answer these questions positively. We can change the world, after all, it has been changed in the past.

InterviewGirl.com collects one story at a time to spread diverse perspectives and ideas throughout the world. The Interview Girl Foundation works to provide answers to the above questions and has committed to playing a role in changing the world as we strive to eliminate miseries that exist. The Interview Girl Foundation's project *Operation A²* is working to assist orphans with HIV/ AIDS. Through the Interview Girl Foundation's guiding goal (*C²: Committed Collaboration*), the Interview Girl Foundation has made a commitment to finding social entrepreneurs within the world and bringing them together. By bringing people and organizations together, solutions that work to eliminate miseries will attack problems faster and more efficiently.

When attempting any seemingly complex task in life, always go back to the basics. It was necessary for the Interview Girl Foundation to go back to the basics when it began its work. Who knew that as I sat in the basement a year ago writing questions in my notebook that this was the beginning of a movement to change the world. Changing the world inaugurates with asking the right questions. With cutting edge innovation so much is possible, but to start, the old fashion way made so much sense: Writing out questions and then seeking solutions from there. There is no other way. Begin by doing the right thing, ask the necessary questions, take a pen to paper, make a list, organize that list and turn it into a plan, and from these ostensibly simplistic beginnings, it is here that the world begins to change. In looking at any event in history that we now see as one that altered the world from how it once was, in its inception stage, that event started with people who returned to the basics. It is important to remember to go back to the basics.

InterviewGirl.com—Changing the World One Story at a Time

"There is no greater agony than bearing an untold story inside you."

—Maya Angelou

How can someone actually change the world? The world begins to change as individual lives are altered. It is through helping individuals one by one that overtime preeminent changes eventually take shape in this world. It has been said that if someone can change a life, he/she then begins to change the world. The idea of helping one person at a time seems like it won't achieve much in comparison to the gargantuan problems that plague the world. It is important for us to remember that when an individual continually makes small-scale efforts over time eventually these small efforts completed over and over lead to larger changes. Any out of the ordinary idea takes tenacity and determination to come to fruition. You have to work and keep working. For example, Muhammad Yunus worked steadily and nonstop for two decades before his Grameen Bank caught on. As David Bornstein reveals, "Yunus worked without pause for two decades to develop Grameen's credit delivery system, and to institutionalize and market his idea."[321] It is essential to not give up. Even when the small efforts that are put in day after day do not seem to pay off, it is especially in those moments that we need to keep striving forward.

Determination, perseverance, effort, and hard work are categorically the secrets behind the stories that most influence history. The truth is that there are not any secrets. People need to work hard day in and day out and as they do this, their aspirations can then become a reality. I find myself sending out letter after letter asking people to complete interviews with InterviewGirl.com, in contact with different grassroots organizations on the ground in Africa in an attempt to set up *Operation A²* in an efficient manner,

508

and in an endless search for volunteers to help InterviewGirl.com and the Interview Girl Foundation's cause. There are days that my efforts do not seem to generate any positive momentum forward, but I see Amara's name pinned to the cork board above my desk and of course I notice the piles of books throughout my office that are filled with stories about social entrepreneurs and individuals who are making the world a better place. Even one glance at Amara's name and/or viewing the multitude of books triggers reminding me of how it is possible to make a difference in this world. This encourages me to keep working at creating InterviewGirl.com and the Interview Girl Foundation. Those individuals whom have veritably played a role in shaping our current world or in making our world better in some way inspire me to keep working.

The stories about Saint Francis of Assisi, Nelson Mandela, James Orbinski, Mother Teresa, Pope John Paul II, St. Therese of Liseaux, Father Moreau, Maria Montessori, Florence Nightingale, Aristotle, Socrates, Ashoka, Jean Monnet, Gandhi, Thomas Jefferson, Abraham Lincoln, Lech Walesa, Sir Thomas More, Joan of Arc, Vaclav Havel, General George S. Patton, Lieutenant Giuseppe Petrosino, Charles de Gaulle, Giuseppe Garibaldi, Fiorella La Guardia, Thomas Clarkson, Martin Luther King Jr., Clara Barton, Candy Lightner, Ryan White, Patrick Henry Hughes, Randy Pausch, and Liz Murray (along with countless others) all vivify that making a difference in our world is possible. Although I don't personally know any of these individuals, I feel as if I do because I read their stories. I was moved as I soaked up the stories of these remarkable people.

The news tends to show a great deal of the violence that happens in our world. Bornstein concludes in his book, "The remarkable story of the emerging citizen sector goes untold." Vera Cordeiro, the founder of Associação Saúde Criançar, told Bornstein, "There is an exciting world behind this terrible world we see."[322] InterviewGirl.com wants to spread stories. It will spread stories about social entrepreneurs, people who are making a difference, people who have overcome difficult odds, and ultimately stories about people who make us all want to become better versions of ourselves and inspire us to want to do more. I was galvanized by the questions Amara asked me at the Children's Home that summer. I was touched by Amara's story. What happened to Amara provoked me in a way that I actually sat down each and every day to work on this book. The books that I've read in the past year exposed to me that thousands upon thousands of people are making a positive difference in the world. Their stories infused my head and heart. I decided stories like these need to be told. I am sometimes discouraged because I feel like InterviewGirl.com is not catching on as I had hoped, but then I re-read Bornstein's words,

> "It is that people who solve problems must somehow first arrive at the belief that they can solve problems. This belief does not emerge suddenly. The capacity to cause change grows in an individual over time as small-scale efforts lead gradually to larger ones. The process needs a beginning—a story, an example, an early taste of success—something along the way that helps a person form the belief that it is possible to make the world a better place. Those who act on that belief spread it to others. They are highly contagious. Their stories must be told."[323]

People who solve problems in our world, people who eliminate miseries that exist must somehow first believe that they can solve problems. I believe in this project as a way to eliminate some of the misery that exists in this world. InterviewGirl.com has a passion to tell the stories of those individuals who are making a difference in this world and the Interview Girl Foundation feels a need to bring these individuals into contact with one another because as these people join forces then the world can genuinely begin to change. There is a Haitain proverb that says, "Beyond mountains there are mountains" (Deye mon gen mon), meaning that when we have solved one problem, we need to then solve the next. This reminds us that when we erase one misery, we must then move onto the next misery because every person deserves the recognition of his or her humanity. There is always another misery to help eliminate and there is always another story to hear.

The Gift of Perspective

Michael Michalko unfolds the importance of learning to see things from different perspectives through discussing Einstein as he describes, "Einstein's theory of relativity is, in essence, a description of the interaction between different perspectives."[324] Einstein did not invent the concepts of energy, mass, or speed of light. He combined these concepts in a new way to make his famous equation: $E=mc^2$. Einstein was able to look at the same world as everyone else and see something different. Hearing stories transmits to us the gift of perspective.

My volunteer trip to Africa challenged my perspective about our world. As we hear peoples' stories, we understand from a different place. During my trip, when I was not at the Children's Home, I would sit outside the little hut where I slept at night and talk to all of my neighbors. They would tell me their stories. They would answer my questions. My neighbor, Charity would stir her food over the open fire. She would heat water over the fire as I queried thirsting to hear her stories.

In *Six Months In Sudan*, a humanitarian doctor describes how he attempted to share with an audience about what it was like in Sudan once he returned to the USA, "I want to bring them there, to erase the distance until it is invisible and only the moment remains. I want to get them close, as near as I can without taking them there."[326] Telling stories was the vehicle that this doctor used to bring the individuals to experience what it was like in Sudan. Stories are the best way to allow us to see the world the way that someone else does. As the popular phrase goes, "To walk in their shoes." As the Zulu in Africa say, not hello, but I *see* you. For someone to look beyond themselves and to care about the needs of another is an act of empathy. Empathy matters in our lives. A quote Mr. Rogers always kept in his wallet said, "Frankly, there isn't anyone you couldn't learn to love once you've heard their story." Jesus spent his days traveling around the countryside. Sometimes he healed people; other times, he told people stories. As people share their stories with one another, they learn to appreciate one another. Hearing different stories compels individuals to view life from a new perspective. The more that you read, hear, and come into contact with, in these encounters, your perspective widens and as this happens, newfangled notions emerge for people. As individuals gain different perspectives, they become more empathetic and this in itself changes the world. Stories transmit to us the gift of perspective and as we gain this gift, we begin to see the world in which we live and reconsider our engagement with the world. When we shift our perspective, we see that all humans deserve a life filled with dignity and when there is misery that some experience—we *see* that we should do something to change this.

One Story at a Time: There is no other way

As you go through life, you never know what will change you. I'll always remember that day when Edem uttered, "Because the Medicines Ran Out." From those five words, my life's purpose would be altered. All the back and forth, the "Renaissance" soul that I was, finally "focus" seemed as if it came to me. I decided to share peoples' stories because we are touched by stories and from these stories we could help someone experiencing a form of misery. I verily believe that hearing a story has the possibility to turn a life around. I have confidence in this project: InterviewGirl.com. I have faith in this project because I think that it's going to serve the public in two ways. 1.) The compilations that we put together at InterviewGirl.com will improve one's life as one learns about different areas. 2.) The revenues that InterviewGirl.com's various projects bring in will help to eliminate some of the miseries that people experience. With the bequests that are raised through *Operation A²*, we can bring health care, education, and other changes that will lead to sustainability and a way to eliminate some of the miseries that some people are facing. Through its initiatives, the Interview Girl Foundation is playing a role in helping to eliminate miseries (such as: helping to break the cycle of poverty that exists in parts of our world and aiding AIDS victims).

We all have a story. Why not share yours and change the world in the process? I challenge you to share a story and/or read a story. Doing either will affect your life in more of a way than you can imagine. Nobody in the history of human civilization has something that you have: your voice, *your story*. As Interview Girl, I have listened to hundreds and hundreds of stories and I hope to listen to millions more. What is your story? Do your part and contribute to one of InterviewGirl.com's projects and one story at a time, we will change the world.

Person to person we can make a difference in this world. Each project at InterviewGirl.com will target a different, specific misery and with doing this, we will help to alleviate the miseries that people experience. You can donate to the Interview Girl Foundation's *Operation A²—Aiding AIDS* project with a monetary donation or you can share a story on InterviewGirl.com. Either way you will be helping to slice off a piece of the misery on our planet. Set some time aside this week and look at the projects on InterviewGirl.com. What can you contribute? What are your messages, ideas, or thoughts? Make your mark today. If you share a story with us, we will be slicing off a piece of the misery in today's world. One story at a time, we will make the world a better place.

A movement to change the world, one story at a time. Could it be possible? Man was told that he would never form a piece of machinery that could fly long distances through the air and people living in the day and time of the slave trade thought that slavery itself would never cease to exist, but as individuals took steps (one action step at a time) toward flying a plane and ending slavery, over time, those challenges that were viewed as impossible (flying airplanes and ending slavery) were overcome. Stories change lives. It happens day in and day out. Now through a project that is specifically created to distribute stories: InterviewGirl.com—we will use a power that was already inherent in stories and as we share one story at a time, we will as they say, change the world, by striving to make miseries that exist no longer exist.

"Stories are the vicissitudes of human intention."

—Jerome Bruner

The Power of a Story

"Stories you read when you're the right age never quite leave you. You may forget who wrote them or what the story was called. Sometimes you'll forget precisely what happened, but if a story touches you it will stay with you, haunting the places in your mind that you rarely ever visit."

—Neil Gaiman, *M is for Magic*

I knew through stories, I too could help to make the world a better place. I personally and solely could not eliminate poverty, nor could any one organization, but with all of us doing something, together we could make meaningful changes. Each of has a unique role on this planet. Mine is to hear and then share stories and from doing this to make a difference. As new studies in neuroscience clarify, telling stories builds empathy and also when someone tells a good one, people act as if they are watching it unfold before them.

InterviewGirl.com comes down to the power of a story. Stories matter. They always have since the beginning of time. Yann Martel declares,

"We are story animals. Stories at their greatest define who we are as a species. We are story animals. Leopards, pandas, kawolsa, lizards are not story animals. They have no stories. We have stories. That makes us unique. That's what we are entirely about. We are not economic animals, although we do have economies. We are not political animals, although we do have politics. As soon as you engage yourself in being human you start developing stories."[325]

When we see ourselves in this world as part of this nation of humanity, yet we understand that each of us has our unrivaled story, we come to understand humanity's interconnectedness. We need to share these stories with one another. When we focus on our interdependence, the world becomes better. Stories help us to get inside other people's heads and hearts. They are the most effective form of human communication, more powerful than any other way of packaging information. As Peter Guber illuminates, "Reams of data rarely engage people to move them to action. Stories, on the other hand, are state-of-the-heart technology—they connect us to others." Our interpersonal relationships, our connections to others are what will allow us to make this world a better place. Through the depths of peoples' stories, we come to understand this world better as we *see* those around us.

Stories are powerful because they prompt us to want to act. Stories entertain while at the same time invite us to perceive the world from outside ourselves. Stories also help us to understand what is best for ourselves. And what I love best about stories is not that preeminent stories offer answers, but more importantly, the greatest stories help us to rightly frame questions. It is only from asking the right questions that we can begin to change anything. As we have seen throughout history, when we ask those tough questions, it is from there that progress is made. Stories challenge us to ask better questions. As we ask better questions, we become closer to achieving what it is that needs to be done. When we ask the right questions, the world can start to change.

Chapter Endnotes and Bibliographies
Chapter One Endnotes

1   "World Poverty Statistics," *Statistic Brain*, Statistic Brain Research Institute, 23 July 2012, Oct. 2013 <>.

2   AIDS is the more advanced stage of HIV infection. When the immune system CD4 cells drop to a very low level, a person's ability to fight infection is lost. In addition, there are several conditions that occur in people with HIV infection with this degree of immune system failure—these are called AIDS—defining illnesses. Amara's body could not fight the infection inside of her body.

3   *WWII Stories* is a compilation of stories from InterviewGirl.com. InterviewGirl.com's first compilation of stories is an oral history project about WWII. From 2008 to 2014, individuals who were alive during the war years were interviewed for this compilation of stories. All of these stories are presented in InterviewGirl.com's compilation: *WWII Stories.*

4   HIV and AIDS Health Center," *WebMD,* WebMD, LLC., 2013. Oct. 2013 <http://www.webmd. com/hiv-aids/ guide/sexual-health-aids>.

5   *A Heart for Justice*, http://www.aheartforjustice.com (2013).

6   Nicholas D. Kristof and Sheryl WuDunn, *Half the Sky: Turning Oppression into Opportunity for Women Worldwide* (New York: Vintage, 2009).

7   "Hunger and World Poverty," http://www.poverty.com (2013).

8   "HIV & AIDS Information from AVERT.org." *http://www.avert.org* (2013).

9   "Catholic Relief Services," http://www.catholiccharitiesusa.org/ (2013).

10 George Ellison, *Learning from HIV and AIDS*, (Cambridge: Cambridge University Press, 2003), 3-4.

11 Peter Schwab, Africa: *A Continent Self-Destructs*, (New York: Palgrave for St. Martin's Press, 2001), 112.

12 "150 Basic AIDS Facts," *GlobalAIDSDay.org*, World Storehouse, 2007, Oct. 2013 <http://www. globalaidsday.org/ html/150_basic_aids_facts.html>.

13 Abhijit V. Banerjee and Esther Duflo, *Poor Economics: A Radical Rethinking of the Way to Fight Global Poverty* (New York: Public Affairs, 2011), 38.

14 Dean Karlan and Jacob Appel, *More Than Good Intentions* (New York: Dutton, 2012), 2.

15 Martin E. P. Seligman, *Authentic Happiness: Using the New Positive Psychology to Realize Your Potential for Lasting Fulfillment* (New York: Atria, 2004).

16 Epicurus, *A Guide to Happiness* (London: Weidenfeld & Nicolson History, 2005).

17 Jean Vanier, *Becoming Human* (Mahwah, NJ: Paulist, 2008).

18 Jean Vanier, *Letters to My Brothers and Sisters in L'Arche.* (L'Arche Internationale, 1996), Introduction, 11.

19 Bill Gates, "The Power of Catalytic Philanthropy." http://www.thegatesnotes.com/Personal/ The-Power-of- Catalytic-Philanthropy (19 Sept. 2012).

    "While the private sector does a phenomenal job meeting human needs among those who can pay, there are billions of people who have no way to express their needs in ways that matter to markets. And so they go without. And while private markets foster many stunning innovations in medicine, science, and technology, the private sector still under-invests in innovation—dramatically. There are huge opportunities for innovation that the market ignores because those taking the risk capture only a small subset of the returns."

20 Peter Singer, "Peter Singer: The Why and How of Effective Altruism." *TED: Ideas worth spreading,* TED Conferences, LLC., May 2013. Oct. 2013 <http://www.ted.com/talks/peter_singer_the_why_and_how_of_effective_altruism. html>.

21 Albert Einstein, *Ideas And Opinions* (New York: Broadway, 1995).

22 Charles Darwin and Sir Francis Darwin, *The Life and Letters of Charles Darwin* (New York: D. Appleton & Co. 1911).

23 David Kord Murray, *Borrowing Brilliance* (New York: Gotham Books, 2009), 34.

24 Murray, 36.

25 Michael Novak, "Benedict: The Quiet Pope, the Scholar." *The Huffington Post,* TheHuffingtonPost. com, Inc., 18 Feb 2013, Oct. 2013 <http://www.huffingtonpost.com/michael-novak/pope-benedict-xvi-resignation_b_2712806. html>.

26 Esther Duflo is the Abdul Latif Jameel Professor of Poverty Alleviation and Development Economics in the Department of Economics at *MIT* and a founder and director of the *Abdul Latif Jameel Poverty Action Lab.*

27 Esther Duflo, "Esther Duflo: Social Experiments to Fight Poverty." *TED: Ideas worth spreading,* TED Conferences, LLC., May 2010, Oct. 2013 <http://www.ted.com/talks/esther_duflo_social_experiments_to_fight_poverty.html>.

28 "Esther Duflo," *Innovations for Poverty Action,* Innovations for Poverty Action, 2011, Oct. 2013 <>.

29 Terry Pratchett, *Mort* (New York: Harper, 2013).

30 Banerjee and Duflo, *Poor Economics,* 1.

31 Maskalyk, James. *Six months in Sudan: a young doctor in a war-torn village.* (New York: Spiegel & Grau, 2009)

32 As my journey through research continued and it eventually turned into founding The *Interview Girl Foundation,* with time, I narrowed down which area I wanted to first help. The *Interview Girl Foundation's Operation A²* was created to focus on the plight of AIDS. We had to start somewhere when it came to "eliminating misery."

33 Michael Gelb and Sarah Caldicott, *Innovate Like Edison: The Five-Step System for Breakthrough Business Success* (New York: Dutton, 2007) 54.

Chapter One Bibliography

"World Poverty Statistics," *Statistic Brain,* Statistic Brain Research Institute, 23 July 2012, Oct. 2013 <http://www. statisticbrain.com/world-poverty-statistics/>.

Matthew Kelly, *Our Lives Change When our Habits Change* (Hebron, KY: Dynamic Catholic, 2008).

I Am Because We Are, Dir. Nathan Rissman (Virgil Films and Entertainment, 2009).

"HIV and AIDS Health Center," *WebMD*, WebMD, LLC, 2013. Oct. 2013 <http://www. webmd.com/hiv-aids/ guide/sexual-health-aids>.

Nicholas D. Kristof and Sheryl WuDunn, *Half the Sky: Turning Oppression into Opportunity for Women Worldwide* (New York: Vintage, 2009).

Abhijit V. Banerjee and Esther Duflo, *Poor Economics: A Radical Rethinking of the Way to Fight Global Poverty* (New York: Public Affairs, 2011) 2.

"150 Basic AIDS Facts," *GlobalAIDSDay.org*, World Storehouse, 2007, Oct. 2013 <http:// www.globalaidsday.org/ html/150_basic_aids_facts.html>.

Martin E. P. Seligman, *Authentic Happiness: Using the New Positive Psychology to Realize Your Potential for Lasting Fulfillment* (New York: Atria, 2004).

Seligman, *Learned Optimism: How to Change Your Mind and Your Life* (New York: Vintage, 2006).

Epicurus, *A Guide to Happiness* (London: Weidenfeld & Nicolson History, 2005).

Kathryn Spink, *The Miracle the Message the Story: Jean Vanier and L'Arche* (Mahwah, NJ: Paulist, 2006).

Jean Vanier, *Becoming Human* (Mahwah, NJ: Paulist, 2008).

Peter Singer, "Peter Singer: The Why and How of Effective Altruism." *TED: Ideas worth spreading*, TED Conferences, LLC, May 2013. Oct. 2013 <http://www.ted.com/talks/ peter_singer_the_why_and_how_of_effective_altruism. html>.

Albert Einstein, *Ideas And Opinions* (New York: Broadway, 1995).

Max Born, *The Born-Einstein Letters* (New York: Macmillan, 1971).

Einstein, *Einstein on Humanism* (New York: Carol, 1993).

Einstein, *Autobiographical Notes* (Peru, IL: Carus, 1979).

Einstein and Leopold Infeld, *The Evolution of Physics* (New York: Touchstone, 1967).

Michael Novak, "Benedict: The Quiet Pope, the Scholar." *The Huffington Post*, TheHuffingtonPost.com, Inc., 18 Feb 2013, Oct. 2013 <http://www.huffingtonpost. com/michael-novak/pope-benedict-xvi-resignation_b_2712806. html>.

Esther Duflo, "Esther Duflo: Social Experiments to Fight Poverty." *TED: Ideas worth spreading*, TED Conferences, LLC, May 2010, Oct. 2013 <http://www.ted.com/talks/ esther_duflo_social_experiments_to_fight_poverty.html>.

Banerjee and Duflo, "Poor Economics: A Radical Rethinking of the Way to Fight Global Poverty." *Poor Economics*, Poor Economics, 2011, Oct. 2013 <http://pooreconomics. com/about-book>.

"Esther Duflo," *J-PAL: Translating Research into Action*, MIT, 2013, Oct. 2013 <http:// www.povertyactionlab.org/ duflo>.

"Esther Duflo," *Innovations for Poverty Action*, Innovations for Poverty Action, 2011, Oct. 2013 <http://www. poverty-action.org/node/148>.

Terry Pratchett, *Mort* (New York: Harper, 2013).

Banerjee and Duflo, *Poor Economics* 1.

Michael Gelb and Sarah Caldicott, *Innovate Like Edison: The Five-Step System for Breakthrough Business Success* (New York: Dutton, 2007) 54.

Seligman, *Learned Optimism*.

Chapter Two Endnotes

33   Douglas McGray, "Dambisa Moyo: Cut Off Aid to Africa," *Wired.com*, Wired Magazine: 17:10, 21 Sept. 2009.Oct. 2013 <http://www.wired.com/techbiz/people/magazine/17-10/ff_smartlist_moyo>.

34   Stephanie Nolen, *28: Stories of AIDS in Africa* (New York: Walker, 2007).

35   Jeffrey Sachs, *The End of Poverty* (New York: Penguin, 2005) 361.

36   Craig Timberg and Daniel Halperin, *Tinderbox: How the West Sparked the AIDS Epidemic and How the World Can Finally Overcome It* (New York: Penguin, 2012), 28.

37   "World Poverty Statistics."

38   David Bornstein, *How to Change the World* (Oxford: Oxford University, 2007), 130.

39   Therese of Lisieux, *The Story of a Soul: The Autobiography of The Little Flower* (Charlotte, NC: Saint Benedict, 2010).

40   "Paying it forward" is discussed later in this book. As individuals share stories with InterviewGirl.com, they are "Paying it Forward."

41   Anup Shah, "Today, around 21,000 children died around the world." *GlobalIssues.com*, Global Issues, 24 Sept. 2011. Oct. 2013 <http://www.globalissues.org/article/715/today-21000-children-died-around-the-world>.

42   "AIDS," *Poverty.com*, Poverty.com, n.d. Oct. 2013 <http://www.poverty.com/aids.html>.

43   My graduate research and subsequent World War Two Stories interview project is discussed later in this book.

44   This notion is discussed later in the book, but the Western notion that Africans are helpless and they need "the white folk to save them" is not the case nor is it a solution to eliminating miseries that exist in Africa. Africa is filled with stories besides stories of misery and despair.

45   James Orbinski, *Imperfect Offering* (New York: Walker, 2008), 65.

46   "Who Will Be the First to Help?" *Motivateus.com*, Motivating Moments LLC, 4 Feb. 2011. Oct. 2013. <>.

47   Bortolotti, Dan. *Hope In Hell: Inside the World of Doctors Without* Borders (Altona: Firefly Books, 2004), 136.

48   Sachs, *End of Poverty*, 364.

Chapter Two Bibliography

Douglas McGray, "Dambisa Moyo: Cut Off Aid to Africa," *Wired.com*, Wired Magazine: 17:10, 21 Sept. 2009. Oct. 2013 <http://www.wired.com/techbiz/people/magazine/17-10/ff_smartlist_moyo>. Stephanie Nolen, *28: Stories of AIDS in Africa* (New York: Walker, 2007). Dambisa Moyo, *Dead Aid* (New York: Farrar, Straus and Giroux, 2009). Jeffrey Sachs, *The End of Poverty* (New York: Penguin, 2005) 361. Craig

Timberg and Daniel Halperin, *Tinderbox: How the West Sparked the AIDS Epidemic and How the World Can*

Finally Overcome It (New York: Penguin, 2012) 28. Edward Hooper, *The River: A Journey to the Source of HIV and AIDS* (Boston: Little, Brown, 1999). Hooper, "Michael Worobey's Possession of 1950s Tissue Samples from Stanleyville (Kisangani)," *AIDSOrigins.com*, AIDS Origins, 19 March 2008. Oct. 2013 <http://www.aidsorigins.com/ michael-worobey-possession-1950s-tissue-samples>. "HIV/AIDS in Africa," AfricaAlive. org, Africa Alive, n.d. Oct. 2013 <http://www.africaalive.org/>. "World Poverty Statistics."

David Bornstein, *How to Change the World* (Oxford: Oxford University, 2007) 130. "Dr. Vera Cordeiro." *Ashoka Innovators for the Public*, Ashoka, n.d. Oct. 2013 <https:// www.ashoka.org/

Vera_Cordeiro>. Leah L. Laxamana, "Saude Crianca: Snapshots from the Inside," *The Huffington Post*, TheHuffingtonPost.com, Inc.,

7 Oct. 2013. Oct. 2013 <http://www.huffingtonpost.com/tag/vera-cordeiro>. "Associacao Saude Crianca Renascer," *Idealist*, Action Without Borders/Idealist.org, 2013, Oct. 2013 <http://www.

idealist.org/view/org/bJwSW5GGbZMD/>. "2008 Best Practices Database: Associacao Saude Crianca Renascer—an integral perspective of health," *Best Practices*

Database in Improving The Living Environment, UN-Habitat, 2008. Oct. 2013 <http://www. unhabitat.org/

bestpractices/2008/mainview04.asp?BPID=1914>. Therese of Lisieux, *The Story of a Soul: The Autobiography of The Little Flower* (Charlotte, NC: Saint Benedict, 2010). "St. Therese of Lisieux," *Sttherese.com*, St. Therese National Office, n.d. Oct. 2013 <http://www.sttherese.com/>. "The Life of Saint Therese of Lisieux," Vatican.va, The Holy See, n.d. Oct. 2013 <http://www.vatican.va/news_services/liturgy/documents/- ns_lit_doc_19101997_stherese_en.html>. "Saint Therese of Lisieux, Virgin," *EWTN/ Global Catholic Network*, Eternal Word Television Network, Inc., 2013.

Oct. 2013 <http://www.ewtn.com/therese/therese1.htm>. Constant Tennelier, *Through the Year with Saint Thérèse of Lisieux: Living the Little Way* (Liguori, MO: Liguori

Publications, 1998). Therese de Lisieux, *Autobiography of St Therese of Lisieux* (Create Space Independent Publishing Platform, 2010). Therese de Lisieux, *Comfort in Hardship* (Philadelphia, PA: Pauline, 2011). Gretchen Rubin, *The Happiness Project* (New York: Harper, 2011) 210-15. Anup Shah, "Today, around 21,000 children died around the world." *GlobalIssues.com*, Global Issues, 24 Sept. 2011.

Oct. 2013 <http://www.globalissues.org/article/715/today-21000-children-died-around- the-world>. "AIDS," Poverty.com, Poverty.com, n.d. Oct. 2013 <http://www.poverty. com/aids.html>. *Triage: Dr. James Orbinski's Humanitarian Dilemma*, Dir. Patrick Reed (Docurama, 2009). "Democracy in Action: Ghana's 2008 Elections," *Cartercenter.org*, The Carter Center, 2008. Oct. 2013. <http://www.cartercenter.org/news/multimedia/ PeacePrograms/ DemocracyinActionGhanas2008Elections.html>. Nic Cheeseman, "'An African Election': Reflections on Ghana's 2008 Elections," *DemocracyinAfrica. org*, Democracy in Africa, 29 Jan. 2012. Oct. 2013 <http://democracyinafrica.org/an-african-election/>.

Ghana, Final Report, Presidential and Parliamentary Elections 2008, European Union Election Observation Mission, Feb. 2009. PDF file.

James Orbinski, *Imperfect Offering* (New York: Walker, 2008) 65.

"Who Will Be the First to Help?" *Motivateus.com*, Motivating Moments LLC, 4 Feb. 2011. Oct. 2013. <http://www.motivateus.com/stories/be-godlike.htm>.

Sachs, *End of Poverty* 364.

"Abolition of the Slave Trade," *Black Presence Exhibition/Rights*, The National Archives (UK). Oct. 2013 <www.nationalarchives.gov.uk/pathways/blackhistory/rights/abolition.htm>.

The Schomburg Center for Research in Black Culture, *The Abolition of the Slave Trade*. The New York Public Library, 2012. Oct. 2013 <http://abolition.nypl.org/home/>.

John Simkin, "1807 Abolition of Slavery Act." *Spartacus Educational*, Spartacus Educational, June 2013. Oct. 2013 <http://www.spartacus.schoolnet.co.uk/Lslavery07.htm>.

Charlotte Hodgman, "The Abolition of the British Slave Trade," *HistoryExtra.Com*, Immediate Media Co., Ltd., 23 Aug. 2012. Oct. 2013 <http://www.historyextra.com/slavery>.

Shah. "Racism." *GlobalIssues.org*, Global Issues, 8 Aug. 2010. Oct. 2013 <http://www.globalissues.org/article/165/ racism>.

Madeline Drexler, "How Racism Hurts – Literally," *Boston.com*, Boston Globe Media Partners, LLC, 15 July 2007. Oct. 2013 <http://www.boston.com/news/globe/ideas/articles/ 2007/07/15/ how_racism_hurts literally/?page=full>.

Ehiedu E. G. Iweriebor, "The Colonization of Africa," *Africana Age*, The Schomburg Center for Research in Black Culture/New York Public Library, 2011. Oct. 2013 <http://exhibitions.nypl.org/africanaage/essay-colonization-of-africa.html>.

Leander Heldring and James A. Robinson, "Colonialism and Development in Africa." *VoxEU.org*, 10 Jan. 2013. Oct. 2013 <http://www.voxeu.org/article/colonialism-and-development-africa>.

Susan M. Pojer, *European Colonialism in Africa*, Chappaqua, NY: Susan M. Pojer, n.d. PDF file.

Mots Pheko, "Africa: Effects of Colonialism on Africa's Past and Present," *AZAPO Commemoration of African Liberation Day*, Pimville Community Hall Soweto, 26 May 2012. Oct. 2013 <http://allafrica.com/stories/201206010988. html>.

Adam Hochschild, *King Leopold's Ghost: A Story of Greed, Terror, and Heroism in Colonial Africa* (Boston: Houghton Mifflin/Mariner, 1999).

Bertrand Taithe, *The Killer Trail: A Colonial Scandal in the Heart of Africa* (New York: Oxford University, 2009). A. Adu Boahen, *African Perspectives on Colonialism* (Baltimore, MD: Johns Hopkins University, 1989). *New York Times UpFront Magazine*, Feb. 2012.

Chapter Three Endnotes

48 Erica Purdue, "What's Next? Social Media Is Changing the Way We Communicate."*Heritage Newspapers*. Journal Register, http://heritage.com/articles/2012/03/21/heritagewest/news/doc4f69ce46f3375121907051. txt?viewmode=default (21 Mar. 2012).

49 Steve Addison, "Movements That Change the World." http://www.movements.net/books/movements-that- change-the-world/movements-synopsis(2012).

50 Editors of Conari Press, *Random Acts of Kindness* (San Francisco: Conari, 2002), 2.

51 Dov Greenberg, "Changing the World, One Person at a Time," *AskMoses.com*, AskMoses.com, 2013. Oct. 2013 <http://www.askmoses.com/en/article/485,1995839/Changing-the-World-One-Person-at-a-Time.html>.

52 This concept is discussed in the book *SNAP: Seizing Your Aha! Moments* by Katherine Ramsland.

53 Examples of a process include 1.) A recipe or 2.) Robert's Rules of Order for parliamentary procedure.

54 Morgan D. Jones, *The Thinker's Toolkit: 14 Powerful Techniques for Problem Solving* (New York: Three Rivers, 1998).

55 Jack Harich, "Welcome to Jack Harich's Personal Page," *Thwink.org*, Thwink.org, 2009. Oct. 2013 <>.

56 Michael Michalko, *Cracking Creativity* (New York: Ten Speed Press, 2001), 82.

57 Mark Hayward, "How to Achieve Your Goals Through Reverse Engineering," *LateralAction.com*, Lateral Action, 2011. Oct. 2013 <http://lateralaction.com/articles/how-to-achieve-your-goals-through-reverse-engineering/>.

58 Michael Zenn, *The Self Health Revolution* (New York: Free, 2012), 136.

59 This concept is further discussed in Chapter 14: *Lessons from Interview Girl*.

60 Greenberg, "Unifying the Universal and Particular Approaches," *Lubavitch.com*, Merkos L'Inyonei Chinuch Inc., 2012. Oct. 2013. <http://lubavitch.com/video/2030515/Unifying-the-Universal-and-Particular-Approaches-Rabbi- Dov-Greenberg.html>.

61 Michalko, *Cracking Creativity*, 137.

62 I didn't want this book to read like a scholarly journal, so the research is in the back for those who are interested.

Chapter Three Bibliography

Editors of Conari Press, *Random Acts of Kindness* (San Francisco: Conari, 2002) 2.

Dov Greenberg, "Changing the World, One Person at a Time," *AskMoses.com*, AskMoses.com, 2013. Oct. 2013 <http://www.askmoses.com/en/article/485,1995839/Changing-the-World-One-Person-at-a-Time.html>.

"Finding and Resolving the Root Causes of the Sustainability Problem," *Thwink.org*, Thwink.org, 2012. Oct. 2013 <http://www.thwink.org/>.

"No Solutions to Problems Like These:" *Thwink.org*, Thwink.org, 2012. Oct. 2013 <http://www.thwink.org/sustain/articles/020_NoSolutionsToProblemsLikeThese/index.htm>.

"A Little Story about Corporate Dominance and the Occupy Movement," *Thwink.org*, Thwink.org, 2012. Oct. 2013 <http://www.thwink.org/sustain/articles/016/CorporateDominanceLoop.htm>.

"The IPAT Equation," *Thwink.org*, Thwink.org, 2012. Oct. 2013 <http://www.thwink.org/sustain/articles/011_IPAT_Equation/index.htm>.

"Sustainability," *epa.gov*, United States Environmental Protection Agency, n.d., Oct. 2013 http://www.epa.gov/ sustainability/>.

"Goal 7: Ensure Environmental Sustainability," *We Can End Poverty*, United Nations, 2013. Oct. 2013 <http://www.un.org/millenniumgoals/environ.shtml>.

Bruce Hamilton, *Environmental Sustainability*, National Science Foundation, n.d. Oct. 2013 <http://www.nsf.gov/ funding/pgm_summ.jsp?pims_id=501027>.

Morgan D. Jones, *The Thinker's Toolkit: 14 Powerful Techniques for Problem Solving* (New York: Three Rivers, 1998).

Jack Harich, "Welcome to Jack Harich's Personal Page," *Thwink.org*, Thwink.org, 2009. Oct. 2013 <http://thwink. org/personal/>.

Harich, *Analytical Activism: A New Approach to Solving the Sustainability Problem and Other Difficult Problems* (Clarkston, GA: Thwink.org, 2006).

Harich, *The Dueling Loops of the Political Powerplace: Why Progressives Are Stymied and How They Can Find Their Way Again* (Clarkston, GA: Thwink.org, 2007).

"Jack Harich," *Solutions for a sustainable and desirable future*, TheSolutionsJournal.com, n.d. Oct. 2013 <http://www. thesolutionsjournal.com/user/12104>.

Keiren Fox, "Environment," *InspirationGreen.com*, n.d. Oct. 2013 <http://www.inspirationgreen.com/environment. html>

Michael Michalko, *Cracking Creativity* (New York: Ten Speed Press, 2001) 82.

Mark Hayward, "How to Achieve Your Goals Through Reverse Engineering," *LateralAction.com*, Lateral Action, 2011.Oct. 2013 <http://lateralaction.com/articles/how-to-achieve-your-goals-through-reverse-engineering/>.

Michael Zenn, *The Self Health Revolution* (New York: Free, 2012) 136.

Gordon S. Wood, *The American Revolution: A History*. Modern Library Ed. (New York: Random, 2002).

Edmund S. Morgan, *The Birth of the Republic, 1763-89* (Chicago: University of Chicago, 2013).

Robert Middlekauff, *The Glorious Cause: The American Revolution, 1763-1789* (New York: Oxford University, 2005). Greenberg, "Unifying the Universal and Particular Approaches," *Lubavitch.com*, Merkos L'Inyonei Chinuch Inc., 2012. Oct. 2013. <http://lubavitch.com/video/2030515/Unifying-the-Universal-and-Particular-Approaches-Rabbi-Dov-Greenberg.html>.

Greenberg, "Rabbi Dov Greenberg's Articles," *Arutz Sheva*. IsraelNationalNews.com, n.d. Oct. 2013 <http://www.israelnationalnews.com/Articles/Author.aspx/202>.

Michalko 137.

Moyo.

William Easterly, *The White Man's Burden* (New York: Oxford University Press, 2006).

IPA: Innovations for Poverty Action, Poverty-Action.org, 2011. Oct. 2013 <http://www.poverty-action.org/>.

Abdul Latif Jameel Poverty Action Lab, Massachusetts Institute of Technology, 2013. Web. Oct. 2013 <http://www.povertyactionlab.org/>.

CRS.org, Catholic Relief Services, 2013. Oct. 2013 <http://crs.org/>.

Care.org, CARE, 2013. Oct. 2013 <http://www.care.org/>.

NelsonMandela.org, Nelson Mandela Foundation, 2013. Oct. 2013 <http://www.nelsonmandela.org/>.

Data.gov, The United States Government, 2013. Oct. 2013 <http://www.data.gov/>.

ClintonFoundation.org, The Clinton Foundation, 2013. Oct. 2013 <http://www.clintonfoundation.org/>. *TheGlobalFund.org*, The Global Fund to Fight AIDS, Tuberculosis, and Malaria, 2013. Oct. 2013 <http://www.theglobalfund.org/en/>.

UNAIDS.org/en, United Nations/UNAIDS, n.d. Oct. 2013 <http://www.unaids.org/en/>.

Avert.org, AVERT: AVERTing HIV and AIDS, 2013. Oct. 2013 <http://www.avert.org/>.

MissionariesOfAfrica.org,

Missionaries of Africa, 2008. Oct. 2013 <http://www.missionariesofafrica.org/>.

WHO.int/en, World Health Organization, 2013. Oct. 2013 <http://www.who.int/en/>.

We Can End Poverty, United Nations, 2013. Oct. 2013 <http://www.un.org/millenniumgoals/>.

Chapter Four Endnotes

[63] James Orbinski, *An Imperfect Offering*, 37-91.

[64] There is always hope (Jane). We should take actions (Sister Mary Theophane). The importance of listening (John Gardner).

[65] "Mother Teresa—Biography." *Biography.com*. A&E Television Networks LLC, 2013. Oct. 2013 <http://www.biography.com/people/mother-teresa-9504160?page=3>.

Chapter Four Bibliography

Michael J. Gelb, *How to Think Like Leonardo DaVinci* (New York: Delta Trade Paperbacks, 2004). *Triage*.

"James Orbinski, Background," *CIGIonline.org*, The Center for International Governance Innovation, n.d. Oct. 2013 <http://www.cigionline.org/person/james-orbinski>.

Orbinski, *Imperfect Offering*.

"Triage: Dr. James Orbinski's Humanitarian Dilemma," *Distributorships.org*. Doctors Without Borders/Medecins Sans Frontieres, n.d. Oct. 2013 <http://www. doctorswithoutborders.org/aboutus/page.cfm?id=6002>.

James Orbinski Official Website, JamesOrbinski.com, 2012. Oct. 2013 <http://jamesorbinski.com/>

Stacey Gibson, "A Doctor in Kigali," *UofTMagazine*, University of Toronto, 2008. Oct. 2013 <http://www.magazine.utoronto.ca/cover-story/james-orbinski-profile-doctors-without-borders-canadians-in-rwanda/>.

Daniel Gross, "Obama Taps Esther Duflo, Poverty's 'Rock Star,'" *Newsweek.com*, IBT Media Inc., 14 Jan. 2013. Oct. 2013 <http://www.thedailybeast.com/newsweek/2013/01/13/obama-taps-esther-duflo-poverty-s-rock-star.html>.

"Esther Duflo: Papers," *MIT Economics*, Massachusetts Institute of Technology Department of Economics, 2013. Oct. 2013 <http://economics.mit.edu/faculty/eduflo/papers>.

"Esther Duflo." *J-PAL*. Banerjee and Duflo, *Poor Economics*.

Jacqueline Novogratz, *The Blue Sweater: Bridging the Gap Between Rich and Poor in an Interconnected World* (New York: Rodale, 2009).

Acumen.org. Acumen, 2013. Oct. 2013 http://acumen.org/.

"Jacqueline Novogratz," *The Huffington Post*, TheHuffingtonPost.com, Inc., 2013. Oct. 2013 <http://www.huffingtonpost.com/jacqueline-novogratz/>.

Jacqueline Novogratz, "When Humility and Audacity Go Hand in Hand." Interviewed by Adam Bryant. *Business Day*. The New York Times Company, 29 Sept. 2012. Oct. 2013. <http://www.nytimes.com/2012/09/30/ business/jacqueline-novogratz-of-acumen-fund-on-pairs-of-values.html? _r=0>.

"Mother Teresa – Biography." *Biography.com*. A&E Television Networks LLC, 2013. Oct. 2013 <http://www.biography.com/people/mother-teresa-9504160?page=3>.

Jose Luis Gonzalez-Balado, *Mother Teresa: In My Own Words* (Liguori, MO: Liguori Publications, 1997).

Teresa of Calcutta, *Seeking the Heart of God: Reflections on Prayer* (New York: HarperOne, 1993).

Teresa of Calcutta, *Where There Is Love, There Is God: A Path to Closer Union with God and Greater Love for Others* (New York: Doubleday Religion, 2010).

Teresa of Calcutta, *No Greater Love* (Novato, CA: New World Library, 2002).

Teresa of Calcutta, *Mother Teresa: Come Be My Light: The Private Writings of the Saint of Calcutta* (New York: Image, 2007).

"Portrait: Bishop Macram Gassis of Sudan," *Guard Duty*, Blog at WordPress.com, 21 Jan. 2007. Oct. 2013 <guardduty.wordpress.com/2007/01/21/portrait-bishop-macram-gassis-of-sudan/>.

Kathryn Jean Lopez, "Revolutionary Father," NationalReview.com. National Review Online, 2013. Oct. 2013 <http://www.nationalreview.com/articles/243534/revolutionary-father-kathryn-jean-lopez>.

"Bishop Macram Gassis," BishopGassis.org, n.p., n.d. Oct. 2013 <http://bishopgassis.org/about/bishop-macram-gassis.php>.

Matthew Arnold and Matthew LeRiche. *South Sudan: From Revolution to Independence* (New York: Columbia University, 2012).

Philip Steele, *Sudan, Darfur and the Nomadic Conflicts* (New York: Rosen, 2012).

Tayeb Salih, *Season of Migration to the North* (New York: New York Review of Books, 2009).

Halima Bashir, *Tears of the Desert: A Memoir of Survival in Darfur* (New York: Random House Reader's Circle, 2009).

John Bul Dau with Michael S. Sweeney, *God Grew Tired of Us: A Memoir* (Washington, DC: National Geographic, 2007). James Maskalyk, *Six Months in Sudan: A Young Doctor in a War-Torn Village* (New York: Doubleday, 2009).

Mary Williams, *Brothers in Hope: The Story of the Lost Boys of Sudan* (New York: Lee and Low, 2005).

Gerard Prunier, *Darfur: The Ambiguous Genocide* (New York: Cornell University, 2005).

John Paul II, *Crossing the Threshold of Hope* (New York: Knopf, 1994).

John Paul II, *The Way to Christ* (New York: HarperCollins, 1994).

"John Paul II: The Millennial Pope" *Frontline*, WGBH Educational Foundation, 2013. Oct. 2013 <http://www.pbs.org/wgbh/pages/frontline/shows/pope/>.

George Weigel, *Witness to Hope: The Biography of Pope John Paul II* (New York: Harper Perennial, 2005).

Luigi Accattoli, *Life in the Vatican with John Paul II* (New York: Universe, 1998). Karol Wojtyla, *Love and Responsibility* (San Francisco: St. Ignatius, 1993).

Joseph Ratzinger, *The Legacy of John Paul II: Images and Memories* (San Francisco: St. Ignatius, 2005).

Benedict XVI, *Jesus of Nazareth: The Infancy Narratives* (New York: Image, 2012).

Benedict XVI, *Doctors of the Church* (Huntington, IN: Our Sunday Visitor, 2005).

Benedict XVI, *Saved in Hope: Spe Salvi* (San Francisco: St. Ignatius, 2008).

Benedict XVI, *The Virtues* (Huntington, IN: Our Sunday Visitor, 2010).

Benedict XVI, *God Is Love: Deus Caritas Est* (San Francisco: St. Ignatius, 2006).

Stanley Meisler, *Kofi Annan: A Man of Peace in a World of War* (Hoboken, NJ: Wiley, 2007).

Kofi Annan, *Interventions: A Life in War and Peace* (New York: Penguin, 2013).

Abiodun Williams, ed., *The Brilliant Art of Peace: Lectures from the Kofi Annan Series.* (New York: United States Institute of Peace, 2013).

Annan, *KofiAnnanFoundation.org*, Kofi Annan Foundation, 2013. Oct. 2013 <http://kofiannanfoundation.org/>.

"Former Secretary-General: Kofi Annan," *UN.org*, United Nations, 2012. Oct. 2013 <http://www.un.org/sg/formersg/annan.shtml>.

"Kofi Annan," *TheElders.org*, The Elders, 2013. Oct. 2013 <http://theelders.org/kofi-annan>.

"Kofi Annan – Biographical," *NobelPrize.org*, Nobel Foundation, 2013. Oct. 2013 <http://www.nobelprize.org/nobel_prizes/peace/laureates/2001/annan-bio.html>.

"Finding and Resolving the Root Causes."

Harich, *Analytical*.

Chapter Five Endnotes

66   Sheila Llanas, *Jonas Salk* (Mankato, MN: Abdo, 2013).

67   *DZDock.com*, DZ Dock, 2011. Oct. 2013 <http://www.dzdock.com/aboutus.php>.

68   *PaulMcCartney.com*. MPL Communications Ltd./Paul McCartney, 2013. Oct. 2013 <http://www.paulmccartney.com/>.

69   "Philo T. Farnsworth – Biography," *Biography.com*, A&E Television Networks LLC, 2013. Oct. 2013 <http://www.biography.com/people/philo-t-farnsworth-40273>.

70   J. K. Rowling, "Welcome to J.K. Rowling's Website" *Jkrowling.com.* 2012. Oct. 2013. <http://www.jkrowling.com/>.

71   Michalko, *Cracking Creativity*, 154.

72   Scott Belsky, *Making Ideas Happen*, (New York: Portfolio Penguin, 2010), 3.

73   Murray, *Borrowing Brilliance*, 24.

74   "Mark Zuckerberg."*Mark Zuckerberg News*, http://topics.nytimes.com/topics/reference/people/z/mark_e_zuckerberg/index.html (12 Sept. 2012).

75   Nick Bilton and Evelyn M. Rusli, "Facebook Fever," *The New York Times Upfront*, http://upfront.scholastic.com/issues/03_12_12/book#/6 (12 Mar. 2012), 7.

76   Dina Spector, "Facebook Facebook Http://www.facebook.com,"*Business Insider*, http://www.businessinsider.com/blackboard/facebook (26 Sept. 2012).

77   Jonah Lehrer, *Imagine: How Creativity Works* (New York: Houghton Mifflin, 2012).

78   Dean Keith Simonton, *Scientific Genius: A Psychology of Science* (New York: Cambridge University, 1988).

79   Andy Boynton and Bill Fischer, *The Idea Hunter: How To Find the Best Ideas and Make Them Happen* (San Francisco, CA: Jossey-Bass, 2011), 62-3.

80   Boynton and Fischer, *The Idea Hunter*, 63.

81   David Kord Murray, *Borrowing Brilliance* (New York: Gotham Books, 2009).

82   Tom Standage, *A History of the World in 6 Glasses* (New York: Walker, 2005), 51.

83   Michalko, *Cracking Creativity*, 97.

84   Dan Pallotta, "HBR Blog Network: Start with an Idea,"*Harvard Business Review*. http://blogs.hbr.org/pallotta/2010/07/start-with-an-idea.html (28 July 2010).

85   Katie Patton, "Katie Patton," *YouTube.com*, YouTube, n.d. Oct. 2013 http://www.youtube.com/playlist?list=UU9WAHCZjaVqdnA7eEkMaiDw>.

86   Katherine Ramsland, *SNAP: Seizing Your Aha! Moments* (Amherst, NY: Prometheus, 2012), 119.

87   Michalko, *Cracking Creativity*, 111.

88   Scott Belsky, *Making Ideas Happen*, (New York: Portfolio Penguin, 2010), 3.

89   Mac Anderson, *What's the Big Idea?* (Naperville, IL: Simple Truths, 2010), 114-115.

90   Scott Belsky, *Making Ideas Happen*, (New York: Portfolio Penguin, 2010), 12.

91   Lehrer, *Imagine*, xy.

92   Dean Keith Simonton Dean Keith Simonton, *Origins of Genius: Darwinian Perspectives on Creativity* (New York:Oxford University, 1999).

93   Michalko, *Cracking Creativity*, 12.

94   Michalko, *Cracking Creativity*, 11.

95   Michalko, *Cracking Creativity*, 21.

96   Michalko, *Cracking Creativity*, 107.

97   Anderson, *What's The Big Idea*, 115.

98   Caldicott and Gelb, *Innovate Like Edison*, 157.

99   "Harry Potter." *The New York Times*, http://topics.nytimes.com/top/reference/timestopics/complete_coverage/harry_potter/index.html (18 July 2011).

100 Ben Fritz, "Hunger Games sells 3.8 million DVDs, Blu-rays on first weekend." *Los Angeles Times.* http://articles.latimes.com/2012/aug/21/entertainment/la-et-ct-hunger-games-dvd-sales-20120820 (21 Aug. 2012).

101 David Brin, "Worlds of David Brin," *DavidBrin.com*, David Brin, 2013. Oct. 2013 <http://www.davidbrin.com/>.

102 Foster, *How to Get Good Ideas*, 174-175.

103 Keld Jensen, "How Great Leaders Triumph over Failure." *Forbes.* http://www.forbes.com/sites/keldjensen/2012/08/08/rock-bottom-how-great-leaders-triumph-over-failure/ (8 Aug. 2012).

104 Srinivas Rao, "The Power of Hitting Rock Bottom." *Life Optimizer.* http://www.lifeoptimizer.org/2010/08/24/the-power-of-hitting-rock-bottom/ (24 Aug. 2010).

105 "Liu Wei, Armless Pianist," *China.org.cn*, China.org.cn, 14 Feb. 2012. Oct. 2013 <http://www.china.org.cn/video/2012-02/14/content_24630732.htm>.

106 Adam Ludwig, "Ashoka Chairman Bill Drayton on the Power of Social Entrepreneurship," *Techonomy: Revolutions in Progress*, Forbes.com LLC, 12 March 2012. Oct. 2013 <http://www.forbes.com/sites/techonomy/2012/03/12/ashoka-chairman-bill-drayton-on-the-power-of-social-entrepreneurship/>.

Chapter Five Bibliography

DZDock.com, DZ Dock, 2011. Oct. 2013 <http://www.dzdock.com/aboutus.php>.

Sheila Llanas, *Jonas Salk* (Mankato, MN: Abdo, 2013).

PaulMcCartney.com. MPL Communications Ltd. /Paul McCartney, 2013. Oct. 2013 <http://www.paulmccartney.com/>.

Kaplan, James. *Paul McCartney: The Legend Rocks On* (New York: Time, 2012).

J. K. Rowling, "Welcome to J.K. Rowling's Website" *Jkrowling.com.* 2012. Oct. 2013. <http://www.jkrowling.com/>.

Jim Crocker, "Jim Crocker on Systems Engineering," Interviewed by Ask the Academy, *NASA Academy3:9 (2010)*. National Aeronautics and Space Administration, 30 Sept. 2010. Oct. 2013 <http://www.nasa.gov/offices/oce/appel/ask-academy/issues/volume3/AA_39_SF_interview.html>.

"Philo T. Farnsworth – Biography," *Biography.com*, A&E Television Networks LLC, 2013. Oct. 2013 <http://www.biography.com/people/philo-t-farnsworth-40273>.

Stephanie Sammartino McPherson, *TV's Forgotten Hero: The Story of Philo T. Farnsworth* (Minneapolis, MN: Carolrhoda, 1996).

David Kirkpatrick, *The Facebook Effect: The Inside Story of the Company That Is Connecting the World* (New York: Simon & Schuster, 2010).

Ben Mezrich, *The Accidental Billionaires: The Founding of Facebook: A Tale of Sex, Money, Genius and Betrayal* (New
York: Doubleday, 2009).

Jonah Lehrer, *Imagine: How Creativity Works* (New York: Houghton Mifflin, 2012).

Dean Keith Simonton, *Scientific Genius: A Psychology of Science* (New York: Cambridge University, 1988).

Andy Boynton and Bill Fischer, *The Idea Hunter: How To Find the Best Ideas and Make Them Happen* (San Francisco, CA: Jossey-Bass, 2011) 62-3.

Tom Standage, *A History of the World in 6 Glasses* (New York: Walker, 2005) 51. Michalko 97.

Katie Patton, "Katie Patton," *YouTube.com*, YouTube, n.d. Oct. 2013 <http://www.youtube.com/playlist?list=UU9WAHCZjaVqdnA7eEkMaiDw>.

Katherine Ramsland, *SNAP: Seizing Your Aha! Moments* (Amherst, NY: Prometheus, 2012) 119. Michalko 111.

William James, *The Principles of Psychology*, Volume 1 (New York: Cosimo, 2007).

James, *The Will To Believe and Other Essays In Popular Philosophy, and Human Immortality* (Mineola, NY: Dover, 1956).

"Richard Restak," *The Great Courses*, The Teaching Company LLC, 2013. Oct. 2013 <http://www.thegreatcourses.com/tgc/professors/professor_detail.aspx?pid=412>.

Richard Restak, *Mysteries of the Mind* (Washington, D.C.: National Geographic, 2000).

Restak, *Modular Brain* (New York: Touchstone, 1995).

Restak, *Think Smart: A Neuroscientist's Prescription for Improving Your Brain's Performance* (New York: Riverhead, 2009).

Bill Welter and Jean Egman, *The Prepared Mind of a Leader* (San Francisco, CA: Jossey-Bass, 2006).Lehrer.

Jim Donovan, "Farewell to my friend Charlie 'Tremendous' Jones," *JimDonovan.com*, Jim Donovan, 21 Oct. 2008. Oct. 2013 <http://www.jimdonovan.com/farewell-to-my-friend-charlie-tremendous-jones/>.

George Lois, *George Lois On His Creation of the Big Idea* (New York: Assouline, 2008).

John Cleese and Connie Booth, *The Complete Fawlty Towers* (Cambridge, MA: DA Capo, 2001).

Dean Keith Simonton, *Origins of Genius: Darwinian Perspectives on Creativity* (New York: Oxford University, 1999).

Michalko 11.

Michalko 21.

"Michelangelo (1475-1564)," *BBC.co.uk/history*, British Broadcasting Corporation, 2013. Oct. 2013 <http://www.bbc.co.uk/history/historic_figures/michelangelo.shtml>.

Sarah Hall, *The Electric Michelangelo* (New York: Harper, 2004).

Giorgio Vasari, *The Lives of the Artists* (New York: Oxford University, 2008).

William E. Wallace, *Michelangelo: The Artist, The Man and His Times* (New York: Cambridge University, 2010).

George Mandler, *Mind and Body: Psychology Of Emotion And Stress* (New York: W. W. Norton, 1984).

Mandler, *Consciousness Recovered: Psychological Functions and Origins of Conscious Thought* (Philadelphia: John Benjamins, 2002).

Gelb and Caldicott 157.

David Brin, "Worlds of David Brin," *DavidBrin.com*, David Brin, 2013. Oct. 2013 <http://www.davidbrin.com/>.

Ji Chen, "Liu Wei, Armless Pianist, Plays With His Toes, Wows Audience (Video)," *Huff Post World*, TheHuffingtonPost.com, Inc., 25 May 2011. Oct. 2013 <http://www.huffingtonpost.com/2010/08/27/chinese-musician-with-no-_n_696914.html>.

"Liu Wei, Armless Pianist," *China.org.cn*, China.org.cn, 14 Feb. 2012. Oct. 2013 <http://www.china.org.cn/

video/2012-02/14/content_24630732.htm>. Adam Ludwig, "Ashoka Chairman Bill Drayton on the Power of Social Entrepreneurship," *Techonomy: Revolutions in Progress*, Forbes.com LLC, 12 March 2012. Oct. 2013 <http://www.forbes.com/sites/techonomy/2012/03/12/ashoka-chairman-bill-drayton-on-the-power-of-social-entrepreneurship/>.

Chapter Six Endnotes

[107] Hannah B. Harvey and Dalton Kehoe, "The Art of Storytelling: From Parents to Professionals," in *The Great Courses*, ed. The Teaching Company, LLC. (North Carolina: University of North Carolina at Chapel Hill Press, 2013), course 9314, tracks 1-4.

[108] Peter Guber, "Peter Guber on Sharing Stories, Not Just Information, to Communicate Effectively," Interviewed by Steve Ennen, *Knowledge@Wharton*, Wharton School of the University of Pennsylvania, 24 June 2009. Oct. 2013 <http://knowledge.wharton.upenn.edu/article.cfm?articleid=2269>.

[109] "Bible study changing lives of prisoners in India," *World*, Christian Today, 17 April 2013. Oct. 2013 <http://www.christiantoday.com/article/ bible.study.changing.lives.of.prisoners.in.india/32161.htm>.

[110] Robert McKee, *Story: Substance, Structure, Style and the Principles of Screenwriting* (New York: HarperCollins, 1997), 11-30.

[111] Leo Widrich, "The Science of Storytelling: Why Telling a Story is the Most Powerful Way to Activate our Brains." *Lifehacker.com*. Lifehacker.com, 5 Dec. 2012. Oct. 2013. <http://lifehacker.com/5965703/the-science-of-storytelling-why-telling-a-story-is-the-most-powerful-way-to-activate-our-brains>.

[112] "Michael S. Gazzaniga," *BigThink.com*, Big Think, n.d. Oct. 2013. <http://bigthink.com/users/michaelgazzaniga>.

[113] Joshua Gowin, "You, Illuminated," *PsychologyToday.com*, Sussex Publishers, LLC, 6 June 2011. Oct. 2013 <http://www.psychologytoday.com/blog/you-illuminated>.

[114] Jill Bolte Taylor, *My Stroke of Insight* (New York: Viking, 2008).

[115] Annie Murphy Paul, "Your Brain on Fiction," *New York Times Sunday Review*, The New York Times Company, 17 March 2012. Oct. 2013. <http://www.nytimes.com/2012/03/18/opinion/sunday/the-neuroscience-of-your-brain- on-fiction.html?pagewanted=all&_r=0>.

[116] Da Vinci and Suh, *Leonardo's Notebooks*, 23-34.

[117] Caldicott and Gelb, *Innovate like Edison*, 122.

[118] Alexander K. McClure, *Lincoln's Yarns and Stories* (Project Gutenberg, 2012).

[119] Masur, *The Civil War: A Concise History* (New York: Oxford University, 2011). <http://opinionator.blogs.nytimes.com/2012/01/27/lincoln-tells-a-story/>

[120] "History of Hinduism." All About Religion, http://www.allaboutreligion.org/history-of-hinduism-faq.htm (2013).

[121] Tom Kelley and Jonathan Littman, *The Ten Faces of Innovation* (New York: Currency Doubleday, 2005), 242.

[122] Storytellingday.net shared this history of storytelling on their website.

[123] Arthur Demarest, *Ancient Maya: The Rise and Fall of a Rainforest Civilization* (England: Cambridge University Press, 2004).

[124] Kelley and Littman, *The Ten Faces of Innovation*, 242.

[125] "Storytelling: Scientist's Perspective: John Seeley Brown," *Storytelling: Passport to the 21st Century*, Larry Prusak, 2001. Oct. 2013 <http://www.creatingthe21stcentury.org/JSB5-descartes.htm>.

[126] "How We Found Ourselves in the World of Storytelling," *Storytelling: Passport to the 21st Century*, Stephen Denning, 2001. Oct. 2013 <http://www.creatingthe21stcentury.org/Intro4a-How-Larry&JSB.html>.

Chapter Six Bibliography

Peter Guber, "Peter Guber on Sharing Stories, Not Just Information, to Communicate Effectively," Interviewed by Steve Ennen, *Knowledge@Wharton*, Wharton School of the University of Pennsylvania, 24 June 2009. Oct. 2013 <http://knowledge.wharton.upenn.edu/article.cfm?articleid=2269>.

"Bible study changing lives of prisoners in India," *World*, Christian Today, 17 April 2013. Oct. 2013 <http://www.christiantoday.com/article/bible.study.changing.lives.of.prisoners.in.india/32161.htm>.

Navpress.com. n.d. Oct. 2013 <http://www.navpress.com/magazines/archives/article.aspx?id=11009>.

Robert McKee, *Story: Substance, Structure, Style and the Principles of Screenwriting* (New York: HarperCollins, 1997) 11-30.

Jason Gots, "Your Storytelling Brain," *BigThink.com*, Big Think, 15 Jan. 2012. Oct. 2013 <http://bigthink.com/think-tank/your-storytelling-brain>.

Leo Widrich, "The Science of Storytelling: Why Telling a Story is the Most Powerful Way to Activate our Brains." *Lifehacker.com*. Lifehacker.com, 5 Dec. 2012. Oct. 2013. <http://lifehacker.com/5965703/the-science-of-storytelling-why-telling-a-story-is-the-most-powerful-way-to-activate-our-brains>.

Joshua Gowin, "You, Illuminated," *PsychologyToday.com*, Sussex Publishers, LLC, 6 June 2011. Oct. 2013 <www.psychologytoday.com/blog/you-illuminated>.

"Uri Hasson, 'Brain-to-Brain Coupling: A Mechanism for Creating and Sharing a Social World'—Followed by a Roundtable Discussion," *Events*, John Hope Franklin Humanities Institute at Duke University, 21 March 2012. Oct. 2013 <http://fhi.duke.edu/events/uri-hasson-lecture>.

U. Hasson, E. Yang, I. Vallines, D.J. Heeger, N. Rubin, "A Hierarchy of temporal receptive windows in human cortex." *Journal of Neuroscience* (2008) 28(10):2539-50.

Y. Lerner, C.J. Honey, L.J. Silbert, U. Hasson, "Topographic mapping of a hierarchy of temporal receptive windows using a narrated story." *Journal of Neuroscience* (2011) 31(8):2906-15.

Y. Nir, U. Hasson, I. Levy, Y. Yeshurun, R. Malach, "Widespread functional connectivity and fMRI fluctuations in human visual cortex in the absence of visual stimulation." *NeuroImage* (2006) 30:1313-24.

M. Regev, C.J. Honey, U. Hasson, "Modality-selective and modality-invariant neural responses to spoken and written narratives." *Journal of Neuroscience* (2013) 33(40):15978 –88.

C.J. Honey, C.R. Thomson, Y. Lerner, U. Hasson, "Not lost in translation: Neural responses shared across languages," *Journal of Neuroscience* (2012) 32(44):15277-83.

"Michael S. Gazzaniga," *BigThink.com*, Big Think, n.d. Oct. 2013. <http://bigthink.com/users/michaelgazzaniga>.

Michael S. Gazzaniga, ed., *The Cognitive Neurosciences*, Third ed. (Cambridge, MA: MIT, 2004).

Jill Bolte Taylor, *My Stroke of Insight* (New York: Viking, 2008).

Annie Murphy Paul, "Your Brain on Fiction," *New York Times Sunday Review*, The New York Times Company, 17 March 2012. Oct. 2013. <http://www.nytimes.com/2012/03/18/opinion/sunday/the-neuroscience-of-your-brain-on-fiction.html?pagewanted=all&_r=0>.

Gelb and Caldicott 122.

Abraham Lincoln, Emancipation Proclamation, 1863.

Doris Kearns Goodwin, *Team of Rivals: The Political Genius of Abraham Lincoln* (New York: Simon & Schuster, 2006).

Alexander K. McClure, *Lincoln's Yarns and Stories* (Project Gutenberg, 2012).

Ben Cleary, "Where Was Stonewall?" *Opinionator*, The New York Times Company, 22 June 2012. Oct. 2013 <opinionator.blogs.nytimes.com/category/disunion/page/37/?scp=2-b&sq=ontherepublic&st=nyt>.

Leonardo DA Vinci and H. Anna Suh, *Leonardo's Notebooks* (New York: Leventhal Publishers, 2005).

Ralph Waldo Emerson, *Character and Heroism* (New York: Ulan, 2012).

Walt Whitman, *The Complete Writings of Walt Whitman, Volume I* (Hong Kong: Forgotten Books, 2012).

George S. Boutwell, *Reminiscences of Sixty Years in Public Affairs, Volume 2* (New York: Fili-Quarian Classics, 2011).

Louis P. Masur, "The Whale in a Tank," *Opinionator*, The New York Times Company, 5 Dec. 2012. Oct. 2013 <http://opinionator.blogs.nytimes.com/2012/12/05/the-whale-in-a-tank/?_r=0>. McClure.

Masur, *The Civil War: A Concise History* (New York: Oxford University, 2011).

John McCain, *Character is Destiny* (New York: Random, 2005).

Timberg and Halperin.

"Storytelling Day," *storytellingday.net*, www.storytellingday.net, 2013. Oct. 2013. <http://storytellingday.net/>. Arthur Demarest, *Ancient Maya: The Rise and Fall of a Rainforest Civilization* (England: Cambridge University Press, 2004).

The Epic of Gilgamesh (New York: Penguin, 1960).

Tom Kelley and Jonathan Littman, *The Ten Faces of Innovation* (New York: Currency Doubleday, 2005) 242.

John Piper, *Seeing and Savoring Jesus Christ* (Wheaton, IL: Crossway, 2004).

Timothy Keller, *King's Cross: The Story of the World in the Life of Jesus* (New York: Dutton, 2011).

Benedict XVI, *Jesus of Nazareth: Holy Week: From the Entrance into Jerusalem to the Resurrection* (San Francisco: St. Ignatius, 2011).

Ken Burns, "Books," Interviewed by Amy Sutherland, *BostonGlobe.com*, Boston Globe Media Partners, LLC, 11 May 2013. Oct. 2013. <http://www.bostonglobe.com/arts/books/2013/05/11/interview-with-bibliophile-ken-burns/GfEshMNYikLnYj19vYn8SO/story.html>.

"George Lucas – Biography," *Biography.com*, A&E Television Networks LLC, 1996-2013. Oct. 2013 <http://www.biography.com/people/george-lucas-9388168>.

Walter Isaacson, *Steve Jobs* (New York: Simon & Schuster, 2011).

William Allan Neilson and Ashley Horace Thorndike, *The Facts About Shakespeare* (New Zealand: Aeterna, 2011).

Daniel H. Pink, *A Whole New Mind* (New York: Riverhead, 2006).

John Seeley Brown, *johnseeleybrown.com*. n.p., n.d. Oct. 2013 <http://www.johnseeleybrown.com/>.

"Biography." *laurenceprusak.com*. n.p., n.d. Oct. 2013 <http://www.laurenceprusak.com/bio.html>.

"Katalina Groh," *katalinagroh.com*, Chicago, IL: Groh, 2011. Oct. 2013 <http://www.katalinagroh.com/>.

Stephen Denning, *The Leader's Guide to Storytelling: Mastering the Art and Discipline of Business Narrative* (San Francisco: Jossey-Bass, 2011).

"Business Story Telling," *elibrary*. Al-Athaiba Muscat, Sultanate of Oman: The Research Council, n.d. Oct. 2013 <https://el.trc.gov.om/htmlroot/K12/.../Business%20Story%20Telling.pdf>.

"Storytelling: Scientist's Perspective: John Seeley Brown," *Storytelling: Passport to the 21st Century*, Larry Prusak, 2001. Oct. 2013 <http://www.creatingthe21stcentury. org/JSB5-descartes.htm>.

William Shakespeare, *Hamlet* (New York: Simon & Schuster, 2003).

Jim Rohn, *The Art Of Exceptional Living* (New York: Simon & Schuster Audio, 2003).

Burstein, Julie. "4 Lessons in Creativity." *TED: Ideas worth spreading*. TED Conferences, LLC, Nov. 2013. Oct. 2013 <http://www.ted.com/talks/julie_burstein_4_lessons_in_ creativity.htm>.

"How We Found Ourselves in the World of Storytelling," *Storytelling: Passport to the 21st Century*, Stephen Denning,

2001. Oct. 2013 <http://www.creatingthe21stcentury.org/Intro4a-How-Larry&JSB.html>.

Chapter Seven Endnotes

[127] "Storytelling: Scientist's Perspective: John Seeley Brown," *Storytelling: Passport to the 21st Century*, Larry Prusak, 2001. Oct. 2013 <http://www.creatingthe21stcentury.org/JSB5-descartes.htm>.

[128] Michiko Kakutani, "It's True: Success Succeeds, and Advantages Can Help," review of *Outliers*, by Malcolm Gladwell, New York Times, November 17, 2008, Books of the Times, http://www.nytimes.com/2008/11/18/ books/18kaku.html?pagewanted=all&_r=0.

[129] U. Hasson and C.J. Honey, "Future trends in neuroimaging: Neural processes as expressed within real-life contexts." *NeuroImage* (2012) 62:1272-8.

[130] "Pinterest," *Mashable.com*, Mashable, 2013. Oct. 2013

[131] Gots, "Your Storytelling Brain."

[132] Josh Kron, "The Africa You Haven't Heard About: Why Africa Is No Longer the Disaster Zone Many Americans Think It Is" *New York Times Upfront*, 10 Dec. 2012. *The Free Library*. Oct. 2013 <http://www.thefreelibrary.com/The+Africa+you+haven't+heard+about% 3A-+why+Africa+is+no+longer+the...-a0312725868>

[133] Nicholas D. Kristof, "The Africa You Haven't Heard About," *The New York Times*, December 10, 2012, 9.

[134] George Friedman, *The Next Decade: Empire and Republic in a Changing World* (New York: Doubleday, 2011), 3.

[135] Pink, *A Whole New Mind*, 22-34.

[136] Pink, *A Whole New Mind*, 50.

[137] Pink, *A Whole New Mind*, 106.

[138] Tim Berners-Lee with Mark Fischetti, *Weaving the Web: The Original Design and Ultimate Destiny of the World Wide Web by Its Inventor*, 3

[139] See *Chapter 12*.

[140] David Bornstein, *How to Change the World* (Oxford: Oxford University, 2007), 37.

[141] Discussed in Chapter Nine: *Stand for Africa* explains that in America a dollar can: sit on your

dresser as change, get lost in the bottom of your purse, buy a pack of gum, buy an inexpensive cup of coffee, buy a cheap toy in a dollar store, and buy a small box of french fries, but in Africa, a dollar can pay for a doctor's visit, purchase Malaria cure for three people, feed one child three meals for a day, buy a pair of pants, a shirt and some underpants for a small child, and buy enough water for a family of three to drink for a week.

142   In Chapter Twelve, *Who exactly are the proceeds from the compilations helping?* InterviewGirl. com's strategy to help others is discussed.

Chapter Seven Bibliography

U. Hasson and C.J. Honey, "Future trends in neuroimaging: Neural processes as expressed within real-life contexts." *NeuroImage* (2012) 62:1272-8.

Maria Montessori, *The Montessori Method* (Provo, UT: Renaissance Classics, 2012).

E. M. Standing, *Maria Montessori: Her Life and Work* (New York: Plume-Penguin, 1998).

Montessori, *The Absorbent Mind* (New York: Henry Holt, 1995).

Paula Polk Lillard, *Montessori: A Modern Approach* (New York: Schocken, 1988).

Alex Nicholls, ed., *Social Entrepreneurship: New Models of Sustainable Social Change* (New York: Oxford University, 2006). Nikki Stone, "Bill Drayton," *When Turtles Fly: Secrets of Successful People Who Know How to Stick Their Necks Out* (New York: Morgan James, 2010) 175-180.

Brendon Burchard, *The Millionaire Messenger: Make a Difference and a Fortune Sharing Your Advice* (New York: Free, 2011).

Chalene Johnson, Push: 30 Days to Turbocharged Habits, a Bangin' Body, and the Life You Deserve! (New York: Rodale, 2012).

Brian Tracy, *No Excuses: The Power of Self-Discipline* (New York: Vanguard, 2010).

Tracy, The Psychology of Achievement (New York: Simon & Schuster Audio, 2002).

Tracy, *Focal Point: A Proven System to Simplify Your Life, Double Your Productivity, and Achieve All Your Goals* (New York: AMACOM, 2004).

Aristotle, *Rhetoric* (Stanley Frost, 2013).

Aristotle, *Introduction to Aristotle* (New York: Modern Library, 1992).

Aristotle, *Politics* (Mineola, NY: Dover Thrift, 2000).

Aristotle and Hugh Lawson-Tancred, ed., *The Art of Rhetoric* (New York: Penguin Classics, 1992).

Aristotle, *The Categories* (Melbourne, Australia: Book Jungle, 2007).

Plato, *The Symposium* (New York: Penguin Classics, 2003).

Plato, *The Republic* (New York: Simon & Brown, 2012).

Plato, *Apology* (New York: International Business Publications, USA, 2010).

Peter Kreeft, *Socrates Meets Descartes: The Father of Philosophy Analyzes the Father of Modern Philosophy's Discourse on Method* (San Francisco: Ignatius, 2007).

Christopher Phillips, *Socrates Cafe: A Fresh Taste of Philosophy* (New York: W.W. Norton & Company, 2001). Donald Kagan, *The Peloponnesian War* (New York: Penguin, 2004).

Edith Hamilton, *The Greek Way* (New York: Penguin, 1993).

Robin Osborne, *Greece in the Making 1200-479 BC* (New York: Routledge, 2009).

Martin Heidegger, *Early Greek Thinking* (San Francisco: Harper San Francisco, 1985).

Reginald E. Allen, ed., *Greek Philosophy: Thales to Aristotle* (New York: Free, 1991).

I Am Because We Are.

Orbinski, *Imperfect Offering.*

Chris Abani, *GraceLand* (New York: Farrar, Straus, Giroux, 2004).

Abani, *The Virgin of Flames* (New York: Penguin, 2007).

Mark Joyner, *Integration Marketing: How Small Businesses Become Big Businesses—And Big Businesses Become Empires* (Hoboken, NJ: Wiley, 2009).

Simpleology: Simplifying Your Complicated Life, Simpleology, 2012. Oct. 2013 <http://www.simpleology.com/>.

"Pinterest," *Mashable.com*, Mashable, 2013. Oct. 2013 <http://mashable.com/follow/topics/pinterest/>.

Gots, "Your Storytelling Brain."

"Chimamanda Ngozi Adichie: The danger of a single story," *TED: Ideas Worth Spreading*, TED Conferences, LLC, Oct. 2009. Oct. 2013 <http://www.ted.com/talks/chimamanda_adichie_the_danger_of_a_single_story.html>.

Chimamanda Ngozi Adichie, *Americanah* (New York: Knopf, 2013).

Josh Kron, "The Africa You Haven't Heard About: Why Africa Is No Longer the Disaster Zone Many Americans Think It Is" *New York Times Upfront*, 10 Dec. 2012. *The Free Library*. Oct. 2013 <http://www.thefreelibrary.com/The+Africa+you+haven't+heard+about%3A-+why+Africa+is+no+longer+the...-a0312725868>.

George Friedman, *The Next Decade: Empire and Republic in a Changing World* (New York: Doubleday, 2011) 3. Pink.

Tim Berners-Lee with Mark Fischetti, *Weaving the Web: The Original Design and Ultimate Destiny of the World Wide Web* (New York: HarperCollins, 2000) 3.

Susan Conley, *The Foremost Good Fortune* (New York: Vintage, 2011).

Bornstein.

Ashoka Innovators for the Public, Ashoka, n.d. Oct. 2013 <https://www.ashoka.org/>.

Harper Lee, *To Kill a Mockingbird* (New York: HarperCollins, 1988).

Jane Austen, *Pride and Prejudice* (New York: Penguin Classics, 2009).

J.D. Salinder, *Catcher in the Rye* (Boston: Little, Brown, 1991).

Vladimir Nabokov, *Lolita* (New York: Vintage, 1997).

Truman Capote, Breakfast at Tiffany's (New York: Modern Library, 1993).

Antoine de Saint-Exupery, *The Little Prince* (New York: Harcourt Brace, 1971).

Ernest Hemingway, *The Old Man and the Sea* (New York: Scribner, 1995).

Michael Ondaatje, *The English Patient* (New York: Vintage, 1992).

Gabriel Garcia Marquez, *Love in the Time of Cholera* (New York: Vintage, 2007).

Joseph Conrad, *Heart of Darkness* (New York: Penguin Classics, 2012).

F. Scott Fitzgerald, *The Great Gatsby* (New York: Scribner, 2004).

Chapter Eight Endnotes

143   I am writing a book on this topic, so if it interests you, stay tuned. You can visit: www. rememberfiume.com for more information. Information about when the documentary will be released can be found on the website, as well.

144   Matthew Kelly is a motivational speaker and author. He has inspired millions with the message that there is genius in Catholicism, but if the Church is to avoid falling into obscurity, individual Catholics must demonstrate its relevance through a dedication to becoming the best version of themselves.

Chapter Nine Endnotes

145   Web Team, "Poverty Questions. . . and Answers," *Blog on Child Poverty*, Compassion International, 9 Mar. 2009. Oct. 2013 <http://blog.compassion.com/poverty-questions/?gclid= CMa7z6j9nrkCFWpk7AodBDQAKg>.

146   Novogratz, *Blue Sweater*, xi.

147   Economic Freedom Team, "In the News: The Good Samaritan Effect: The Virtuous Cycle of Private Charity," *Economic Freedom*, Charles Koch Institute, 28 Jan 2013. <http://www. economicfreedom.org/2013/01/28/ the-virtuous-cycle-of-private-charity/>.

148   Doug Bandow, "Poverty and Personal Choice," *cato.org*, Cato Institute, 14 May 2002. Oct. 2013 <http://www.cato.org/publications/commentary/poverty-personal-choice>.

149   *Ashoka Innovators for the Public*, Ashoka, n.d. Oct. 2013 <https://www.ashoka.org/>.

150   *Exercise Secrets from Around the World* is another compilation in progress at InterviewGirl. com. The secrets to toned arms, shoulders, legs, and other trouble areas for people are shared in this compilation where personal trainers and exercise physiologists from around the world were consulted for their advice and expertise.

151   BJ Fogg, "BJ Fogg: Innovator, Social Scientist, Teacher," *BJ Fogg*, 2013. Oct. 2013 <http://www. bjfogg.com/>.

152   Matthew Kelly is a motivational speaker and author. He has inspired millions with the message that there is genius in Catholicism, but if the Church is to avoid falling into obscurity, individual Catholics must demonstrate its relevance through a dedication to becoming the best version of themselves.

153   Brett and Kate McKay, "The Pocket Notebooks of 20 Famous Men." http://artofmanliness. com/2010/09/13/ the-pocket-notebooks-of-20-famous-men/2/ (13 Sept. 2010).

154   Michalko, *Cracking Creativity*, 258.

155   Josh Linkner, *Disciplined Dreaming: A Proven System to Drive Breakthrough Creativity*. (San Francisco: Jossey-Bass, 2011), 137.

156   "Recipient of SBC's Lifetime Achievement in Sustainability Award: Van Vlahakis," *Sustainable Business Council of Los Angeles*, Sustainable Business Council of Los Angeles, 2013. Oct.

2013 <http://www.sustainablebc.org/events/ bio/-recipient_sbcs_lifetime_achievement_ sustainability_award_van_vlahakis.html_0>.

[157]   Erica O'Grady, "Everything Changes." *medium.com*, 14 Nov. 2012. Oct. 2013 <https://medium. com/ what-i-learned-today/55694ab243c7>.

[158]   "Contributing Authors," *The Code*, John Spencer Ellis, 2013. Oct. 2013 <http://www. thecodeebook.com/ contributors.html>, 283.

[159]   Kristof, *Half the Sky*, 126-128.

[160]   *Operation A*² was formed with a mission to eliminate some of the misery that HIV/AIDS creates. See *Chapter Twelve* for details about *Operation A*².

[161]   Paul M. Lubeck, "The Crisis of African Development: Conflicting Interpretations and Resolutions," *Annual Review of Sociology*, (1992) 18:519-40, *Annual Reviews*. Oct. 2013 <http://-www.annualreviews.org/doi/abs/10.1146/ annurev.so.18.080192.002511?journalCo de=soc>.

[162]   New Statesman, "Does Aid Work?" *New Statesman*, New Statesman, 20 June 2012. Oct. 2013 <>.

[163]   J. Haavard Maridal, "The Good Samaritan Effect: The Virtuous Cycle of Private Charity," *Huff Post Impact*, 24 Jan. 2013. Oct. 2013. <http://www.huffingtonpost.com/j-haavard-maridal/ the-good-samaritan-effect_b_2545630.html>.

[164]   *New Statesman*.

Chapter Nine Bibliography

Web Team, "Poverty Questions. . . and Answers," *Blog on Child Poverty*, Compassion International, 9 Mar. 2009. Oct. 2013 <http://blog.compassion.com/poverty-questi ons/?gclid=CMa7z6j9nrkCFWpk7AodBDQAKg>.

Novogratz. *Blue Sweater* xi.

Banerjee and Duflo, *Poor Economics*.

Economic Freedom Team, "In the News: The Good Samaritan Effect: The Virtuous Cycle of Private Charity," *Economic Freedom*, Charles Koch Institute, 28 Jan 2013. Oct. 2013 <http://www.economicfreedom.org/2013/01/28/ the-virtuous-cycle-of-private-charity/>.

Doug Bandow, "Poverty and Personal Choice," *cato.org*, Cato Institute, 14 May 2002. Oct. 2013 <http://www.cato.org/publications/commentary/poverty-personal-choice>.

Ashoka Innovators for the Public.

Ruth A. Shapiro, *The Real Problem Solvers: Social Entrepreneurs in America* (Stanford, CA: Stanford Business, 2012).

Peter Karoff, et al. *The World We Want: New Dimensions in Philanthropy and Social Change* (Lanham, MD: AltaMira, 2006).

Bill Drayton, ed. *Leading Social Entrepreneurs Changing the World (Activist Biographies)* (Arlington, VA: Ashoka Innovators for the Public, 2009).

William D. Eggers, and Paul Macmillan, *The Solution Revolution: How Business, Government, and Social Enterprises Are Teaming Up to Solve Society's Toughest Problems* (Boston: Harvard Business, 2013).

Social Entrepreneurship: Skoll Foundation, Bill Drayton, Charityvillage.Com, Echoing Green, Schwab Foundation for Social Entrepreneurship (Memphis, TN: General Books LLC, 2010).

Jakob Lauring and Charlotte Jonasson, *Group Processes in Ethnically Diverse Organizations: Language and Intercultural Learning* (Hauppauge, NY: Nova Science, 2010).

Danielle Sampson, *Social Entrepreneurship* (Hauppauge, NY: Nova Science, 2011).

BJ Fogg, "BJ Fogg: Innovator, Social Scientist, Teacher," *BJ Fogg*, 2013. Oct. 2013 <http://www.bjfogg.com/>.

Jeffrey Kluger, *Splendid Solution: Jonas Salk and the Conquest of Polio* (New York: Berkley, 2004).

Edward Hallet Carr, *What is History?* (New York: Palgrave-Macmillan, 2001).

Wood, The Purpose of the Past: Reflections on the Uses of History (New York: Penguin, 2009).

Ernst Breisach, *Historiography: Ancient, Medieval and Modern* (Chicago: University of Chicago, 2007).

Keith Jenkins, Re-thinking History (New York: Routledge, 2003).

Eric Hobsbawm, *On History* (New York: New, 1998).

George G. Iggers, *A Global History of Modern Historiography* (Old Tappan, NJ: Pearson Education, 2008).

Josh Linkner, *Disciplined Dreaming: A Proven System to Drive Breakthrough Creativity.* (San Francisco: Jossey-Bass, 2011) 137.

"Recipient of SBC's Lifetime Achievement in Sustainability Award: Van Vlahakis," *Sustainable Business Council of Los Angeles*, Sustainable Business Council of Los Angeles, 2013. Oct. 2013 <http://www.sustainablebc.org/events/bio/-recipient_sbcs_lifetime_achievement_sustainability_award_van_vlahakis.html_0>.

Michalko, *Cracking Creativity* 258.

Erica O'Grady, "Everything Changes." *medium.com*, 14 Nov. 2012. Oct. 2013 <https://medium.com/what-i-learned-today/55694ab243c7>.

"Contributing Authors," *The Code*, John Spencer Ellis, 2013. Oct. 2013 <http://www.thecodeebook.com/contributors.html>.

Kristof 126.

Rohn, *Take Charge of Your Life* (Wheeling, IL: Nightingale-Conant, 1991).

Rohn, *The Day That Turns Your Life Around* (Wheeling, IL: Nightingale-Conant, 2003).

Rohn, *The Five Major Pieces to the Life Puzzle* (Sydney: Angus & Robertson, 1991).

George S. Clason, *The Richest Man in Babylon* (CreateSpace Independent Publishing Platform, 2012).

"Stand for Africa." *Standforafrica.org*, 2012. Oct. 2013 <http://www.standforafrica.org/>.

Paul M. Lubeck, "The Crisis of African Development: Conflicting Interpretations and Resolutions," *Annual Review of Sociology*, (1992) 18:519-40, *Annual Reviews*. Oct.

2013 <http://www.annualreviews.org/doi/abs/10.1146/annurev.so.18.080192.0025
11?journalCode=soc>

New Statesman, "Does Aid Work?" *New Statesman*, New Statesman, 20 June 2012. Oct. 2013 <http://www.newstatesman.com/2012/06/does-aid-work>.

Moyo.com

J. Haavard Maridal, "The Good Samaritan Effect: The Virtuous Cycle of Private Charity," *Huff Post Impact*, 24 Jan. 2013.

Oct. 2013. <http://www.huffingtonpost.com/j-haavard-maridal/the-good-samaritan-effect_b_2545630.html>.

New Statesman.

Paddy Ashdown, *A Fortunate Life: The Autobiography of Paddy Ashdown* (London: Aurum, 2009). Ashdown,

Swords and Ploughshares: Bringing Peace to the 21st Century (San Diego: Phoenix, 2008).

Chapter Ten Endnotes

[165] *Mind Brain Behavior Interfaculty Initiative*, Harvard University. 2013. Oct. 2013. <http://mbb.harvard.edu/>.

[166] "What is Depression?" *Healthy Living*, http://healthyliving.msn.com/diseases/depression?cp-documentid=100167285 (2013).

[167] Robert M. Sherfield, *The Everything Self Esteem Book: Boost Your Confidence, Achieve Inner Strength, and Learn to Love Yourself* (Avon, MA: F&W, 2004).

[168] Laura Oliver, *The Story Within: New Insights and Inspiration for Writers* (New York: Alpha-Penguin, 2011).

[169] Stephen G. Post, "Help Others: How helping others helps you," http://www.liveyourlifewell.org/go/live-your-life-well/others (2013).

[170] Rochelle Melander, *Write-a-thon*. (Cincinnati, OH: Writer's Digest Books, 2011), 24.

[171] Beth Pennington, "Dealing with Life After Combat—Sharing leads to healing," http://voiceofwarriors.com/2012/02/dealing-with-life-after-combat-sharing-leads-to-healing/ (23 Feb. 2012).

[172] David W. Moore, "Close to 6 in 10 Americans want to lose weight," *Gallup Well Being*. http://www.gallup.com/poll/21859/close-americans-want-lose-weight.aspx (10 Mar. 2006).

Chapter Ten Bibliography

Mind Brain Behavior Interfaculty Initiative, Harvard University. 2013. Oct. 2013. <http://mbb.harvard.edu/>.

Norman Doidge, *The Brain That Changes Itself: Stories of Personal Triumph from the Frontiers of Brain Science* (New York: Penguin, 2007).

Joseph LeDoux, *Synaptic Self: How Our Brains Become Who We Are* (New York: Penguin, 2003).

David Eagleman, *Incognito: The Secret Lives of the Brain* (New York: Pantheon, 2011).

Kunhardt McGee Productions, *This Emotional Life* (Boston: NOVA/WGBH Science Unit & Vulcan Productions, 2009).

Mario J. Paredes, "What Makes Us Happy? Balancing Success and Salvation," *Mr. Mario's Reflections on Faith, Culture and Religion,* blogspot.com, 30 Jan. 2011. Oct. 2013 <http://mariojparedesen.blogspot.com/2011_01_01_archive.html>.

"Austin Michelle Cloyd," *We Remember: Biographies,* Virginia Polytechnic Institute and State University, 2007. Oct.2013 <http://www.remembrance.vt.edu/2007/biographies/austin_michelle_cloyd.html>. "Austin Michelle Cloyd," *Vt-memorial. org,* VT-Memorial.org, 2007. Oct. 2013 <http://www.vt-memorial.org/profiles/Cloyd.html>.

"Austin Michelle Cloyd," *Cbsnews.com,* CBS Interactive, 18 April 2007. Oct. 2013. <http://www.cbsnews.com/2100-501803_162-2698537.html>.

"Shootings at Virginia Tech," *washingtonpost.com,* The Washington Post, n.d. Oct. 2013. <http://www.washingtonpost.com/wp-srv/metro/vatechshootings/>.

CNN Library, "Virginia Tech Shooting Fast Facts," *CNN U.S.* Cable News Network-Turner Broadcasting System, Inc., 31 Oct. 2013. Oct. 2013 <http://www.cnn.com/2013/10/31/us/virginia-tech-shootings-fast-facts/>.

Elizabeth Scott, "How Helping Others Can Reduce Stress and Increase Happiness," *About.com Stress Management,* About.com, 29 Dec. 2011. Oct. 2013 <http://stress.about.com/od/positiveattitude/qt/helping.htm>.

Todd Beeler, *The Seven Hidden Secrets of Motivation: Unlocking the Genius Within* (Prince Frederick, MD: Your Coach in a Box, 2006). Abraham H. Maslow, *Motivation and Personality* (Old Tappan, NJ: Pearson, 1997).

Robert M. Sherfield, *The Everything Self Esteem Book: Boost Your Confidence, Achieve Inner Strength, and Learn to Love Yourself* (Avon, MA: F&W, 2004).

Catherine Ryan Hyde, *Pay It Forward* (New York: Pocket, 2010).

Laura Oliver, *The Story Within: New Insights and Inspiration for Writers* (New York: Alpha-Penguin, 2011).

Kathryn Shafer and Fran Greenfield, *Asthma Free in 21 Days: The Breakthrough Mind-Body Healing Program* (New York: HarperCollins, 2000).

Gareth Cook, "The Secret Language Code," ScientificAmerican.com, Scientific American, Inc., 16 Aug. 2011. Oct. 2013 <http://www.scientificamerican.com/article.cfm?id=the-secret-language-code>.

James W. Pennebaker, *Opening Up: The Healing Power of Expressing Emotions* (New York: Guilford, 1997).

Rohn, *Art*.

Rudolf H. Moos, and Bernice S. Moos, "Treatment plus Alcoholics Anonymous may work best for those with drinking problems," *Research and Development*, United States Department of Veterans Affairs, 22 Oct. 2009. Oct. 2013 <http://www.research. va.gov/ news/research_highlights/alcoholism-101105.cfm#.Uoeq6sjnb4g>.

"Finding Forrester (2000)," *rottentomatoes.com*, Fixter, Inc., n.d. Oct. 2013 http://www. rottentomatoes.com/m/finding_forrester/.

Hammurabi, *The Code of Hammurabi* (Huntington, MA: Seven Treasures, 2008).

Charles F. Horne, *The Code of Hammurabi* (London: Forgotten Books, 2007).

Chapter Eleven Endnotes

[173]   Brad McCarty, "6 Stories of Life-changing Social Media Connections," *Social Media*, http://thenextweb.com/socialmedia/2011/09/03/6-stories-of-life-changing-social-media-connections/ (2013).

[174]   Natasha Burgert, "How Social Media has Changed my Medical Practice," http://www.kevinmd.com/blog/2011/08/ social-media-changed-medical-practice.html (18 Aug. 2011).

[175]   "Social Media Bootcamp," *ChaleneJohnson.com*, ChaleneJohnson.com, n.d. Oct. 2013 <http://www.chalenejohnson.com/>.

[176]   *The Social Habit: Social Media Research Redefined*, The Social Habit, 2012. Oct. 2013 <http://socialhabit.com/>.

[177]   Melanie Notkin, "How Social Media Changed my Life," http://bub.blicio.us/how-social-media-changed-my-life/(22 Apr. 2011).

[178]   Stelzner, Michael. "2012 Social Media Marketing Industry Report." *Social Media Examiner*, Social Media Examiner, 3 April 2012. Oct. 2013 <http://www.socialmediaexaminer.com/social-media-marketing-industry-report-2012/>.

[179]   Alice Yoo, "Top 6 Technologies That Are Revolutionizing How We Socially Connect," *Mylifescoop.com*, Federated Media, 2013. Oct. 2013 <http://mylifescoop.com/2013/05/13/top-6-technologies-that-are-revolutionizing-how-we-socially-connect/>.

[180]   "The 100 Most Influential People in the World," *Time Magazine*, 6 May 2013.

[181]   Phil Ament, "Assembly Line," *Ideafinder.com*, Troy, MI: The Great Idea Finder, 16 May 2005. Oct. 2013 <http://www.ideafinder.com/history/inventions/assbline.htm>.

Chapter Eleven Bibliography

Merriam-Webster, *The Merriam-Webster Dictionary* (Springfield, MA: Merriam-Webster, 2008).

"Social Media Bootcamp," *ChaleneJohnson.com*, ChaleneJohnson.com, n.d. Oct. 2013 <http://www.chalenejohnson.com/>.

The Social Habit: Social Media Research Redefined, The Social Habit, 2012. Oct. 2013 <http://socialhabit.com/>.

Stelzner, Michael. "2012 Social Media Marketing Industry Report." *Social Media Examiner*, Social Media Examiner, 3 April 2012. Oct. 2013 <http://www.socialmediaexaminer.com/social-media-marketing-industry-report-2012/>.

Elizabeth F. Thompson, *Justice Interrupted: The Struggle for Constitutional Government in the Middle East* (Boston: Harvard University, 2013).

Joshua Stacher, *Adaptable Autocrats: Regime Power in Egypt and Syria* (Stanford, CA: Stanford University, 2012).

Bahgat Korany and Rabab El-Mahdi, eds., *Arab Spring in Egypt: Revolution and Beyond* (New York: American University in Cairo, 2012).\

"Profile: Hosni Mubarak," *BBC News Middle East*, British Broadcasting Corporation, 22 Aug. 2013. Oct. 2013 <http://www.bbc.co.uk/news/world-middle-east-12301713>.

Elizabeth Dickinson, "Anatomy of a Dictatorship: Hosni Mubarak," *Foreignpolicy.com*, Foreign Policy Group, LLC, 3 Mar. 2011. Oct. 2013 <http://www.foreignpolicy.com/articles/2011/02/04/anatomy_of_a_dictatorship_hosni_mubarak>.

"Zine al-Abidine Ben Ali," *The Guardian*, Guardian News and Media Limited, n.d. Oct. 2013 <http://www.theguardian.com/world/zine-al-abidine-ben-ali>.

"Zine El-Abidine Ben Ali," *Topics.nytimes.com*, The New York Times Company, 11 Jan. 2004. Oct. 2013 <topics.nytimes.com/top/reference/timestopics/people/b/zine_elabidine_ben_ali/>.

Alice Yoo, "Top 6 Technologies That Are Revolutionizing How We Socially Connect," *Mylifescoop.com*, Federated Media, 2013. Oct. 2013 <http://mylifescoop.com/2013/05/13/top-6-technologies-that-are-revolutionizing-how-we-socially-connect/>.

"The 100 Most Influential People in the World," *Time Magazine*, 6 May 2013.

"Joel Selanikio," *Lemelson-MIT*, Massachusetts Institute of Technology/MIT School of Engineering, n.d. Oct. 2013 <http://web.mit.edu/invent/a-winners/a-selanikio.html>.

"Joel Selanikio, MD," Speaker Biography, *Worldcongress.com*, n.d. Oct. 2013 <http://www.worldcongress.com/speakerBio.cfm?speakerID=4117>.

Joel Selanikio, "Spotlight on DataDyne: Dr. Joel Selanikio," Interviewed by Fatima, *Designmeasurechange.com*, Evalu, n.d. Oct. 2013 <http://www.designmeasurechange.com/spotlight-on-datadyne-dr-joel-selanikio/>.

Selanikio and Paul Margie, "Data Collection Improving World—Dr. Joel Selanikio Explains," *YouTube.com*, YouTube, n.d. Oct. 2013 <http://www.youtube.com/watch?v=JtAcEpCUFCw>.

Phil Ament, "Assembly Line," *Ideafinder.com*, Troy, MI: The Great Idea Finder, 16 May 2005. Oct. 2013 <www.ideafinder.com/history/inventions/assbline.htm>.

"The Life of Henry Ford," *The Henry Ford*, Dearborn, MI: The Henry Ford, 2013. Oct. 2013 <http://www.hfmgv.org/exhibits/hf/>.

Henry Ford, *My Life and Work* (New York: CruGuru, 2008).

Ann Thomas, *Henry Ford's Dream: Car Assembly Lines* (Flinders Park SA, Australia: Era, 2007).

Chapter Twelve Endnotes

[182] John Konia and Mark Kramer, "Collective Impact," *Ssireview.org*, Stanford Social Innovation Review, Winter 2011. Oct. 2013 <http://www.ssireview.org/articles/entry/collective_impact>.

[183] Dean Karlan and Jacob Appel, *More Than Good Intentions* (New York: Dutton, 2012) 38.

[184] "Questions and Answers," *Real Clear World*, RealClearWorld, 2012. Oct. 2013 <http://hiv-stats.realclearworld.com/q/21/8056/How-many-orphans-are-there-in-Ghana-as-a-result-of-AIDS>.

[185] Sachs, "Aid Ironies," *Huff Post World*, TheHuffingtonPost.com, Inc., 24 May 2009. Oct. 2013 <http://www.huffingtonpost.com/jeffrey-sachs/aid-ironies_b_207181.html>.

[186] Appel and Karlan, *More than Good Intentions*, 267.

[187] "What Does Thwink.org Have to Offer?" *Thwink.org*, 2012. Oct. 2013 <http://www.thwink.org/sustain/general/WhatDoesThwinkHave.htm>.

[188] Anne Hunsaker Hawkins, *A Small, Good Thing* (New York: W.W. Norton, 2000).

[189] Friedman, *The Next Decade*, 220.

[190] Sachs, "Aid Ironies," *Huff Post World*, TheHuffingtonPost.com, Inc., 24 May 2009. Oct. 2013 <http://www.huffingtonpost.com/jeffrey-sachs/aid-ironies_b_207181.html>.

[191] Friedman, *The Next Decade*, 220.

[192] "5 Minutes with Jacqueline Novogratz," *PTPI Blog*, People to People International, 26 Feb. 2013. Oct. 2013 <http://blog.ptpi.org/2013/02/26/5-minutes-with-jacqueline-novogratz/>.

[193] Appel and Karlan, *More than Good Intentions*, 37-43.

[194] When we compare current statistics about AIDS to statistics from the early 1990's, progress has been made compared to where the disease once was.

[195] Appel and Karlan, *More than Good Intentions*, 267.

[196] Novogratz, *The Blue Sweater*, 142.
John Gardner was a Professor at Stanford whom with Novogratz formed a friendship. From the 1960s onward, Gardner played a major role in civil rights enforcement, education reform and campaign finance reform. He was instrumental in creating Medicare, establishing the public television network and supporting community volunteer service. In 1964, Gardner received the Presidential Medal of Freedom, the nation's highest civil honor. He founded Common Cause and headed the Urban Coalition, chaired numerous presidential task forces and commissions, and mentored many public service organizations.

[197] "Jeffrey Sachs," *jeffsachs.org*, New York: The Earth Institute, Columbia University, 2013. Oct.

2013 <http://jeffsachs.org/>.

198   *I Am Because We Are.*

199   "Jeffrey Sachs," *The Huffington Post*, TheHuffingtonPost.com, Inc., 2013. Oct. 2013 <http://www.huffingtonpost. com/jeffrey-sachs/>.

200   Orbinski, *An Imperfect Offering*, 352.

201   Orbinski, *An Imperfect Offering*, 352.

202   "Jeffrey Sachs," *Project Syndicate.*

203   "Human Development Reports," *UNDP.org*, United Nations Development Programme, 2013. Oct. 2013 <http://hdr.undp.org/en/reports/global/hdr2013/>.

204   Hawkins, *Reconstructing Illness* (West Lafayette, IN: Purdue University, 1999).

205   "Poverty Reduction," *UNDP.org*. United Nations Development Programme, 2013. Oct. 2013 <http://www.undp.org/content/undp/en/home/ourwork/povertyreduction/overview.html>.

206   Miguel Helft, "The Class That Built Apps, and Fortunes," *Technology*, The New York Times Company, 2011.Oct. 2013 <http://www.nytimes.com/2011/05/08/technology/08class.html?_r=0>.

207   "A Road to Somewhere," *The Economist*, The Economist Newspaper Limited, 21 July 2011. Oct. 2013 <http://www.economist.com/node/18989203>.

Chapter Twelve Bibliography

Brian Tracy, *21 Great Ways to Manage Your Time and Double Your Productivity* (Solana Beach, CA: Brian Tracy International, 2008).

John Konia and Mark Kramer, "Collective Impact," *Ssireview.org*, Stanford Social Innovation Review, Winter 2011. Oct. 2013 <http://www.ssireview.org/articles/entry/collective_impact>.

Dean Karlan and Jacob Appel, *More Than Good Intentions* (New York: Dutton, 2012) 38.

"Speakers: Jacqueline Novogratz: Philanthropist," *TED: Ideas Worth Spreading*, TED Conferences LLC, n.d. Oct.2013 <http://www.ted.com/speakers/jacqueline_novogratz.html>.

Tina Seelig, *InGenius: A Crash Course on Creativity* (New York: HarperOne, 2012).

"Questions and Answers," *Real Clear World*, RealClearWorld, 2012. Oct. 2013 <http://hiv-stats.realclearworld.com/q/21/8056/How-many-orphans-are-there-in-Ghana-as-a-result-of-AIDS>.

Sachs, *End of Poverty.* "Jeffrey D. Sachs," *Project Syndicate*, Project Syndicate, 2013. Oct. 2013 <http://www.project-syndicate.org/contributor/jeffrey-d—sachs>.

Sachs, *Common Wealth: Economics for a Crowded Planet* (New York: Penguin, 2009).

Sachs, *The Price of Civilization: Reawakening American Virtue and Prosperity* (New York: Random, 2012).

Sachs, "Global Development's Winning Goals," *Project Syndicate*, Project Syndicate, 27 Aug. 2013. Oct. 2013 <http://www.project-syndicate.org/commentary/ensuring-the-success-of-the-un-s-sustainable-development-goals-by-jeffrey-d—sachs>.

Moyo. *DambisaMoyo.com*. Dambisa Moyo, 2013. Oct. 2013 <http://www.dambisamoyo.com/>.

Paul Collier, *The Bottom Billion* (New York: Oxford University, 2007).

Helen Epstein, *The Invisible Cure* (New York: Picador, 2007).

Karlan 37-43.

"What Does Thwink.org Have to Offer?" *Thwink.org*, 2012. Oct. 2013 <http://www.thwink.org/sustain/general/WhatDoesThwinkHave.htm>.

Anne Hunsaker Hawkins, *A Small, Good Thing* (New York: W.W. Norton, 2000).

Friedman 220.

Sachs, "Aid Ironies," *Huff Post World*, TheHuffingtonPost.com, Inc., 24 May 2009. Oct. 2013 <http://www.huffingtonpost.com/jeffrey-sachs/aid-ironies_b_207181.html>.

Friedman 222.

"5 Minutes with Jacqueline Novogratz," *PTPI Blog*, People to People International, 26 Feb. 2013. Oct. 2013 <blog.ptpi.org/2013/02/26/5-minutes-with-jacqueline-novogratz/>.

Karlan 37-43.

Crs.org. The United States President's Emergency Plan for AIDS Relief, U.S. State Department, 2013. Oct. 2013 <http://www.pepfar.gov/>.

Karlan 267. "Jeffrey Sachs," *jeffsachs.org*, New York: The Earth Institute, Columbia University, 2013. Oct. 2013 <http://jeffsachs.org/>.

I Am Because We Are. "Jeffrey Sachs," *The Huffington Post*, TheHuffingtonPost.com, Inc., 2013. Oct. 2013 <http://www.huffingtonpost.com/jeffrey-sachs/>.

"Jeffrey Sachs," *Project Syndicate*.

Orbinski, *Imperfect Offering* 352. Sachs, "Global Development's Winning Goals." Hawkins, *Reconstructing Illness* (West Lafayette, IN: Purdue University, 1999).

Mothers2mothers.org, Mothers2mothers South Africa, n.d. Oct. 2013 <http://www.m2m.org/>.

SkollFoundation.org. The Skoll Foundation, 2013. Oct. 2013 <http://www.skollfoundation.org/>.

"Mitchell Besser," *Ashoka Innovators for the Public*, Ashoka, n.d. Oct. 2013 <https://www.ashoka.org/fellow/mitchell-besser>.

"Poverty Reduction," *UNDP.org*. United Nations Development Programme, 2013. Oct. 2013 <http://www.undp.org/content/undp/en/home/ourwork/povertyreduction/overview.html>. Miguel Helft, "The Class That Built Apps, and Fortunes," *Technology*, The New York Times Company, 2011. Oct.2013 <http://www.nytimes.com/2011/05/08/technology/08class.html?_r=0>.

"A Road to Somewhere," *The Economist*, The Economist Newspaper Limited, 21 July 2011. Oct. 2013 <http://www.economist.com/node/18989203>.

Chapter Thirteen Endnotes

[208]   "Bono: The Good News on Poverty (Yes, There's Good News)," *TED: Ideas Worth Spreading*, TED Conferences, LLC, Mar. 2013. Oct. 2013 <http://www.ted.com/talks/ bono_the_good_news_on_poverty_yes_there_s_good_news.html>.

[209]   Amartya Sen, *Development as Freedom* (New York: Knopf, 1999).

[210]   Sen, "Amartya Sen: The Taste of True Freedom," Interviewed by Tonkin Boyd, *The Independent*, Independent.co.uk, 5 July 2013. Oct. 2013 <http://www.independent.co.uk/arts-entertainment/art/features/amartya-sen-the-taste-of-true-freedom-8688089.html>.

[211]   Appel and Karlan, *More Than Good Intentions*, 37.

[212]   How A Little Bit Makes a Big Difference is explained in *Chapter 10* in *Lesson Eleven: A Little Bit Makes a Big Difference*.

[213]   Steve Chapman, "World Poverty in Retreat," *Chicago Tribune News*, Chicago Tribune, 29 Mar. 2012. Oct. 2013 <http://articles.chicagotribune.com/2012-03-29/news/ct-oped-0329-chapman-20120329_1_poverty-rate-poverty-reduction-world-bank>.

[214]   Taziana C. Dearing, *Tiziana C. Dearing, Consultant*, Yola.com, n.d. Oct. 2013 <http://www.tizianadearing.com/about-me.php>.

[215]   McKinsey & Company, "The Rise of Social Entrepreneurship Suggests a Possible Future for Global Capitalism," *Skoll World Forum*, Forbes.com LLC, 2 May 2013. Oct. 2013 <http://www.forbes.com/sites/skollworldforum/2013/05/02/the-rise-of-social-entrepreneurship-suggests-a-possible-future-for-global-capitalism/>.

[216]   Novogratz, *The Blue Sweater*, 142.

[217]   *Success.org*, Success Magazine, 2013. Oct. 2013 <http://www.success.com/articles/print/850>.

[218]   Masur, "Lincoln Tells a Story," *Opinionator*, The New York Times Company, 27 Jan. 2012. Oct. 2013 <http://opinionator.blogs.nytimes.com/2012/01/27/lincoln-tells-a-story/?_r=0>.

[219]   David Bohm, *On Dialogue* (New York: Routledge, 2004).

[220]   Standage, *History of the World in 6 Glasses*, 256.

[221]   More information on the website: InterviewGirl.com. Check out the *People Making a Difference in the World* compilation of stories.

Chapter Thirteen Bibliography

"Bono: The Good News on Poverty (Yes, There's Good News)," *TED: Ideas Worth Spreading*, TED Conferences, LLC, Mar. 2013. Oct. 2013 <http://www.ted.com/talks/ bono_the_good_news_on_poverty_yes_there_s_good_news.html>.

Michael D. Coe and Rex Koontz, *Mexico: From the Olmecs to the Aztecs*, 6th ed. (New York: Thames & Hudson, 2008).

Alice Albinia, *Empires of the Indus: The Story of a River* (New York: W.W. Norton, 2010).

Yunus Centre, YunusCentre.org, 2011. Oct. 2013 <http://www.muhammadyunus.org/>.

Grameen-Info.org, Network Solutions, 2013. Oct. 2013 <http://www.grameeninfo.org/index.php?option=com_content&task=view&id=329&Itemid=363>.

Mohammad Yunus, *Banker to the Poor: Micro-Lending and the Battle against World Poverty* (New York: PublicAffairs, 2007).

Yunus and Karl Weber, *Creating a World Without Poverty: Social Business and the Future of Capitalism* (New York: PublicAffairs, 2007).

Joseph E. Stiglitz, Amartya Sen and Jean-Paul Fitoussi, *Mismeasuring Our Lives: Why GDP Doesn't Add Up* (New York: New, 2010).

Mahbub Ul Haq, *The Poverty Curtain* (New York: Columbia University, 1976).

Amartya Sen, *Development as Freedom* (New York: Knopf, 1999).

"Human Development Reports," *UNDP.org*, United Nations Development Programme, 2013. Oct. 2013 <hdr.undp.org/en/reports/global/hdr2013/>.

Sabina Alkire and Severine Deneulin, "The Human Development and Capability Approach," *IDRC.ca*, International Development Research Centre, n.d. Oct. 2013 <http://web.idrc.ca/openebooks/470-3/#page_22>.

Sen, "Amartya Sen: The Taste of True Freedom," Interviewed by Tonkin Boyd, *The Independent*, Independent.co.uk, 5 July 2013. Oct. 2013 <http://www.independent.co.uk/arts-entertainment/art/features/amartya-sen-the-taste-of-true-freedom-8688089.html>.

Yunus, *Building Social Business: The New Kind of Capitalism that Serves Humanity's Most Pressing Needs* (New York: Public Affairs, 2010).

"Capability Poverty Measure (CPM)," *Women Aid International*, London: Women Aid International, 2000. Oct. 2013 <http://www.womenaid.org/press/info/poverty/cpm.html>.

"A Wealth of Data," *The Economist*, The Economist Newspaper Limited, 29 July 2010. Oct. 2013 <http://www.economist.com/node/ 16693283?zid=295&ah=0bca374e65f2354d553956ea65f756e0>.

Amartya Sen, "How to Do It Better," *The Economist*, The Economist Newspaper Limited, 6 Aug. 2007. Oct. 2013<http://www.economist.com/node/4164449?zid=295&ah=0bca374e65f2354d553956ea65f756e0>.

Karlan.

Novogratz, *Blue Sweater*.

Missionary Society of St. Paul, Houston, TX: Missionary Society of St. Paul, 2013. Oct. 2013 <http://www.mspfathers.org/>.

Steve Chapman, "World Poverty in Retreat," *Chicago Tribune News*, Chicago Tribune, 29 Mar. 2012. Oct. 2013 <http://articles.chicagotribune.com/2012-03-29/news/ct-oped-0329-chapman-20120329_1_poverty-rate-poverty-reduction-world-bank>.

McKinsey & Company, "The Rise of Social Entrepreneurship Suggests a Possible Future for Global Capitalism," *Skoll World Forum*, Forbes.com LLC, 2 May 2013. Oct. 2013 <http://www.forbes.com/sites/skollworldforum/2013/05/02/the-rise-of-social-entrepreneurship-suggests-a-possible-future-for-global-capitalism/>.

Taziana C. Dearing, *Tiziana C. Dearing, Consultant*, Yola.com, n.d. Oct. 2013 <http://www.tizianadearing.com/about-me.php>.

Veronica Weis, "Tiziana Dearing, CEO of Boston Rising, Shares Her Post-Assets Learning Conference Ideas," *Cfed.org*, Corporation for Enterprise Development, 30 Oct. 2012. Oct. 2013 <http://cfed.org/blog/inclusiveeconomy/assets_learning_conference_reflections_profile_tiziana_dearing_of_boston_rising/>.

Novogratz 142.

Success.org, Success Magazine, 2013. Oct. 2013 <http://www.success.com/articles/print/850>.

Masur, "Lincoln Tells a Story," *Opinionator*, The New York Times Company, 27 Jan. 2012. Oct. 2013 <opinionator.blogs.nytimes.com/2012/01/27/lincoln-tells-a-story/?_r=0>.

Moyo.

J. Krishnamurti and David Bohm, *The Ending of Time* (New York: HarperCollins, 1985).

David Bohm, *On Dialogue* (New York: Routledge, 2004).

Lee Nichol, ed., The Essential David Bohm (New York: Routledge, 2003).

Sarah Davey Chesters, *The Socratic Classroom: Reflective Thinking Through Collaborative Inquiry* (Rotterdam: Sense, 2012).

Standage 256.

Chapter Fourteen Endnotes

[222] *Farmers.com*, Farmers Insurance Group, 2012. Oct. 2013 <http://www.farmers.com/>.

[223] "John D. Rockefeller," *Artofmanliness.com*, The Art of Manliness, 2010. Oct. 2013 <http://artofmanliness.com/2010/09/13/the-pocket-notebooks-of-20-famous-men/2/>.

[224] Susan Love, "Thomas Alva Edison (1847—1931)." *Patentdrafting.com*, Morgan Hill, CA: Technographics, n.d.Oct. 2013 <http://www.patentdrafting.com/edison.htm>.

[225] "Martha Graham: About the Dancer," *American Masters*, Thirteen/WNET/PBS, 16 Sept. 2005. Oct. 2013 <http://www.pbs.org/wnet/americanmasters/episodes/martha-graham/about-the-dancer/497/>, page 79.

[226] Susan Love, "Thomas Alva Edison (1847—1931)." *Patentdrafting.com*, Morgan Hill, CA: Technographics, n.d.Oct. 2013 <http://www.patentdrafting.com/edison.htm>.

[227] "Atul Gawande," Harvard School of Public Health, Boston, MA: Harvard, 2013. Oct. 2013 <http://www.hsph.harvard.edu/atul-gawande/>.

[228] David Kord Murray, *Borrowing Brilliance* (New York: Gotham, 2009), 37.

[229] Murray, *Borrowing Brilliance*, 488.

[230] Michalko, *Cracking Creativity*, 23.

[231] "Finding and Resolving the Root Causes".

[232] Russell Freedman, *The Wright Brothers: How They Invented the Airplane* (New York: Holiday House, 1994).

[233] Lola M. Schaefer, *Thomas Edison* (North Mankato, MN: Capstone, 2002).

[234] Foster, *How To Get Ideas*, 163.

[235] (c.1900)

[236] Alfred Lansing, *Endurance: Shackleton's Incredible Voyage* (New York: Basic-Perseus, 2007).

[237] "The Choice is Yours," *TeamBuilding-Leader.com*, teambuilding-leader.com, 2012. Oct. 2013 <http://www.teambuilding-leader.com/the-choice-is-yours.html>.

[238] "Famous People Who Found Success Despite Failures," *Getbusylivingblog. com*, Get Busy Living, 2013. Oct. 2013 <http://getbusylivingblog.com/famous-people-who-found-success-despite-failures/>.

[239] Hugh Thomas, *The Slave Trade: The Story of the Atlantic Slave Trade: 1440 – 1870* (New York: Touchstone, 1997).

[240] William Wilberforce's full story is shared in the conclusion.

[241] These references were pointed out by Michael Zenn in *Self Help Revolution*.

[242] Steve Crawshaw and John Jackson, "10 Everyday Acts of Resistance That Changed the World," *Yesmagazine.org*, Positive Futures Network, 1 April 2011. Web. Oct. 2013 <http://www.yesmagazine.org/people-power/10-everyday-acts-of-resistance-that-changed-the-world>.

[243] Steve Crawshaw and John Jackson, "10 Everyday Acts of Resistance That Changed the World," *Yesmagazine.org*, Positive Futures Network, 1 April 2011. Web. Oct. 2013 <http://www.yesmagazine.org/people-power/10-everyday-acts-of-resistance-that-changed-the-world>.

[244] "Compassion International," *MinistryWatch.com*, Wall Watchers.org, 2013. Oct. 2013 <http://www.ministrywatch.com/profile/compassion-international.aspx>.

[245] "Famous People."

[246] Seth Godin, Interviewed by Ryan and Tina Essmaker, *Thegreatdiscontent.com*, TGD, 14 Aug. 2012. Oct. 2013 <http://thegreatdiscontent.com/seth-godin>.

[247] Ruud Kluivers, "No Success Without Failure: How to Get It Right," *Wolters Kluwer: The Intelligent Solutions Blog,* Wolters Kluwer, 12 Nov. 2010. Oct. 2013 <>.

[248] Sam Parker, *212: The Extra Degree* (Dallas, TX: Walk the Talk, 2005), page 21.

[249] Michalko, *CrackingCreativity*, 10.

[250] Michalko, *Cracking Creativity*, 10.

[251] Nakkia Gray, "Turn Your Life Around, One Day at a Time," *Beliefnet.com*, Beliefnet, Inc., 2012. Oct. 2013 <http://blog.beliefnet.com/fromthemasters/2012/01/turn-your-life-around-one-day-at-a-time.html#ixzz1jLVJ4zZX)>.

[252] Foster, *How to Get Ideas*, 179.

[253] "Ancient Rome," *The History Channel*, A&E Television Networks, LLC, 2013. Oct. 2013 <http://www.history.com/topics/ancient-rome>.

[254] Natan Sharansky, *Defending Identity: Its Indispensable Role in Protecting Democracy* (New York: PublicAffairs, 2008).

[255] Dan Green, *Finish Strong* (Nashville, TN: Thomas Nelson, 2012) 41-2.

[256] Gillian Gill, *Nightingales: The Extraordinary Upbringing and Curious Life of Miss Florence Nightingale* (New York: Random, 2005).

[257] Sam Parker, *212: The Extra Degree* (Dallas, TX: Walk the Talk, 2005), page 10.

[258] Nonna Bannister, *The Secret Holocaust Diaries: The Untold Story of Nonna Bannister* (Carol Stream, IL: Tyndale, 2010), page 3.

[259] Nonna Bannister, *The Secret Holocaust Diaries: The Untold Story of Nonna Bannister* (Carol Stream, IL: Tyndale, 2010), page 9.

[260] Bannister, *The Secret Holocaust Diaries: The Untold Story of Nonna Bannister*, page 204.

[261]   Bannister, *The Secret Holocaust Diaries: The Untold Story of Nonna Bannister*, page 208.

[262]   Abby Johnson, *Unplanned: The Dramatic True Story of a Former Planned Parenthood Leader's Eye-Opening Journey Across the Life Line* (Carol Stream, IL: Tyndale, 2010).

[263]   Michalko, *Cracking Creativity*, 56.

[264]   Ramsland, *Snap*, page 101.

[265]   Ramsland, *Snap*, page 102.

[266]   Jacob Bronowski, *The Ascent of Man* (London: BBC, 2011), page 133.

[267]   Sherwin Nuland, *Leonardo da Vinci* (New York: Penguin Lives, 2000), page 73.

[268]   Martin Kemp, *Leonardo* (New York: Oxford University, 2004), page 115.

[269]   "Leader of the Month for February 2006: Charlie 'Tremendous' Jones." *LeaderNetwork.org: The Resource for Leaders*. Leadernetwork.org, n.d. Oct. 2013 <http://www.leadernetwork.org/charlie_jones_february_06.htm>.

[270]   Richard Koch, *The 80/20 Principle: The Secret to Achieving More with Less* (New York: Doubleday, 2008).

[271]   Charles Duhigg, *The Power of Habit: Why We Do What We Do in Life and Business* (New York: Random, 2012).

[272]   BJ Fogg, *TinyHabits.com*, BJ Fogg, 2013. Oct. 2013 <http://tinyhabits.com/>.

[273]   Charles Duhigg, *The Power of Habit: Why We Do What We Do in Life and Business* (New York: Random, 2012). 7777

[274]   Eileen Barker, "What Would Gandhi Do?" *Mediate.com*, Resourceful Internet Solutions, Inc., 2013. Oct. 2013 <http://www.mediate.com/articles/ebarker4.cfm>.

[275]   Alwine de Vos van Steenwijk, *Father Joseph Wresinski: voice of the poorest* (Goleta, CA: Queenship, 1996).

[276]   Russell Kirk, "The Moral Imagination," *The Russell Kirk Center for Cultural Renewal*, The Russell Kirk Center, 2013. Oct. 2013 <http://www.kirkcenter.org/index.php/detail/the-moral-imagination/>.

[277]   Mark Turner, *The Literary Mind: The Origins of Thought and Language* (New York: Oxford University, 1998), 4-5.

[278]   Pink, *A Whole New Mind*, 115.

[279]   Pink, *A Whole New Mind*, 113—115.

Chapter Fourteen Bibliography

Farmers.com, Farmers Insurance Group, 2012. Oct. 2013 <http://www.farmers.com/>.

Florence Nightingale, *Notes on Nursing: What it is and What it is not (1860)* (Mineola, NY: Dover, 1969).

Lytton Strachey, *Eminent Victorians* (New York: Penguin, 1990) 102-105.

Bernard Cohen, "Florence Nightingale," *Scientific American* (1984) 250(3):128-136.

Connie Ann Kirk, *Mark Twain: A Biography* (Westport, CT: Greenwood, 2004).

Peter Messent, *The Cambridge Introduction to Mark Twain* (New York: Cambridge University, 2007).

James Gleick, *Isaac Newton* (New York: Vintage, 2003).

Ron Chernow, Titan: The Life of John D. Rockefeller, Sr. (New York: Vintage, 2004).

"John D. Rockefeller," *Artofmanliness.com*, The Art of Manliness, 2010. Oct. 2013 <http://artofmanliness.com/2010/09/13/the-pocket-notebooks-of-20-famous-men/2/>.

Susan Love, "Thomas Alva Edison (1847 – 1931)." *Patentdrafting.com*, Morgan Hill, CA: Technographics, n.d. Oct. 2013 <http://www.patentdrafting.com/edison.htm>.

Michalko 79.

"Martha Graham: About the Dancer," *American Masters*, Thirteen/WNET/PBS, 16 Sept. 2005. Oct. 2013 <www.pbs.org/wnet/americanmasters/episodes/martha-graham/about-the-dancer/497/>.

Leonard DeGraaf, *Edison and the Rise of Innovation* (New York: Sterling Signature, 2013).

Atul Gawande, *Better: A Surgeon's Notes on Performance* (New York: Picador, 2007).

Gawande, *The Checklist Manifesto: How to Get Things Right* (New York: Metropolitan, 2009).

"Atul Gawande," Harvard School of Public Health, Boston, MA: Harvard, 2013. Oct. 2013 <http://www.hsph.harvard.edu/atul-gawande/>.

Gawande.com, Atul Gawande, n.d. Oct. 2013 <http://gawande.com/>. David Kord Murray, *Borrowing Brilliance* (New York: Gotham, 2009).

Michalko 23.

Paul Johnson, *Socrates: A Man for Our Times* (New York: Penguin, 2011).

George Sullivan, *Thomas Edison* (New York: Scholastic, 2002).

Caryn Jenner, *Thomas Edison: The Great Inventor* (New York: DK Children, 2007).

Jan Adkins, *Thomas Edison* (New York: DK Children, 2009).

Lola M. Schaefer, *Thomas Edison* (North Mankato, MN: Capstone, 2002).

Charles Darwin and Frederick Burkhardt, ed. *Charles Darwin's Letters: A Selection, 1825-1859* (New York: Cambridge University, 1996).

"Finding and Resolving the Root Causes".

Quentin Reynolds, *The Wright Brothers: Pioneers of American Aviation* (New York: Random House, 1950).

Russell Freedman, *The Wright Brothers: How They Invented the Airplane* (New York: Holiday House, 1994).

Johnson, *Socrates*.

Ernest Shackleton, *Escape from the Antarctic* (New York: Penguin, 2007).

Alfred Lansing, *Endurance: Shackleton's Incredible Voyage* (New York: Basic-Perseus, 2007).

David Herbert Donald, *Lincoln* (New York: Touchstone, 1995). Goodwin.

James M. McPherson, *Abraham Lincoln* (New York: Oxford University, 2009).

Mark Roskill, ed., *Letters of Vincent van Gogh* (New York: Touchstone, 2008).

Nienke Bakker, Leo Jansen and Hans Luijten, eds., *Vincent van Gogh: The Letters: The Complete Illustrated and Annotated Edition (Vol. 1-6)* (New York: Thames & Hudson, 2009).

"The Choice is Yours," *TeamBuilding-Leader.com*, teambuilding-leader.com, 2012. Oct. 2013 <http://www.teambuilding-leader.com/the-choice-is-yours.html>.

"Famous People Who Found Success Despite Failures," *Getbusylivingblog.com*, Get Busy Living, 2013. Oct. 2013 <http://getbusylivingblog.com/famous-people-who-found-success-despite-failures/>.

Hugh Thomas, *The Slave Trade: The Story of the Atlantic Slave Trade: 1440 – 1870* (New York: Touchstone, 1997).

Thomas, *An Unfinished History of the World* (New York: Papermac, 1995).

Steve Crawshaw and John Jackson, "10 Everyday Acts of Resistance That Changed the World," *Yesmagazine.org*, Positive Futures Network, 1 April 2011. Web. Oct. 2013 <http://www.yesmagazine.org/people-power/10-everyday-acts-of-resistance -that-changed-the-world>.

"Compassion International," *MinistryWatch.com*, Wall Watchers.org, 2013. Oct. 2013 <http://www.ministrywatch.com/profile/compassion-international.aspx>.

Donald McKim, "Cy Young: A Life in Baseball," *Baseball-almanac.com*, Baseball-Almanac, 2013. Oct. 2013 <www.baseball-almanac.com/dugout0e.shtml>.

Marie Hammontree, *Albert Einstein: Young Thinker* (New York: Aladdin, 1986).

Mike Venezia, *Albert Einstein: Universal Genius* (New York: Scholastic, 2009).

Robert Frost and Edward Connery Lathem, ed., *The Poetry of Robert Frost, Completed and Unabridged* (New York: Henry Holt, 1969).

Richard J. Foster, *The Extraordinary Life of an Olympic Champion* (Solana Beach, CA: Santa Monica Press, 2008).

Miguel de Cervantes and Edith Grossman, tr, *Don Quixote* (New York: Harper Perennial, 2005).

Robert W. Creamer, *Babe: The Legend Comes to Life* (New York: Simon & Schuster, 1992).

"Famous People."

Seth Godin, Interviewed by Ryan and Tina Essmaker, *Thegreatdiscontent.com*, TGD, 14 Aug. 2012. Oct. 2013 <http://thegreatdiscontent.com/seth-godin>.

Ruud Kluivers, "No Success Without Failure: How to Get It Right," *Wolters Kluwer: The Intelligent Solutions Blog*, Wolters Kluwer, 12 Nov. 2010. Oct. 2013 <>.

Max Tollens, Jr., "An Evening With an American Hero: Admiral Bob Shumaker," *Patriot Action Network*, Grassfire Nation, 21 Apr. 2011. Oct. 2013 <http://patriotaction.net/ profiles/blogs/an-evening-with-an-american?xg_source=activity>.

Brian Albrecht, "Navy veteran Robert Schumaker talks about surviving as POW during Vietnam," *Cleveland.com*, Northeast Ohio Media Group LLC, 21 Sept. 2012. Oct. 2013 <http://www.cleveland.com/metro/index.ssf/2012/09/ vietnam_pow_robert_shumaker_sp.html>.

Sam Parker, *212: The Extra Degree* (Dallas, TX: Walk the Talk, 2005).

Michalko 10.

Lewis Timberlake, *First Thing Every Morning* (Naperville, IL: Simple Truths, 2003).

Bornstein.

Nakkia Gray, "Turn Your Life Around, One Day at a Time," *Beliefnet.com*, Beliefnet, Inc., 2012. Oct. 2013 <blog.beliefnet.com/fromthemasters/2012/01/turn-your-life-around-one-day-at-a-time.html#ixzz1jLVJ4zZX)>.

Jack Foster, *How to Get Ideas* (San Francisco: Berrett-Koehler, 2007) 179.

"Meet Fred Culick," *Quest.nasa.gov*, NASA Quest, 11 Mar. 1999. Oct. 2013 <http://quest.nasa.gov/people/bios/aero/culick.html >.

Fred Charters Kelly, *The Wright Brothers: A Biography* (Mineola, NY: Dover, 1989).

"Ancient Rome," *The History Channel*, A&E Television Networks, LLC, 2013. Oct. 2013 <http://www.history.com/topics/ancient-rome>.

Aubrey J. Sher, *Romulus & Remus: The Imperfect Murders* (Bloomington, IN: AuthorHouse, 2010).

Christopher S. Mackay, *Ancient Rome: A Military and Political History* (New York: Cambridge University Free Press,2004).

Anneapplebaum.com, WordPress, 2013. Oct. 2013 <http://www.anneapplebaum.com/>.

Anne Applebaum, *Between East and West: Across the Borderlands of Europe* (New York: Pantheon, 1994).

Natan Sharansky, *Defending Identity: Its Indispensable Role in Protecting Democracy* (New York: PublicAffairs, 2008).

Sharansky and Ron Dermer, *The Case for Democracy: The Power of Freedom to Overcome Tyranny and Terror* (New York: PublicAffairs, 2006).

Sharansky, *Defending Identity*.

Richard Pipes, *The Concise History of the Russian Revolution* (New York: Vintage, 2005).

Robert Conquest, *Stalin: Breaker of Nations* (New York: Penguin, 1992).

A. Kemp-Welch, *Poland Under Communism: A Cold War History* (New York: Cambridge University, 2008).

Michael Checinski, *Poland, Communism, nationalism, anti-semitism* (New York: Karz-Cohl, 1982).

Dan Green, *Finish Strong* (Nashville, TN: Thomas Nelson, 2012) 41-2.

Montessori, *The Montessori Method*.

Standing.

Montessori, *Discovery of the Child* (New York: Ballantine, 1986).

Lillard.

"Vinoba Bhave," *vinobabhave.org*, VinobaBhave.org, n.d. Oct. 2013 <http://www.vinobabhave.org/en/>.

Vinoba Bhave, *Democratic Values and the Practice of Citizenship* (Uttar Pradesh, India: Sarva Seva Sangh Prakashan, 1962).

The Editors of Encyclopaedia Britannica, "Vinoba Bhave," *Britannica.com*, Encyclopaedia Britannica, Inc., 2013.Oct. 2013 <http://www.britannica.com/EBchecked/topic/64103/Vinoba-Bhave>.

"Maria Montessori," *amshq.org*, American Montessori Society, 2013. Oct. 2013 <https://www.amshq.org/Montessori-Education/History-of-Montessori-Education/Biography-of-Maria-Montessori.aspx>.

The Jean Monnet Association, "Jean Monnet 1888-1979," *Historiasiglo20.org*, Juan Carlos Ocana, 2003. Oct. 2013 <http://www.historiasiglo20.org/europe/monnet.htm>,

Mark Bostridge, *Florence Nightingale: The Woman and her Legend* (New York: Penguin, 2009).

Gillian Gill, *Nightingales: The Extraordinary Upbringing and Curious Life of Miss Florence Nightingale* (New York: Random, 2005).

Barbara Montgomery Dossey, *Florence Nightingale: Mystic, Visionary, Healer* (Philadelphia, PA: F. A. Davis, 2009).

John Muir, *The Eight Wilderness Discovery Books* (Seattle, WA: The Mountaineers, 1992).

Jean Monnet, *Memoirs* (New York: Doubleday, 1978).

"International Compassion Ministry," *Friar Rookey ICM.org*, The Servants of Mary, 2010. Oct. 2013 <frrookeyicm.org/about_icm>.

Kathleen E. Quasey, *Healer of Souls: The Life of Father Peter Mary Rookey and the International Compassion Ministry* (Bloomington, IN: Xlibris, 2008).

Heather Parsons, *Father Peter Rookey: Man of Miracles* (New York: Robert Andrews Press, 1994).

Parker.

Anthony Robbins, *Awaken the Giant Within: How to Take Immediate Control of Your Mental, Emotional, Physical and Financial Destiny* (New York: Free, 1991).

Gawande, *Better.*

Mette Bastholm Jensen, "Solidarity in action: A comparative analysis of collective rescue efforts in Nazi-occupied Denmark and the Netherlands," *Udini.* Proquest, LLC, 2013. Oct. 2013 <http://udini.proquest.com/view/solidarity-in-action-a-comparative-goid:304781033/>.

Jewish Telegraphic Agency, "Danish Jews to Travel to Malmo, Sweden in Solidarity Visit Against Anti-Semitic Attacks," *Jspace.com*, Jspace LLC, 20 Sept. 2012. Oct. 2013 <http://www.jspace.com/news/articles/danish-jews-to-travel-to-malmo-sweden-in-solidarity-visit-against-anti-semitic-attacks/10845>.

YadVashem.org. Yad Vashem The Holocaust Martyrs' and Heroes' Remembrance Authority, 2013. Oct. 2013 <www.yadvashem.org>.

Nonna Bannister, *The Secret Holocaust Diaries: The Untold Story of Nonna Bannister* (Carol Stream, IL: Tyndale, 2010).

Abby Johnson, *Unplanned: The Dramatic True Story of a Former Planned Parenthood Leader's Eye-Opening Journey Across the Life Line* (Carol Stream, IL: Tyndale, 2010).

AbbyJohnson.org, Pro Life Web Design, n.d. Oct. 2013 <http://www.abbyjohnson.org/>.

Ramsland.

Michalko 56.

Jim Glenn, *The Complete Patents of Nikola Tesla* (New York: Barnes & Noble, 1994).

Leland I. Anderson, *Nikola Tesla on His Work with Alternating Currents and Their Application to Wireless Telegraphy, Telephony, and Transmission of Power: An Extended Interview* (Minneapolis, MN: Twenty-First Century-Lerner, 2002).

Tas Anjarwalla, "Inventor of Cell Phone: We knew someday everybody would have one," *CNNTech*. Cable News Network/Turner Broadcasting System, Inc., 2013. Oct. 2013 <http://www.cnn.com/2010/TECH/mobile/07/09/cooper.cell.phone.inventor/>.

Jacob Bronowski, *The Ascent of Man* (London: BBC, 2011).

Roberta Edwards and True Kelley, *Who Was Leonardo da Vinci?* (New York: Grosset & Dunlap, 2005).

Sherwin Nuland, *Leonardo da Vinci* (New York: Penguin Lives, 2000).

Martin Kemp, *Leonardo* (New York: Oxford University, 2004).

Matthew Josephson, *Edison: A Biography* (Hoboken, NJ: Wiley, 1992).

Margaret Cousins, *The Story of Thomas Alva Edison* (New York: Random, 1993).

"Leader of the Month for February 2006: Charlie 'Tremendous' Jones." *LeaderNetwork. org: The Resource for Leaders.*Leadernetwork.org, n.d. Oct. 2013 <http://www. leadernetwork.org/charlie_jones_february_06.htm>.

"Charlie 'Tremendous' Jones: The People You Meet and the Books You Read." *YouTube. com.* You Tube, n.d. Oct. 2013 <http://www.youtube.com/watch?v=Cp—2fvuTRE>.

Charlie E. Jones, *Life is Tremendous* (Carol Stream, IL: Tyndale, 1981).

Voltaire and Peter Constantine, *Candide: or Optimism* (New York: Modern Library, 2005).

Richard Koch, *The 80/20 Principle: The Secret to Achieving More with Less* (New York: Doubleday, 2008).

Perry Marshall, *80/20 Sales and Marketing: The Definitive Guide to Working Less and Making More* (Irvine, CA:Entrepreneur, 2013).

S. G. Tallentyre, *The Life of Voltaire* (London: Smith, Elder, 1903).

Charles Duhigg, *The Power of Habit: Why We Do What We Do in Life and Business* (New York: Random, 2012).

BJ Fogg, *TinyHabits.com*, BJ Fogg, 2013. Oct. 2013 <http://tinyhabits.com/>.

Fogg, *Persuasive Technology: Using Computers to Change What We Think and Do* (San Francisco: Morgan Kaufmann, 2003).

Nicholas Croce, *Newton and the Three Laws of Motion* (New York: Rosen, 2005).

Eileen Barker, "What Would Gandhi Do?" *Mediate.com*, Resourceful Internet Solutions, Inc., 2013. Oct. 2013 <http://www.mediate.com/articles/ebarker4.cfm>.

Alwine de Vos van Steenwijk, *Father Joseph Wresinski: voice of the poorest* (Goleta, CA: Queenship, 1996).

Gilles Anouil, *The Poor Are the Church: A Conversation with Father Joseph Wresinski* (New London, CT: Twenty-third Publications, 2002).

Quentin Wodon, ed., "Extreme Poverty and Human Rights: Essays on Joseph Wresinski." *WorldBank.org*. World Bank, 9 Mar. 2000. Oct. 2013 <http://www-wds.worldbank. org/external/default/WDSContentServer/WDSP/IB/2004/02/25/000265513_200402 25165617/Rendered/PDF/wdr27915.pdf>.

Jonathan Jones, "Defining 'Moral Imagination,'" *Postmodern Conservative*, FirstThings.com, 1 July 2009. Oct. 2013 <http://www.firstthings.com/blogs/ postmodernconservative/2009/07/01/defining-moral-imagination/>.

Edmund Burke, *Reflections on the Revolution in France* (New York: Burke, 2013).

Russell Kirk, "The Moral Imagination," *The Russell Kirk Center for Cultural Renewal*, The Russell Kirk Center, 2013. Oct. 2013 <http://www.kirkcenter.org/index.php/detail/the-moral-imagination/>.

Mark Turner, *The Literary Mind: The Origins of Thought and Language* (New York: Oxford University, 1998).

Chapter Fifteen Endnotes

[280] S. Dick, "Prison was a tough teacher," *Greater Seattle area's AA Intergroup*, 2013. Oct. <http://www.seattleaa.org/ stories/floyd_c.html/>.

Chapter Fifteen Bibliography

S. Dick, "Prison was a tough teacher," *Greater Seattle area's AA Intergroup*, 2013. Oct. <http://www.seattleaa.org/ stories/floyd_c.html/>.

Chapter Seventeen Endnotes

[281] Tom Crouch, *First Flight: The Wright Brothers and the Invention of the Airplane* (Washington, DC: National Park Service, U.S. Department of the Interior, 2002) 8-11.

[282] The examples given earlier in this book include weight loss, accumulating wealth, and writing a book. If you want to lose weight, you eat a little bit less and exercise a little bit more day after day after day. You lose weight pound by pound. If you want to write a book, you write a page of that book day after day after day. People who strive to become wealthy become wealthy if they save their money little by little day after day.

[283] Gary Ryan Blair, *Everything Counts: 52 Remarkable Ways to Inspire Excellence and Drive Results* (Hoboken, NJ: John Wiley & Sons, 2010), xvii.

[284] Novogratz, *The Blue Sweater,* 15.

[285] Orbinski, *An Imperfect Offering,* 64.

[286] "Jon Berkeley." *Behance.net.* Adobe Systems, Inc., 2013. Oct. 2013 <http://www.behance.net/jonberkeley>.

[287] "Toward the end of poverty," *The Economist*, The Economist Newspaper Limited, 1 June 2013.

Oct. 2013 <http://www.economist.com/news/leaders/21578665-nearly-1-billion-people-have-been-taken-out-extreme-poverty-20years-world-should-aim>.

[288] Donna Hicks, *Dignity: Its Essential Role in Resolving Conflict* (Boston: Yale University, 2011).

[289] *Robertsherfield.com*. Las Vegas, NJ: Robert M. Sherfield, n.d. Oct. 2013 <http://www.robertsherfield.com/>.

[290] Orbinski, *An Imperfect Offering*, 65.

[291] Orbinski, *An Imperfect Offering*, 60-69.

[292] "Give your voice to the 2.5 billion people without access to a toilet," *Global Citizen*, The Global Poverty Project, 17 Dec. 2013. Dec. 2013 <http://www.globalcitizen.org/Content/Content.aspx?id=592eeaa7-8945-4d61-9128-e47abb06d317>.

[293] "Global Hunger," *Bread.org*, Washington, D.C.: Bread for the World, n.d. Oct. 2013 <http://www.bread.org/hunger/global/>.

[294] "Statistics: Worldwide," *Amfar.org*, AMFAR, The Foundation for AIDS Research. Oct. 2013. Oct. 2013 <http://www.amfar.org/about-hiv-and-aids/facts-and-stats/statistics-worldwide/>.

[295] Kristof and WuDunn, *Half the Sky*, 69.

[296] Kristof and WuDunn, *Half the Sky*, 237.

[297] Mark Johnson, *Moral Imagination: Implications of Cognitive Science for Ethics* (Chicago: University of Chicago, 1993).

[298] Gandhi and Louis Fischer, ed., *The Essential Gandhi: An Anthology of His Writings on His Life, Work, and Ideas* (New York: Vintage, 2002), 64.

[299] Novogratz, *The Blue Sweater*, 145.

[300] The prevailing opinion among the clergy of France in his time took the moral formation of students far more seriously than their intellectual development. Of course, because of the destruction of Catholic education in the French Revolution, priests themselves were often very badly educated. While he emphasized the importance of forming the Christian heart in the love of God and neighbor, Father Moreau insisted that his priests should be well educated. In fact, he sent Holy Cross students to one of the greatest universities in the world, the Sorbonne.

[301] Hawkins, *A Small, Good Thing*, 259.

[302] Amanda Ripley, *The Unthinkable: Who Survives When Disaster Strikes—and Why* (New York: Crown, 2008), xi.

[303] Orbinski, "Transcript for James Orbinski on his Time with Doctors Without Borders," Interviewed by Jim Fleming, *To the Best of our Knowledge*, TTBook, n.d. Oct. 2013 <http://ttbook.org/book/transcript/transcript-james-orbinski-his-time-doctors-without-borders>.

[304] Orbinski, "Transcript."

[305] Orbinski, "Transcript."

[306] Bernie S. Siegel, *Love, Medicine and Miracles* (New York: HarperCollins, 1986), 173.

[307] Halperin and Timberg, *Tinderbox*, 9.

[308] James Orbinski, "Nobel Lecture," *nobelprize.org*, Nobel Media AB, 10 Dec. 1999. Oct. 2013 <http://www.nobelprize.org/nobel_prizes/peace/laureates/1999/msf-lecture.html>.

[309] Bortolotti, Dan. *Hope In Hell: Inside the World of Doctors Without Borders* (Altona: Firefly Books, 2004), 136.

Chapter Seventeen Bibliography

Tom Crouch, *First Flight: The Wright Brothers and the Invention of the Airplane* (Washington, DC: National Park Service, U.S. Department of the Interior, 2002) 8-11.

Gary Ryan Blair, *Everything Counts: 52 Remarkable Ways to Inspire Excellence and Drive Results* (Hoboken, NJ: John Wiley & Sons, 2010) xvii. Robert M.

Sherfield and Patricia G. Moody, *Cornerstones for Community College Success*, 2nd ed. (Upper Saddle River, NJ: Prentice Hall, 2013). Sherfield, *The Everything Self Esteem Book*.

Sherfield and Moody, *Solving the Professional Development Puzzle: 101 Solutions for Career and Life Planning* (Upper Saddle River, NJ: Prentice Hall, 2008).

Sherfield, *Cornerstone: Discovering Your Potential, Learning Actively, and Living Well.* Concise 5th ed. (Upper Saddle River, NJ: Prentice Hall, 2007).

Robertsherfield.com. Las Vegas, NJ: Robert M. Sherfield, n.d. Oct. 2013 <http://www.robertsherfield.com/>.

Novogratz 15.

Orbinski, *Imperfect Offering* 64.

"Toward the end of poverty," *The Economist*, The Economist Newspaper Limited, 1 June 2013. Oct. 2013 <www.economist.com/news/leaders/21578665-nearly-1-billion-people-have-been-taken-out-extreme-poverty-20-years-world-should-aim>.

"Jon Berkeley." *Behance.net.* Adobe Systems, Inc., 2013. Oct. 2013 <http://www.behance.net/jonberkeley>.

Donna Hicks, *Dignity: Its Essential Role in Resolving Conflict* (Boston: Yale University, 2011).

Orbinski, *Imperfect Offering* 65.

Clayborne Carson, "American Civil Rights Movement," *Britannica.com.* Encyclopaedia Britannica, 2013. Oct. 2013 <http://www.britannica.com/EBchecked/topic/119368/American-civil-rights-movement>.

Taylor Branch, *Parting the Waters: America in the King Years 1954-63* (New York: Simon & Schuster, 1988).

Charles M. Payne, *I've Got the Light of Freedom: The Organizing Tradition and the Mississippi Freedom Struggle* (Berkeley, CA: University of California, 2007).

Martin Luther King, Jr., *The Autobiography of Martin Luther King, Jr.* (New York: Warner, 1998).

Jervis Anderson, *Bayard Rustin: Troubles I've Seen* (New York: HarperCollins, 1997).

Rachel Carson, *Silent Spring* (Boston: Houghton Mifflin, 1962).

Mohandas Karamchand (Mahatma) Gandhi, *Autobiography: The Story of My Experiments With Truth* (CreateSpace Independent Publishing Platform, 2012).

Charles J. Shields, *Mohandas K. Gandhi (OA) (Z) (Overcoming Adversity)* (New York: Chelsea House, 2001)

Gandhi, *All Men Are Brothers* (New York: Continuum, 1980).

Howard Gardner, *Creating Minds: An Anatomy of Creativity Seen Through the Lives of Freud, Einstein, Picasso, Stravinsky, Eliot, Graham, and Gandhi* (New York: Basic, 2011).

Mary King, *Mahatma Gandhi and Martin Luther King, Jr.: The Power of Nonviolent Action* (New York: United Nations Education, Scientific, and Cultural Organization, 1999).

Patricia Cronin Marcello, *Mohandas K. Gandhi: A Biography* (Westport, CT: Greenwood, 2006).

Thomas Clarkson, "An essay on the impolicy of the African slave trade," *Archive.org*. San Francisco: Internet Archive, 2008. Oct. 2013 <https://archive.org/details/essayonimpolicyo00clariala>.

Clarkson, *The History of the Rise, Progress, and Accomplishment of the Abolition of the African Slave-Trade, by the British Parliament*. 2 Vol. Frank Cass, 1808.

Clarkson, *History*.

Anne Moore Mueller, "Thomas Clarkson," *Quakers and Slavery Project*, Institute of Museum and Library Services, 2007. Oct. 2013 <http://trilogy.brynmawr.edu/speccoll/quakersandslavery/commentary/people/clarkson.php>.

William Wilberforce, *William Wilberforce: Greatest Works*. Alachua, FL: Bridge-Logos, 2007).

William Hague, *William Wilberforce: The Life of the Great Anti-Slave Trade Campaigner* (Orlando, FL: Harcourt, 2007).

Stephen Tomkins, *William Wilberforce: A Biography* (Grand Rapids, MI: Eerdmans, 2007).

Ellen Gibson Wilson, *Thomas Clarkson: A Biography* (New York: Palgrave Macmillan, 1990).

Earl Leslie Griggs, *Thomas Clarkson: The Friend of Slaves* (New York: Negro Universities, 1970).

Clarkson, *History*, Vol. 2.

Clarkson and Mary-Antoinette Smith, ed., *Thomas Clarkson and Ottobah Cugoano: Essays on the Slavery and Commerce of the Human Species* (Peterborough, Ontario: Broadview, 2010).

"Give your voice to the 2.5 billion people without access to a toilet," *Global Citizen*, The Global Poverty Project, 17 Dec. 2013. Dec. 2013 <http://www.globalcitizen.org/Content/Content.aspx?id=592eeaa7-8945-4d61-9128-e47abb06d317>.

"Global Hunger," *Bread.org*, Washington, D.C.: Bread for the World, n.d. Oct. 2013 <http://www.bread.org/hunger/global/>.

"Statistics: Worldwide," *Amfar.org*, AMFAR, The Foundation for AIDS Research. Oct. 2013. Oct. 2013 <www.amfar.org/about-hiv-and-aids/facts-and-stats/statistics—worldwide/>.

Kristof 237.

Mark Johnson, *Moral Imagination: Implications of Cognitive Science for Ethics* (Chicago: University of Chicago, 1993).

Gandhi and Louis Fischer, ed., *The Essential Gandhi: An Anthology of His Writings on His Life, Work, and Ideas* (New York: Vintage, 2002) 64.

Novogratz 145.

"Our Founder," *Congregation of Holy Cross*, Notre Dame, IN: United States Province of Priests and Brothers, 2013. Oct. 2013 <http://www.holycrossusa.org/spirituality/our-founder-blessed-basil-moreau-csc/>.

Gary MacEoin, *Father Moreau: Founder of Holy Cross* (Whitefish, MT: Literary Licensing, LLC, 2012).

"Janine Di Giovanni," *Janinedigiovanni.com*, Squarespace, n.d. Oct. 2013 <http://www.janinedigiovanni.com/>.

Janine di Giovanni, "What a Sad Little Empire Britain Has Become," *TheDailyBeast.com* The Daily Beast Company LLC., 22 Mar. 2013. Oct. 2013 <http://www.thedailybeast.com/articles/ 2013/03/22/what-a-sad-little-empire-britain-has-become.html>.

di Giovanni, "I Watched Iraq Fall," *TheDailyBeast.com*, The Daily Beast Company LLC, 17 Mar. 2013. Oct. 2013 <http://www.thedailybeast.com/articles/2013/03/17/i-watched-iraq-fall.html>.

di Giovanni, "Syria: When Nonviolent Revolutions Spin into Bloodshed," *Newsweek.com*, IBT Media Inc., 11 Mar. 2013. Oct. 2013 <http://www.newsweek.com/syria-when-nonviolent-revolutions-spin-bloodshed-62809>.

di Giovanni, "The World's Most Vulnerable Mayor," *TheDailyBeast.com* The Daily Beast Company LLC, 2 Mar. 2013. Oct. 2013 <http://www.thedailybeast.com/articles/2013/03/02/the-world-s-most-vulnerable-mayor.html>.

di Giovanni, "How France Got So Lazy," *TheDailyBeast.com*, The Daily Beast Company LLC, 22 Feb. 2013. Oct. 2013 <http://www.thedailybeast.com/articles/2013/02/22/how-france-got-so-lazy.html>.

di Giovanni, "Seven Days in Syria," *Granta.com*. Granta, Spring 2013. Oct. 2013 <http://www.granta.com/Archive/122/Seven-Days-in-Syria>.

di Giovanni, *Madness Visible: Kosovo* (New York: Knopf, 2003).

di Giovanni, *The Place at the End of the World: Essays from the Edge* (London: Bloomsbury, 2006).

di Giovanni, *Ghosts by Daylight: Love, War, and Redemption* (New York: Knopf, 2011).

"Janine di Giovanni: What I saw in the war," *TED: Ideas Worth Spreading*. TED Conferences, LLC, Jan. 2013. Oct. 2013 <http://www.ted.com/talks/janine_di_giovanni_what_i_saw_in_the_war.html>.

Hawkins, *A Small, Good Thing* 259.

"Jacqueline Novogratz: An Escape from Poverty," *TED: Ideas Worth Speading*, TED Conferences, LLC, Mar. 2009. Oct. 2013 <http://www.ted.com/talks/jacqueline_novogratz_on_an_escape_from_poverty.html>.

Bill Gates, Sr., and Mary Ann Mackin, *Showing Up for Life: Thoughts on the Gifts of a Lifetime* (New York: Broadway, 2009).

Amanda Ripley, *The Unthinkable: Who Survives When Disaster Strikes—and Why* (New York: Crown, 2008).

Banerjee and Duflo, *Poor Economics*.

Orbinski, "Transcript for James Orbinski on his Time with Doctors Without Borders," Interviewed by Jim Fleming, *To the Best of our Knowledge*, TTBook, n.d. Oct. 2013 <http://ttbook.org/book/transcript/transcript-james-orbinski-his-time-doctors-without-borders>.

Orbinski, *Imperfect Offering* xi.

Triage: Dr. James Orbinski's Humanitarian Dilemma, Dir. Patrick Reed (Docurama, 2009).

Orbinski, "Transcript."

Orbinski, "Transcript."

Albert Camus, *The Plague* (New York: Penguin, 2008).

J.R.R. Tolkien, *The Two Towers* (New York: Del Rey, 2012).

Bernie S. Siegel, *Love, Medicine and Miracles* (New York: HarperCollins, 1986) 173. "Bono."

David Schaffer, *People in the News: Bono* (Farmington Hills, MI: Lucent, 2003).

Timberg and Halperin 9.

James Orbinski, "Nobel Lecture," *nobelprize.org*, Nobel Media AB, 10 Dec. 1999. Oct. 2013 <http://www.nobelprize.org/nobel_prizes/peace/laureates/1999/msf-lecture.html>.

"Triage: Dr. James Orbinski's Humanitarian Dilemma," *DoctorsWithoutBorders.org*. Doctors Without Borders/Medecins Sans Frontieres, n.d. Oct. 2013 <http://www.doctorswithoutborders.org/aboutus/page.cfm?id=6002>.

Chapter Eighteen Endnotes

[309] Orbinski, *Imperfect Offering*, 34.

[310] Orbinski, *Imperfect Offering*, 35.

[311] Novogratz, *The Blue Sweater*, 183.

[312] "Albert Cairo: There are no scraps of men." *TED: Ideas worth spreading*. TED Conferences, LLC, Dec. 2011. Oct. 2013. <http://www.ted.com/talks/alberto_cairo_there_are_no_scraps_of_men.html>.

[313] Bornstein, *How to Change the World*, 47.

[314] Their stories and many others will be shared in InterviewGirl.com's *WWII Stories* project.

[315] Orbinski, *An Imperfect Offering*, 34.

[316] Yunus, *Banker to the Poor*, 70.

[317] Yunus, *Banker to the Poor*, 69.

[318] Bornstein, *How to Change the World*, 13.

[319] Bornstein, *How to Change the World*, 16.

[320] Bornstein, *How to Change the World*, 17.

[321] Bornstein, *How to Change the World*, 1-20.

[322] Bornstein, *How to Change the World*, 302-305.

[323] Bornstein, *How to Change the World*, 291.

[324] Michalko, *Cracking Creativity*, 212.

[325] Bill Kenower, "Yann Martel Interview," *YouTube.com*, YouTube. 13 May 2010. Oct. 2013 <http://www.youtube.com/watch?v=B29tigyBJIQ>.

[326] Maskalyk, James, *Six Months in Sudan*, 336.

Chapter Eighteen Bibliography

Ernesto Sirolli, *Ripples from the Zambezi: Passion, Entrepreneurship and the Rebirth of Local Economies* (Gabriola Island, BC, Canada: New Society, 1999).

"Ernesto Sirolli: Want to help someone? Shut up and listen!" TED: Ideas worth spreading. TED Conferences, LLC, Nov. 2012. Oct. 2013 <http://www.ted.com/talks/ernesto_sirolli_want_to_help_someone_shut_up_and_listen.html>.

Orbinski, *Imperfect Offering* 34.

Orbinski, *Imperfect Offering* 35.

Novogratz 183.

John W. Gardner, *On Leadership* (New York: Free, 1990).

Robert D. McFadden, "John W. Gardner, 89, Founder of Common Cause and Adviser to Presidents, Dies." *NYTimes.com*. The New York Times Company, 18 Feb. 2002. Oct 2013 <http://www.nytimes.com/2002/02/18/us/john-w-gardner-89-founder-of-common-cause-and-adviser-to-presidents-dies.html?pagewanted=all&src=pm>.

"Albert Cairo: There are no scraps of men." *TED: Ideas worth spreading*. TED Conferences, LLC, Dec. 2011. Oct. 2013. <http://www.ted.com/talks/alberto_cairo_there_are_no_scraps_of_men.html>.

"Honorary Planetary Citizen of the Month: Dr. Alberto Cairo, The Angel of Kabul." *Gccalliance.org*, Global Community Communications Alliance, n.d. Oct. 2013 <http://gccalliance.org/planetaryhonor/16>.

"Alberto Cairo." *Great Thoughts Treasury*. Alan Smolowe, 2013. Oct. 2013 <http://www.greatthoughtstreasury.com/author/alberto-cairo>.

John F. Burns, "A Foreign Face Beloved by Afghans of All Stripes," *NYTimes.com*, The New York Times Company, 2009. Oct. 2013 <http://www.nytimes.com/2008/12/25/world/asia/25afghan.html?_r=0>.

Landmine Monitor Report (New York: Human Rights Watch, n.d.).

Bornstein 47.

Drayton, *Leading*. Beverly Schwartz, *Rippling: How Social Entrepreneurs Spread Innovation Throughout the World* (San Francisco, CA: Jossey-Bass, 2012).

"Bill Drayton," *Social Entrepreneurship in the Age of Atrocities: Changing our World*, Zachary D. Kaufman, 2013. Oct. 2013 <http://www.socialentrepreneurship-book.com/contributors/bill-drayton/>.

Bill Drayton, "The World Needs More Social Entrepreneurs" *Harvard Business Review*. Harvard Business School Publishing, 30 Mar. 2010. Oct. 2013 <http://blogs.hbr.org/2010/03/the-world-needs-more-social-entrepreneurs/>.

Gregory M. Lamb, "Bill Drayton sees a world where 'everyone is a change maker,'" *CSMonitor.com*, The Christian Science Monitor, 16 May 2011. Oct. 2013 <http://www.csmonitor.com/World/Making-a-difference/Change-Agent/2011/0516/Bill-Drayton-sees-a-world-where-everyone-is-a-changemaker>.

Shapiro. Simon Mainwaring, *We First: How Brands and Consumers Use Social Media to Build a Better World* (New York: Palgrave-Macmillan, 2011).

Pankaj Ghemawat, *Redefining Global Strategy: Crossing Borders in a World Where Differences Still Matter* (Boston, MA: Harvard Business, 2007).

Bornstein and Susan Davis, *Social Entrepreneurship: What Everyone Needs to Know* (New York: Oxford University, 2010).

Yunus, *Banker to the Poor.*

Yunus, *Creating a World.*

Yunus. *Building Social Business.*

Kevin Danaher, *Fifty Years is Enough: The Case Against the World Bank and the International Monetary Fund* (San Francisco, CA: Global Exchange, 1994).

Yunus and Aradhana Parmar, *South Asia: A Historical Narrative* (New York: Oxford University, 2003).

Patrick U. Petit, *Creating a New Civilization through Social Entrepreneurship* (Piscataway, NJ: Transaction, 2010).

Zebiba Shekhia, *Healing Bridges* (New York: Morgan James, 2008).

Mohammed Iqbal and Mohammed Yunus, eds., *Plant Response to Air Pollution* (Hoboken, NJ: Wiley, 1996).

Bornstein, *How to Change* 13-14, 16-17, 69, 291.

Yann Martel, "Conversation: *Life of Pi*," Interview by Ray Swarez, *PBS Newshour*, MacNeil/Lehrer Productions, 11 Nov. 2002. Web. Oct. 2013 <http://www.pbs.org/newshour/bb/entertainment/july-dec02/martel_11-11.html>.

"Interview with Yann Martel." *Goodreads.com.* Goodreads Inc., Feb. 2013. Oct. 2013 <https://www.goodreads.com/topic/show/1202294-interview-with-yann-martel>.

Bill Kenower, "Yann Martel Interview," *YouTube.com,* YouTube. 13 May 2010. Oct. 2013 <http://www.youtube.com/watch?v=B29tigyBJIQ>.

Martel, "'May Richard Parker be always at your side.'" *Theguardian.com*, Guardian News and Media Limited, 26 Nov. 2002. Oct. 2013 <http://www.theguardian.com/books/2002/nov/26/fiction>.

"Michael Michalko," *Creativitypost.com*, The Creativity Post, 2013. Oct. 2013 <http://www.creativitypost.com/authors/profile/33/mmichalko>.

Michalko, *Creative Thinkering* (Novato, CA: New World, 2011).

Michalko, *Cracking Creativity.*

Michalko, *Thinkertoys: A Handbook of Business Creativity* (Berkeley, CA: Ten Speed, 1991).

CreativeThinking.net. Michael Michalko, 2013. Oct. 2013 <http://creativethinking.net/WP01_Home.htm>.CH 18

Ernesto Sirolli, *Ripples from the Zambezi: Passion, Entrepreneurship and the Rebirth of Local Economies* (Gabriola Island, BC, Canada: New Society, 1999).

"Ernesto Sirolli: Want to help someone? Shut up and listen!" TED: Ideas worth spreading. TED Conferences, LLC, Nov. 2012. Oct. 2013 <http://www.ted.com/talks/ernesto_sirolli_want_to_help_someone_shut_up_and_listen.html>.

Orbinski, *Imperfect Offering* 34.

Orbinski, *Imperfect Offering* 35.

Novogratz 183.

John W. Gardner, *On Leadership* (New York: Free, 1990).

Robert D. McFadden, "John W. Gardner, 89, Founder of Common Cause and Adviser to Presidents, Dies." *NYTimes.com.* The New York Times Company, 18 Feb. 2002. Oct 2013 <http://www.nytimes.com/2002/02/18/us/john-w-gardner-89-founder-of-common-cause-and-adviser-to-presidents-dies.html?pagewanted=all&src=pm>.

"Albert Cairo: There are no scraps of men." *TED: Ideas worth spreading*. TED Conferences, LLC, Dec. 2011. Oct. 2013. <http://www.ted.com/talks/alberto_cairo_there_are_no_scraps_of_men.html>.

"Honorary Planetary Citizen of the Month: Dr. Alberto Cairo, The Angel of Kabul." *Gccalliance.org*, Global Community Communications Alliance, n.d. Oct. 2013 <http://gccalliance.org/planetaryhonor/16>.

"Alberto Cairo." *Great Thoughts Treasury*. Alan Smolowe, 2013. Oct. 2013 <http://www.greatthoughtstreasury.com/author/alberto-cairo>.

John F. Burns, "A Foreign Face Beloved by Afghans of All Stripes," *NYTimes.com*, The New York Times Company, 2009. Oct. 2013 <http://www.nytimes.com/2008/12/25/world/asia/25afghan.html?_r=0>.

Landmine Monitor Report (New York: Human Rights Watch, n.d.).

Bornstein 47.

Drayton, *Leading*.

Beverly Schwartz, *Rippling: How Social Entrepreneurs Spread Innovation Throughout the World* (San Francisco, CA: Jossey-Bass, 2012).

"Bill Drayton," *Social Entrepreneurship in the Age of Atrocities: Changing our World*, Zachary D. Kaufman, 2013. Oct. 2013 <http://www.socialentrepreneurship-book.com/contributors/bill-drayton/>.

Bill Drayton, "The World Needs More Social Entrepreneurs" *Harvard Business Review*. Harvard Business School Publishing, 30 Mar. 2010. Oct. 2013 <http://blogs.hbr.org/2010/03/the-world-needs-more-social-entrepreneurs/>.

Gregory M. Lamb, "Bill Drayton sees a world where 'everyone is a changemaker,'" *CSMonitor.com*, The Christian Science Monitor,16 May 2011. Oct. 2013 <http://www.csmonitor.com/World/Making-a-difference/Change-Agent/2011/0516/Bill-Drayton-sees-a-world-where-everyone-is-a-changemaker>

Shapiro.

Simon Mainwaring, *We First: How Brands and Consumers Use Social Media to Build a Better World* (New York: Palgrave-Macmillan, 2011).

Pankaj Ghemawat, *Redefining Global Strategy: Crossing Borders in a World Where Differences Still Matter* (Boston, MA: Harvard Business, 2007).

Bornstein and Susan Davis, *Social Entrepreneurship: What Everyone Needs to Know* (New York: Oxford University, 2010).

Yunus, *Banker to the Poor*.

Yunus, *Creating a World*.

Yunus. *Building Social Business*.

Kevin Danaher, *Fifty Years is Enough: The Case Against the World Bank and the International Monetary Fund* (San Francisco, CA: Global Exchange, 1994).

Yunus and Aradhana Parmar, *South Asia: A Historical Narrative* (New York: Oxford University, 2003).

Patrick U. Petit, *Creating a New Civilization through Social Entrepreneurship* (Piscataway, NJ: Transaction, 2010).

Zebiba Shekhia, *Healing Bridges* (New York: Morgan James, 2008).

Mohammed Iqbal and Mohammed Yunus, eds., *Plant Response to Air Pollution* (Hoboken, NJ: Wiley, 1996). Bornstein, *How to Change* 13-14, 16-17, 69, 291.

Yann Martel, "Conversation: *Life of Pi,*" Interview by Ray Swarez, *PBS Newshour*, MacNeil/Lehrer Productions, 11 Nov. 2002. Web. Oct. 2013 <http://www.pbs.org/newshour/bb/entertainment/july-dec02/martel_11-11.html>.

"Interview with Yann Martel." *Goodreads.com.* Goodreads Inc., Feb. 2013. Oct. 2013 <https://www.goodreads.com/topic/show/1202294-interview-with-yann-martel>.

Bill Kenower, "Yann Martel Interview," *YouTube.com,* YouTube. 13 May 2010. Oct. 2013 <http://www.youtube.com/watch?v=B29tigyBJIQ>.

Martel, "'May Richard Parker be always at your side.'" *Theguardian.com*, Guardian News and Media Limited, 26 Nov. 2002. Oct. 2013 <http://www.theguardian.com/books/2002/nov/26/fiction>.

"Michael Michalko," *Creativitypost.com*, The Creativity Post, 2013. Oct. 2013 <http://www.creativitypost.com/authors/profile/33/mmichalko>.

Michalko, *Creative Thinkering* (Novato, CA: New World, 2011).

Michalko, *Cracking Creativity.*

Michalko, *Thinkertoys: A Handbook of Business Creativity* (Berkeley, CA: Ten Speed, 1991).

CreativeThinking.net. Michael Michalko, 2013. Oct. 2013<http://creativethinking.net/WP01_Home.htm>.

Maskalyk, James. *Six months in Sudan: a young doctor in a war-torn village.* (New York: Spiegel & Grau, 2009).

Chapter Nineteen Endnotes

[326] "What is Human Trafficking?" United Nations Office on Drugs and Crime. http://www.unodc.org/unodc/en/human-trafficking/what-is-human-trafficking.html (accessed June 19, 2013).

[327] "Human Trafficking Fact Sheet | Proposition 35: The CASE Act PASSED!." Vote Yes On Prop 35: The CASE Act. http://www.caseact.org/learn/humantrafficking/ (accessed June 19, 2013).

[328] "What Is Human Trafficking?"

[329] Ibid.

[330] "allAfrica.com: Southern Africa: Human Trafficking." allAfrica.com: Home. http://allafrica.com/stories/201304100442.html (accessed June 19, 2013).

[331] United Nations Office on Drugs and Crime, Human Trafficking: an overview (Vienna: United Nations, 2008).

[332] Alexis, A. Aronowitz, *Human Trafficking, Human Misery: The Global Trade in Human Beings* (Westport, CT: Praeger, 2009), 11-12.

[333] Department of Children services; ANPPCAN 2005.

[334] United Nations Office on Drugs and Crime, Human Trafficking: an overview (Vienna: United Nations, 2008).

[335] *Situation of TIP in Uganda report to the National steering committee 2008*

[336] "Ugandan girl tells of living horror of Asian sex-slavery." Safe World for Women. http://www.asafeworldforwomen.org/trafficking/ht-africa/2144-ugandan-girl-tells-of-living-horror-of-asian-sex-slavery.html (accessed June 19, 2013).

[337]"Human Trafficking Law Project." The University of Michigan Law School. http://www.law.umich. edu/clinical/humantraffickingclinicalprogram/humantraffickingproject/Pages/default.aspx (accessed June 19, 2013).

[338] "Search." United Nations Office on Drugs and Crime. http://www.unodc.org/cld/search.jspx? (Accessed June 19, 2013).

[339] "International Project Methodology & Global Impact – Not For Sale: End Human Trafficking and Slavery." Not For Sale: End Human Trafficking and Slavery. http://www.notforsalecampaign. org/global-initiatives/international-projects-methodology/ (accessed June 19, 2013).

[340] Ibid.

[341] "The 100 Most Influential People in the World," *Time Magazine*, 6 May 2013.

[342] Nolen, *Stories of Aids in Africa*, 28.

[343] "11 Facts About Global Poverty | Do Something." Do Something | Largest organization for teens and social cause. http://www.dosomething.org/tipsandtools/11-facts-about-global-poverty (accessed June 19, 2013).

[344] "Maternal and Child Health | ONE." ONE.org | Join the fight against extreme poverty. http:// www.one.org/c/international/issue/951/ (accessed June 19, 2013).

[345] Ibid.

[346] "Agriculture | ONE." ONE.org | Join the fight against extreme poverty. http://www.one.org/c/ international/ issue/1115/ (accessed June 19, 2013).

[347] "Education | ONE." ONE.org | Join the fight against extreme poverty. http://www.one.org/c/ international/ issue/948/ (accessed June 19, 2013).

[348] "Debt Cancellation | ONE." ONE.org | Join the fight against extreme poverty. http://www.one. org/c/international/issue/1116/ (accessed June 19, 2013).

[349] "ONE Millennium Development Goals." ONE.org | Join the fight against extreme poverty. http://www.one.org/international/mdg/ (accessed June 19, 2013).

[350] Ibid.

[351] Ibid.

[352] Category. "Charitable Giving—Best Charities for Combating Global Poverty." Nonprofit: Starting Up, Marketing, Fundraising, Volunteers, Careers. http://nonprofit.about.com/od/fordonors/ tp/globalpovertygiving.htm (accessed June 19, 2013).

[353] "What Is Social Entrepreneurship?" Schwab Foundation. www.schwabfound.org/content/ what-social-entrepreneur (accessed June 19, 2013).

[354] Ibid.

[355] "Forbes' List of the Top 30 Social Entrepreneurs—Forbes." Information for the World's Business Leaders—Forbes.com. http://www.forbes.com/sites/helencoster/2011/11/30/forbes-list-of-the-top-30-social-entrepreneurs/ (accessed June 19, 2013).

[356] "What Is HIV/AIDS?" Welcome to AIDS.gov. http://aids.gov/hiv-aids-basics/hiv-aids-101/what-is-hiv-aids/ (accessed June 19, 2013).

[357] Ibid.

[358] "Opportunistic Infections." Welcome to AIDS.gov. http://aids.gov/hiv-aids-basics/staying-healthy-with-hiv-aids/potential-related-health-problems/opportunistic-infections/ (accessed June 19, 2013).

[359] "What is HIV/AIDS?"

[360] "Signs & Symptoms." Welcome to AIDS.gov. http://aids.gov/hiv-aids-basics/hiv-aids-101/signs-

and-symptoms/index.html (accessed June 19, 2013).

361 "How Do You Get HIV or AIDS?" Welcome to AIDS.gov. http://aids.gov/hiv-aids-basics/hiv-aids-101/how-you-get-hiv-aids/index.html (accessed June 19, 2013).

362 "How Do You Get HIV or AIDS?" Welcome to AIDS.gov. http://aids.gov/hiv-aids-basics/hiv-aids-101/how-you-get-hiv-aids/index.html (accessed June 19, 2013).

363 George Ellison, Melissa Parker, Catherine Campbell. *Learning from HIV and AIDS.*

364 Fru Doh, Emmanuel. *Stereotyping Africa: Surprising Answers to Surprising Questions.*

365 Orbinski, *An Imperfect Offering*, 352.

366 Joint United Nations Programme on HIV/AIDS (UNAIDS), World AIDS Day Report, (Geneva: United Nations, 2011).

367 "HIV/AIDS in Africa." HIV/AIDS in Africa. http://www.africaalive.org/ (accessed June 19, 2013).

368 "HIV and AIDS in Africa." HIV & AIDS Information from AVERT.org. http://www.avert.org/hiv-aids-africa.htm#contentTable1 (accessed June 19, 2013).

369 "Children orphaned by HIV and AIDS." HIV & AIDS Information from AVERT.org. http://www.avert.org/aids-orphans.htm#contentTable0 (accessed June 19, 2013).

370 Ibid.

371 Nolen, *28 Stories of Aids in Africa*, 28-33.

372 Nolen, *28 Stories of Aids in Africa*, 246.

373 Nolen, *28 Stories of Aids in Africa*, 248.

374 Epstein, *The Invisible Cure.*

375 "Avert HIV-AIDS."

376 Shah, Anup. *AIDS in Africa.* http://www.globalissues.org/article/90/aids-in-africa#ActionbyotherAfricanLeaders

377 Nolen, *28 Stories of Aids in Africa*, 361.

Chapter Nineteen Bibliography

"United Nations Office on Drugs and Crime." *What is Human Trafficking?* 19 June 2013. <http://www.unodc.org/unodc/en/human-trafficking/what-is-human-trafficking.html>.

"What is Human Trafficking?" *Human Trafficking Fact Sheet.* N.p., n.d. Web. 19 June 2013. <http://www.caseact.org/learn/humantrafficking/>. PDF file

"What Is Human Trafficking?" *Ibid.*

"Southern Africa: Human Trafficking." *allAfrica.com.* N.p., n.d. Web. 19 June 2013. <http://allafrica.com/stories/201304100442.html>.

Quantifying human trafficking, its impact and the responses to it 024 workshop: the Vienna Forum to Fight Human Trafficking, 13-15 February 2008, Austria Center Vienna: background paper. Vienna, Austria: Anti-Human Trafficking Unit, United Nations Office on Drugs and Crime, 2008.

Aronowitz, Alexis A. "Delete." *Human trafficking, human misery the global trade in human beings*. (Westport, Conn.: Praeger, 2009). 11-12.

"Department of Child and Services." *ANPPCAN*. 2005. N.p., n.d. 19 June 2013. <http://www.anppcan.org/files/File/08_ChildLabour.pdf>.

Quantifying human trafficking, its impact and the responses to it 024 workshop: the Vienna Forum to Fight Human Trafficking, 13-15 February 2008, Austria Center Vienna: background paper. Vienna, Austria: Anti-Human Trafficking Unit, United Nations Office on Drugs and Crime, 2008. PDF file

"Situation of TIP in Uganda report to the National steering committee." 2008. N.p., n.d. 19 June 2013. PDF file

"Ugandan girl tells of living horror of Asian sex-slavery." *Safe World for Women*. N.p., n.d. 19 June 2013. <http://www.asafeworldforwomen.org/trafficking/ht-africa/2144-ugandan-girl-tells-of-living-horror-of-asian-sex-slavery.html>.

"Human Trafficking Law Project." *Human Trafficking Law Project*. The University Michigan Law School., n.d.2013. <http://www.law.umich.edu/clinical/humantraffickingclinicalprogram/humantraffickingproject/Pages/default.aspx>.

"United Nations Office on Drugs and Crime." *Search*. N.p., n.d. 19 June 2013. <http://www.unodc.org/cld/search.jspx?>.

"International Project Methodology & Global Impact." *International Project Methodology & Global Impact –Not For Sale: End Human Trafficking and Slavery*. NotForSaleCampaign.org, n.d. 19 June 2013. <http://www.notforsalecampaign.org/global-initiatives/international-projects-methodology/>.

Ibid.

"The 100 Most Influential People in the World." *Time Magazine*. Time Magazine. n.d. 6 May 2013.

Nolen, *28: stories of AIDS in Africa*.

"11 Facts About Global Poverty." *DoSomething.org| Largest organization for teens and social cause*. N.p., n.d. 19 June 2013. <http://www.dosomething.org/tipsandtools/11-facts-about-global-poverty>.

"The Issues Affecting Global Poverty: Maternal & Child Health." *ONE*. N.p., n.d. 19 June 2013. <http://www.one.org/c/international/issue/951/>.

"The Issues Affecting Global Poverty: Agriculture." *ONE*. N.p., n.d. 19 June 2013. <http://www.one.org/c/international/issue/1115/>.

"Education | One." *ONE.org | Join the fight against extreme poverty*. N.p., n.d.19 June 2013. <http://www.one.org/c/international/issue/948>.

"The Issues Affecting Global Poverty: Debt Cancellation." *ONE*. N.p., n.d. 19 June 2013. <http://www.one.org/c/international/issue/1116/>.

"ONE Millennium Development Goals." *ONE.org | Join the fight against extreme poverty*. N.p., n.d. 19 June 2013. <http://www.one.org/international/mdg/>.

Ibid.

Ibid.

Fritz, Joan. "Global Poverty and Charitable Giving—Best Charities for Combating Global Poverty." *About.com Nonprofit Charitable Orgs.* N.p., n.d. 19 June 2013. <http://nonprofit.about.com/od/fordonors/tp/ globalpovertygiving.htm>.

"What is a social entrepreneur?." *Home.* Schwab Foundation, n.d.19 June 2013. <http://www.schwabfound.org/ content/what-social-entrepreneur>.

Ibid.

Coster, Helen. "Forbes' List of the Top 30 Social Entrepreneurs." *Forbes.* Forbes Magazine, 30 Nov. 2011. Web. June 2013. <http://www.forbes.com/sites/helencoster/2011/11/30/forbes-list-of-the-top-30-social-entrepreneurs/>.

"What Is HIV/AIDS?." *Welcome to AIDS.gov.* N.p., n.d. 19 June 2013. <http://aids.gov/hiv-aids-basics/hiv-aids-101/ what-is-hiv-aids/>.

Ibid.

"Opportunistic Infections." *Welcome to AIDS.gov.* N.p., n.d. Web. 19 June 2013. <http://aids.gov/hiv-aids-basics/ staying-healthy-with-hiv-aids/potential-related-health-problems/opportunistic-infections/>.

"What is HIV/AIDS?"

"Signs & Symptoms." *Welcome to AIDS.gov.* N.p., n.d. Web. 19 June 2013. <http://aids.gov/hiv-aids-basics/hiv-aids-101/signs-and-symptoms/index.html>.

"How Do You Get HIV or AIDS?" *Welcome to AIDS.gov.* N.p., n.d. Web. 19 June 2013. <http://aids.gov/hiv-aids-basics/hiv-aids-101/how-you-get-hiv-aids/index.html>.

"How Do You Get HIV or AIDS?" *Welcome to AIDS.gov.* N.p., n.d. Web. 19 June 2013. <http://aids.gov/hiv-aids-basics/hiv-aids-101/how-you-get-hiv-aids/index.html>.

Ellison, George, Melissa Parker, and Catherine Campbell. *Learning from HIV/AIDS.* (Cambridge: Cambridge University Press, 2003).

Doh, Emmanuel Fru. *Stereotyping Africa surprising answers to surprising questions.* (Mankon, Bamenda, Cameroon: Langaa Research & Pub. CIG, 2009).

Orbinski, *An imperfect offering,* 352.

(UNAIDS) World AIDS day report 2011. (Geneva: UNAIDS, 2011).

"HIV/AIDS in Africa." *HIV/AIDS in Africa.* N.p., n.d. 19 June 2013. <http://www.africaalive.org/>.

"HIV and AIDS in Africa." *HIV and AIDS information and resources.* Avert.org, n.d. 19 June 2013. <http://www. avert.org/hiv-aids-africa.htm#contentTable1>.

"Children Orphaned by HIV and AIDS." *HIV and AIDS information and resources.* Avert.org, n.d. 19 June 2013. <http://www.avert.org/aids-orphans.htm#contentTable0>.

Ibid.

Nolen, *28: stories of AIDS in Africa.*

Nolen, *28: stories of AIDS in Africa* .

Nolen, *28: stories of AIDS in Africa* .

Epstein, *The invisible cure.*

"Avert HIV-AIDS."

Shah, Anup. "AIDS in Africa."—*Global Issues.* N.p., n.d. 19 June 2013. <http://www.globalissues.org/article/90/ aids-in-africa#ActionbyotherAfricanLeaders>.

Nolen, *28: stories of AIDS in Africa* .

Bibliography

"Mark Zuckerberg." *Mark Zuckerberg News*. New York Times, 12 Sept. 2012. Web. Jan. 2013. <http://topics.nytimes.com/topics/reference/timestopics/people/z/mark_e_zuckerberg/index.html>.

—-. "'May Richard Parker be always at your side.'" Theguardian.com. Guardian News and Media Limited, 26 Nov. 2002. Web. Oct. 2013 <http://www.theguardian.com/books/2002/nov/26/fiction>.

—-. "Global Development's Winning Goals." Project Syndicate. Project Syndicate, 27 Aug. 2013. Web. Oct. 2013 <http://www.project-syndicate.org/commentary/ensuring-the-success-of-the-un-s-sustainable-development-goals-by-jeffrey-d—sachs>.

—-. "How France Got So Lazy." TheDailyBeast.com. The Daily Beast Company LLC, 22 Feb. 2013. Web. Oct. 2013 <http://www.thedailybeast.com/articles/2013/02/22/how-france-got-so-lazy.html>.

—-. "How to Do It Better." The Economist. The Economist Newspaper Limited, 6 Aug. 2007. Web. Oct. 2013 <http://www.economist.com/node/ 14164449?zid=295&ah=0bca37 4e65f2354d553956ea65f756e0>.

—-. "I Watched Iraq Fall." TheDailyBeast.com. The Daily Beast Company LLC, 17 Mar. 2013. Web. Oct. 2013 <http://www.thedailybeast.com/articles/2013/03/17/i-watched-iraq-fall.html>.

—-. "Lincoln Tells a Story." Opinionator. The New York Times Company, 27 Jan. 2012. Web. Oct. 2013 <opinionator.blogs.nytimes.com/2012/01/27/lincoln-tells-a-story/?_r=0>.

—-. "Nobel Lecture." Nobelprize.org. Nobel Media AB, 10 Dec. 1999. Web. Oct. 2013 <http://www.nobelprize.org/nobel_prizes/peace/laureates/1999/msf-lecture.html>.

—-. "Poor Economics: A Radical Rethinking of the Way to Fight Global Poverty." PoorEconomics.com. Poor Economics, 2011. Web. Oct. 2013 <http://pooreconomics.com/about-book>.

—-. "Rabbi Dov Greenberg's Articles." Arutz Sheva. IsraelNationalNews.com, n.d. Web. Oct. 2013 <http://www.israelnationalnews.com/Articles/Author.aspx/202>.

—-. "Seven Days in Syria." Granta.com. Granta, Spring 2013. Web. Oct. 2013 <http://www.granta.com/Archive/122/Seven-Days-in-Syria>.

—-. "Syria: When Nonviolent Revolutions Spin into Bloodshed." Newsweek.com. IBT Media Inc., 11 Mar. 2013. Web. Oct. 2013<http://www.newsweek.com/syria-when-nonviolent-revolutions-spin-bloodshed-62809>.

—-. "The Whale in a Tank." Opinionator. The New York Times Company, 5 Dec. 2012. Web. Oct. 2013 <opinionator.blogs.nytimes.com/2012/12/05/the-whale-in-a-tank/?_r=0>.

—-. "The World Needs More Social Entrepreneurs." Harvard Business Review. Harvard Business School, 30 Mar. 2010. Web. Oct. 2013 <http://blogs.hbr.org/2010/03/the-world-needs-more-social-entrepreneurs/>.

—-. "The World's Most Vulnerable Mayor." TheDailyBeast.com. The Daily Beast Company LLC, 2 Mar. 2013. Web. Oct. 2013 <http://www.thedailybeast.com/articles/2013/03/02/the-world-s-most-vulnerable-mayor.html>.

—-. "Today, around 21,000 children died around the world." Global Issues. 24 Sept. 2011. Web. Oct. 2013 < www.globalissues.org/article/715/today-21000-children-died-around-the-world>.

—-. "Transcript for James Orbinski on his Time with Doctors Without Borders." Interviewed by Jim Fleming. To the Best of our Knowledge. TTBook, n.d. Web. Oct. 2013 <http://ttbook.org/ book/transcript/transcript-james-orbinski-his-time-doctors-without-borders>.

—-. "Unifying the Universal and Particular Approaches." Lubavitch.com, n.d. Web. Oct. 2013. Video. <lubavitch.com/video/2030515/Unifying-the-Universal-and-Particular-Approaches-Rabbi-Dov-Greenberg.html>.

—-. "Welcome to Jack Harich's Personal Page." Thwink.org, Thwink.org. 2009. Web. Oct. 2013 <http://thwink.org/personal/>.

—-. "When Humility and Audacity Go Hand in Hand." Interviewed by Adam Bryant. Business Day. The New York Times Company, 29 Sept. 2012. Web. Oct. 2013 <http://www.nytimes.com/2012/09/30/business/jacqueline-novogratz-of-acumen-fund-on-pairs-of-values.html?_r=0>.

—-. 21 Great Ways to Manage Your Time and Double Your Productivity. Solana Beach, CA: Brian Tracy International, 2008. CD.

—-. A Small, Good Thing. New York: W.W. Norton, 2000. Print.

—-. An Unfinished History of the World. New York: Papermac, 1995. Print.

—-. Autobiography: The Story of My Experiments With Truth. CreateSpace Independent Publishing Platform, 2012. Print.

—-. Building Social Business: The New Kind of Capitalism that Serves Humanity's Most Pressing Needs. New York: PublicAffairs, 2010. Print.

—-. Comfort in Hardship. Philadelphia, PA: Pauline, 2011. Print.

—-. Common Wealth: Economics for a Crowded Planet. New York: Penguin, 2009. Print.

—-. Creative Thinkering. Novato, CA: New World, 2011. Print.

—-. Development as Freedom. New York: Knopf, 1999. Print.

—-. Discovery of the Child. New York: Ballantine, 1986. Print.

—-. Einstein on Humanism. New York: Carol, 1993. Print.

—-. God Is Love: Deus Caritas Est. San Francisco: St. Ignatius, 2006. Print.

—-. Ideas And Opinions. New York: Broadway, 1995. Print.

—-. Introduction to Aristotle. New York: Modern Library, 1992. Print.

—-. Jesus of Nazareth: Holy Week: From the Entrance into Jerusalem to the Resurrection. San Francisco: St. Ignatius, 2011. Print.

—-. Jesus of Nazareth: The Infancy Narratives. New York: Image, 2012. Print.

—-. KofiAnnanFoundation.org. Kofi Annan Foundation, 2013. Web. Oct. 2013. <http://kofiannanfoundation.org/>.

—-. Learned Optimism: How to Change Your Mind and Your Life. New York: Vintage, 2006. Print.

—-. Madness Visible: Kosovo. New York: Knopf, 2003. Print.

—-. Mind and Body: Psychology Of Emotion And Stress. New York: W. W. Norton, 1984. Print.

—-. Mysteries of the Mind. Washington, DC: National Geographic, 2000. Print.

—-. No Excuses: The Power of Self-Discipline. New York: Vanguard, 2010. Print.

—-. No Greater Love. Novato, CA: New World Library, 2002. Print.

—-. Persuasive Technology: Using Computers to Change What We Think and Do. San Francisco, CA: Morgan Kaufmann, 2003. Print.

—-. Politics. Mineola, NY: Dover Thrift, 2000. Print.

—-. Rhetoric. Staley Frost, 2013. Print.

—-. Saved in Hope: Spe Salvi. San Francisco: St. Ignatius, 2008. Print.

—-. Seeking the Heart of God: Reflections on Prayer. New York: HarperOne, 1993. Print.

—-. Solving the Professional Development Puzzle: 101 Solutions for Career and Life Planning. Upper Saddle River, NJ: Prentice Hall, 2008. Print.

—-. Swords and Ploughshares: Bringing Peace to the 21st Century. San Diego: Phoenix, 2008. Print.

—-. Take Charge of Your Life. Wheeling, IL: Nightingale-Conant, 1991. CD.

—-. The Checklist Manifesto: How to Get Things Right. New York: Metropolitan, 2009. Print.

—-. The Day That Turns Your Life Around. Wheeling, IL: Nightingale-Conant, 2003. CD

—-. The Dueling Loops of the Political Powerplace: Why Progressives Are Stymied and How They Can Find Their Way Again. Clarkston, GA: Thwink.org, 2007. Print.

—-. The End of Poverty. New York: Penguin, 2005. Print.

—-. The Everything Self Esteem Book: Boost Your Confidence, Achieve Inner Strength, and Learn to Love Yourself. Avon, MA: F&W, 2004. Print.

—-. The Five Major Pieces to the Life Puzzle. Sydney, Australia: Angus & Robertson, 1991. Print.

—-. The History of the Rise, Progress, and Accomplishment of the Abolition of the African Slave-Trade, by the British Parliament. 2 Vol. Frank Cass, 1808. Print.

—-. The Montessori Method. Provo, UT: Renaissance Classics, 2012. Print.

—-. The Place at the End of the World: Essays from the Edge. London: Bloomsbury, 2006. Print.

—-. The Price of Civilization: Reawakening American Virtue and Prosperity. New York: Random, 2012.

—-. The Psychology of Achievement. New York: Simon & Schuster Audio, 2002. CD.

—-. The Purpose of the Past: Reflections on the Uses of History. New York: Penguin, 2009. Print.

—-. The Republic. New York: Simon & Brown, 2012. Print.

—-. The River: A Journey to the Source of HIV and AIDS. Boston: Little, Brown, 1999. Print.

—-. The Story of a Soul: The Autobiography of The Little Flower. Charlotte, NC: Saint Benedict, 2010. Print.

—-. The Symposium. New York: Penguin Classics, 2003. Print.

—-. The Virgin of Flames. New York: Penguin, 2007. Print.

—-. The Virtues. Huntington, IN: Our Sunday Visitor, 2010. Print.

—-. The Way to Christ. New York: HarperCollins, 1994. Print.

—-. The Will To Believe and Other Essays In Popular Philosophy, and Human Immortality. Mineola, NY: Dover, 1956. Print.

—-. Think Smart: A Neuroscientist's Prescription for Improving Your Brain's Performance. New York: Riverhead, 2009. Print.

—-. Thinkertoys: A Handbook of Business Creativity. Berkeley, CA: Ten Speed, 1991. Print.

—-. TinyHabits.com. BJ Fogg, 2013. Web. Oct. 2013 <http://tinyhabits.com/>.

—-. What a Sad Little Empire Britain Has Become." TheDailyBeast.com. The Daily Beast Company LLC, 22 Mar. 2013. Web. Oct. 2013 <http://www.thedailybeast.com/ articles/ 2013/03/22/what-a-sad-little-empire-britain-has-become.html>.

—-. Where There Is Love, There Is God: A Path to Closer Union with God and Greater Love for Others. New York: Doubleday Religion, 2010. Print.

"150 Basic AIDS Facts—Global AIDS DAY." Global AIDS Day. World Storehouse, 2007. Web. Oct. 2013 <www.globalaidsday.org/html/150_basic_aids_facts.html>.

"2008 Best Practices Database: Associacao Saude Crianca Renascer—an integral perspective of health." Best Practices Database in Improving The Living Environment. UN-Habitat, 2008. Web. Oct. 2013 <http://www.unhabitat.org/bestpractices/2008/ mainview04.asp?BPID=1914>.

"5 Minutes with Jacqueline Novogratz." PTPI Blog. People to People International, 26 Feb. 2013. Web. Oct. 2013 <http://blog.ptpi. org/2013/02/26/5-minutes-with-jacqueline-novogratz/>.

"A Little Story about Corporate Dominance and the Occupy Movement." Thwink.org. Thwink.org, 2012. Web. Oct. 2013 <http://www.thwink.org/sustain/articles/016/ CorporateDominanceLoop.htm>.

"A Road to Somewhere." The Economist. The Economist Newspaper Limited, 21 July 2011. Web. Oct. 2013 <www.economist.com/node/18989203>.

"A Wealth of Data." The Economist. The Economist Newspaper Limited, 29 July 2010. Web. Oct. 2013 <www.economist.com/node/16693283?zid=295&ah=0bca374e65f2354d5 53956ea65f756e0>.

"Abolition of the Slave Trade." Black Presence Exhibition/Rights. The National Archives (UK). Web. Oct. 2013 <http://www.nationalarchives.gov.uk/pathways/blackhistory/ rights/abolition.htm>.

"AIDS." Poverty.com. Poverty.com. n.d. Web. Oct. 2013. <http://www.poverty.com/aids. html>.

"Alberto Cairo." Great Thoughts Treasury. Alan Smolowe, 2013. Web. Oct. 2013 <http:// www.greatthoughtstreasury.com/author/alberto-cairo>.

"Alberto Cairo: There are no scraps of men." TED: Ideas worth spreading. TED Conferences, LLC, Dec. 2011. Web. Oct. 2013. <http://www.ted.com/talks/alberto_cairo_there_are_no_scraps_of_men.html>.

"Ancient Rome." The History Channel. A&E Television Networks, LLC, 2013. Web. Oct. 2013 <http://www.history.com/topics/ancient-rome>.

"Associacao Saude Crianca Renascer." Idealist. Action Without Borders/Idealist.org, 2013. Web. Oct. 2013 <www.idealist.org/view/org/bJwSW5GGbZMD/>.

"Atul Gawande." Harvard School of Public Health. Boston, MA: Harvard, 2013. Web. Oct. 2013 <http://www.hsph.harvard.edu/atul-gawande/>.

"Austin Michelle Cloyd." Cbsnews.com. CBS Interactive, 18 April 2007. Web. Oct. 2013. <http://www.cbsnews.com/2100-501803_162-2698537.html>.

"Austin Michelle Cloyd." Vt-memorial.org, 2007. Web. Oct. 2013 <http://www.vt-memorial.org/profiles/Cloyd.html>.

"Austin Michelle Cloyd." We Remember: Biographies. Virginia Polytechnic Institute and State University, 2007. Web. Oct. 2013 <http://www.remembrance.vt.edu/2007/biographies/austin_michelle_cloyd.html>.

"Bible study changing lives of prisoners in India." World. Christian Today, 17 April 2013. Web. Oct. 2013 <www.christiantoday.com/article/bible.study.changing.lives.of.prisoners.in.india/32161.htm>.

"Bill Drayton." Social Entrepreneurship in the Age of Atrocities: Changing our World. Zachary D. Kaufman, 2013. Web. Oct. 2013 <http://www.socialentrepreneurship-book.com/contributors/bill-drayton/>.

"Biography." laurenceprusak.com. n.p., n.d. Web. Oct. 2013 <http://www.laurenceprusak.com/bio.html>.

"Bishop Macram Gassis." BishopGassis.org, n.p., n.d. Web. Oct. 2013 <http://bishopgassis.org/about/bishop-macram-gassis.php>.

"Bono: The Good News on Poverty (Yes, There's Good News)." TED: Ideas Worth Spreading. TED Conferences, LLC, Mar. 2013. Web. Oct. 2013 <http://www.ted.com/talks/bono_the_good_news_on_poverty_yes_there_s_good_news.html>.

"Business Story Telling." elibrary. Al-Athaiba Muscat, Sultanate of Oman: The Research Council, n.d. Web. Oct. 2013 <https://el.trc.gov.om/htmlroot/K12/.../Business%20Story%20Telling.pdf>.

"Capability Poverty Measure (CPM)." WomenAid International. London: WomenAid International, 2000. Web. Oct. 2013 <http://www.womenaid.org/press/info/poverty/cpm.html>.

"Catholic Relief Services." Baltimore, MD: Catholic Relief Services, 2013. Web. Jan. 2013.

"Charlie 'Tremendous' Jones: The People You Meet and the Books You Read." YouTube.com. You Tube, n.d. Web. Oct. 2013 <http://www.youtube.com/watch?v=Cp—2fvuTRE>.

"Chimamanda Ngozi Adichie: The danger of a single story." TED: Ideas Worth Spreading. TED Conferences, LLC, Oct. 2009. Web. Oct. 2013 <http://www.ted.com/talks/chimamanda_adichie_the_danger_of_a_single_story.html>.

"Compassion International." MinistryWatch.com. Wall Watchers.org. 2013. Web. Oct. 2013 <http://www.ministrywatch.com/profile/compassion-international.aspx>.

"Contributing Authors." The Code. John Spencer Ellis, 2013. Web. Oct. 2013 <http://www.thecodeebook.com/contributors.html>.

"Democracy in Action: Ghana's 2008 Elections." Cartercenter.org. The Carter Center, 2008. Web. Oct. 2013. Video. <http://www.cartercenter.org/news/multimedia/PeacePrograms/DemocracyinActionGhanas2008Elections.html>.

"Dr. Vera Cordeiro." Ashoka Innovators for the Public. Ashoka. n.d. Web. Oct. 2013 <https://www.ashoka.org/Vera_Cordeiro>.

"Ernesto Sirolli: Want to help someone? Shut up and listen!" TED: Ideas worth spreading. TED Conferences, LLC, Nov. 2012. Web. Oct. 2013 <http://www.ted.com/talks/ernesto_sirolli_want_to_help_someone_shut_up_and_listen.html >.

"Esther Duflo." Innovations for Poverty Action, 2011. Web, Oct. 2013 <http://www.poverty-action.org/node/148>.

"Esther Duflo." J-PAL: Translating Research into Action. Massachusetts Institute of Technology, 2013. Web. Oct. 2013 <http://www.povertyactionlab.org/duflo>.

"Esther Duflo: Papers." MIT Economics. Massachusetts Institute of Technology Department of Economics, 2013. Web. Oct. 2013 <http://economics.mit.edu/faculty/eduflo/papers>.

"Famous People Who Found Success Despite Failures." Getbusylivingblog.com. Get Busy Living, 2013. Web. Oct. 2013 <http://getbusylivingblog.com/famous-people-who-found-success-despite-failures/>.

"Finding and Resolving the Root Causes of the Sustainability Problem." Thwink.org, Thwink.org, 2012. Web. Oct. 2013 <http://www.thwink.org/>.

"Finding Forrester (2000)." rottentomatoes.com. Fixter, Inc. n.d. Web. Oct. 2013 <http://www.rottentomatoes.com/m/finding_forrester/>.

"Former Secretary-General: Kofi Annan." UN.org. United Nations, 2012. Web. Oct. 2013. <http://www.un.org/sg/formersg/annan.shtml>.

"George Lucas – Biography." Biography.com. A&E Television Networks LLC, 1996-2013. Web. Oct. 2013 <www.biography.com/people/george-lucas-9388168>.

"Give your voice to the 2.5 billion people without access to a toilet." Global Citizen. The Global Poverty Project, 17 Dec. 2013. Web. Dec. 2013 <http://www.globalcitizen.org/ Content/Content.aspx?id=592eeaa7-8945-4d61-9128-e47abb06d317>.

"Global Hunger." Bread.org. Washington, D.C.: Bread for the World, n.d. Web. Oct. 2013 <http://www.bread.org/hunger/global/>.

"Goal 7: Ensure Environmental Sustainability." We Can End Poverty. United Nations, 2013. Web. Oct. 2013 <www.un.org/millenniumgoals/environ.shtml>.

"Harry Potter." The New York Times. New York: The New York Times Company, 18 July 2011. Web. Jan. 2013.

"History of Hinduism." All About Religion. Allaboutreligion.org, 2002-2013. Web. Jan. 2013.

"HIV & AIDS Information from AVERT.org." AVERT.org. West Sussex, England (UK), 2013. Web. Jan. 2013.

"HIV and AIDS Health Center." WebMD.com. WebMD, LLC. Web. Oct. 2013 <http://www.webmd.com/hiv-aids/guide/sexual-health-aids>.

"HIV/AIDS in Africa." AfricaAlive.org. Africa Alive. Web. Oct. 2013. <http://www.africaalive.org/>.

"Honorary Planetary Citizen of the Month: Dr. Alberto Cairo, The Angel of Kabul." Gccalliance.org. Global Community Communications Alliance, n.d. Web. Oct. 2013 <http://gccalliance.org/planetaryhonor/16>.

"How We Found Ourselves in the World of Storytelling." Storytelling: Passport to the 21st Century. Stephen Denning, 2001. Web. Oct. 2013. <http://www.creatingthe21stcentury.org/Intro4a-How-Larry&JSB.html>.

"Human Development Reports." UNDP.org. United Nations Development Programme, 2013. Web. Oct. 2013 <http://hdr.undp.org/en/reports/global/hdr2013/>.

"Hunger and World Poverty." Poverty.com. 2007-2013. Web. Jan. 2013.

"Improving Health in Africa." TheWaterProject.org. The Water Project, 2013. Web. Oct. 2013 <thewaterproject.org/health.asp>.

"International Compassion Ministry." Friar Rookey ICM.org. The Servants of Mary, 2010. Web. Oct. 2013 <frrookeyicm.org/about_icm>.

"Interview with Yann Martel." Goodreads.com. Goodreads Inc., Feb. 2013. Web. Oct. 2013 <https://www.goodreads.com/topic/show/1202294-interview-with-yann-martel>.

"Jack Harich." Solutions for a sustainable and desirable future. TheSolutionsJournal.com, n.d. Web. Oct. 2013 <http://www.thesolutionsjournal.com/user/12104>.

"Jacqueline Novogratz." The Huffington Post, TheHuffingtonPost.com, Inc., 2013. Web. Oct. 2013 <http://www.huffingtonpost.com/jacqueline-novogratz/>.

"Jacqueline Novogratz: An Escape from Poverty." TED: Ideas Worth Speading. TED Conferences, LLC. Mar. 2009. Web. Oct. 2013 <http://www.ted.com/talks/jacqueline_novogratz_on_an_escape_from_poverty.html>.

"James Orbinski, Background." CIGIonline.org. The Centre for International Governance Innovation, n.d. Web. Oct. 2013 <http://www.cigionline.org/person/james-orbinski>.

"Janine Di Giovanni." Janinedigiovanni.com. Squarespace, n.d. Web. Oct. 2013 <http://www.janinedigiovanni.com/>.

"Janine di Giovanni: What I saw in the war." TED: Ideas Worth Spreading. TED Conferences, LLC, Jan. 2013. Web. Oct. 2013 <http://www.ted.com/talks/janine_di_giovanni_what_i_saw_in_the_war.html>.

"Jeffrey D. Sachs." Project Syndicate. Project Syndicate, 2013. Web. Oct. 2013 <http://www.project-syndicate.org/contributor/jeffrey-d—sachs>.

"Jeffrey Sachs." jeffsachs.org. New York: The Earth Institute, Columbia University, 2013. Web. Oct. 2013 <jeffsachs.org/>.

"Jeffrey Sachs." The Huffington Post. TheHuffingtonPost.com, Inc., 2013. Web. Oct. 2013 <http://www.huffingtonpost.com/jeffrey-sachs/>.

"Joel Selanikio, MD." Speaker Biography. Worldcongress.com, n.d. Web. Oct. 2013 <http://www.worldcongress.com/speakerBio.cfm?speakerID=4117>.

"Joel Selanikio." Lemelson-MIT. Massachusetts Institute of Technology/MIT School of Engineering, n.d. Web. Oct. 2013 <http://web.mit.edu/invent/a-winners/a-selanikio.html>.

"John D. Rockefeller." Artofmanliness.com. The Art of Manliness, 2010. Web. Oct. 2013 <http://artofmanliness.com/2010/09/13/the-pocket-notebooks-of-20-famous-men/2/>.

"John Paul II: The Millennial Pope." Frontline. WGBH Educational Foundation, 2013. Web. Oct. 2013 <www.pbs.org/wgbh/pages/frontline/shows/pope/>.

"Jon Berkeley." Behance.net. Adobe Systems, Inc., 2013. Web. Oct. 2013 <http://www.behance.net/jonberkeley>.

"Katalina Groh." katalinagroh.com. Chicago, IL: Groh, 2011. Web. Oct. 2013 <http://www.katalinagroh.com/>.

"Kofi Annan – Biographical." NobelPrize.org. Nobel Foundation, 2013. Web. Oct. 2013 <http://www.nobelprize.org/nobel_prizes/peace/laureates/2001/annan-bio.html>.

"Kofi Annan." TheElders.org. The Elders, 2013. Web. Oct. 2013 <http://theelders.org/kofi-annan>.

"Leader of the Month for February 2006: Charlie 'Tremendous' Jones." LeaderNetwork. org: The Resource for Leaders. Leadernetwork.org, n.d. Web. Oct. 2013 <http://www.leadernetwork.org/charlie_jones_february_06.htm>.

"Liu Wei, Armless Pianist." China.org.cn. China.org.cn, 14 Feb. 2012. Web. Oct. 2013 <http://www.china.org.cn/video/2012-02/14/content_24630732.htm>.

"Maria Montessori." Amshq.org. American Montessori Society, 2013. Web. Oct. 2013 <https://www.amshq.org/Montessori-Education/History-of-Montessori-Education/Biography-of-Maria-Montessori.aspx>.

"Martha Graham: About the Dancer." American Masters. Thirteen/WNET/PBS, 16 Sept. 2005. Web. Oct. 2013 <http://www.pbs.org/wnet/americanmasters/episodes/martha-graham/about-the-dancer/497/>.

"Meet Fred Culick." Quest.nasa.gov. NASA Quest, 11 Mar. 1999. Web. Oct. 2013 <http://quest.nasa.gov/people/bios/aero/culick.html>.

"Michael Michalko." Creativitypost.com. The Creativity Post, 2013. Web. Oct. 2013 <http://www.creativitypost.com/authors/profile/33/mmichalko>.

"Michael S. Gazzaniga." BigThink.com. Big Think, n.d. Web. Oct. 2013. <http://bigthink.com/users/michaelgazzaniga>.

"Michelangelo (1475-1564)." BBC.co.uk/history. British Broadcasting Corporation, 2013. Web. Oct. 2013 <www.bbc.co.uk/history/historic_figures/michelangelo.shtml>.

"Mitchell Besser." Ashoka Innovators for the Public. Ashoka, n.d. Web. Oct. 2013 <https://www.ashoka.org/fellow/mitchell-besser>.

"Mother Teresa – Biography." Biography.com. A&E Television Networks LLC, 2013. Web. Oct. 2013 <http://www.biography.com/people/mother-teresa-9504160?page=3>.

"No Solutions to Problems Like These:." Thwink.org. Thwink.org, 2012. Web. Oct. 2013 <http://www.thwink.org/sustain/articles/020_NoSolutionsToProblemsLikeThese/index.htm>.

"Our Founder." Congregation of Holy Cross. Notre Dame, IN: United States Province of Priests and Brothers, 2013. Web. Oct. 2013 <http://www.holycrossusa.org/spirituality/our-founder-blessed-basil-moreau-csc/>.

"Philo T. Farnsworth – Biography." Biography.com. A&E Television Networks LLC, 2013. Web. Oct. 2013 <www.biography.com/people/philo-t-farnsworth-40273>.

"Pinterest." Mashable.com. Mashable, 2013. Web. Oct. 2013 <http://mashable.com/follow/topics/pinterest/>.

"Pinterest." *Mashable.com*. New York: Mashable, 2013. Web. Jan. 2013.

"Portrait: Bishop Macram Gassis of Sudan." Guard Duty. Blog at WordPress.com, 21 Jan. 2007. Web. Oct. 2013 <http://guardduty.wordpress.com/2007/01/21/portrait-bishop-macram-gassis-of-sudan/>.

"Poverty Reduction." UNDP.org. United Nations Development Programme, 2013. Web. Oct. 2013 <http://www.undp.org/content/undp/en/home/ourwork/povertyreduction/overview.html>.

"Profile: Hosni Mubarak." BBC News Middle East. British Broadcasting Corporation, 22 Aug. 2013. Web. Oct. 2013 <http://www.bbc.co.uk/news/world-middle-east-12301713>.

"Questions and Answers." Real Clear World. RealClearWorld, 2012. Web. Oct. 2013 <http://hiv-stats.realclearworld.com/q/21/8056/How-many-orphans-are-there-in-Ghana-as-a-result-of-AIDS>.

"Recipient of SBC's Lifetime Achievement in Sustainability Award: Van Vlahakis." Sustainable Business Council of Los Angeles. Sustainable Business Council of Los Angeles, 2013. Web. Oct. 2013 <http://www.sustainablebc.org/events/bio/recipient_sbcs_lifetime_achievement_sustainability_award_van_vlahakis.html_0>.

"Richard Restak." The Great Courses. The Teaching Company LLC, 2013. Web. Oct. 2013 <http://www.thegreatcourses.com/tgc/professors/professor_detail.aspx?pid=412>.

"Saint Therese of Lisieux, Virgin." EWTN/Global Catholic Network. Eternal Word Television Network, Inc. 2013. Web. Oct. 2013 <http://www.ewtn.com/therese/therese1.htm>.

"Shootings at Virginia Tech." Washingtonpost.com. The Washington Post. n.d. Web. Oct. 2013. <http://www.washingtonpost.com/wp-srv/metro/vatechshootings/>.

"Social Media Bootcamp." ChaleneJohnson.com. n.d. Web. Oct. 2013 <http://www.chalenejohnson.com/>.

"Speakers: Jacqueline Novogratz: Philanthropist." TED: Ideas Worth Spreading. TED Conferences LLC, n.d. Web. Oct. 2013 <http://www.ted.com/speakers/jacqueline_novogratz.html>.

"St. Therese of Lisieux." StTherese.com. St. Therese National Office. n.d. Web. Oct. 2013 <http://www.sttherese.com/>.

"Stand for Africa." Standforafrica.org, 2012. Web. Oct. 2013 <http://www.standforafrica.org/>.

"Statistics: Worldwide." Amfar.org. AMFAR, The Foundation for AIDS Research. Oct. 2013. Web. Oct. 2013 <http://www.amfar.org/about-hiv-and-aids/facts-and-stats/statistics—worldwide/>.

"Storytelling Day." *Storytellingday.net*, 2013. Web. Jan. 2013. <http://www.storytellingday.net/>.

"Storytelling Day." StorytellingDay.net. www.storytellingday.net, 2013. Web. Oct. 2013. <http://storytellingday.net/>.

"Storytelling: Scientist's Perspective: John Seeley Brown." Storytelling: Passport to the 21st Century. Larry Prusak, 2001. Web. Oct. 2013 <http://www.creatingthe21stcentury.org/JSB5-descartes.htm>.

"Sustainability." Epa.gov. United States Environmental Protection Agency, n.d. Web. Oct. 2013 <http://www.epa.gov/sustainability/>.

"The 100 Most Influential People in the World." Time Magazine, 6 May 2013. Print.

"The Choice is Yours." *Teambuilding-leader.com*. SBI, 2008-2012. Web. Jan. 2013. <http://www.teambuilding-leader.com/the-choice-is-yours.html>.

"The Choice is Yours." TeamBuilding-Leader.com. Teambuilding-leader.com, 2012. Web. Oct. 2013 <http://www.teambuilding-leader.com/the-choice-is-yours.html>.

"The IPAT Equation." Thwink.org, Thwink.org, 2012. Web. Oct. 2013 <http://www.thwink.org/sustain/articles/011_IPAT_Equation/index.htm>.

"The Life of Henry Ford." The Henry Ford. Dearborn, MI: The Henry Ford, 2013. Web. Oct. 2013 <http://www.hfmgv.org/exhibits/hf/>.

"The Life of Saint Therese of Lisieux." Vatican.va. The Holy See. n.d. Web. Oct. 2013 <http://www.vatican.va/news_services/liturgy/documents/ns_lit_doc_19101997_stherese_en.html>.

"The Nobel Peace Prize." Msf.org.uk. Medecins Sans Frontieres/Doctors Without Borders, n.d. Web. Oct. 2013 <http://www.msf.org.uk/nobel-peace-prize>.

"Toward the end of poverty." The Economist. The Economist Newspaper Limited, 1 June 2013. Web. Oct. 2013 <http://www.economist.com/news/leaders/21578665-nearly-1-billion-people-have-been-taken-out-extreme-poverty-20-years-world-should-aim>.

"Triage: Dr. James Orbinski's Humanitarian Dilemma." DoctorsWithoutBorders.org. Doctors Without Borders/Medecins Sans Frontieres, 2013. Web. Oct. 2013 <http://www.doctorswithoutborders.org/aboutus/page.cfm?id=6002>.

"Uri Hasson, 'Brain-to-Brain Coupling: A Mechanism for Creating and Sharing a Social World'—Followed by a Roundtable Discussion." Events. John Hope Franklin Humanities Institute at Duke University, 21 March 2012. Web. Oct. 2013 <http://fhi.duke.edu/events/uri-hasson-lecture>.

"Vinoba Bhave." vinobabhave.org. VinobaBhave.org, n.d. Web. Oct. 2013 <http://www.vinobabhave.org/en/>.

"What Does Thwink.org Have to Offer? Thwink.org. Thwink.org, 2012. Web. Oct. 2013 <http://www.thwink.org/sustain/general/WhatDoesThwinkHave.htm>.

"What is Depression?" *Healthy Living*. Seattle, WA: Microsoft/MSN, 2013. Web. Jan. 2013. <http://healthyliving.msn.com/diseases/depression?cp-documentid=100167285>.

"Who Will Be the First to Help?" Motivateus.com. Motivating Moments LLC, 4 Feb. 2011. Web. Oct. 2013. <www.motivateus.com/stories/be-godlike.htm>.

"World Poverty Statistics." Statistic Brain Research Institute. Statistic Brain, 23 July 2012. Web. Oct. 2013 <www.statisticbrain.com/world-poverty-statistics/>.

"You Can Help Provide Clean, Safe Drinking Water." *Thewaterproject.org*. The Water Project, Inc., 2006-2013. Web. Jan. 2013.

"Zine al-Abidine Ben Ali." The Guardian. Guardian News and Media Limited, n.d. Web. 2013 <http://www.theguardian.com/world/zine-al-abidine-ben-ali>.

"Zine El-Abidine Ben Ali." Topics.nytimes.com. The New York Times Company, 11 Jan. 2004. Web. Oct. 2013 <http://topics.nytimes.com/top/reference/timestopics/people/b/zine_elabidine_ben_ali/>.

A Heart for Justice. Black Hills Web Works, 2009-2013. Aheartforjustice.com. Web. Jan. 2013.

Abani, Chris. GraceLand. New York: Farrar, Straus, Giroux, 2004. Print.

AbbyJohnson.org. Pro Life Web Design, n.d. Web. Oct. 2013 <http://www.abbyjohnson.org/>.

Abdul Latif Jameel Poverty Action Lab. Massachusetts Institute of Technology, 2013. Web. Oct. 2013 <http://www.povertyactionlab.org/>.

Accattoli, Luigi. Life in the Vatican with John Paul II. New York: Universe, 1998. Print. Acumen.org.

Acumen, 2013. Web. Oct. 2013 http://acumen.org/.

Addison, Steve. "Movements That Change the World."Movements That Change the World Synopsis Movements That Change the World Comments. KWD, 2012. Web. Jan. 2013. <http://www.movements.net/books/movements-that-change-the-world/movements-synopsis>.

Adichie, Chimamanda Ngozi. Americanah. New York: Knopf, 2013. Print.

Adkins, Jan. Thomas Edison. New York: DK Children, 2009. Print.

Albinia, Alice. Empires of the Indus: The Story of a River. New York: W.W. Norton, 2010. Print.

Albrecht, Brian. "Navy veteran Robert Schumaker talks about surviving as POW during Vietnam." Cleveland.com. Northeast Ohio Media Group LLC, 21 Sept. 2012. Web. Oct. 2013 <http://www.cleveland.com/metro/index.ssf/2012/09/vietnam_pow_robert_shumaker _sp.html>.

Alkire, Sabina and Severine Deneulin. "The Human Development and Capability Approach." IDRC.ca. International Development Research Centre, n.d. Web. Oct. 2013 <http://web.idrc.ca/openebooks/470-3/#page_22>.

Allen, Reginald E., ed. Greek Philosophy: Thales to Aristotle. New York: Free, 1991. Print.

Ament, Phil. "Assembly Line." Ideafinder.com. Troy, MI: The Great Idea Finder, 1997-2007. 16 May 2005. Web. Jan. 2013.

Anderson, Jervis. Bayard Rustin: Troubles I've Seen. New York: HarperCollins, 1997. Print.

Anderson, Leland I. Nikola Tesla on His Work with Alternating Currents and Their Application to Wireless Telegraphy, Telephony, and Transmission of Power: An Extended Interview. Minneapolis, MN: Twenty-First Century-Lerner, 2002. Print.

Anderson, Mac. What's the Big Idea? Naperville, IL: Simple Truths, 2010. Print.

Anjarwalla, Tas. "Inventor of Cell Phone: We knew someday everybody would have one." CNNTech. Cable News Network/Turner Broadcasting System, Inc., 2013. Web. Oct. 2013 <http://www.cnn.com/2010/TECH/mobile/07/09/cooper.cell.phone.inventor/>.

Annan, Kofi. Interventions: A Life in War and Peace. New York: Penguin, 2013. Print.

Anneapplebaum.com. WordPress, 2013. Web. Oct. 2013 <http://www.anneapplebaum.com/>.

Anouil, Gilles. The Poor Are the Church: A Conversation with Father Joseph Wresinski. New London, CT: Twenty-third Publications, 2002. Print.

Applebaum, Anne. Between East and West: Across the Borderlands of Europe. New York: Pantheon, 1994. Print.

Aristotle and Hugh Lawson-Tancred, ed. The Art of Rhetoric. New York: Penguin Classics, 1992. Print.

Aristotle. The Categories. Melbourne, Australia: Book Jungle, 2007. Print.

Arnold, Matthew and Matthew LeRiche. South Sudan: From Revolution to Independence. New York: Columbia University, 2012. Print.

Ashdown, Paddy. A Fortunate Life: The Autobiography of Paddy Ashdown. London: Aurum, 2009. Print.

Ashoka Innovators for the Public. Ashoka. n.d. Web. Oct. 2013 <https://www.ashoka. org/>.

Austen, Jane. Pride and Prejudice. New York: Penguin Classics, 2009. Print.

Avert.org. AVERT: AVERTing HIV and AIDS, 2013. Web. Oct. 2013 <http://www.avert.org/>.

Bakker, Nienke, Leo Jansen and Hans Luijten, eds. Vincent van Gogh: The Letters: The Complete Illustrated and Annotated Edition (Vol. 1-6). New York: Thames & Hudson, 2009. Print.

Bandow, Doug. "Poverty and Personal Choice." Cato.org. Cato Institute, 14 May 2002. Web. Oct. 2013 <www.cato.org/publications/commentary/poverty-personal-choice>.

Banerjee, Abhijit V. and Esther Duflo. Poor Economics: A Radical Rethinking of the Way to Fight Global Poverty. New York: PublicAffairs, 2011. Print.

Bannister, Nonna. The Secret Holocaust Diaries: The Untold Story of Nonna Bannister. Carol Stream, IL: Tyndale House, 2010. Print.

Barker, Eileen. "What Would Gandhi Do?" Mediate.com. Resourceful Internet Solutions, Inc., 2013. Web. Oct. 2013 <http://www.mediate.com/articles/ebarker4.cfm>.

Bashir, Halima. Tears of the Desert: A Memoir of Survival in Darfur. New York: Random House Reader's Circle, 2009. Print.

Beeler, Todd. The Seven Hidden Secrets of Motivation: Unlocking the Genius Within. Prince Frederick, MD: Your Coach in a Box, 2006.

CD. Belsky, Scott. *Making Ideas Happen.* New York: Portfolio Penguin, 2010. Print.

Benedict XVI. Doctors of the Church. Huntington, IN: Our Sunday Visitor, 2005. Print.

Berners-Lee, Tim with Mark Fischetti. Weaving the Web: The Original Design and Ultimate Destiny of the World Wide Web. New York: HarperCollins, 2000. Print.

Bhave, Vinoba. Democratic Values and the Practice of Citizenship. Uttar Pradesh, India: Sarva Seva Sangh Prakashan, 1962. Print.

Bilton, Nick and Evelyn M. Rusli. "Facebook Fever." *The New York Times Upfront.* 12 Mar. 2012. Web. Jan. 2013. <http://upfront.scholastic.com/issues/03_12_12/book#/6>.

Blair, Gary Ryan. Everything Counts: 52 Remarkable Ways to Inspire Excellence and Drive Results. Hoboken, NJ: Wiley, 2010. Print.

Boahen, A. Adu. African Perspectives on Colonialism. Baltimore, MD: Johns Hopkins University, 1989. Print.

Bohm, David. On Dialogue. New York: Routledge, 2004. Print. Born, Max. The Born-Einstein Letters. New York: Macmillan, 1971. Print.

Bornstein, David and Susan Davis. Social Entrepreneurship: What Everyone Needs to Know. New York: Oxford University, 2010. Print.

Bornstein, David. How to Change the World. Oxford: Oxford University, 2007. Print.

Bortolotti, Dan. Hope In Hell: Inside the World of Doctors Without Borders. Altona: Firefly Books, 2004. 136. Print.

Bostridge, Mark. Florence Nightingale: The Woman and her Legend. New York: Penguin, 2009. Print.

Boutwell, George S. Reminiscences of Sixty Years in Public Affairs, Volume 2. New York: Fili-Quarian Classics, 2011. Print.

Boynton, Andy and Bill Fischer. The Idea Hunter: How To Find the Best Ideas and Make Them Happen. San Francisco: Jossey-Bass, 2011. Print.

Branch, Taylor. Parting the Waters: America in the King Years 1954-63. New York: Simon & Schuster, 1988. Print.

Breisach, Ernst. Historiography: Ancient, Medieval and Modern. Chicago: University of Chicago, 2007. Print.

Brin, David. "Worlds of David Brin." DavidBrin.com. David Brin, 2013. Web. Oct. 2013 <http://www.davidbrin.com/>.

Bronowski, Jacob. The Ascent of Man. London: BBC, 2011. Print.

Brown, John Seeley. johnseeleybrown.com. n.p., n.d. Web. Oct. 2013 <http://www.johnseelybrown.com/>.

Bul Dau, John with Michael S. Sweeney. God Grew Tired of Us: A Memoir. Washington, DC: National Geographic, 2007. Print.

Burchard, Brendon. The Millionaire Messenger: Make a Difference and a Fortune Sharing Your Advice. New York: Free, 2011. Print.

Burgert, Natasha. "How Social Media has Changed my Medical Practice." KevinMD.com. OutThink Group, 18 Aug. 2011. Web. Jan. 2013.

Burke, Edmund. Reflections on the Revolution in France. New York: Burke Press, 2013. Print.

Burns, John F. "A Foreign Face Beloved by Afghans of All Stripes." NYTimes.com. The New York Times Company, 2009. Web. Oct. 2013 <http://www.nytimes.com/2008/12/25/world/asia/25afghan.html?_r=0>.

Burns, Ken. "Books." Interviewed by Amy Sutherland. BostonGlobe.com. Boston Globe Media Partners, LLC, 11 May 2013. Web. Oct. 2013. <http://www.bostonglobe.com/arts/books/2013/05/11/-interview-with-bibliophile-ken-burns/GfEshMNYikLnYj19vYn8SO/story.html>.

Burstein, Julie. "4 Lessons in Creativity." TED: Ideas worth spreading. TED Conferences, LLC. Nov. 2013. Web. Oct. 2013 <http://www.ted.com/talks/julie_burstein_4_lessons_in_creativity.htm>.

Camus, Albert. The Plague. New York: Penguin, 2008. Print.

Capote, Truman. Breakfast at Tiffany's. New York: Modern Library, 1993. Print.

Care.org. CARE, 2013. Web. Oct. 2013 <http://www.care.org/>.

Carr, Edward Hallet. What is History? New York: Palgrave-Macmillan, 2001. Print.

Carson, Clayborne. "American Civil Rights Movement." Britannica.com. Encyclopaedia Britannica, 2013. Web. Oct. 2013 <http://www.britannica.com/EBchecked/topic/119368/American-civil-rights-movement>.

Carson, Rachel. Silent Spring. Boston: Houghton Mifflin, 1962. Print.

Cervantes, Miguel de and Edith Grossman. Don Quixote. New York: Harper Perennial, 2005. Print.

Chapman, Steve. "World Poverty in Retreat." Chicago Tribune News. Chicago Tribune, 29 Mar. 2012. Web. Oct. 2013 <http://articles.chicagotribune.com/2012-03-29/news/ct-oped-0329-chapman-20120329_1_poverty-rate-poverty-reduction-world-bank>.

Checinski, Michael. Poland, Communism, nationalism, anti-semitism. New York: Karz-Cohl, 1982. Print.

Cheeseman, Nic. "'An African Election': Reflections on Ghana's 2008 Elections." DemocracyinAfrica.org. Democracy in Africa, 29 January 2012. Web. Oct. 2013 <http://democracyinafrica.org/an-african-election/>.

Chen, Ji. "Liu Wei, Armless Pianist, Plays With His Toes, Wows Audience (Video)." Huff Post World. TheHuffingtonPost.com, Inc., 25 May 2011. Web. Oct. 2013 <http://www.huffingtonpost.com/2010/08/27/ chinese-musician-with-no-_n_696914.html>.

Chernow, Ron. Titan: The Life of John D. Rockefeller, Sr. New York: Vintage, 2004. Print.

Chesters, Sarah Davey. The Socratic Classroom: Reflective Thinking Through Collaborative Inquiry. Rotterdam: Sense, 2012. Print.

Clarkson, Thomas and Mary-Antoinette Smith, ed. Thomas Clarkson and Ottobah Cugoano: Essays on the Slavery and Commerce of the Human Species. Peterborough, Ontario: Broadview, 2010. Print.

Clarkson, Thomas. "An essay on the impolicy of the African slave trade." Archive. org. San Francisco: Internet Archive, 2008. eBook. <https://archive.org/details/essayonimpolicyo00clariala >.

Clason, George S. The Richest Man in Babylon. CreateSpace Independent Publishing Platform, 2012. Print.

Cleary, Ben. "Where Was Stonewall?" Opinionator. The New York Times Company, 22 June 2012. Web. Oct. 2013 <http://opinionator.blogs.nytimes.com/category/disunion/page/37/?scp=2-b&sq=ontherepublic&st=nyt>

Cleese, John and Connie Booth. The Complete Fawlty Towers. Cambridge, MA: Da Capo, 2001. Print.

ClintonFoundation.org. The Clinton Foundation, 2013. Web. Oct. 2013 <http://www.clintonfoundation.org/>.

CNN Library. "Virginia Tech Shooting Fast Facts." CNN U.S. Cable News Network-Turner Broadcasting System, Inc. 31 Oct. 2013. Web. Oct. 2013 <http://www.cnn.com/2013/10/31/us/virginia-tech-shootings-fast-facts/>.

Coe, Michael D. and Rex Koontz. Mexico: From the Olmecs to the Aztecs. 6th ed. New York: Thames & Hudson, 2008. Print.

Cohen, Bernard. "Florence Nightingale." Scientific American (1984) 250(3):128-136. Print.

Collier, Paul. The Bottom Billion. New York: Oxford University, 2007. Print.

Conley, Susan. The Foremost Good Fortune. New York: Vintage, 2011. Print.

Conquest, Robert. Stalin: Breaker of Nations. New York: Penguin, 1992. Print.

Conrad, Joseph. Heart of Darkness. New York: Penguin Classics, 2012. Print.

Cook, Gareth. "The Secret Language Code." ScientificAmerican.com. Scientific American, Inc. 16 Aug. 2011. Web. Oct. 2013 <http://www.scientificamerican.com/article. cfm?id=the-secret-language-code>.

Cousins, Margaret. The Story of Thomas Alva Edison. New York: Random, 1993. Print.

Crawshaw, Steve and John Jackson. "10 Everyday Acts of Resistance That Changed the World." Yesmagazine.org. Positive Futures Network, 1 April 2011. Web. Oct. 2013 <http://www.yesmagazine.org/ people-power/10-everyday-acts-of-resistance-that-changed-the-world>.

Creamer, Robert W. Babe: The Legend Comes to Life. New York: Simon & Schuster, 1992. Print.

CreativeThinking.net. Michael Michalko, 2013. Web. Oct. 2013 <http://creativethinking. net/WP01_Home.htm>.

Croce, Nicholas. Newton and the Three Laws of Motion. New York: Rosen, 2005. Print.

Crocker, Jim. "Jim Crocker on Systems Engineering." Interviewed by Ask the Academy. NASA Academy 3:9 (2010). National Aeronautics and Space Administration, 30 Sept. 2010. Web. Oct. 2013 <http://www.nasa.gov/offices/oce/appel/ask-academy/issues/ volume3/AA_3-9_SF_interview.html>.

Crouch, Tom. First Flight: The Wright Brothers and the Invention of the Airplane. Washington, DC: National Park Service, U.S. Department of the Interior, 2002. Print.

CRS.org. Catholic Relief Services, 2013. Web. Oct. 2013 <http://crs.org/>.

DambisaMoyo.com. Dambisa Moyo, 2013. Web. Oct. 2013 <http://www.dambisamoyo. com/>.

Danaher, Kevin. Fifty Years is Enough: The Case Against the World Bank and the International Monetary Fund. San Francisco: Global Exchange, 1994. Print.

Darwin, Charles and Frederick Burkhardt, ed. Charles Darwin's Letters: A Selection, 1825-1859. New York: Cambridge University, 1996. Print.

Darwin, Charles, and Sir Francis Darwin. The Life and Letters of Charles Darwin. New York: D. Appleton & Co., 1911. Web.

Data.gov. The United States Government, 2013. Web. Oct. 2013 <http://www.data.gov/>.

de Saint-Exupery, Antoine. The Little Prince. New York: Harcourt Brace, 1971. Print.

Dearing, Tiziana C. Tiziana C. Dearing, Consultant. Yola.com, n.d. Web. Oct. 2013 <http:// www.tizianadearing.com/about-me.php>.

DeGraaf, Leonard. Edison and the Rise of Innovation. New York: Sterling Signature, 2013. Print.

Denning, Stephen. The Leader's Guide to Storytelling: Mastering the Art and Discipline of Business Narrative. San Francisco: Jossey-Bass, 2011. Print.

di Giovanni, Janine. Ghosts by Daylight: Love, War, and Redemption. New York: Knopf, 2011. Print.

Dickinson, Elizabeth. "Anatomy of a Dictatorship: Hosni Mubarak." Foreignpolicy.com. Foreign Policy Group, LLC, 3 Mar. 2011. Web. Oct. 2013 <http://www.foreignpolicy. com/ articles/2011/02/04/anatomy_of_a_dictatorship_hosni_mubarak>.

Doidge, Norman. The Brain That Changes Itself: Stories of Personal Triumph from the Frontiers of Brain Science. New York: Penguin, 2007. Print.

Donald, David Herbert. Lincoln. New York: Touchstone, 1995. Print.

Donovan, Jim. "Farewell to my friend Charlie 'Tremendous' Jones." JimDonovan. com, Jim Donovan, 21 Oct. 2008. Web. Oct. 2013 <http://www.jimdonovan.com/ farewell-to-my-friend-charlie-tremendous-jones/>.

Dossey, Barbara Montgomery. Florence Nightingale: Mystic, Visionary, Healer. Philadelphia, PA: F. A. Davis, 2009. Print.

Drayton, Bill, ed. Leading Social Entrepreneurs Changing the World (Activist Biographies). Arlington, VA: Ashoka Innovators for the Public, 2009. Print.

Drexler, Madeline. "How Racism Hurts — Literally." The Boston Globe, 15 July 2007. Web. Oct. 2013 <http://www.boston.com/news/globe/ideas/articles/2007/07/15/ how_racism_hurts__literally/?page=full>

Duflo, Esther. "Esther Duflo: Social Experiments to Fight Poverty." TED: Ideas worth spreading. TED Conferences, LLC. May 2010. Web. Oct. 2013 <http://www.ted.com/ talks/esther_duflo_social_experiments_to_fight_poverty.html>.

Duhigg, Charles. The Power of Habit: Why We Do What We Do in Life and Business. New York: Random, 2012.Print.

DZDock.com. DZ Dock, 2011. Web. Oct. 2013 <http://www.dzdock.com/aboutus.php>.

Eagleman, David. Incognito: The Secret Lives of the Brain. New York: Pantheon, 2011. Print.

Easterly, William. The White Man's Burden. New York: Oxford University, 2006. Print.

Economic Freedom Team. "In the News: The Good Samaritan Effect: The Virtuous Cycle of Private Charity." Economic Freedom. Charles Koch Institute, 28 Jan 2013. Web. Oct. 2013 <http://www.economicfreedom.org/2013/01/28/ the-virtuous-cycle-of-private-charity/>.

Edwards, Roberta and True Kelley. Who Was Leonardo da Vinci? New York: Grosset & Dunlap, 2005. Print.

Eggers, William D. and Paul Macmillan. The Solution Revolution: How Business, Government, and Social Enterprises Are Teaming Up to Solve Society's Toughest Problems. Boston: Harvard Business, 2013. Print.

Einstein, Albert and Leopold Infeld. The Evolution of Physics. New York: Touchstone, 1967. Print.

Einstein, Albert. Autobiographical Notes. Peru, IL: Carus, 1979. Print.

Ellison, George. Learning from HIV and AIDS. Cambridge: Cambridge University Press, 2003. Print. United Nations Office on Drugs and Crime. Human Trafficking: an overview. Vienna: United Nations, 2008. Web.

Emerson, Ralph Waldo. Character and Heroism. New York: Ulan, 2012. Print.

Ennen, Steve. "Peter Guber on Sharing Stories, not just Information, to Communicate Effectively." *Knowledge@Wharton*, The Wharton School of the University of Pennsylvania, 24 June 2009. Web. Jan. 2013.

Epicurus. A Guide to Happiness. London: Weidenfeld & Nicolson History, 2005. Print.

Epstein, Helen. The Invisible Cure. New York: Picador, 2007. Print.

Farmers Insurance. Web. Jan 2013. <http://www.farmersinsurance.com/>.

Farmers.com. Farmers Insurance Group, 2012. Web. Oct. 2013 <http://www.farmers. com>.

Fitzgerald, F. Scott. The Great Gatsby. New York: Scribner, 2004. Print.

Fogg, BJ. "BJ Fogg: Innovator, Social Scientist, Teacher." BJ Fogg, 2013. Web. Oct. 2013 <http://www.bjfogg.com/>.

Ford, Henry. My Life and Work. New York: CruGuru, 2008. Print.

Foster, Jack. How to Get Ideas. San Francisco: Berrett-Koehler, 2007. Print.

Foster, Jack. *How to Get Ideas*. San Francisco: Berrett-Koehler Publishers, Inc., 2007. Print.

Foster, Richard J. The Extraordinary Life of an Olympic Champion. Solana Beach, CA: Santa Monica, 2008. Print.

Fox, Keiren. "Environment." InspirationGreen.com, n.d. Web. Oct. 2013 <http://www. inspirationgreen.com/environment.html>.

Freedman, Russell. The Wright Brothers: How They Invented the Airplane. New York: Holiday, 1994. Print.

Friedman, George. The Next Decade: Empire and Republic in a Changing World. New York: Doubleday, 2011. Print.

Fritz, Ben. "*Hunger Games* sells 3.8 million DVDs, Blu-rays on first weekend." *Los Angeles Times.* Los Angeles: Los Angeles Times, 21 Aug. 2012. Web. Jan. 2013.

Frost, Robert and Edward Connery Lathem, ed. The Poetry of Robert Frost, Completed and Unabridged. New York: Henry Holt, 1969. Print.

Gandhi, Mahatma and Louis Fischer, ed. The Essential Gandhi: An Anthology of His Writings on His Life, Work, and Ideas. New York: Vintage, 2002. Print.

Gandhi, Mohandas K. All Men Are Brothers. New York: Continuum, 1980. Print.

Gardner, Howard. Creating Minds: An Anatomy of Creativity Seen Through the Lives of Freud, Einstein, Picasso, Stravinsky, Eliot, Graham, and Gandhi. New York: Basic, 2011. Print.

Gardner, John W. On Leadership. New York: Free, 1990. Print.

Gates, Bill, Sr. and Mary Ann Mackin. Showing Up for Life: Thoughts on the Gifts of a Lifetime. New York: Broadway, 2009. Print.

Gates, Bill. "The Power of Catalytic Philanthropy."*Thegatesnotes.com*. The Gates Notes, LLC., 19 Sept. 2012. Web. 20 Jan. 2013.

Gawande, Atul. Better: A Surgeon's Notes on Performance. New York: Picador, 2007. Print.

Gawande.com. Atul Gawande, n.d. Web. Oct. 2013 <<http://gawande.com/>>.

Gazzaniga, Michael S. "Your Storytelling Brain." *Bigthink.com*. New York: Big Think, n.d. Web. Jan. 2013.

Gazzaniga, Michael S., ed. The Cognitive Neurosciences, Third ed. Cambridge, MA: MIT Press, 2004. Print.

Gelb, Michael J. and Sarah Miller Caldicott. *Innovate Like Edison*. New York: Dutton, 2007. Print.

Gelb, Michael J. and Sarah Miller Caldicott. Innovate Like Edison: The Five-Step System for Breakthrough Business Success. New York: Dutton, 2007. Print.

Gelb, Michael J. How to Think Like Leonardo DaVinci. New York: Delta, 2004. Print.

Ghana, Final Report, Presidential and Parliamentary Elections 2008. European Union Election Observation Mission, Feb. 2009. PDF file.

Ghemawat, Pankaj. Redefining Global Strategy: Crossing Borders in a World Where Differences Still Matter. Boston, MA: Harvard Business, 2007. Print.

Gibson, Stacey. "A Doctor in Kigali." UofTMagazine. University of Toronto, 2008. Web. Oct. 2013 <http://www.magazine.utoronto.ca/cover-story/james-orbinski-profile-doctors-without-borders-canadians-in-rwanda/>.

Gill, Gillian. Nightingales: The Extraordinary Upbringing and Curious Life of Miss Florence Nightingale. New York: Random, 2005. Print.

Gleick, James. Isaac Newton. New York: Vintage, 2003. Print.

Glenn, Jim. The Complete Patents of Nikola Tesla. New York: Barnes & Noble, 1994. Print.

Godin, Seth. Interviewed by Ryan and Tina Essmaker. Thegreatdiscontent.com. TGD, 14 Aug. 2012. Web. Oct. 2013. <http://thegreatdiscontent.com/seth-godin>.

Gonzalez-Balado, Jose Luis. Mother Teresa: In My Own Words. Liguori, MO: Liguori, 1997. Print.

Goodwin, Doris Kearns. Team of Rivals: The Political Genius of Abraham Lincoln. New York: Simon & Schuster, 2006. Print.

Gots, Jason. "Your Storytelling Brain." BigThink.com. Big Think, 15 Jan. 2012. Web. Oct. 2013 <http://bigthink.com/think-tank/your-storytelling-brain>.

Gowin, Joshua. "You, Illuminated." PsychologyToday.com. Sussex Publishers, LLC, 6 June 2011. Web. Oct. 2013 <http://www.psychologytoday.com/blog/you-illuminated>.

Grameen-Info.org. Network Solutions, 2013. Web. Oct. 2013 <http://www.grameen-info.org/index.php?option=com_content&task=view&id=329&Itemid=363>.

Gray, Nakkia. "Turn Your Life Around, One Day at a Time." Beliefnet.com. Beliefnet, Inc., 2012. Web. Oct. 2013 <http://blog.beliefnet.com/fromthemasters/2012/01/turn-your-life-around-one-day-at-a-time.html#ixzz1jLVJ4zZX >.

Green, Dan. Finish Strong. Nashville, TN: Thomas Nelson, 2012. Print.

Greenberg, Dov. "Changing the World, One Person at a Time." AskMoses.com. 2013. Web. Oct. 2013. <www.askmoses.com/en/article/485,1995839/Changing-the-World-One-Person-at-a-Time.html>.

Griggs, Earl Leslie. Thomas Clarkson: The Friend of Slaves. New York: Negro Universities, 1970. Print.

Gross, Daniel. "Obama Taps Esther Duflo, Poverty's 'Rock Star.'" Newsweek.com. IBT Media, 14 Jan. 2013. Web. Oct. 2013 <http://www.thedailybeast.com/newsweek/2013/01/13/obama-taps-esther-duflo-poverty-s-rock-star.html>.

Guber, Peter. "Peter Guber on Sharing Stories, Not Just Information, to Communicate Effectively." Interviewed by Steve Ennen. Knowledge@Wharton. Wharton School of

the University of Pennsylvania, 24 June 2009. Web. Oct. 2013 <http://knowledge.
wharton.upenn.edu/article.cfm?articleid=2269>.

Hague, William. William Wilberforce: The Life of the Great Anti-Slave Trade Campaigner.
Orlando, FL: Harcourt, 2007. Print.

Hall, Sarah. The Electric Michelangelo. New York: Harper, 2004. Print.

Hamilton, Bruce. Environmental Sustainability. National Science Foundation, n.d. Web.
Oct. 2013 <http://www.nsf.gov/funding/pgm_summ.jsp?pims_id=501027>.

Hamilton, Edith. The Greek Way. New York: Penguin, 1993. Print.

Hammontree, Marie. Albert Einstein: Young Thinker. New York: Aladdin, 1986. Print.

Hammurabi. The Code of Hammurabi. Huntington, MA: SevenTreasures, 2008. Print.

Haq, Mahbub Ul. The Poverty Curtain. New York: Columbia University, 1976. Print.

Harich, Jack. Analytical Activism: A New Approach to Solving the Sustainability Problem
and Other Difficult Problems. Clarkston, GA: Thwink.org, 2006. Print.

Hasson, U. and C.J. Honey. "Future trends in neuroimaging: Neural processes as expressed
within real-life contexts." NeuroImage (2012) 62:1272-8. Print.

Hasson, U., E. Yang, I. Vallines, D.J. Heeger, N. Rubin. "A Hierarchy of temporal receptive
windows in human cortex." Journal of Neuroscience (2008) 28(10):2539-2550. Print.

Hawkins, Anne Hunsaker. Reconstructing Illness. West Lafayette, IN: Purdue University,
1999. Print.

Hayward, Mark. "How to Achieve Your Goals Through Reverse Engineering," LateralAction.
com. Lateral Action, 2011. Web. Oct. 2013 <http://lateralaction.com/articles/
how-to-achieve-your-goals-through-reverse-engineering/>.

Heidegger, Martin. Early Greek Thinking. San Francisco: Harper San Francisco, 1985. Print.

Heldring, Leander and James A. Robinson. "Colonialism and Development in Africa."
VoxEU.org, 10 Jan. 2013. Web. Oct. 2013 <http://www.voxeu.org/article/
colonialism-and-development-africa>.

Helft, Miguel. "The Class That Built Apps, and Fortunes." Technology. The New York
Times Company, 2011. Web. Oct. 2013 <http://www.nytimes.com/2011/05/08/
technology/08class.html?_r=0>.

Hemingway, Ernest. The Old Man and the Sea. New York: Scribner, 1995. Print.

Hicks, Donna. Dignity: Its Essential Role in Resolving Conflict. Boston: Yale University,
2011. Print.

Hobsbawm, Eric. On History. New York: New, 1998. Print.

Hobsbawm, Eric. On History. New York: New, 1998. Print.

Hochschild, Adam. King Leopold's Ghost: A Story of Greed, Terror, and Heroism in Colonial
Africa. Boston: Mariner-Houghton Mifflin, 1999. Print.

Hodgman, Charlotte. "The Abolition of the British Slave Trade." HistoryExtra.Com,
Immediate Media Co., Ltd., 23 Aug. 2012. Web. Oct. 2013 <http://www.historyextra.
com/slavery>.

Honey, C.J., C.R. Thomson, Y. Lerner, U. Hasson. "Not lost in translation: Neural responses
shared across languages." Journal of Neuroscience (2012) 32(44):15277-83. Print.

Hooper, Edward. "Michael Worobey's Possession of 1950s Tissue Samples from Stanleyville (Kisangani)." AIDSorigins.com. AIDS Origins, 19 March 2008. Web. Oct. 2013 <http://www.aidsorigins.com/michael-worobey-possession-1950s-tissue-samples>.

Horne, Charles F. The Code of Hammurabi. London: Forgotten, 2007. Print.

Hsu, Benjamin. "Famous People Who Found Success Despite Failures." *Getbusylivingblog. com*. Get Busy Living, 2013. Web. Jan. 2013.

Hyde, Catherine Ryan. Pay It Forward. New York: Pocket, 2010. Print.

I Am Because We Are. Dir. Nathan Rissman. Perf. Bill Clinton and Madonna. Virgil Films and Entertainment, 2009. DVD.

Iggers, George G. A Global History of Modern Historiography. Old Tappan, NJ: Pearson Education, 2008. Print.

IPA: Innovations for Poverty Action. Poverty-Action.org, 2011. Web. Oct. 2013 <http://www.poverty-action.org/>.

Iqbal, Mohammed and Mohammed Yunus, eds. Plant Response to Air Pollution. New York: Wiley, 1996. Print.

Isaacson, Walter. Steve Jobs. New York: Simon & Schuster, 2011. Print.

Iweriebor, Ehiedu E. G. "The Colonization of Africa." Africana Age. The Schomburg Center for Research in Black Culture/New York Public Library, 2011. Web. Oct. 2013 <http://exhibitions.nypl.org/africanaage/essay-colonization-of-africa.html>.

James Orbinski Official Website. JamesOrbinski.com, 2012. Web. Oct. 2013 <http://jamesorbinski.com/>.

James, William. The Principles of Psychology, Volume 1. New York: Cosimo, 2007. Print.

Jenkins, Keith. Re-thinking History. New York: Routledge, 2003. Print.

Jenner, Caryn. Thomas Edison: The Great Inventor. New York: DK Children, 2007. Print.

Jensen, Keld. "How Great Leaders Triumph over Failure." *Forbes*. Forbes.com LLC., 8 Aug. 2012. Web. Jan. 2013.

Jensen, Mette Bastholm. "Solidarity in action: A comparative analysis of collective rescue efforts in Nazi-occupied Denmark and the Netherlands." Udini. Proquest, LLC, 2013. Web. Oct. 2013 <http://udini.proquest.com/view/solidarity-in-action-a-comparative-goid:304781033/>.

Jewish Telegraphic Agency. "Danish Jews to Travel to Malmo, Sweden in Solidarity Visit Against Anti-Semitic Attacks." Jspace.com. Jspace LLC, 20 Sept. 2012. Web. Oct. 2013 <http://www.jspace.com/news/articles/danish-jews-to-travel-to-malmo-sweden-in-solidarity-visit-against-anti-semitic-attacks/10845>.

John Paul II. Crossing the Threshold of Hope. New York: Knopf, 1994. Print.

Johnson, Abby. Unplanned: The Dramatic True Story of a Former Planned Parenthood Leader's Eye-Opening Journey Across the Life Line. Carol Stream, IL: Tyndale, 2010. Print.

Johnson, Chalene. Push: 30 Days to Turbocharged Habits, a Bangin' Body, and the Life You Deserve! New York: Rodale, 2012. Print. Johnson, Mark. Moral Imagination: Implications of Cognitive Science for Ethics. Chicago: University of Chicago, 1993. Print.

Johnson, Paul. Socrates: A Man for Our Times. New York: Penguin, 2011. Print.

Joint United Nations Programme on HIV/AIDS (UNAIDS). *World AIDS Day Report*. Geneva: United Nations, 2011. Web.

Jones, Charlie E. Life is Tremendous. Carol Stream, IL: Tyndale, 1981. Print.

Jones, Jonathan. "Defining 'Moral Imagination.'" Postmodern Conservative. FirstThings.com, 1 July 2009. Web. Oct. 2013 <http://www.firstthings.com/blogs/postmodernconservative/2009/07/01/defining-moral-imagination/>.

Jones, Morgan D. The Thinker's Toolkit: 14 Powerful Techniques for Problem Solving. New York: Three Rivers, 1998. Print.

Josephson, Matthew. Edison: A Biography. Hoboken, NJ: Wiley, 1992. Print.

Joyner, Mark. Integration Marketing: How Small Businesses Become Big Businesses—And Big Businesses Become Empires. Hoboken, NJ: Wiley, 2009. Print.

Kagan, Donald. The Peloponnesian War. New York: Penguin, 2004. Print.

Kaplan, James. Paul McCartney: The Legend Rocks On. New York: Time, 2012. Print.

Karlan, Dean and Jacob Appel. More Than Good Intentions. New York: Dutton, 2012. Print.

Karoff, Peter, et al. The World We Want: New Dimensions in Philanthropy and Social Change. Lanham, MD: AltaMira, 2006. Print.

Keller, Timothy. King's Cross: The Story of the World in the Life of Jesus. New York: Dutton, 2011. Print.

Kelley, Tom and Jonathan Littman. The Ten Faces of Innovation. New York: Currency Doubleday, 2005. Print.

Kelly, Fred Charters. The Wright Brothers: A Biography. Mineola, NY: Dover, 1989. Print.

Kelly, Matthew. Our Lives Change When Our Habits Change. Hebron, KY: DynamicCatholic, 2008. Audio CD.

Kemp, Martin. Leonardo. New York: Oxford University, 2004. Print.

Kemp-Welch, A. Poland Under Communism: A Cold War History. New York: Cambridge University, 2008. Print.

Kenower, Bill. "Yann Martel Interview." YouTube.com. YouTube. 13 May 2010. Web. Oct. 2013 <http://www.youtube.com/watch?v=B29tigyBJlQ>.

King, Martin Luther, Jr. The Autobiography of Martin Luther King, Jr. New York: Warner Books, 1998. Print.

King, Mary. Mahatma Gandhi and Martin Luther King, Jr.: The Power of Nonviolent Action. New York: United Nations Education, Scientific, and Cultural Organization, 1999. Print.

Kirk, Connie Ann. Mark Twain: A Biography. Westport, CT: Greenwood, 2004. Print.\

Kirk, Russell. "The Moral Imagination." The Russell Kirk Center for Cultural Renewal. The Russell Kirk Center.2013. Web. Oct. 2013 <http://www.kirkcenter.org/index.php/detail/the-moral-imagination/>.

Kirkpatrick, David. The Facebook Effect: The Inside Story of the Company That Is Connecting the World. New York: Simon & Schuster, 2010.

Print. Kluger, Jeffrey. Splendid Solution: Jonas Salk and the Conquest of Polio. New York: Berkley, 2004.Print.

Kluivers, Ruud. "No Success Without Failure: How to Get It Right." Wolters Kluwer: The Intelligent Solutions Blog. Wolters Kluwer, 12 Nov. 2010. Web. Oct. 2013 <http://solutions wolterskluwer.com/blog/2010/11/ no-success-without-failure-how-to-get-it-right/>.

Koch, Richard. The 80/20 Principle: The Secret to Achieving More with Less. New York: Doubleday, 2008. Print.

Konia, John and Mark Kramer. "Collective Impact." Ssireview.org. Stanford Social Innovation Review, Winter 2011. Web. Oct. 2013 <http://www.ssireview.org/articles/ entry/collective_impact>.

Korany, Bahgat and Rabab El-Mahdi, eds. Arab Spring in Egypt: Revolution and Beyond. New York: American University in Cairo, 2012. Print.

Kreeft, Peter. Socrates Meets Descartes: The Father of Philosophy Analyzes the Father of Modern Philosophy's Discourse on Method. San Francisco: Ignatius, 2007. Print.

Krishnamurti, J. and David Bohm. The Ending of Time. New York: HarperCollins, 1985. Print.

Kristof, Nicholas D. and Sheryl WuDunn. Half the Sky: Turning Oppression into Opportunity for Women Worldwide. New York: Vintage, 2009. Print.

Kron, Josh. "The Africa You Haven't Heard About: Why Africa Is No Longer the Disaster Zone Many Americans Think It Is." New York Times Upfront. 10 Dec. 2012. The Free Library. Web. Oct. 2013. <http://www.thefreelibrary.com/The+Africa+you+haven't+ heard+about%3A+why+Africa+is+no+longer+the...-a0312725868>.

Kunhardt McGee Productions. This Emotional Life. Boston: NOVA/WGBH Science Unit & Vulcan Productions, 2009. Film.

Lamb, Gregory M. "Bill Drayton sees a world where 'everyone is a changemaker.'" CSMonitor.com. The Christian Science Monitor, 16 May 2011. Web. Oct. 2013 <http://www.csmonitor.com/World/Making-a-difference/Change-Agent/2011/0516/ Bill-Drayton-sees-a-world-where-everyone-is-a-changemaker>.

Landmine Monitor Report. New York: Human Rights Watch, n.d. Print.

Lansing, Alfred. Endurance: Shackleton's Incredible Voyage. New York: Basic-Perseus, 2007. Print.

Lauring, Jakob and Charlotte Jonasson. Group Processes in Ethnically Diverse Organizations: Language and Intercultural Learning. Hauppauge, NY: Nova Science, 2010. Print.

Laxamana, Leah L. "Saude Crianca: Snapshots From the Inside." The Huffington Post. TheHuffingtonPost.com, Inc., 7 Oct. 2013. Web. Oct. 2013 <http://www. huffingtonpost.com/tag/vera-cordeiro>.

LeDoux, Joseph. Synaptic Self: How Our Brains Become Who We Are. New York: Penguin, 2003. Print.

Lee, Harper. To Kill a Mockingbird. New York: HarperCollins, 1988. Print. Lehrer, Jonah. Imagine: How Creativity Works. New York: Houghton Mifflin, 2012. Print.

Lerner, Y., C.J. Honey, L.J. Silbert, U. Hasson. "Topographic mapping of a hierarchy of temporal receptive windows using a narrated story." Journal of Neuroscience (2011) 31(8):2906-2915. Print.

Lillard, Paula Polk. Montessori: A Modern Approach. New York: Schocken, 1988. Print.

Lincoln, Abraham. Emancipation Proclamation. 1863.

Linkner, Josh. Disciplined Dreaming: A Proven System to Drive Breakthrough Creativity. San Francisco: Jossey-Bass, 2011. Print.

Llanas, Sheila. Jonas Salk. Mankato, MN: Abdo, 2013. Print.

Lois, George. George Lois On His Creation of the Big Idea. New York: Assouline, 2008. Print. Lopez,

Kathryn Jean. "Revolutionary Father." NationalReview.com. National Review Online, 2013. Web. Oct. 2013 <http://www.nationalreview.com/articles/243534/revolutionary-father-kathryn-jean-lopez>.

Love, Susan. "Thomas Alva Edison (1847 – 1931)." Patentdrafting.com. Morgan Hill, CA: Technographics, n.d. Web. Oct. 2013 <http://www.patentdrafting.com/edison.htm>.

Love, Susan. "Thomas Alva Edison." Patentdrafting.com. n.d. Web. Jan. 2013. <http://www.patentdrafting.com/edison.htm>.

Lubeck, Paul M. "The Crisis of African Development: Conflicting Interpretations and Resolutions." Annual Review of Sociology. (1992) 18:519-40. Annual Reviews. Oct. 2013 <http://-www.annualreviews.org/doi/abs/10.1146/annurev.so.18.080192.002511?journalCode=soc>.

Ludwig, Adam. "Ashoka Chairman Bill Drayton on the Power of Social Entrepreneurship." Techonomy: Revolutions in Progress. Forbes.com LLC, 12 March 2012. Web. Oct. 2013 <http://www.forbes.com/sites/techonomy/2012/03/12/ashoka-chairman-bill-drayton-on-the-power-of-social-entrepreneurship/>.

MacEoin, Gary. Father Moreau: Founder of Holy Cross. Whitefish, MT: Literary Licensing, LLC, 2012. Print.

Mackay, Christopher S. Ancient Rome: A Military and Political History. New York: Cambridge University Free Press, 2004. Print.

Mainwaring, Simon. We First: How Brands and Consumers Use Social Media to Build a Better World. New York: Palgrave-Macmillan, 2011. Print.

Mandler, George. Consciousness Recovered: Psychological Functions and Origins of Conscious Thought. Philadelphia: John Benjamins, 2002. Print.

Marcello, Patricia Cronin. Mohandas K. Gandhi: A Biography. Westport, CT: Greenwood, 2006. Print.

Maridal, J. Haavard. "The Good Samaritan Effect: The Virtuous Cycle of Private Charity." Huff Post Impact. 24 Jan. 2013. Web. Oct. 2013 <http://www.huffingtonpost.com/j-haavard-maridal/the-good-samaritan-effect_b_2545630.html>.

Marquez, Gabriel Garcia. Love in the Time of Cholera. New York: Vintage, 2007. Print.

Marshall, Perry. 80/20 Sales and Marketing: The Definitive Guide to Working Less and Making More. Irvine, CA: Entrepreneur, 2013. Print.

Martel, Yann. "Conversation: Life of Pi." Interview by Ray Swarez. PBS Newshour. MacNeil/Lehrer Productions, 11 Nov. 2002. Web. Oct. 2013 <http://www.pbs.org/newshour/bb/entertainment/july-dec02/martel_11-11.html>.

Maskalyk, James. Six Months in Sudan: A Young Doctor in a War-Torn Village. New York: Doubleday, 2009. Print.

Maslow, Abraham H. Motivation and Personality. Old Tappan, NJ: Pearson, 1997. Print.

Masur, Louis P. The Civil War: A Concise History. New York: Oxford University, 2011. Print.

McCain, John. Character is Destiny. New York: Random, 2005. Print.

McCarty, Brad. "6 Stories of Life-changing Social Media Connections." *Social Media.* The Next Web, Inc., 2001-2013. Web. Jan 2013. <http://thenextweb.com/ socialmedia/2011/09/03/6-stories-of-life-changing-social-media-connections/>.

McClure, Alexander K. Lincoln's Yarns and Stories. Project Gutenberg, 2012. eBook.

McFadden, Robert D. "John W. Gardner, 89, Founder of Common Cause and Adviser to Presidents, Dies." NYTimes. com. The New York Times Company, 18 Feb. 2002. Web. Oct 2013 <http://www.nytimes.com/2002/02/18/us/john-w-gardner-89-founder-of-common-cause-and-adviser-to-presidents-dies.html?pagewanted=all&src=pm>.

McGray, Douglas. "Dambisa Moyo: Cut Off Aid to Africa." Wired Magazine 17:10 21 Sept. 2009, Web. Oct. 2013 <http://www.wired.com/techbiz/people/magazine/17-10/ ff_smartlist_moyo>.

McKay, Brett and Kate. "The Pocket Notebooks of 20 Famous Men." *Theartofmanliness. com.* DIYThemes.com, 13 Sept. 2010. Web. Jan. 2013.

McKee, Robert. *Story.* Sedona, AZ: Storylogue.com, 2010. Web. Jan. 2013. <http://www. storylogue.com/>.

McKee, Robert. Story: Substance, Structure, Style and the Principles of Screenwriting. New York: HarperCollins, 1997. Print.

McKim, Donald. "Cy Young: A Life in Baseball." Baseball-almanac.com. Baseball-Almanac, 2013. Web. Oct. 2013 <http://www.baseball-almanac.com/dugout0e.shtml>.

McKinsey & Company. "The Rise of Social Entrepreneurship Suggests a Possible Future for Global Capitalism." Skoll World Forum. Forbes.com LLC, 2 May 2013. Web. Oct. 2013 <http://www.forbes.com/sites/skollworldforum/2013/05/02/the-rise-of-social-entrepreneurship-suggests-a-possible-future-for-global-capitalism/>.

McPherson, James M. Abraham Lincoln. New York: Oxford University, 2009. Print.

McPherson, Stephanie Sammartino. TV's Forgotten Hero: The Story of Philo T. Farnsworth. Minneapolis, MN: Carolrhoda, 1996. Print.

Meisler, Stanley. Kofi Annan: A Man of Peace in a World of War. Hoboken, NJ: Wiley, 2007. Print.

Melander, Rochelle. *Write-a-thon.* Cincinnati, OH: Writer's Digest Books, 2011. Print.

Merriam-Webster. The Merriam-Webster Dictionary. Springfield, MA, Merriam-Webster, 2008. Print.

Messent, Peter. The Cambridge Introduction to Mark Twain. New York: Cambridge University, 2007. Print.

Mezrich, Ben. The Accidental Billionaires: The Founding of Facebook: A Tale of Sex, Money, Genius and Betrayal. New York: Doubleday, 2009. Print.

Michalko, Michael. Cracking Creativity. New York: Te n Speed, 2001. Print.

Middlekauff, Robert. The Glorious Cause: The American Revolution, 1763-1789. New York: Oxford University, 2005. Print.

Mind Brain Behavior Interfaculty Initiative. Harvard University. 2013. Web. Oct. 2013. <http://mbb.harvard.edu/>.

MissionariesOfAfrica.org. Missionaries of Africa, 2008. Web. Oct. 2013. <http://www. missionariesofafrica.org/>.

Missionary Society of St. Paul. Houston, TX: Missionary Society of St. Paul, 2013. Web. Oct. 2013 <http://www.mspfathers.org/>.

Monnet, Jean. Memoirs. New York: Doubleday, 1978. Print.

Montessori, Maria. The Absorbent Mind. New York: Henry Holt, 1995. Print.

Moore, David W. "Close to 6 in 10 Americans want to lose weight." *Gallup Well Being.* Gallup, Inc.: 10 Mar. 2006. Web. Jan. 2013. <http://www.gallup.com/poll/21859/close-americans-want-lose-weight.aspx>.

Moos, Rudolf H. and Bernice S. Moos. "Treatment plus Alcoholics Anonymous may work best for those with drinking problems." Research and Development. United States Department of Veterans Affairs, 22 Oct. 2009. Web. Oct. 2013 <http://www.research. va.gov/ news/research_highlights/alcoholism-101105.cfm#.Uoeq6sjnb4g>.

Morgan, Edmund S. The Birth of the Republic, 1763-89. Chicago: The University of Chicago, 2013. Print.

Mothers2mothers.org. Mothers2mothers South Africa, n.d. Web. Oct. 2013 <http://www. m2m.org/>.

Moyo, Dambisa. Dead Aid. New York: Farrar, Straus and Giroux, 2009. Print.

Mueller, Anne Moore. "Thomas Clarkson." Quakers and Slavery Project. Institute of Museum and Library Services, 2007. Web. Oct. 2013 <http://trilogy.brynmawr.edu/ speccoll/quakersandslavery/commentary/people/clarkson.php >.

Muir, John. The Eight Wilderness Discovery Books. Seattle, WA: The Mountaineers, 1992. Print.

Murray, David Kord. Borrowing Brilliance. New York: Gotham, 2009. Print.

Murray, David Kord. *Borrowing Brilliance.* New York: Gotham Books, 2009. Print.

Nabokov, Vladimir. Lolita. New York: Vintage, 1997. Print.

Navpress.com. NavPress.com. n.d. Web. Oct. 2013 <http://www.navpress.com/magazines/ archives/article.aspx?id=11009>.

Neilson, William Allan and Ashley Horace Thorndike. The Facts About Shakespeare. New Zealand: Aeterna, 2011. Print.

NelsonMandela.org. Nelson Mandela Foundation, 2013. Web. Oct. 2013 <http://www. nelsonmandela.org/>. New Statesman. "Does Aid Work?" New Statesman.

New Statesman, 20 June 2012. Web. Oct. 2013 <http://www.newstatesman.com/2012/06/ does-aid-work>.

New York Times UpFront Magazine. Feb. 2012. Print.

Nichol, Lee, ed. The Essential David Bohm. New York: Routledge, 2003. Print.

Nicholls, Alex, ed. Social Entrepreneurship: New Models of Sustainable Social Change. New York: Oxford University, 2006. Print.

Nightingale, Florence. Notes on Nursing: What it is and What it is not (1860). Mineola, NY: Dover, 1969. Print.

Nir, Y., U. Hasson, I. Levy, Y. Yeshurun, R. Malach. "Widespread functional connectivity and fMRI fluctuations in human visual cortex in the absence of visual stimulation." NeuroImage (2006) 30:1313-24. Print.

Nolen, Stephanie. 28: Stories of AIDS in Africa. New York: Walker, 2007. Print.

Notkin, Melanie. "How Social Media Changed my Life." *Bub.blicio.us.* Bub.blicio.us, 22 Apr. 2011. Web. Jan. 2013.

Novak, Michael. "Benedict: The Quiet Pope, the Scholar." The Huffington Post. TheHuffingtonPost.com, Inc.,18 Feb 2013. Web. Oct. 2013 <http://www. huffingtonpost.com/michael-novak/pope-benedict-xvi-resignation_b_2712806. html>.

Novogratz, Jacqueline. The Blue Sweater: Bridging the Gap Between Rich and Poor in an Interconnected World. New York: Rodale, 2009. Print.

Nuland, Sherwin. Leonardo da Vinci. New York: Penguin Lives, 2000. Print.

O'Grady, Erica. "Everything Changes." *What I Learned Today.* Medium.com, 14 Nov. 2012. Web. Jan. 2013.

O'Grady, Erica. Everything Changes. medium.com. 14 Nov. 2012. Web. Oct. 2013 <https:// medium.com/what-i-learned-today/55694ab243c7 >.

Oliver, Laura. The Story Within: New Insights and Inspiration for Writers. New York: Alpha-Penguin, 2011. Print.

Ondaatje, Michael. The English Patient. New York: Vintage, 1992. Print.

Orbinski, James. Imperfect Offering. New York: Walker, 2008. Print.

Osborne, Robin. Greece in the Making 1200-479 BC. New York: Routledge, 2009. Print.

Pallotta, Dan. "HBR Blog Network: Start with an Idea." Web log post. *Harvard Business Review.* Harvard Business School Publishing, 28 July 2010. Web. Jan. 2013.

Paredes, Mario J. "What Makes Us Happy? Balancing Success and Salvation." Mr. Mario's Reflections on Faith, Culture and Religion. blogspot.com, 30 Jan. 2011. Web. Oct. 2013 <http://mariojparedesen.blogspot. com/2011_01_01_archive.html>.

Parker, Sam. 212: The Extra Degree. Dallas, TX: Walk the Talk, 2005. Print.

Parsons, Heather. Father Peter Rookey: Man of Miracles. New York: Robert Andrews Press, 1994. Print.

Patton, Katie. "Katie Patton." YouTube.com, YouTube, n.d. Web. Oct. 2013 <http://www. youtube.com/ playlist?list=UU9WAHCZjaVqdnA7eEkMaiDw>.

Paul, Annie Murphy. "Your Brain on Fiction." New York Times Sunday Review. The New York Times Company, 17 March 2012. Web. Oct. 2013. <http://www.nytimes. com/2012/03/18/opinion/sunday/the-neuroscience-of-your-brain-on-fiction. html?pagewanted=all&_r=0>.

PaulMcCartney.com. MPL Communications Ltd./Paul McCartney, 2013. Web. Oct. 2013 <http://www. paulmccartney.com/>.

Payne, Charles M. I've Got the Light of Freedom: The Organizing Tradition and the Mississippi Freedom Struggle. Berkeley, CA: University of California, 2007. Print.

Pennebaker, James W. Opening Up: The Healing Power of Expressing Emotions. New York: Guilford, 1997. Print.

Pennington, Beth. "Dealing with Life After Combat—Sharing leads to healing." *Voiceofwarriors.com.* WordPress, 23 Feb. 2012. Web. Jan. 2013.

Petit, Patrick U. Creating a New Civilization through Social Entrepreneurship. Piscataway, NJ: Transaction, 2010. Print.

Pheko, Mots. "Africa: Effects of Colonialism on Africa's Past and Present." AZAPO Commemoration of African Liberation Day, Pimville Community Hall Soweto, 26 May 2012. Address. Oct. 2013 <http://allafrica.com/ stories/201206010988.html>.

Phil Ament. "Assembly Line." Ideafinder.com. Troy, MI: The Great Idea Finder, 16 May 2005. Web. Oct. 2013 <http://www.ideafinder.com/history/inventions/assbline. htm>.

Phillips, Christopher. Socrates Cafe: A Fresh Taste of Philosophy. New York: W.W. Norton, 2001. Print.

Pink, Daniel H. A Whole New Mind. New York: Riverhead, 2006. Print.

Pink, Daniel H. *A Whole New Mind: Why Right-Brainers will Rule the Future.* New York: The Berkley Publishing Group, 2006. Print.

Piper, John. Seeing and Savoring Jesus Christ. Wheaton, IL: Crossway, 2004. Print.

Pipes, Richard. The Concise History of the Russian Revolution. New York: Vintage, 2005. Print.

Plato. Apology. New York: International Business Publications, USA, 2010. Print.

Pojer, Susan M. European Colonialism in Africa. Chappaqua, NY: Susan M. Pojer, n.d. PDF file.

Post, Stephen G. "Help Others: How helping others helps you." *Liveyourlifewell.org.* Alexandria, VA: Mental HealthAmerica, 2013. Web. Jan. 2013.

Pratchett, Terry. Mort. New York: Harper, 2013. Print.

Prunier, Gerard. Darfur: The Ambiguous Genocide. New York: Cornell University, 2005. Print.

Purdue, Erica. "WHAT'S NEXT?: Social Media Is Changing the Way We Communicate."*Heritage Newspapers.* Journal Register, 21 Mar. 2012. Web. Jan. 2013.

Quasey, Kathleen E. Healer of Souls: The Life of Father Peter Mary Rookey and the International Compassion Ministry. Bloomington, IN: Xlibris, 2008. Print.

Ramsland, Katherine. SNAP: Seizing Your Aha! Moments. Amherst, NY: Prometheus, 2012. Print.

Rao, Srinivas. "The Power of Hitting Rock Bottom." *Life Optimizer.* Word Press, 24 Aug. 2010. Web. Jan. 2013.

Ratzinger, Joseph. The Legacy of John Paul II: Images and Memories. San Francisco: St. Ignatius, 2005. Print.

Regev, M., C.J. Honey, U. Hasson. "Modality-selective and modality-invariant neural responses to spoken and written narratives." Journal of Neuroscience (2013) 33(40):15978 –88. Print.

Restak, Richard. Modular Brain. New York: Touchstone, 1995. Print.

Reynolds, Quentin. The Wright Brothers: Pioneers of American Aviation. New York: Random, 1950. Print.

Ripley, Amanda. The Unthinkable: Who Survives When Disaster Strikes—and Why. New York: Crown, 2008. Print.

Robbins, Anthony. Awaken the Giant Within: How to Take Immediate Control of Your Mental, Emotional, Physical and Financial Destiny. New York: Free, 1991. Print.

Robertsherfield.com. Las Vegas, NJ: Robert M. Sherfield, n.d. Web. Oct. 2013 <http://www.robertsherfield.com/>.

Rohn, Jim. The Art Of Exceptional Living. New York: Simon & Schuster Audio, 2003. CD.

Roskill, Mark, ed. Letters of Vincent van Gogh. New York: Touchstone, 2008. Print.

Rowling, J. K. "Welcome to J.K. Rowling's Website." Jkrowling.com. 2012. Web. Oct. 2013. <http://www.jkrowling.com/>.

Rubin, Gretchen. The Happiness Project. New York: Harper, 2011. Print.

Sachs, Jeffrey D. "Aid Ironies." Huff Post World. TheHuffingtonPost.com, Inc., 24 May 2009. Web. Oct. 2013 <http://www.huffingtonpost.com/jeffrey-sachs/aid-ironies_b_207181.html>.

Salih, Tayeb. Season of Migration to the North. New York: New York Review of Books, 2009. Print.

Salinger, J.D. Catcher in the Rye. Boston: Little, Brown, 1991. Print.

Sampson, Danielle. Social Entrepreneurship. Hauppauge, NY: Nova Science, 2011. Print.

Schaefer, Lola M. Thomas Edison. North Mankato, MN: Capstone, 2002. Print.

Schaffer, David. People in the News: Bono. Farmington Hills, MI: Lucent, 2003. Print.

Schwab, Peter. Africa: A Continent Self-Destructs. New York: Palgrave for St. Martins Press, 2001. Print.

Schwartz, Beverly. Rippling: How Social Entrepreneurs Spread Innovation Throughout the World. San Francisco: Jossey-Bass, 2012. Print.

Scott, Elizabeth. "How Helping Others Can Reduce Stress and Increase Happiness." About.com Stress Management. About.com. 29 Dec. 2011. Web. Oct. 2013 <http://stress.about.com/od/positiveattitude/qt/helping.htm>.

Seelig, Tina. InGenius: A Crash Course on Creativity. New York: HarperOne, 2012. Print.

Selanikio, Joel and Paul Margie. "Data Collection Improving World – Dr. Joel Selanikio Explains." YouTube.com. You Tube, n.d. Web. Oct. 2013 <http://www.youtube.com/watch?v=JtAcEpCUFCw>.

Selanikio, Joel. "Spotlight on DataDyne: Dr. Joel Selanikio." Interviewed by Fatima. Designmeasurechange.com. Evalu, n.d. Web. Oct. 2013 <http://www.designmeasurechange.com/spotlight-on-datadyne-dr-joel-selanikio/>.

Seligman, Martin E. P. Authentic Happiness: Using the New Positive Psychology to Realize Your Potential for Lasting Fulfillment. New York: Atria, 2004. Print.

Sen, Amartya. "Amartya Sen: The Taste of True Freedom." Interviewed by Tonkin Boyd. The Independent. Independent.co.uk, 5 July 2013. Web. Oct. 2013 <http://www.independent.co.uk/arts-entertainment/art/features/amartya-sen-the-taste-of-true-freedom-8688089.html>.

Shackleton, Ernest. Escape from the Antarctic. New York: Penguin, 2007. Print.

Shafer, Kathryn and Fran Greenfield. Asthma Free in 21 Days: The Breakthrough Mind-Body Healing Program. New York: HarperCollins, 2000. Print.

Shah, Anup. "Racism." Global Issues, 8 Aug. 2010. Web. Oct. 2013 <http://www.globalissues.org/article/165/racism>.

Shakespeare, William. Hamlet. New York: Simon & Schuster, 2003. Print.

Shapiro, Ruth A. The Real Problem Solvers: Social Entrepreneurs in America. Stanford, CA: Stanford Business, 2012. Print.

Sharansky, Natan and Ron Dermer. The Case for Democracy: The Power of Freedom to Overcome Tyranny and Terror. New York: PublicAffairs, 2006. Print.

Sharansky, Natan. Defending Identity: Its Indispensable Role in Protecting Democracy. New York: PublicAffairs, 2008.

Shekhia, Zebiba. Healing Bridges. New York: Morgan James, 2008. Print.

Sher, Aubrey J. Romulus & Remus: The Imperfect Murders. Bloomington, IN: AuthorHouse, 2010. Print.

Sherfield, Robert M. and Patricia G. Moody. Cornerstones for Community College Success. 2nd ed. Upper Saddle River, NJ: Prentice Hall, 2013. Print.

Sherfield, Robert M. Cornerstone: Discovering Your Potential, Learning Actively, and Living Well. Concise 5th ed. Upper Saddle River, NJ: Prentice Hall, 2007. Print.

Shields, Charles J. Mohandas K. Gandhi (OA) (Z) (Overcoming Adversity). New York: Chelsea House, 2001. Print.

Siegel, Bernie S. Love, Medicine and Miracles. New York: HarperCollins, 1986. Print.

Simkin, John. "1807 Abolition of Slavery Act." Spartacus Educational. Spartacus Educational, Sept. 1997 – June 2013. Web. Oct. 2013 <http://www.spartacus. schoolnet.co.uk/Lslavery07.htm>.

Simonton, Dean Keith. Origins of Genius: Darwinian Perspectives on Creativity. New York: Oxford University, 1999. Print.

Simonton, Dean Keith. Scientific Genius: A Psychology of Science. New York: Cambridge University, 1988. Print.

Simpleology: Simplifying Your Complicated Life. Simpleology, 2012. Web. Oct. 2013. <http://www.simpleology.com/>.

Singer, Peter. "Peter Singer: The Why and How of Effective Altruism." TED: Ideas worth spreading. TED Conferences, LLC. May 2013. Web. Oct. 2013 <http://www.ted.com/ talks/peter_singer_the_why_and_how_of_effective altruism.html>.

Sirolli, Ernesto. Ripples from the Zambezi: Passion, Entrepreneurship and the Rebirth of Local Economies. Gabriola Island, BC, Canada: New Society, 1999. Print.

SkollFoundation.org. The Skoll Foundation, 2013. Web. Oct. 2013 <http://www. skollfoundation.org/>.

Social Entrepreneurship: Skoll Foundation, Bill Drayton, Charityvillage.Com, Echoing Green, Schwab Foundation for Social Entrepreneurship. Memphis, TN: General Books LLC, 2010. Print.

Spector, Dina. "Facebook Facebook Http://www.facebook.com."Business Insider. Business Insider, Inc., 26 Sept. 2012. Web. Jan. 2013. <http://www.businessinsider.com/ blackboard/facebook>.

Spink, Kathryn. The Miracle the Message the Story: Jean Vanier and L'Arche. Mahwah, NJ: Paulist, 2006. Print.

Stacher, Joshua. Adaptable Autocrats: Regime Power in Egypt and Syria. Stanford, CA: Stanford University, 2012. Print.

Standage, Tom. A History of the World in 6 Glasses. New York: Walker, 2005. Print.

Standing, E. M. Maria Montessori: Her Life and Work. New York: Plume-Penguin, 1998. Print.

Steele, Philip. Sudan, Darfur and the Nomadic Conflicts. New York: Rosen, 2012. Print.

Stelzner, Michael. "2012 Social Media Marketing Industry Report." Social Media Examiner. Social Media Examiner, 3 April 2012. Web. Oct. 2013 <http://www.socialmediaexaminer.com/social-media-marketing-industry-report-2012/>.

Stiglitz, Joseph E., Amartya Sen and Jean-Paul Fitoussi. Mismeasuring Our Lives: Why GDP Doesn't Add Up. New York: New, 2010. Print.

Stone, Nikki. "Bill Drayton." When Turtles Fly: Secrets of Successful People Who Know How to Stick Their Necks Out. New York: Morgan James, 2010. Print.

Strachey, Lytton. Eminent Victorians. New York: Penguin, 1990. Print.

Success.org. Success Magazine, 2013. Web. Oct. 2013 <http://www.success.com/articles/print/850>.

Sullivan, George. Thomas Edison. New York: Scholastic, 2002. Print.

Taithe, Bertrand. The Killer Trail: A Colonial Scandal in the Heart of Africa. New York: Oxford University, 2009. Print.

Tallentyre, S. G. The Life of Voltaire. London: Smith, Elder, 1903. Print.

Taylor, Jill Bolte. My Stroke of Insight. New York: Viking, 2008. Print.

Teresa of Calcutta. Mother Teresa: Come Be My Light: The Private Writings of the Saint of Calcutta. New York: Image, 2007. Print.

The Editors of Conari Press. Random Acts of Kindness. San Francisco: Conari, 2002. Print.

The Editors of Encyclopaedia Britannica. "Vinoba Bhave." Britannica.com. Encyclopaedia Britannica, Inc. 2013. Web. Oct. 2013 <http://www.britannica.com/EBchecked/topic/64103/Vinoba-Bhave>.

The Epic of Gilgamesh. New York: Penguin Classics, 1960. Print.

The Jean Monnet Association. "Jean Monnet 1888-1979." Historiasiglo20.org. Juan Carlos Ocana, 2003. Web. Oct. 2013 <http://www.historiasiglo20.org/europe/monnet.htm>.

The Schomburg Center for Research in Black Culture. The Abolition of the Slave Trade. The New York Public Library, 2012. Web. Oct. 2013 <http://abolition.nypl.org/home/>.

The Social Habit: Social Media Research Redefined. The Social Habit, 2012. Web. Oct. 2013 <http://socialhabit.com/>.

The United States President's Emergency Plan for AIDS Relief. U.S. State Department, 2013. Web. Oct. 2013 <http://www.pepfar.gov/>.

TheGlobalFund.org. The Global Fund To Fight AIDS, Tuberculosis, and Malaria, 2013. Web. Oct. 2013 <www.theglobalfund.org/en/>.

Therese, de Lisieux. Autobiography of St Therese of Lisieux. CreateSpace Independent Publishing Platform, 2010. Print.

Thomas, Ann. Henry Ford's Dream: Car Assembly Lines. Flinders Park SA, Australia: Era, 2007. Print.

Thomas, Hugh. The Slave Trade: The Story of the Atlantic Slave Trade: 1440 – 1870. New York: Touchstone, 1997. Print.

Thompson, Elizabeth F. Justice Interrupted: The Struggle for Constitutional Government in the Middle East. Boston: Harvard University, 2013. Print.

Timberg, Craig and Daniel Halperin. Tinderbox: How the West Sparked the AIDS Epidemic and How the World Can Finally Overcome It. New York: Penguin, 2012. Print.

Timberlake, Lewis. First Thing Every Morning. Naperville, IL: Simple Truths, 2003. Print.

Tolkien, J.R.R. The Two Towers. New York: Del Rey, 2012. Print.

Tollens, Jr., Max. "An Evening With an American Hero: Admiral Bob Shumaker." Patriot Action Network.

Grassfire Nation, 21 Apr. 2011. Web. Oct. 2013 <http://patriotaction.net/profiles/blogs/an-evening-with-an-american?xg_source=activity>.

Tomkins, Stephen. William Wilberforce: A Biography. Grand Rapids, MI: Eerdmans, 2007. Print.

Tonnelier, Constant. Through the Year with Saint Thérèse of Lisieux: Living the Little Way. Liguori, MO: Liguori, 1998. Print.

Tracy, Brian. Focal Point: A Proven System to Simplify Your Life, Double Your Productivity, and Achieve All Your Goals. New York: AMACOM, 2004. Print.

Tracy, Brian. Reinvention: How to Make the Rest of Your Life the Best of Your Life. New York: AMACOM, 2009. Print.

Triage: Dr. James Orbinski's Humanitarian Dilemma. Dir. Patrick Reed. Perf. Dr. James Orbinski. Docurama, 2009. DVD.

Turner, Mark. The Literary Mind: The Origins of Thought and Language. New York: Oxford University, 1998. Print.

UNAIDS.org/en. United Nations/UNAIDS, n.d. Web. Oct. 2013 <http://www.unaids.org/en/>.

van Steenwijk, Alwine de Vos. Father Joseph Wresinski: voice of the poorest. Goleta, CA: Queenship, 1996. Print.

Vanier, Jean. "Fragility."Jean Vanier. Ed. Isabelle Aumont. L'Arche Internationale, n.d. Web. 20 Jan. 2013. <http://www.jean-vanier.org/en/home>.

Vanier, Jean. Becoming Human. Mahwah, NJ: Paulist, 2008. Print.

Vanier, Jean. Letters to My Brothers and Sisters in L'Arche. L'Arche Internationale, 1996.

Vasari, Giorgio. The Lives of the Artists. New York: Oxford University, 2008. Print.

Venezia, Mike. Albert Einstein: Universal Genius. New York: Scholastic, 2009. Print.

Voltaire, Peter Constantine. Candide: or Optimism. New York: Modern Library, 2005. Print.

Wallace, William E. Michelangelo: The Artist, The Man and His Times. New York: Cambridge University, 2010. Print.

We Can End Poverty. United Nations, 2013. Web. Oct. 2013 <http://www.un.org/millenniumgoals/>.

Web Team. "Poverty Questions. . . and Answers." Blog on Child Poverty. Compassion International. 9 Mar. 2009. Web. Oct. 2013 <http://blog.compassion.com/poverty-questions/?gclid=CMa7z6j9nrkCFWpk7AodBDQAKg>.

Weigel, George. Witness to Hope: The Biography of Pope John Paul II. New York: Harper Perennial, 2005. Print.

Weis, Veronica. "Tiziana Dearing, CEO of Boston Rising, Shares Her Post-Assets Learning Conference Ideas." Cfed.org. Corporation for Enterprise Development, 30 Oct. 2012. Web. Oct. 2013 <http://cfed.org/blog/inclusiveeconomy/assets_learning_conference_reflections_profile_tiziana_dearing_of_boston_rising/>.

Welter, Bill and Jean Egman. The Prepared Mind of a Leader. San Francisco: Jossey-Bass, 2006. Print.

Whitman, Walt. The Complete Writings of Walt Whitman, Volume I. Hong Kong: Forgotten Books, 2012. Print.

WHO.int/en. World Health Organization, 2013. Web. Oct. 2013 <http://www.who.int/en/>.

Widrich, Leo. "The Science of Storytelling: Why Telling a Story is the Most Powerful Way to Activate our Brains." Lifehacker.com. Lifehacker.com, 5 Dec. 2012. Web. Oct. 2013 <http://lifehacker.com/5965703/the-science-of-storytelling-why-telling-a-story-is-the-most-powerful-way-to-activate-our-brains>.

Wilberforce, William. William Wilberforce: Greatest Works. Alachua, FL: Bridge-Logos, 2007. Print.

Williams, Abiodun, ed. The Brilliant Art of Peace: Lectures from the Kofi Annan Series. New York: United States Institute of Peace Press, 2013. Print.

Williams, Mary. Brothers in Hope: The Story of the Lost Boys of Sudan. New York: Lee and Low, 2005. Print.

Wilson, Ellen Gibson. Thomas Clarkson: A Biography. New York: Palgrave-Macmillan, 1990. Print.

Wodon, Quentin, ed. "Extreme Poverty and Human Rights: Essays on Joseph Wresinski." WorldBank.org. World Bank, 9 Mar. 2000. PDF/Web. <http://www-wds.worldbank.org/external/default/WDSContentServer/WDSP/IB/2004/02/25/000265513_20040225165617/Rendered/PDF/wdr27915.pdf>.

Wojtyla, Karol. Love and Responsibility. San Francisco: St. Ignatius, 1993. Print.

Wood, Gordon S. The American Revolution: A History. Modern Library Ed. New York: Random, 2002. Print.

YadVashem.org. Yad Vashem The Holocaust Martyrs' and Heroes' Remembrance Authority, 2013. Web. Oct. 2013 <www.yadvashem.org>.

Yoo, Alice. "Top 6 Technologies That Are Revolutionizing How We Socially Connect." Mylifescoop.com. Federated Media, 2013. Web. Oct. 2013 <http://mylifescoop.com/2013/05/13/top-6-technologies-that-are-revolutionizing-how-we-socially-connect/>.

Yunus Centre. YunusCentre.org, 2011. Web. Oct. 2013 <http://www.muhammadyunus.org/>.

Yunus, Mohammad and Karl Weber. Creating a World Without Poverty: Social Business and the Future of Capitalism. New York: PublicAffairs, 2007. Print.

Yunus, Mohammad. Banker to the Poor: Micro-Lending and the Battle against World Poverty. New York: PublicAffairs, 2007. Print.

Yunus, Mohammed and Aradhana Parmar. South Asia: A Historical Narrative. New York: Oxford University, 2003. Print.

Zenn, J. Michael. The Self Health Revolution. New York: Free, 2012. Print.

CHAPTER NINETEEN

STATISTICS: The Data to prove why InterviewGirl. com Desires to make a Difference in this World

Research Revealed

The purpose of this chapter is to expound upon the statistics mentioned in Chapter One and throughout the book. Collecting interesting stories through InterviewGirl.com and my mission to continue to interview people whenever I can are being completed in order to make a difference in this world: to eliminate miseries that exist. As John McCain told us, "Shared stories help to strengthen the bonds between generations. Through stories we impart the wisdom of our experience and pass along our values." InterviewGirl.com is targeting any and all misery and completing the projects that we are in order to eliminate the misery that someone is experiencing. Currently, the Interview Girl Foundation has projects started with the intent to fight poverty, AIDS, and human trafficking in Africa. As this book revealed, I decided to start making a difference (start eliminating misery for people) by making life better for orphans in Africa through *Operation A²*. This chapter is meant to enlighten you further about some of the gross miseries that the Interview Girl Foundation is working to eliminate: poverty, children living with HIV, and children who are trafficked into slavery-like conditions. The empirical evidence shared in this chapter illuminates why the Interview Girl Foundation hopes to start with eliminating the misery that the orphans in Africa experience. The proceeds from InterviewGirl. com's first two compendiums to be released hope to change some of the statistics you will read about in this chapter.

Part I: Human Trafficking

The United Nations officially defines trafficking as:

> "The recruitment, transportation, transfer, harboring or receipt of persons, by means of the threat or use of force or other forms of coercion, of abduction, of fraud, of deception, of the abuse of power or of a position of vulnerability or of the giving or receiving of payments or benefits to achieve the consent of a person having control over another person, for the purpose of exploitation. Exploitation shall include, at a minimum, the exploitation of the prostitution of others or other forms of sexual exploitation, forced labor or services, slavery or practices similar to slavery, servitude or the removal of organs."[326]

Human trafficking is not limited to women in developing countries. In fact, in almost every country human trafficking takes place and every year thousands of men, women and children are abducted, abused and sold. Human trafficking, sometimes referred to as modern slavery, traps 12.3 million people worldwide. Unfortunately, less than 1% (.4% exactly) of victims are identified. Even among those who are successfully identified, their captors are only convicted 8.5% of the time, leaving millions of victims and offenders invisible to the legal system. Many people in the sex trade are minors—children—being forced to enter the sex trade between 12 and 14 years old. Many female victims were sexually abused by family members, ran away, and were snatched by traffickers. The Internet has intensified the trade by offering almost total anonymity to people buying and selling women and children online.[327]

Organized Crime

Human trafficking is often not facilitated by one person in isolation, but by an organized network of traffickers coordinating the capture, transport and exploitation of victims. With the rise of globalization, human trafficking has spread as offenders take their victims through multiple countries and even to multiple continents. The trade is often wrapped up with other illegal goods, such as weapons, narcotics and money laundering.[328]

Offenders pursue human trafficking for two major reasons: risk and profit. Compared to other crimes, trafficking has low risk and high profit because, as the adage goes, sex sells. While 18% of victims are forced into nonconsensual labor, 79% are forced into the sex trade, where patrons pay generously for sexual acts. Their victims are rarely identified and recovered by the police, partly because traffickers intimidate their slaves, and partly because slaves fear that police will prosecute the slave -and not the offender—for illegal sex work and illegal immigration, even though the slave committed those acts against his or her will.[329]

Human Trafficking in Africa

Human trafficking occurs in almost all countries, including many of those in Africa. For example, during the 2010 World Cup in South Africa, the number of women and children trafficked for sex work into the country increased. Mozambique was one of the major hubs. In 2011, police discovered a trafficking ring that sold forty women per month and girls to patrons in South Africa, which is only the tip of the iceberg because so much trafficking goes unnoticed. In Angola, traffickers transferred women between West Africa and China, while in Madagascar, traffickers transport women to the Middle East.[330] Human trafficking is evidenced within all regions in Africa. According to USAID (2007), the devastation of poverty is a primary push factor for trafficking in persons and is what leads people into unsafe situations and what has persuaded parents to sell their children into slavery. Other factors that have greatly contributed to the vulnerability and risks of women and children include; social and cultural prejudices, divorce, and separation, just to mention a few. As a representative from UNICEF (2004) says, "This heinous crime is said to be intertwined, clandestine and secretive in nature hence the need for holistic approaches in interventions." Poverty, unemployment, armed conflict, socio cultural practices, weak legislation and enforcement and weak capacities in programs addressing trafficking are some of the other factors that have been associated with trafficking.[331] Numerous root causes have been identified for the existence of human trafficking. They include lack of employment opportunities, poverty, economic imbalances among regions of the world, corruption, decline of border controls, gender and ethnic discrimination, and political instability and conflict. These push factors are combined with the pull factors of demand for workers, the possibilities of higher standards of living, and the perceptions of many in poor communities that better opportunities exist in larger cities abroad.[332]

To further understand human trafficking within Africa, we will examine examples in Kenya and Uganda. According to the United Nations, in Kenya, a high number of children are trafficked internally from the rural areas to urban centers to work as domestic servants. These children are often molested, physically, sexually, abused by their employers and in some cases resold.[333] In addition, the HIV/AIDS problem has rendered an estimated 1.7 million children orphans. This has triggered many local and international adoptions giving potential traffickers an easy way to get involved in trafficking the children because they can pretend to be loving families interested in adoption. Some Kenyan children are adopted by foreigners and they are moved out of the country; yet there is no proper monitoring system. Due to this, potential perpetrators can take advantage of the situation. Unfortunately these uncertainties in the Kenyan law, have made the country an attractive destination for inter—country adoptions and human trafficking.[334]

According to the U.S. Department of State's *Trafficking in persons report 2008*, Uganda is a source country for men, women and children trafficked for forced labor and sexual exploitation. There is little information on the actual number of trafficked victims in Uganda; however a high number of boys are trafficked at an early age and they mainly fall under the bracket 10-14 years while girls are moved slightly higher between the ages of 15—19 years. While the overall ratio of female to male trafficked victims remains unclear, the number appears to be steadily growing due to an increase in wars, migration, displacement poverty and disintegration of families.[335]

Tales of human trafficking are tales of lying, corruption and abuse. For example, Marta, a seventeen-year-old girl from Uganda, traveled to southern China to be a secretary at a Chinese company. The company had assured her that she had the position. However, upon arrival, Marta was told that she owed thousands of dollars in debt for her travel, and had to work off the debt as a prostitute in a brothel. First in China and then Vietnam, traffickers forced her to sleep with five people per day in order to repay her "debts." Eventually, she escaped to Indonesia to seek help from human rights organizations, and she now works as a maid. Marta is expecting a child. One of the men she was forced to sleep with got her pregnant. Marta's story is tragic, but unique only in that she escaped; many girls do not. In the past few years, six hundred girls just like Marta living in Uganda have been sold into slavery.[336]

Child Trafficking

The worst glaring form of human trafficking is the child soldier trafficking which has recruited many children into combat, hard labor and also exchanged children into wives and domestic workers. Children are sacrificed in animist Sudan and in the Middle East for guns and food. For example, 25,000—30,000 children were abducted and recruited into the Lord's Resistance Army ranks. These child soldiers were subjected to intolerable, inhuman and the worst forms of degrading treatment. Children are forced to fight as combatants and are also involved in other hazardous activities including carrying heavy luggage, ammunitions, wounded soldiers, merchandise and loot. Girls are subjected to sex slavery and forced marriage. Other children are used to torture, kill and do reconnaissance missions in Uganda and Sudan. There are reports of a small number of children serving in the Uganda Peoples Defense Forces (UPDF) and various local militias.

Each day, more children are trafficked into slavery-like conditions. These include: prostitution, forced labor, child marriage and other atrocious activities. Every day we see the growth of skills and experience of traffickers and those who purchase trafficked persons. Each day, the challenges grow greater for those who seek to prevent child trafficking and provide care for children who have been trafficked.

Activism and Legal Issues

In 2011, in order to better facilitate the prosecution of offenders and the end of trafficking, Michigan Law School's Human Trafficking Clinic created the first public database of U.S. case law concerning the illegal trade. The clinic hopes that this database will "strengthen anti-traffic laws in the United States and... support government officials, law enforcement agencies and practitioners who are working on behalf of human trafficking victims." In order to offer a comprehensive picture of trafficking, the Clinic published criminal and civil cases from before and after the Trafficking Victims Protection Act of 2000. The database records begin in 1980.[337]

The United Nations Office on Drugs and Crime published a similar database. Unlike that of Michigan Law, the UN database includes cases from seventy-seven different countries (although most concern the United States). It also lets lawyers and researchers search by nationality, gender, verdict, appellate decision, legal system and more. Whether these databases have significantly helped lawyers prosecute human traffickers is unclear.[338]

In recent years, nonprofits, NGOs and international governments have intensified the fight against human trafficking. Governments have passed stricter laws against trafficking, and nonprofits work to spread awareness about the problems. One of the most prominent organizations is *Not For Sale*, which "is at the forefront of creating innovative, replicable and sustainable solutions to fight modern-day slavery."[339] *Not For Sale* fights trafficking in three stages: stability/safety, life skills/job training, and dignified work/sustainable future. With this model, *Not For Sale* helps provide food, shelter and legal services to communities (such as refugee camps and slums) who are at high risk for human trafficking. Next, *Not For Sale* provides both victims and at-risk communities with formal and non-formal education, such as cooking, self-worth and sewing. Finally, *Not For Sale* helps create new businesses to hire members of at-risk communities, and works with business owners to improve working conditions. This three-part plan is designed to prevent human trafficking from occurring and to help victims recover.[340] There is hope in the fight against human trafficking because in recent years, nonprofits, NGOs and international governments have increased measures to stop human trafficking. Within this heinous problem, there is hope because individuals are taking actions to make a difference and stop human trafficking.

One of the most hopeful examples in the fight to end human trafficking is Jared Cohen's story. In 2010, Cohen founded Google Ideas, which focuses on how technology can make the world better. In April 2013, he led Google in donating $3 million to create a database system to connect 65 independent hotlines used to report human trafficking. Google chair, Eric Schmidt and Jared Cohen published *The New Digital Age*. The book analyzes this global transformation.[341] Cohen's idea about creating a database system to connect independent hotlines in order to report human trafficking is an action that an individual started in order to help this dreadful crime. People like Cohen who take actions to better the issue provide hope amidst the debauched statistics about how and why human trafficking exists.

Human trafficking exists because of poverty, unemployment, armed conflict, socio cultural practices, weak legislation, weak enforcement and weak capacities in programs addressing trafficking. As the policies within communities and eventually countries become better, ills like child trafficking will weaken. As Anne Mumbi states about Zambia, "it's a beautiful country, a peaceful country—with a terrible policy."[342] For child trafficking to be ceased, progress needs to happen within different areas of a society. Multi-pronged solutions are needed to address problems such as human trafficking, poverty, and AIDS. As poverty, unemployment, and armed conflict go down within communities, so too will unpleasantries like child trafficking. That's why *Operation A²* stresses the importance of education and programs that help individuals to develop skills, businesses, and ultimately solutions people seek within their own communities. The philosophy responsible for the Interview Girl Foundation and the larger goals behind *Operation A²* (diversified solutions are needed in order to eliminate misery in the world) will help in the movement to stop human trafficking as well because as one segment of a society eliminates a misery, other miseries are then also eliminated.

Part II: Global Poverty

Worldwide wealth inequality lowers the standard of living for billions of people. More than 3 billion people, actually, live on less than $2.50 a day, while more than 1.3 billion live on less than $1.25 a day, which is extreme poverty. Of the global poor, 1 billion are children, 22,000 of whom die due to poverty—daily. 165 million children under the age of 5 suffer reduced physical growth and development because of chronic malnutrition. Yearly, 2 million children die because of preventable diseases, such as diarrhea and pneumonia, because their families cannot afford health care.[343]

More than 1 billion people (including 400 million children) do not have and cannot attain clean drinking water. This causes children to miss school. A quarter of the world's population -1.6 billion people -lack electricity, while 80% of the world's population must survive on less than $10 a day. Hunger is the global leading cause of death, stealing the lives of more people than malaria, tuberculosis, and even HIV/AIDS combined. Poverty causes hunger. Below details some of the ways that poverty is felt within Africa:

Maternal/Child Health

Lack of access to technology results in hundreds of thousands of pregnancy-related deaths annually. 287,000 mothers die from pregnancy and childbirth and millions more are affected by complications. According to nonprofit *ONE*, in sub-Saharan Africa, the mortality rate is 24 times higher than the mortality rate in developed countries, while women living in the world's poorest countries are 300 times more likely than their industrialized counterparts to die from complications related to pregnancy or childbirth. If these women could access health care, they could save their lives and their children's lives and lower the rate of birth defects. However, health care systems in many areas of Africa lack sufficient numbers of health care workers, lack adequate basic equipment, and lack adequate infrastructure.[344]

Simple, low-cost solutions would make a big difference. Possibilities include antenatal care, health care during birth, and postpartum and newborn care during the first few weeks after childbirth. According to *ONE*, "research indicates that if women had access to basic maternal health services, 80% of maternal deaths could be prevented. Vitamin A supplementation, which costs only $1.25 per year per child, could save over a quarter of a million young lives annually by reducing the risk and severity of diarrhea and infections."[345] Maternal health and child health are affected when someone lives in poverty.

Other Devastating Results from Poverty

- *Agriculture:* Due to decline in global investment in and developmental assistance for sub-Saharan Africa, poor farmers are struggling to farm enough to feed their families and make money. Many Africans cannot afford to eat because the price of food is rapidly rising locally and worldwide. Since 2011, another 44 million people have been pushed into poverty as a result.[346]

- *Education:* Lack of education traps many people in extreme poverty. Currently, 61 million children are out of school; most of them live in poor countries, in conflict zones, or in rural areas, and are girls. Although primary school is often free, poor families cannot afford to send their children due to test fees and cost of uniforms. Subsequently, millions of children are kept at home to work. The children that do get to attend school face overcrowded buildings, lack of school supplies and countless barriers to secondary schooling, and so many of them drop out. In sub-Saharan Africa, 30% of children who enroll in first grade will maintain their schooling and eventually graduate.[347]

- *Debt:* Under corrupt leadership in the mid-twentieth century, many developing countries accumulated millions of dollars in debt, which they have been struggling for decades to repay. Forced to take on new loans to repay the debts, these countries (such as Lesotho and Kenya) cannot focus on stimulating their economies or improving health care and education for their citizens. In 1996, the Highly Indebted Poor Country Initiative (HPIC) facilitated the cancellation of $94.4 billion of debt, most of which was for sub-Saharan Africa. Although this helped in the short term, not all developing countries received debt cancellation, and are still struggling, and, due to a deficit of promised development funds, the countries that had their debts cancelled are rapidly accumulating new ones. Donors and developed countries are advised to extend subsequent rounds of debt cancellation.[348]

Progress

Millennium Development Goals: In the year 2000, 189 countries made a bold decision to sign the Millennium Development Goals, which are "a set of poverty-busting goals designed to significantly reduce global poverty and disease by 2015."[349]

These goals are:

- "Eradicate extreme hunger and poverty

- Achieve universal primary education

- Promote gender equality and empower women

- Reduce child mortality

- Improve maternal health

• Combat HIV/AIDS, malaria and other diseases

• Ensure environmental sustainability

• Develop a global partnership for development."[350]

Although the goals have not been realized, significant progress has been made. In 1970, only 76% of people had enough to eat, while today that percentage is 87%. Between 1999 and 2010, the number of children in sub-Saharan Africa able to attend school increased by 51 million. Between 2000 and 2011, immunizations of children prevented 5.5 million child deaths. Since 1990, the number of women dying from pregnancy and child-related complications has decreased by 47%. In the past twelve years, the rate of new infections for HIV and AIDS has decreased (or at least stabilized) in 33 countries, most of which are in sub-Saharan Africa. Unfortunately, out of the almost 200 countries who should donate 0.7% of their gross national income to developmental assistance (according to UN goals), only 5 countries have done so.[351]

Outside of the government, individuals are taking matters into their own hands. Thousands of charities have started worldwide in order to combat poverty at home and abroad. Major charities include Oxfam International, Global Giving, Fistula Foundation and Partners in Health.[352] Entrepreneurs have also turned to social entrepreneurship, a relatively new phenomenon where one uses business techniques in order to "build strong and sustainable organizations, which are either set up as not-for-profits or companies."[353] According to the Schwab Foundation, which has a history of working for social change, "social entrepreneurship is about applying practical, innovative and sustainable approaches to benefit society in general, with an emphasis on those who are marginalized and poor."[354] In 2011, for the first time ever, Forbes published a list of the top 30 social entrepreneurs in the world.[355]

Although miseries still need to be eliminated when it comes to Global Poverty, people and organizations have taken many steps forward to make the misery better. The positive steps taken thus far to alleviate the poverty that exists is hope that poverty can be overcome. The Interview Girl Foundation is proud to play a role in helping the world to meet the Millennium Development Goals.

Part III: The AIDS Dilemma What is HIV/AIDS?

Human Immunodeficiency Virus (HIV) is an infection that leads to Acquired Immunodeficiency Syndrome (AIDS). The two are often confused because they are so closely related, however, they are quite distinct. HIV only infects humans, and weakens immune systems by killing T-cells, which combat disease and infection. HIV reproduces itself by latching onto these cells and then destroying them. Although HIV is similar to relatively harmless viruses, such as ones that cause the flu or the cold, HIV has one fatal distinction: the human immune system cannot overcome it, so HIV stays permanently in the body of the infected person. Why? Scientists do not know. Therefore, HIV continues to destroy T-cells until the body can no longer fight off *any* infection or disease. That's when the infected person acquires AIDS.[356]

AIDS is a syndrome, and not a virus or a disease, because it's a complex web of complications and symptoms that often lead to death.[357] When HIV has ravaged the body so much that it's vulnerable to any and all infections, then opportunistic infections (OIs) exploit the weakened immune system and cause fatal sicknesses.[358] When someone has one or more OIs, cancers such as lymphoma or Kaposi's sarcoma, or a low number of T-cells, they will be diagnosed with AIDS.[359]

One reason that HIV/AIDS is so deadly is that it takes a long time to detect: Most HIV-positive people do not have any symptoms until they start to develop AIDS, which can take longer than ten years. In the meantime, they are not receiving treatment, and they can unknowingly infect others with the virus.[360] HIV is most known for being transmitted through sexual contact, but it can also be spread through pregnancy and breastfeeding, drug use by injection, occupational exposure and even (but rarely) blood transfusions and organ transplants. The body fluids that contain enough HIV to transmit the virus include blood, semen, pre-seminal fluid, breast milk, vaginal fluids and rectal mucous.[361]

The Difference Between HIV and AIDS

Let's take a closer look at these words and what they mean: HIV stands for the Human Immunodeficiency Virus. "H" is for Human, meaning that only humans get this virus. People cannot get infected from a pet or a mosquito. "I" is for Immunodeficiency, meaning that this virus causes your immune system to have some serious problems. The immune system is what fights off diseases and infections. When your immune system has problems, it makes it easier for you to get sick and harder for you to get well. "V" is for Virus, which refers to the specific type of germ or antigen. Other types of germs are bacteria, fungi, and parasites. Fortunately, all of those types of germs can be killed with specific medications. Unfortunately, viruses can't be killed. You can't take a medicine like an antibiotic and get rid of HIV. Viruses stay with us forever. Sometimes we are able to create conditions where they don't cause us any problems, and that is where a strong and healthy immune system comes in handy. HIV is found in the body fluids of an infected person (semen and vaginal fluids, blood and breast milk). The virus is passed from one person to another through blood-to-blood and sexual contact. In addition, infected pregnant women can pass HIV to their babies during pregnancy, delivering the baby during childbirth, and through breast feeding.

AIDS (Acquired immune deficiency syndrome or acquired immunodeficiency syndrome) is a disease caused by a virus called HIV (Human Immunodeficiency Virus). The illness alters the immune system, making people much more vulnerable to infections and diseases. This susceptibility worsens as the disease progresses.

AIDS is a syndrome, and not a virus or a disease, because it's a composite of various complications and symptoms that often lead to death.[362]

AIDS Dilemma

The World Health Organization estimates that 36.1 million people are infected with HIV. Every day, nearly 15,000 previously healthy men, women, and children contact the virus. This figure becomes even higher as the disease gathers momentum in China and India, the world's most populous nations. In South Africa, one in four adults already carries HIV. The spread of AIDS seems to be surrounded by poverty, inequality, and instability, both political and economic. Most of its victims are poor people who live in developing countries where HIV infection goes undetected until they come down with the terrible symptoms of AIDS. By that point, they have inadvertently affected their loved ones. Once they do become sick, more than 95% of the world's AIDS patients will die without ever being treated with the antiretroviral drugs that have made life so much better, and longer, for infected people in the industrialized world.[363]

AIDS was initially observed in 1981. In 1983 researchers in Maryland and Paris isolated the HIV/AIDS virus. The same year the first reported cases were observed in Central Africa. In December 1982, two AIDS cases were diagnosed in South Africa. By 1989 each African country reported at least one AIDS case. Within a decade 25.2 million sub-Saharan Africans, in a region that had 10% of the earth's population, were infected with the HIV virus. 70% of those contaminated worldwide were from this region. Africa is without a doubt the epicenter of an AIDS pandemic.[364] By 1999, HIV/AIDS had become a global catastrophe. Worldwide, 19 million people had already died of the disease, and nearly 3 million more were dying every year. Thirty-three million were infected with the virus, and millions of infections were added to the toll each year.[365]

The HIV virus, which causes AIDS, spreads very fast. According to, Michel Sidibé, the UNAIDS Executive Director Under Secretary-General of the United Nations, in 2000, 3.8 million new HIV-infections were reported in sub-Saharan Africa alone. That means 10,500 cases per day. Thirteen percent were children. The first state of HIV may last from 1 to 10 years. Most people are unaware that they have been infected since they often have no disabling symptoms. As AIDS takes on its full blown capacity, pulmonary tuberculosis, prolonged diarrhea, fever, weight loss, bacterial pneumonia, cancers, and fatigue set in. In the final phase, the individual with AIDS experiences chronic fever, severe weight loss, and infections. At that point, often times the patient is unable to care for himself/herself. Due to the state of health care in Africa, patients and their families are left to fend for themselves. The Declaration of Commitment to combat AIDS approved by the General Assembly of the United Nations on June 27, 2001, recognized "accountability as vital; without it the destruction of Africa by the equivalent of a nuclear bomb will be ensured."

HIV / AIDS causes immense suffering to millions of people. Recent figures published by UNAIDS (the joint United Nations program on HIV / AIDS) show that HIV / AIDS has been diagnosed in every continent on the globe, but its distribution is far from even. North America has 950,000 people living with HIV / AIDS, while an estimated 28.5 million people are infected with HIV in sub-Saharan Africa, and 11 million African children are thought to have been orphaned by AIDS.

Statistics about Africa

Before further detailing the AIDS epidemic in Africa, below are some general statistics about the continent. With an area of

30,310,000 square km, Africa is the third largest continent on Earth, after Asia and America. It is home to more than 770 million Africans, and a wide variety of traditions and civilizations. It is made up of more than 50 independent states.

In the Whole of Africa:

- Over 12,000,000 adults have died of AIDS and 13,200,000 children have been orphaned.

- It is estimated that the African economy loses more than $12 billion USD a year because of malaria.

- Wood and other biomass generate 90 to 98% of household energy in most African countries.

- About 65% of Africa's agricultural land suffers from soil degradation.

- Africa has the highest deforestation rate in the world, and lost 13 million acres (5.3m hectares) of forest each year in the 1990s.

- Almost half of all Africans live on less than $1 (USD) a day— the number of people living in poverty grew from 220,000,000 in 1990 to 300,000,000 in 1998.

- Africa's share of world trade fell from 2.7% in 1990 to 2.1% in 2000. A 1% increase in Africa's share of world trade would generate five times more than the continent receives in aid and debt relief.

- Over the last decade, Africa's annual percentage growth rate for exports was 3.8%, as compared to a world average growth rate of 6%.

- The consumption expenditure for the average African household is 20% less than it was 25 years ago.

- The population of Africa is expected to reach 1.3 billion in 2025. The countries with the largest populations are Nigeria, Egypt, Ethiopia, the Democratic Republic of Congo, and South Africa. Roughly 45% of Africans are under the age of 15.

- An estimated 2,000 languages and dialects are spoken in Africa, some by a few million people, others by only a few thousand.

- Christianity is growing in a very large number of African countries. At present, there are more than 325 million Christians in Africa, including 123 million Catholics. Islam is the second most widespread religion in Africa, with more than 300 million Muslims. Traditional religion—also sometimes called Animism—is still practiced by more than 15% of Africans.

In Sub-Saharan Africa:

- About a third of the population is undernourished.

- Sub-Saharan Africa has the world's highest proportion of people living in poverty, about 48%.

- Estimated 24,500,000 people are living with HIV/AIDS. It has almost 90% of the world's fatal Malaria cases.

- About 30% of children die or are disabled due to acute respiratory infections—60% are caused by air pollution.

- Fewer than one in five people have electrical power.

- Over 500,000,000 people depend on firewood as basic fuel, leading to deforestation and soil erosion.

HIV/AIDS in Africa

At the end of 2001, it was estimated that only 30,000 of the 28.5 million people living with HIV / AIDS in Africa had access to antiretroviral drugs. By 2006, some twelve million African children have lost at least one parent to AIDS. A small fraction received help from dedicated, community-based organizations, but there were not nearly enough of such programs to reach all needy children.[366] Africa has more cases of AIDS than any other continent, and is singularly responsible for 65% of HIV and AIDS cases that occur worldwide. In Africa, one out of every twelve people is carrying the virus, which has devastating consequences for the continent in terms of education, gender equality and health care.

Impact of AIDS on Africa

According to *Avert*, a nonprofit organization dedicated to ending HIV and AIDS worldwide, AIDS has had several distinct effects on the continent of Africa. After decades of increase, life expectancy has declined sharply to between 48 and 55 years. While the average European lives 78 years, life expectancy in parts of southern Africa has dropped to 49.[367] Households lose money when AIDS prevents someone from working, or when families have to care for sick relatives or orphans. As the AIDS epidemic worsens, the demand for health care rises, straining the health sector increasing the number of health care workers accidentally infected with HIV. Schools often close, eliminating opportunities for community HIV education and support, which could decrease infection rates. Because most people infected with HIV are between 15 and 49 years old, which is the prime time to be working, each country's production slows, which prevents social progress and economic growth.[36]

AIDS Orphans in Africa

The number of children who have lost parents due to AIDS is massive, which leads to emotional distress, poverty and stigmatization in the countries most affected. In 2009, Nigeria had 2.5 million AIDS orphans, South Africa had 1.9 million, and Zimbabwe, Kenya, Uganda and Tanzania had between 1 and 1.3 million. In Malawi, Lesotho, Swaziland, Zimbabwe and Botswana, 65% or more of orphans had been orphaned because of AIDS— this means that if not for AIDS, these children would still have their parents. Demographically, 15% of orphans are 0-4 years old, 35% are age 5-9, and 50% are age 10-14. Not only do these children suffer the trauma associated with watching their parents die, they also suffer physical and emotional neglect, are thrust into unfamiliar situations with no support, and are particularly vulnerable to exploitation and abuse. AIDS orphans experience more anxiety, depression and anger than other children, and according to a 2005 study in Uganda, 12% wished they were dead (compared to 3% of the general child population).[369]

After the death of their parents, orphans are usually also separated from their siblings and are sent to live in large households where many people are dependent on few incomes; consequently, in order to contribute financially, orphans work, beg or steal food. Many either stop attending school, or receive low marks due to psychological trauma, malnutrition and unstable households. A culture of fear and rejection surrounds HIV and AIDS, so society stigmatizes AIDS orphans, sometimes denying them schooling and health care, and sometimes even inheritance and property. People assume that the children are also infected with HIV, leading to lifelong discrimination.[370]

Africa's Orphan Crisis Worsens

Thirty-four Million without Parents

With diseases such as AIDS, malaria and tuberculosis continuing to claim the lives of millions of Africa's poorest adults, millions more children are being left homeless and orphaned. "Africa needs more than one billion dollars each year to care for the millions of orphans on the continent," an official spokesman for the United Nations recently stated. "In less than five years," the official continued, "there will be more than 50 million orphans in just 16 of Africa's 53 countries." "Such a situation," an African Union spokesman explained, "will easily destabilize countries because these children are vulnerable and they can be exploited. Funds will be needed for education and healthcare, but we don't know at the moment where the money is coming from." "In the past, people used to care for the orphans and loved them," a woman whose husband recently died from disease explained. "But these days they are so many, and many people have died who could have assisted them, and therefore orphan hood is a common phenomenon, not strange. The few who are alive cannot support them."

- Every day, 14,000 people contract HIV

- 40.3 million people now live with HIV/AIDS

- AIDS kills 1 child every minute

- AIDS has orphaned 15 million children

"The epidemic of diseases such as AIDS and malaria in sub-Saharan Africa has already orphaned a generation of children," explains Fr. John Lynch of the Missionaries of Africa. "Now it seems set to affect future generations. Official reports estimate that, at the moment, there are more than 34 million orphans in the region today and some 11 million of them have been orphaned by AIDS. Eight out of every 10 children in the world whose parents have died of AIDS live in sub-Saharan Africa. During the last decade, the proportion of children who are orphaned as a result of AIDS rose from 3.5% to 32%," Fr. Lynch continues. "Unless we reach out and act now, a whole generation of children could die before our eyes."

Stories about AIDS

Tigist's story

As it is InterviewGirl.com's mission to collect stories, in order to understand what the statistics detailed above in reality mean, learning a few stories will allow us to better understand why the Interview Girl Foundation was created to help eliminate this misery (HIV/AIDS). The General Assembly of the United Nations predicted that AIDS could take the amount of lives equal to the amount of lives that a nuclear bomb could take. We have seen millions of lives taken by the AIDS pandemic. Tigist's story and other "child-headed households" reveal how many lives are being taken by AIDS. In *28 Stories of AIDS in Africa*, Stephanie Nolen discloses a story about Tigist, a child in Kazachis, a crowded Addis Ababa slum, who was left to care for her younger brother when her Mom died. When Tigist's mother died, she was ten and her brother was six. Nolen elucidates that 10 or 15 years ago, it would not have been up to Tigist to take care of herself and her 6 year old brother, but someone in the community would have stepped forward to take care of the orphaned children. In sharing Tigist's story, Nolen writes, "It would have been as unthinkable in Addis Ababa as it would be in Toronto or Dallas for two small children to set up house on their own. But in the age of AIDS, the net of family and community that once cared for children such as these has frayed and worn and finally unraveled altogether." When the commonness of AIDS in Ethiopia hit 5%, it had a devastating effect on families. At first, when parents died, their children would be taken in by an aunt or uncle. Then the children would go to other aunts and uncles. Then they went to grandparents and neighbors. Eventually there was nowhere left for them to go. As you can imagine each move was difficult on these children. It is now common to see "little families" of children living on their own because there was no one left to take them in. In the language of AIDS, they are called "child-headed households." Nolen describes that it is difficult to imagine a nine-year old gathering firewood, cooking, washing, and telling bedtime stories to the seven, five, three, and one year old left in his/her hands because he/she was the oldest. AIDS has created realities such as this.

Learning Tigist's story gives us perspective as we try to understand why we must work to change the statistics and research revealed about AIDS in this chapter. Tigist's story allows us to understand what life is accurately like for an orphan who has AIDS. Imagining a young girl caring for her six year old brother and the two of them living all by themselves in a house is difficult to fully wrap our minds around. Statistics like: "AIDS has orphaned 15 million children" take on a new dimension as personal stories are learned in order to help us to better understand these disheartening statistics. Changing these statistics is the impetus behind *Operation A²* through the Interview Girl Foundation.

Anne Mumbi's Story

Anne Mumbi's story is motivating because she is someone trying to help the AIDS problem in Zambia. Anne Mumbi runs an organization called Children in Distress (CINDI). It was founded in 1994 by women alarmed by the growing number of "grimy, barefoot children" living in the streets in Kitwe. They started to register the orphans and to organize community caregivers in the slums and villages because no state agency was doing it. In *28 Stories of AIDS in Africa*, Stephanie Nolen chronicles how Anne Mumbi showed her the many ways that the disease has hit Kitwe. Nolen explains the time when Mumbi walked her through Kitwe Central Hospital, "the director showed me his staffing charts— more than half his jobs for nurses were vacant. Sixteen patients had died in the past twenty-four hours, all but one of AIDS."[371] Learning that fifteen patients died of AIDS in one day in one hospital, the "dilemma, pandemic, epidemic, problem," and the many other terms that AIDS spreading in Africa is referred to as by various authors becomes evident. There is no denying the legitimacy of an AIDS dilemma in Kitwe along with many other places in Africa.

Anne Mumbi's perspective is of value because she sees the bigger picture in Zambia. In seeking solutions, *Operation A²'s* philosophy is to see the whole picture. As one reads about AIDS spreading in Africa, it is apparent that there is not a magic bullet solution to the issue, but rather it is a multifaceted problem, so in trying to solve it, we cannot just come up with a one dimensional solution. Anne Mumbi explained to Stephanie Nolen that a 25 percent prevalence rate would be devastating anywhere, but "a complex mix of factors has made the impact of AIDS on Zambia even worse. Factors that have made people poor and thus at greater risk of exposure to the disease. There are factors that have undermined the ability of their country to respond. This part of the picture is much harder to see; it takes a thoughtful observer such as Anne, someone who works in the eye of the pandemic but retains the ability to step back and assess the larger picture."[372] Anne believes the three main variables in the AIDS equation to be: debt, aid, and trade.

In sharing Anne's story, Stephanie Nolen explains how she could see the varying problems that led to the crisis in Zambia. Stephanie divulges, "In a couple days spent with Anne in Kitwe, I could see the intersection of all these things—the impact of international trade policy, of external debt, of aid and the lack thereof—in one grim package." Anne told Stephanie,

"In this country, only people with a bit of money have a life. We're just in a terrible state. People die in their houses because they know that if they go to the hospital there is no one there—they die without even a little Tylenol to relieve the pain because they can't even afford that. It's so heartbreaking, this beautiful country with all its rich resources, its good land and good rain. It's a beautiful country, a peaceful country—with a terrible policy."[373]

Anne Mumbi, who is in charge of, Children in Distress (CINDI), understands that public health problems cannot be addressed without considering their social and political causes. One of the Interview Girl Foundation's larger questions, *How does a country's public policy affect the AIDS pandemic?* highlights this issue. The only cure to help AIDS victims is to take everything into consideration, to break down the social and political causes of peoples' situations. Africa struggles to cope with many scourges, including winner-take-all economic development, political corruption, civil conflict and AIDS. Social movements that change things for the better are needed to help stop AIDS from spreading. The science and medicine are important in the fight against AIDS, but positive social movements are the key to moving forward in Africa as we try to help those suffering from AIDS. The story shared about Anne Mumbi reveals that Dr. Epstein's basic point in *The Invisible Cure* is quite true: the drugs alone will never save those suffering from AIDS in Africa. Prevalence and transmission rates are too high, the health care infrastructure is too weak, there are too many other threatening diseases, and the costs are impossible. The hope to change the AIDS dilemma lies in what seems like a still-distant vaccine, and in the "invisible cure" of Epstein's title: dramatic behavioral changes to prevent new infections. Anne Mumbi tells Stephanie Nolen, "If Zambia can raise a generation that remains HIV-negative, then there is much to be hopeful about."[374]

Progress

"Success seems to be connected with action. Successful people keep moving. They make mistakes but don't quit."

—Conrad Hilton

This chapter has exposed that the statistics remain dire, but let us not forget the headway that has been made in the fight against AIDS in Africa. Wonderful organizations like PEPFAR, Catholic Relief Services, Children in Distress, Grandmothers to Grandmothers Campaign, Stop-SIDA, the Nelson Mandela Foundation, Pan-African Treatment Access Movement, the Global Fund to Fight AIDS, Tuberculosis and Malaria, and Oxfam America have undoubtedly completed beneficial work to combat the AIDS epidemic. When it comes to advocacy for AIDS in Africa, Access to essential medicines, AIDS Vaccine Advocacy Coalition, DATA: Debt, AIDS, Trade, Africa, and International AIDS Vaccine Initiative have also all made a difference in the AIDS dilemma. The Interview Girl Foundation has closely studied the best practices from all of these organizations currently making a difference. It is important for us to recognize the good that these organizations have done, but we must not remain complacent because even with useful organizations like these, more needs to be done in order to eliminate the miseries that HIV/ AIDS creates and this is where the Interview Girl Foundation can help. Numerous international charities are already doing meaningful work in Africa and I want InterviewGirl.com to share the stories about all of these charities doing lifesaving work, but there is still misery throughout the world, so *Operation A²* can join in and try to slice off some of the remaining misery that HIV/AIDS creates.

In order to effectively combat the HIV/AIDS epidemic in Africa, international governments and NGOs have stepped up. Developed countries have donated to the Global Fund, an initiative that streamlines international funding; this fund has given billions of dollars in grants for AIDS treatment and prevention. The US government has created the President's Emergency Plan For AIDS Relief, or PEPFAR, which fights AIDS in fifteen countries. However, the AIDS crisis demands not only billions of dollars, but also a developed health, education and communication infrastructure within African countries, in order to promote the overall health of the continent.[375] The Interview Girl Foundation works to help develop health, education and communication infrastructure within African countries.

Although the AIDS epidemic looms large still today, we must not lose hope because as we have seen progress has been made within the last decade in combating the misery of AIDS and the Interview Girl Foundation will continue to work toward further progress. To detail some of the epidemic's progress, certain countries in Africa have responded quickly to the AIDS crisis, with high success. For example, Senegal recognized the epidemic early and funneled many resources to fighting HIV/AIDS. The government used multimedia to reduce stigma surrounding the disease, promoted prevention strategies and offered universal access to anti-retroviral drugs that help prevent HIV from progressing to AIDS. Uganda, Ethiopia, Tanzania, and Zambia have also had success through measures that include "governments working with NGOs and their own people to deal with gender issues, recognizing the role of grandparents in high cases of orphaned children, using the mainstream media to raise awareness, providing universal access to health care in many cases, and improving children's access to education."[376]

Another aspect to be hopeful about is modern day technology and medicine and what it can do to support the AIDS victims. Both HIV infection and AIDS are considered to be chronic illnesses managed with both pharmaceutical (pharmacy drugs) therapies and complementary (alternative) therapies. In most cases, people can live for many years with HIV infection and with AIDS if they are fortunate enough to have access to the resources that allow the disease to become manageable. It is usually impossible to know just how long a person will live with AIDS. Today's HIV therapies are extending the lives of people living with AIDS as well as helping to improve their quality of life. Thanks to modern medicine, drugs have been created to make the AIDS disease, to use the words of James Orbinski, "as manageable as diabetes."

Revealing the research concerning the AIDS dilemma seems overwhelming and unfair, however, we must remain hopeful about the future of the AIDS pandemic because of the positive changes that have been achieved thus far. The Interview Girl Foundation is stepping in and hoping to help with continuing to make these types of progressive changes in helping to eliminate the miseries that people with AIDS experience. In playing its role to eliminate some of the miseries that AIDS creates, especially for orphans, the Interview Girl Foundation began by attempting to identify where certain loopholes are and why despite relief efforts, there are still many individuals who are experiencing misery. For example, there are trained doctors in Africa who cannot use their training because there is not enough money for the proper resources that the doctors need in order to implement their training. One of the Interview Girl Foundation's desires is to get the doctors the resources that they need.

Conclusion

Patricia Thomas designated, "Science has been described as a special kind of storytelling, with no right or wrong answers, just better and better stories." Thomas wrote *Big Shot: AIDS Vaccine* in which she chronicles the search for an AIDS vaccine. Meeting the children in Africa at the Children's Home and then researching "this story" about AIDS spreading in Africa for this book, it hit a nerve. AIDS was first observed in the 1980's and within a decade 25.2 million people living in sub-Saharan Africa were infected with the HIV virus. Only 10% of the Earth's population lives in sub-Saharan Africa, yet 25.2 million people were infected.

The HIV virus spread at an accelerated rate in that decade. My research prompted me to decompound even further those statistics that unfolded within that decade that I first read about as I wrote this book, started InterviewGirl.com and founded the Interview Girl Foundation. I had disparate statistics written on note cards and placed under my guiding questions spread out across my parent's basement. As I made sense of the research, specifically what happened with the AIDS epidemic during the decade of the 1980's, I came up with a new question. What if positive changes could spread like that? What if turning the AIDS pandemic around could have the same story? In learning about Africa and why the AIDS epidemic has spread there, stories surface. These are stories that need better endings.

The Interview Girl Foundation hopes to help with creating these endings. If it weren't for the time that I spent in Africa volunteering with children, many of whom suffer from AIDS, maybe "AIDS has orphaned 15 million children" would just be a statistic that I read on a page, but I made a connection with 20 some orphans and to think there are millions more, well that makes me more than think. It makes it necessary to *take action*, which is what I am attempting to do in creating InterviewGirl. com and the Interview Girl Foundation. Stephanie Nolen ends her book, "Each day in Africa, six thousand people die of HIV/AIDS—a treatable, preventable disease illness. We have twenty-eight million reasons to act." Action is needed to combat the AIDS epidemic. Meeting those children that summer had an indelible effect on me in profound ways. When Edem shared Amara's story with me that day, it imparted upon me what became a quest to figure out what could I do across the world to help eliminate the misery of someone like Amara. I became versed in many new topics and discussions thanks to the children whom I met that summer in Ghana. Those beautiful children were able to transmit an exemplification of multiplied lessons to me. They taught me many things that I cannot even begin to do justice to as I attempt to put into words what they taught me. Above all, as I learned the stories of the children at the Children's Home, I learned about empathy. *Operation A²* is working hard to chip away at this reality, this misery (AIDS) in Africa. Like all considerable and extensive projects throughout human history, *Operation A²* always goes back to the larger questions to guide its direction: Was there something that could be done to ensure that these children get the medicine that Edem explained ran out as he described Amara's death? Was there a way to prevent these children from ending up with AIDS and needing medicine in the first place? From *Operation A²'s* questions, we will continue to make improvements in what many consider an impossible problem. The problem is undoubtedly immense in scope, but we must not sojourn in seeking solutions.

"Do not let what you cannot do interfere with what you can do."

—John Wooden

My initial intentions, thoughts, and plans for how to sincerely help to eliminate the misery of someone living with AIDS has been turned on its head. As I told you earlier in the book, I don't know why it was that I really went to Kpando, Ghana that summer. At the time, it was something along the lines of I wanted to go to Africa "to help" that summer. The truth is since then I have learned that this does more harm than good. As Stephanie Nolen details how we can help the AIDS crisis, she writes, "First, people want to go to Africa to help in a hands-on way and they ask me to suggest a community or organization they can assist. It is a commendable idea, but not always the best solution. I have seen how volunteering in Africa can be a fantastic experience for volunteers, but often a less than terrific one for the project or community they join, which may be a high price for the skills the volunteers bring."[377]

When I first came home from Africa and I was saddened by Amara's story, at that point, I wanted to collect money to "help" the orphans, but thankfully I am trained to research, so that's exactly what I did and as I did this, my initial plan and intentions changed. I now know that providing medicine is not enough to solve the misery of someone living with AIDS. It's a solution, but a temporary one. I've read enough about how top down aid has its limitations. I know that *Operation A²'s* plans will constantly change and I know that all our efforts may not be as hopeful as we anticipate, but I understand that it's okay to fail—this is one of history's greatest lessons. As Samuel Beckett says in *Worstward Ho*, "All of old. Nothing else ever. Ever tried. Ever failed. No matter. Try again. Fail again. Fail better." *Operation A²* will always move forward and learn from what it tries even if what we try does not work as we had hoped it would. The Interview Girl Foundation has the philosophy that not every endeavor will work perfectly, but in our larger plan, we need to continually look at what's worked, what has not, and what needs to be tried differently. This is where *Operation A²* is doing its work.

The Interview Girl Foundation will never give up. InterviewGirl.com will continue to collect stories and from the proceeds that come from our stories, we will keep progressing forward. We will continue to try to eliminate miseries where they are happening in the world. We will do this because there are grim statistics and sad stories, but beyond that, we know that there is hope and we will continue to bring people this hope through our instrument: sharing stories.

Acknowledgments

Thank you to all of society's unsung heroes. Your stories are what will allow this nonprofit organization to make a difference in our world. Your selfless sacrifices and acts of courage make our world a better place.

Thank you to every Italian, Istrian, Fiuman, Dalmatian, and WWII veteran who has shared a story with me. The countless hours that we have spent together have allowed me to perfect my craft: interviewing.

To Nonno Giannese, Nonna Giannese, Grandpa Spiering, and Grandma Rita —In memory of lives so beautifully lived and hearts so deeply loved.

To Amara—Your soft tone, inquisitive spirit, and gentle face will always be a part of me. The Indo-European root of the word hope means: change in direction, going in a different way. I believe that there is *hope* that *all* children throughout the world can have access to medicine.

To Jim Mallers—You are one of the best friends that I have ever had. I love when you read Henry Van Dyke and Rudyard Kipling poems to me, I love when we debate the greatest players and the best moments in the history of the game of baseball, I love when we go through the various presidential regimes from U.S. History and of course I love your war stories.

To all my current and former students—Your indomitable spirit makes me believe that all things are possible if we put our minds to achieving them.

To my esteemed colleagues at the high school—It is a privilege to work with everyone. A special thank you to my colleagues in the Social Studies department—I admire your passion for your subject matter, your creative ideas and the hard work that you put into teaching day in and day out. Bill Bell, Karen Castelli, Steve Galovich, Ty Gorman, Kevin Kaplan, Eric Kuffel, Nate Newhalfen, Tim Rife, John Roncone, Kelley Sohler, Cary Waxler, and Kurt Weisenburger -you have all been exceptional mentors to me and I am grateful for the friendships that we share. Patty Baumann, Derek Gablenz, Heidi Rockwell, and Al Strobl – thank you for everything that you have done for me. I admire and appreciate you all more than you know. To Mr. Tim Dunn - thank you for believing in me and giving me the opportunity of a lifetime to work in the best department in the world. A very special thank you to my dear friends Pat Wire and Kathe Keeler - Flavia Weedn puts what I would like to say to you two best, "Some people come into our lives and leave footprints on our hearts and we are never ever the same."

Thank you to all of my friends. You each have your own stories and I am privileged to know all of you. Each of you brightens my life in your own way. I am so grateful to have all of you in my life. Of course there are numerous others to mention; unfortunately space constraints do not allow me to mention everyone. Thank you to: Claire Ackerman, Marcella Bellini, Brittany Berleman, Franco Biloslavo, Giuseppe Budicin, Lyz Carmody, Dr. Peter Checca, Dr. Celeste Chamberland, Dr. Chris Chulos, Lisa Cristiano, Jackie Cuisnier, Luciano DiPalermo, Leslie Duff, Brother Ed Foken, Valerie Galgan, Cristina Garizio, Lindsay Gayle, Melissa Glorioso, Leah Gonzalez, Gilberto Gonzalez, Bridget Gottlieb, Kyle Hansen, Alan Hartman, Jen Healy, Tim Iding, Kelly Goranson Kelty, Brian Kroes, Stacey Lezon, Ed Lucero, Lora Martinez, Beth Moore, Liz Mulherin, Bridget Nora, Mike Nora, Dr. Marco Pignotti, Adam Pike, Jeanette Reifenberg, Allie Reninger, Carrie Rose, Beth Ruland, Gordon Shick, Elaine Stapleton, Eva

Stradinski, Courtney Sturgess, Giulia Tellini, Hallie Tenenbaum, Teresa Thomas, Stefanie Valcarenghi, and Amy Yentes.

A special thank you to my forever friends: Sara Campo, Stacey Compton, Lisa DiMichelle, Katy Hackett, Nicole Retzlaff, Katie Sard, Jen Sizemore, Jessica Sloan and Nicole Ursetta.

To my family: thank you for your love and support. To my Mother's family (Giannese family) and my Father's family (Spiering family)—you are all a part of me and each and every one of you has a part of my heart. To the Hagerty family and the Sciaccotta family—it is such a blessing to be a part of your wonderful family. A special thank you to Mom and Dad Hagerty and Grandma and Grandpa Sciaccotta - thank you from the bottom of my heart for your welcoming kindness and love. Grandma Sciaccotta - I will always be grateful for your help in obtaining interviews for my WWII book. To my Godmother and Godfather (Aunt Cindy and Uncle Mike)—thank you for everything that you have done for me throughout the years. To Grandma Spiering—I appreciate you and miss you greatly. I love you. God Bless all of my aunts, uncles, cousins, nieces, nephews, and in-laws. Carter and Bennett—you both warm my heart and you are the greatest nephews on the planet. I am grateful to be a part of such a loving family. Spending time and sharing momentous life occasions with my family truly has been one of life's greatest joys.

To Uncle Nino and Uncle Vince—I didn't know it at the time, but when I look back …… those Saturday mornings that we spent together at my parent's house will end up being some of the most memorable moments of my lifetime—"Them Were The Days." Thank you for having the patience to tell me the same story over and over. All these years later, hearing your story still doesn't get old. "You Better Believe It!" Uncle Nino, nobody says those four words like you. Thank you for everything that you do for me and for the conversations that we share, Uncle Nino. Uncle Vince—in the *Dictionary* next to the word, *straordinario*, there should be a picture of you (and one of my Mom to represent the feminine version of the word). You genuinely are straordinario. Uncle Frank,

Uncle Dino, and Uncle Mario—you are amazing uncles whom I am proud to call my family.

To Zio Angelo, Zia Clara, Uncle Vince, Uncle Nino, Uncle Frank, Uncle Mario, Uncle Dino, and Mamma—Sono fiera di essere di una famiglia italiana. Di tutte le cose che ho fatto nella mia vita, imparare l'Italiano era una delle migliori esperienze della mia vita.

God Bless my godchildren. I love you both. To Lucca: In Italian, your name means: "bringer of light." You bring light to all of us. To Madeleine—You are a little darling. The world awaits precious you. You are the perfect little niece.

To Christopher, Stefanie, Kristen, Nathan, Carter, Bennett and Madeleine—Thank for your love and support. You all mean the world to me. As Susan Scarf Merrell says, "Our siblings. They resemble us just enough to make all their differences confusing, and no matter what we choose to make of this, we are cast in relation to them our whole lives long." You each inspire and encourage me. I appreciate all of the memories that we share. I look forward to making many more memories in the future, as well. I love you all.

To Chris—You are one of the most intelligent individuals I know. Most of us pale in comparison to your brainpower. On top of that, you are also an admirable and caring person. Everyone will always remember the day that you gave the gift that keeps on giving. "Because I have a brother I will always have a friend."

To Stef—You too, have a brilliant mind and you are beyond question a gem of a person. I don't know where I'd be without you. Thank you for being loving, caring, gracious and absolutely wonderful you—as they say in Italy, "squisita." They say that sisters have been where you have been. They say that you can call your sister when things aren't going right. As Isadora James impeccably puts it, "A sister is a gift to the heart, a friend to the spirit, a golden thread to the meaning of life." You are more than just family—you are the perfect best friend.

To Mom and Dad—Your sacrificial love has been constant through the years. I am able to do what I do because of the sacrifices that you have made for me. You have allowed me to see the world from a very young age. When I was just five, I was fortunate enough to travel to Italy and since then I have never gone more than a few years without going back. Outside of Italy, I appreciate all of my other travel experiences, as well. There is not a trip that I have been on where you haven't taken me to and from the airport. You have been there through it all. You have allowed me to experience a world class education because you sent me to *St. Mary's*. You instilled within me the power that comes from stories from a very young age and as Stef and Nathan lovingly say, "you created a monster." I remember in elementary school when the books from *Scholastic* would arrive; I had to go out to the bus early so the patrol could help me to carry my books because you ordered so many for me. I remember coming down on Christmas morning and seeing stacks and stacks of books in front of my stocking. Thank you for putting up with all of my books throughout your basement and thank you for driving to various libraries to pick up my inter-library loan books that I ordered from all over the world. I appreciate when you would check out books for me on your library card because I had checked out more books than I could on my own card. I am grateful for all the times that you paid my steep library late fees.

Who knew that your daughter who for years and years could not make it through a doctor's visit or even hear the word needle in Health class without fainting would write her first book filled with references to Antiretroviral Aids medication? Who would have guessed that your daughter who tirelessly worked and traveled to learn Italian and capture stories from the WWII generation for the past decade would not have written her first book about History, Italy, or Fiume? Life has a funny way of fulfilling our desires in unexpected ways. I never did relax my dream of being a doctor; yet I kept signing up for more classes in the Humanities. Although given my queasiness around needles and blood, I may never be the person in the operating room; when I wrote the story that I did about *Grace* over the past two years, I myself wasn't the doctor, but I finally felt at peace. I know it's just a story, but to me, it's more than a story. There are many Grace(s) in our world and their stories need to be told. That's the thing. Through the pages of books as my eyes glance from one side of the page to the other, I am transported to no end of different places. Sometimes I travel back into History, sometimes I traverse to places very diverse from my own subculture at home, and always the books are filled with treasures of wisdom and knowledge that allow me to understand or see something that I didn't previously know. Centering this nonprofit organization around *stories* was not an accident. I authentically believe that stories can have a transformative effect on us. I believe that because I have lived it time and time again as I read stories and *good* literature. You have always believed in me. I remember when I was a little girl and I wrote *Perky the King of the Penguins*. I was disappointed when I did not win the Young Authors Conference; you told me not to give up on my dream of being a writer. I have written many things since that contest. Most of them are unread and saved to a computer at your house. Who knows what will happen with the Interview Girl Foundation, but I am reminded of *Field of Dreams:* "If You Build It—He Will Come." It's built—maybe now it will lead to helping others within in our world. Most of all, thank you for the gift of showing me Christ's love through our faith and our family. Thank you for unceasingly sacrificing for me through the years. Your love and "caritas" allow me to have the marvelous life that I do.

To Joe—Thank you to my best friend (Beppe) for your loving support and encouragement. What I am sure seem like my crazy ideas are always met with a "sure, you can try that" and a smile. Thank you for making my dreams come true and making everyday life special: "Only love lets us see normal things in an extraordinary way." I love spending each and every one of my ordinary days with you. Every day that we share together is the gift of an ordinary day. I am incredibly grateful that you built me my very own library. Thank you for helping me address hundreds of letters, buying the stamps, putting up with my note taking and videotaping obsession, purchasing external hard drives, and above all for just getting me. I appreciate your willingness to debate and discuss all of my "topics of the day." Your loving and generous heart is unparalleled. You have what Dante Alighieri wrote about, "un gentil cuore." One day I will write *An Irving And Cumberland Love Story*, but for now, it's just a fun story to live. I love you.

Please Connect With Interview Girl:
www.InterviewGirl.com

Twitter: @InterviewGirl
Instagram: @interviewgirltori
Facebook: https://www.facebook.com/InterviewGirl
YouTube: https://www.youtube.com/user/MsToriStory
Podcast: https://itunes.apple.com/us/podcast/InterviewGirl.
      com-life-lesson-series
Pinterest: http://www.pinterest.com/interviewgirl
WWII Stories: https://www.worldwartwostories.com
Google Plus: @InterviewGirl
Skype: storytori05
E-mail: info@InterviewGirl.com

**What story can you share with
InterviewGirl.com to make
the world a better place?**